THE *ULTIMATE* GAME DEVELOPER'S SOURCEBOOK

Ben Sawyer

Publisher	*Keith Weiskamp*
Editor	*Jenni Aloi*
Proofreader	*Diane Green Cook*
Cover Art	*Gary Smith*
Cover Design	*Anthony Stock*
Interior Design	*Michelle Stroup and Bradley Grannis*
Layout Production	*Chris Fadley*
Indexer	*Sat-Kartar Khalsa and Diane Green Cook*

The Coriolis Group
7339 E. Acoma Drive, Suite 7
Scottsdale, AZ 85260
Phone: (602) 483-0192
Fax: (602) 483-0193
Web address: http://www.coriolis.com

ISBN 1-883577-59-4 : $44.99

Printed in the United States of America

10 9 8 7 6 5 4 3 2 1

This book is dedicated to the memory of three close people in my life: Walter Ramsey, Richard G. Sawyer, and Louise Gibson, who all shared an eternal determination to succeed in every way.

Ben Sawyer (*73522.1470@compuserve.com*) is a leading author and market and publishing consultant who is heavily involved in the interactive entertainment industry. He writes about games and interactive multimedia industries for *Interactive Update* published by Alexander & Associates. He is also a moderator of CompuServe's Game Developers forum.

Dean Gloster (*glosterd@hooked.net*) is a multimedia attorney and partner in the San Francisco law firm Farella, Braun & Martel, where he represents and advises numerous game developers, designer, and publishers, and many online ventures. He has extensive experience in publishing and distribution deals, financing, joint ventures, intellectual property licensing, company formation, and sales of software and technology companies. Dean is a regular speaker at industry conferences.

Contents

Part 3 Designing Different Types of Games 141

Chapter 7 Tips for Game Design Success 143

Chapter 8 Game Development Categories 157

Part 5 Game Players and Development Issues 377

Chapter 15 A Technical Overview of Game Development 379

Chapter 16 Windows Game Programming: Up Close and Personal 401

Chapter 27 Game Market Analysis and Resources 575

Chapter 28 Game Company Startups: Finding the Critical Mass 597

Chapter 30 The Art of Computer Game Publishing, Selling, and Promotion 647

Introduction

The idea for this book came about almost a year ago after I attended the annual Computer Game Developers conference in California. While hanging out with hundreds of fellow game developers, I realized that numerous books had been written on game programming but few books or articles had been published to really help game developers perfect their craft and tap into the vast sea of resources available. After zillions of hours of research and discussions with leading developers, programmers, artists, musicians, designers, packagers, marketing folks, publishers, and tool development companies, the end result is this book. My goal was to create a book that provided "everything you ever wanted to know about game development but were afraid to ask." (A quote graciously sent my way by Phil Steinmeyer, an amazing game developer who did the major programming work for New World's mega-hit, Heroes of Might and Magic.) Of course, not every single thing in this book will be useful to every single person. But I guarantee you will find a lot of information in these pages that will help you in your specific endeavors.

Before we get too far, I want to explain that in doing the research for this book, I came across many different game companies. Each one had a slightly different way of approaching game design, development, marketing, packaging, production, and so on. Few people in this business do everything by the book. You'll find there are more ways of creating and selling games than there are for creating and selling any other type of software product.

I've tried to factor in this creative diversity in a few ways. First, I gathered and incorporated hundreds of comments, tips, advice, and specific practices from the many companies I spoke to and worked with while writing this book. Throughout, you'll find unique sidebars, interviews, and tips from experienced game developers and market leaders around the world. While I haven't covered every different approach possible, I think that you'll find more than enough ideas and techniques to keep you busy for quite some time.

In addition, I tried to cover the entire spectrum of the game development process, from market research to design to development. You'll not only get a book full of hands-on "how-tos" but an in-depth guide that puts the *entire* industry in perspective.

My hope is that no matter what your experience level, you'll really benefit from the material presented, which is designed to help you make better games and achieve greater success.

No matter what tools you choose to develop with or processes you plan to follow, creating awesome games is what this book is all about.

Finally, this book works on a few different levels. If you are relatively new to game development, you'll really benefit from the general discussions and ideas on development, design, tools, and more. I've also included coverage of a number of topics like how to get a job in the game industry, how to make money with shareware distribution, how to design different types of games, how to select development platforms, and so on—all which should be helpful for anyone trying to break into the game business.

If you are a game developer with lots of experience, you'll benefit from the hundreds of key contact information and addresses of leading game companies and multimedia publishers, venture capital and investment firms, trade organizations, tool development companies, and much more. In addition, you'll find chapters on legal issues, market research, console development, venture capital, and putting deals together with major publishers. I've included tons of Web sites and pointers, magazine listings, and bibliographies that will help both veteran and novice developers learn even more about the game industry.

How This Book Works

When I set out to write this book, I envisioned it as the first and most detailed book you might read on game development, not the last. I had many of the same questions typical of novices and veterans alike:

- How do I document my design ideas?
- Where can I learn about AI for my wargame product?
- How do I deal with a publisher?
- What should I be reading and studying?
- Where should I go to meet other game developers?
- How do I raise money for my game development company?
- What are the hottest selling games in the industry?
- Do shareware games really make money?
- How do leading game development companies like Electronic Arts develop games?
- How doI find better tools and resources to develop games?
- Where are the best places to go on the Internet and the World Wide Web to get game development ideas, tools, code examples, art samples, game engines, and other resources?
- How do I put a deal together with a major publisher?
- What is the best way to distribute games?

I found answers to questions like these by investigating hundreds of resources, including other developers, books and periodicals, and Web sites. While attempting to further my own education, I started collecting everything I could get my hands on. This book represents the best of everything I gathered, discovered, and developed. The bottom line is that there's a lot of relevant information out there; you just need to know where to get it. And hopefully I can take you there.

A World of Tradeoffs

At a recent conference, I enjoyed a great speech given by Noah Fahlstein, who worked at coin-op giant Williams Electronics (where he authored one of the best early coin-op arcade games, Sinistar), as well as LucasArts, and now at Dreamworks Interactive. His key philosophy on game development is this: "Creating games involves a continuous stream of decisions, or more succinctly, tradeoffs."

Whether it be over budgets, graphics, gameplay issues, storyline, artwork, and so on, a good developer is able to properly work through hundreds of tradeoffs that will come up during the process of constructing a game. This is really the most succinct description of game development that I have heard. The one thing I hope you get out of this book is the knowledge to help you better manage the tradeoffs effectively. You need to identify areas where tradeoff decisions have to be made, and purposefully learn about your options once you have identified those junctures.

There's No Single Path

Another axiom I believe strongly is that there is no one way to approach the field of game development. Sure you can identify some right and wrong ways to accomplish certain tasks, but finding a "one right way" isn't easily accomplished. So, in the end, there are a lot of different ways to attack designing and producing a game. Any book that presents a "my way is it" premise would be misleading at best.

My approach is to present many different options and show you how they apply to the thought processes needed for game construction. Thus, the book is meant to complement your own ideas and processes as much as possible, and not give you any cast-in-concrete method. I've included tips, outlines, and guidelines, but all of these ideas are presented as concepts for you to adapt to your own ways of doing things.

Understanding All the Options

Building on my previous axiom, the more you understand all the options, the better you will understand what's available to you at any decision point. But you need to know more than just what tools and techniques exist. You need to understand how to select different tools and techniques for different areas of the game development process—and that's exactly what this book is devoted to doing.

Even with hundreds of pages describing resources and ideas for game development, there is so much more I'd like to cover. Over time, I plan to expand and revise this book a few times. (So tell your friends to buy lots of copies!) As newer approaches and technology emerge, I'll plan to cover them. I'm also preparing a Web site to debut sometime in 1996 to help supplement the book and provide live links to many of the Web sites mentioned in the book.

What's Really Inside

Whether you use this book as a starting point or you pick it up while you are in the middle of a game development project, it should prove to be an invaluable resource. If you are counting on this book to solve all of your development problems, forget it. Think of this book as a road map; it's up to you to use it to help you get from one place to the next. Specifically, here are some of the ways this book will help you.

Contacts, Contacts, Contacts

For every company or product mentioned, I've provided full addresses and phone information—no product or resource is included without giving you the exact information you need to find out everything about it. You'll also learn how to use the Web to track down additional valuable resources. In addition, I've provided names of venture capitalists for the industry, key publishing contacts, and more. Special industry publications and reports that provide this kind of information usually cost hundreds of dollars. If you compiled this stuff on your own, it would take you hundreds of hours.

Advanced Topics: Dealing with Publishers and Financial Backers

I recruited one of the top game industry lawyers and business experts, Dean Gloster, who has dealt with numerous top publishers representing developers. He's written a few wonderful chapters on how to put publishing deals together and how to take your talents and create your own game development company.

Market Analysis and Resources

Some of the key questions that permeate the industry include:

- What is going on out there?
- Who buys what games?
- What's the state of the console industry?
- How can I find out how many copies of a particular type of game has sold?
- Where can I turn for marketing advice?

- What should I be reading to keep up on the industry?

After you read the business section of this book, you'll find the answers you've been searching for to questions like these.

Lots of Learning Aids

Another goal I had for this book was to provide hundreds of the best learning aids. Whether you're just starting to program games or you have lots of experience, you'll find resources of value. Whether you are developing for Windows, DOS, the Macintosh, consoles, or other platforms, you'll be able to use much of what is presented in the book. In addition, master CD-ROM developer Anthony Potts at The Coriolis Group has put together a CD-ROM full of shareware, demos, and source examples that would take hours and hours to download. Throughout this book I've listed and *described* almost every important book, magazine, organization, trade show, and Web site that I could possibly think of. Whatever game development experience you already have, this book will put in front of you a complete course-load of material that could help you immensely.

We Covered Everything the Other Books Don't

From day one of the development of this book I stuck to one mantra, "Cover everything the others don't." I learned a lot about programming games from some of the technical game development books that have been published. Many of them are very good, but the fact is that if game development were only about programming, companies would be entirely made up of only programmers and we all know that's not the case. Thus, this book covers hard-to-find information on artwork creation, sound tools, design ideas, marketing, shareware distribution, getting hired, and much more.

The Big Picture View of the Industry

I've been playing games since Pong, programming since my first 8-bit Atari (with tape drive!) and writing about the industry over the past few years. Drawing on my experience, I've tried to provide a look at the history and future of the industry as I see it throughout this book. You'll find an entire chapter about the history of games and game development. In many of the other chapters, I've tried to point out new trends and future trends. Hopefully, you'll find some unique ideas (and not only my own) about what's going on in the world of game development.

It's Business But Let's Have Fun

Games are meant to be fun. Whether you're playing them, writing them, creating artwork for them, writing scripts, or selling them to retailers, you should strive to

balance the business (and seriousness) of making money with the need to have fun. (If you are the type of person who gets the paycheck first and has fun next, you might want to reconsider being a game developer!) But make no mistake, this is also a serious business as I say, "It's first about fun, and second about the rent!" This book tries to show you both sides of the business—how interesting and exciting it is, how much promise it has, but also how serious and dedicated the people are who are involved.

Acknowledgments

This book has had a lot of friends. From the day it was conceived to the final weekend of writing and edits, many people including my publisher at The Coriolis Group, fellow developers in the game industry, as well as personal friends and family pitched in ideas and support. I couldn't have asked for a better group to help me see this idea through to completion.

Specifically I'd like to thank a number of people individually. By *not* thanking my publisher Keith Weiskamp, I've thanked him enough—instead I should announce that a shrine I'm building to him is almost complete—with daily prayer vigils beginning very soon. Nothing would have happened if it weren't for him.

I also should thank the members of my "Lobstah club," the folks who will be receiving a shipment of fresh soft-shell Maine lobsters from me this coming July. On that list is my copy editor and virtual partner Jenny Aloi, Dean Gloster, esquire extraordinary, who wrote three great chapters on key business and legal issues, and Karen Crowther who originally boosted this idea and helped with some of the writing in the design chapters.

I also will be sending some lobsters and fresh Maine beer to the entire Coriolis gang, Tony Stock, Tony Potts, Michelle Stroup, Chris Fadley, Shannon Bounds-Karl, Tom Mayer, Jeff Duntenman, and company—one couldn't imagine a better team housed under one roof.

I'd also like to thank Phil Steinmeyer, Kenny Tannebaum, Bob Alexander, Sally Plourde, Ken Lemieux, Diana Gruber, Marta Daglow, Darin Reed, and Scott Douglas, as well as Ian Firth, all of whom have helped me by contributing ideas, contacts, or actual writing for the book.

I can't forget my personal friends and family who were from day one confident that I could actually write a book of such magnitude as this, much less one paragraph. The list includes Gritty McDuff's of Portland Maine, Erica G. Sawyer, Alan Sawyer, Leon Schiffman, Dave B. Blanchard, Francis X. Brady, Adam Mattesich, Barbara Holt, and my mother, Paula Sawyer, who made every sacrifice conceivable to give me the brains and skills that made this book possible.

Ben Sawyer
February 1996

PART 1

Getting Started with Game Development

1

Game development is the Renaissance Art of the information age.

Game Development FAQs

What Is Game Development?

Game development is the combination of stories, art, music, sound effects, animation, and programming techniques to create a dynamic, interactive form of electronic entertainment. For those who pursue it, game development requires a lot of long nights, hard work, and never-ending passion. Once you get hooked, there's no turning back!

The game development field is so new and unique that very few books have been published on it. (That's why I've written this one.) And you certainly won't find any correspondence courses on game development advertised in the back of computer magazines. The best way to get started in game development is to just jump in and learn as you go.

What Kinds of Games Can You Create?

Just about anything you can dream up—adventure games, simulation games, role-playing games, sports games, shoot-em-up arcade games, flight simulators, card games, awesome 3D games, and even kids' games. The best part about the game field is that it is bursting at the seams with creativity. This is one area of technology where you can let your imagination go. If you come up with a new game form and it catches fire, you might be headed for early retirement.

But don't fool yourself. Creating a successful game is a lot of hard work. You'll need to develop a lot of skills—from programming, to sound effects design, to story writing—or you'll need to get really good at bringing highly-creative people together to create great games.

What Game Platforms Can You Develop Games For?

There are many, but we can arrange them into a few groups: computer games, video games, and multiplayer games. Let's take a closer look.

Computer Games

Computer games are basically games created to run on personal computers. This market is enormous, since there are more PCs out there than there are movie theaters or amusement parks. Obviously, the leader of the PC pack is the MS-DOS/Windows machine. Previously, several major PC platforms were aggressively supported by game

developers. The original platforms included the Atari 800/400/XL series, Commodore 64, and Apple II series. (You don't still have one of these machines hiding in your closet, do you?) Later on, these early platforms were replaced by the Atari ST, Commodore Amiga, Apple Macintosh, and the surging IBM PC. Today, aside from the Mac's relatively modest share of the PC market, the MS-DOS/Windows platform is the only major computer platform for which large numbers of games are developed.

Of course, within the IBM PC-clone world there are significant platform variations. These variations are caused by the fact that there has never been a "standard" PC; and with technology changing near the speed of light, there probably never will be one. PCs feature all kinds of different graphics cards, sound cards, video cards, and network cards. Developing software that can run on as many of these machines as possible is one heck of an undertaking.

To solve the compatibility problem, game developers identify a minimum platform standard for every game they make. Today, the platform that companies are developing for is a PC equipped with at least 8MB of RAM, CD-ROM drive, Soundblaster compatible sound card, Super-VGA graphics, and a 486-66Mhz CPU. Soon (probably by the time this book hits the shelves), the minimum hardware standard is likely to become an 8MB PC, with quad-speed CD-ROM drive, 16-bit sound card, Pentium 60Mhz or faster CPU, and a specialized 3D graphics acceleration card. Are you sure you still want to be a PC game developer?

What about the DOS versus Windows war? Battle lines are being drawn as I'm writing this book. With the emergence of Windows 95, Microsoft is pushing hard to get game developers to convert their blockbuster DOS games to Windows. Many game developers have taken the bait. It's likely that you'll see hundreds of amazing games, from 3D adventures to realistic simulations, available for Windows 95 sooner than you think. If you want to create successful games for the PC market and you only know DOS programming, you'd better get your hands on a good Windows programming book. Check out the book reference section in Part V for some suggestions.

One technology that promises to open the door wide for Windows games development is Microsoft's new Windows Games SDK. This programming library includes the DirectDraw DLL for performing fast animation, the DirectSound DLL for adding sound effects and music to Windows applications, and the DirectPlay DLL for creating fast-action, network-playable games.

Video Games

Video games are a little more complicated to develop than PC games because they require specialized hardware. But this market is huge (many times larger in sales of software than PCs!) and it's growing every day. There are already several major

competing platforms; and in the near future there will be more video game platforms than flavors of ice cream. Unless, of course, a big shakeout occurs.

Originally, the video game platforms of choice included the Atari 2600 with Intellivision, Colecovision, and a few small stragglers. (Anyone remember the Vectrex or Oddessy?) After the first shakeout, the platforms became the Nintendo Entertainment System and the Sega Master System. Later, the Sega Genesis and Super Nintendo dominated.

Today, however, it's a completely different story. As consoles move to 32-bit and even 64-bit levels, the customer base for these systems is exploding. Currently, there are five major platforms fighting it out to see who will dominate the market. These platforms include the Atari Jaguar, 3DO (and the new M2 version), Sony PSX Playstation, Sega Saturn, and the soon-to-be-announced Nintendo Ultra 64.

To develop games for any of these platforms, you'll need access to specialized hardware and software. Development is done by using what is called a *cross compiler* or *cross development system.* This is basically a C language compiler that lets you write code and create artwork on a PC or Mac, and then download them into a specially adapted version of the console hardware. Of course, most cross development systems are more than a language; and many programs include developer support, art creation tools, and music editors, which is why they are expensive. When you complete the game, you take the master out for duplication and distribution.

The trick in developing video games is learning about the hardware requirements, cross development systems, and developer programs from the different video game platforms. Then you have to actually qualify for development status by contacting the company (or an approved publisher) and getting approval to develop for it.

Video game development requires a much higher startup cost than PC-based development because of the hardware requirements involved, the licensing fees, and other associated costs you must pay to begin developing programs. From my research, which you will read later, the average cost to get a development setup going seems to be around $25,000. This investment will get you just a bare bones system and pay the required developer fees. In addition, you may have to qualify in other ways with the company for whose machine you want to produce software.

What's amazing is that the cost for 16-bit development used to be as much as four times more than it is now. Many companies have created lower-cost entrance fees and systems to encourage more development companies to create games for their platforms. So, while still expensive, video game development is getting cheaper every day.

Multiplayer Games

Multiplayer games are divided into three main sub-categories: peer-to-peer modem games, PC-network games, and client/server games.

Peer-to-peer modem games allow two people to play games over a modem. This is a great way to play a game with a friend who lives in your neighborhood or at least in the same local calling zone. (If you are playing a peer-to-peer game with someone long distance, you'd better watch your phone bill.) Peer-to-peer games have been around for a while, but they are just starting to become very popular. In the past, many players avoided these games because they didn't have high-speed modems, and these games were slow to play. Today, most people who purchase PCs for playing games are likely to buy fast modems. Some of the popular games that provide peer-to-peer connections include wargames like Empire Deluxe, action games like Doom II, and most flight simulators.

PC-network games allow multiple players to play against or with each other over a local area network, such as Windows 95 or Windows NT. The main benefit here is that you can play with others without tying up a phone line. The only problem is that most local area networks are installed in offices. This means that you run the risk of getting caught by your boss. If you design PC network games, try to look out for your fellow gamers and include a "boss" safety feature. Whenever the boss comes near anyone in the office who is playing the game across the network, the game will turn into an annual budget report or something equally boring.

Client/server games provide a machine that "serves" dynamic game information to client computers that log in. This is the wave of the future. If you haven't heard about it yet, you are either living in a cave or you were selected as an alternate juror for the O.J. Simpson trial. Many client/server type games are being set up on the Internet or World Wide Web. The advantage is that client computers can log in from all over the world, and they can save big bucks in phone charges. The big challenge with client/server games is coming up with techniques to quickly transfer information so that game players can get fast response. The new DirectPlay API, which is provided with Microsoft's new Game SDK for Windows, provides a complete feature-rich development tool for creating client/server games for Windows.

How Hot Is Game Development?

It's hotter than Death Valley in the summer. In 1994, the entire industry pulled in over $6 billion worldwide! In 1995, sales are projected to exceed $8 billion. In 1994, the game company Acclaim grossed $50 million in a single day on Mortal Kombat II, a feat it announced in full page ads in the *Daily Variety.* (The message sent to movie executives was "the game industry is huge!") The 1995 computer games developer conference—an annual event attended by leading game developers—attracted over 2,500 people, twice the number of developers who attended the year before. This conference is expected to attract over 4,500 dedicated game developers in 1996. In the U.S. alone, estimates indicate that over 50,000 people are employed in some aspect of the game development industry.

One of the best ways to gauge how hot the game development field has become is to consider the number of people who have grown up playing computer games. Currently, that number in the U.S. alone is projected to be 15 million. By the year 2010 this number should exceed 100 million. Now that's a heck of a lot of households—all waiting to play your latest game. (Keep in mind that movies have been around for over 60 years and computer games have only been around in earnest for 15!)

Recently, many of the major media conglomerates have started to spend large sums of money to establish interactive divisions. These guys don't exactly do it right all the time, but the fact that they are actively building up large development teams shows they smell money to be made on a rapidly expanding market. With online services and interactive networks expanding like crazy, there are opportunities out there for game developers that have never existed before. One might say that this is the best time to enter the game development field in a big way. But you'd better move fast because the competition is really heating up.

What Does It Take to Be a Game Developer?

There is no other profession on the planet quite like that of a game developer. Being a game developer takes a certain edge. Creating a game requires a lot of work and many types of skills. Even if you are working with a team and are only responsible for one part of the game, creating a game requires a lot of thinking, artistry, creativity, and discipline. And if you don't like working long hours with little sleep, you should consider another occupation.

Can You Do It Alone?

Originally, games were mainly developed by very small teams such as FreeFall Associates (John Freeman and Anne Westfall with Paul Reiche III, who wrote Archon among other notable games) or Ozark Softscape, which developed the big hit Seven Cities of Gold. Many popular games were even created by "lone-wolf" developers like Bill Budge (Pinball Construction Set) and Chris Crawford (Eastern Front 1941 and Balance of Power). Today, many games feature a design created by one person, but the underlying work is performed by an entire team. The creative lone-wolf developer is becoming an endangered species (although you can still find them on exhibit at specialized industry trade shows such as The Computer Game Developers Conference). The days of one person having the time, talent, and cash to create a state-of-the-art product are almost gone. Games require too much professional quality artwork, music, and programming techniques for one person to handle. That means teamwork skills and organization and management skills are very, very important in this business.

What Programming Experience Do You Need?

You'll need lots of experience or lots of time to learn. Game programming will challenge you significantly. Today's computer games are developed using cutting-edge programming techniques. Not only do you need to know the basics of writing programs, you'll need to know how to write highly optimized code, tricky graphics and animation, hardware interface code (mouse, joystick, keyboard, and so on), game play algorithms, and much more.

Think about it. What other software product requires state-of-the-art full-motion video, fast-action animation, high-quality music, way-cool sound effects, and artificial intelligence? Because of these requirements, game programming can even be a handful for highly trained programmers. Becoming a great game programmer is a life-long pursuit. Just when you think you know everything about a certain area of game development, such as 3D rendering, someone is bound to come along and show you up. If you adopt an attitude early on that you can always learn more and improve your skills, your chances of becoming really good at programming games will increase by 200 percent.

To get started with game programming, you'll want to learn a programming language like C or Visual Basic. (I'll have more to say about programming languages shortly.) Another set of skills that will become very important is a good working knowledge of the hardware platform for which you are planning to develop games. Unlike developing other types of computer programs, such as recipe managers or sales trackers, you can't just stand back and write high-level code using the latest whiz-bang auto code generator. Game programming demands that you unscrew the cover of your computer and get under the hood. Eventually, you'll want to add features to your games that can only be programmed by performing hardware tricks and working with a low-level language like assembly.

But before you get overwhelmed by all of the things you need to learn, keep in mind that with the new tools becoming available and the plethora of other developers who are out there willing to give you a hand and share their experiences, it gets a little easier to master the hard stuff every day.

What Programming Language Should You Use?

C? C++? Pascal? Assembly? Visual Basic? Delphi? Actually, any of these will work. Just stay away from languages like COBOL. Unless of course you are planning to write a game called *Revenge of the MIS Dweebs.*

Some highly-accomplished game programmers will tell you that there is only one language for game development—assembly language. Other programmers will tell you that you must program in C/C++ because it is the language that all of the other game programmers use. This is like telling someone that they should drive a Ford Escort because everyone else drives an Escort. And if you break down on the highway some day, another Escort driver will stop, pull some spare parts out of his or her trunk, and fix your car for you. Sure thing!

C/C++ is a powerful language because of its speed, portability, and flexibility. There are also a wide variety of C/C++ tools, libraries, and sample source code available for you to use when writing applications. But if you have a passion for using another programming environment, such as Delphi or Visual Basic, follow your instinct. As PC game development is moving from DOS to Windows, many developers are looking for alternatives for writing applications because of the complexities and inefficiencies of C/C++. Development environments like Delphi and Visual Basic are rapid Windows-based development tools. These products not only give you programming languages that are widely supported in the software industry, but they also provide powerful development tools to help you program Windows applications using the latest object-oriented and visual programming techniques.

The question of what language to use is often asked by both new programmers and experienced programmers moving into game development, and I'll address it more in depth later in this book. For now, Table 1.1 provides a summary of the pros and cons of some of the more popular languages.

Table 1.1 Pros and Cons of Different Programming Languages for Game Development

Language	Pro	Con
Assembly	The fastest language you can use.	The most difficult language to use, very hard to master, not very portable.
C	Fast, portable, must be used for consoles.	More difficult to learn; takes time to debug and program.
C++	Highly portable and reusable code. Future of C language, quite fast.	Slightly more difficult to program than C.
Delphi (Pascal)	Fast (though not as fast as C or Assembly) and somewhat easier to learn than C.	Not portable to other platforms. Windows Only.
Visual Basic	Easy to learn. Easy to develop interfaces.	Not portable to other platforms. Windows only. Interpreted code can be slow.

C/C++ is the major language to use; it's fast and it's portable. Delphi and VB, only available for MS-DOS/IBM clone machines, are interesting alternatives that have specific advantages and drawbacks compared to C/C++, especially relating to speed and portability. So, in short, C/C++ is the language of choice. VB and Delphi are alternatives that you may decide are advantageous to the type of game you want to develop, and also work well as back office development tools for creating components like level editors.

What About Programming Libraries, Engines, and Other Development Tools?

As game programming and hardware becomes more complex and consumers become more demanding (especially for new products), more and more developers are turning to off-the-shelf tools, libraries, and engines to speed up the development process.

Libraries are available like FastGraph from Ted Gruber Software, which handles graphical functions, or DiamondWare's Sound Tool Kit, which handles MIDI and sound file playback.

Engines are complete skeletons for creating various types of games. Some examples include Lary Myers' ACK-3D kit, which helps developers easily create 3D raycasting style games, or Lucas Arts' SCUMM system, which developers use to create graphical adventures like Sam and Maxx.

While some of the bigger development companies can afford to build and maintain their own engines, you can purchase others relatively cheaply. This book contains lots of descriptions of various game engines available for purchase and licensing. You'll even find a number of shareware engines included on the companion CD-ROM.

For video game development, you'll need to contact the various manufacturers of the consoles to see how you can become an authorized developer. You'll need to acquire a developer's kit that includes software and tools to create the necessary code for those specific machines.

What Is the Best Way to Develop Game Programming Skills?

You need a good, fundamental understanding of programming. But this isn't as difficult as you might think because people are figuring out new ways to make game programming easier. Later in this book, for example, you'll find a good skills checklist

to help you become a skilled game programmer. In addition, spend some time pouring over the resource sections and the sidebars to see the products and processes major developers are using to create their leading games.

After that, the best way to master game programming is to practice, practice, practice. But start simple. One of the best ways to learn is to create copies of other games (like Lode Runner or Pac-Man). Then, taking what you learn from that exercise, you'll be ready to move on and create something more original and complex.

What Are Some of the Major Programming Trends in Game Development?

Many types of technologies from multimedia to 3D animation to realtime video are all converging in the game development industry but there are a few significant trends that really stand out.

3D, 3D, and 3D Noted graphics programming expert, Michael Abrash, said it best at a talk at the CGDC (The Computer Games Developers Conference): "Someday computers will be really, really fast." That day is upon us now. Today's top of the line PCs and the new 32-bit consoles allow developers to create awesome 3D-looking graphics, including both point-of-view and third person products. The entire industry is working to bring out the ultimate in 3D games. Products like Sega's Virtua Fighter, or Crystal Dynamics' 3D Baseball, or Origin's Bioforge and Looking Glass's Flight Unlimited show us a glimpse of what possibilities are in store for 3D technology. For an even more eye-opening look at the future, check out technologies like Motion Capture, which allow users to create animated skeletons and wrap digital actors onto them to create lifelike human movement.

Virtual Reality Hardware is finally getting cheap enough to allow developers to combine lifelike 3D and video to create virtual reality (VR) environments for consumer-oriented games. Only just a few years ago, VR could be experienced only by visiting expensive high-tech gaming centers that employ costly computer systems and specialty hardware. Today, you can purchase relatively low-cost hardware and peripherals, such as VR helmets and glasses, to turn your home PC into a VR powerhouse. Game companies like Seattle Startup Zombie are constructing innovative PC-based VR games like Locus, which take full advantage of new VR hardware that is hitting the market.

Really Good Artificial Intelligence In the early 80s, computer scientists around the world predicted that we would all soon have computers on our desks that could think and reason like humans. A few years later, many of these "technology experts" were run out of town and the AI industry came apart at the seams. Fortunately, AI researchers developed a number of useful technologies that have been perfected over the years to make them suitable for the game industry. Today, game development companies like Bullfrog (Magic Carpet, Populous) are leading a major trend by incorporating artificial intelligence into their games such as Dungeon Keeper and Syndicate II.

Specialized Game Play Hardware Developing a computer game in the past simply meant that you would need to support the basic input and output devices including the mouse, joystick, keyboard, speakers, and so on. But unlike other forms of software development, game technology always tries to push the limits of the available hardware. New gadgets that game players can plug into their home computers are appearing at an accelerated pace. The bottom line is that the games you develop in the near future will need to support everything from specialized 3D accelerator cards to VR devices to custom input devices that are still on the drawing board. Whether it's more memory, faster processors, or new graphics acceleration chips, game software is never far behind in pushing the available hardware to the max.

Internet and the World Wide Web Meet Interactive Games The big headline in today's technology news is the Internet and the World Wide Web. The Internet is growing faster than any other computer technology invented to date. As the Internct and the Web are becoming more mature, many leading game development companies are looking for ways to tie their interactive products into this dynamic communication system. The Web provides full support for multimedia components including sound, video, music, animation, and hypertext, making it possible for developers to create highly interactive games that can be played across the Web. Newer 3D technologies like VRML will allow Web-based games to provide VR- and 3D-like worlds where game players can move about and interact with each other. If you haven't experienced the Web yet, you should get an Interact account as soon as you can and start surfing.

What Design Experience Do You Need?

Well, design is the essential artistic ingredient for game development. Despite all the new hardware and software now available, design is still very much an art form. As many artists will tell you, getting better means practice, practice, practice. Writing your own games, stories, and so on will help you to become a better designer. Here are some other tips to help you gain design experience:

- Attend the major game developer conferences. The list and explanations of the major conferences available are presented in Part V.

- Read as much as you can about game design. (You'll find a list of helpful magazines in the reference section of this book.)
- Try modifying a game that has an editor. Games like Klik n Play, Empire, Doom, Heretic, and Abuse allow you to modify them to create whole new experiences. This is a good way to help you to learn to create interesting environments with puzzles and challenges. Without having to do any programming, you can learn some of the thought process game designers need to have.
- Check out the ideas in this book. This book devotes over 100 pages to discussing creating interactive designs and challenging puzzles for players to enjoy and experience.
- Finally, develop the proper mindset.

Understand that games design is different from every other form of design. Games are *interactive*, making them very different from passive forms of art like movies and music. Not only do you have to give your players a good experience or an interesting world to interact with, but you need to make sure your players receive interesting reactions to whatever actions they take. This means you need to anticipate a player's every move as you are designing your game. Game worlds also need to be as realistic as possible—players demand to go anywhere and try anything, and they want to do it any time. This is essentially a non-linear process. At the same time players want a story that, no matter how you tell it, is a linear process. Combining the need for realism and linearity effectively is one of the biggest dilemmas many game designers must face.

Designing games is like no other form of design. Understanding this principle is your first step to becoming a good game designer.

Can You Make a Game?

Sure—why not?

Even though many companies spend a lot of time and money creating games that everyone in the world loves to play, it is still possible for you to learn, design, and write a game people will play. And perhaps people will even give you some money for it. You might not create the next MYST the first time out of the gate, but not all enjoyable games are as complex as MYST. For example, one of MVP software's best selling products is the collection of EGA poker games created over three years ago by game developer Diana Gruber. Remember, not all money-making games are huge hits that the game-playing public remembers for years to come.

We've talked about big budgets and big programming teams, but writing a good game is still easier for anyone to do than, say, making a good movie. So while the big shots push the industry forward, you can still find a niche in the game business easier than you can in other industries. If you get good enough, getting a job with one of your favorite game development companies could also be a good career move since most developers working at these companies earn a comfortable living.

Whatever you do, don't let the lure of fame and riches cloud your judgment. Many of today's successful game developers had been working at their craft for years before their big hit came along. Don't be surprised if your early attempts are failures that end up in the remainder bins. But don't get discouraged by these failures—treat each one as an important step in the learning process. If your ideas are good and you cultivate your game programming and design talents, you'll eventually meet with success.

Can Game Development Be a Hobby?

As I was learning about game development, one of the first things I did was take everything I had discovered on my own or from working with other game developers and turn it into a Game Developer's FAQ. I figured that many people had the same basic questions I had when I started to develop my first game: "Where do I start?" "How do I design my game?" "How do I sell my creations?" and so on. After I published my FAQ, I received a lot of email from other developers who were trying to create games (or interactive multimedia) as a hobby. Some of these developers were mixing in some shareware publishing to make some money, mostly to fund more hardware and software purchases, but hey! that's part of the fun, isn't it?

So yes, game development makes a great hobby. I also think in the future, with engines, tools, and books on game development becoming commonplace, that more artists, writers, and just plain creative people will start to produce more games for people to play simply because they enjoy doing it. If you already have a job you enjoy and simply find game development fun, by all means keep having fun! For a growing number of people, constructing cool software is like building a neat model airplane; it's just a craft that takes a lot of skill but provides even more enjoyment in return.

Can You Sell Your Games?

Well, now things get complicated….

Selling a game means committing to a level of sophistication in design, programming, artistry, and business. Remember, above all, *this is a business.* Creating games may be a dream business—but it is a business. Lots of money rides on the line for hits, and the pressure of a Christmas deadline can be overwhelming. I don't want to scare you, but if you want to make money with your games, you need to prepare yourself for the realities of the business world as you transition from creating games for fun to creating games for profit.

There are many ways to sell a game. Let's take a look at some of the more "tried-and-true" methods.

Selling Games in Retail Channels

Selling your games in retail involves creating packaging and sales and promotional materials. It also means you need a well-conceived strategy for getting your software on the shelf in major retail outlets. This involves the traditional process of selling software and gives your product the widest exposure. Of course, shelf space is at a premium; so getting your product on the shelf means having an awesome product as well as finding a publisher who is capable of getting your product out to retailers. *No small task.* You could also elect to publish your game yourself, but be prepared for the tough road that lies ahead. Most game developers I know find it literally impossible to get adequate distribution for products they self-publish.

Computer games originally were sold through various independent computer stores around the country as well as through mail order. Today, though, the computer game and video game retail market is very different. Large chains (both computer oriented and not so computer oriented) are now the dominant sellers of software. While ten years ago the key software outlets were places like "Earl's Software Shack," today's outlets are places like WAL-MART, Toy's 'Я' Us, and Software, Etc.

So the retail market has become very mass market and very demanding and very expensive. Don't expect to see a self-published game on the retail shelve unless you hook up with an experienced publisher, and that means it better be good. However, this isn't the only way to earn money from your work; there are alternatives.

Selling Games in Shareware Channels

Shareware is a software marketing concept that works like this: You give away a portion of your game (say levels 1-8 of a 32 level game) and if the player gets hooked on it, he or she can order the upgrade version, getting access to all the levels and features in return. (I've heard software marketing people refer to this concept as heroin-ware—an appropriate description since the goal is to get the player hooked on your product so that you can keep selling him or her more.) Several major titles have been marketed by the shareware method. A few of the more recent success stories include Id Software's Doom and Interplay's Descent. You can also find several major software publishers, such as MVP, Apogee, and Epic Megagames, who exclusively sell using the shareware method.

The advantage of the shareware method is that you can go after a niche market much easier. Your marketing costs are extremely low; and your margins, because you are selling directly to the consumer, are high.

Of course, there are many more issues to discuss about shareware's benefits and limitations, which we'll cover in much more depth later in this book. At this stage, I've tried to simplify how shareware works to introduce this important concept, but as you'll see, executing the shareware method, in conjunction with the LCR concept described next, is a sophisticated process.

Selling Games in Low Cost Retail

Low cost retail (LCR) is sort of a mix between shareware and full retail. This approach involves various companies that package and sell, by retail or mail order, the shareware version, or a variation of it, at retail at a very low cost. So if you have a game, an LCR company might sell the shareware version at retail for, say, $5.95. Or they may sell a special version of the full game for $24.95.

While it was long considered a small business, LCR is now known as a major component of the software and especially game business. This business may at first sound enticing, but be careful because LCR publishing is fraught with fly-by-night publishers, who can rob you blind if you don't watch out. By protecting your rights to resell even the shareware copy of your game, you can control the flow of your shareware as sold with the LCR method. Licensing of your shareware software to LCR vendors can be a nice source of income. As more and more people get computers, their appetite for lower cost software should increase, making LCR software even bigger than it is today.

Other Opportunities

You can also make big money with your games even if they never appear in a retail outlet or are sold as shareware. One company I've worked with is doing some major development for sponsored games. Several advertising agencies are looking for games, sponsored by their clients, to be developed and given away. Although the games are not sold, they still need to be first rate and as enjoyable to play as other commercial games. The company sponsoring the games will usually pay handsomely to ensure that the game becomes a big hit. Imagine K2, a major Ski marketer, giving away a downhill racing game at Ski Shops. Or, how about Descent brought to you by Chrysler? Don't laugh, these types of games and deals are being created as I write.

The "sponsored" game development business model is very much in its infancy. I suspect it will become a growing trend and could develop over the next five to ten years as a major source of revenue, especially for smaller shops looking for their first break. Even major software companies like Microsoft are commissioning small development groups to create games to promote their new operating systems (Windows 95). After all, Bill Gates would rather open his wallet and fund a few outside developers than allow his internal programmers and engineers to develop and play with games all day!

Developers are getting as sophisticated at selling their products as they are at developing them. I'll be discussing more about how you can sell your games, from a full retail blitz to shareware and licensing, throughout the later sections of this book.

Do Games Make Money?

Let's just say $8 billion isn't chicken feed.

Sure games make money; but just like movies and books, not *every* game makes money. People are spending a lot of money these days on computer games; but as they do, more companies are trying to make games, so competition is fierce, to say the least.

However, there is no denying that there is money to be made with stuff you create. How much depends on the quality and timeliness of your game, your marketing, promotional, and distribution strategy, and a number of other intangibles that only economic theorists and fortune tellers know.

How Can You Get a Job Creating Games?

Getting a job in the industry requires strong creative skills, a good ability to communicate, and (if you're looking for a programming or any creative job) a portfolio or demo of your work. Several headhunting firms have sprung up, and the CGDC (Computer Game Developers Conference) sponsors a very active job fair each year. In addition, through avenues like Compuserve's game developers forum (GAMDEV) and user groups and postings on the Internet and World Wide Web, you can find help wanted ads from some of the world's greatest development houses. In Part VII, you'll find a complete discussion about how to get a job in the industry or find a publisher for your games.

Making game development a full time occupation is as difficult as any job hunt. It takes desire, skill, effort, and luck. The industry is definitely growing; and if you have the talent, you can land a job. Just make sure you go about it in a deliberate, organized, professional manner, or you're going to find more roadblocks than open doors.

In short, don't quit your day job yet, but yes, there are plenty of opportunities.

Do You Have What It Takes to Create the Next Blockbuster Game?

Whoa! Slow down for a second. Let's try walking before we compile. Take a look at the screenshot shown in Figure 1.1.

Guess who created this game? The Beaver Brothers? Nope. Microsoft? Nope. Try Id Software, which created the megahit Doom. Big difference, huh? Do you think that when the guys at Id created their first game, they were thinking about all of the fame and money they were going to make from Doom? Of course not. Id built their skills and market sense over time.

Figure 1.1 Id Software's Commander Keen.

Very few programmers are able to create a big hit on their first or second attempt. It takes time to build the skills required. So start simple (at the bottom), write a game you are capable of doing, and work your way up to the top. Always try to finish what you start. Finishing a game is important because it can impress companies looking to fund future projects or hire developers. After you write one game, take a short break, then write your next game. Each time you'll know a little more than you did before.

How Much Time Does It Take to Develop Game Development Skills?

If you're a pro already, you're well aware of the time it took you to build the skills you already have. A lot of people, mostly outside of the business (and even a few in this business) think anyone can create a game. The fact is, though, whether you're the designer, artist, producer, programmer, or any combination of those roles, it takes a lot of time to build the necessary skills to make a game. If you take your time and put in the effort to listen and learn from others (for example, books, magazines, example code, art, music, and design), you will in time start to make enjoyable games.

How Long Does It Take to Make a Complete Game?

Like I said, it can take a while. Obviously, the actual amount of development time required depends on the type of game you plan to create. Developing a card game may take time, but not nearly as much time as a complete adventure game or a 3D multiplayer game. Much of the work (and time) involved in creating a game is spent testing and polishing the game and working on the artwork. The complexity of the programming and the amount of artwork are the two biggest factors that determine how much time must be set aside.

At an established game company, a development team may take three to four months to flesh out an entire idea before programming even begins. Then, they set up a timeline to write the code and create the artwork and music for the product. When the product is complete, it goes into a testing period. The first testing phase is called *Alpha*, where design changes and other more substantive problems are addressed. At the next stage, called *Beta*, only bugs and minor design flaws are fixed.

Testing is usually performed over a period of 8-12 weeks, depending on the complexity of the game. In some cases, the testing period can take quite a bit longer. When the testing is done, the product goes Gold, which signifies it is ready for duplication. Taken altogether, games may take from 12 to 24 months to complete.

What Kinds of Resources Do You Need?

Time and money. If you don't have much money, you'll need a heck of a lot of time. Creating a game takes time because programming computers is such an inexact science. Games are also incredible time sinks because they require a lot of creative thinking. If you try to rush the creative process, and you don't allow enough time for experimentation and feedback from your potential customers, you're likely to end up with a game that will be sold only in the discount bins. Even with big teams, most game development companies spend one to two years making a game, spending as much as four to six months just designing the game before even a single piece of code or artwork is started. If the game is really complex, they might still be working on it when the company files for Chapter 11.

A large budget is ideal if you can swing it. Wing Commander III took $3 million to develop. Many companies try to budget $1 million as a ballpark figure for the cost of developing a typical game. As consumers require more live video, art, music, and realism from their games, budgets will surely go up.

If you don't have a large budget, don't panic. There are many ways that you can cut corners and still create great games. Throughout this book, we'll provide you with tools, techniques, and common sense advice gathered from many leading game development experts to help you create games on a limited budget. Even if you are working by yourself, there are proven techniques that you can put to work to help you build really cool games.

So, What Exactly Do You Need to Make a Game?

You mean aside from this book?

Understand that many companies use very high-end software and hardware and have dozens of tools available for their development teams. That doesn't mean these are requirements. Even among some of the most successful companies there are still many low end tools, like Deluxe Paint, used to create games. Whether it costs $20,000 or $20, here are the basic products you need to develop games.

Hardware

You obviously need some sort of computer. It may seem obvious to you that the faster the better, since compiling code and creating artwork (especially 3D rendered images) is time-consuming. What is not so obvious is the fact that for video games you might not use a IBM PC but instead use a Mac, or if you can afford it, a workstation.

Many of the more well-funded game companies use Silicon Graphic workstations, as well as Macs and PCs, to do development. These systems are very high-end and out of the reach for most lone-wolf developers. Still, that doesn't mean you can't create awesome games without state-of-the-art hardware. The decision of what hardware you use comes down to the system or consoles you want to develop for and what sort of capital you have available.

For the software side of the equation you need several things...

Selecting a Programming Language

The majority of games are written in C/C++. If you want to follow the industry standard, you'll need a version (several exist) of a C/C++ compiler.

There are other language options, though, especially for the MS-DOS/Windows environment. Development environments like Delphi from Borland and Visual Basic from Microsoft are rapid Windows-based development tools. And while they offer an ease of use factor over C/C++, there are several major trade-offs you should consider.

The question of what language to use is often asked, and I'll address it more in depth later. The thing you should most understand is that the consumer doesn't care what

language you used. They don't know C++ from Basic; what they do know is whether a game is good or not. Thus, while to us the language selected is important, you should learn to select the language that allows you to build the product you want—and the product that your users will like. You don't select the language first and then the game; you select the game first, then the language. If you can create the final product perfectly using a higher-level development tool like Director, in place of a lower-level language like C++, by all means use Director. Many people in the game development community use C/C++ for good reason. It's fast, it's portable and most of the games require it. On the other hand, don't be fooled by the language zealots; there are many alternatives, that when applied in the right situation work extremely well. Knowing when and where to use a certain development language is important, knowing only one language to use is short-sighted.

Do You Need Programming Libraries, Engines, and Development Tools?

The short answer is yes. Why? Because you shouldn't spend your precious time and money reinventing the wheel. Your goal is to make a finished game, so why get bogged down in the trial and error of low-level sound or graphics programming? A productive game programmer is a person who quickly learns how to meld the right libraries and fundamental engines into a final product. Using tools and engines properly means faster development, lower costs, and (potentially) an easier job making games.

While some of the bigger development companies can afford to build and maintain their own engines, you can purchase third-party engines relatively cheaply. This book actually contains lots of descriptions of various game engines available for purchase and licensing.

For video game development, you'll need to contact the various manufacturers or approved software publishers to get information on their consoles and discuss how you can become an authorized developer. You'll also need to acquire a developer's kit, which includes software and tools to create the necessary code for those specific platforms.

Which Artwork Creation Products Do You Need?

Several major art packages for creating 2D and 3D artwork exist. You will need at least a 2D editor. If you want to have a 3D game, you will need a 3D rendering package such as 3D Studio.

There are also image processing products like DeBabelizer and Adobe Photoshop that can be extremely useful. You will need some sort of conversion program, since not all artwork programs output the type of format you may need for your games.

Optional artwork creation tools may include a scanner and a digital camera to acquire graphics from the real world or from art created by the more traditional art forms (for example, sculpture or pen and paper). You might also consider texture makers and libraries for 3D graphical programs.

On the high-end, using workstations like the Silicon Graphics Indigo and such super-software as Alias, Wavefront, or SoftImage, is now the main way large game companies produce artwork for their products. These packages not only render astounding 3D images but have amazing animating features, especially for live action figures from humans to horses.

If you have deep pockets, you can purchase full digital production of real time live actors shot mostly on Blue Screens, then merged with computer created backgrounds.

We will discuss a number of art creation techniques and products, from art creation on a budget to full digital production, in Part IV of this book.

Sound Digitizer Hardware and Software

Many game programmers are not sound engineers; they tend to use canned sounds from sound libraries and such. If you can't find ones you like, you're going to have to record your own. To do this, you'll need to acquire a good digitizing card (which is usually built into your sound card). If you also plan to digitize sounds live, you'll need a really good microphone.

For software, you need a program to record sound as well as one that will allow you to edit and transform the sounds. Good digitizations are rarely used straight up. Some form of editing and remixing will be needed.

Music Editor/Sequencer

Even if you expect to work just with a file, you may need to have some form of music editor available to you to make changes to the file at program time, depending on issues like instruments or re-orchestrating for a different sound card.

If you are going to create music in-house for your game, you will need a complete MIDI setup including midi card, sequencing software, and a keyboard that is MIDI compatible.

How Big of an Army Do You Need?

Hey, if you're a beginner you're starting to catch on. While the lone-wolf developer used to be prevalent on the plains of development, he or she is becoming a dying breed. Most of today's sophisticated multimedia styled apps require multiple developers along with artists, musicians, and producers to manage the entire task.

That's not to say there isn't still room for a lone wolf or two out there—many games might not require a huge development team. For example, the huge hit Tetris doesn't require the same team approach used to create a game like Origin's Wing Commander III.

How Can You Learn to Be a Game Developer?

Until educators create a major in game development (don't laugh; there are plans—besides what other $8 billion dollar industry doesn't have an associated college major?) much of the learning involved takes place in the school of *Trial & Error.*

Game development takes incredible patience and persistence. Until recently much of the information about programming games was passed around like folklore, from developers just talking to other developers.

Are More Resources Becoming Available to Help You Learn Game Development?

Yes! As more people have taken up game development either for fun or profit, an industry has sprouted up to support them and help them learn more. The Coriolis Group, the publisher of this book, has already published five books on game development and more are on the way. Many other publishers are getting in on the act and publishing books, magazines, and software tools to help game developers master their craft.

Microsoft has created a game developer's SDK; so has IBM. Several Internet sites devoted to game development have emerged. Many of the major online networks have sections devoted to it, and there are several magazines such as *Visual Developer* and *Game Developer*, which regularly feature articles on game development.

This book was started in part to collect a listing of all the information out there to help game developers and provide as many resources as possible in one place. You could say that there is now enough material on game development available that this book is a result of that.

So, What Does This Book Offer?

Quite simply, this book offers everything to help you master every key aspect of game development. I have put together a single source that covers as much about the entire process of creating and selling computer games as humanly possible in book format. This book attempts to do the teaching and provide the resources and reference information every game developer needs to learn how to get involved in this incredible industry.

In addition, I've included a CD-ROM full of all kinds of goodies you can use to create games. You'll find demos of high-end graphics libraries like Argonaut's BRender, a database of industry contacts, and hours worth of resource material.

What Should You Do Next?

Read, experiment, design, develop, play, and most important of all, have fun. In the end, having fun is what games are all about.

Good Luck!

CHAPTER 2

The colorful history of a colorful industry.

The History of Computer Games

From Humble Beginnings

In the beginning giant machines roamed the earth and only a few lucky souls got a chance to play with software as exotic as games on them. In secret government labs, large corporations, and large universities, the first computer games were created, tested, and re-engineered. The only thing anyone knew about these software creations was that some programmers were spending a lot of late nights doing something other than work.

In the early 1970s a man named Nolan Bushnell was the first to really show the world what a computer game was. Nolan started a company called Syzygy in 1972 to sell a game called Computer Space, which was originally known as SpaceWar. (The game was created on some of the first computers at MIT.) Bushnell assumed these new electronic games would be great for bars and pizza joints as a substitute for pinball machines. Initially, SpaceWar failed. It was considered too different from conventional pinball and other sorts of machines. In 1972, Nolan was just a little bit ahead of his time.

Always the entrepreneur, Bushnell started over and came back with Pong. Players used primitive paddles to bat a small electronic ball back and forth. The game was an instant hit. Even the machines the software ran on broke down from overuse! Bushnell followed up with a more complex game called Tank Command. Millions of quarters started disappearing from peoples' pockets, and Bushnell renamed his company Atari.

Atari, which is the name of a move in the ancient game of Go, certainly went— straight to the top. The corporate logo as shown in Figure 2.1 was the Japanese character for Mount Fuji. Seemingly from the start, the sky was indeed the limit for Atari. Nolan Bushnell, although not a genius, had the luck, vision, and timing to set the seeds in place for a multibillion dollar industry that we call *interactive entertainment* today. Certainly computer gaming was destined to happen; Nolan just made sure it happened with him at the center of the universe.

The Rise and Fall of Atari

Atari started hiring fast and furiously, adding employees weekly. Among some of Atari's hires over its years were such computer and game industry stars as Steve Jobs, Alan Kay, and Chris Crawford.

Figure 2.1 Atari's Japanese-style corporate logo using the character representing Mount Fuji, Japan's largest peak.

In 1976 Bushnell sold controlling interest in Atari to Warner Communications—parent of Warner Brothers Studios. The price was $26 million, with Bushnell personally making $15 million on the deal. With Warner now in the driver's seat, Atari's products started to move into the homes of America. Atari achieved this by developing specialized hardware units that could plug into people's TV sets. These units featured Atari's hit games like Pong and they sold well. The only problem with them was that they were hardwired to play only one game. Later in 1977, Atari removed this limitation and hit the jackpot by unleashing a cartridge system that offered new games with every new cartridge. This new system was called the Atari VCS 2600.

Designing for the 2600 wasn't exactly easy. The machine had 2K (yes, 2K) of ROM for program code and 128 bytes of RAM (yes 128 *bytes!*) to hold all the variables. Still, designers were able to create some amazing products with it. Who remembers Yar's Revenge or Pitfall or Adventure? The designs were ingeniously simple. Without fancy graphics and sound, it was the game above all that mattered.

Needless to say, Atari went ballistic. In 1976 it had revenues of $36 million, but by 1980 it was doing over a billion dollars a year (close to $2.2 billion in 1995 dollars). However, trouble *was* on the horizon. Bushnell was no longer in charge, since Warner, being the corporate parent it was, had brought in a new CEO. Bushnell had been forced out in 1978. The man at the helm in 1982 was Ray Kassar. He had previously worked as a top executive at Burlington Mills—the textile manufacturer—a far cry from Sunnyvale, California, and the high-tech creations of Silicon Valley.

While Atari had built a small empire making products for people's homes, the Japanese had quickly moved into the arcade industry. Soon, companies like Nintendo (with Donkey Kong) and Namco (with Pac-Man) dominated the arcades. Pac-Man become a phenomenon transcending all others. In one year Pac-Man did one billion dollars in business. Pac-Man became a symbol for the entire video game movement. Licensing of this facsimile put the character everywhere, even in a Saturday morning cartoon (perhaps one of the worst cartoons of all time too!).

Certainly, the world took notice of all the money being made, and many business experts predicted that video games would soon be everywhere—laundromats, movie theaters, restaurants, you name it. Still, video games were considered just toys for kids or geeky adults—something that seemed, well, not very enlightening or mature to most people.

Still, the growth rate was phenomenal and Atari was at the center of most of it. Soon other companies joined in trying to grab as much of the money as possible. Giant toy companies like Mattel with its Intellivision, and Coleco Toys with Colecovision, started fighting it out.

Figures 2.2 through 2.4 show the original major video game consoles including the Atari 2600, the Mattel Intellivision, and the Colevision. Who thought that all three systems would lead a revolution in how Americans spent their free time and money?

Figure 2.2 The Atari 2600 game console.

Figure 2.3 The ColecoVision game console.

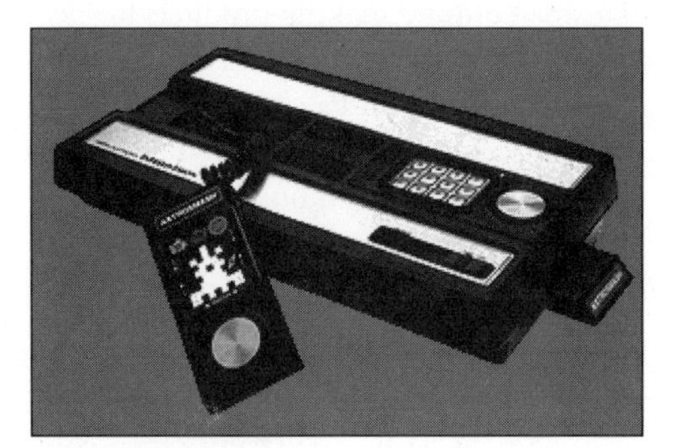

Figure 2.4 The Intellivision game console.

The biggest competition for Atari was from Intellivision. Mattel Toys, makers of Barbie and Hot Wheels, had originally wanted only to do software. They had tried to get other hardware companies to develop a competing machine, for which they would sell the software. No manufacturer could be found, so they went ahead on their own. The machine was technically superior to the Atari VCS, but it was saddled with a horrible "paddle like" controller. Still Mattel produced some amazing software for the machine, especially great sports games, which helped sell it.

Despite a poor controller and Atari's dominance, sales climbed. Mattel hired like crazy; the electronics division was almost a complete company in its own right, growing from 100 to over 1,000 in 1983. Despite the success though, Mattel remained on the periphery. In 1982 Atari still controlled 80 percent of the U.S. home market for electronic entertainment products.

Then it all fell apart.

The First Shakeout

In 1983 the market crashed hard. Mattel's electronic division almost destroyed the entire company when it posted a loss of $166.7 million in the first six months of 1983. In December the figure was revised to over $225 million, which was equal to the entire profit the company had made from Intellivision for the four prior years! Mattel laid off over 700 employees nearly as fast at it had hired them.

1n 1983 Atari spent wildly. Kassar, seemingly enjoying the position as the CEO of the world's fastest growing company, lost focus buying expensive houses and jets. Game geniuses like Bob Whitehead and David Crane left to form their own company called Activision. A famous outburst between one of Activision's founders, Larry Kaplan, and Kassar had Kassar telling Kaplan "You're a dime a dozen. You're not unique. Anybody can do a cartridge." Man, was he ever wrong.

Kassar had made the single biggest assumption that to this day plagues many companies in the game development industry: The industry is no more unique than auto parts—game development is not a different form of art and engineering from those used to create other types of consumer products.

In the resulting fallout, Kassar was replaced by James Morgan, an executive from tobacco giant Phillip Morris. It seems like they never learn.

Soon other software-only companies started springing up—many founded by programmers who had worked for Atari and wanted credit for their work. The new games featured credits, and pictures of the programmers appeared in the manuals or on the box. Stars like David Crane (Pitfall) became best-selling authors overnight. Activision began what became a trickle and then a flood of third-party cartridge developers. Software became the key.

Atari started losing its edge. The market was flooded with software (most of it garbage) from such huge media conglomerates and corporations as Quaker Oats, Fox, CBS, and even later Mattel. Games like Pac-Man from Atari were rushed to market and looked nothing like their arcade counterparts. In its most famous gaff, Steve Ross, Warner's Chairman, had paid $22 million to Steven Speilberg for the video game rights to E.T.

The game was rushed to market. Poorly designed and downright awful, it sat on the shelves. After a number of failures like this, the market crashed.

Companies like Activision and Imagic crashed with it. The public had had enough for now, and their attention had turned elsewhere. In 1984 sales of video game software and hardware dropped below $800 million. The industry had only recently had sales figures of over $6 billion dollars; stock markets haven't crashed as hard.

Personal computers—the little mammals among the dinosaurs—had come of age. The desktop computer revolution and, importantly with it the computer games, had emerged.

While the new CEO James Morgan and Atari were licking their wounds, the computer industry was maturing at a nice clip. Personal computers like the Apple II, Commodore 64, and even the Atari 800, started taking off. Not only could these machines play games, but they could also perform tasks like word processing and number crunching (spreadsheets) as well.

The Rise of the Computer Game

Personal computers had been around since the early 70s, but until the great video game crash, the PCs and the games associated with them hadn't received the type of attention that video games had gotten. PCs offered much more than video game systems, so people flocked to them. With their higher income level and more mature market, personal computers brought in a whole new group of people. Users who, like their video game counterparts, also wanted to play games.

While major producers were concentrating on the video game market, many start-up companies concentrated on producing computer-only games. Companies like Sierra On-Line, BudgeCo, and Broderbund were founded without a single product being developed for video game consoles. During the period 1980 through 1982, these companies worked hard to build the growing business of computer game software. As the sales of computers grew, other companies began to take notice—and soon the industry took off like a rocket.

These new computers offered game designers more powerful CPUs, more RAM, and devices like keyboards to introduce more options for player input. This, coupled with a more mature consumer base, meant more sophisticated games. Sure, simple arcade games were ported to personal computers but essentially an entirely new set of games was created to take advantage of the new technology at hand. Products such as the Infocom and Scott Adams text adventures were created; roleplaying games, some with 3D dungeons, like Wizardry and Ultima appeared. Designers began creating sophisticated products, and a new era in gaming began. At this point, many computer users began to see the value in being entertained by

computer games. Many gamers who had been playing AD&D and other role-playing-games migrated to computers; people who enjoyed strategy-based games like chess, wargames, and puzzles also found interesting computer-based products waiting for them.

The growth was rapid and accelerated the demise of video games. Video game manufacturers tried to convert their consoles to computers. Mattel's Aquarius and Coleco's Adam were some of the more noteworthy attempts. But all of them failed. No video game system's computer adaptation ever made it into the big leagues. Consumers saw the difference between them, and rejected the products.

The Next Generation on the Rise

With consumers flocking to computers, the existing computer software developers became much more serious and sophisticated. Long an industry where packaging was synonymous with Ziplock bags, these companies began to wake up. In 1982 Trip Hawkins, with help from several major Apple employees like Steve Wozniak, and some good venture capital, started what was to become the first modern age computer game company, Electronic Arts (EA).

Hawkins was a unique visionary for the entertainment software market. His background was business based but always with a certain technological and game edge. While studying for his MBA at Harvard, Hawkins convinced his professors to let his Masters thesis be on game strategy. After school, he joined Apple as one of its earliest employees. He served as product manager for the ill-fated Lisa, which was the precursor for the Macintosh.

Electronic Arts was hot from the start. Activision had introduced the original concept of an artist-oriented environment and approach for game development. EA took this to the next level, and incorporated an artist-oriented marketing effort into their operations. One of EA's early metaphors was the idea of producing computer games like major record labels sold records. Products were sold in album-style packaging, with slick art work and artist liner notes. EA promoted its authors with full page portraits and fold-out posters in leading game magazines.

Some industry veterans saw this as gimmick and hype, and Hawkins' slogan for EA software of "Simple, Hot, and Deep" sometimes seemed missing in EA's early games. EA pressed on, though, and proved that the company had much more to offer than just marketing hype. Products like Archon, Pinball Contruction Kit, M.U.L.E., Seven Cities of Gold, and Skyfox became huge hits, both critically and in units sold. Today, EA is the leading independent entertainment software company in the world.

Certainly, EA represented not only the arrival of the computer game industry but its instant maturing as well. Existing computer companies and new spinoffs joined EA to create successful environments for both creating and marketing first-class com-

puter games. Veterans like Activision, Sierra On-Line, and Broderbund, along with other start-ups like Synapse, Sirrus, and Epyx, turned into major multi-million dollar companies by 1984.

During this golden age some of the biggest hits in computer games were created. Richard Garriot, otherwise known as Lord British, created the first major RPG hit, Ultima. Sir-Tech Software published another major RPG hit, Wizardry. Bruce Artwick published the first of many versions of the venerable Flight Simulator. These hits showed the world how mature and feature-rich games had become.

The Return of the Video Game Console

As 8-bit computers started biting the dust, and the Atari ST, Commodore Amiga, Apple Macintosh, and IBM clones began setting the pace for 16-bit computers, a little known Japanese company surfaced and in one fell swoop recreated the entire home video game market from its smoldering ashes of 1984.

Nintendo had been an early creator of such arcade classics as Donkey Kong, Super Mario Brothers, and Kung-Fu. As it quietly watched the computer industry switch to newer computers and studied the consumer market, it saw an opening for a new video-game system. Of course, the prospect for recreating the video game craze of the late 70s/early 80s was difficult, but in 1986 roughly 36 months after the previous shakeout, Nintendo felt it not only had a better machine, but a better plan, too.

Nintendo is probably the most ancient game company in the game development arena. It was founded over 100 years ago. Nintendo opened up shop in Japan, manufacturing Hanafuda playing cards. When video games became the rage, Nintendo dove right in, concentrating first on Arcade games, and hitting paydirt bigtime with the release of Donkey Kong in the early 1980s.

Once home video games became the rage in the late 1970s and early 80s, Nintendo stuck to arcade consoles. Then, in the mid 80s as computer games were rising, Nintendo re-entered the market, becoming the number one video game company in the world. It started first in Japan, where PCs had never taken off. After a successful rollout there, they brought their system to the U.S. Their plan was simple: Reintroduce video games with a more sophisticated platform and a far better level of quality control on the software level. Do it at a low price point so it could co-exist with computers or be purchased by those who couldn't afford the far costlier new computers. Buttressing Nintendo would be a bunch of third party licensees that read like a who's who of the Japanese coin-op makers. Companies like Namco, Konami, and Cap-Com pumped out good translations of their coin-op hits.

Ironically, as computer users went for machines with more horsepower than their previous computer, trading in Commodore 64s for Amigas and Atari 800s for Macs and Atari 1040STs, they were actually trading down the technology ladder, or in parallel with the Nintendo, which featured a 6502 chip (albeit with some co-processing graphics chips).

Lessons Learned Lead to Tight "Quality" Control

Nintendo clearly felt that software was the key, and it exerted incredible control over it. Companies developing for Nintendo could only produce five titles every year. Nintendo did all the manufacturing. Companies were prevented from creating and manufacturing their own cartridges because Nintendo had created a special "lockout" chip to prevent companies from making unsanctioned games. In addition, to get the manufacturing go-ahead, developers had to submit their product to Nintendo for quality review, which would result in Nintendo sending back the game with changes to be made before a seal of approval would be given.

Later on, Atari Games, a former remnant of the original video game giant, would create a process around the lockout chip, resulting in a major exchange of lawsuits. While most developers had no problem with the lockout process (or at least didn't voice their frustrations in public), some developers really didn't like it and they moved on to other platforms.

Ironically, early in the Nintendo introduction, many American computer game companies stayed away from the hardware. Many of the people at these companies had seen what had happened to the video game industry and were determined not to get burned twice. Some couldn't afford the entry fee. Many notable developers who had built their companies on the backs of computer games, such as Sierra and Broderbund, stayed the course as computer game makers. Others, most notably Electronic Arts slowly (and later quickly) began developing for them.

Nintendo manufacturing, being cartridge based and requiring major mass-market campaigns, demanded large capital expenditures other companies weren't willing or able to extend. Many companies instead opted for licensing their products to Japanese companies for porting to the Nintendo.

Where There's a Market, There's a Rival

Nintendo may have begun the resurgence of video game consoles, but soon they were not alone. Nintendo's crosstown rival Sega Enterprises launched its Sega Master System in competition. The story of Sega is perhaps one of the more amazing stories

in the history of game development. While Sega is mostly thought of as a Japanese company, its history of over 40 years shows it has deep U.S. roots.

Sega was founded in Japan in 1954, but not by a Japanese citizen. A former American G.I. named David Rosen started it as a company called Service Games Co. He started the company to develop amusement games. With his Army background and contacts, Rosen started importing mechanical coin-operated games. He had learned about their popularity on U.S. military bases in Japan. Not content with just importing other peoples' machines, Sega began manufacturing its own product. Sega was born as a manufacturer; and its name, shortened from Service Games, became well known.

In 1957, Sega's big hit "Periscope," a submarine shooter, hit the market. Seeing the growth of the company, Gulf & Western Industries (later going on to become Paramount, and now part of Viacom) bought the company. They kept Rosen on as CEO. Sega kept up its strong growth and by 1982 was earning over $214 million in revenues. When the video game market crashed, Gulf & Western divested itself of Sega and sold the U.S. assets to Bally Manufacturing.

Strangely, though, the Japanese division of Sega kept going. One reason was that back in 1979, Rosen had acquired a distribution company founded by a Japanese entrepreneur, Hayao Nakayama. Following the crash, Rosen joined Nakayama and other Japanese investors to buy the Japanese assets of Sega for $38 million. Nakayama became chief executive and Rosen headed the U.S. subsidiary. From this point forward, the company vowed to not stick with one thing too long, realizing that each generation of technology has a life and a death.

In 1984, Sega Enterprises was bought by a partnership of Sega Enterprises Japan management and CSK, forming Sega Enterprises Ltd., a Japanese-based company. In 1986, Sega Enterprises Ltd.'s stock was listed over-the-counter on the Tokyo Stock Exchange. Also in 1986, Sega of America, Inc., was established to adapt and market video game products to a rapidly expanding American market. It was subsequently given the charter to develop software products specifically for the American market.

The Sega Master System was a graphically superior product; but it suffered in sales to Nintendo. This happened because Sega had not aggressively courted third party licensees, some of which had to do with Nintendo's clamping down on its licensees. Sega entered the market aggressively, but only managed to get about 15 percent of the market when all was said and done. Nonetheless, Sega survived, and began to build a brand image as a top quality game machine and software maker; and it learned from its mistakes. All of this prepared Sega for the next round.

As Nintendo and Sega nibbled away at the low end and IBM clones moved in to offer better graphics and unbelievable price points, the Atari ST and the Amiga started to feel the pressure. With much weaker corporate parents and a dearth of major applications software, these machines slowly started to lose out. VGA and SVGA hardware brought PC graphics up to par—and ahead. Macintosh continued to build on its successful niche—Apple's success helped to support it, but even then Macintosh still found itself to be a step-child despite its abilities.

Shakeout II

The second wave of the computer shakeout hit in the 1989-1991 stretch. With it, several companies bit the dust. Epyx, long a staple Commodore 64 producer, fell into bankruptcy. Cinemaware, a large Amiga producer with interesting products, also fell on hard times. Activision, still spending, was crippled and entered bankruptcy. Consolidation took place. Software Toolworks purchased Mindscape and others.

At the same time, producers who had bet big on IBM or who had the resources to cover all bases of the market pulled out even stronger. Broderbund, with its core bestsellers; EA, which had made a major move into the PC and new 16-bit cartridge business; and Sierra On-Line, which had bet big on the success of MS-DOS, saw earnings climb to new highs. Game software companies had really matured as they had emerged from some niche business into the business mainstream. All three of these companies later in this stretch completed major public offerings. Today there are well over a dozen computer/video game-oriented companies that are listed on the Nasdaq stock market.

As with the previous computer shakeout and, before that, the video game shakeout, the survivors emerged to see a new level of maturity. They were able to push not only their games to new heights, but the industry as well. After the failure of the Amiga and the Atari, the MS-DOS platform took off. It had actually begun earlier; but once it became apparent that the Amiga wasn't going to reach a critical share of the market, game companies and consumers knew what the dominant computer was going to be for the home: MS-DOS based PCs had won.

Although it seemed that the problem of multiple machines was ending, others had just begun. The MS-DOS world was, and still is, riddled with problems, many of which plague game development. While IBM PC clones had won the war, due to its "dumb box" architecture, there were (and are) thousands of different platforms within the PC world. Developers quickly found themselves dealing with all kinds of different sound cards, video cards, memory configurations, and CPU speeds.

Console Wars II

Computers got more sophisticated and so did video games, which shifted to more complex 16-bit consoles. These fueled major game developments. Games required far

more art, sound, music, and programming code. As the business grew, more and more game development capability was brought in-house. EA, which had traditionally worked with lone-wolf individual or small-team developers, began assembling large in-house teams to better manage its people. Game design now required these large teams, comprised of programmers, artists, musicians, writers, and producers not only because of the more complexities of the game but because deadlines like Christmas became far more critical. The goal wasn't just to finish a game any longer; it was to finish it by a set date because large dollars and lots of marketing plans were riding on the right games and their deadlines.

Many U.S. companies started producing cartridges. Trip Hawkins, EA's president, who had previously sworn he would never do a cartridge, finally gave in to the demands of others at the company and EA began producing cartridges for Sega's new Genesis machine. Other companies, like Accolade, joined in as well. With the consoles' 16-bit graphics, and with competition's slightly more relaxed third-party standards, many developers who had traditionally done PC development were enticed into the console arena.

The most significant factor of the 16-bit generation was the early domination by Sega over Nintendo, which had waited to release a 16-bit machine. Hired in 1990 as the chief executive of Sega's U.S. subsidiary, Tom Kalinske was a marketer with a vision. He aimed Sega at a slightly older market than its main competitor, Nintendo.

The biggest weapon in this consumer battle was advertising, and Sega struck gold with some very witty advertisements that portrayed Nintendo as outdated kids' games and Genesis as the Generation X console. Sega hired a young San Francisco ad agency, Goodby, Berlin & Silverstein, which created MTV-paced, wacky TV spots featuring what became know as the "Sega Scream." At the end of the ad in a funny shot, the feature character, whether it be a goofy-looking kid, Joe Montana, or a T-Rex, would yell "Se-ga!" Goodby also created a cool recognizable slogan as well, a code-like layout of Sega's tag line:

WELCO

METOT

HENEX

TLEVEL

It was a smart move, since as the nine- to thirteen-year-olds started getting older, they wanted a machine that was aimed at their age level. Sega's wild marketing campaign drove them in. With early sports hits from Electronic Arts like John Madden Football, many older people also bought the consoles. Sega's demographic profile, while including many young or pre-teens, included a wealth of people in their 20s and even 30s, who had taken to the higher level of the sophisticated sports simulations.

A Brief Game History Timeline

Early 1960s

Using mainframe computers, a small band of programmers create games while others think they are working. SpaceWar and other early games are developed in the labs at MIT.

1973 to 1975

Nolan Bushnell forms Syzygy. He markets "Arcade" version of SpaceWar, which fails. Later in 1974, he introduces Pong, which becomes a major hit. He renames the company to Atari and they give quick birth to the games industry as we know it today.

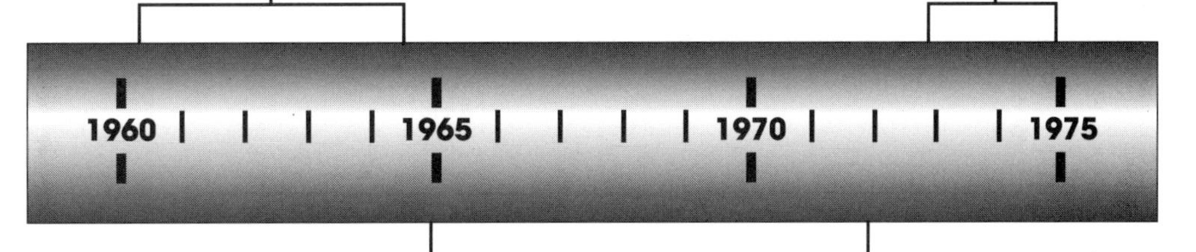

Late 1960s to Early 1970s

More programmers use large computers to create games; William Crowther creates the "huge" hit Adventure.

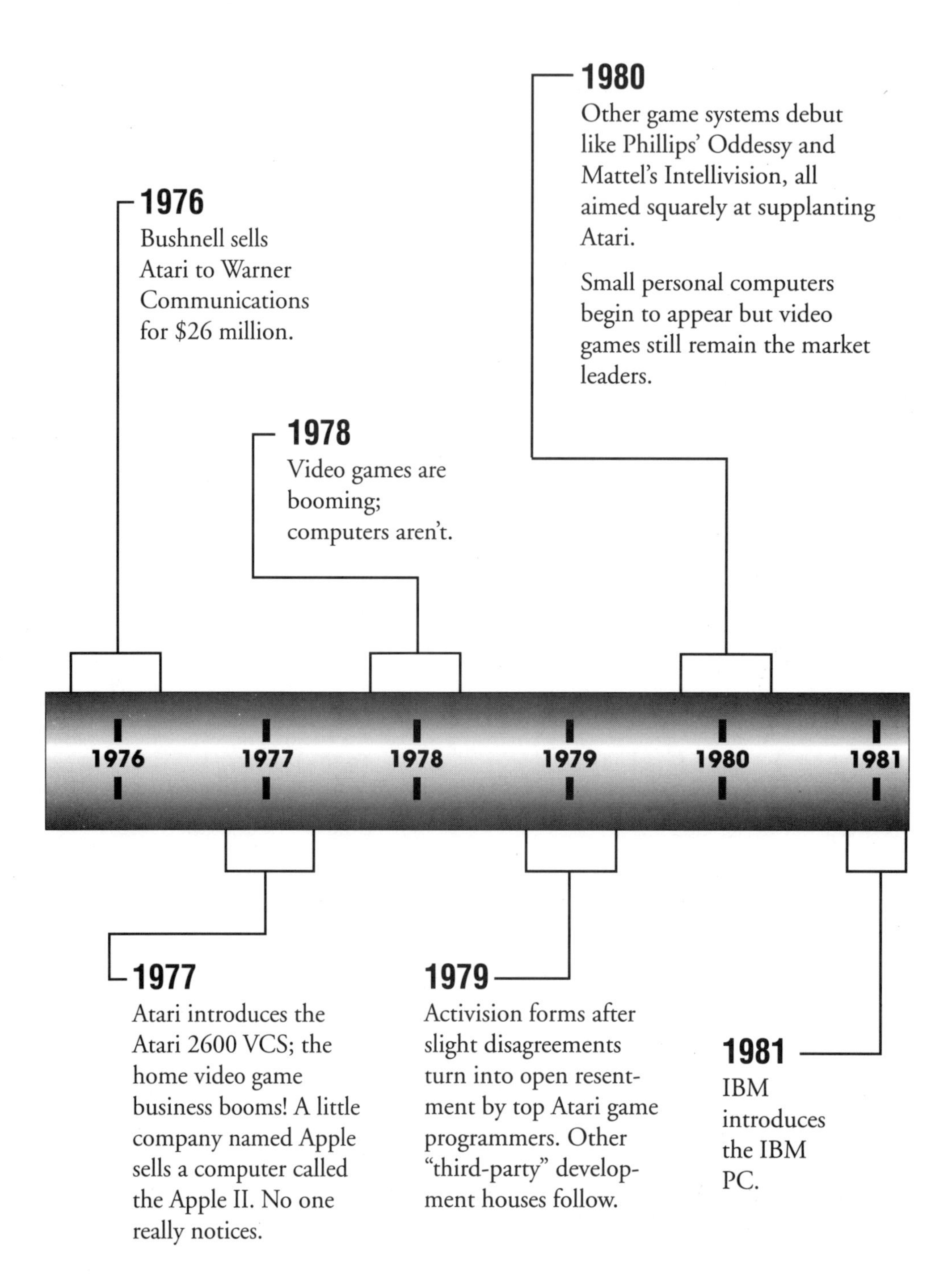
1976
Bushnell sells Atari to Warner Communications for $26 million.
1977
Atari introduces the Atari 2600 VCS; the home video game business booms! A little company named Apple sells a computer called the Apple II. No one really notices.
1978
Video games are booming; computers aren't.
1979
Activision forms after slight disagreements turn into open resentment by top Atari game programmers. Other "third-party" development houses follow.
1980
Other game systems debut like Phillips' Oddessy and Mattel's Intellivision, all aimed squarely at supplanting Atari.
Small personal computers begin to appear but video games still remain the market leaders.
1981
IBM introduces the IBM PC.
1976
1977
1978
1979
1980
1981

1982

Atari loses; the video game market crashes big-time. Ray Kassar, chairman of Atari, announces sales have fallen over 50 percent.

Personal computers are emerging big time. Many new computer game developers start up or emerge from humble beginnings to become major players. The new leading companies include Sierra On-Line, Broderbund, Synapse, Sirius, and Strategic Simulations.

Electronic Arts forms and becomes the model of a modern day game publisher.

1984

Apple introduces the modern computer with the release of the Macintosh. The system is plagued by a slow start, and games are not a priority for its buyers or software developers.

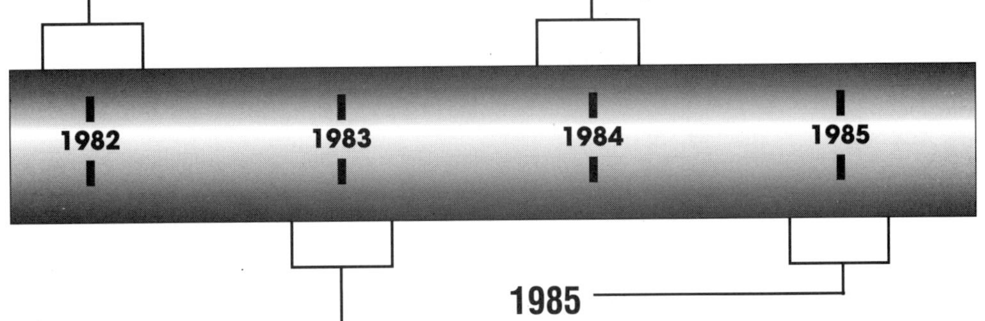

1983

The great video game crash reaches full force. Mattel announces a loss of $225 million due to its Intellivision product.

1985

Nintendo recreates the home video game market by introducing a new video game unit called the Nintendo Entertainment System.

The 16-bit computer revolution continues; Atari beats Commodore to the punch and launches the Atari ST.

1986

Commodore ships large numbers of the Amiga computer to rave reviews. The computer designed by longtime Atari hardware master Jay Miner was originally slated to be a next generation video game system. Funded by Commodore, it instead becomes the successor to their Commodore 64. Unfortunately, massive marketing miscues and other developments sink the machine's long-term prospects.

Sega ships the Sega Master System, which was technically superior to the Nintendo Entertainment System. The product fails to obtain much market share because Sega ignores third-party developers and doesn't muster enough software to sell the machine.

1988

Shifting forces in the computer industry from 8-bit computers to 16-bit systems and new emerging video game consoles cause more consolidation. Companies like Cinemaware, Epyx, and others hit hard times.

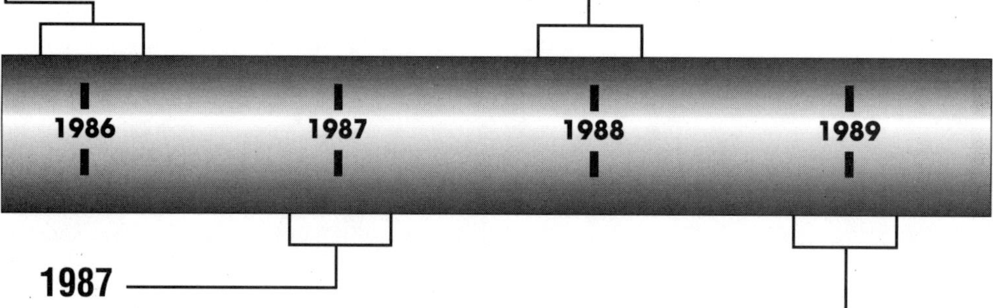

1987

Games become more complex. More publishers begin moving development in-house. Electronic Arts releases the first of their in-house developed products called "Skate or Die."

IBM PC's, fueled by better graphic adapters, begin to emerge as viable computer gaming platforms.

1989

Newer 16-bit systems debut, most notably Sega's Genesis.

Nintendo comes in late making a costly mistake, as Sega rushes to the top of the console market fueled by hot advertising and major EA sports titles.

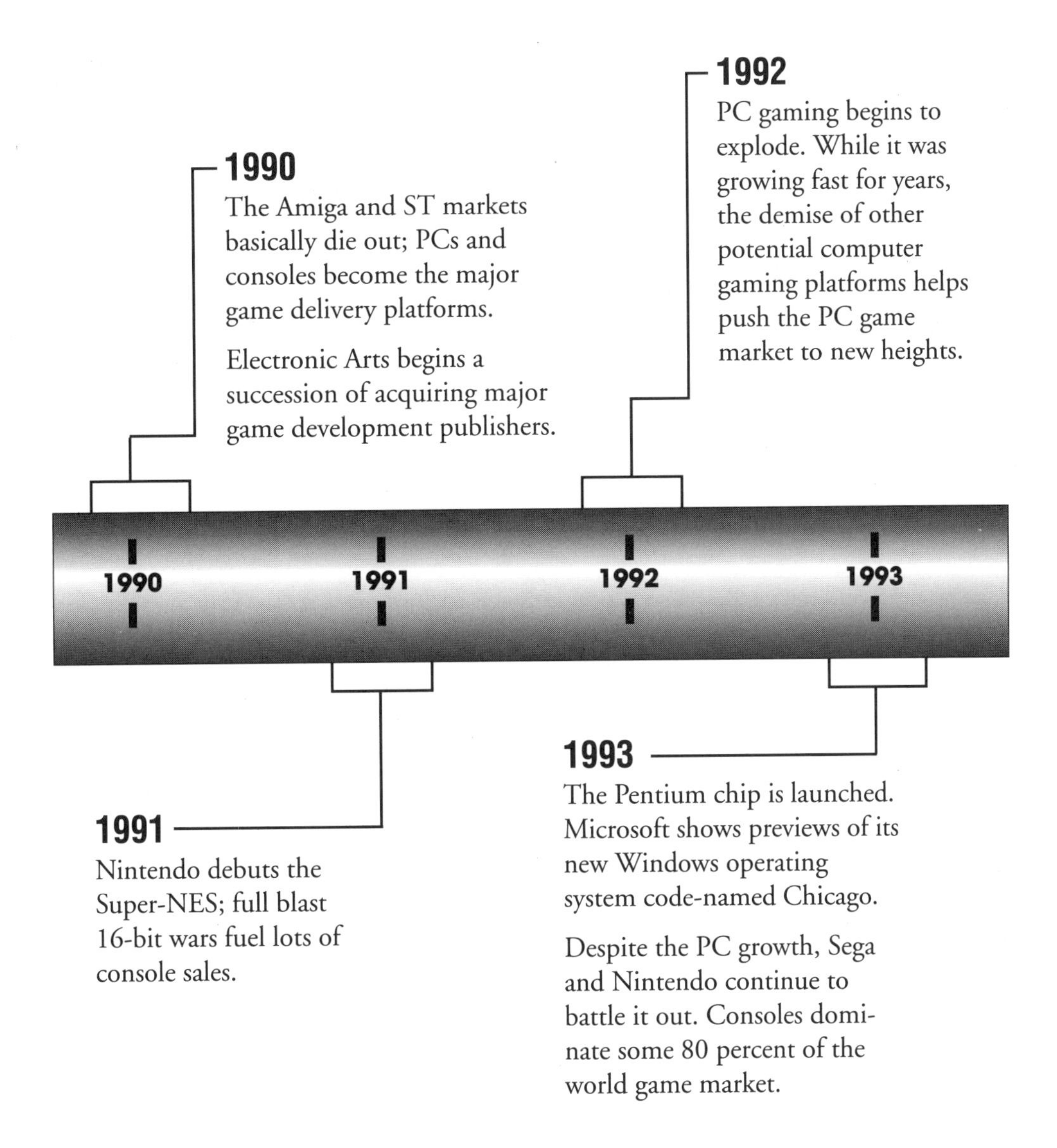
1990
The Amiga and ST markets basically die out; PCs and consoles become the major game delivery platforms.
Electronic Arts begins a succession of acquiring major game development publishers.
1992
PC gaming begins to explode. While it was growing fast for years, the demise of other potential computer gaming platforms helps push the PC game market to new heights.
1990
1991
1992
1993
1991
Nintendo debuts the Super-NES; full blast 16-bit wars fuel lots of console sales.
1993
The Pentium chip is launched. Microsoft shows previews of its new Windows operating system code-named Chicago.
Despite the PC growth, Sega and Nintendo continue to battle it out. Consoles dominate some 80 percent of the world game market.

1996

Nintendo set to release the Ultra 64.

Birth of widespread multiplayer gaming expected.

Multimedia, 3D, and virtual reality features are poised to take over the World Wide Web with the release of new technology and products such as Java, ShockWave, JavaScript, Netscape 2, and a host of others.

1994

Panasonic ships the Real-3DO player, ushering in the 32-bit console.

Atari ships the Jaguar 32-bit game player. Both products (especially the 3DO) don't fair too well.

Id Software releases Doom, which awakens people to the emerging shareware distribution method.

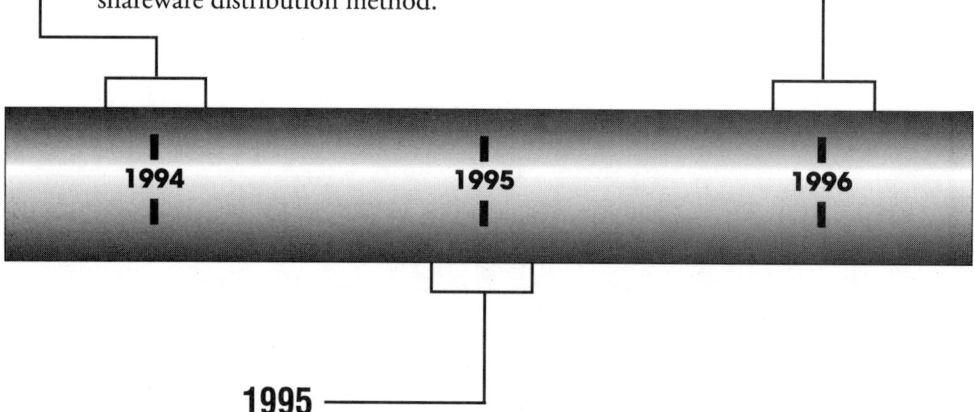

1995

Sega ships the Sega Saturn 32-bit console.

Sony ships the Sony Playstation 32-bit console.

Microsoft releases Windows 95 and the Windows Game SDK, bringing major game performance to the Windows platform.

The Internet and World Wide Web explode, leading millions of users online.

CHAPTER 3

A future moving at the speed of light....

The New Age of Game Development

Moving Fast, Breaking Ground

With 16-bit platforms booming in the 1990s, PCs with sharp graphics (finally!), professional-quality sound capabilities, and CD-ROMs started to become commonplace. This technology ushered in a new age of game development. Game development teams grew in size almost overnight, and the amount of animation, art work, and other visual features that were added to the average game jumped significantly. I don't think anyone in the industry at this time was fully aware of the impact that the new and emerging hardware and software technologies were going to have on the game industry. In looking back, this period seems not unlike the fast-paced creativeness and excitement of today's climate with the emergence and commercialization of the Internet and the World Wide Web.

Shareware Comes of Age

While shareware was not a new concept (it had been around for years), Id Software turned the concept of shareware into a sophisticated and extremely profitable marketing tool with the release of their innovative game, Doom (see Figure 3.1). Id's success was unanticipated, not in the sense that Doom was not an incredible game, but that the marketing approach worked so well. Think about it, if a couple of young and crazy game programmers came to you with a business plan that stated, "our company will give away our product and we think our product is so good that thousands of people all over the globe will get so hooked on it that they'll send us money just to get new updates (levels)," would you have opened your wallet to fund the development? Probably not.

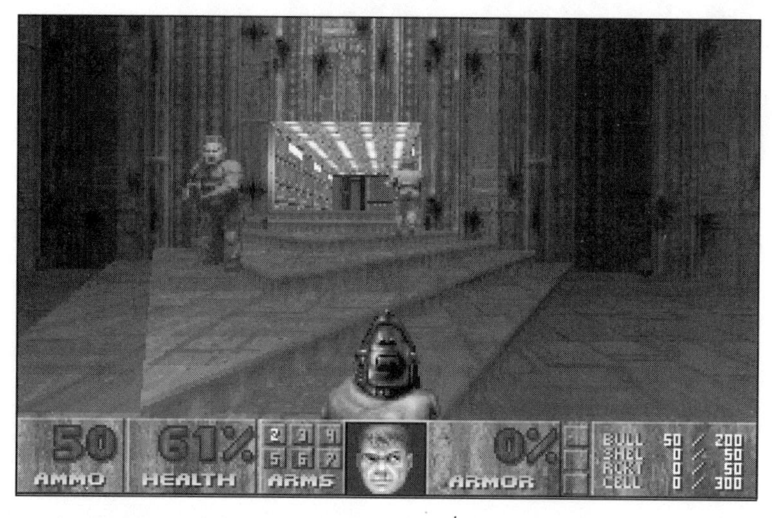

Figure 3.1 While other games started the trend, Id Software's Doom proved that shareware games were not only good, they were great!

The marketing concept of shareware complemented Doom's technological prowess really well. Doom was a unique game and its features would have been hard to get across on the back of a static software box. Id's strategy made much more sense—get the game in the hands of potential customers as fast as possible so that they could directly experience the amazing animation and smoothness of the raycasting engine Id had built. Id chose to go with a comprehensive shareware release instead of a playable demo so that their customers could *immediately* be exposed to everything Doom had to offer. Playable demos are useful and effective, but fully-operational shareware takes the playable demo concept a step further and offers a self-contained game with a beginning, middle, and climatic outcome. What would you rather have? Doom didn't only set a new standard for 3D programming and game play, it also brought to prominence a marketing concept previously never truly thought of as a serious enterprise. In industry terms, Doom will probably go down as *the* game that established shareware as a viable commercial marketing and distribution technique for the game industry.

CD-ROMs Finally Show Promise; DVD on the Horizon

I heard Bill Gates, the founder of Microsoft, speaking at a business meeting recently and he made a remark that really caught my attention. While discussing his visions of the consumer acceptance and commercial success of CD-ROM and multimedia technology, he stated, "We at Microsoft were always right, we were just off by five or so years." Microsoft early on took the position that CD-ROMs and multimedia would become a dominant force in the personal computer industry. As you probably remember, this technology got off to a very slow start and for a while many industry pundits predicted that CD-ROMs would never make it.

When it comes to the game industry, the ascendancy of CD-ROMs as a distribution vehicle has had a tremendous impact on both the type and quality of games being developed. Of course, CD-ROMs haven't totally replaced disk-based distribution; but after all the years of promise, CD-ROMs have finally became the development standard the majority of publishers choose to support.

Just as we are seeing the promise of CD-ROMs, the powers that be are getting ready to replace CDs with DVDs (Digital Video Discs). This new storage device offers a storage capacity of over six gigabytes (yes, gigabytes), and while CDs took time to make it into the mainstream, DVD won't take nearly as long.

In the computer business, memory (RAM) and storage space is everything. The sudden amount of storage capacity that CD-ROMs provided allowed game developers to use media, such as stereo music, video clips, true 3D animation, and so on,

that they couldn't use before. Games like LucasArts' Rebel Assault and 7th Level's The Seventh Guest gave game players a glimpse of what was to come—games that could break the barriers between the more two-dimensional and static world of computer screens to the realism found in everyday life.

Enter Multimedia Developers and Non-Traditional Development

Also during this time, game development became the pursuit of many people who hadn't traditionally made games. Many of these people were not programmers by profession, but artists, designers, musicians, and animators. Yet, just as early game fanatics were driven to the exciting field of game development in the 1980s, these people became infatuated with game creation, also. This new talent pool brought a myriad of creative ideas that quickly changed the game industry for good.

What is especially significant about these new "multimedia" entrants is that a number of them began creating games and interactive stories with non-traditional development products and techniques. While most game developers had learned Assembly, then C, these newer developers gravitated toward development products and tools that were easier to use, like Hypercard, Macromedia Director, ToolBook, and Visual Basic.

A New Round of "Consolidation"

Consolidation occurred during this period too, well sort of.... While the number of companies and developers grew very rapidly, many major deals took place. Publishers and development houses merged in attempts to secure retail channels, consolidate skills, and create stronger companies to be more competitive. For example, Bullfrog and Origin were bought by Electronic Arts; Mindscape purchased SSI; Nintendo bought into a 25 percent stake of RARE, the British based outlet that created Donkey Kong Country; Acclaim purchased Iguana; and two giants of the industry almost got together. (EA and Broderbund tried to join forces but the merger failed because of a stock slump.) In fact as this book was being written, over ten major purchases and mergers took place in the game industry!

Other non-traditional companies got into the act also, including some movie studios and media conglomerates. The multimedia elements that were starting to show up in games led some movie executives to believe that the game industry was rapidly becoming an extension or derivative of the movie industry. Sony started Sony Imagesoft and bought Pysgnosis, MCA took a 25 percent stake of Interplay, and Viacom purchased ICOM and started Viacom Interactive. Many companies finally saw that interactive entertainment was becoming a mainstream, big dollar business. The difference between the $6 to $8 billion made today in the industry to the much smaller industry that existed in 1982 was a direct result of interactive technology entering the consumer marketplace. Instead of a distribution system that was just focused on selling games in software stores, games were starting to sell in record numbers in high-traffic retail outlets—record stores, discount warehouses and clubs, and even Kmart. (Although, I have to admit. I've yet to see a Kmart feature a computer game in one of their famous "blue light" specials. But maybe this too is coming.) The bottom line was that consumers in large numbers wanted to play games. As market research showed, they wanted all types of games and they were willing to spend a good chunk of their disposal income. In short, support for gaming became broad *and* deep.

Some enterprising publishers and investors saw that developing the talent to produce games would take time. Even more time would be needed to develop the systems and skills needed to produce the top-notch games with lots of 3D, animation, and multimedia goodies that consumers were demanding. And time is something that is especially precious when a hungry market is standing at your doorstep ready to buy. While these publishers and investors could see that there wouldn't be much immediate payoff, they were able to extrapolate and predict that there were big bucks to be made in the future. So many companies and investors started setting up shop to put groups of developers together to create games quickly.

Consoles Wars III

Another factor involved in this booming growth period was the arrival of consoles into the 32-bit world. Until the 3DO and Jaguar were available, consoles were for the most part inferior to their PC counterparts. Sure, both the SNES and Genesis had sprite and arcade response superiority, but the fact is both were inferior, although cheaper, platforms. With the 32-bit movement, consumers had, for the first time, consoles that actually become architectural equals to their PC cousins. For game developers, the 3DO/Jaguar, and now the Sony/Saturn/Ultra 64, represented a change of pace for consoles.

Microsoft sought to design the next generation Sega operating system, and many major computer-oriented software development houses, who never before had produced a console product, began to show interest in consoles. The possibility of console/PC coexistence had been predicted before, but with these newer platforms the idea took on new significance. Game developers have reacted by looking to support the new console platforms in record numbers.

Figure 3.2 through 3.4 show the three top consoles that will duke it out in Console Wars III: the Sony PlayStation, Sega Saturn, and Nintendo Ultra 64. As you can see, these consoles represent a big step up from the early video game trio of the Atari 2600, Mattel Intellivision, and CBS/Colecovision!

Figure 3.2 The Sony PlayStation console.

Figure 3.3 The Sega Saturn console.

Figure 3.4 The Nintendo Ultra 64 console.

The State of Game Development Now

Today in 1996 gaming is again in a transitional stage. New 32-bit game consoles are beginning to hit, ushering in an age of even more advanced arcade-oriented entertainment. Windows, once scorned, then accepted for applications, is becoming a growing force in the IBM clone world, which for now seems to be the only computer left, albeit in hundreds of flavors.

Game development for sure is also in transition. The emerging success of shareware has brought back the notion of smaller development houses. Companies are popping up all over the country from Kansas to Texas, all hoping to duplicate the success of Doom. Even the lone-wolf developer seems to have made a slight comeback using techniques like shareware and better authoring tools like sound libraries and complex multimedia development environments.

The large media conglomerates, always searching for new growth, are looking once again at games, this time with a decidedly more advanced, market-oriented approach. It isn't yet apparent whether they will finally see the success they have sought for so long in interactive entertainment. Time Warner, Viacom, and MCA have made major moves into interactive entertainment. With the cash on hand at some of these places, one can only wonder what influence they will have on the industry. For now, small development companies are still leading the pack when it comes to creativity and innovation. For example, SimTex, based in the Austin, Texas area, made a major success of games called Master of Orion and Master of Magic, both done on shoestring budgets.

Certainly, though, some very significant developments are in store for gaming's immediate future. Let's take a closer look.

Multiplayer Games

Already beginning to become more prevalent, multiplayer games seem to be catching on faster than anything else these days. Doom became the first big net-game, and it only scratched the surface. Modem games had been created before, but Doom could actually be played on a local area network in addition to a modem. This meant you could have many players fighting it out. So many, some players found out, that the game was banned from some offices. Notably, there was a decree from the heads of Intel's internal network demanding that employees stop playing Doom because it was slowing down and crashing the network due to the volume of game players! (One humorous comment that game players used to make on online services such as CompuServe and the Internet was that whenever a new update of Doom was released, productivity in the workplace would take a dive for a week or two. Apparently, Id had more power over the workplace than Wall Street.)

In the future, multiplayer games will become standard fare.With the proliferation of the Internet and commercial online networks, the possibility of not just multiplayer games but multiplayer worlds is quickly becoming a reality. Multiplayer online games have been around for a while. CompuServe's Sniper! and Genie's Air Warrior are two

of the more well-known multiplayer games. What will be different in the future is that with Internet connections and more programs allowing people to set up their own servers, the need for networks and for special software in addition to a user's regular log on software will decline. Players will simply load the game and sign on to a local server and play away!

One of the reasons that very few multiplayer games have been created is due to the fact that network programming is very tricky and few game developers know how to take advantage of this technology. But one new development product that offers great potential for multiplayer game developers is Microsoft's DirectPlay API. This API was released in late 1995 after the introduction of Windows 95 as part of the Windows Game SDK. DirectPlay is a specialized set of function calls that allow developers to add networking, multiplayer capabilities to their games. The best part is that networking support can be added just by using a few functions. If you are interested in learning more about this technology, pick up a copy of the book *Visual Basic 4 Network Gaming Adventure Set* (Coriolis Group Books, 1996). In it, author David Allen, a former developer at Microsoft, shows you how to use DirectPlay with Visual Basic to create games that can be played over a number of different types of networks.

Right now several big-time startups like Mpath and T.E.N. (The Total Entertainment Network) are creating incredible Internet-based gaming network backbones. These companies, who have specialized code libraries and tools, are planning on giving game developers a system where there is no excuse for not adding awesome multiplayer capabilities to their current and future hit games.

Certainly, gamers will cry out for more and more multiplayer games as they search for the most challenging opponent ever invented to date—the human mind. They

Figure 3.5 The world eagerly awaits Quake. Id Software's next major effort is expected to break new ground in the multiplayer game field.

won't be disappointed. On the horizon is Id Software's Quake! (see Figure 3.5), a multiplayer game with wide area dial-up client-server technology that will blow people away (pardon the pun!).

Realtime Polygon-Based Animation

Graphically, we're currently seeing the emergence of the polygon! Long used for flight simulators, polygon graphics technology is being used by game developers to create fully rendered, realtime 3D environments. Polygon animation is now in full swing, with not just plain polygons but fully shaded, texture mapped polygons. Routines and games, which only a few years ago would have been relegated to workstation environments, are becoming standard in today's PC market. As the installed base of Pentium machines and next generation video game consoles achieve a higher level of performance, we will see even higher levels of graphical realism due to state-of-the-art polygon graphical engines.

Sega's Virtua Fighter 2 (as shown in Figure 3.6) continues to push the graphics edge by using the same awesome polygon animation of its predecessor Virtua Fighter—a game that became a symbol of the polygon revolution. Virtua Fighter has shown the market the incredible realism of high-tech, polygon-based products. Id Software's Quake and products like Argonaut's Brender technology seem to indicate that 1996 will indeed be the year polygon games hit big time success, both in technical achievement and in game units sold.

Besides the number of APIs and systems like Open/GL, 3D chipsets and boards are appearing that give the PC awesome, silicon level 3D graphics capabilities. These boards will quickly add similar chip-level 3D capabilities like those now used in next generation console machines like the 3DO and Sony PSX/Playstation.

Figure 3.6 Sega's Virtua Fighter 2.

Gaming Platforms and Increased Hardware Specs

The standard is becoming 32-bit platforms and will soon yield to 64-bit platforms. Already the next Nintendo, called the Ultra 64, is promising a full 64-bit platform. Along with this we will also see the rapid rise of major co-processor technology, chip, and hardware technology. DSPs and the 3D Labs' Glint Chip will become regular buzzwords among consumers, game players, and especially developers. The speed at which 64-bit consoles and computers are hitting is half the time it took for 16-bit consoles to take over from 8-bit, and a third of the time to it took 32-bit machines to start taking over from 16-bit machines.

The PC Platform and Microsoft

There is a large push, spurred by Microsoft, to finally make PCs as enticing a game platform as the new consoles from Sony, Sega, and Nintendo. Microsoft, the behemoth of the computer software industry, has decided that entertainment software is the next big thing. They have developed some significant tools, and put into Windows 95 some significant features to make PC games easier to install, faster to run, and more enjoyable. Microsoft has bought Canadian-based SoftImage for its high end SGI-based animation tools, rolled out its own Windows Game Development SDK, begun full scale production of its own game titles, and in an interesting move formed a joint venture with Japanese software giant SoftBank. The task of this new company will be to fund and translate major Japanese-produced video games to the Windows 95 platform.

In other areas of software production, Microsoft has had a bigger impact than the Shoemaker Comet that crashed into Jupiter. Microsoft, now aggressively setting its sites on the PC gaming market, is starting a new trend.

This situation, of course, sets up a battle that many have been wondering about: Whether consoles and PCs will finally have it out for the dominant games platform honors. In terms of revenue, consoles have been winning by a margin of better than three to one. However, as more and more people take the plunge into buying a $2,000 to $3,500 multimedia computer system, the PC market will grow. The biggest problem has always been that PCs are very expensive and, due to configuration problems, have been a pain to play games on. (What do you mean that I've got to get 750 bytes more free to hear sound!) Now with technologies like Autoplay for CD-ROMs, plug-and-play architecture, and 3D graphics performance, some of the issues that have plagued games on the platform may cease and let PCs catch up.

In the hardware department, Intel and other hardware companies like Creative and Diamond are working on keeping pace with new console technology. There are now

3D chipsets, surround sound technology, and virtual reality hardware. While the next generation consoles (like M2 from 3DO) promise to leapfrog today's PC standards, companies like Intel now are trying to keep the PC platform up with, if not ahead of, consoles.

In addition, one has to factor in the effect of online gaming. If there is a secret weapon the PC world can bring to bear on console-based entertainment, it's the World Wide Web, VRML, and online services. These technologies will evolve very quickly to offer dynamic game playing opportunities far faster than the consoles.

Whatever happens—the continued dominance of consoles, the co-existence of both, or the final supremacy of PCs—it will be almost as exciting to watch the war as it will be to participate in its battles!

High Tech Workstation Technology

It's also certain that, as computers and consoles approach the domain of today's graphical workstations, traditional computer companies like Hewlett-Packard, IBM, DEC, and Silicon Graphics will play increasing roles in providing consumers with the hardware on which to play tomorrow's games.

Already much has been made of Silicon Graphics as the hardware collaborator for Nintendo. It's only natural that as the entertainment platform increases in sophistication to the level at which companies already have backgrounds, they will get more and more involved. Today SGI workstations and DEC Alphas are popping up all over the game development landscape. SGI has even taken out ads for its hardware in gaming magazines, and Nintendo is running two-page ads hyping its SGI development technology for titles like Donkey Kong Country. With PCs trying to usurp console dominance, how long will it be before consumers follow the direct path to this technology instead?

Virtual Reality Becomes Reality

As hardware power increases, the ability for game developers to create immersive environments will also expand. Whereas three to four years ago virtual reality was a hypothesized or rarely seen concept in the micro/consumer world, today (and certainly in the near future) it is a sure bet. Game development is certainly on a collision course with virtual reality development on one front: graphical realism. But on another front, game development promises to revolutionize virtual reality. Up until now, virtual reality has been consumed by the ability to use hardware and software to render point of view 3D graphical engines, which to some extent were interactive. Game development, on the other hand, has been obsessed with interaction. As the two collide, the benefits game developers (with world build-

ing, interaction, and especially artificial intelligence) promise to bring to virtual reality are the other components beyond graphical realism, which true virtual reality will require. VR is definitely an interesting concept developers will want to explore.

While much has been written about the virtues of virtual reality, the future promises to bring us closer than ever to the realization of complete immersion in a computer-rendered environment. Certainly game development not only will be on this cutting edge, but will most likely lead the effort.

Figure 3.7 shows scenes from the VR game Zombie Show by Locus. This PC-based game supports a wide range of emerging PC virtual reality hardware.

The History Is Rich and the Future Richer

Looking back, one sees the rich history that computer games have already compiled. Everything essential is there—the giant discoveries, the absolutely mesmerizing mistakes, the incredible personalities, and tall tales. It all makes for fascinating reading.

As you learn to appreciate the history of games and game development, you will quickly place yourself in awe of the future. To realize that computer games are still in their infancy is almost as mind boggling as contemplating the size of the universe and other life in it. Despite its quiet beginnings in the labs where SpaceWar was first programmed, games are roughly 25 years old, consumer gaming 20 years, and PC gaming (as we know it) 10 years! Film, books, and music have been around for 5 to 600 times longer! A decade from now, if I'm still writing updates to this book, this history and future of games section will probably comprise not a chapter but a complete volume!

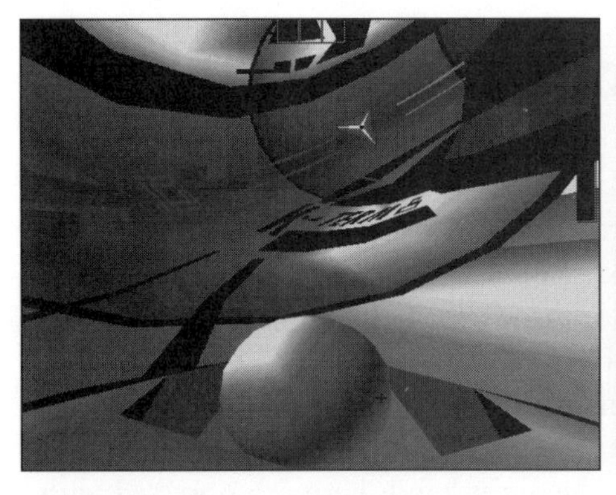

Figure 3.7 Locus trail blazing PC virtual reality game by Zombie Interactive.

What Do We Get from All This?

Having discussed the past and present, and taken a brief look at the future, what did we learn? What is the big picture for game development? Well, I see several things worth discussing.

What Is Hardware?

The concept of what will be the delivery system for interactive entertainment has been in a state of flux from the beginnings of the industry. It's not just a matter of improving hardware, such as the move from 8-bit to 16-bit. Instead, it's the actual nature of the hardware. First we started with dedicated consoles, then cartridge-based consoles, then computers, then consoles came back, then newer computers came about and consoles coexisted. Now we have computers selling faster than ever, CD-ROM is the delivery standard, and consoles have leaped in power, exceeding or matching computers for the first time. On the horizon we have a massive battle in set-top boxes, which could deliver games over cable and get rid of CD-ROMs and consoles altogether.

The point I am making is that, as game developers, the choices for the ultimate delivery system is growing. It will take a keen eye to make sure a company can cover all the bases until a clear picture emerges. High production budgets are needed as companies seek to cover all the outlets and have products in the pipeline for each. The uncertainty has already resulted in the mergers and acquisitions that I discussed earlier.

What Is a Game? What Is a Good Game?

Over time, as games have grown in complexity and artistry, it has become more apparent that the definition of what is a game is central to the medium. Products like Sewer Shark and Rocket Science's Loadstar have been examples of incredibly sophisticated graphics married to an extremely linear product. Other non-gaming products have taken on increasingly game-like interactive experiences such as The Residents Freak Show and Peter Gabriel's Explora. These examples seem to cloud the issue of the exact definition of a game.

The Relationship between Large Companies and Small Producers

Every year I hear developers complain about the large conglomerates seeking to create games, and I have joined their chorus on a number of occasions. Every time this happens, the majority of the complaints seem to indicate that these large companies have never been involved in this business. The fact is they've been here all along. Since Warner Communications bought Atari, large corporations have been involved (for better or worse) with game development.

The schism really lies in the fact that game development is unlike any other form of product development we've seen before. Even the huge leverage these big companies have, with the skills they've spent years honing, they haven't avoided making some amazingly large failures. Their extensive prior knowledge of making movies, records, or producing television and books hasn't been transferable to game development. This knowledge has been best built by individuals or small companies that approached game development from an entirely different view.

Now, over time, the relationship has improved. Many large companies now see development of interactive entertainment as a different form of production. That concession alone has helped companies like Viacom and yes, even Time Warner, start to achieve some success. Even Microsoft seems to approach interactive development differently; many of its well-known interactive titles are produced outside the company, a testament to the scarcity of the good talent it takes to create and produce entertainment products. Still, many newcomers appear every day seeking to do game development; and even if they are armed with tons of capital, they learn quickly that they need much more than capital and marketing know-how.

So the life of big companies and game development will continue, but over time it will be more and more apparent to them that game development is a new form of production. In that respect they will play a new, more important role in helping to grow the market.

The Big Integration—Multimedia, Games, and Online Services Come Together

Up until now, games have been games, multimedia has been reference-based, "documentary" like products, and online services have been cyberspace databases of information from newspapers and special interest forums. As all three mediums move forward, the lines between them are getting blurred. What will emerge will be a more hybrid level of product. Already many games are being developed by companies long known as traditional multimedia developers, like Byron Preiss Multimedia or Voyager. Online development tools and technology like Microsoft's Blackbird, VRML, and Macromedia extensions for the Web will allow major development of gaming and combined local content and online content for hybrid games.

Games in the future will be products with multimedia components, game components, and online components all woven together into a seamless hybrid. As the three main interactive disciplines grow closer together, it's inevitable that some very novel combinations will be developed. So, keep your eyes out for new opportunities.

The Big Integration II—Society Completely Accepts Interactive Entertainment

Over time we'll increasingly see the integration of interactive entertainment into society. This integration represents, at some point, the total acceptance by most people that money spent on entertainment products includes some portion of interactive entertainment.

As people become more accepting of games, and games become more accommodating of people, this trend will continue until it is a universal staple of consumers' entertainment appetites. It will first happen, of course, in the U.S. and Europe, soon after in Japan, and then the rest of the world. The growth potential is absolutely enormous if not downright scary.

Game History References

This section contains a description of useful books, online references, and even museums that you can explore to learn more about the history of the game development industry. If you have a connection to the Internet and a Web browser, you'll especially enjoy exploring some of the Web sites I've listed.

Books Covering Gaming History

Software People by Doug Carlston (Simon & Schuster, New York, NY; ISBN 0-671-50971-3)

This is a great book, albeit a little dated, about the early days of the computer biz and the computer game biz specifically. Doug Carlston is president of Broderbund Software and one of the original founders, makers of such hits as Karateka, Print Shop, Lode Runner, Living Books, and of course Myst!

Zap!—The Rise and Fall of Atari by Scott Cohen (McGraw Hill Press, New York, NY 1984; ISBN 0-070-11543-5)

One can't but wonder how different the game industry might have been if Atari hadn't 5blown it. Would we even have heard of companies like Nintendo, Sega, or even Microsoft? The fact is that Atari was the only game in town for the consumer marketplace, at least at one moment in time. However, they did blow it big time and if you want a hardcore look at the people, problems, and mistakes that caused Atari to "buy the farm," check out this book. Hopefully, others will learn from Atari's mistakes.

Phoenix—The Fall and Rise of Home Videogames by Leonard Herman (Rolenta Press)

Did Atari's failure poison the industry? Well, yes and no. Other companies were there trying to stake out turf and still others today have revived the entire industry to a new era. This book presents as complete a history of the video game industry as one could possibly get. It covers all the major machines and their associated stories including Magnavox (remember Vectrex?), Nintendo, Sony, Sega, and more.

Hackers by Steven Levy (DELTA, 1994; ISBN 0-385-31210-5

Longtime new technology journalist Steven Levy wrote this infamous accounting of many of the early digital pioneers. It's one of the classics books of the personal computer age. Watch out though; once you start it, you won't be able to put it down.

Online References

Classic game and game history buffs are in full action on the World Wide Web. I could kill myself for giving away my old video games and computer systems (actually I gave them away to kids who couldn't afford any type of computer or video game) because there are now tons of folks collecting and still playing many of the older systems.

Some of these people even have systems I've never heard of, like the Fairchild F or the Aquarius from Mattel. Well, if you want to catch up with these video game preservers, check out the following cool Web sites that will give you tons of information and pointers to pictures of the old systems, reviews of the games, historical information, and complete FAQs about the hardware and more!

USENET Newsgroup
`rec.games.video.classic`

Video Games Nexus
`http://iquest.com/~lkseitz/remote_cvg.html`

This site is really at the epicenter of the classic video game movement. Start here and you'll be set for an entire week of classic video and computer game Web surfing.

The Classic Arcades Game Page
`http://sharkie.psych.indiana.edu/rynersw/vids/vids.html`

This is a great site, created by Stephen Ryner, for starting your exploration of all the neat games you might remember from your childhood.

The Classic Videogames Page
`http://www.ecst.csuchico.edu/~gchance/`

This site provides tons of information including all kinds of cool pointers, pictures, and FAQs about some of the most classic video games of all time.

Video Arcade Preservation Society
`http://www.vaps.org/`

This is an online organization that you can join, which is dedicated to preserving video game history. Check out this site to explore membership.

Blue Sky Rangers Home Page
`http://www.webcom.com/~makingit/bluesky/companies.html`

This page is devoted to the band of programmers known as the Blue Sky Rangers. The Blue Sky Rangers were the original in-house game developers for Mattel's Intellivision game system.

Other Site Ideas

There are also tons of Web sites set up that are devoted to classic computers like the Atari 400/800, Apple II, Commodore 64, and Vic 20, as well as such distant memories as the Commodore Pet and TRS-80. The sites are too numerous to list here but a simple search at Webcrawler, Lycos, or Yahoo should have you exploring in no time.

Emulators and Retro Games

Retro gaming is big these days and it's a great way to have fun and explore the early days of the game industry. Microsoft produced the Windows Arcade Pack, which contains four class Atari video games like Asteroids and Centipe complete with histories in the help file. Activision has produced not one but two complete CD-ROMs that have tons of their awesome Atari 2600 classics like River Raid and Chopper Command.

Additionally, several emulators are floating around the Net that can help you play your old computer games on your IBM PCs. I've come across an Atari 8-bit emulator and a Commodore 64 emulator.

ATARI 8-bit Emulator
Branch Always Software
14150 N.E. 20th Street, Suite 302
Bellevue, WA 98007

Phone: 206 236-0540 **Fax:** 206 236-0257

The best thing to do is visit their Web page at:

```
http://www.halcyon.com/brasoft/
```

Here you can find downloadable versions of some of their emulators and much more information about how to play Atari 8-bit software on your IBM PC.

Commodore 64 Emulator
Seattle Lab
9606 Northeast 180th Street
Bothell, WA 98011

Seattle Lab is located at the following web site:

```
http://www.seattlelab.com/prodc64s.html
```

They make a Commodore 64 emulator, and also sell the various cabling to hook up to old C-64 drives as well.

Apple II+/IIe Emulator
Michael O'Brien
292 Portico
Irvine, CA 92714
Email: mobrien@netcom.com

Vist the following ftp site:

```
ftp.netcom.com/pub/ap/applewin
```

This company creates a Windows 95 Apple IIe/II+ emulator that really runs well. The help file will even point you to tons of old games to run with the emulator.

Museums

The National Video Game and Coin-OP Museum
801 North Second Street
St. Louis, MO 63012

Phone: 314-621-2900

If you don't believe games have an illustrative history, visit this place. I haven't visited it myself, but from reports on the Web (listed below) I hear it's a really wonderful place to explore all sorts of old arcade, computer, pinball, and video games. They also have displays about associated artwork (posters and such) and all the games are hands on! This is a museum where touching isn't allowed but playing is!

You can virtually visit Stephen Ryner's trip to the museum by surfing over to:

```
http://sharkie.psych.indiana.edu/rynersw/vids/coinop/coinop.html
```

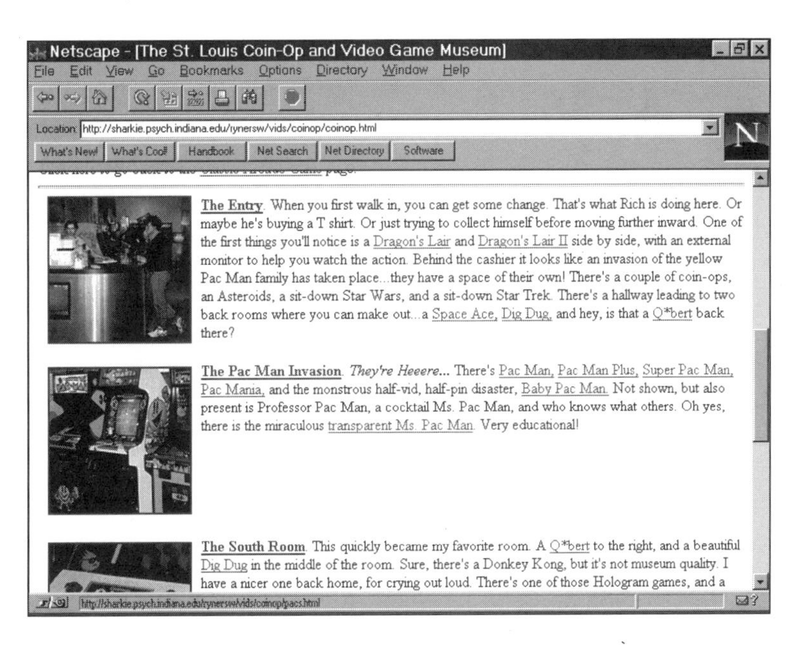

The Boston Computer Museum

The history of game development isn't chronicled here as much as it is at the National Videogame Museum but the history of computers is the history of computer games, and for the history of computers there is no better place than the Boston Computer Museum.

PART 2

The Art of Game Design

CHAPTER 4

Game design is a very deliberative frontloaded process.

Essentials of Game Design

Introducing the Design Elements

Designing computer games is much more of an art form than a science. But as an art form it has an inherent engineering element to differentiate it from other art forms like painting or music. So here's the million dollar question: What exactly is game design? Is it simply interactive storytelling? Is it puzzle or strategy design? Is it character development? Or is it interface design? Truth be told, it's none of these and it's all of these. Game design is a never-ending process of creating interactive situations, whether they are created from puzzles, characters, real-world events, or stories. Philosophically speaking, game design is fun!

Ever since people started "playing," either as a ritual or simply for enjoyment, game designers have existed. While early game designers like baseball inventor Abner Doubleday didn't exactly have a set of digital tools to create their wonders, many of the world's greatest games (baseball, football, Monopoly, chess, checkers, and so on) were still designed, manufactured, and enjoyed billions of times over. Many computer games are simply electronic extensions or adaptations of their earlier low-tech counterparts. So game design is rooted in many things not developed by the computer or electronics industry. Sure, there are some very big differences between an electronic game and a board game, sports game, or pen and paper RPG, but the design skills and creative elements are fundamentally the same, as you'll soon see in this chapter.

Understanding the Medium and Its Dynamic Forms

Most designers maintain scrapbooks, notes, and journals of interesting ideas and other tidbits. For game designers, this practice can be incredibly important. As an artistic medium that encompasses many different forms of media, collecting potential game material involves cataloging all sorts of different ideas, videos, movies, pictures, stories, character descriptions, music clips, sound effects, animation sequences, interface techniques, and much more.

Understanding the medium means mastering the art of maintaining a steady flow of game play. Playing games, even ones you aren't terribly fond of, can influence the games you produce, even if they are of a totally different type. Many game companies actually set aside time during the week for the entire development staff to get together and evaluate new games to see what other developers are creating. (This is a good way to avoid creating a game concept you think is totally original only to find that the game has already been developed, as well as to keep pace with the competition.)

Brainstorming and Creating New Ideas

Among game designers, the brainstorming process is especially important and interesting, to say the least! If you ever get a chance to sit in on a brainstorming session with a group of professional game designers, jump at the chance because you'll find it to be a very stimulating and revealing process. Many people outside of the game development field seem to think that creating games is very similar to the creative process of developing movies. In some cases, you'll find some parallels; however, there are many more differences than similarities. In the movie business, for example, many of the most successful films (*Jurrassic Park*, *Batman*, and *Superman*) have been spawned from licensed properties or existing books. In the game industry, on the other hand, the most successful games (Carmen Sandiego, Monkey Island, and Donkey Kong Country) were original ideas and not designs adapted from movies or books. These games introduced entirely new characters, stories, and other elements. Original ideas, stories, and characters are far more interesting to game players than digital incarnations of existing products. That doesn't mean licensing isn't an effective game development strategy. However, the fact remains that gaming is a unique medium that relies on a constant stream of fresh ideas.

The best way to come up with new ideas is to get a group of creative people together in a monitored (and somewhat organized) brainstorming season. Brainstorming provides an interactive method for enabling new ideas to bubble to the surface in a determined manner. The goal is to get all of the creative designers together to come up with as many new ideas for characters, stories, animation sequences, interface design, market-related issues, and so on. But keep in mind that the best brainstorming sessions are those in which every member of the design team can freely contribute his or her ideas without being criticized. In a well-run brainstorming session, one idea (even if it is a weak one) will often lead to another idea.

Here's a helpful brainstorming checklist you can use to help organize and conduct your sessions:

1. Make sure that everyone who is involved in the design process of your game attends. (If a key member doesn't attend, he or she might resent the fact that they were not able to participate—you don't want to end up with unhappy creative people on your hands!)
2. Make it clear up front to everyone who attends that the purpose of the brainstorming session is to have a free exchange of ideas. (More than likely, you'll need to constantly remind the group of this issue during the session—it's hard for people to put their judgmental thoughts aside for a few hours.)

3. Keep the session as focused as possible. (You might find that your group starts out by discussing character development and ends up discussing white water rafting in the Grand Canyon.)
4. Don't let some members of the design team (the more aggressive ones) dominate the session while other members watch in silence.
5. Even though the purpose of the session is to be as creative as possible, make sure that you have a set of goals for the meeting and that your goals are clear to everyone who attends.
6. Bring food and sodas to the session—this always seems to help relax people to get the creative juices flowing when they are placed in a group session.

Hang up a sign in your brainstorming session that says something like this, "Leave your judgments outside this room." Also, make sure that you designate someone to take detailed notes. (Some companies even videotape the meetings!) Often, unique ideas will come up that don't get recorded and then they get lost forever. Putting a wipe board in the brainstorming room is always a good idea.

Experimenting and Evaluating New Design Ideas

Brainstorming is a great way to come up with new ideas but once you have them, what do you do next? If you are really in a hurry, you'll probably want to take some of the better ideas and start creating the code and graphics for your game right way. Stop right there! *Resist this temptation.* Before you become too committed (or attached) to any of your ideas, you'll need a method to test them to make sure they work (and that you have the skills to properly implement them). I wish I had the time to tell you the hundreds of horror stories I've come across of developers who made too many assumptions in the early stages of their game design process only to find out later that most of the time-consuming early work they created needed to be thrown away.

Like any type of software design and development, game design requires prototyping. Think about it; interface designs are only truly tested once they are implemented in some way. In addition, technical details like optimizing frame rates and sound quality issues require a constant evaluation of products and services, as well as the ability to produce the types of sequences or program code your designs need.

Whether good or bad, the results of your early testing will affect the direction your designs may take. You might find out that an idea is impossible after you try to implement it. For example, while trying to implement an animation sequence, you might discover that the frame rate you are using is too fast and your important detailed graphical objects don't show up the way you intended. Such a test might cause you to rethink the type of animations you want to use in your game, and save you or your artist a lot of wasted time. Whatever the outcome, the only way you'll discover if new or modified ideas really work is to test them. If you develop methodical systems for testing your ideas, you'll be able to make the required adjustments early and select the technology and tools that are better suited for the actual game you are building.

I don't want to encourage you to write too much code in the early stages of your design process, but if you feel insecure or compelled to test some of your technical ideas, then go ahead. A lot of companies will test game ideas using a multimedia development tool like Director, or they may create simple demos in C/C++ to test technical realities. For example, they might write some code to see how fast they can move polygons around. What they won't do is dive in head first to do the entire project.

Assembling Disparate Pieces of Information into a Completely New Form

Here's an important point to keep in mind as a game designer: People may purchase a game for its amazing graphics or incredible sound and music, but they play a game because it's fun and the flow of the game engages and stimulates them. No single element can make a game repeatedly fun. To make a game fun, game designers need to know how to combine art, music, sound, text, video, and other elements to create a single interactive experience. This means designers need to know exactly what they can use to construct a game and understand how and when to use the various components.

As an exercise, take one of your favorite games and isolate the different components that the game uses. Perhaps you'll want to make a chart and catalog and rate features such as sound effects, music, animation, video clips, and so on. Once you do this, take a step back and visualize how all of these elements are combined to make the game really work. This type of reverse engineering process can often help you see things in a new perspective.

Careful Planning and Pre-Construction Preparation

If you were going to build a house, would you just start nailing wood together and digging a hole for the foundation? Of course not. You'd plan it out on paper first. Today, some architects render a complete walk-through 3D model before they build their structures. Good design takes a deliberate pre-construction process.

Game design is no different. With today's large investments, the game design process needs to be treated as the primary pre-constructive process—and that means planning. Much of a game's design is accomplished in meetings and simply sitting down and sketching out scripts, storyboards, and design documents.

Figure 4.1 shows a sample storyboard used to aid the game design process. The storyboard shows the flow pattern of the game, and it outlines the major elements that are required—characters, animation, video clips, and so on. In a sense, the storyboard plays a similar role to the blueprints that an architect uses to design and create a house.

Figure 4.1 Using a storyboard to help design a game.

Developing an Implementation Plan and Guidelines

Another good design technique you should get in the habit of following is to come up with a plan for designing the process (game plan) to construct your game product. In game design, this means project management. As you design your products, it's important to plan and budget for implementing the design as well. I'll have more to say later about developing an actual plan to complete your game.

Amending and Constructing the Product until It's Completed

We can learn a valuable lesson from football coaches here. They design, implement a plan, and then produce a product—their game plan. Every good coach knows, though, that no matter how much preparation goes into the game, there's always a need for a half-time adjustment. Good designers are able to amend ideas on the fly.

Most companies make sure that by the time they are in their main production phase, the game they want to produce is fleshed out and documented on paper. As you develop your games, it's important not only to look for changes that can be made yourself, but also to set up proper testing strategies to help find changes that need to be made.

Certainly even more skills are involved in designing games, but I think that the ones we discussed earlier should give you a good foundation for the types of skills that you need to construct a finished game. Keep in mind one of the first issues I presented in the introduction to this book—game development is the art and science of trade-offs. The more skilled you get in some of the basic design areas, the more ability you'll have to make correct judgments about the trade-off decisions you need to make.

One thing should already be apparent. Game development is a medium very much unto itself, and the more you hone your skills toward the specifics of game development, the better.

Designing in the Real World

So far I've outlined the various skills and mindsets that the game design and development process entails; but as useful as they may sound, the advice doesn't exactly get down to the nitty gritty and isn't extremely practical. So, let's dig in and discuss some practical advice collected from various sources around the industry.

How Do Game Developers Come Up with Ideas?

Coming up with ideas is not an exact science—ideas often come from thin air and certainly not from some sort of "book of ideas." Coming up with ideas is a very subjective process for the designer and also at times a very quantitative process for a publisher.

There are two main ways to come up with a basic concept. First would be simply coming up with an idea through a process of brainstorming and idea generation. Second would be to research the market and see what it is people want to play. Either way, the process of generating an idea can be a very deliberate one.

Creative Brainstorming

Earlier in this chapter, I introduced the technique of brainstorming and discussed some basic guidelines for putting brainstorming concepts to work. Because of the importance of this powerful "idea generation" approach, let's discuss the process in a little more detail and look at some of its limitations.

It always amazes me that very few people understand the process of brainstorming. I'm also surprised at how little attention it is given in the process of developing any creative product. My first formal introduction to brainstorming was my freshman English course in college. I had always been a "day dreamer" student and I was chided for it throughout my earlier school days. So imagine my surprise when I had a college professor who actually encouraged me to engage in free-flowing lateral thinking.

At first, I was a little apprehensive. Our classroom brainstorming sessions seemed to me like a New Age initiation rite. After a while, though, I began to appreciate the notion of brainstorming as a very deliberate process that, when approached properly, can be the essential development tool for all creative design.

There is no right way to brainstorm. Many techniques exist (some of which we've previously discussed) and most designers and other creative types try out a variety of brainstorming sessions. In the following sections, I have compiled some more ideas to help you get more out of your own brainstorming sessions.

Brainstorming Tips

Here are some more useful tips to help you brainstorm:

- Brainstorming sessions should be arranged into two parts: New product brainstorming and then brainstorming that embellishes or fleshes out an existing idea.

- Set aside specific times for totally new brainstorming sessions.
- Brainstorming by using a computer is not as effective as getting people together in a room with a wipe board. Perhaps the only time brainstorming on a computer is relevant is in the artwork creation process, where prototyping and experimentation can help.
- Videotaping brainstorming sessions can be great! You don't need to take notes and you can incorporate visuals like stuff on a wipe board as well.
- Create the most relaxed atmosphere possible; stretching and breathing exercises really do help.
- Incorporate play-testing into your sessions as well. You might want to videotape your team as they play other games and critique them.

Brainstorming Constraints

During a brainstorming process, you'll want to try to dream up ideas, no matter how fanciful. But don't get carried away; the whole point is to come up with ideas that are both produceable and marketable. The trick is to balance the generation of ideas with actual constraints such as budget, production ability, and probable market success. No one said it was going to be easy.

You can approach the application of constraints in two ways, before or after the brainstorming process. In most situations, you'll want to employ both types of brainstorming.

Defining Constraints Before

With the "before" approach you set constraints on the brainstorming process, defining some common "rules" of thought. For example, take the following ideas and list them on a wipe board or piece of paper and then try to brainstorm. Here's an example of some constraints you might start with:

- We must produce a game for under $100,000.
- The game must be completed in six months.
- The game must be a "diversionary" 15-20 minute game.
- The game can't have tons of artwork and should sell for under $20.

Then, brainstorm away. Using the above constraints, you might come up with some sort of puzzle or card game. Here you've first generated an idea of what the game will be without specifically thinking of a game. Then, you brainstormed to create an idea that worked within the chosen constraints.

Placing Constraints After

With the "after" approach, you go back through your unconstrained ideas and search for one that seems feasible. For example, you might start by listing all kinds of wacky ideas:

- A game about river rafting, with 3D point of view on all kinds of different rivers.
- A fanciful arcade game about skydive surfing where the player performs all kinds of wild air stunts and other tricks.
- A murder mystery adventure, featuring digital actors that takes place in the Capital.

Without the constraints, the ideas may be more wild. Hopefully, one will be really unique and could be produced within the production means you have available. This process also works well for generating ideas that might be doable in the future. For example, the arcade game idea might be more feasible and, if successful, could generate the cash flow to hire all the additional artists needed to do the murder mystery adventure.

The lesson here is that constraints do play an important role in the brainstorming process. The technique of applying them up front or at the back end can dynamically alter the actual brainstorming process. In generating ideas, you want to use as wide a range of techniques as possible.

Market Research

One very deliberate way to come up with game ideas is to do market research. If you are more of a creative type person, you might not be inclined to take a market-oriented approach. However, you should consider it because it offers some real benefits. After all, if you are about to spend thousands, hundreds of thousands, or millions of dollars on a project, some market research could help you from spending your money foolishly. From my conversations with both big and small developers, I found it quite interesting that they spend little time on market research. When done correctly (and believe me many people do a lot of poor market research these days), market research can be a most effective tool for generating and fine-tuning your ideas—especially because your ideas will more likely be in synch with what consumers want.

Game market research can be done in many ways, each with a level of exactness and associated cost:

- **Research which games are currently selling well.** This is easy to determine by either scanning through various trade magazines or by obtaining a specialized report from a market research firm. Sometimes these reports are expensive, but heck, if they are good, they can save you from wasting a lot of money.

- **Survey gamers.** Certainly this is quite expensive, depending on your sample size and the length of the questionnaire. Costs will also be higher if you use a firm to perform and tabulate the survey. In any case, you will want to have a professional market research firm help you design a questionnaire unless you have some experience in this area. One note here: If you set up a forum on the World Wide Web or one of the commercial online services to do such a poll, your results may be skewed more than a professional poll would be, but the associated costs will be much smaller.
- **Organize a focus group.** Again, my advice would be to hire a professional market research firm to handle this for you. They can ensure that the chosen group is well moderated and that you get a diverse set of opinions through correct screening procedures.
- **Collect feedback from current customers.** If you're designing a game as a sequel or a similar product to one you've already published, you should have (and probably have) received lots of feedback from your existing customers to help incorporate into the new product. For example, Maxis, the designers of SimCity, spent a lot of time going over online customer responses and phone call records that generated over 1,000 new ideas for a new version of SimCity. It's important to note that many customers, if given the proper outlets (for example, reader response cards, online sites, and so on), can provide not only ideas for improvements but entire product ideas too!

Make sure you set up a good way to catalog all the consumer feedback you have. If you create a simple database with keywords and stuff, you could continually monitor requests and organize them in a fashion that shows the top requests and patterns of thought your players will share.

As the game market continues to mature, the use of market research will grow, especially as companies try to create products to be purchased by the largest possible game audience.

Beginners' Mistakes

Let's discuss a few issues that will be especially useful to you if you are just starting out as a game designer. You're probably bursting at the seams with fanciful ideas—sequels to Doom, full-blown flight simulators, golf games that take place on the moon, and so on. But before you get too far, make sure that the ideas you are generating are ones that you can do. Far too often, the biggest mistake most novice (and even experienced) game designers make is to overestimate what they can realistically produce. Even developers with good art and programming skills lose sight of what they can do.

In the end, the brainstorming and market research processes are meant to help you generate successful products. They must be products that fit your or your company's skill level. And that includes programming and artwork ability. You also must make sure you have the budget.

The difference between success and failure in the business most often translates to the ability to finish a project. The game development landscape is riddled with cool ideas that ended up unfinished. Most people will tell you that success is based on a good or bad game. What that message fails to remind you of is in order for a game to get a good or bad review, it actually has to ship.

Get It on Paper, Make It Real

At any major game development company, a game is more than a game; it's an investment. Actually, it's also more than an investment; it's a living. It's no wonder that designers at large companies spend a lot of time in the planning stages working out their ideas on paper. As game development becomes more complex and much more expensive, you can expect "paper" planning to play an even more significant role.

Probably the most shocking aspect to most people who have examined or done a major game project is the amount of upfront planning that professional developers put into their games. Pre-planning for many major projects can take several months before the actual work begins.

For this section, I've assembled examples of various game designs in their paper state to illustrate how presentations and designs look as they are prepared prior to creating the digital incarnation. These examples can help you format and organize your designs on paper to make for smooth construction once the actual development process has begun.

We've already explored the process of developing ideas and brainstorming. Once that's done (if you stay on the formal path), there are essentially three major stages of design documentation that need to be created:

- Design Treatment
- Design Document
- Game Script/Storyboard or Prototype

Let's examine each one in detail.

Creating the Design Treatment

Many computer games played today were not originally created as electronic games. This is one important reason that electronic games should start out on paper. Another reason is that it is much less expensive to design a game on paper than it is to jump in and design and create its digital components.

Games are about so much more than their digital composition. At this stage, the designer should not be as concerned with digital content as he or she is with the rules and the who, what, and where of the game being designed.

The first step in designing a game for most companies is the composition of a project or design treatment. A *treatment* is a conceptual idea laid out in more detail. A treatment takes an idea from the stage of notes, words, and doodles to a more detailed summary description where the early plot of the project is sketched out. Of course, the treatment shouldn't try to discuss the development process for the project in its entirety—that will come later. Instead, the treatment presents a cohesive idea that management and marketing people can look at and conclude "this is a great idea for game; let's develop it."

Here are a few guidelines to help you compose a design treatment for one of your projects:

1. Try to keep your treatment as short and simple as possible.
2. Don't try to lay out every detail, or show how the game branches to different scenarios; but do make sure you show a beginning, middle, and main ending. (If there are several possible outcomes, simply state them; don't explain them.)
3. Don't try to explain every character or object. In short, your treatment should be a simple overview.

A treatment should talk about the basic plot of the game, how gameplay would take place, the age group or general discussion of the target audience, and other basic features. In addition, you might include a shorter technical treatment to present the basics of how you would construct the game. For example:

This game will feature our new 3D engine, coupled with animated 3D backgrounds. There are roughly 50 scenes we are constructing, each with several views; these scenes will be rendered with 3D Studio Maxx. We will use an IBM development platform and later port to the Mac. The development language will be C++, using several APIs developed in and out of house. Overall, we expect a development time of roughly 10-16 months.

Figure 4.2 shows a sample treatment for a game I came up with called x. Notice that the treatment conveys the essence of the game idea, with the plot and design treatment included to flush out the game idea. The development section presents the basics of how you see the development process coming together. Again, the goal isn't to tell the reader about all of the development details but rather to give a good overview of what tools and techniques may be needed to implement the game. But even at this stage it's important for people reading this to understand some of the basic assumptions like whether you plan to code in C or use a higher-level tool like Director.

As you can see, a treatment is basically an idea on paper with enough embellishment to communicate effectively to other potential project people exactly what you want the game to be. Anyone who understands the game industry should be able to read your treatment and immediately understand what the game is.

The basic rule of thumb here is to design your treatment well enough to warrant further development without writing a complete design document and wasting time if the project ultimately isn't worth pursuing.

Once your treatment is nailed down and you (or the people you answer to!) are satisfied with the initial concepts, you'll be ready to start designing the game in earnest. The next step is to create a *design summary* or *design document*. This is basically a blueprint for the game. It can take many forms, but overall it must be very readable. It must tell the reader exactly what it is you intend to build. (Even the marketing folks must be able to understand it.)

A design document is much more formal and complete than a design treatment. It has to be since it is the document people will read and decide if they want to spend money on your project. And money people follow the golden rule of finance—the one who has the gold, rules. The design document is where you spell out specifically what the person who has the money will get. If you can't tell a convincing story, you'll have to go back to programming accounting software, washing dishes, or some other exciting profession.

Again, if you're new to game design and development, you may be surprised at the amount of upfront planning put into a game by professionals. LucasArts will develop an idea on paper for up to four or five months before a single piece of artwork or code is created. If you're on your own, spending four to five months planning a game seems sort of crazy. On the other hand, if you're looking to take a prototype project out to investors to get funding, and you don't already have a track record, a good design document can be extra helpful.

Dear Jim:
We've looked at the two major 3D action games to hit the world by storm, Id's Doom and Sega's Virtua Fighter and we also remembered a Sega "3D" game from the mid 80's called Space Harrier. We feel a game which combines elements from them into a new game would be cool.

Game Story
It's 2025, 5 years after a major nuclear war has destroyed many things. Australia has been divided into three segments, a penal colony , the badlands a swath of land made up of villages of policed mutants, and other crazed beings and the "free zone" where group of outcasts are reestablishing democracy. It is up to you the player to escape and make it to the free zone. You have only martial arts expertise to help you. You must run a foot race to the freezone to lead a revolution.

Game Play and Look
The game features 3D graphics which scroll toward the player (the movement somewhat like a raycaster like Doom except the movement is 180 degrees not 360. Imagine "Auto Racing Doom") The player is represented by a third person polygon figure (Like in Virtua Fighter) controlled with a joystick. The faster you run and avoid obstacles, the better chance you have to survive. Too slow a pace allows your chasers to catch up to you.

The player runs through a continuos stream of towns, forest, brush and other settings attempting to maintain speed jumping onto, over and around, while mutants and securtity guards and more enemies attack them. At your disposal are weaponry you pickup, water and food for health and a series of "Virtua fighter" like martial arts moves including flips and summorsaults.

The trick is to use the flips and roles to jump over things, on to building rooftops (in towns) and to use kicks, punches and weaponry to take out oncoming enemies. Again all this takes place while also trying to racing forward. A guage on the screen and sound will indicate to the player how close they are to being caught from behind. Players will have to make split second decisions on whether to take on an attacker or try and avoid them. Attacks, especially martial arts ones cause the player to loose time on their pursuers. This motivates the player to be fast attackers part of the allure of the game. The game is won when the player makes it to the "free zone."

Development Spec
We'll be using C++ and a 3D engine we've been developing for a while that uses the very portable Argonuat BRender library. The Windows 95 platform will be the first developed. Our expanded art staff will be making use of higher end 3D art tools like Microsoft's SoftImage and motion capture for our 3D polygon figures in the game. I expect a development time of 1 year for Windows 95 and several months morefor Sony's Playstation and Sega's Saturn ports.

Figure 4.2 A design treatment for a sample game.

Any upfront planning you do early on will pay off ten-fold; so the more you do, the better. And a design document is one of the best planning tools you can use because it effectively communicates important ideas to others. Whenever you are trying to get funding for a project (or trying to make your boss happy), try to follow this general rule: The less of a track record you have, the more detailed your project needs to be planned to get others interested in it.

As game development changes and matures as an industry, the more you'll see developers using formal design documents. Why? Because games are becoming

more sophisticated, and formal techniques have been developed to help manage projects that require large teams for the production process. And of course as games become more costly to develop, the people who finance them will demand more accountability.

A design document, as I said, can have many different formats. The format you use depends on your product, your publisher, and your own preferences. Some situations may call for a fairly simple design document and others, especially interactive fiction, are going to require very extensive design documents.

Design documents can include complete game scripts, complete technical specifications, storyboards, character bibles, and more. We'll break down some of the basic components of design documents in a moment, but first let's look at a sample design document. Figure 4.3 shows a document I came up with for the sample game for which we earlier created a design treatment.

Starting with the Basic Idea of the Game

Provide a concise but detailed explanation of the gameplay and the interface the player uses. Basically, this is a more mature version of the design treatment you wrote earlier. First and foremost, everyone in game development will ask you about your design: "What does the player do?"

In addition to the "basic idea" summary, there are all kinds of different things you can put into your design document. Most large design documents are associated with

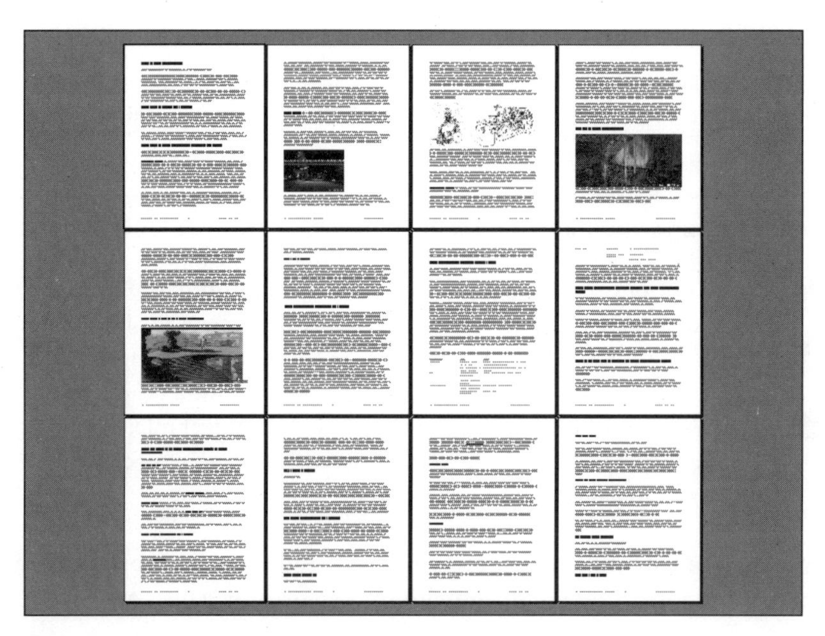

Figure 4.3 Creating a design document for a sample game.

adventure games or interactive fiction titles. As more and more storage becomes available with CD-ROMs and compression techniques, these games will be able to become even bigger than they are now. This means a lot more planning, and thus a more extensive design document. With these types of projects, design documents can borrow and adapt many ideas used in TV/movie scripts and production notes. But because your work is interactive, you'll need to approach things a little differently.

Detailing the Plot Line

Right up front include a detailed story of the game's plot. Be careful not to turn it into a novel. Later on you will break it out into more detail, but here you want to give the reader of the document just enough detail to understand all of the elements you will present later in the document.

Detail the achievements the player will have to make to complete the game. The goal of every game is for the player to "achieve" something, whether it be to get to the end of the story or become the supreme ruler of the cosmos. Many games have major achievements and smaller achievements the player must make along the way to get to the big stuff. Thinking in these terms, detail in your design document the stages the player will go through to complete the game:

Major Achievement: What is the final act the player must do to finish the game?

Smaller Achievements: What sub-goals must the player achieve to progress to the final section?

I started, though, with the final goal: Save evil. (Incidentally, the idea came from flipping on its head the entire premise of most RPGs.) From there I asked myself, how does the player in the game finally "save evil"? Working backwards, creating the story that way, the sub-goals and their associated tasks were derived from their results. A game must "come together" at the end; and an easy way to insure yourself of no loose ends is to start from the end.

Detailing the Game Itself

Almost every game is "sectionalized" in some form. Arcade games have levels; RPGs and adventures have plots, scenes, and maps; sports games have quarters and innings. In addition, every game has a startup process, perhaps some additional option screens, and some selection menus. While creating your design document, you'll need to break apart your game into its components and detail every single last ounce of your game the fullest extent possible and then some.

Easier said than done, huh? Well, let's break this down a little to show you how detailed is detailed. First, here's an overview of the elements.

Developing a System of Naming and Organizing

Because of the number of production elements involved in a game, good organization is a must. Without it, you're bound to get lost in the woods. This is why design documents are so important. They force you to organize your game and the depth and quality of this organization carries through right to the last days of development. You must have an extremely organized design document.

Make sure you use a good outlining system, either with numbers or a naming convention to make it easy to break apart the elements in the game. Games can have hundreds of different elements, especially when they later go into actual production. As you break your game into different sections, make sure that everything you talk about is appropriately and logically named.

Everything Means Everything

You should have a plan to detail everything you can. The design document is not a hand waving guide full of generalities. If a rock can be moved, describe that it can be moved, how it's moved, and what the result is. If you're creating an RPG and the player can buy armor, list all the armors and other goodies. Be as detailed as possible. For example, list the price of the armor, the resulting features, whatever else you can think of that's relevant.

Try to draft your game design in "waves of detail," especially if you are designing a complex game like an RPG or a Wargame. For a game I've been working on, I spent too much time on just a few sections detailing them early on. After a couple weeks of work, I had an amazing level of detail but it was just in one segment of a very big project. The rest of the game was very uneven. Instead, it's better to build all of your detail into your document evenly. (Obviously, I don't always practice what I preach.) If you design your game evenly, you'll get a sense of completeness for your game design document. Go through the document and build it up in even stages, just like you would a building, first doing the framing, then the electrical, then go put up the walls on all the sides, and then the windows. You get the picture. Eventually you will end up with a complete design that has the right balance.

Describing Through Comparison

One of the best ways to talk about the features, sections, and ideas in your game's design document is to cite other games and products as being similar or different. (I didn't tell you to play all kinds of games just for fun, did I?) Some people disagree with this approach because they don't want to end up making their game sound unoriginal. I don't share this viewpoint. Just because a game is like a few other games doesn't mean it's not original. In many ways Doom is like Pac-Man. (Both games place the player in a maze where monsters rule the day.) Comparing your game to others is not a bad thing to do, since it can also show your knowledge of the market.

In some cases, your comparison can also show what features were poorly implemented in other games.

All of the games you have played in the past should help you describe your game, and don't be afraid to talk about your game in terms of others. Just be sure to do it in a way that shows how your game is different, not the same. When comparing your game to others, your best bet is to stick to major benchmark games (Doom, Descent, Wing Commander, SimCity, and so on), recent games, and ones that were fairly popular. Keep in mind that an extensive comparison to every similar game type could be key in convincing someone that the game is indeed a neat idea.

Outlining Your Game

So far we've talked about the three general components of the design document: organization and naming, detail, and comparisons to other games. Now let's talk about some specific outline strategies you can use to carry them out.

Describing the Universal Elements

Many games have events and features that happen in every part of the game. I like to call these the *universal elements.* Get your universal elements down first and the details should flow from there. Before I start thinking about the specifics of any section in detail, I first define anything that is universal for that section or for the game itself. For example, if you're creating a game where the main character can morph into another creature at any time, pull this description out and make sure that it is up front. You might want to designate an early section in your document to list and clearly define your universal elements. Some examples of these elements might be scoring rules, names of main characters, types of monsters, how characters are destroyed, and so on.

Detailing the Sections of Your Game

Once you've established the universal elements of your game and included a section to document them, the details take over. In most cases games have obvious subdivisions, where the real detail of your game is placed. A level or a scene is the typical division. As you lay out your game, you will find most of your time being spent on "level/scene" design.

In some cases, the real meaty details of a game come out as part of the actual production process. For example, I doubt the designers of Doom spent much time writing down the details of their levels. They probably did that work once they had a level designed and most of the game up and running. Still, they did probably design on paper how a level would be constructed and the main elements that make up a level. For example, raising platforms and doors with color-coded locks were probably

details that were determined prior to actual production; the actual shape of the levels themselves weren't.

Some games, however, require that you define the gritty details during development. For example, the designers for a graphical adventure like LucasArts Full Throttle may actually sketch out all the various scenes up front, storyboarding them from a written script. Every detail in a game like this might be determined on paper.

The first key to detailing your game is to figure out exactly what level of detail you can pre-define. In your game design document, your ability to detail as much information as you can in this section will be the most helpful part of the document.

Pre-Programming and Post-Design Details

I first determine what level of detail I can pre-define. That is, what is it I know up front about this section of the game. Here's an example:

"This section of the game involves a complex puzzle of figuring out the proper sequence of levers and pulleys to use to...."

Second, I define what detail will be determined later, for example:

"The overall level design will occur during a later-level designing process."

I also describe in general how levels will be constructed and what they'll look like. For example, you might be designing an RPG with a big map, which will have various dungeons and towns. Now, you're not going to map out every single town or dungeon until you have a town editor. However, you should detail some of the elements that will be in the towns, such as pubs (my favorite!), shops, inns, and so on. Again, detail everything you can.

The more story-centric your game is, the more likely you'll be doing the majority of your level design on paper and storyboard first. The more open-ended the game, the more you'll bring out the fine details during a "level" editing process.

An Outline of a Section Description

Here's a template for creating the description of a section. You can use it as is or modify it to fit the game you are designing.

Name of the Section/Level/Scene

Summarize this part of the game with several sentences stating its purpose.

Detail

Here's where you describe the segments (in detail) of this part of your game. List everything the programmers, artists, and musicians will need to know to turn your game into a digital product. The more you leave out, the more headaches you'll have later on.

Physical and Audio Appearance

Describe the look of the screen and what views are implemented here. Also include a description of the audio features. (What kinds of sounds and music will the player hear?) These items can be divided into subcategories for exacting detail. If the game is more of a map or multiple screens, draw it out.

Background

Describe the background playfield that the game has at this point. You can use descriptive words or pictures (if you're co-producing a storyboard or other visual aids).

Foreground Objects and Characters

Describe objects like moving sprites or "hotspots" from the background. What actions do they perform? How are these actions initiated? Can they be picked up, thrown, and so on? It's important to maintain a consistent naming convention for these objects as well.

Animation

Make sure that all the animations are listed. For example, if a player can open a chest, describe the animation of the chest opening. Make sure to describe the type of animation you plan to use. Is it digitized video, hand drawn, or 3D rendered?

Music and Sound Effects

Describe what music is playing in this part of the game. What sounds are associated with the actions the player makes in this section. Does the chest creak open?

Scripts for Characters

If the characters speak at this point in the game, what do they say? If the game is interactive, what will the player do to further the conversation? You might move all the scripts to a separate part of the document, but make sure you describe in some way that some sort of dialogue takes place.

Scenes and Transitions

If your story is branching, make a flowchart with little boxes for each scene and a one sentence description of what happens. The goal is to make each scene as independent

as possible. By doing that, your game becomes more non-linear, meaning you could rearrange those boxes and still have the same outcomes you want.

Include descriptions of non-game sequences such as the opening introduction, credits, and the ending (or endings) of the game.

It's easily overlooked, but don't forget that a significant portion of your game deals with things like opening screens, boxes, credits at the end of the game, saving and loading game routines, sound setup, and so on. As a designer, try to make these things clear to the user, but also try to be creative. The more you integrate these things into the whole of the game, the less "computer-like" the game will be. This integration contributes to the entire gaming experience.

Optional Design Document Sections

We've already discussed some of the formal techniques companies use to design games, but aside from the design document, we haven't gone into much depth about techniques like scripting and storyboarding. Most of these concepts are more closely associated with television and film. However, many game companies use these techniques as well, especially when they design products like interactive fiction adventure games.

In creating design documents, game developers have borrowed many ideas from script-writers and programmers to help embellish their explanations for what a game will be and how it should work. Again, using some implementation examples from major game companies, let's discuss what exactly these sections are and how they work.

Storyboarding

As the artwork, animation, and overall size of computer games have increased, a useful movie and animation technique called *storyboarding* has been used by artists and programmers to document exactly how games will look sequence by sequence. A storyboard is typically built after the elements of the game have been scripted. The storyboard artist works up a mockup of the screen and subsequent animations that will take place in that "scene." This can range from rough sketches to very exact drawings. In the case of a game like Dynamix's Willy Beamish, which entailed a lot of hand drawn animation, a very detailed storyboard might have been developed to properly give the animators the information they would need.

If you'll be enlisting outside talent for tasks like art and animation, your storyboards may need to have more detail. A detailed storyboard can be among the most needed design documents when working with content providers outside your company.

Flowcharting

Flowcharts usually conjure up those ideas of boring steps in a process control system. Nevertheless, they can be really useful for designing games. The concept of story telling and interaction need to collide at some point, and many times that collision is a flowchart. Flowcharts are great diagrams to show the branching process stories take in games. They can help to make sure that the game branches all end up at the right places. Flowcharts can help storyboarders take your script and create a visual representation of what your game will look like.

Flowcharts can be maps, or traditional looking logic charts (like those found in college programming textbooks, yuk!). Anything that details the actual sequence or placement of events in a game is a flowchart.

Using Character Bibles

Many of today's games have very complex characters with whom the player will interact. To keep track of all of the characters used and to help organize scripts and dialogs, developers use what are called *character bibles.* A character bible is a journal where the designer simply writes a bio and profile of the characters they intend to script later. Writers have traditionally used character bibles to help them design the characters for their novels and other literary works.

A character bible can include anything you want. Some designers will write two to three pages about a character's life, how they feel about things, who they're married to, and so on. The general rule is to write as much as you think you need to draw out the character. The description can be a as simple as a short synopsis. For example, Sonic from Sega's Sonic the Hedgehog could be described as follows:

> Sonic is a speedy blue hedgehog with a love for animals; he wants them all to be free from Dr. Robotnik. Sonic can run really fast and he can spin in a tumbleweed fashion as a way of attacking his foes. In addition, Sonic can jump. By combining his jump with a spin, he can land on top of opponents and attack his foes. Sonic is also somewhat impatient: He taps his toes whenever he isn't moving faster than the speed of sound!

Now armed with this short description, you should be able to come up with all sorts of ideas for how you want to use the character in your game.

Also keep in mind that many interactive game characters have gone on to fame when licensed for movies, cartoons, comic books, books, and various other products. This is an important aspect for you, the designer, to consider. The characters, especially the main characters you create, need to be well defined on paper, sometimes further than they will be in the game. A memorable game character can lead not only to offshoot products, but many (like Humongus's Freddi Fish, Sega's Sonic, or Broderbund's Carmen Sandiego) can become corporate symbols for you as well. Your characters could even become movie stars. But don't count on it and go out and buy that Ferrari just yet.

Scripting

The concept of scripting as it applies to computer games is one of great debate. Traditional scripts for plays, television, and film are linear in nature. A game can be linear; but for the most part, the linear approach doesn't work especially well for game flow. While a game can have a distinct beginning and a distinct end, what happens enroute to that ending (or endings) is up for grabs.

Therefore, scripting in the traditional sense is not entirely possible. I say *not entirely* because certain aspects of any game have traditionally scripted elements. In essence, a non-linear script is a series of interchangeable scripted "nodes" in a network. So just in case you thought all that traditional scripting knowledge was about to be blown out of the water, relax. We're just going to add some different twists.

The main process is the notion of branching. In its simplest form, a computer game can offer a player the ability to choose A or B. Of course, in a more complex form many more choices can be available at any one point, so designers use scripts to make sure they have documented every choice the player can make.

Computer game scripts are frequently much longer than movie scripts, a fact that sometimes catches traditional script writers off guard. I once told a Broadway playwriter friend of mine that the script for Wing Commander III was three hundred pages and he literally fell off his stool!

Prototyping

Prototyping in game design takes one of two forms: a demo of a particular technology or an interactive storyboard metaphor. In each instance, a development team tries to investigate an idea more fully than can be done with pen and paper. Overall, prototyping isn't used extensively as a way to show off a design idea, since many people in the business can easily envision a game from paper.

Prototyping technology is important, though, as your development team investigates whether they can implement an idea. Rebel Assault started out as a prototype of some new digital video replay technology developer Vince Lee was working on. It later evolved into a hit CD-ROM. Typically, this type of prototyping is an ongoing process by the developers in your company, or at times a more deliberate process, if a designer calls for a new idea.

You could create a prototype that functions as a storyboard by using a high-level multimedia scripting product such as ScriptX, Director, or even Visual Basic. This type of prototype could help you pitch your game to another company or investor. The prototyping process may simply involve trying to create an interactive storyboard concept to test the combination of art, video, and sound that cannot be done with a more conventional storyboarding process.

The goal of prototyping is to answer the following questions: What will this product look like when it's done? What do we need to do? Should we even produce this product at all?

The Designer as Engineer

A basic design document can be created by a non-technical person (after all it's a story, really). A design specification, on the other hand, is more technical in nature and requires the input of the programming team, art staff, and producer. The designer also needs to participate in its construction as well.

One important aspect of the design process is to make sure that your game doesn't require features that can't be implemented, are too ambitious, too expensive, and so on. At a large company, this is easily done in two stages:

1. The designer suggests features that he or she would like to see in the game (fast 3D graphics, interactive video clips, stereo images, and so on).
2. The key programmers tell the designer to stuff it! Oh, just kidding. The programmers actually get together with the producer to determine if the design ideas can be implemented. (This is where they get all worked up and remark, "You want it out by Christmas? you're crazy!") The programming team needs to set aside time to test ideas that they haven't implemented before.

At a smaller company, a large staff won't be available. Thus, it's important to make sure that your design is "doable." For whatever constraints the situation has, a design needs to push right up against them without bursting the bubble. Many products slip because the company, producer, designer, or someone pushed at the beginning for too much.

Good designers know when to put on their engineering caps to ensure that what they suggest can be implemented both technically (the easier part) and financially (the hard part). This is where designers with technical backgrounds can be especially effective. Without constant feedback and contact with some technically oriented member of the project (either the producer or more likely the lead programmer), the designer will need to fill in the gaps.

As a designer, it is also important to make sure you are familiar with what's technically been done by your programming staff or other companies. You should know exactly what your development team is capable of doing. That way you'll begin to produce designs that don't outstrip the development team's abilities, to the detriment of the project.

The Design Spec

Once you have created the basic part of your design document, you can start to flesh it out to incorporate a more detailed assessment of the breadth of your project. Unlike a lot of software creation, games have a lot of other pieces included. This means that your design document needs to include what some people might call the design specification, or *design spec.*

A design spec is sort of a technical version of the design document. While the design document tells you what the game will be like, the design spec is a road map for how you will actually construct the game. We'll explore some of the details that it might provide next.

Materials Needed

At the beginning of your design process, you'll need to come up with a list of materials and people you will need to put together your game. A game is perhaps 10 percent (or even less) programming code, and the rest is artwork, stories, music, and sound. This is why your design document is so important. Once you have created it, the picture of all the additional materials you will need becomes clear. From here, the producer can start to divide the work and get the content and programming creation underway.

For each item you need, you'll want to not just say what it is, but where it will come from, who will create it, and so on. This would be a specific list of the content items you need to create, most of which would be defined from the detail work of a script and storyboard. For example, list fifty 320×200 Backgrounds, 200 Objects (then provide a list of each).

For each object it's important to provide a name and a pre-defined file name. When you're constructing a game, the amount of artwork can climb so fast that if you're not careful, things will get out of hand. Even for a smaller game, take the time to organize all the file names ahead of time. You'll thank yourself considerably later.

Data Structures Defined

A key aspect to any game (or any program for that matter) is the various data structures you are going to employ. Especially with RPGs, wargames, and other strategy products, you'll need to have a ton of various objects with associated data structures. The best strategy is to define these components even before you begin programming, and that's where the design spec comes in.

Creating the Timeline

You'll want to establish your development timeline up front. This is very important especially if you have outside people investing in your project or you have an impatient boss. Here are a few of the questions you need to ask yourself:

- When is your art going to be done?
- How much time is needed to write the text?
- How long will the sound and programming take?
- Will the development process speed up if more people are added?

Good design documents include a section, usually as part of the technical spec, that provides as detailed a schedule as possible. The typical development cycle is one to two years, with an average of about one year.

As a design moves closer to actual implementation, most developers will start laying out an actual project schedule. This responsibility will usually fall into the producer's hands. Working with the lead programmer, artists, and musicians, the producer draws up a schedule to make sure that the content and programming are being produced at the right time. For example, the producer will make sure that the artwork for the sprites in a game is done before the programmers commit in earnest to completing the corresponding section of code.

You should plan when things are going to get done over the course of a year. Any good plan must have an associated timeline, especially when you're dealing with a team that needs to focus on a collective goal. Some companies then take this part of the design document and use a project management program like Microsoft Project.

In addition, you also need to deal with considerations for outside sources. For example, if you're using a voice actor and you want a certain actor, say Patrick Stewart (who has supplied voice-overs for several major games), you may not have the luxury of getting him when you most want him. That means you'll need to adjust your schedule or you'll need to find someone else who is available, and hopefully not your brother-in-law!

The extent of planning required depends significantly on the number of different types of media (movies, sounds, narrations, music, writing, programming, background and foreground animations, and so on) you will be combining in your game, as well as the amount of content. Because each type of media involves different production methods, you'll need to approach the scheduling for each one in a different manner.

Equipment and Tools to Employ

An important aspect of your design spec is detailing exactly what you are going to use to construct a game. What hardware are you going to need? Do you need any programming libraries? Some of this stuff will need to be evaluated up front.

People to Involve

Once you've figured out what you need to make your game, you'll need to determine what help you need. Even if you're a small developer, you'll probably need at least one artist, one programmer, and some sort of musical talent. Try to take the time in your design spec phase to determine the required skills of the people you will need.

Can I Sell Just My Designs?

This is a common question novice game developers often ask. At every online conference I've been involved in, someone always remarks: "I've got this great idea for a game I want to get developed and make millions from it," and 99 percent of the time the person continues with the remark, "but I don't want to program it. I just want to design it." Dream on!

Of course, there are people employed in the industry who don't do anything but think up ideas and get paid for them. Let's look at what it takes to be a successful designer.

Game Development Experience Required

The majority of professional designers who are making money just off their designs have developed a game (or more!) on their own or were a programmer, artist, or producer prior to becoming a designer.

Most of the successful designers you read about in magazines have been around for quite some time. So if your goal is to be more a designer than a programmer or artist, you're going to have to be an awesome designer right off the bat, and impress a lot of people. The other route (and much more realistic one) is to get your foot in the door as an artist, playtester, assistant producer, or programmer and develop your design skills. The bottom line is that you'll need to *pay your dues and prove yourself.*

The Challenge of Selling Ideas

Selling a game idea is a very tough sell and requires a lot of luck and skill.

Coming up with ideas for marketable games is tricky, and companies spend millions on market research, technical R&D, and other work to ensure they produce playable, profitable games. The odds that an idea coming from an outside party will be better than the ideas an established company will develop are slim at best. Your idea has to be so good that they will want to shift resources to your idea over other ideas. That's a tall order, to say the least.

In addition, the majority of industry people have heard it all; they've played hundreds of games, and seen just as many ideas. Many of them, frankly, aren't that great or marketable; they're either too similar to other ideas, too far-fetched technically, or not fleshed out enough. The fact is most people pitching ideas really have no clue about game development—and it shows.

Noah Fahlstein, formerly of Williams, LucasArts, and now with Dreamworks, knows more about game design and development than most of us, and at a talk he gave, he described a typical conversation he had with a "game pitcher":

Caller: Hi, I've got this great idea for a game and I want some money, programmers, and artists to make it.

Producer: That's not really done, but what experience do you have?

Caller: Well none, actually, I don't even really play games that much, but most of the games I see aren't very good and my idea is *so* original it's going to be awesome.

Producer: So you don't play games much...

Caller: Well, enough to know my idea is great.

The caller then rapidly pitches the product only to have the producer tell him that there are several similar games already out.

This sounds like a scene from the movie *The Player* (the film that spoofed Hollywood where people were always pitching wacky film ideas).

So is it impossible to sell a game idea? Not exactly, but pretty close. Some people have sold outright designs to companies but it's really rare. I heard one story about a producer from a large company who said they had bought only one novice designer's idea outright in all their years. The odds were probably one in three thousand. Many companies don't even look at suggestions because they don't want to get involved in a lawsuit for stealing ideas.

Some Techniques That Work

If I haven't discouraged you too much and you are still anxious to try to sell your ideas, here are some tips to help you get started.

Track records count. I know I'm starting to sound like a broken record but this is really important. Always remember: *Success breeds success.* Get the experience you need before you try to pitch your ideas to some giant company or an investor. If you were going to fund a game, whom would you bet on, a developer who had experience creating commercially successful games or a programmer who took a few programming courses at a school for truck drivers?

So often the rebuttal is "Well, if no one takes a chance on me, how do I get the experience?" The fact is that many people saying this don't want to settle for the menial "starter" often required to make it to the good stuff. Get off your high horse, take the stars out of your eyes, and start where you need to start.

Make sure your idea is original, feasible, and as detailed as a space shuttle technical manual. So, you really think your idea is a killer? Well, good for you; at least you're determined. If you are that determined, you shouldn't have any trouble getting your idea down on paper *in great detail.* You definitely have a fighting chance if you can approach a company with a polished design, complete with detailed, well thought-out design documents, scripts, storyboards, the works—and even this is no guarantee.

Focus on ideas that fit your skill level. When you hear about a company buying a design from an outsider, the idea usually comes from someone who has real-world background in the subject matter. For example if you've been a rock/mountain climber all your life, maybe you really could design a cool game on rock climbing. You then are selling more than an idea; your entire knowledge about the subject matter helps to make a really cool game.

Start a company; gather resources to back up the game design idea. Pitch a company, not an idea. This is the most common advice given; if you've got an idea, develop it yourself. The fact is most outside designs get a green light when a company can pitch not only the design but most of the means to turn that design into an actual product. If you've got a cool idea, get other programmers and artists interested in it, produce a prototype and design document, then pitch the company with your company, not just the idea.

Choose your targets carefully. If you're pitching an idea to a company, choose a company that buys game ideas from outsiders. Don't mail out hundreds of letters to every company. Read all the trade publications and game magazines, become acutely familiar with the industry, see who buys outside designs more often, match your ideas with companies who are receptive to not only outside ideas but the type of game you want to make. Don't pitch an interactive story game to a company that only makes fast action 3D games.

In the End

In the end the design only approach to getting a publisher interested is just about the toughest road to game development success. It has been done, but the work put into getting it done is substantial. Rome wasn't built in a day, and neither is a game or game design. If you're determined, you might make it, but the hurdles are high, hard, and frequent.

CHAPTER 5

For many people in the game development industry, making games is first a love, and then it's the rent.

Getting Your Designs Just Right

Game Design Meets Marketing

In Chapter 4, we examined the basic techniques used by game designers to come up with ideas. We also looked at how ideas are committed to paper before they are implemented in digital form. As you recall, this process can get rather involved, but it is certainly worth the effort especially because it can save you a lot of time and money in the end.

We're now ready to take the next step and explore some of the other unique and important issues that game designers confront as they develop their creations. Our focus now is to look at how marketing issues influence the design process. The considerations we're about to look at are very important because you don't want to get in the habit of designing your games in a vacuum.

Concerns about Game Design

What are the major concerns you need to address as you design your games? Many of them are marketing and sales related, such as:

- Who is the audience?
- What can be done to differentiate your game?
- Where and how will your game be sold?
- What category is your game? This is important because it will determine how your game is cataloged and sold in retail channels.
- What is the competition and demand like?
- Will you need to use sophisticated graphics and interactivity (realistic 3D, virtual reality, and so on) to entice players to buy your game?
- What will be your game's sale price? Will you create updates?
- Are there features you can add to possibly expand the market for your game?
- Can you design add-on components for your game, such as additional levels, scenes, or stories? (For example, if you a creating a simulation type game such as a flight simulator, you could create other settings and landscapes that the player can fly over. These additional settings could be sold as a separate pack.)
- Can you design your game so that it can be ported to other environments (especially consoles without keyboards!) without costing you a fortune?
- Can you afford to license unique material for your game or pay for celebrity endorsements?

- Will your game have much international appeal?
- Are there ways to design your game so it possibly will have a longer shelf life?
- If the game sells well, is it the type of game which you could create a sequel?
- Does the game serve solely as an entertainment product or can it be used as an educational tool?
- Is your game one that can work as a multiplayer game? Can it work on a network?

Some of these concerns will resolve themselves later in the design process, but you still need to think about them as you begin developing your design. If you don't, you'll probably regret it later on. The issues that relate to how your game will ultimately be marketed are very important no matter how convinced you are that your new game is going to set the world on fire. After all, no matter how good your game design is, if the game doesn't eventually sell, you won't feel very good about all of the hard work you did.

Your checklist of concerns should definitely include the questions listed above as well as other concerns that are unique to your development situation. Certainly these questions aren't the only ones you'll need to answer, but they sort of stress the point I want to make. When I've talked to other developers, one of the biggest question they have is "Can I afford to make this product?" The answer to that question is made up of three major issues:

- The cost of producing the game, which is also linked to the time it takes to develop it
- The ability for the game to sell and thus recoup the expenses of making it
- The ability of a developer to know those answers (as much as possible) before committing significant funding

As you examine the questions, you'll see that they fall into two groups:

- Questions that address cost and marketing issues
- Questions that address creative issues

Let's discuss a few of the more important marketing-related issues in a little more detail.

What Type of Game Are You Going to Make?

First and foremost, you need to answer this question. And certainly you need to answer it by the time you've taken your idea to the design treatment stage. Essentially, your guiding question should be: "What do I want to end up with when I'm done?"

If you can visualize to some degree your end result first, you can better answer the more detailed questions like the ones I've described above.

Most developers determine which type of game they want to create by both selecting one that interests them and one they think will be a big seller. If you like wargames, you might tend to say "I want to make a wargame." Or if you see that a new sport, say Ultimate Frisbee, is becoming a huge sport, maybe you'll decide "Let's make an Ultimate Frisbee Game." In both cases you aim for the desired end result. Next, it's time to think about the details required to carry out your goal.

What Is the Age Range and Gender of Your Audience?

As more and more people purchase computers and consoles, there is an increasing need to tailor a game to different age ranges. The industry can no longer just produce games for a target audience of 13-year-old boys. A lot of discussion has taken place recently about the need to produce games that females will purchase and enjoy. You need to make some decisions and identify exactly the audience you want to target your game for right up front. Be careful that you don't fall into the trap of thinking "my game is so hot, everyone will want to buy it and play it." If you are really that good of a designer, you probably don't need to be reading this book. Although it is possible to create a game that has a wide age appeal, most games that are successful target a certain age group. This is important because if your game is too challenging (or not challenging enough) for a certain age group, your game won't be played very often.

Designing a game in this respect is no different from writing a book. If you were writing a sci-fi novel about life in another galaxy, you'd have a clear idea of who your reader is. If you were writing the book for young adults, you'd make sure that you used shorter sentences and that you carefully explained technical concepts that are important to your story.

How Many Hours of Play Will Your Game Allow?

Is your game a diversion game that is meant for a quick 20 minute play during office breaks? (Hopefully, no one will get caught playing it during work hours.) Or is it a mega long adventure game that is meant to last a good 100 hours? Or is it a arcade or sports game that is meant for hour upon hour of repetitive play?

Hours of play are determined by consumers in several ways. First, *value* is considered. That is, what is the cost per hour of play that a game delivers? Other consumers don't want games that take forever to finish. Again, you need to decide where your product will fall.

What Systems Will Work with Your Game?

Is your game a single platform game, or will you port it to every known platform in existence? This decision will affect greatly your technical decisions later in the process. A game developed just for Windows can take technical liberties over a project that is designed to be ported to multiple platforms.

What Price Point Do You Want Your Game Delivery to Meet?

Just as with deciding the platforms for your game, your choice of price point will have significant technical implications. Certainly a low priced product will dictate a smaller development budget. This isn't a question of ultimate profit, but more a question of what budget will produce the best game for the price target you want to deliver. Price is a major consumer concern, and many people are becoming "price shocked" when they see games that reach upwards of $70 or $80. If you want to sell higher volume, try to create lower cost entertainment products. This fact makes your price point a major decision, and one that will certainly affect your design.

What Distribution Method Will You Use for Your Game?

Distribution is everything in the game business. Even the best produced games will fall flat on their face without a well thought-out distribution plan that matches the game itself. Try to invest as much time and resources up front as you can to make sure the game you plan to develop can be distributed with the resources you have at hand. The three major distribution systems you'll want to consider include retail, shareware, and direct mail, or a combination of any of these.

If you plan to use shareware, you will want to do a different design and game than if you were creating a major retail product. Explore the differences among products distributed in various ways and adjust your design to maximize what people expect. There are many different ways to distribute your product, and for each one consumers look for distinct features.

You can learn a lot by listening to the distribution horror stories told by other game developers. David Allen, an accomplished game designer and author, developed a fun to play adventure/strategy game called MORDOR in early 1995. He showed the game to a number of other developers and gamers during the course of the game's development and

early feedback was very positive. After the game was published, one of his main distributors who was planning to put the game in the Software Etc. chain decided not to take on the game because it didn't have enough flashy graphics. (Remember, 1995 was the year of "shoot-'em-up" 3D games like Doom.) This response sent David and his team back to the drawing board to update the game and make it more salable. Unfortunately, MORDOR didn't make it onto the big league shelves for the Christmas season. The moral of the story here is: Talk to your distributor and sales force early in your development cycle.

Is Your Game Interactive Enough?

It may sound crazy, but I see a lot of games with a low level of interactivity. If your game doesn't let the player interact enough with the environment, you're in big trouble. For example, if you have a city with people in it and the player can't talk to the people, this will restrict the interactivity. Taking this principle one step further, if you have a city full of people, but you can only talk to a few of them, you are still restricting the interactivity. So as you design your game and add components, make sure that they contribute to the interactive nature of the game. You may not realize it but it is very easy to end up with a low-level of interactivity in your game if you aren't actively looking to develop it at every turn of the design process.

Addressing the Concerns

As I said earlier, you should start with the biggest creative issue first: "What do I want to make?" Then, flesh out your ideas some. Finally, you should go straight to the cost and marketing issues, which will lay out the parameters for your final creative decisions. Let's talk about this some more.

For example, let's assume you decide to make a basketball game. Your first goal might be to create a five-on-five action oriented game with cut scenes. The scenes could include some digital video footage of various dunks and cool shots. Next, you should think about the cost and marketing issues. Who is the audience? Can you afford to buy or license the video? Can you afford to use Magic Johnson or Charles Barkley to do some voice-overs? For what platforms are you going to write? Do sports games like this sell better as PC games or as cartridge games? To answer these questions you'll need to do some creative thinking, but more or less the goal is to determine how much it's going to cost, how long it will take to make, what technical obstacles are involved, and so on.

Let's say that after much discussion you decide to go ahead with this product. But after considering the market and cost factors, you decide to develop for three platforms (Sega, Sony, and Windows) and design the game for three-on-three play instead of five-on-five (to save time and money). Now that you've laid down the parameters under which further creativity can be accomplished, you can start to shoehorn your original ideas into your parameters.

Design and planning are coexistent: They depend so much on each other. Designing a game, especially a major commercial product, requires a fine balance. True design creativity is making sure that you create an artistic and appealing game within the real-world framework of costs and other technical parameters. Creative design is not done with a blank slate.

So as we discuss various game design ideas, dilemmas, and issues, you've got to understand the context for applying these ideas. They aren't always being done in some sort of design nirvana where anything you intend to design into a game is actually doable. It may sound cool to do an RPG with 3000 NPCs all with cool personalities and their own conversational engines. It's another thing to pull it off technically and even more to do it in a feasible time and budget framework.

What Makes Games Really Work?

Are there fundamental principles that can be applied to help you succeed at game design? You bet. There are some specific elements that shape games in general, and interactive computer games in particular. Let's investigate them next so that you can quickly master the art of creating successful interactive games.

The Notion of Interactivity

Game design concerns one thing that takes center stage to everything else—*interaction.* The component that separates games from other creative mediums (such as art, movies, music, and books) is found in the way the player interacts with the medium. The driving force for the medium is the player's decisions, in other words, the player's actions, not the medium itself.

You don't stare at or just listen to a game—*you control it.* Designers must create a product that entices people to play, and at the same time, provides the storyline, emotional feel, realistic tone, and the other qualities other creative media give us. This is a tall order, but it is the challenge that makes game development so much fun!

Playing games means making decisions. Therefore, our games need to create situations where the player has to decide what to do, and then he or she can perform the desired action. This can be as simple as Pac-Man where the player has to decide whether to go up, down, left, or right, or as complex as a game like Balance of Power

where the player needs to make key strategic decisions. In some cases, the more challenging the decisions are, the more appealing the game will be. In addition, the more players can affect the outcome of the game, the more the game will lure them in.

When sitting down to design a game, try to create *entertaining* interaction and try to provide an *easy* way for the player to make decisions about the situation you put him or her in. Then, provide interesting outcomes that in turn lead to *new* situations. This whole process can start again and again until the final outcome is achieved.

Affecting the Outcome

One of the most important aspects of interaction is the notion that players can have the final say in affecting the outcome of your game. A player expects that he or she can advance from last to first, save the world, or reach the final level when he or she sits down to play the game. In designing a game, you must make it clear to the player early on, to what extent he or she can change the outcome of the game. You don't need to tell players up front what outcome they can change or how they can change it; you just need to make it clear that they *can* affect the outcome.

One important concept game designers use to create more playable games is called *multiple-outcome* or *endings*. Years ago, most games only provided two outcomes—win or lose. For example, a video game like Asteroids or Pac-Man has but two outcomes, either the player finishes the game as a winner or the player gets wiped out. However, many of today's games, especially interactive stories or RPGs, can have several entirely different outcomes. These outcomes might involve taking the player on an entirely new adventure or introducing new interactive stories. For instance, if you are playing a wargame and you are successful in a certain battle, you could receive a promotion in rank to Captain, Major, or General.

A great example of how a player can affect the outcome of a game can be found in Microprose's Pirates! by Sid Meir. In this game, you take on the role of a pirate captain as you lead your fleet of ships around the Spanish Caribbean battling other pirates, Spanish Galleys, and such. The goal is not only to become rich and famous, but rescue your lost siblings, marry a beautiful woman, and climb in the social ranks back in your home country. At the end of the game, either by retirement or forced retirement, the computer tells you a story about what you had accomplished during the game and how this has made you a rich, famous, healthy, and happy person in your years after. The outcome changes each time you play the game and thus makes the game more fun and interesting to play.

Again, in designing games, the ability to give the players a variable outcome determined by *their* gameplay is key to getting them to spend time playing the game.

The Role of Achievement

The underlying goal in playing any game is to achieve something. Success is an ingredient in every game no matter how it's designed. Success can take on many different forms. It can be as simple as defeating a major opponent, accumulating more points, or moving up to higher levels. When you design achievement into a game, it works on many levels. You can offer multiple achievement goals, like the ones indicated in the Pirates game we just discussed, or you can provide progressive achievements, such as a special opponent at the end of a level followed every three levels by a "main monster" style opponent, and finally by some "master monster" style opponent at the end.

Whatever forms of achievement your game offers, achievement is a major cornerstone of a game's process. Achievement doesn't only mean winning. It also involves the complete natural progression of increased success in finally getting really good at a game. Some games offer actual finishes that can be achievement; other games (like many sports titles) have definite achievements like winning a game or the championship, but also can have achievement levels like getting really good at pitching or beating friends and such.

What's important about this notion is that achievement in a game shouldn't happen in sudden large jumps. It's a progressive process that happens over a defined amount of time. Additionally, I think it's important to understand that a game has to allow for 100 percent achievement by at least three-quarters of its potential players. After all, a game isn't supposed to be anti-climatic simply because it's too tough. Players want to have challenges they can see as clearly surmountable.

Basic human nature pushes us to want to achieve. It is not in human nature to take on an event if there is no perceivable form of achievement that can be gained by doing so. Moral: Don't design games to deliberately sell cluebooks!

The Role of Failure

The phrase "Game over" is probably the most infamous one introduced by computer games. From their early days, games based on competitive achievement, or simply achievement, have contained varying degrees of failure.

The role of failure in games is an interesting one. Chris Crawford in his game, Balance of Power, didn't present players with a nuclear explosion. Instead they got a black screen and terse note saying blowing up the world was not a reward he gave players. In Cinemaware's King of Chicago, a very chilling scene of a player getting the electric chair is presented. The scene has the screen fading to a bright white screen. The first time I encountered this scene, I knew that I had failed and lost the game.

In many games failure is treated more as a setback to the ultimate outcome. In the game Ultima, for example, dying finds you transported back to the castle of Lord British for a quick resurrection. This evolved out of people saving games and then restarting them, thus making ultimate failure sort of moot. It also developed from what I described above. Games need to ultimately succumb to a player's progress; they can't be insurmountable.

Changing the Circumstances

Many games allow the player to control or change the circumstances or parameters of play. Players often like or need to be able to modify the playability of their games, whether this involves simply changing the number of "lives" they can have or changing all the statistical elements in a wargame.

By changing the circumstances, designers can offer players features like:

- The ability to modify the difficulty of the game
- The ability to change the environment of play
- The ability to modify levels or game characters

Problem Solving

We've spent some time talking about achievement and failure. One actual instance of that paradigm is found in problem solving. While problem solving is most often associated with products like *puzzles*, it also is a key ingredient in other types of games including adventure, RPG, and strategy games.

Problem solving is about clearly defining some sort of challenge for the player and communicating the means by which the problem can be solved. Thus, a major challenge of game design is creating interesting and challenging problems that have logical solutions that the player can eventually figure out by playing the game. If the solutions are too easy, the player will finish too quickly and go on to someone else's games (your major competitor, perhaps). On the other hand, if the solutions are too difficult to figure out, the player will give up in frustration.

This may sound easy, but the fact is many games still have illogical or just too difficult puzzles or challenges for the players. The appeal of problem solving in a game is directly related to the roles of achievement and failure. People don't mind the risk of failure (it's part of the challenge). But if achievement is impossible or just simply not available, a problem becomes unsolveable and is no longer a problem; it's a roadblock.

One interesting take on presenting problem solving in games is to construct problems that require the players to bring their existing knowledge on how the world works and use that to solve the problem. Many games' problem solving knowledge is confined to your knowledge of the game itself, and for most games this is fine.

However, there are many games, particularly adventure games or "interactive stories," where you can present puzzles of the real world knowledge type. An easy example of this type of approach is the old puzzle of being trapped in a giant pit with a board and a rock; and there's a stream of water dropping into the pit and then down into some sort of drain. The player takes the rock and covers the drain, filling the pit with water and using the board to float to the top. A very simple example, but again, when designing games, especially when trying to challenge people who aren't avid gamers, consider constructing these types of puzzles.

Whenever you can make the player an integral part of the problem solving process, the better chance you'll have at getting players hooked on your game. An example of a game that does this well is SimCity.

Role Playing and Entering Other Worlds

Perhaps the most fundamental appeal of computer and video games is escapism. Most games are role-playing games, casting you into an imaginary world or situation. People play games for the same reason they go to movies or read books: Humans have an imagination, and most people need to have their imaginations stimulated. While movies and books do that, games take imagination one step further and actually allow players to participate.

What this means from a game design standpoint is that it is an important responsibility for you to convey to the players the idea that they have crossed over to another world. Game design in this role tries to create a different here and now aura. Whether it's as simple as a shoot-em-up or as complex as Broderbund's new court case product, In the First Degree, one of the goals is to create a world, and within it a role that the player assumes.

Suspension of Disbelief

We just talked about entering other worlds and the distinct human trait of imagination. The ultimate incarnation of this idea is a common design term heard in the game development crowd, "suspension of disbelief." When game designers talk about the "suspension of disbelief," they are describing what I call an "imaginative state." This is the point where a player's consciousness lapses into the world of the game environment, where he or she is not playing a game but actually experiencing another place.

Now, one could laugh at this notion, or on the opposite end, one could say it's entirely possible when virtual reality hardware arrives. Of course they are both very wrong. Authors, and before the written word, story tellers, were able to create the same state in their audience. Have you ever been in front of a camp fire in the middle of the woods and start telling ghost stories? Do it well enough, and your eyes will start seeing shadows.

Personal Experiences

Another core component of game design is the personal experience the player has with the product. In working on my game this year, I have focused on three core components of a player's personal experience when playing a game.

Having Fun

I don't think you have to be a rocket scientist (or work at Rocket Science Games) to understand that a game has to be fun. Defining fun is, of course, a subjective experience. Only play testing will determine whether a product is indeed fun. It's important to understand that a game only needs to be fun for those people who will play it. If you're designing a game for women specifically, you won't add the same elements that make a game fun for many young boys.

Learning

I don't think every game needs to be a total learning experience in the pure educational sense of the term. Instead I think all good games require you to learn in order to conquer a game, either learning weaknesses of opponents or figuring out the answer to a puzzle in a game. In both cases you want to deliberately plan these events. If you want the player to have to learn the computer's weaknesses, you deliberately plan what those weaknesses are.

Exploring

The most important component beyond fun is the personal experience of exploring an alternate reality. We all go to movies or read fictional books for one major reason: escapism. Games offer the chance to give people the ultimate in escapism through amazing graphics, artificial intelligence, 3D sound, and wild imaginations married to the interactive component of games. The biggest aspect of this in my mind is the principal of exploration. Here is my game, explore it, become consumed in it, cast away the world you're in, and assume a life exploring my world. Exploring is a key component. Above all when you're constructing a game, you are in essence exploring a new world.

Is That All There Is?

There is much more to game design than these basic notions. Game design is incredibly subjective, and so far you've been exposed to only a few of my thoughts on design. Like any good student, you should always search and explore more to broaden your knowledge. At the end of Chapter 6, you'll find a list of additional resources to help you understand other ideas about game design.

In addition, understand that all reading and inspiration for game development doesn't just come from reading about game design or playing other games. Many of the developers I've talked to tend to be people who enjoy consuming thoughts and ideas from all kinds of sources.

Game design is the renaissance art of the information age. A true renaissance artist is is a jack of all trades, and that very persona consumes massive amounts of thought from diverse sources. Search for design ideas and stimuli beyond just the small amount of written material specifically about game design.

Game Design: A Constant Series of Trade-offs...

A simple way of looking at game design and development is as a constant series of trade-offs. Whether it's graphics vs. gameplay or strategy vs. arcade action, you'll always have to choose one direction in your quest for the perfect game.

The problem with this method is that for every decision you make, nine times out of ten you'll have to give up an equally desirable trait that you also want in your game. That's the essence of a trade-off. How you handle these crucial development dilemmas will have a big impact in your game's success.

I've outlined some of the more infamous game trade-off decisions commonly encountered. This outline could not possibly cover the potentially thousand possible decisions you'll have to make that qualify as trade-offs. However, as you design your game, consider the trade-offs you will eventually face and determine, if at all possible, what direction you will take.

In any trade-off situation there are four possible options for you to consider, as shown in Figure 5.1.

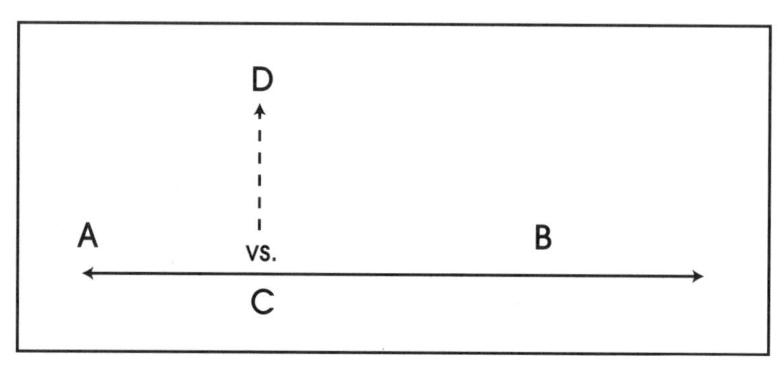

Figure 5.1 Game design dilemmas.

Options A and B are polar opposites in the design scheme; as you begin to favor one, the other option becomes unusable. The other two options are C and D. Choice C represents finding a workable balance between options A and B. However, just because it's a balance doesn't mean that it's a good option. Finally, we come to option D, which is the most desired option, but also the hardest to attain. Option D represents a solution that allows both A and B. In most cases, the route to D is paved through an awesome technical solution or a very clever design. More often than not, though, trying to breakthrough to option D all the time isn't going to get your game done in a reasonable amount of time or keep it within budget.

Now that we've got the logistics out of the way, let's apply the diagram in Figure 5.1 to some real life examples. Here are some of the more classic trade-off situations you're likely to encounter.

Dilemma 1: Graphics vs. Gameplay

This dilemma just keeps cropping up and it's a tough one to solve; the classic case of fancy graphics or in-depth gameplay. We all want to have both; after all, isn't that what a killer game is all about? So do you spend your time creating cool digital video or a wide open world? Or do you spend time and resources with intricate gameplay, level design, and interactive elements? Believe it or not, there is success on both sides of the equation. Dragon's Lair for example, took the graphic road and ended up with a highly addictive game because of the amazing animation; however, the gameplay was simply joystick sequence memorizations. On the gameplay side of the equation, there are products such as Civilization or Master of Magic, hardly graphical masterpieces, but fluid awesome gameplay have made both of these big hits.

Dilemma 2: Linear vs. Non-Linear

Does your game take a very linear approach (1 to 2 to 3) or does it offer the player an open sequence of steps to complete the game? Sometimes you need a little linearity to maintain the storyline or to make it easier to develop. Other times the less linear the better; giving the player more control and the chance to explore.

Dilemma 3: Features vs. Time

You want to add all kinds of cool features but you're under a deadline. Do you take the time to add more features and let your deadline slip, or do you opt for fewer features and stay on track? If you choose to sacrifice features, which ones should go away with last month's turkey leftovers?

Dilemma 4: Arcade vs. Strategy

Some players prefer only one type of game, others like both types, but most folks tend to shy away from the games that combine both arcade elements and traditional strategy. Among strategy enthusiasts, you can doom your game by adding any arcade elements.

Dilemma 5: Core Market vs. Wider Audience

We talked about this in detail earlier. But this point is hardly minor. You don't want to lose your hard-core enthusiasts, but you also don't want to kill your potentially new audience before they get a chance to see what you have to offer. Whoever said this stuff was easy, never dealt with this rising dilemma!

Dilemma 6: New Technology vs. Wider Base

A fundamental problem in the gaming industry, if there ever was one. While you may be privy to the hottest new technology, your consumers probably aren't. Herein lies the dilemma. Do you forsake features like super hi-res implementations and large sound files to reach more consumers? Or do you push the limits, ignore the plight of the standard consumer, and be hailed in the market as being the first developer with stunning new graphics and gameplay? Trailblazers have broken through big time, but also have gone down in blazes of glory. What will happen to you?

Dilemma 7: Platform Specific vs. Highly Portable

This little gem is a variation of dilemma 4. In this situation do you code very specifically—adding all the bells and whistles—for your platform because your code isn't very portable? Or do you spend additional time and relax the design and other features to make the product more conducive to rapid porting to other platforms?

As you can see, there are clear strategic decisions you will face in making your game. Unfortunately, these dilemmas don't come with a clear answer; what works best is *never* universal. Your ability to properly weigh the advantages and disadvantages will determine, up to a point, your success. Spend some time creating a variety of game dilemma situations and determine how you would handle them; the more you think about these dilemmas, the more you'll develop a sound overall philosophy about game design.

CHAPTER 6

Don't reveal everything until it is time!

Storytelling, Design Details, and Interface Design

The Art of Storytelling

Storytelling is one of the most basic human activities. Perhaps the most demonstrable difference between humans and animals is the ability to imagine things and describe them to other people. (After all, when was the last time your cat told you a good story!) Cave paintings created 100,000 years ago were perhaps the first type of recorded stories. From these humble beginnings, we have evolved into creatures capable of telling interactive stories—perhaps the most sophisticated story tool in the history of storytelling.

Most games use some sort of storyline in one of two ways: either as a simple background tale to enhance the game or as an entire script to create the interactive flow of the game. In games that use a storyline to embellish or explain the circumstances of the game, the story adds a nice element but it is not really essential. For example, most arcade side-scrolling games like Donkey Kong Country or Sonic are based on some sort of simple storyline that gives the game a little more depth and makes the game more fun to play. However, if the story were removed, the game could still stand on its own. The action in the game turns out to be the interactive element that makes players want to play the game. Game stories are presented in these types of games in the manual or perhaps by some "cut scene" animations and text sprinkled throughout the game.

The second category, games that are stories themselves, use stories as the central interactive element. Some examples include Sierra's Quest games or Origin's Ultima series. In these games, the main goal for the player is to advance through the story. The game designer's job is to create (or use) a story that gets the reader hooked on the game. Often, the player becomes one of the characters in the story, which greatly contributes to the interactive nature of the game.

In creating interactive fiction games, you can draw on many of the effective concepts used in theater, television, and movies to create more dynamic games. An interactive fiction game should be based on a much more involved story and script.

A simple variation of games completely based on stories are games that use stories to string together various sections of the game. For example, many simulation type games now incorporate storylines to enhance the action. Here a player might fly a series of missions in a flight simulator connected together with a storyline. This technique can help make a game seem more like a cohesive adventure instead of a series of separate activities. The overriding goal is to use a storyline to enhance the game play and keep the player as stimulated as possible.

How Games Make Stories Interactive

When designing a game that is essentially a story, it's important to understand what makes a story interactive. In the previous chapter we spent a considerable amount of time discussing some of the more fundamental game design features, including achievement, failure, changing the outcome, and so on. By combining these concepts with a story, you can create very effective and entertaining interactive stories.

In thinking about interactive stories, you might be asking the question, what comes first, the story or the game? For a true interactive story, the story comes first. For a game that uses a story as embellishment, both components should be developed at the same time. Although, some semblance of the game has to be generated in order to define the story.

The other ingredients that help make stories more interactive are the essential gameplay components including decisions, skills, puzzles, problem solving, and so on. Without them, your game will come across as a dull electronic book. The story requires a level of input and response for the player so that the story can unfold and progress. In a sense, the player controls how the story is told.

Linear and Non-Linear Storytelling

Two common concepts used by game designers who create interactive stories are *non-linear* and *linear* storytelling. These design concepts are actually used in all areas of game design; however, they are most applicable when we discuss the techniques of game storytelling.

A game that is based on a linear story is essentially a game whose story is essentially a straight line with no deviation or variants. The story is told, some interaction takes place, and depending on the outcome, more story is given. This process continues until the final story element is presented. This linear approach is used by a majority of interactive story games.

Non-linear story games, on the other hand, are games where the player doesn't necessarily follow a specific order to complete the game. Multiple routes through the game are possible and along the way the player must solve various puzzles or problems. In many cases, not every route needs to be investigated. Unlike a linear story, the object of a non-linear story is to maintain some sort of overall story, but allow the players the freedom to pursue various paths as *they* wish.

Currently, game designers frequently debate what exactly is and isn't a true non-linear storyline. Some designers feel that a story having multiple routes or variable outcomes and such, is not really different from a linear storyline. The player still follows a mostly pre-defined route even if the sequence may differ from game to game.

For our purposes though, you just need to understand that a linear storyline offers no choice to the player as to the route and outcome of a game. A non-linear storyline, on the other hand, always offers choices so that the player can feel that he or she can constantly change the outcome of the story. The best way to think of any game, in relation to these two concepts, is to view them as opposite forces, then figure out what mix of the two your game will have as shown in Figure 6.1.

Creating Good Game Stories

Some amazing and highly entertaining stories have been made into games. For example, Raymond Feist's Betrayal at Krondor was a major adaptation of a book Mr. Feist wrote. On the other hand, we have some great stories that are only known as games. Ultima IV falls into this category. Both game stories are excellent, yet they were created by two different processes: One was a story turned into a game and the other began as a game story.

How Well Can an Existing Story Be Adapted to an Interactive Game?

Many games are built from original works of fiction for marketing and sales reasons. Think about it; books become popular because they present good (or at least entertaining) stories. Once a game developer knows that a particular story is popular, he or she can justify doing the hard work to adapt the story to the computer screen. This is what you might call a safe bet. After all, the game developer should have a ready market for the game—the diehard fans of the original book! Keep in mind, though, that the key to success is in picking a story (or book) that can properly be turned into an interactive game. As with movies, games that are based on books, usually must must make changes to the story to make it work in a different medium.

Recall that in the previous chapter we discussed the importance of being able to affect the outcome of a game. The challenge is that stories are linear; they start on page one and always finish on the last page. A game doesn't necessarily do that. It may end on page 20, 145, 542, or 234. Where it ends depends on the player. So right

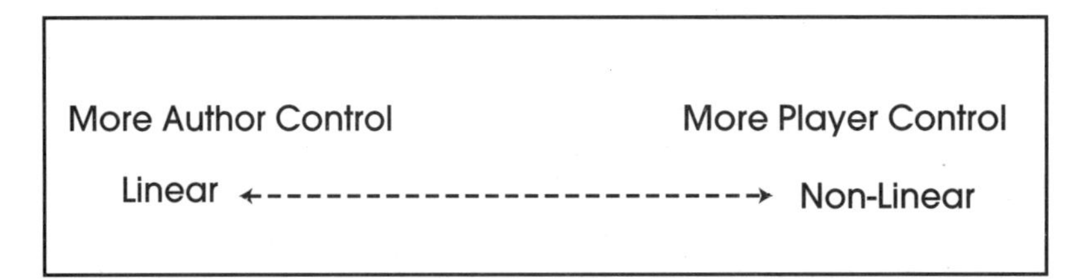

Figure 6.1 Using techniques of linear and non-linear storytelling to create interactive games.

off the bat, any book will need some adapting. Even if the final outcome of your game is the same as the book, you will need to add plot twists, pitfalls, obstacles along the way, and so on. Additionally, you might need to change to ending or provide different levels of endings. Then, people familiar with the original work won't be predisposed to the game's final ending. Wouldn't it be cool to take a tragic ending of say a Shakespearean type tragedy and make the player's goal to overcome the fatal flaw of the central character? Games are great vehicles for placing the players into a familiar storyline and giving them a "What If?" potential outcome.

How Well Can a Story Emerge from a Game?

This is a crucial factor to good game stories. In my opinion, from a player's prespective, I have never seen a good interactive story game that is driven by the story. Instead, every great game story I have experienced is driven by the gameplay. The story emerges from the game; the game doesn't emerge from the story.

The very notion of interactivity means that the decisions and skills of the player will move the story in a certain direction. Thus, the game becomes the interface for the story. The player interacts with the game, which then results in the game presenting back to the player the actual underlying story. This is a very different approach from writing a book or reading one from beginning to end. While a writer may indeed divide a book into component scenes, he or she never has to think about the book being read in a different order or having to compose multiple outcomes for the story. In addition, a book writer doesn't have to worry about how the players' skills will affect any part of the story.

Understand that successful game stories can draw upon other successful stories or can be entirely new. Either way, how you present the story and allow the game to drive it back to the player is going to determine the success of the story. Toward those ends, I've compiled some ideas and advice for presenting stories as games.

Dramatic Unfolding

One thing I've encountered in many games that I absolutely can't understand is that the game tells me everything about the story up front. This is typically done in the manual or with the game's opening sequence. For example, a manual might tell you something like this in the introduction:

"Mort the evil wizard has reigned darkness on the land and now it's up to you to get the great pink staff from the bottom of dungeon Dweezil and use it to take Mort out!"

Did you ever see a murder mystery where the detective knows at the start who killed the victim? This would make the show rather boring since you would just be watching the detective fill out paperwork or something instead of learning how to solve the who, what, where, and when of the crime.

Too few game designers use techniques of dramatic unfolding. My sense is that many game designers are overly concerned about making their game stories easy to understand, and thus they don't think about using techniques to keep the player in suspense. A well designed game places the player in a situation where something is wrong and lets the player spend time finding out exactly what is wrong. Then, as it becomes clear exactly what has gone wrong, the player logically can start to figure out how to change the outcome. This creates an excellent sense of drama and mystery that too few games tend to adopt.

The Art of Design Details

Let's take a moment to discuss some of the more detailed issues of game design. We're not going to discuss them all right now since some of them, such as sound, are best left for later chapters. Here, we'll look at some of the more specific decisions you'll need to make during your early design stages. I'll present a number of different options so that you can make the right choices.

Graphical Design Decisions

The most important initial decision to make while designing your game is how the graphical display should be created. Ninety percent of human sensory perception is through sight. And, for a more mundane fact, good graphics sell games (even bad games, unfortunately). The graphical abilities of hardware have improved dramatically. Therefore, many games are rapidly incorporating sophisticated high resolution graphics. This is true even for games that typically don't require a lot of graphics.

The design concerns of realistic graphics lie mostly with fictional games. In presenting most non-fictional material, such as sports events, incorporating graphical realism using techniques like motion capture and digital video is straightforward. But for fictional type products, there are many different ways to go about designing graphics, interfaces, animation, background scenes, and so on.

In many situations art is better than realism. People enjoy games as works of art, and just as better graphics have allowed for more realistic images, they have allowed for even more impressive artwork. For example, I have always wanted to design a game about the middle ages, where the characters were animated tapestry representations instead of digitized actors. This is the type of creative decision making that you can incorporate in your designs. Don't assume that rendering reality is necessarily the best option. The resurgence of animation in the movie industry is a great indicator that the public has a large appetite for characterized or artistic forms of imagery in storytelling.

One of the most crucial decisions you need to make is what view (or mix of view types) a game will have. Before computers became as powerful as they are today, this decision used to be very simple. But today the added power of computers and consoles allows designers to create very different games with different view types. Let's explore the various types and identify some key points about each one.

2D Side Scrollers

Side scrollers are basically used for arcade-style games. Figure 6.2 shows a screen shot of a more traditional 2D side scroller. These games provide multiple levels that the player can advance to as he or she progresses through the game. Typically, each level has its own unique artwork and often new characters (or bad guys) are introduced at each level.

2D Top Down

Top down games can come in two flavors: top down view and top down/side view. With the standard top down view, the player looks at everything top down. This is like standing on top of a tall building and looking down on the ground. With top down/side view, a map is rendered in 2D and the objects on the map are rendered as side or front views. Figure 6.3 shows two of Sid Meir's games, Colonization and Civilization, which are strategic games that work well in the top down mode because they are based on a map navigational system.

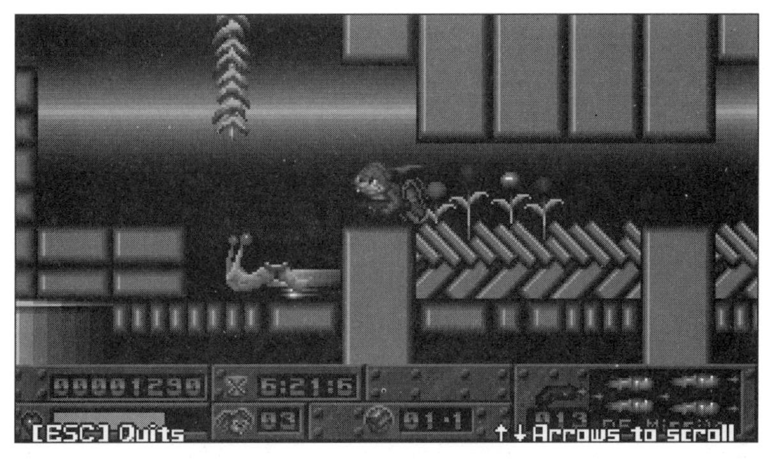

Figure 6.2 Jazz Jackrabbit is a good example of your standard side scroller with multiple levels of adventure.

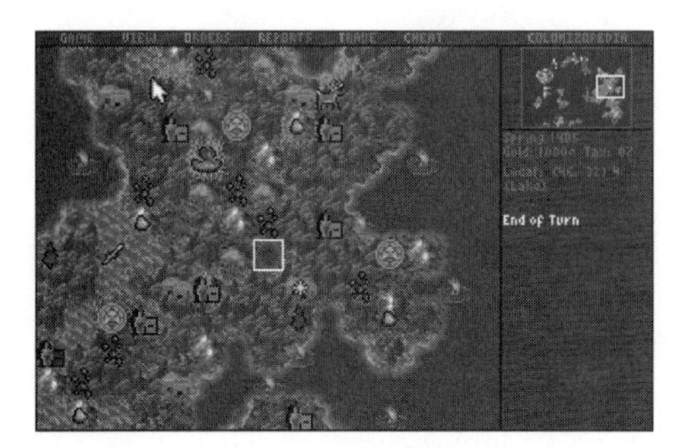

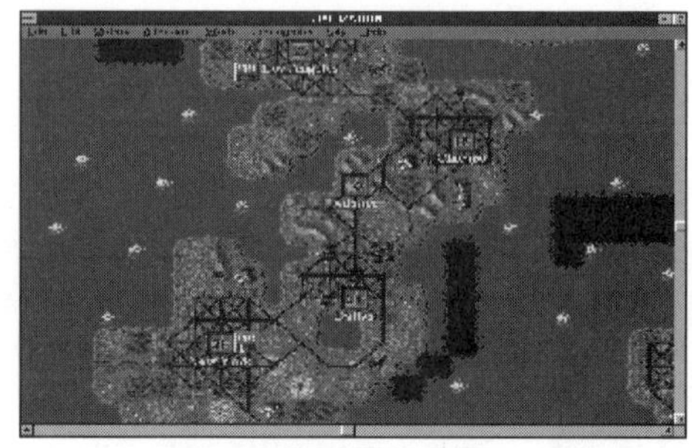

Figures 6.3 These screens illustrate a common view for wargames, RPGs, and other strategy map oriented games like these games from Microprose.

Third-Person 3/4 View

This view is basically a cousin of the top down view, but it has much more of a 3D look. The graphics are drawn at an angle to the floor to show a 3/4 view. Origin has been using this view quite successfully in its latest Ultima games. As an example, Figure 6.4 shows how Ultima VIII uses this view. Games like SimCity and Bullfrog's Syndicate have been using 3/4 views from the start.

3D Point-of-View "Step Engine"

This view is perhaps the precursor to what we now call the *raycaster*. Basically, the "walls" of the view are pre-rendered to certain angles, sizes, and lighting. Then, they are drawn on the screen depending on the x,y and n,s,e,w position of the character. Movement is limited to 90 degree turns and the depth may take 3 to 5 steps to reach the furthest displayed object. This view was used in such early classics as Ultima, Wizardry, Dungeon Master, and The Bards Tale. Once faster

Figure 6.4 This view from Origin's Ultima VIII shows a really nicely drawn 3/4 view.

machines came along making raycasting possible, this relatively simpler graphical view was left by the wayside.

Point-of-View Polygonal/Raycaster

This is the type of view made popular by many games like Castle Wolfenstein, Doom, Shadow Caster, and System Shock. It consists of a 3D view containing walls and floors, which moves smoothly with lighting and line of sight in real time. Despite the ascendancy of polygonal based 3D graphics, raycasters will continue to play a prominent role in gaming. Next generation 3D raycasting engines like Bethesda's Xengine and Id Software's Quake, as shown in Figures 6.5, are about to bring further levels of detail and resolution to this graphical view.

First-Person 3D Point-of-View Polygonal

This view is used by your generic flight-simulator game, as shown in Figure 6.6. Of course, most flight simulators can also display a third-person point of view, but the main simulator view is the first-person one.

Third-Person Point of View Polygonal or Pre-Rendered

With fast machines becoming available almost overnight, this view is quickly turning into the view of choice for most new games. Either by rendering on the fly (Virtua Fighter) or pre-rendering the animations and then just blitting them to the screen (Origin's Bioforge), this view presents a third-person view of any number of potential

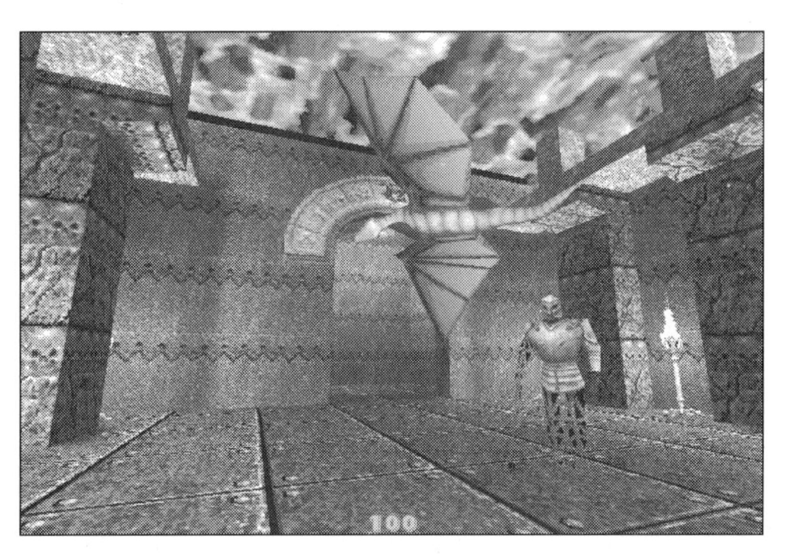

Figure 6.5 This shot from Doom's successor Quake is actually a polygonal version of the traditional raycaster view. By using polygons instead of raycasted tiles, they are able to create far more realistic shapes for their game.

Figure 6.6 Here you see a classic "flight-simulator" from Microsoft Flight Simulator 5.1.

angles. Programmers like to call this technique true 3D rendering "on the fly." This is an excellent view for fighting games or games that need to animate multiple characters on the screen at the same time.

Figure 6.7 shows an example of how awesome graphical animations are created in Origin's BioForge by combining motion capture with third-person views. This game is a real cinematic adventure where you take the role of a Cyborg being. By using a third-person view, Origin was able to create different "camera angles" and produce a more "movie-like" look and feel to the product.

Character Creation

In the early days, few game designers were able to create characters or personalities out of the crude objects that players interacted with or controlled. Nevertheless, a few games did succeed in bringing personalities to life such as Floyd the Robot from Infocom's Planetfall. But for the most part, creating a real character with a computer game was tough. After all, what sort of attitude or personality was conveyed by Pac-Man?

Today, computer games have the ability to render high quality artwork and display dazzling animation. Armed with large storage capacity, these machines offer designers a powerful tool for creating highly in-depth characters. And these characters are not

Figure 6.7 Third-person point of view graphics created with Origin's BioForge.

just limited to interactive story games. Sega's Sonic the Hedgehog incorporates lots of little animated parts to bring out a more character-like persona. For example, when left alone, Sonic looks at the screen and, rather peeved, taps his foot waiting for action. In the Ultima series, Origin has worked over a long series of titles to bring out the character in its world's inhabitants, many of whom like Dupre and Iolo, span across multiple works and have become household names among fans of the series.

Game designers can no longer get away creating one-dimensional static characters. Not only are players frowning on 2D graphics but on 2D characters as well. So let's discuss some ways for designing better characters for interactive games.

Give Your Characters Depth

As you are developing your characters, write down everything in a journal or character bible and include as much background information as you possibly can. Here are some of the questions you'll want to ask yourself:

- What is their life like?
- Are they married?
- What things do they like and dislike?
- Are they friendly or mean?
- How do they interact with other characters?
- What personality quirks do they have?
- What kind of emotions do they express?

- Do they have any special talents?
- Are they generally happy or sad?
- Do they make people laugh or do they scare the heck out of people?
- Do they communicate well or do they have problems expressing themselves?

Come up with anything you can that will add to the character's persona. Of course, not all of these traits will probably make their way into your game, but they will help you make your characters much more interesting. Your detailed personality descriptions will also help your art staff come up with ideas.

Give Your Characters Attitude

People tend to relate to characters that express a distinct attitude. Try to go for extremes—make your character especially angry or happy or impatient. The attitude you project greatly helps define the "motion" for the character and how the character interacts with the player and other characters and objects in the game. For ideas, look at a game like Sonic or Shiny's hit product Earthworm Jim, as shown in Figure 6.8. Through ample use of whimsical animation, the main character has an attitude to which players really respond. Here we find a earthworm named Jim ready to take on the

Figure 6.8 Here is an artist's test sketch from the developers of Earthworm Jim, which illustrates the type of attitude conveyed just by the way the artist drew this material.

world with his edgy style. In Sonic, the main character is impatient and he taps his foot constantly. He's got a certain speedy style.

Use Multimedia Sound to Add Depth

In RPGs or interactive stories, you can make use of voice-overs with good actors to give your characters' voices the proper stress. Voice is, in my opinion, ten times better than video for adding depth to a character in a story.

Level Design

Well, if you haven't done it before, play around with some of the games that let you make your own levels. Certainly your game might be different, but the conceptual techniques and issues for designing levels are similar. Here are some of the more important ones to consider:

- What new characters and objects will be introduced?
- What new obstacles will be added?
- What is the basic layout?
- What will be the new level of difficulty (for example, will enemies multiply or come at the main character faster?)
- What is the design and color scheme?
- What will the background artwork look like?
- What new animation techniques will be incorporated?
- How will the player move from the current level to the next one?
- What problems and puzzles need to be solved?

Getting good at level design takes quite a bit of practice. The first key to successful level design is to get your hands on a good level editor. A level editor is basically a graphical program that allows you to interactively create all of the key components for your level. Fortunately, many tools and examples are available to help you develop your skills. We'll look at a few of the more popular ones in a moment.

Level design is a world unto itself. Programming a game and designing levels for it should not be considered the same skill set (although one person may possess both skills). I have heard many a story about developers making a fantastic game engine and level editor, but bringing in the skills, or having another person develop the specific skills, of level design. It's a specialty and should be treated as such in your development plans.

Level design is the art of taking the resources provided by the complete game engine and applying the essential ingredients of puzzles and challenges that actually form the game. A game engine is not a game; the actual levels and challenges designed to be played using the game engine are the game, and that's why many companies have people who program the game engines and other people who design levels with those engines.

Doom II

The cool thing about Doom is that Id Software released the spec for their level files, giving rise to all kinds of third party applications for modifying and editing new levels for Doom. If you want to experiment with level design skills and look at various level design examples, check out some of the various Doom editors like DOOMCAD.

Abuse

The game Abuse, as shown in Figure 6.9, was created by a new company, Crack Dot Com. This game has a completely cool level editor filled with all kinds of wild scripting/AI functionality. It's perhaps the most open ended level editor released; and it's no wonder, since Dave Taylor, a member of Id Software, helped fund this company.

Abuse's level editing requires a lot of work, but you can learn a lot about level editing and game design in general just by trying to construct one good level. It's not easy, despite a really well done editor, simply because good level editing is hard to do. Abuse is probably one of the best examples of a well constructed game engine with editor.

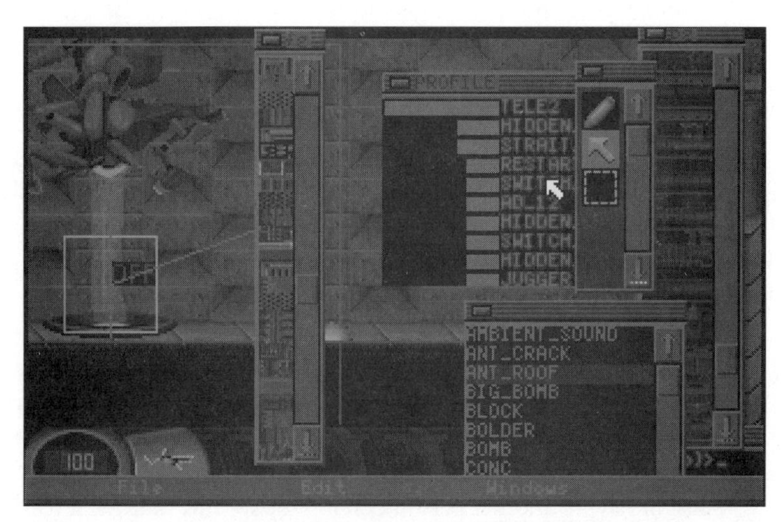

Figure 6.9 Using Abuse's level editor you can add detailed levels to the game.

The developers created a complete WYSIWYG editing environment that makes the complex task of level editing much easier with windowing, menus, and other GUI goodies. Many companies are including level editors with their products to allow players to become game designers, creating an unending supply of new challenges.

Simulating Environments

As games become more complex and developers seek to build entire worlds and self-contained systems, the notion of simulating entire environments comes more into play. During my research, I noticed that many of the leading developers in the business (Peter Molyneux of Bullfrog, Sid Meir of Microprose, Chris Crawford, Richard Garriot and company) are now talking more about not only building games with realistic graphics, but realistic underlying systems.

There are two distinct types of simulation. The first requires the use of readily available statistical databases and easy to define formulas. One example of a game built on this model is baseball, in particular Electronic Arts' Earl Weaver Baseball. The world of baseball can be realistically simulated because loads of statistical data is available to use. You can devise formulas for concepts like the physics of a hit ball or the speed of a shortstop fairly easily. The other type of simulation is represented in games like SimCity, which are much harder to create. The data used in a game like this is much harder to gather and model into a coherent simulative system.

The challenge of simulation games is in creating algorithmic representations of the world. So instead of having a table of set prices in an RPG game for swords and shields, you would need to include an entire economic system based on the real world principles of classic supply and demand, and then have the game determine the prices dynamically.

From a design standpoint, simulation games require ingenuity and research—there aren't exactly books filled with formulas of this stuff! A great example of algorithmic representation of environments that can help you explore the thought process behind this is Chris Crawford's book about his experience making the game Balance of Power. For those of you not familiar with it, BoP was a game about geopolitical war between the U.S. and U.S.S.R. To create the game, Chris Crawford had to come up with algorithmic systems that determine success of insurgents in a given country, and many other factors. In the book, he spends a lot of time explaining the actual formulas he developed and the research and reasoning behind them. If you take the time to look at the bibliographies associated with some of the more simulation-intensive games like SimCity, you'll discover the extensive research that these developers did to create their games.

Simulating entire worlds takes extensive thought and care. After all, "playing God" is not easy. From the humble beginning of a game called Life, computer programmers have been charging forward to create artificial systems. Even looking back at games from the mid 80s, I can easily see that game developers have perhaps a unique passion and approach to this problem and perhaps may even be the ones doing the most groundbreaking work, whether they know it or not!

Algorithmic/Artificial Intelligence Compared to Scripting

Creating interesting game environments and especially interesting non-player-characters or opponents is one of the goals game developers have only recently begun to master. There are two techniques you can use to do this: Artificial Intelligence (AI) and scripting.

The difference between them is similar to the difference between pre-rendered graphics and on-the-fly rendering. Scripting is easier to implement and has exacting detail. AI-based processing, on the other hand, is much harder to implement but it offers some amazing possibilities.

Deciding exactly how to use these techniques will probably take some serious time. If you're just a pure designer, you'll probably leave some of this up to the programming staff, concerning yourself with just the desired end result.

If you are determined to tackle some of these issues on your own, you've got a lot of learning to do. I've been working on some of these issues for a never-ending RPG product I was working on before I started this book. Chris Crawford, who has over ten professional games to his credit, has been tackling a highly AI-type storytelling scheme for over three years.

Most games use a combination of scripting and AI. Scripting is used to define the actions and responses of characters, and more specialized AI routines and algorithms are used to embellish the action and make the characters appear to have more intelligence and human-like qualities.

Consistency of Design

In the movie business, continuity experts are used to make sure that all of the scenes in a movie are accurate. This person or group of people participates during the entire shooting process to keep mistakes from being made. During the editing process, the continuity expert watches each scene closely and takes close notes so that scenes can be fixed. (And despite this, mistakes are always made, such as an actor walking out of the pouring rain into a salon to have a quick drink and then walking out into a bright sunny day.)

Good games also demand consistent designs. Puzzles must be well integrated into a story, the artwork must be clean and accurate, sprites must be fine tuned and their movements must be adjusted, sound effects must be accurately timed, and so on. In short, nothing should appear out of place. The logic or strategy necessary to finish or excel at the game must be consistent throughout the game. Overall, the game should have a good sense of balance.

Some Design Dilemmas

One common way to approach game design is to think of it as a series of questions you have to answer. These questions deal with the key dilemmas of game design. Game development, as I've said earlier, is best described as engineering oriented, and engineering is geared toward answering questions and solving problems.

How Much Detail Do You Need?

Chris Crawford, in his book *The Balance of Power*, provides a very interesting comparison of designing simulations and games. As a designer, it is very important to understand the differences and challenges.

In the book Chris talks about the main dilemma in creating a simulation. He calls it "*verisimilitude in detail.*" The dilemma is this: How much detail is needed to make a simulation a good simulation? Put too much in, and it might be too simulative. Put in too little, and people will see it as "less real" and more game-like. To take this idea further, consider the example of a simulation of a presidential election. Having a background in campaigning, I would love a game that had all kinds of detail in it, that really simulated every mundane detail in running a campaign. That detail is important to me, since I have such a deep understanding of the process. Now take the same product and put it in front of school teachers and their classes. The amount of detail they would want and accept is totally different. The additional content I might require would push it away from being a "game" that people would enjoy for its play value.

Certainly some of this is a market decision. You will have to define early on the parameters of the market you want to reach. Even then you must consider technical and implementation issues. To produce an election game of the detail I would find appealing would take a large amount of research and statistical data to be compiled.

In designing your game, you must decide up front exactly what amount of detail is required. Some game designers work this out by putting in the detail where it is most needed. For example, consider a submarine simulation. If you were going to make it very detailed in one area, what might that be? Of course the "Torpedoing Section." You might make it easy to move the sub around and find ships to blast; but once you've

found a ship, the game could allow you to get very involved in the process of firing torpedoes, since this is the focal point of a sub game anyway.

When Is a Task a Chore?

In some situations, a game can become so real that the tasks in the game turn into chores. I remember a game called Falcon from Spectrum Holybyte, an incredible simulation that allowed you to pilot an F-16 fighter. The simulation was so real that the player had to do many of the tasks a real pilot would do to take off. The work was so extensive that it took a lot of fun out of the game. Other examples of this defect can be found in some RPG games where the player finds that he or she spends more time running "errands" than he or she does in real life. This isn't to say these games aren't good. Falcon is an amazingly accurate simulation, and many simulation fans crave this level of detail. Understand, though, that many games do take the objective of realism a little too far.

The biggest problem for me is when "tasks" become more like chores. Although I can see how they contribute to the sense of realism, to me they end up being more of an impediment to playing the game. Again, this is a dilemma of having fun contrasted to stressing accuracy and realism. The most elegant games solve this problem by adding settings for people to control the realism factors. The higher the setting, the more realistic a game becomes.

It's important to test simulation games during the game development cycle to see how people react to the tasks you put them through. If your tasks turn out to be too simple or complex, you can always adjust them during the testing stage.

Task Bottlenecks

Look for "task bottlenecks" in your games. Task bottlenecks are of two types, *necessary* and *hidden*. The necessary task bottlenecks are the worst kind. These are the activities that a game requires you to perform over and over to progress through the game. An example of this might be found in an adventure game that adds some sort of gambling element as a way for players to increase cash. In this case, you might spend an entire day playing various stupid gambling games for the sole purpose of raising cash. Not exactly a fun day, and it creates a bottleneck toward the true goal of the game.

Hidden tasks are game flaws that allow players who spend time repeatedly doing something to gain a strategic advantage, even if the designer never actually intended this. While it's definitely not the designer's intention, gameplay still requires a period of "chores." A great example of this is in Ultima III. In this game, a town is provided called Death Gulch, which has some 35 chests of gold in it. In order to raise money quickly, a player can simply rob the gold over and over. It probably wasn't meant to be done, but again it became the de facto way to play the game. In my playing of that game, I must have gone through that cycle over 100 times.

Another similar example is in the original SimCity. It became obvious to me how to set up a city so that it would survive in a constant year after year state, not really growing or worsening. Subsequently I would collect a net of $3,000 to $4,000 in a cycle. I'd just leave my computer on overnight and wake up in the morning with $200,000 in my bank. Again the designers never meant that to be an element of gameplay, yet it existed.

The trick is to be vigilant for both types and put in place things that discourage this type of play. In the example of the Ultima town, they simply could have made the towns not regenerate the chests over and over. In the case of SimCity they could have done several things; one was to add random events to keep me from doing this. (The game does have this feature, but it was optional.) Or they could have had the cash generate faster thus not requiring the long waits to generate major cash.

The bottom line here is testing the product, and seeing where players find repetitive tasks they hate or use to circumvent various game problems. Most of the problems you find will be easily solvable and will prevent the game from devolving into a series of "chore like" repetitions.

Applying Market Concerns to Game Design

Many times your designs will need to be altered to fit the demands of the marketplace. When you are designing a game to be sold, it's important to remember that you must ultimately please your market, and not yourself or the other people working on the game. Your personal goal may be to please both, thus pleasing yourself, but make no mistake. You can't buy your own game, someone else has to, and they may have requirements and expectations different from yours.

When incorporating market considerations into your designs, the first step is to know your market. This is essentially asking: "Who is the average buyer of this game?" Then, try to make sure you consider their requirements. For example, let's plan out a deep sea diving game and walk through the market considerations:

> **Game Summary:** Deep Dive: A game about deep sea diving and searching for buried treasure. The object is to find all of the loot you can before the evil underwater lost souls get you.
>
> **The Market:** People who like diving, people who like adventure games, people who enjoy the ocean.

Here I've made some general assumptions. For example, this game should appeal to people who like adventure games. Thus, the game needs a detailed story—an essential requirement of adventure game fans. To appeal to people who like diving, we'd better make sure that we give them a convincing simulation of deep sea diving. After all, people who like diving are experts and they can't be easily fooled.

The idea here is that as you design your game and evolve your target player profile, you will be forced to adapt your ideas and designs to their requirements. This may at times take the game in different directions. Perhaps your original design didn't have a story really, it was a just a diving simulation. Well, the market for adventure games is much bigger overall, so here you may find yourself forced into adding a detailed story of mystery and intrigue.

In today's competitive game market, many game companies are working hard to create games large numbers of people want to play. You can bet they are combining market research with market driven design adjustments to help create the software that people are telling them they want.

Your personal views and opinions are certainly applicable. Just be sure not to make them in a world that you believe to be inhabited by people all like you. Assumptions like that can lead to disasters.

Pleasing Hard-Core Gamers—the Pros and Cons

As you are designing your game, make sure you consider the most important group of gamers out there—the hard-core gamers. High-tech marketing doctrine tells us that the rule of thumb is to please the hard-core people, and they will in turn generate the enthusiasm to help sale the product. They will recommend the product to other people who may be less "hard-core" and look to this group for help in making their purchasing decisions.

Understand as well that by following this path you might find yourself so eager to please a hard-core game fanatic that you fail to make a game that might be enjoyed by people who are more casual players. For example, people might not enjoy a wargame that takes 400 hours to complete or has over 100 different kinds of tanks. Instead, they might enjoy a really good, more linear oriented story game, or a game about relationships between people, rather than a blood fest. Sure there's overlap, but more and more developers are looking to define breakthrough games that appeal beyond the core gaming audience. The very fact that only a few games accomplish this each year shows the difficulty in doing this.

There really isn't a right or wrong approach here. As you design a game, you've got to figure out who the audience will be. It's important to think about both sides of the issue. It's also tough if you're like most people who enjoy developing games, because 99 percent of the time they themselves are members of the hard-core group! Thus, for many designers, only thinking deliberately about this issue forces them to think beyond what previously was standard practice.

If you really look to make a break from the types of games typically enjoyed by hard-core gamers, be careful not to leave out some key features for which hard core gamers and reviewers will crucify you. While features like modem play or networking might only be used by a small percentage of the game market, reviewers and other hard-core gamers who have considerable influence will look for them. It can cost an otherwise great game to be faulted in reviews and word of mouth.

Overall, make sure you understand the types of elements and features that please the game experts. Then, purposefully decide where it makes sense to implement those features and where it doesn't. The key word here is *purposefully.* Don't guess or assume; define what is specifically needed and you'll give yourself the maximum ability to create games that please hard-core gamers and perhaps also break out and find newer audiences beyond these folks.

The Art of the Interface

Bill Volk, a veteran game developer, once wrote that the equation for a game is "Interface + Production Elements = Games." This is similar in spirit to the classic equation penned by the famous programming language designer Nicholas Wirth, "Algorithms + Data Structures = Programs." Obviously Volk's goal was not to say that putting a game together is as simple as addition, but to stress the importance of the interface in game design. His point is essentially this:

Your game is your interface.

The interface is the gatekeeper of all of the interaction in a game. Whether you are using a simple joystick scheme or a complete windowing interface with multiple input devices, your interface is the link between the production elements and the player.

Interfaces can make or break games. When I first saw Dungeon Master on the Atari ST nearly 10 years ago, I was much more amazed by the interface than the game, which was nice in its own right. The interface made the game fun and interesting to play. To feed a player, you dragged and dropped a piece of food onto the player. To arm a player, you dragged a weapon into the player's hand. These are interface

techniques we take for granted today but back then they were very innovative concepts. This was the first game (and the first software program for that matter) that proved to me how useful a point and click interface could be.

Now that I've sold you on the importance of having a great interface, what are the ingredients and techniques you need to create one? We could fill this entire book with discussions just trying to answer this question. But there are some basic issues we can discuss to help you create more effective interfaces for your games.

Housekeeping Issues

Housekeeping issues are the tasks you need to perform to set up or prepare a person to play a game. These include the initial setup, loading and saving games, configuring a game, and any online instructions or general documentation.

Player Involvement Issues

The player involvement factor is probably the most important ingredient that goes into the interface. Essentially, it affects how the player controls the play in the game. Is it by keyboard, joystick, mouse, or a combination of these? Or could another type of input device be used? How do they ready a missile to fire? Is there a sequence of moves that launch a special move? Is there more than one way to do things? All of those questions are player involvement issues that need to be addressed.

Input Devices

This is also an issue of player involvement , but because devices like keyboards, mice, and joysticks are so crucial, their use should be considered in much detail. It's important to look at the range of devices available to control the play in a game. Among PCs there are many types of joysticks, some with digital input, some which are analog, some with two buttons, and some with one. Newer devices are available like full flight controls, steering wheels, and devices that hook up to consoles to add as many as four to six joysticks.

As you design your interface, make sure you explore the range of devices capable of feeding input into the game. Consider a wide range of flexibility and type of devices that can be applied to your game.

Getting a Player Started Fast!

When was the last time you picked up a new game and read the users manual cover to cover before you started up the game? If you are like most game players, you probably jumped in head first and tried to figure out how the game works by interacting with the game's interface. Game players aren't typical software users. They aren't interested in learning a lot of new features—they simply want to play! So when you're designing your interface, make it easy for people to jump right in. Your number one goal should be to make the game and the interface as intuitive as possible. Sure, you can provide a manual but don't expect all of your users to read it.

Let's look at some guidelines to help you design interfaces that encourage users to jump right in.

Reducing the Effect of Using a Computer

One of the more abstract concepts of interactivity, and also one of the components of the "suspension of disbelief" concept, is reducing the effect of using a computer. Certainly, when we sit down to use a computer, we are aware that what we are doing is using the computer to place ourselves in another world. However, when designing a game, especially its interface, the success you achieve in reducing the players' feeling that they are using a computer will contribute positively to the players' experience. I remember reading an interview with a developer who was asked why the game came without a manual describing all the monsters and stuff the player might encounter. The designer's answer was that every time the players took their eyes off the screen and referenced a manual, they left the designer's world, thus losing whatever suspension of disbelief they may have acquired.

Try to make the startup of your game fast and easy. The longer a player works to get into a game the more apparent that's what it is—a game. You'd think this would be a no brainer, but you still see it day in and day out.

Integrating Help into a Game

Incorporate your manuals into the game as much as possible. Reduce the need for the players to pull themselves away from the screen and the input device to access written text. This can be accomplished mostly through elegant design, but if needed, incorporate the text into the game. For example, if you are creating an adventure game, have the screen open up to a book of weapons or monsters or whatever. Or how about a flight simulator that uses voice-over to tell the pilot what to do like a real trainer would? "OK—ease back on the stick...." The idea here is to integrate the help into the game and make it part of the overall experience.

For example, if you have a map you want the player to use, don't make it part of the documentation, incorporate it as a graphic on the screen.

Avoiding the Standard Interface

Microsoft will probably kill me for saying this, but for most games designed in the Windows environment, try not to use the conventional Windows interface. If you do, you are again reminding them that they are using a computer. Use other objects for buttons and customize the dialogs. Avoid menus and such that remind people they're using computers.

Integrating the Interface

The key message that's been presented here is simple. For many application products an interface is an absolute gateway to the product's features. But for games, the goal is to drive the interface more and more into the fabric of the game itself. As more people take to games, some with little if any traditional computer experience, interface issues become more and more important.

How Does Game Design Evolve?

Game design will move forward just as it always has. Developers will continue to push out new ideas and more refined versions of existing games. How do you and I become better designers? It's becoming harder to find games that truly "break the mold" or ones that don't make the same basic mistakes. The trick is to become far more deliberate in expanding your ideas and knowledge about game design. Here are some ideas about how you can enhance, build upon, and refine your game design ideas and skills.

Keep a Journal

Writing down things (thinking out loud on paper) helps me refine many ideas and thoughts. A journal is an essential development tool for every creative endeavor. Painters, writers, and musicians all use them. As a game designer, you can't afford not to use one.

A journal needn't contain only game design ideas; it should serve as a place to store ideas in general. When you write down any idea, it begins to take shape and come alive. The process of writing helps you organize your thoughts and refine them.

Some artists have actually turned their journals into publications. Chris Crawford publishes a monthly journal, which I assume comes from other more personal journals he keeps himself.

I like those black artist books with the thick paper you can find in any good art supply house. I also fold in a few sheets of graph paper to sketch out ideas or interface designs.

You've Got to Read

I'll keep saying this over and over. It's the most common mistake I see made by lots of people, no matter what it is they're doing. The plain fact is that there is a ton of stuff to read and keep up on. Although I've presented a lot of game-related material in this sourcebook, you shouldn't confine yourself just to that.

Increase Your Interaction

In several sections of this book you will find listings for online sites, conferences, and associations that are frequented by other developers. Whether you attend any of these just to listen or to participate, it's increasingly important to make sure you're interacting with people in this business. I can tell you I attended several roundtable discussions on game design at the Computer Game Developers Conference last year and learned a lot of things. Especially if you are a beginner, it's important to be out there where you can gain from the experiences of people who have years of experience.

Even for those of you who are old pros, there is more of a need now to help share ideas with the industry in an effort to grow the pie for everyone involved.

Study People and the Market More

One factor that will help move game design into new areas is for developers to study people and markets more. It's important to understand that games are a product, and people who buy products have opinions and ideas that they're willing to share. As any good marketing person knows, this information can provide keen insight and ideas for game design.

As games move more toward mass markets, it's important to understand that as artistic and creative as they may be, the needs of the marketplace drive the industry. Thus, it's important to listen to the end users more and find out what's on their minds and in their dreams. You may find it presents entirely new opportunities.

Keep Up with the Industry

Finally, it's important to keep up with the computer and game industry. A lot of new design ideas and games are directly linked to the technology advances that enable them. If you're not keeping up with what's going on out there, how do you expect to implement or come up with new ideas? For example, some hardware company might announce tomorrow that it has a new technology that renders complete human actors in 3D. This includes perfect lip synching and actually a complete speech engine, too, all available in a complete API. If you were up on this, you might design a game that could only be possible with this technology, or look at an existing game design and reapply it to this fantastic new technology. If you don't keep up, well just remember, someone else is.

Do a Game

I would be in a lot of trouble if I didn't finally say that the best way to move game design forward is simply to develop, design, and construct a game. And make sure you finish it. No matter how bad, how simple, how slow, how great your finished product is, you will learn an immense amount simply by building a game on your own.

So game design moves forward really by your ability to surround yourself with the information, tools, and ideas that allow you to build your skills, and collectively the industry as a whole, too. Aside from an amazing enabling technology gain, there is no cut and dried sign of advancement in game design. It's all a slow methodical process whereby developers learn, test their knowledge by practicing their craft, gain from the experience, and then start all over.

The Process of Evolutionary Design

The process of evolutionary design teaches us that Rome wasn't built in a day. A simple lesson, but let's talk more about what it means to evolve a design.

For most developers, evolving a design means specialization. Looking around at the industry, it's easy to see that there are very few companies that don't specialize in one or several types of games. Even among the bigger companies, it's obvious they specialize as well. Broderbund, as big as it is, tends to focus on broad-based edutainment titles. Electronic Arts, which probably is the most diverse company in the industry, is actually a conglomeration of specific units dedicated to different types of games. For example, EA Canada produces most of the company's major sports titles, while the Origin unit focuses on major role-playing games, and the subsidiary Bullfrog focuses on cutting edge strategy games.

Additionally, specialization in the industry means that more and more companies are focusing on game engine development. In this development strategy, companies focus on designing various games from an ever improving underlying engine. Sometimes this means that existing code is upgraded, or it's scrapped and started from scratch; but in both cases the company attempts to build on the knowledge it gained from doing a specific type of game. This is mostly achieved by specifying a series of improvements that will generate a new game of higher quality.

PART 3

Designing Different Types of Games

CHAPTER 7

The best designed games are the ones players want to play over and over.

Tips for Game Design Success

The Game Design Puzzle—Breaking It Down

From all the fantastic games out there you'd think that game design is a breeze! Let me be the first to tell you: It ain't! When you undertake a complex task such as developing a blockbuster game, you'll have many issues to consider. We've covered many of them already, though one can never cover enough. Before we move on and carve up the types of games you can create and discuss some key design ideas and tradeoffs associated with different game types, we'll look at a few issues related to the final plateau of good game design.

Playability—The Holy Grail of Game Development

The most crucial element to a game is playability. Unfortunately, this is not fully evident in any specific component of a game; only after every piece of development is in place can you truly gauge the strength of a game's playability.

Playability isn't just a measurement of how much fun a game is to play, or how cool the graphics are; it's the sum of how fun, easy, challenging, and responsive the game is, and how much depth, cool sounds, stimulating graphics, and so on are provided. The key to playability is to strive for the best out of every facet of your game. While a game's ultimate playability cannot be fully determined until you ship your game, testing and adjusting it during development will have a big effect. Every little detail can lead to an improvement in playability.

Final Playability Doesn't Become Apparent until the End

You'll never know exactly how playable your game is until it's done. This is a two-fold lesson. First, you should make sure you finish your game, unless the people who test your game *all* tell you that the game really sucks. You won't ever find out how playable your game really is until you've completed all the artwork, sound, graphics, and everything else. Second, the end result always proves that every little detail really counts. Players will nit pick everything in a game, from the out of place pixel on the introduction screen to the inappropriate sound effects. Anything that potentially detracts from a player's overall gaming experience can harm the perceived playability of the game.

Test Early and Often—The Halftime Adjustment

When your idea is on paper, it probably looks fantastic, but once you start to implement it, things change and usually for the worse! Because of this, every major game goes through an extensive testing process. Even after a completed game document has been approved, companies will constantly monitor a game's development and make many adjustments throughout the development process.

So try not to feel stuck with your design even when you have spent months developing it on paper. Something on the screen might not work the way you originally thought, or your perfectly planned animation might be too slow or awkward. Sometimes your testers are going to come back and tell you that your game is too easy, too stupid, too boring, and then some.

Be prepared to alter your game plan based on the feedback you receive. Sometimes the criticisms will be helpful and offer you actual suggestions to make your game more playable. Other times they won't be helpful. You'll have to be the judge. Just understand that you should test your game's playability during development, not after it's too late to make crucial changes.

Designing Content: Know Your Target Audience

The best way to increase the playability of a game is to make sure that it is designed for a target audience. What works for one player may not work for another due to age, gender, educational background, and so on. Thus, one of the most important activities involved in designing successful games is researching and understanding the concerns, wants, and needs of your target audience.

Let's look at some issues involved in targeting games for age and gender. We'll look at some examples of how designers approach targeting their games and incorporating features that lead to more playable games.

Targeting the Appropriate Age Group

The game market is wide open. You can design games for 2-to 4-year-olds, college educated adults, or for any age in between. Your considerations here revolve not only around the maturity of the situation presented (complex sophisticated stories that address themes not commonly found in other games would not be for a preteen, for example), but also around such basic issues as manual dexterity (learning games for preschoolers, for example). Let's look at some age distinctions first.

Early Preschool (ages 2 to 4) This group has problems controlling the mouse, let alone the keyboard and other complex input devices. Thus, standard adult joysticks are beyond them. They can't type or read. So how do you design a game for them?

Preschool kids can use the arrow keys and find single letters on the keyboard, and they can use a mouse if you design the hotspots to be very large. In fact, the hotspots should not be smaller than about 1/12th of the screen. However, speech is the biggest boon for early preschool games. Here are some rules for using speech wisely:

- Your game should be so simple that it does not require instructions. But *do not* use spoken instructions as a substitute for an obvious interface. That said, do use simple phrases to lead the child through the gameplay.
- When there has been no input activity for a while, play a phrase telling the player what to do like "Click on the cat" or "Press the *A* key."
- Use speech as a pay-off. After the child has performed a task say "That's great," "Good work," or "You did it!"
- Use speech in telling stories.
- Have the characters in your game talk. Young kids especially like silly noises and words.

Young children like bright colors and simple shapes. Unfortunately, publishers like detailed, high-resolution graphics—since their adult taste is quite different. Adults tend to equate complexity with a high price and thus quality. Your job as the game developer is to somehow satisfy both constituencies.

Do not make the interface too busy and complicated. The preschooler's brain has not yet had a lot of experience making sense of complicated and detailed pictures. Use surprises such as pop-ups, random animation, clever sounds, and so on. Your players are kids who last year thought peek-a-boo was completely entrancing and now love jack-in-the-boxes. Avoid frightening images. Kids at this age are not ready to handle concepts like injury, death, separation, violence, monsters, witches, and bad guys. In fact, almost anything that is not friendly should be avoided.

Preschool (ages 4 to 6) Many of the principles that apply to early preschool apply to this age group. These kids are becoming more coordinated and can recognize words (although you can't count on reading). Some have become experts with the joystick and can manage a mouse better, so simplified arcade games are within their abilities. However, it is still a good idea to provide a keyboard interface as well as joystick or mouse controls. Since you can't count on them reading, a word recognition game is appropriate for this age.

Early Elementary (ages 5 to 8) At this age, children may enjoy monsters and other bad guys as long as the enemies are "safe." For example, in the game Word Rescue the enemies are blobs that the player "slimes." However, in Treasure Mountain, the pixies are also friendly and humorous even when they are sneaking up on the player to steal a coin. It goes without saying that violence, injury, blood, and gore are out for these kids.

Elementary/Middle (ages 7 to 11) These kids have reached "The Age of Reason." They are starting to develop their own peer culture and can think for themselves. At this age, kids begin to identify with the group that is older than they are. You, the designer, must be careful not to present material that is too "babyish." Your characters should be just a little older than your target player.

You can assume that this group reads, although not fluently. There is some controversy over whether the vocabulary should be watered down so that it is well within the child's resources or whether one should aim higher. There are arguments for both sides; use your best judgment. Age-appropriate vocabulary (a policy in U.S. education) appears to have created a generation of adults who feel the need for tapes guaranteed "to increase your vocabulary so you can win the job you deserve," implying that the policy has not worked well. You are on solid ground whichever philosophy you choose to follow.

Teens (ages 12 and up) This age group is acknowledged to be *the* hardest audience with which to achieve success. About the only games that have done it are the Carmen San Diego games. Here, the more non-traditional edutainment titles can be effectively developed and marketed to parents.

"Cool" is king with this group. Boys are heavy into games like Doom and Mortal Kombat where they can indulge in testosterone feats. Girls are more interested in social activities and sitting down at the computer is not often high on their list. These teens are essentially adults in their abilities and brain power. In fact, they probably have *superior* computer skills than many adults.

Games that have the best chance at hitting this market are ones that involve cooperative/competitive play among a group. And yes, you've got the thumbs up with monsters, blood, and gore! What would Mortal Kombat be without these elements? Multiplayer and modem games fit the bill also.

Adults (ages 17 and up) These players tend to be well-educated adults, and their ability to both enjoy and deal with more sophisticated stories and content allows you to pursue non-traditional themes—storylines that would garner a PG13 or R rating in a movie. Despite the call for ratings, there is far more opportunity to create adult-level content. This isn't an advocacy for a slew of soft-porn games, but think of some of the more sophisticated movies of the past few years, such as *Pulp Fiction*, *Seven*, *Basic Instinct*, *Falling Down*, *Disclosure*, and try to imagine games that push the edge in a similar fashion.

Targeting Gender Considerations

I have just a few pointers when it comes to this topic. If you want your game to span the ever-divided gender lines, take these considerations to heart:

- Games should have both male and female protagonists. Some even allow the player to choose whether to play a male or female character.
- You should not feature significant blood and gore.
- You should not feature significant fighting.
- Try to avoid gender stereotypes; the male should not always be the leader, the female should not always be portrayed as a sex symbol.
- Try to include humor (but not gross-out body function humor).

Acquiring Your Own Targets

Although game design can be a very intuitive and creative field, you can employ a very calculated and deliberate approach to many of the design and development tasks. For example, targeting a distinct audience and tailoring your game for this audience is one area in which you can research the market, come up with a detailed plan of action, and execute your plan based on the guidelines your research unfolds.

That doesn't mean you can't be creative in how you approach producing a game that your target audience is going to enjoy. Your job is to creatively develop an appealing product. But in order to make a product appealing, you have to work to understand exactly what it is that appeals to your audience. How do designers do that? Here's a list of suggestions:

- They usually make games that they like themselves—serving as their own target audience.
- They talk online and in person with the audience to which they want to appeal. They find out the things both in games and outside of games that interest their audience.
- They carefully ask for and catalog consumer feedback from previous game efforts.
- They religiously play and evaluate other games, constantly reading the reviews and opinions found on online services and in magazines.
- They attend conferences to exchange ideas and meet with market researchers whose job it is to inform them what interests people.

Games are very subjective experiences. That's what makes them exciting to play as well as to make. No one will ever come up with the 100 percent proven formula for game development success. However, if you're careful, creative, and passionate about creating great games, I think you'll find some formula for success that works for you and your target audience.

Design Resources

Although nothing helps you to understand the ins and outs of game design as well as experience, the second best way to spend your development time is with the vast amount of literature available on the subject. Unfortunately, with the exception of Chris Crawford's two books and his *Journal of Interactive Entertainment Design*, it's not easy to obtain a good selection of professional game design ideas and experiences. So I decided to do a little leg work for you and compile a list of the various resources available.

Reading Material

Read, read, read. I can't say it any better than that. There are a lot of articles and books out there for your perusal. Take advantage of the experts who have taken the time to lay down their insights into game development. This book is crammed with websites, books, magazines, and conferences, which means there are more pointers to reading material than you probably have time to explore. But if you're going to be a serious game developer, you've got to make the time.

Magazines

As you might guess, there is an overflow of magazines devoted to the subject of gaming. The majority of these contain mostly consumer reviews, but even reviews can be useful learning tools. Among the many magazines though, several stand out for their attention to game design concepts:

- *Game Developer*
- *Interactivity*
- *New Media*
- *Next Generation*
- *Computer Gaming World*

For a complete listing of every conceivable useful game development magazine, peruse the magazine bibliography in the back of this book. There you will find complete contact and subscription information.

Books

Here is a list of relevant game design books and publications. Some are out of print but you may still be able to locate a copy.

The Journal of Interactive Game Design
5251 Sierra Road
San Jose, CA 95132

$36.00, Payable by check

This is Chris Crawford's monthly newsletter that focuses exclusively on game design and interactive storytelling. Chris writes the majority of the articles, but other notable game designers like Talin have contributed as well. You can order back issues for $5.00 each or purchase an entire eight volume set for $150.00—a real bargain! Although some of the writing is as dated as the paper it's printed on, the material is still relevant in today's game development environment.

The Art of Computer Game Design by Chris Crawford
5251 Sierra Road
San Jose, CA 95132

This title was originally published by McGraw Hill in the early 1980s. Although the book is now out of print, it is available at the above address directly from Chris Crawford for a price of $25.00.

Balance of Power—International Politics as the Ultimate Global Game by Chris Crawford (Microsoft Press, Redmond, WA, 1986; ISBN 0-914845-97-7)

Yet another reading extravaganza from Chris Crawford. This book chronicles Crawford's experience and design philosophy behind the construction of his best selling game of the same name. The game was an amazing work of art; its focus on geopolitical concerns of the superpowers was enlightening for its true-to-life lessons and programming prowess.

What's really useful about this now out of print text is examining Crawford's thought process as he devises the many formulas used in the game to simulate various real-world events—like the success of insurgents in a country or how one superpower might react to a move by another.

Behind the Scenes at Sega by Nicholas Lavroff (Prima Publishing, Rocklin, CA, 1995; ISBN 1-55958-525-0)

Written for the children's market, this book allows kids to see how all their favorite arcade games are made. Although it doesn't go into too much detail, the many pages of sample storyboards and the overall presentation of the behind-the-scenes look at game development (especially stuff from the hit cartridge Earth Worm Jim) make this book a worthy resource for beginning gamers.

Entertainment in the Cyber Zone—Exploring the Interactive Universe of Multimedia by Chris McGowan and Jim McCullaugh (Random House, New York, NY, 1994; ISBN 0-679-75804-6)

A very interesting book that covers a broad range of games and interactive multimedia titles. *Entertainment in the Cyber Zone* includes interviews with designers, writers, and producers, a look at various hot games, coverage of the hardware you can use to play games, and more. While this book is written for players, developers will also find it useful.

Computer Gamesmanship, Elements of Intelligent Game Design by David Levy (Simon & Schuster, New York, NY; ISBN 0-67149-532-1)

This textbook-style book focuses on the basics of AI and includes discussions on fundamental game design issues. You'll also get some inside information on the various algorithms for such programs as chess, checkers, and poker.

The Complete Wargame Handbook by James Dunnigan (William Morrow and Co.; ISBN 0-688-10368-5)

This handbook is a really interesting, albeit dated, book on wargame design. It doesn't cover any programming issues, but discusses general issues concerning wargame design.

The Interactive Writers Handbook by Jon Samsel and Darryl Wimberley (ISBN 1-885452-02-9)

This handbook includes interviews with tons of writers, producers, and designers who are constructing interactive media. The book covers topics like idea evaluation, creating proposals, scripting, and title design structure. A useful resource for anyone making games.

Developer's Conferences

If you ever get a chance to attend a gaming conference, go! And you should have plenty of opportunity; every time I turn around there seems to be a new conference on some aspect of computers, software, or the Internet popping up. However, you should be aware of several key conferences:

- The Computer Game Developers Conference (CGDC) sponsored by the Computer Game Developers Association is *the* conference to attend if you are at

all serious about game design and development. Whenever a large group of commercial developers get together you're bound to learn something!

- The Interactive/Game Developers conference in New York City has been produced the past two years by Alexander and Associates.
- E3 (The Electronic Entertainment Expo) debuted last year. While mostly a trade show for retailers, E3 does have sessions on development (though not like those found at the CGDC) and has become the show for commercial developers to announce their products to the public.

You can find a complete listing of game development-related products with the registration info in the back of this book.

Next Stop...the Web: Online Game Design Resource

There are few places where you can immerse yourself in tons of game-related information. Regardless of what kind of information you're looking for, the online universe can provide you with a multitude of resources. From code examples to discussion groups to various Web sites with white papers and other materials, there are many ways to learn more about game design. I've spent a lot of time online and gathered some of the best sources for you to check out. At the end of the book, I've included a more comprehensive listing of cool online sites covering a wide range of game development issues.

CompuServe's GamDev Design Theory Section

Compuserve's Game Developers' section (GO GAMDEV) is a great resource to bat around ideas. A frequent contributor (and official instigator) on the site is game legend Chris Crawford.

I've found that this a great place to talk about theory as well as practice. Often discussions that deal with traditional topics, such as interactive storytelling, drift to other game themes and more leading-edge subjects.

rec.games.design

This Internet Usenet newsgroup is devoted to the discussion of computer and interactive game design. As with many newsgroups, you can get divergent and sometimes ugly conversation, but the interesting and thought provoking posts help you to weather the storm.

The OZ Project

http://www.cs.cmu.edu/afs/cs.cmu.edu/project/oz/web/oz.html
The OZ Project is a Carnegie Mellon University computer science project that focuses on creating incredibly realistic interactive stories and characters. Its associated Web site has a ton of interesting material concerning their research into these fascinating areas of game design and development. This site is well worth checking out.

These sites are oriented toward the design of games. There are at least a dozen or more sites and cyberspace stops oriented toward development issues, especially programming. These sites are covered later, so don't worry.

The Art of Learning Game Design

So you've never really designed a game and you want to learn how it's done! Well, join the club. I hope that this book has at least started you on the path to finding the resources you'll need to learn and explore more about game design. Although the best way to learn good game design is to practice, practice, practice, let's take a look at the places you can go to formally learn the skills to be a designer.

Game Design Schools

Game design as a formal study is in its infancy. Although most gamers are self taught, there are a few places you can go to receive formal game design training. Canada has two schools that are actually setting up curriculum to "teach" game development. (They're listed below.) The curriculum revolves around three main ideas—read up on the field, play games until your fingers fall off, and experiment with your own games. Sage advice if I've ever heard it. After all, it's the same advice I will give you throughout this book!

Game Schools

DigiPen Applied Computer Graphics School
500-530 Hornby Street
Vancouver, B.C., Canada V6C 2E7

Phone: 604 682-0300
Fax: 604 682-0310
E-mail: programming@digipen.com

The DigiPen Applied Computer Graphics School is located in Vancouver, B.C., Canada and is registered with the B.C. Private Post-Secondary Education Commission. The mandate of the school is to provide comprehensive programs

for students who are interested in becoming either video game programmers or 3D computer animators.

NBCC Miramichi
P.O. Box 1053
Miramichi, New Brunswick E1N 3W4

Phone: 506 778-6044
Fax: 506 778-6001
E-mail: learntec@mailserv.nbnet.nb.ca

Digipen is on the west coast of Canada, NBCC is on the east coast. While the two schools are not related, they pursue the same goal of teaching people how to program and design interactive games. The NBCC program is geared mostly toward residents of the New Brunswick area. The college's hope is that after students graduate from this two-year program they stay in the area to start their own design shops. However, that isn't to say they don't accept outside applications. Contact them for complete details about the program and how to apply to the school. If you find a structured environment works best to learn how to make games, maybe a slew of college course is in the works for you.

Additionally, I know that the directors of the NBCC school are looking to help advise other colleges around the world about how to set up their own programs for teaching game development. If you're looking to add a major in interactive entertainment development, contact them for more assistance.

Reading

There aren't many books that dive extensively into computer game design techniques. However, you can always count on Chris Crawford to offer his expertise and insight. Take a look at the *Reading Materials* section presented earlier in this chapter to get an idea of what's available to you.

You can also find some helpful articles in various magazines like *Morph's Outpost*, *New Media*, and *Interactivity*, which provide information about the design elements of game development. In addition, there are a couple of industry newsletters that you can check out. While these periodicals provide the most coverage, you should regularly read other magazines, too. I found a cool level-editing article in a CD-ROM magazine once.

The only other source is the Computer Game Developers Conference (CGDC) proceedings and tapes. The conference is held every year and all attendees get a big book filled with papers and other presentations on many aspects of the game-development process, including design processes and opinions. In addition, you can order tapes of the various speeches and roundtables held at the conference. See the *Design Resources* section of this chapter for more information.

A final source is online content. Again, see the *Design Resources* section of this chapter for details.

Practice with Editable Games

Rather than develop your own game completely from scratch to learn about game development, you might want to start out playing with games that are modifiable. They can rapidly set you up to explore ideas like puzzle creation and other inherent design practices. Here are a list of personal favorite products you can modify to learn more about game design:

Abuse Abuse is a multilevel, platform game that's a cross between Konami's Contra, Aliens the movie, and Metroid. However, what makes this game interesting is that it has a fantastic level editor, complete with all kinds of cool scripting/AI functionality. Abuse provides one of the most open-ended level editors released; no wonder, anything connected with Id Software is usually top-notch.

What's also cool is that Abuse's creators, Crack dot Com, plan to accept, evaluate, and publish submitted levels on quarterly CDs available from the company. The authors of the levels could potentially pick up a few bucks for their work.

Abuse can be downloaded from their Web site at http://www.crack.com and from CompuServe's Action Games forum (GO ACTION).

Klik n Play This title from Maxis allows you to create a wide range of simple but impressive arcade-style games in Windows. The games can be shipped with a runtime module, which means you can distribute the finished product online for others who don't have Klik n Play to use.

Doom/Heretic Using the many shareware editors and modification programs to design your own levels and create your own graphics and sounds, you can design an almost completely different game than Doom (Alien Doom being a case in point). There are several CDs and books with CDs that can give you all the editors and advice you need to begin experimenting with level editing for Doom and Heretic.

DoMark's Flight Simulator Toolkit DoMark sponsored a contest to see who could make the coolest flight simulator with this product, and wow! Did they get some awesome entries. One contestant entered an entire recreation of the Hoth battle scene from *Star Wars: The Empire Strikes Back!* complete with the AT Walkers, snowspeeders, and everything. This is a wonderful tool to experiment with modeling techniques and other flight simulator attributes.

Empire Deluxe Available from New World Computing, this wargame, based on the venerable mainframe version, has a full editor attached to the game. It allows you to design the terrain and place forces.

Needless to say, there are many more games that allow you to modify the scenarios and levels or design completely new versions. Check online to see which ones are most popular; most of the distribution of new designs is exchanged over forums and Internet sites. You can also find design FAQs, fancier level editors, and great examples online as well.

Practice, Practice, Practice!

Any time you write down an idea, pick up an editable game, or start developing your own game, you're practicing. Game developers are always learning; it's a trait all professions share, especially ones that are involved in a creative pursuit. My best piece of advice is to *consciously* practice. Push yourself to learn and try new ideas and share your games, while in development, with your friends. You'll learn a lot from their comments—they're often brutally honest.

CHAPTER 8

There are memorable games that might help you make yours just as memorable.

Game Development Categories

3D "Point-of-View" Games

Almost every category of game (you'll learn about all the categories in this chapter) is going 3D these days, but 3D point-of-view games are built around a unique 3D model. These games, such as Doom and Heretic, are also known as *3D raycasting* games. The idea is to put players in a 3D-like atmosphere where they can walk, turn at any angle, and move forward and backward in a fluid motion of unbelievable speed. Although you could also include these games in other categories (for example, Bethesda Software's Arena is a raycasting game that is also an RPG), the number and success of these games has earned them their own category. And as has been evident by the stunning hit status of Doom and Wolfenstein 3D, and the emergence of other major 3D games, this new category of gaming is hot.

The majority of 3D raycasting games have been sci-fi based shoot-outs. Following closely behind are fantasy-based games. Here are some of the benchmark 3D point-of-view games:

Wolfenstein 3D Wolfenstein 3D was the game that put Id Software on the map. It was an instant shareware (and later retail) hit and thus helped prove that shareware games could be as good, and even better than retail games. Wolfenstein 3D also proved that game companies who used shareware marketing techniques could make money. Figure 8.1 shows a screen from this highly popular game. Here we have a free moving first person perspective in a maze-type setting. The walls of this environment are beautifully texture mapped with high-resolution graphics that make people really take notice.

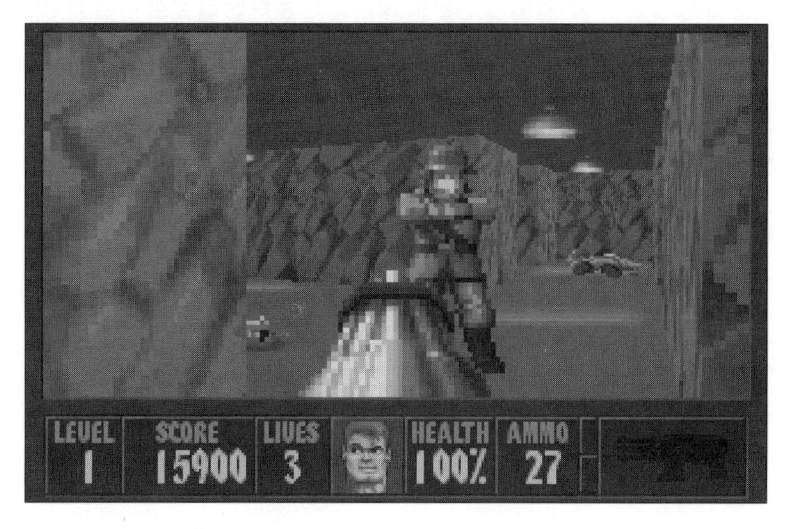

Figure 8.1 Wolfenstein 3D in action.

Doom Doom is perhaps the most often talked about game these days. Developers like it not so much for its awesome speedy graphics, but mostly because it encapsulates so many things that make any game a major hit—it's easy to get hooked on, it supports multiplayer action, it has awesome level design, it is extendible, and, of course, it's fun! Figure 8.2 shows an example of the action-packed Doom.

In the traditional Wolfenstein 3D approach to rendering scenes, walls are treated as individual bitmap images. Walls must be placed at grid points in a 2D map. This type of representation works well for creating scenes that are based on geometric shapes. Doom, on the other hand, treats walls as line segments with endpoints that are no longer restricted to grid points on a 2D map. This allows the 3D rendering to look more realistic and it gives the player more freedom of movement.

Xengine from Bethesda and Quake from Id While the first two waves of raycasting games were developed by using large graphical blocks, this third wave of games incorporated a much smaller polygon graphics engine to do the work. Not only does the engine tremendously increase the flexibility of the shapes you can form, but the lighting and "pixelation" effects are taken to a much higher level.

Figures 8.3 and 8.4 show screen shots from Bethesda's Terminator game and Id's upcoming release called Quake. Both of these games are created from polygon-based 3D engines that redefine the 3D raycasting shooter style game.

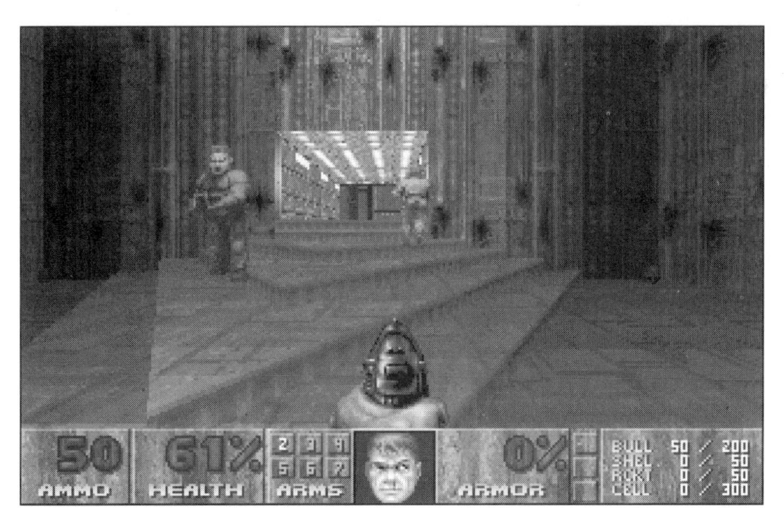

Figure 8.2 Doom, the popular successor to Wolfenstein 3D.

Figure 8.3 Bethesda's Terminator polygon-based 3D game.

Figure 8.4 The upcoming Quake from Id.

3D Raycasting Game Design Issues

Designing 3D raycasting games involves a number of techniques from high-resolution graphics to fast action animation. Although the 3D scenes presented in these different games may vary widely, the basic techniques of both playing and designing these games are similar. The more obvious components include rendered walls, floors, ceilings, movable objects, and stationary objects. Of course, these games also take advantage of a number of other visual and non-visual features including storylines, sound effects and music, story levels, 3D animation, secret doors, and so on.

Speed, Power, and Simplicity

The key factors in designing games like Doom and Rise-of-the-Triad seem basic enough: Marry great 3D-like graphics with a speedy and powerful raycasting engine and provide for a great, but simple gaming system.

Add to it the dynamic multiplayer abilities and excellent level design and let 'er rip. Of course, this is much easier said than done, and that brings us to a key point. Just because Doom *seems* like a relatively simple design doesn't mean it is.

One designer categorized these games in a really succinct way: "They're playground games." She was using the analogy of a big defined space that contains all the apparatus for gameplay within it. The rules are simple and it's designed for interaction between others.

Graphics Power

After Doom debuted, tons of knockoffs appeared. Although some of these games were good in their own right, none seemed to capture the feel and play of Doom. This is an excellent example that proves even in a category dominated by the graphical power of the underlying game engine, attention to design and level editing is crucial.

I once spoke with one of the top-level designers at Id and came away from the conversation really understanding their dedication to superior game design. The designer talked about the attention they put into level design. Despite the number of excellent editors and utilities to design new Doom levels, only a handful (perhaps as little as 1 percent) of the levels were good enough to make it into the actual game.

Far too often, developing a game that emphasizes high "eye-candy" content is often shortsighted. Give your players more credit, and provide them with a superior overall game. I guarantee, they'll keep coming back for more.

It's All in the Rays

Raycasting is a technique of determining where objects should be placed in a scene as a player moves around. You can see how this works by examining Figure 8.5. As the person moves around in the scene, the rays change their position and intersect different points in the scene. The points of intersection are the places where walls and other objects are displayed. Usually, rays are cast in an arc so that the walls and other objects that are directly in front of a player as well as those off to the side can be found.

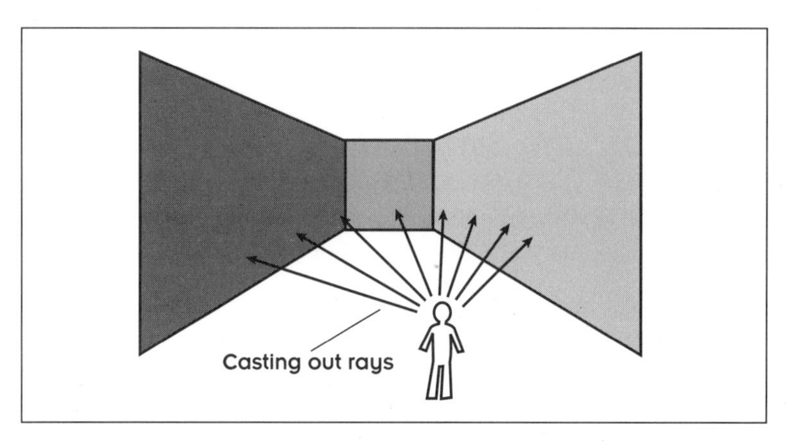

Figure 8.5 Casting out rays to create a 3D scene.

Lost in a Maze

Many game developers refer to 3D raycasting games as maze games because they often take place in a maze-like environment. Creating a 3D game like Doom or Wolfenstein 3D involves building a maze and then deciding where you want to put different objects into the maze. Many developers create design editors, as shown in Figure 8.6, for laying out the borders of the maze. Although the maze is set up as a 2D representation, objects are rendered in a 3D-like atmosphere when the game is played.

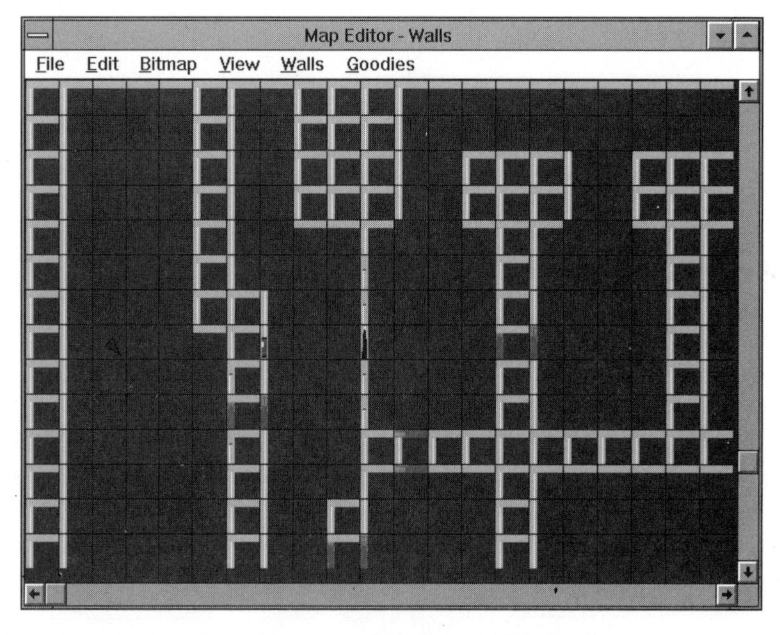

Figure 8.6 Creating a maze for a 3D raycasting game (2D view).

The components that give shape to a maze in a 3D world are rooms, walls, floors, ceilings, and so on. Rooms are constructed by placing walls in a maze. The walls themselves are created out of rendered bitmaps. Essentially, a wall is a stationary object that can be placed only at a boundary point in a maze grid.

Multiple Levels of Adventure

Most 3D raycasting games provide multiple levels of adventure to keep players challenged for hours, days, and even weeks. Each level of a game can be constructed from a different maze. As the player successfully works his or her way to the end of one maze, the game can advance the player to the next level, where he or she can encounter the next maze and take on new obstacles. The levels are important because they give the game a change of scenery and help the game from becoming visually boring. In this respect, many 3D games are not all that different from arcade-style side scrollers where the main goal is to navigate your way through a level until you collect enough points to move up to another level. All of the standard tricks can be used such as having a player locate and pass through a secret door to move to another level or capture a hidden object. If you are really into violence, you can design a game so that the player has to wipe out all of the aggressive villains in order to move up to a new level.

Looking toward the Future

Overall the big move in the future of 3D raycasting games will be not only with multiplayer and polygonal additions, we'll also see an increased speed of the 3D engines being developed. Prepare yourself. The future of this game category is soaring.

Adventure Games and Interactive Fiction

Adventure games are among the oldest and most popular type of game in existence. Ever since William Crowther, a programmer at Stanford University, created what became known simply as Adventure, developers and players have been fostering the interactive story.

Generally, adventure games are "story-based." By this, I mean that the player moves through the game as if he or she is a character in a story. The storyline, which often focuses on current-day scenarios like detective/police stories and horror stories, contains various interactions and puzzles that the player must solve before concluding the adventure. The characters under the player's control tends to maintain his or her (or *its*!) initial characteristics and skill level provided, unlike RPGs, which we will discuss later in the chapter.

Although the story and writing of that story are the most crucial aspects of the game, adventure games also rely on considerable animation to keep players visually involved.

Here are some of the benchmark adventure games:

Infocom Series The original adventure in the series was Zork, a more sophisticated version of the venerable "Adventure" game. Zork was a big success and lead to some of the more memorable titles in this category: Planetfall, Hitchhiker's Guide to the Galaxy, and The Leather Goddesses of Phobos are among my favorites. Although the games were all text—even though other companies were merging text and graphics—they made a huge impact by producing some of the most memorable games and game characters ever.

Check out a fan page for the Infocom games maintained on the Web at *http://www.csd.uwo.ca/~pete/Infocom/*. It has tons of links and information about this awesome series of text adventures.

The Sierra Quest Series Sierra, which has published a number of different games over the years, entered the adventure market with many titles, including Ultima II. Their greatest hit, though, was their Quest series, a product line that continues today. It started with King's Quest and later, as the series progressed and a sophisticated construction engine and interface were created, the series expanded to include other masterful products like Space Quest, Police Quest, and Hero's Quest.

Sierra mastered high-end animated graphics, which, back in the days of the Apple II, were quite impressive. Sierra is currently building the next generation of their Quest series, using not only Disney-like animation but full-motion video as they continue to push the edge of graphic quality that players of their games have come to expect. They are also using authors like former Los Angles Police Chief Daryl Gates to help make games like Police Quest much more realistic.

Figures 8.7 through 8.9 show some of the screen shots from several of Sierra's Quest Series as well as their latest hit Phantasmagoria. Notice the full screen graphics, the well-drawn figures, and almost "Disney-like" artwork. Overall, most of the games have a similar look to the overall game presentation. Finally, look at the latest digital video approach they're embracing in their latest release Phantasmagoria.

Monkey Island/Lucas Arts Series Lucas Arts has had some memorable adventure titles over the years, but the most notable were the two-part series of adventures called Monkey Island. They were scripted by Ron Gilbert, who went on to co-found Humongous Entertainment.

Figure 8.7 A scene from King Quest VI.

Figure 8.8 A scene from Police Quest.

Figure 8.9 A scene from Phantasmagoria.

The series included two games of which Monkey Island I is considered the best. Lucas Arts has also made some other memorable adventure games, including Sam and Max, the Indiana Jones series, the upcoming Dig, and the current Full Throttle.

All of their games have been characterized with excellent graphics and animation, but most of all, from what I've seen and constantly heard from others, the games are noted for their clever stories and excellent writing. Figure 8.10 shows a screen shot from Monkey Island 2; the Monkey Island series was a popular Adventure game series cited by several adventure lovers with whom I talked.

Adventure Game Design Issues

Adventure game design involves several concepts that, while not specific to the games themselves, are essential elements for this category.

Stories and Engines

It's quite interesting to note all of the benchmark games I've listed in this category are complete lines of products and were developed by companies that used internally built game engines and game creation systems.

Although the engines used to create these different games all come from different sources, there are some inherent similarities in style, interface, and presentation in adventure/interactive story games. Both Lucas Arts and Sierra have come up with a common denominator way of building their adventure games. With the engines working out a lot of the graphical and housekeeping issues, the companies can really concentrate on the driving force of an adventure game: the story and characters. In

Figure 8.10 Example from Lucas Arts' Monkey Island 2.

addition, the overall commonality of interface and such can work well for fans of previous efforts, as they can easily understand how the game should be played.

Try to build a core engine first and work out as much of the common traits you would need in an adventure game, including maps, movement, conversation interactions, and so on. Then, build your games on top of that foundation. Remember though, good games created from the same engine must have a fresh and sophisticated story and design to make them stand out from other games in the series. This mean that you've got to design in flexibility to the core engine to accommodate a wide range of ideas and potential upgrades.

In short, build a system to support a number of stories you might create. This is an approach that has worked well for two of the leading developers in the adventure/interactive story game category.

Mature Content

A key design consideration of the adventure game/interactive story category is content. People who play these games tend to be well-educated adults, and they have the ability to both enjoy and deal with more sophisticated stories and content.

Traditionally, the majority of adventure/interactive story games, have, like most games, tended to shy away from these themes, but as gaming becomes more widespread, there is far more opportunity to create adult-level content, despite the call for ratings.

Looking toward the Future

As I've already hinted, the adventure game is really the closest thing to interactive storytelling. So the future of the category is tied to a more enriched form of interactive storytelling.

Adventure games will no doubt continue to be one of the main game staples, and with the interesting code engine ideas being created by developers like Chris Crawford, we'll see even more exciting developments here in the future.

Edutainment Games

When people talk about the great promise of computers and games, many think of what has commonly become known as "edutainment"—the merging of education and entertainment. This area provides a goldmine for game designers and developers who find genuine satisfaction in creating a game that teaches a skill while keeping the player so happily occupied that the learning process goes almost unnoticed. If you

really think about it, though, most games are educational because strategic thinking is an essential skill that every one of us must learn.

One of the best edutainment gamers around, Karen Crowther, has produced numerous educational commercial and shareware games for kids. Chapter 7 presents Karen's thoughts and advice about edutainment game design.

Here are some of the benchmark edutainment games:

Spinnaker Software Spinnaker Software, now part of the entity known as SoftKey, originally started as a cutting edge educational software maker. Many of their early efforts for the Commodore 64, Atari, and Apple produced memorable edutainment titles like Snooper Troops. The games offered lots of great educational value, and, most of all, great gameplay. If you (or your kids) haven't played some of these early packages, you've missed out.

Where in the World Is Carmen Sandiego If you haven't heard of Carmen Sandiego, I think you should strongly reconsider entering the game industry. Not only did this game almost single-handedly establish Broderbund as one of the biggest and most respected game publishers in the world, but it laid the foundation for merging a game with educational content. The series is still immensely popular—check out the PBS children's game show (sing it, Rockapella!) or the Saturday morning cartoon series if you don't believe me. This game has probably done more to educate people about geography in years past than *National Geographic*.

SimCity/Seven Cities of Gold/Tetris/Wolf Often, the phrase edutainment software brings to mind the traditional educational games and publishers. Crossover is a common aspect of the gaming industry. Many games generally promoted solely for their game quality also have educational elements. Numerous games over the years, like EA's Seven Cities of Gold, Maxis' entire Sim series, Spectrum Holybyte's Tetris, and Sanctuary Woods' recent hit Wolf, have all been commended for their high educational content.

The follow-up to Sanctuary Woods' cool edutainment game is Lion, as shown in Figure 8.11. Using the basic design of their hit product Wolf, Sanctuary Woods redesigned the product to simulate a lion pride's life on the African Plains.

Edutainment Game Design Issues

Edutainment game design involves some techniques unique to this category. When developing a game for this category, you must wrestle with many issues, including game type, target age, and target gender. Let's take a detailed look at some of these issues.

Edutainment Game Categories

Edutainment products come in two broad categories: traditional and non-traditional. Let's take a look at the traditional style first, which I've broken down even further by educational content:

Figure 8.11 Scene from the edutainment game, Lion.

Drill and Practice Games In this type of game, drill problems are provided and the child is rewarded with a "pay off" game for correctly completing a certain number of problems—usually an animation at the end of a problem set.

These games are quite successful with children. Young children who have not yet been drilled to death in school perceive the drill as a game.

The Half and Half Game Games such as Where in the World Is Carmen Sandiego (discussed earlier) intermix the educational content with the game. In Carmen Sandiego for example, the situation is a crime scene. The educational portion has the player question suspects and collect geographical clues to determine which geographical location holds the next clue to the investigation. The game portion then presents its challenge: The player has a limited amount of time to locate Carmen's henchmen and solve the crime at hand. For every wrong guess the player makes in determining the geographical location, precious time is wasted. Geography materials are provided with the game.

Content games These games represent a middle ground between drill and exploration games and involve three key elements of regular games: exploration, risk, and collection. (More about these elements later.) The educational content is still clear but it takes a secondary position to the actual game play. The child (especially older kids) perceives the experience to be a game rather than a drill.

Discovery Games The newest fad in U.S. public education today is exploration and problem solving. The idea is that children will acquire academic skills and knowledge on their own if they are given a structured experience in which to discover the information.

In my opinion, this approach is somewhat akin to giving a child a computer and telling them to write a novel...without first teaching them to type. In this type of game, the child clicks on various hot spots and something happens. Either an animation unfolds, a story is read, or a game is begun—a perfect game for pre-schoolers.

A non-traditional edutainment game is one that for one reason or another really stands out for its inherent educational value even though it wasn't actually designed to serve such a role. For example, games like SimCity by Maxis, Seven Cities of Gold from Ozark Softscape/EA, and Wolf from Sanctuary Woods are included in this category.

Age Considerations

Perhaps the single biggest factor in designing edutainment products is in targeting your age group. Children change so quickly that you must have a clear idea of the age group being targeted. A rough breakdown is shown in Table 8.1.

Notice that some categories overlap. Not all kids mature at the same rate and kids will enjoy some games from neighboring age ranges. For a detailed discussion of age concerns with game design, refer to Chapter 7.

Licensed Properties

Games that incorporate Disney characters, the Berenstain Bears, the Power Rangers, or Batman, are developed using what are called *licensed properties.* The publisher has paid a fee—usually 10 percent of the wholesale income of the game—to the trademark holder in order to use the names and likenesses in the game. In return, the developer promises to adhere to their standards for the content, look, and use of their characters. In fact, most trademark holders require that the developer submit art and scripts for approval.

Table 8.1 Age-Related Game Design Considerations

Age	Game Design Considerations
Early Preschool: 2-4 years	Includes fun sound, bright colors and simple shapes, minimal mouse and keyboard use, and lots of surprises
Preschool: 4-6 years	Includes the same considerations as early preschool, with more emphasis on mouse and keyboard use
Early Elementary: 5-8 years	Includes the addition of "safe" monsters and bad guys, emphasis on the mouse and keyboard
Elementary/Middle: 7-12 years	Includes more mature subject matter and characters (older than your target player) and more detailed instructions
Teens: 13 years and up	Characterized by cooperative/competitive play and strategic planning

Why would you use a licensed property when such a large chunk of the profits go to the trademark holder? Licenses confer instant name recognition. Every other incarnation of the licensed character (be it TV, movies, T-shirts, action figures, or whatever) is building name recognition that will translate into potential sales of your computer game. Your publisher will most likely find it easier to get retail distribution because of this name recognition.

Who's Buying This Game Anyway?

Children's edutainment is difficult to target because the person who is going to buy the game (the parent) is not the one who is going to play the game. Consequently, you need to target your game to two very different audiences. This is especially true for the under-seven set.

Additionally, you'll want to appeal to teachers. If your game is picked up by schools, the site licenses may not make you rich, but the recognition and authority imparted by the school is influential in driving consumer sales.

Looking toward the Future

The future of edutainment games will be in the development of captivating learning experiences that meld games and educational content. Toward those ends, expect to see more multimedia content, connections to online elements, and more refined elements of gaming added to all educational software efforts. Perhaps the largest growth in edutainment will come from games that combine all the major software categories into complete learning environments. In the near future, students might find a complete multimedia reference book on a subject, a complete set of online forums and sites to explore for even more content and interaction with other like-minded students, as well as a complete educational game that helps them develop an even deeper understanding of the material.

Fighting Games

Among action-oriented games, fighting games seem to have carved out the most consistently successful niche among all of gaming. With the addition of motion capture and 3D polygon graphical engines in recent years, fighting games have really started to, excuse the pun, kick!

Early versions of fighting games were rooted around basic boxing or Karate-like moves—pretty boring for kids today who get to witness extreme gore and terrifying monsters. And the creativity doesn't stop there. Most fighting games these days include elements like weaponry (swords and clubs) and special "secret moves" that players have to learn. In fact, some of these moves are so secret that a game can be

out for months before the company leaks the move combination or some amazing 12-year-old discovers it while kicking the living daylights out of an "old guy" like myself!

The fighting game category has really blossomed into a full-fledged string of hit products and, as designers continue creating interesting worlds with monsters and secret moves and weapons, the category will continue to grow.

Here are some of the benchmark fighting games:

Karateka Jordan Mechner's Karateka was one of the first major fighting games. This blockbuster established itself as a benchmark fighting game because of its breathtakingly smooth animation, complete storyline, and strong opponents. These gaming techniques were unheard of at the time but are commonplace in many fighting games today.

Mortal Kombat/Street Fighter/Killer Instinct While there have been others—Double Dragon, Kung Fu, Black Belt, Way of the Warrior, and Samurai Showdown, for example—2D sideview fighting game purists would definitely say that Mortal Kombat, Street Fighter, and Killer Instinct stand out the most. What separates these games from the pack are their infamous "finishing/fatality moves" and interesting characters with special moves and backgrounds. Mortal Kombat has been extra successful, spawning a hit movie and stage show. Figure 8.12 shows a scene from Mortal Kombat.

Figure 8.12 Mortal Kombat—one of the most popular fighting games of all time.

Virtua Fighter/Tekken/TohShinDen/Fx-Fighter These games represent the latest in fighting game presentation. Using a high-speed textured polygon engine, these new fighting games provide a true 3D aspect—an incredibly intense experience. Virtua Fighter from Sega lead the way first as an arcade game and now as Saturn's showcase CD. TohShinDen and Tekken, created by Namco, are the Virtua Fighters of the Sony PSX platform. Finally, Argonaut/GTE's Fx-Fighter, while not quite up to the same level as the others (but still great!), brings this specific game type to the PC platform and takes advantage of the power of the 3D API BRender as the underlying technology. Figure 8.13 shows two screen shots from Tekken, which is currently the hot 3D fighting game title.

Fighting Game Design Issues

Fighting game design involves several concepts such as character creation, secret moves, violence, and so on that are essential elements for this category of games.

Character Creation

One striking similarity you'll find among all of the fighting games is the use of solid, convincing characters. As an example, consider Mortal Kombat. The developers showed an incredible amount of motivation and inventiveness in creating a diverse set of opponents, each with a totally different set of strategies, physiques, and characteristics.

Sony took this concept one step farther and made one of the characters from Namco's flagship fighting game, Tohshinden, a key part of their advertising campaign. Although character development is often overlooked by players and is overshadowed by the spectacular graphics and mind-bending combination moves, as a designer you must put considerable thought and care into developing great characters.

Figure 8.13 3D fighting games like Tekkon are based on powerful polygon rendering techniques.

Special or Secret Moves

One of the key design elements in fighting games is the "special move," sometimes called the "fatality move" or the "finishing move." While each character possesses the everyday kicks, spin kicks, punches, and jumps, each character also has one to several special moves to perform in special situations. For example, a character might jump up in the air and twirl around in a flying spinning whirlwind only if he or she is far enough away from the opponent and, at the same time, the player presses three buttons simultaneously while moving up, right, and left quickly. Whew! That's a lot of conditions and key combinations!

Secret moves are similar to special moves with one key exception: They are not documented. And that's a big exception. Some moves are so secret that it may take several weeks or even months before players discover them. This secrecy creates an incredible sense of discovery to the game.

When designing your own games, keep this particular issue in mind. You want your players interested and continually coming back for more. If players learn to identify with some of the characters by becoming particularly adept at manipulating the characters' special or secret moves, you've got them hooked. However, if the game lacks complexity and your players learn how the computer and the specific characters react in a particular game quickly, the game will lose its appeal.

Violence

Needless to say, the majority of fighting games are brutally violent. Is it necessary? Well, I'm not one to make a judgment, so I'll just present the facts. Mortal Kombat with its various "fatality moves," like ripping out beating hearts, was one of the major catalysts behind the recent Senate hearings on game ratings and labeling. If you don't mind having your games labeled, you'll have no problems.

Continued Inventiveness

Here is a thought to keep you pondering over your morning coffee: Fighting games rely on the continued inventiveness of designers to survive. So far, most of fighting games have had little inventiveness on the storyline front, and little has been done to push the games into new areas beyond one-on-one fighting scenario. Maybe you'll be the one to come up with some new innovative ideas and create the next hit fighting game.

Looking toward the Future

I said in the beginning, motion capture and 3D technology promise to bring exciting immediate fun to fighting games; no doubt it already has.

The future for fighting games definitely lies in the following trends:

Online Opponents The virtual bar brawl of the computer age is coming. Multiplayer online fighting games should usher in a new reality in fighting games. Online versions promise players a chance to really test their skills. And fighting games are sure to be one of the most popular online games, once online gaming hits big. Keep your eyes open for the long awaited Quake from ID Software. This polygon-based fighting game promises major online capabilities.

Immersive VR A major move for fighting games is toward allowing players to immerse themselves in fantastic VR fighting simulations, bobbing and weaving to avoid kicks and punches. Certainly all games in the future will find new life in immersive VR environs, but something about the personal mano-a-mano level seems enticing in the immersive VR world.

Integration into Larger Gaming Systems At the Computer Game Developers Conference in 1995, one of the seminars I attended was on the future of RPGs. One idea that made the rounds was producing a game in which the combat system was that of a traditional fighting game. While RPG fans, who don't normally gravitate to action games might not consider this idea with any enthusiasm, the concept definitely shows potential for fighting games to become integrated into complex storylines and serve as an element of a larger game.

God Games: Games That Put You in the Driver's Seat

As you might have guessed, this category of games caters to the egoist in all of us. This concept takes the RPG classification of games to the extreme. In a "God game," players are provided with tremendous control in both the macro and micro concerns of the game. God games are basically strategy games in which the player is more a shaper of systems than an absolute commander. In a well-crafted game, the player plans the various course of actions and manages the resources, and the game—with the help of some algorithms and a few "random" factors (such as rain in Utopia or fire in SimCity)—determines the outcome.

The goal of a typical God game is to sustain the underlying system as long as possible. Many game categories, such as wargames, have been mislabeled as God games; after all, it's hardly a goal of the game to sustain fighting. As a God game progresses, the player is challenged by the actual world of the game. It is the players' responsibility to monitor the reactions of the system they're managing to continually provide and mold the system to further levels of existence.

In most God games—Hamurabi, Populous, Utopia, and SimCity, for example—the system tends to be an actual human society, but as Maxis has proven with products like SimAnt, you can definitely apply the concept to non-human systems as well.

Here are some of the benchmark God games:

Hamurabi Hamurabi was one of the first God games I remember playing. In this game, you assumed the role of the Hamurabi, the ancient Sumerian ruler. Hamurabi's job was to allocate resources and supervise the planting of crops to ensure ten years of survival. Although this was a text game and there was more randomness to the events than in a modeled environment, it still was captivating. The player was in complete control—simulating the choices and reacting to the outcomes of them.

Utopia This is one of my favorite games and the precursor (although not deliberately) to Maxis' SimCity. In this game, you get to be the ruler of one of two islands; the other player or computer rules the other. Your goal is to build the perfect world, providing food, protection, housing, and education for your citizens. However, if you don't do the job, your citizens will revolt. The game includes obstacles, such as tropical storms, that can severely damage the island, and aid, in the form of rain, to help crops along.

Populous When Bullfrog broke through with Populous, they established themselves as a frontrunner in the game-development field. Populous is a benchmark game not only for great gameplay, graphics, and interface, but also because the game proved so successful that it (and perhaps SimCity) really spawned the "God game" label for itself and similar games.

The game casts you in the role of a god, creating a world in which the inhabitants live, work, and battle. As God, it is your goal to provide the inhabitants the type of land they need to reign supreme—easier said than done, as many of us found out.

Today, Bullfrog continues to push the God game metaphor with products like Syndicate and its upcoming Dungeon Keeper, which casts the player in the role of a Dungeon Master trying to keep heroes out of a dungeon. Stay tuned for this one!

SimCity, SimEarth, and Other Maxis Titles We've been mostly talking about benchmark games but Maxis may well be the first benchmark *company*. Starting with the most well-known God game, SimCity, Maxis has capitalized on that success to bring us an entire product line of God games, including SimEarth, SimAnt, SimTower, SimCity 2000, SimFarm, and SimHealth. At the core of all of Maxis' games is a strong research base that has enabled them to accurately model systems like a city or a health-care plan. Figures 8.14 and 8.15 show an example from two of Maxis' popular line of "Sim" products, SimIsle and SimEarth.

On top of this base, Maxis' game developers build an extremely intuitive interface and add the elements to turn this highly simulative environment into a game. In addition, they've built scenarios and stories into their products and added such random events as earthquakes or Godzilla destroying a town to keep the player alert. No company or product has exposed more people to the "God game" category in such a clear presentation than Maxis.

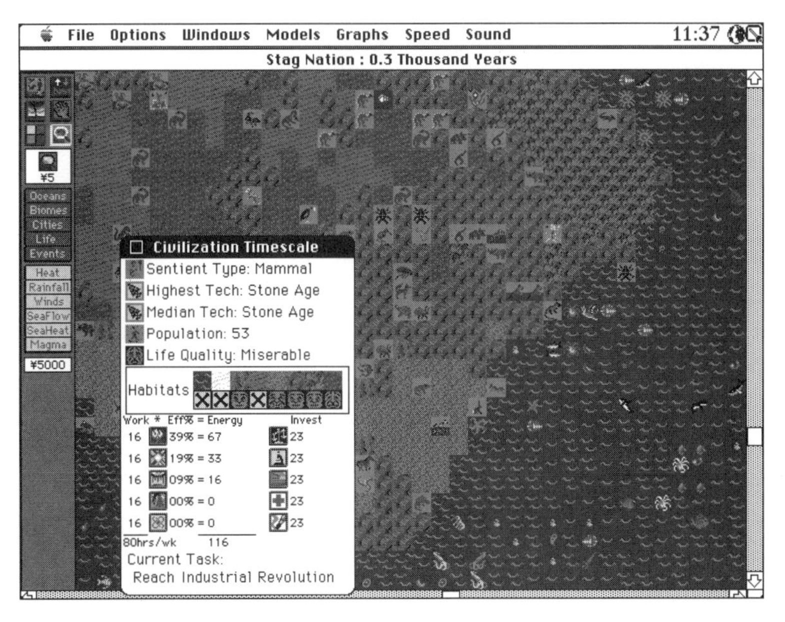

Figure 8.14 Maxis' SimEarth.

Figure 8.15 Maxis' SimIsle.

God Game Design Issues

God game design involves several concepts such as modeling and simulation that, while not specific to the games themselves, are essential elements for this category.

Systems Modeling

God games are the most basic form of simulation games. "Simulation games?" you say, "Aren't those the games like Flight Simulator?" Well, yes, but those type of simulation games are distinct from God games in that they simulate just one piece of military or non-military hardware instead of entire systems, such as a city in SimCity or an ant colony in SimAnt.

As you probably have surmised, the nature of God games makes it difficult for designers to model an accurate simulation. Designers put an enormous amount of time into research—developing accurate data tables and formulas to reflect, for example, why people move into or out of a city, or the effects of people in relationship to food. The effort is not wasted; what you get is a fun and realistic game. But don't feel too sorry for the designers. After all, in designing a God game, the designer really is the ultimate God!

Looking toward the Future

What's awesome about the "God game" concept is that students, teachers, parents, and gamers all see how unique an experience it provides. God Games have found a niche as a novel learning, strategic, and fun gaming experience.

So the future is definitely bright. More sophisticated artificial intelligence and modeling strategies are available, which allows designers to create even more intelligent inhabitants and systems, which leads to even more realistic play. There's no doubt that this gaming category will move into network and wide area network gaming. Count me in when SimCity makes its debut!

Multiplayer Games

Perhaps the hottest buzzword in game development for 1996 and beyond is *multiplayer*, especially when that word refers to games that are structured as large online games. There has been a wealth of startups with enormous venture capital formed to deliver tools and services to build large multiplayer games. Multiplayer games come in many varieties, as shown in Table 8.2

Let's take a look at some of the benchmark multiplayer games:

M.U.L.E. For many game developers, this isn't just a benchmark game for multiplayer games, but a benchmark game *period.* M.U.L.E., developed by

Table 8.2 Multiplayer Game Types

Game Type	Description
Multiplayer in the Same Room	The original multiplayer game in which multiple players play the same game simultaneously on the same hardware.
Multiplayer Modem Games	With two machines and two modems, players hook up long distance to play the same game. Many games today offer some sort of modem-based long distance playing option because it has become expected by many hardcore gamers and reviewers.
Network Game	This game type allows multiple players over a LAN (Local Area Network). Some folks enjoy this so much that they have purchased second and even third computers and created simple, home-based LANs for games. (You laugh, but I used to hook up home LANs for people all the time.) While adding network capabilities to a game is not going to propel it to hit status, it is a small feature that a number of people want.
Remote Access Server Game	The future of multiplayer games starts here. Imagine combining modem-to-modem and Local Area Network games. In this scenario, the players don't have to reside on the same LAN, and even though they use a modem, it's not a one-to-one connection. A remote access server game has two components, a server product and a client product. People "dial up" the remote server with their client package and engage in simultaneous play with multiple players who have dialed in to play. Unlike past remote server setups that had you dialing in directly to a server, many of the new wave of remote server games are using the TCP/IP networking protocol and setting up server sights all over the Internet.
Online Service Multiplayer Network Game	Online multiplayer games are essentially structured like remote access server games, but because the games have the hardware support of a large online service, they can support many more simultaneous players.

Danielle Berry and Ozark Softscape and published by Electronic Arts, was a fun strategy game that on the Atari 800 could handle up to four players. Jockeying for resources, the frantic trading and interaction between the players made this a really fun game to play.

Doom Awesome graphics and vicious gameplay aside, the multiplayer death matches this game spawned are famous around the world. While other games before it offered networking and modem play, Doom broke the format wide open. And the brilliant Id shareware distribution scheme only added to the success of Doom as a multiplayer game.

Air Warrior Of all the early major online service multiplayer games, Genie Air Warrior, developed by Kesmai Corporation, became the first major hit primarily because it offered players multiplayer dogfighting ability. Shooting down enemy planes online is a very cool way to relieve work stress.

The Imagination Network & MPG-NET If you're looking to find a plethora of online multiplayer games to evaluate and learn from, signing on to these two services will do the trick. Imagination Network and MPG-NET combine to form an entire benchmark online game system. Developed by Sierra and owned by AT&T, both Imagination Network and MPG-NET are complete online services that show an example from two of Maxis' popular line of Sim products, SimIsle and SimEarth.

Multiplayer Game Design Issues

Multiplayer game design involves several concepts that, while not specific to the games themselves, are essential elements for this category.

Your Economic Model

One facet of multiplayer games worth mentioning is in the economic model you employ to earn money from your game. For example, when designing a multiplayer network game, you control two software components: the server version and the client version. You can give away the client version and sell the server version, or you could give away the server version and sell the client version, set up a licensing fee with remote access server providers, and charge people for their time online.

For LAN games you need to think about how many people can play off one purchased copy of the game. (Everyone? Two? Three?) You might want to consider setting up your game with multiple keys that unlock the ability to add players; players can then get keys from an 800 number.

The bottom line is that when dealing with multiplayer game development, how you actually expect to earn money from the product can have a substantial impact on the design and the development of the game itself.

Player Interaction

In a recent conference, Richard Mulligan, a veteran online service multiplayer game developer, discussed the importance of chat in games. In his game GemStone, the added chat function proved successful; he once logged on at 2:00 am to find 12 players huddled together in one room, not playing the game, but discussing the best recipe for peanut butter cookies!

The lesson is simple. While the game provides the true interaction for players, the sense of community and heightened player interactivity that comes from chat is an absolute necessity.

Developers seeking to create dynamic multiplayer games need to think about the overall playing environment that multiplayer gaming requires.

Artificial Players

Many developers see the need for artificial opponents diminishing with multiplayer games—with human opponents on the other end of the line, there's no need to create other dynamic opponents, right? Wrong. The fact is that artificial players in many games become even more important in a multiplayer environment. Just because you have multiplayer capability in your game doesn't mean that multiple players will always be logged on. For example, if you create a multiplayer racing game but only one player is logged on, you still need to control the other cars to provide the racing experience. Additionally, if a player logs off in the middle of the race, the car can't just disappear. The bottom line is that in a large scale online game, you still need artificial characters to populate the worlds you create.

Looking toward the Future

The stratosphere is where this category is headed. Perhaps the only thing growing faster than games are online services and the Internet that support them.

Currently, 99 percent of the multiplayer game market revolves around LANs. However, the real potential for multiplayer games is from commercial networks, the Internet, and, someday, interactive television.

In the immediate future, one of the more interesting developments in online gaming will be Quake and its remote access server technology. This style of architecture will allow for people to set up Quake servers and have multiple players dial into them to play against each other in the server's own unique Quake levels. This technology promises to start all kinds of local online gaming services.

The multiplayer game category is still very much in its infancy. New ideas are constantly emerging, but there are equally as many new problems to go with them. If this is the area you choose for development, you can bet that you're in for a great adventure.

Platform Games

Among fundamental game types, shooters came first, then maze games followed. The next evolution introduced a popular category of games which became known as Platform games. Let's reminisce as we take a look at some benchmark platform games:

Donkey Kong Perhaps the most well-known of the early platform games, Donkey Kong was the number two game behind the Pac-Man series in arcades all over the world. But this game "one-upped" Pac-Man by launching the most well-known gaming character of all time: Mario, the plumber whose only mission in life was to get his girlfriend back from some big ape.

Super Mario Brothers This game established Nintendo as the premiere home video game system and went on to become one of the best-known games in all of gaming. Despite all the hype, Super Mario Brothers was, and still is, a great game with lots of secret rooms and tons of tricks hidden in the game.

Sonic The Hedgehog This game did for the Sega Genesis home video game system what Super Mario Brothers did for Nintendo: It became a killer game that launched an entire platform. Although Sonic was most certainly inspired by Super Mario Brothers, it took on a look and feel all unto itself. Especially amazing were the stark differences in play between each level, and the amount of work and number of puzzles built into the game. Figure 8.16 shows a screen shot from one of the series of Sonic The Hedgehog games produced by Sega. Sonic became Sega's "signature" game (like Super Mario was for Nintendo) and helped make Sega's 16-bit system, The Genesis a huge hit.

Jazz Jackrabbit/Abuse/Duke Nuk'em I include all of these games to point out that the PC too can be a great platform for high-paced console-like platform games. Better yet, one of the games is shareware too. Jazz Jackrabbit, a certain Sonic the Hedgehog knockoff, featured some blindly fast graphics and fun play. It's predecessor, Duke Nuk'em, was one of the early success stories in PC shareware arcade games. Abuse, the newest kid on the block, is a truly amazing game with tons of advanced-level editing capability and console quality sound, graphics, and animation.

Prince of Persia I should include several other PC-platform games like the early Data East's Bruce Lee and Miner 2049er (a personal favorite), but for argument's sake I'll leave them out and simply note Jordan Mechner's tour de force, Prince of Persia. This game boasts incredibly fluid animation and excellent puzzles, and while platform in nature, Prince of Persia looks entirely different from most platform games.

Donkey Kong Country Donkey Kong Country, produced by the hot British based software house, Rare, Ltd., utilized a neat graphic trick. Even though the basic veiw of the game is a 2D side scrolling view, the team at Rare, using high-end Silicon Graphics workstations, rendered all the graphics in 3D, then produced a

Figure 8.16 Some action scenes from the popular Sonic The Hedgehog series.

basic sidescrolling look to the game. The result was a 2D game with an awesome 3D feel to it. The graphics and gameplay were such a success the product sold well over ten million plus cartridges world wide! Figure 8.17 shows some of the really cool graphic looks Rare achieved for its next generation side scroller.

Bug! I've only played Bug! a couple of times, and I don't consider it the most amazing game, but I've included it here as a benchmark platform game because it's really one of the first real 3D-oriented platform games. While Marble Madness and a couple of others have been interesting 3D platform type products, Bug! strikes me as

Figure 8.17 The hugely successful Donkey Kong Country series developed by Rare.

a true 3D extension of a 2D platform game. Sega is taking the traditional platform game to whole new heights and depths as shown in Figure 8.18. Bug! is a brand new game for Sega's next generation platform, the Saturn.

Platform Game Design Issues

Platform game design involves several concepts that, while not specific to the games themselves, are essential elements for this category of game.

Level Editing

If you take a look at some of the benchmark products like Super Mario Brothers and Sonic The Hedgehog, you'll surely see that level editing is a key ingredient of platform games. Your levels need to be unique from other games and among the levels in your game itself. Make use of complex puzzles for your players to accomplish tasks.

Character Creation

Any good computer game has a diverse set of characters. Among the most successful platform games, Sonic, Mario, and Donkey Kong have proven to be the most memorable characters. Take a look at the animation used and the characteristics given to these guys as you consider characters for your own games.

Figure 8.18 Unlike previous platform games, Bug! takes place in a full 3D platform world.

Looking toward the Future

Platform games have been the most successful arcade game type of all time. And, if it ain't broke, don't fix it. As computers move more and more toward 3D graphics, platform games are following close behind. For example, Sega's new Bug! shows that with 3D graphics the platform game can offer new dimensions of play while retaining all the great elements that made the 2D side-scrolling platform games great.

Platform games are one of the more mature game categories today, so aside from graphical improvement, gameplay will stay basically the same. But because this category is so popular, expect many more great games in the future.

Puzzle and Card Games

Puzzle and card games don't seem similar enough to be grouped together overall, but they really have quite a bit in common. After all, Klondike Solitaire is as much of a puzzle as Minesweeper—both games emphasize problem solving and strategy. Puzzle and card games are both also thought of as diversional or break type games. Meant to be played in a short single setting, these products are usually designed and sold as suites—a package containing several different types or one with many levels. You might laugh at the seriousness of developing these type of games, but the fact is that these things sell. (And that *is* a consideration, right?) Not only will they make you a tidy profit, but you get the satisfaction of knowing that your game has single-handedly put a cog into even the most efficient office's productivity wheel. Well... maybe not single-handedly.

Here are some of the benchmark puzzle and card games:

Microsoft and Sierra Card Games Among card games, Microsoft's game packs and Sierra's Hoyle series have offered a number of excellent card games. In Hoyles as shown in Figure 8.19, Sierra has added all kinds of quirky characters to play against, each with their own style of playing the various games in the package. In addition, the whimsical animations and sound that Sierra has incorporated strengthens the underlying basic game of cards. This provides more interaction and fun experience for the player. Figure 8.20 shows the popular Solitaire card game published by Microsoft. This is perhaps the world's most played computer game.

The Fools Errand The Fools Errand from Miles Computing offered not only a large array of interesting puzzle games, but packaged them around a simple storyline that lead the player from one game to the next. This is an excellent example of enhancing a plain vanilla puzzle game with a few simple details to create a more interesting overall gaming environment.

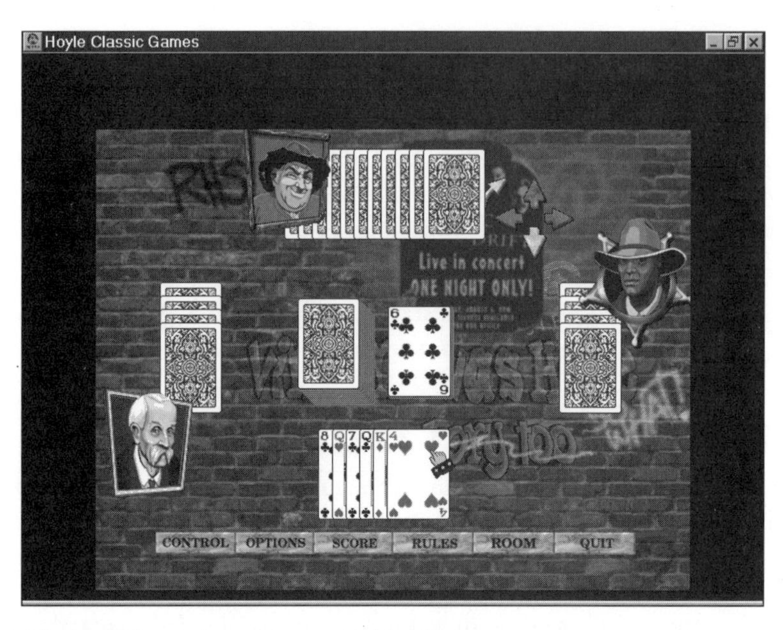

Figure 8.19 Hoyle's card game created by Sierra.

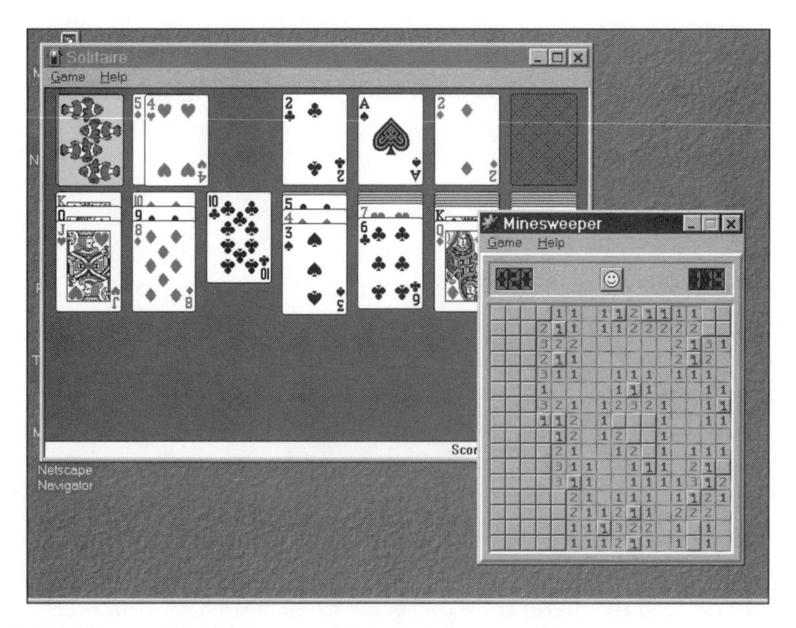

Figure 8.20 Microsoft's highly popular Solitaire card game.

Puzzle and Card Game Design Issues

Most puzzle, card, or basic boardgames are easy enough to create as electronic games. However, the more successful and critically acclaimed versions of these types of games tend to be those that strive to create a unique overall gaming environment. Many times taking a simple game and establishing a more robust version of it with multimedia and other gaming elements can be the simplest formula for success. It is no longer enough to create a simple card game. A better (and certainly more profitable) approach is to create a poker game that takes place in the Old West, chock full of unruly, gunslinging characters and saloon-like settings complete with music and background sounds. Just an idea!

Looking toward the Future

Overall, the major puzzle and card game market will continue in its current role creating enjoyable, diversionary fun and cool brain teasers. More and more though, companies will work to find inventive ways to present these basic games in interesting formats.

Retro Games

Believe it or not, this is a really fast-growing category. In fact, I actually think it's inspiring to see game developers re-introducing classics for newer machines or, in some cases, giving an old classic a complete, modernized facelift.

The fact is that some games are classics for a simple reason: They were spectacular games! Take a moment to think of some of the most amazing games you played 10 and 15 years ago. If they were good then, why wouldn't they be good now? (Some savvy designers thought the same thing.)

Is there any reason a good game of Joust would be any less enjoyable now? Or how about Asteroids? Perhaps a good game of Defender? How about some Tempest? Maybe a little Riverraid? Okay, okay, I'll stop, but I wanted to make plenty sure you got the point.

My definition for a retro game is this: a classic game (10 years or older) that is brought back to life by either creating an exact replica on a new platform or by designing a new version that retains the original game in a recognizable form.

Recently, some companies including Microsoft have released games that fall into the retro category, and these provide the benchmark products other developers can use:

Microsoft Arcade for Windows This product includes four classic Atari games totally rewritten for Windows with the actual sounds digitized from the coin-op versions. They even include entire backgrounds on the games and the original designers—a design must, in my opinion. As this concept takes a stronger foothold, we may even have to start including a "where are they now" segment. Superbly done.

Activision Atari 2600 Game Pack I and II In the early 80s, as cable and video sales started to take off, there were more movie studio takeovers than there were

studios. Why? Because of the vast amount of films that these studios had accumulated, mergers offered incredible potential value through colorization, re-makes, restoration, and reissuing film on video and as pay-per-view movies.

Activision recently added a spin to this concept. By joining a 2600 emulator with old game code from their awesome library of cartridges, they were able to re-market—using CD-ROM—the games that made Activision a household word in the early 1980s.

Tempest 2000 and Defender 2000 When Atari took stock of the vast amount of amazing games stored in their library, they found a rich set of old favorites in need of a new look—perfect for their new Jaguar gaming system. Two of those games—in what hopefully will be an extensive series of re-makes—are Jeff Minter's, Tempest 2000 and Defender 2000. With new high-tech graphics and more modernized gameplay, they set a standard for reintroducing new versions of old hits.

Retro Game Design Issues

The benchmark games I've presented show the various design routes you can take with this category. You can either update the game for a new platform, much like Microsoft did with Microsoft Arcade for Windows, or you can create a new wave version, like Atari did with Defender 2000 and Tempest 2000.

Another approach that we didn't discuss can be equally profitable and fun. Activision's recent Pitfall '95 introduced an entirely new game, but also included the original version of the game upon which Pitfall was based.

Looking toward the Future

The entire computer industry has always had its eye on the future, but retro gaming is sure to be a welcome facet. It's a great thing to preserve the classics. I also like watching a designer like Jeff Minter from Atari take a classic game like Defender and, while preserving all the elements that made it such a classic, give it an entire new lease on life with updated graphics and gameplay.

I look forward to seeing future generations enjoying those early games just as much as I did.

Role Playing Games

If you read Chapter 7, you are already familiar with the concept of a role-playing game. So I won't bore you with too many more details. As you probably know, early RPGs were played with pen, paper, and dice. Once the computer came of age, RPGs naturally moved to this new medium. Through the years, there have been some memorable series, some of which have spawned great RPG engines, and others that have pushed RPGs into one of the most popular overall gaming categories.

Here are some of the benchmark RPGs:

Ultima Perhaps the single most successful RPG ever is the Ultima series, currently entering its ninth episode. The success of Ultima is due to three main reasons: great fantasy world, great role-playing capabilities, and an amazing story. In creating the Ultima series, Richard Garriot (a.k.a. Lord British) has always sought to shape a realistic game world first and then place in it a complex story of good and evil.

Figure 8.21 Shows screens from the latest Ultima, Ultima VIII, and Figure 8.22 shows the title screen to one of the best Ultimas, Ultima IV. Finally, Figure 8.23 shows a screen shot from a rereleased Mac version of Ultima III. (This is a shareware version written, with permission by Leon McNeil.) This amazingly fresh update of the classic is available on the web at: http://www.swcp.com/~beastie/ultima3.html.

Figure 8.21 Action screens from Ultima VIII.

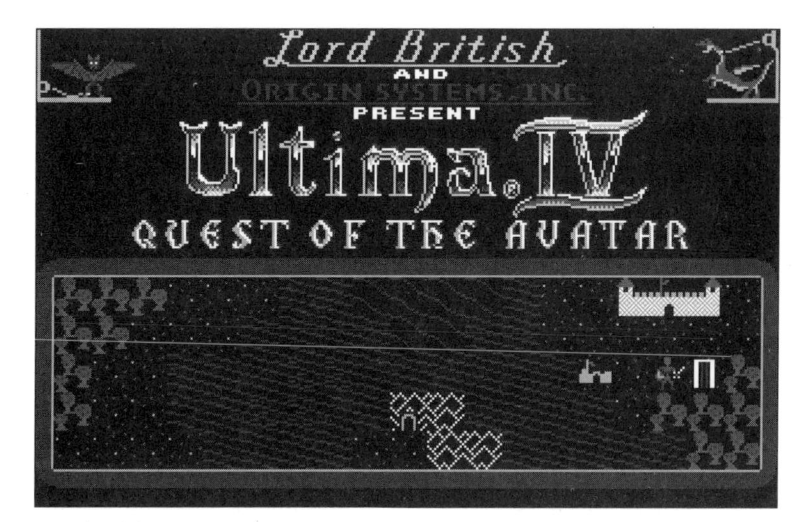

Figure 8.22 The Ultima IV title screen.

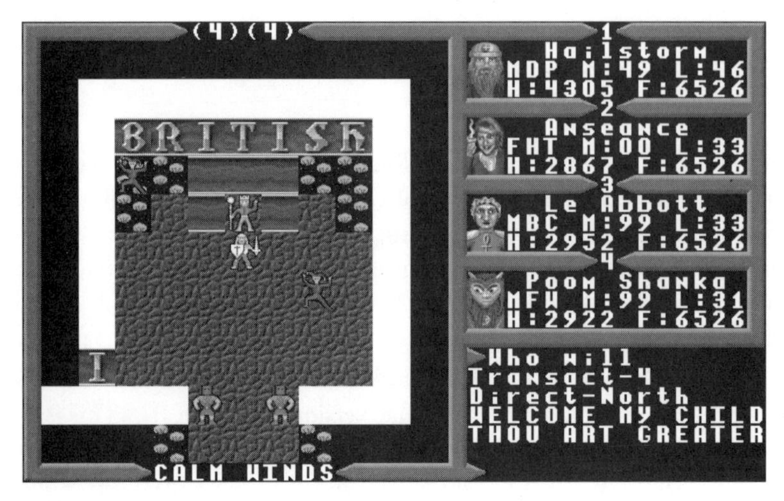

Figure 8.23 Ultima III Mac shareware version.

Dungeon Master Although Dungeon Master was more of an adventure game than an RPG, several elements—the multiple character party and the stats-based advancement of players—were more RPG in style.

The Bard's Tale This game put Interplay on the map. Set in the town of Skara Brae, this game was noted (at the time it was published) for its great 3D graphics. The series eventually expanded to include two sequels.

Wasteland This second Interplay hit explored post-apocolyptic Earth as an RPG backdrop.

Wizardry With the exception of Ultima, no early RPG had the effect on people that Wizardry had. Cavernous 3D dungeons and intense gameplay made this game a favorite among early computer enthusiasts.

Starflight Starflight, a huge success for IBM and one of the first major space-based RPGs, was significant for its advanced game play and incredibly sized game world, which was the result of 1,000 hours of development time. Starflight had one of the largest development teams ever seen in game development before.

SSI AD&D Series At the time SSI won the competitive bid to develop the official Advanced Dungeons & Dragons (AD&D) games, they were best known for their wargames, but had recently branched out into adventure games with their awesome Phantasie series.

Many AD&D players were eager to see how the games would turn out, and they weren't disappointed. SSI employed several innovative ideas, including their licensing strategy and their interesting, and sometimes exhaustive, battle sequences.

Recently the rights to the license reverted back to TSR, who will employ several companies to create products based on the AD&D world. Let's hope that SSI will continue to be included in TSR's stable of developers.

Might and Magic Might and Magic from New World Computing has been, perhaps, the second most successful series of RPG games after Ultima. The series has featured wondrous first-person point-of-view graphics and lots of "hack 'n' slash" fun.

Arena:Elder Scrolls Arena:Elder Scrolls, the latest of major RPGs, combines a raycasting smooth-movement engine with a major RPG game. Arena has an excellent storyline and includes both above and below ground graphics. It has become the latest major RPG product to break through the pack of RPGs. Bethesda, the creators of Arena, are due to release its sequel with a host of hot features sure to breathe new life into the RPG category.

RPG Game Design Issues

RPG design involves several concepts that, while not specific to the games themselves, are essential elements for this category of games.

Stay Tuned for the Next Episode

RPGs are great products to develop because they lend themselves to sequels—of course, your first game has to be successful to warrant a sequel! If you create a dynamic world with a good story, you can return to it over and over to present new ideas and games to people who enjoy your creations. If you look at all the major RPG products—Wizardry, The Bard's Tale, Ultima, and Arena—you'll notice that they are all series.

As you create your initial game, put some thought into ideas that can be expanded in additional versions. For example, you might introduce a character who in a later game becomes an arch-enemy, or you could refer to some sort of lost object that could become the theme for other stories.

You will also want to pay considerable attention to the world you are creating. You want your players to involve themselves in your world and enjoy everything that happens within it. Designing such a fabulous world is our next topic.

A World Unlike Any Other

As computer adventure games have gotten ever more complex, building worlds has become increasingly more important. In world building, the designer seeks to build an entire working society, including all the characters and the storyline involving their "lives." Basically, the idea is to place the story into an environment, not match an environment to a story.

In addition, world building creates a minor dilemma. Although the world is fictitious, it must be realistic. The no-holds-barred approach won't gain you many fans. Players will evaluate your world accordingly:

- Is this new fictitious world different and interesting enough?
- Do certain systems in this world work realistically? (For example, when I sell things into a town's economy, will the price drop?)

NPC Interaction and Conversation

The biggest problem in designing RPGs is Non Player Character (NPC) interaction. Simply put, RPGs can lack depth if characters do not dynamically interact with the game.

The solution is obvious: Incorporate more flexibility into the internal simulative engines and AI facilities in games. For example, instead of hard coding daggers to cost six gold coins, a game could constantly fluctuate the prices of items based on traditional supply and demand algorithms.

The goal is to have NPCs relate to the players based on their previous actions, interact among themselves more, with the players working to involve themselves within the natural order of community interaction among the world being portrayed. Issues like weather and weapons that wear down are also being discussed by developers.

Developers are also hard at work to create better interaction concerning RPG conversations—varying words, implementing characters with memory capabilities, varying conversation according to different contexts, and much more.

As you design your RPGs, give considerable thought to how to implement an increased level of depth and conversational interaction.

Battles and Combat

A key ingredient in almost every type of RPG is some form of combat in the game. Combat is the main distinction when classifying RPGs and adventure games. Although most adventure games might have a combat sequence, it isn't a recurring element.

The combat aspect of the game is really a miniature wargame inside the surrounding RPG game. Players control their characters and arm them with weapons (or spells in fantasy style games). Then, based upon choices and statistical tests, combat takes place. Surviving characters often see improvement in their combat skills.

On a more specific level, the designer needs to decide whether combat will involve decision making on the part of the player or whether tactical skills should be left to the program.

Some developers have found a happy medium and have designed games to allow the player to return control of the combat decisions to the computer at any time during the game. Another approach would be to have the computer offer a variety of tactical options that the player can choose from; for instance, positioning, movement, attack types, and so on.

Heroes of Might & Magic from New World Computing offers the player an "auto" feature, which allows the player to watch the computer control the strategy of his or her troops at any point in a battle. The auto feature has two purposes: Beginning players can learn from watching the computer's tactics, and powerfully situated players—players whose positions are so strong that even bad decisions won't affect the outcome of a battle—can allow the computer to handle combat results with less work on their part and a quicker resolution.

Looking toward the Future

RPGs currently seem to be in somewhat of a state of flux. Perhaps more than any other type of game, RPGs designers are struggling to broaden their market appeal while staying true to the RPG ideal—a struggle that is rampant in the gaming industry these days. The problem is that many games haven't found the proper balance.

Perhaps the biggest move for RPGs will be to large multiplayer gaming systems. RPGs are well suited to multiplayer environments. In fact, several major online RPG games—like Gemstone III and AOL's Neverwinter Nights, for example—are already attracting huge crowds. And, both Interplay and Origin, among other notable RPG producers, are planning major online RPGs for the coming year.

Shooters

It's hard to find a more fundamental arcade game than the pure-hearted shoot 'em up. From Space Invaders to Asteroids to Galaxian to Xenon to 1942 to Gradius to Tempest 2000, there have been more memorable shooters than I can name in a single breath. However, today, most of the pure shooters are being supplanted by 3D shooters like Doom and Battletech.

The majority of shooters are space motifs or some sort of futuristic Earth scenario. However, a few shooters tap into another style, like 1942, which uses a war theme. New ideas are always welcome. For example, how about a shooter based in the old West? The player rides horseback through a stampede trying to take out renegade rustlers. I know it's not the most enticing game idea, but it *is* new!

The older a category is, the more benchmark games it has. Shooters is one of those categories—it has some of the most classic games of all time. I won't bother to discuss

them at great length. Games like Space Invaders, Asteroids, Missile Command, Centipede, Zaxxon, Galaxian, Galaga, and Defender are so classic that if you haven't been exposed to at least one of them you've been taking up residence in a cave for the last 20 years.

Shooter Game Design Issues

Now that more complex systems with 3D graphics have entered the gaming arena, the pure arcade experience provided by shooters has fallen by the wayside—3D is, after all, the current rage!

Still, traditional-looking "top down" shooters are great games, and are still being pumped out by such prestigious gaming companies as Apogee and Epic.

Shoot 'em ups tend to follow a basic "cookie cutter" design of power ups, progressively harder levels, and, at the end of the levels, some sort of major obstacle that long ago became known as the "main monster." So many successful games have used this design that it's hard to argue against it. Of course, designers employ a creative license in the graphics and backgrounds domains.

However, given the number of shooters that have been made and the number of players involved, it's important that you take into account the prevailing ideals and then carve out a successful product niche for yourself.

Looking toward the Future

Overall, this category isn't going anywhere; that's not to say that shooters have run their course, but design-wise it's hard to see them taking large leaps and bounds over time. But then again, isn't that what makes a shooter so much fun? For many of us, it's a basic game that still provides hours of non-productive, mindless amusement.

Simulation Games

Simulation games have been among the strongest category of games ever made, with flight simulators leading the way in the category. Simulations are most often associated with some form of military hardware. Examples include Spectrum Holobyte's F-16, or any of the other tank, submarine, or helicopter simulators. In addition to these warfare simulators, other products like Vette!, a driving simulation, and Scram!, a simulation of a nuclear power plant, have been developed. Also keep in mind that many games have considerable simulative qualities; an average wargame is a simulation of sorts, as are many sports games.

Our discussion will only include simulations based on the "vehicle" track, including flight and other military simulators, driving games, and fictional space ship fighting.

Numerous benchmark games come to mind when I think of simulators, but I've pulled together a few special ones to highlight:

Microsoft Flight Simulator Among the early simulation products, the original Flight Simulator has to be the best if not the longest lived. The original product, which was based on flying a Cessna single engine plane around the United States, has seen numerous implementations over the years. Of those, the version Microsoft purchased the rights to is now known as Microsoft Flight Simulator (see Figure 8.24).

Today, Microsoft Flight Simulator continues to provide countless hours of quality simulated flight for millions of flying enthusiasts. Its biggest strength has been the many scenery disks that offer great fun flying around many of the world's greatest geographic areas, like the Grand Canyon.

Silent Service, F-15 Strike Eagle, Gunship 2000, and M1-Tank Platoon These four titles are only a sampling of the many great simulation products that Microprose has developed. Each of these titles guarantees a simulation that is not only fun, but extremely accurate. Microprose simulations also include some really neat "missions" that game players must complete in order to finish the game.

Chuck Yeager's AFT, FA-18/Interceptor Over the years, Electronic Arts (EA) has provided many interesting simulation products. Two of the earlier simulators were Chuck Yeager's Advanced Flight Trainer and FA-18/Interceptor, an Amiga title.

Figure 8.24 A screen shot from the latest version of the longtime simulation benchmark product, Flight Simulator.

Both games were excellent products combining well-defined flight simulations with excellent graphics and, in the case of AFT, neat training, tons of different planes, and acrobatics. With FA-18/Interceptor, EA used the full power of the Amiga to provide an amazing graphic and sound feast. Additionally, the game strung its missions along in a loosely knit overall storyline, something EA would build upon in future simulation efforts.

Falcon Falcon, by far, represents the ability to really push the detail level in simulations. Originally published early in the PC's history, Falcon's flight and accurate portrayal of the F-16 Falcon jet was even evident with CGA graphics! From these amazing beginnings, Spectrum has gone on to establish itself as a major PC game company, especially with its high-tech simulations.

Falcon was such an accurate simulation that the Air Force worked with Spectrum to create a new low-cost simulation product for its own pilots—the ultimate compliment!

Indy Car Racing/Nascar One thing that is evident in some of the most successful simulation products is detail; specifically, detail evolved from a love of the subject and single pursuit by a company to become *the* top designer of that type of simulation. Great attention to detail is just what Papyrus is all about. And their two racing products are no exception. When it comes to building awesome simulations, this company and these two products are at the top of the list.

Flight Unlimited From the team behind a number of simulations and great games, comes perhaps the latest and greatest in flight simulators. Flight Unlimited from Looking Glass features an amazing graphical engine and incredible accuracy. Right down to determining the actual flight by calculating airflow over the wings using sophisticated aerodynamic formulas, this product was built from scratch to provide unparalleled simulation.

Simulation Game Design Issues

Simulation games involve several concepts that, while not specific to the games themselves, are essential elements for this category of games.

Fly Me to the Moon (Or Is That the Grand Canyon?)

Existing simulations are easily broken down into two categories, but it's important to remember that a simulation needn't be limited to them. Let's take a look:

Military and Non-Military Vehicle Simulations The majority of simulation products center around military vehicle simulations. Entire companies like Microprose and Spectrum Holybyte were founded on the strength of their simulations of major military fighter planes, tanks, and ships.

Simulations of non-military machines tend to be products based on sports car racing and standard flight simulators like Flight Unlimited and Microsoft Flight Simulator.

Space Simulations A lot of simulation products, especially those of a fictional nature, have something to do with space. After all, space *is* the final frontier and space travel makes for an incredibly appealing simulation program. X-Wing and Space Maxx/Microsoft Space Simulator both offer good insight into a well-developed space simulation.

Verisimilitude of Detail

I learned this term from reading Chris Crawford's book about his product Balance of Power, which was a simulation of global politics in the cold war of the mid 1980s. In his book, he explained that a game designer needs to decide how much detail is enough. Sometimes you can have too little detail and sometimes you can have too much. Many simulation designers grapple with this problem all the time. Some designers feel that the word *simulation* indicates that a product must be as realistic and as exciting as possible. However, sometimes striving for this level of real-world detail can make a good game boring or too complex to play.

For example, you might want to create a simulation of an airplane by placing great attention on details such as all sorts of pre-flight checks and stuff, but does that really add to the overall game? Sure, it adds to the simulative accuracy, but it might be overkill.

In the end, you and your testers must determine how much detail to include, but keep in mind that nit picking details in simulations, however accurate they might actually be, might be a turn-off. Don't forget that people play games to escape the menial chores of the real world.

Mission Impossible

A lot of the more popular simulation products design "missions" into their simulations, and I've heard nothing but positive comments on this approach. As you design your simulations, try to think about the various missions and the overriding storylines you could incorporate into your product. LucasArts has embellished this approach by producing exquisite "cut scenes," which enhance and tell the storyline throughout the course of the game.

Ladies and Gentlemen...Start Your Engine

Simulations tend more often than not to be developed around sophisticated 3D graphical engines. It's no surprise that many of the games spawn sequels or that the

engines are used to develop other simulation style games. The key to producing a string of simulation hits is to come up with an excellent 3D graphics engine (easier said than done!) and work to apply that technology to a range of potential simulation situations.

Reinventing the Wheel and Looking for New Opportunities

Simulations tend to be one of the most graphically intensive types of games in the gaming universe. Therefore, it's common to see a new twist on a previously done topic because developers can "easily" and substantially improve these types of games, through major strides in the graphical presentation of the game. You only need to look at the number of flight simulators on the market to see this premise in motion. Each major breakthrough in 3D graphics sparks a new wave of updated simulations of every type of plane out there. However, the more popular simulators have always been the ones that focus on entirely new ideas. Certainly Flight Unlimited is Flight Simulator with a much improved graphic engine, yet the designers chose to focus on aerial acrobatics—a completely new variation on the flying theme. Even though a leap in graphical technology gives you the ability to do the 5th WWII submarine simulator, rack your brain and see if you can come up with something better...something new. Your fans will love you for it!

Looking toward the Future

One thing about simulations is that more than most other game categories, simulations are highly dependent on the latest advancements in graphics programming and hardware technology. Looking at the companies that have produced benchmark games, they're all stocked with heavily experienced programming teams combined with massive resources and money. Many of these companies have been plying their craft for considerable amounts of time.

Still the future for this category is not entirely technology based. There's always room for creativity.

Sports Games

Sports games are bread and butter in the computer game industry. Electronic Arts (EA) has built an entire company around the strongest sports games in the industry. And EA isn't alone. Accolade, Sega, and Dynamix have all built successful sports lines as well. Because sports games are such big profit makers, it certainly follows that this category is the most competitive in the gaming industry. Unfortunately, competing successfully in this arena is going to be almost impossible for anyone but the most well funded and technically adept companies.

Sport games are as old as gaming itself and come in two basic varieties (although one has not been nearly as exploited as the other): fictional and non-fictional. Overall, most of the sports games in existence tend to be simulations of actual sports like football, baseball, and soccer. But there's no reason that this has to be the standard. For example, Lucas Arts created entirely fictional sports games. Now, I'm not sure about you, but I think a hard game of BallBlazer, a futuristic soccer game, would do me good.

And in EA's case, they were able to squeeze extra revenue out of an existing investment (a rarity in the game business) when they developed their Mutant League games from the core engines of their non-fictional games.

The modern sport game first appeared on the Commodore Amiga, and it was quickly followed by John Madden Football for the Apple IIe and Formula One Grand Prix for the Amiga. At that point, sports games took off like a rocket. Sports fanatics (at least the ones I know) can never get enough.

Here are some of the benchmark sports games:

Intellivision Sports In its early battles with Atari and their 2600, Mattel successfully created a slew of sports games that were, for the time, well implemented and immensely playable. Skiing, Boxing, and Football were among my personal favorites.

Microleague and APBA While other early baseball games like the classic Hardball continued to focus on the action element to baseball, two products came along—APBA and Microleague baseball—that were stat-based baseball simulations. These games were a baseball lover's dream long before the rotisserie league craze broke out.

Earl Weaver Baseball Originally produced for the Commodore Amiga, Earl Weaver Baseball was in many ways a groundbreaking product. Designer Eddie Drombower and producer Don Daglow constructed an entirely new category of game. Earl Weaver was not just a game, it was a simulation. Weaver combined arcade-style techniques with stat game techniques to create a game that could be played for hours of enjoyment. Tremendous attention was paid to the detail in the game; ballparks were rendered to exacting scale and wind and actual physical properties were used to determine how far the ball traveled off the bat.

EA Sports "If it's in the game it's in the game" is the tagline for what has become the most successful sports line in all of gaming. EA broke new ground with Earl Weaver Baseball, then they went on to create an entire line of sports titles that they later grouped under the EA Sports label.

Each of the games follows the basic design formula devised for Earl Weaver: a great arcade game that is tied to an awesome statistical database. These games offer all sorts of "general manager" options so that you can construct your own teams. You can even trade players and get rid of them when they don't perform the way you

want. Each game is also presented in a format that resembles an actual television broadcast with multiple camera angles, half-time reports, and so on.

EA's design and execution has lead to a yearly dosage of awesome games like NBA Live, NHL Hockey, PGA Tour Golf, and John Madden Football. As far as sports games go, EA is the market and development leader. Figures 8.25 and 8.26 show screen shots from two of Electronic Arts' biggest sport game hits, the NBA Live series and their NHL Hockey. Notice how the graphic look is very much done from a TV production standpoint.

Figure 8.25 Two action screens from NBA Live.

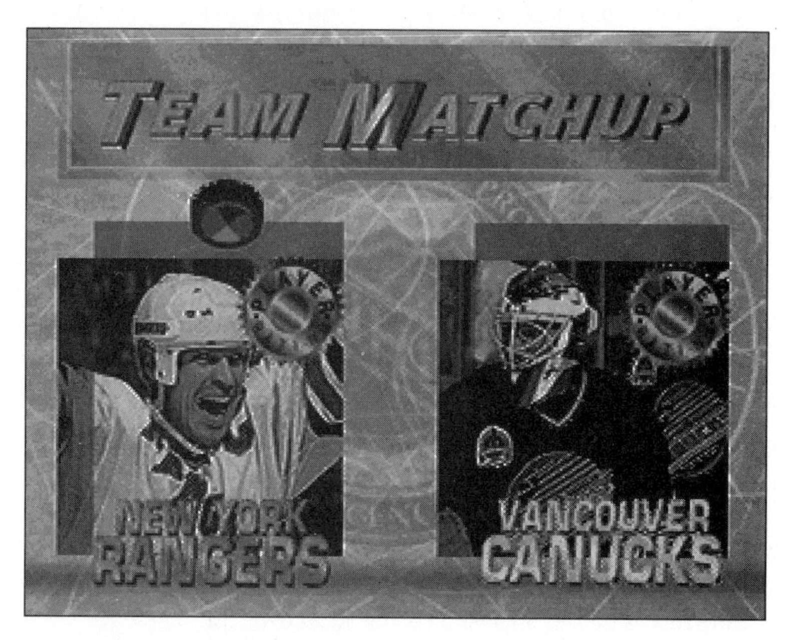

Figure 8.26 Screen from NHL 96.

FIFA Soccer 3DO In 1994 EA added one more notch to their belt with the release of FIFA international soccer. Simply put, FIFA was more than a simulation, it was immersive. From the controllable camera angles to the complete TV-like presentation of all the action, an awesome replay feature, and an incredibly rendered 3D stadium, EA stepped into the 32-bit console market and set the standard for sports games.

Of special note here are the incredible sound effects EA added to this game; the roar of the stadium crowds and the chanting is out of this world.

It's Not All EA... However dominant EA is in the sports gaming arena, there are some other companies that are providing excellent sports titles: Sierra has produced through its Dynamic subsidiary, the Front Page Sports Series; Accolade has provided several great games, including their most memorable Hardball; Crystal Dynamics and Microsoft, which is developing with Stormfront Studios, are both slated to put out next generation baseball games. The Crystal Dynamics game is rumored to feature wild 3D graphics with motion captured animation—certainly a sign of things to come in sports games.

Meanwhile, no doubt EA will continue to build on its past success and continue to bring out the most complete line of major sports titles from Baseball and Basketball to Football, Golf, Hockey, and even Rugby.

Sports Games Design Issues

Sport games involve several concepts that, while not specific to the games themselves, are essential elements for this category of games.

Action and Stats

The key design elements in many sports games are the arcade action and stats-based systems. Back in the old days, most of the sports games focused on one approach or the other. However, once EA hit with Earl Weaver and John Madden, the combined approach took off. Today every major sports game offers itself as an action game where the skills of the players are based on their real-life counterparts.

Packaging the Game

Sports games have recently taken a more interesting approach to the presentation and packaging of both the interface and the overall game. Many of the games now not only try to re-create the look and feel of the actual game, but through the use of announcers, TV-like graphics, half-time scores, and more, they are starting to look like actual television broadcasts.

Sony Imagesoft used a license from well-known sports broadcaster ESPN to add an even more realistic touch. Spectrum Holybyte will do the same with a tie-in to ABC

Sports, and Sega recently debuted a hockey title using Truemotion's Digital Video Sprite software to superimpose announcer Marv Albert over the action. These are wonderful examples of how developers are pushing games into new areas.

Looking toward the Future

Because sports games are the single best-selling category in all of gaming, there's no doubt as to their future. EA built itself into close to a billion dollar company through its sports games.

The biggest new technology that will have an impact on sports gaming is motion capture. Motion capture works really well for sports games because it's good for capturing fluid human movements (not to mention that motion capture technology was initially developed to research and help athletes be better athletes!).

And I haven't even touched on the multiplayer possibilities. Not many other game categories lend themselves to multiplayer situations better than sports. EA has already provided Genesis owners with a four-joystick adapter, allowing for all kinds of cool multiplayer cooperative and opposition play. And I'm willing to bet that complete online football and baseball games, where teams of players compete against each other, are not too far behind.

On a more mundane level, take note of the trend to build the interface around and package the game in a sports-based, TV-like interface. After all, most people absorb their sports through the tube, anyway. I suspect we'll continue to see this interface metaphor pushed so far that it will be indistinguishable from an actual network sports broadcast.

Virtual Reality Games

Virtual reality is the catch phrase of the '90s. We've all heard about it, but what is it exactly? Certainly the intent of virtual reality is to invoke a "suspension of disbelief," and in the area of gaming, that is ultimately a top goal.

For the most part, the focus on virtual reality has been in the area of portraying realistic-looking, 3D environments—sights, sounds, and smells that mimic our reality. For the virtual reality games that exist in labs or in virtual arcades, this means loads of high-tech hardware. Most of the games incorporate head mounting displays (HMDs) or motion tracking equipment to provide an actual "immersive" experience. Of course, only recently has some of the VR equipment become cheap and cool enough for home users to enjoy it.

Today there are several VR hardware setups that work with PCs to bring home VR experiences and certainly VR games to consumers! In the location based entertainment business (amusement parks, arcades, casinos, and so on) VR games are such a big hit that many companies (Sega, DreamWorks, SKG, Virtuality, and Disney among others) have opened "VR-CADES," VR gaming centers that integrate amazing graphical capabilities with either HMDs or large, full-view screens to create wild VR experiences. If you're looking to see actually viable VR games, check your local area for a location-based VR center near you.

So far though the technology while cool is definitely in its infancy. However, as VR technology improves over time, it is sure to garner more widespread use. This means VR gaming will move from a hardware centered entity to gaming centered fun.

So as the graphic and technology wizards at companies like Zombie, Virtual I/O, and Vivid give us the ability to place players into virtual reality schemes, designers and developers must start focusing on the other side of virtual reality—the story, real life-like game characters, and overall world reality, to match VR's heightened graphical and sensual realisms.

Because VR gaming is a relatively new category, there aren't many of benchmark games to pick and choose from, but let's take a look at what's out there now:

> **Zombie Interactive** Zombie Interactive is one of the hotter software startups of the 1990s. Formed by VR wizards Mark Long and Joanna Alexander, formerly VR researchers at the David Sarnoff research center, the company is developing a complete line of VR-enabled games for the PC. Their first games should be in wide release as this book goes to press.
>
> Zombie's game are from the ground up meant to be played with HMDs as full VR experiences. If you're not near a location-based VR center, check out the games this company is constructing as they're built for home PC and VR equipment!

VR Game Design Issues

VR is very much a hardware-driven experience. Therefore, if you're going to design and develop a VR game, you must first start by evaluating the hardware options you have and see what that hardware will allow you to do. Among PC-based VR games, you'll also have several different headset decisions, various input options, and more. I'll go into detail about these options later in the book.

You also have to take into account things like hardware to input movement, the restrictions the hardware imposes (it's hard to type at a keyboard with a large head mounted display), and more.

Looking toward the Future

Again, the question here is hardware. There have been some famous crash and burn stories in creating VR games. Sega spent millions developing some VR hardware only to halt development when beta testers complained about dizziness and other health

problems like eyestrain. Hasbro, the toy giant, reportedly sank $39 million (yes, million) into a much ballyhooed attempt to create a major VR gaming system for the home, only to yank the cord. Nintendo recently has tried its hand with Virtual Boy, which does some novel things to overcome some of the perceived health problems VR introduces, but the amount of tradeoffs it made to deliver Virtual Boy have resulted in what many people consider a completely moronic device.

On the PC side, there are several companies pushing a variety of top-quality VR products, like Virtual I/O, VictorMaxx, and others. The problem is that these much higher quality offerings are also high priced—too high for mass-market appeal. In addition, each of the various major HMDs has a different set of specs, which makes it impossible for the industry to set a standard.

Still, progress is being made. Researchers from many industries are working hard to create next generation hardware that is both safer and cheaper. Game giants like Nintendo and Sega are, despite their failures, still working to develop mass-market VR systems; trailblazers like Zombie Interactive are creating demand simply by offering the games; and location-based VR centers are growing by leaps and bounds, showing people today what they'll have in their homes tomorrow.

VR games are here and they offer truly amazing possibilities, but they're not going to hit the mass market any time soon. For developers who want to push ahead, you'll need to become familiar with a ton of additional and new hardware.

Wargames

Wargames, like their RPG cousins, have had a significant non-computer life (and still do to some extent), and just like RPGs, wargames have been enhanced by computers. Computer-based wargames allow single players and require adherence to a set of rules, which creates a structured gaming environment. Of course, the computer-based versions offer the advantages of multimedia and the sheer speed of computer technology.

Over the years, computer-based wargames have been a staple of traditional wargaming lovers—those who placed a new RISK game at the top of their Christmas list every year. With computers, though, wargames have steadily grown as a game category and include such memorable games as Eastern Front 1941, Empire, Kampfgruppe, Carriers at War, and Gettysburg.

There are several major benchmark wargames to note, but I think a discussion about a few benchmark designers and companies is a more logical way to present the work that you should be familiar with when making a game for this category.

Chris Crawford Chris Crawford, a longtime well-known game designer, developed two very notable works in the wargaming category. Eastern Front 1941 was a historical re-creation of the Russian Front during World War II and featured an incredible (for the time) scrolling map of the action and a very easy-to-use interface. His other game, Patton vs. Rommell, was originally developed for the Macintosh and featured a fantastic re-creation of the tank tactics of two of Europe's greatest generals.

Gary Grigsby and SSI Gary Grigsby is, in my mind (and I'm hardly alone), the single most accomplished wargame designer. He's created over 15 different games, all known for their incredible attention to detail and historical accuracy. Likewise, SSI is the most well-known computer-based wargaming company, having produced all of Grigsby's works, as well as many other notable games. Check out both SSI's and Grigsby's work to see some excellent examples of good wargame design.

Roger Keating and SSG Probably best known for their big hit Carriers at War, Australian-based SSG has been creating awesome wargaming programs for at least ten years. All of their games are known for their attention to detail and flexibility with scenarios. Figure 8.27 shows two screens from Carriers at War.

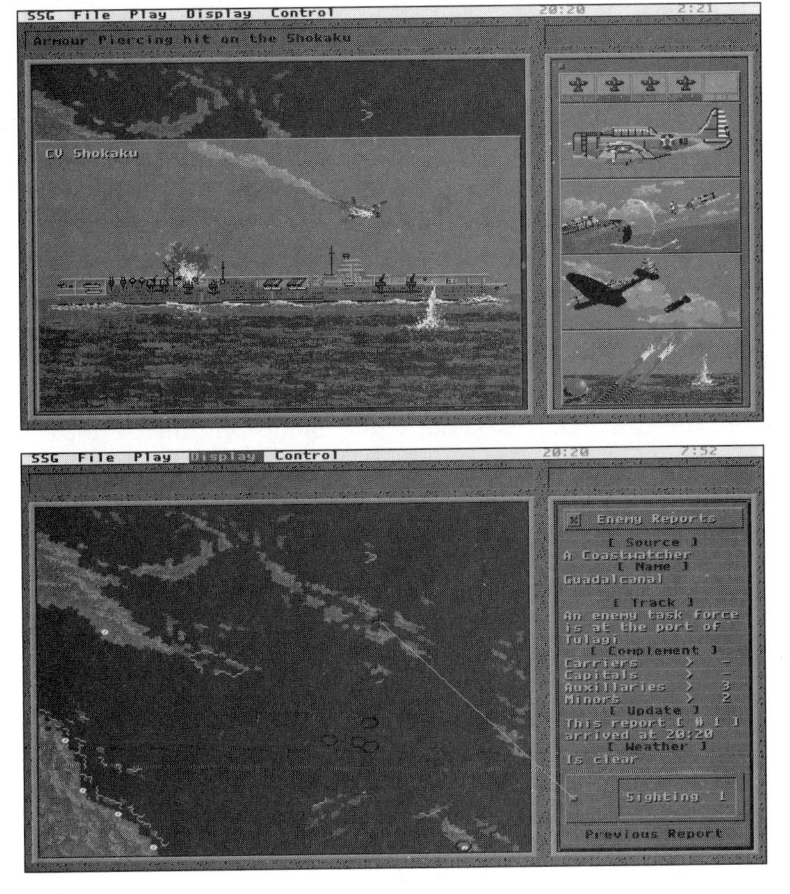

Figure 8.27 Action scenes from Carriers at War.

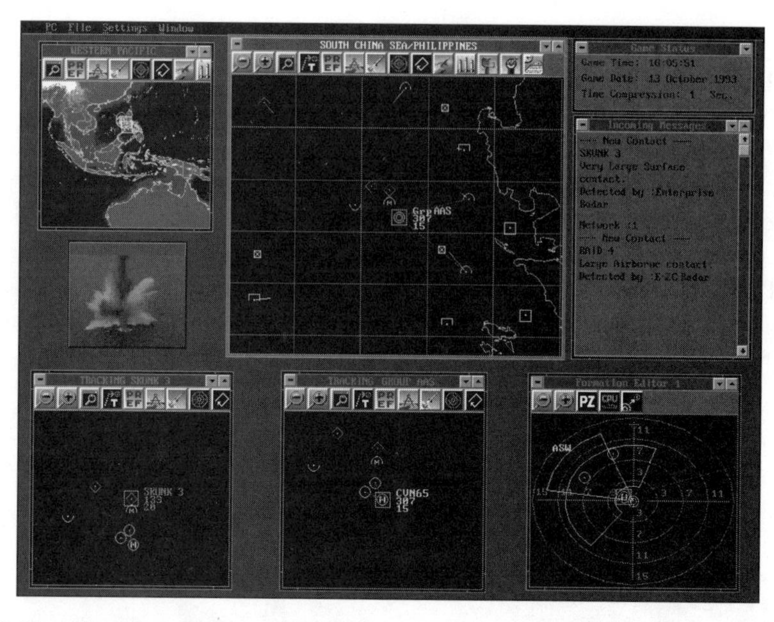

Figure 8.28 Harpoon has seen several incarnations and today still remains one of the most liked wargames.

Empire/Harpoon and Other Notable Products While I've focused on three accomplished wargame designers and companies, there are definitely a few other games and designers whose work is worth researching. Harpoon (Figure 8.28), a game based on the pen and paper masterpiece of the same name, has seen several incarnations through its developer Three-Sixty, and Empire, an original mainframe game, has seen several wonderful PC versions produced by Mark Baldwin and Bob Rakovsky of White Wolf Software. Additionally, there is the work of Jeff Johanningman and Bob Dunnigan, two veteran game developers. Dunnigan even authored a book on wargaming back in the 1980s that you might still find on the shelves.

Wargame Design Issues

Wargame design involves several concepts that, while not specific to the games themselves, are essential elements for this category of games.

Historical Accuracy

There are two types of wargames: those rooted in historical re-creations of our world's history (Gettysburg, Carriers at War, and Eastern Front 1941) and those of a fictitious nature (Roadwars, Warcraft, or Empire).

When a designer sets out to re-create a historically-based game, the market especially in the case of a wargame, expects accurate detail. However, the outcome of the game does not necessarily have to be 100 percent historically accurate. In this case, accuracy could end up ruining the challenge of the game. Take, for example, Eastern Front 1941, a game by Chris Crawford. This game is a re-creation of the German Offensive on the Russian Front in 1941. History tells us it was an unsuccessful attempt. But if the Russians won every time, the game ceases to be a challenge; a player won't play if there isn't a chance to affect the outcome.

When confronted with this design issue, be historically accurate as possible, but create a game engine that allows the player, under the right decisions and circumstances, to change history! After all, one of the appeals of wargame products is that armchair generals get to see if their ideas would have changed the outcome.

Looking toward the Future

Taking into account the historical pen and paper past, wargames have been around for a long time, and over that time they've built up a very strong, dedicated following. Long thought of as very technical and graphically uninteresting products, wargame developers in the last few years have been building increasingly interesting games.

Combining improvements like graphical user interfaces, more interesting computer AI, and far superior graphics, the wargame has found new fans. Additionally, wargames have expanded into realtime with products like Westwood Studios' new Command and Conquer and certainly have a bright future ahead in multiplayer online products as well.

The future for wargames isn't bleak or burning with excitement, but it has a loyal group of players and developers. By increasingly simplifying the play mechanics (though not the games themselves) and increasing the graphical components with more multimedia additions, it's clear that there are even more potential fans to be found.

PART 4

Content Creation

CHAPTER 9

Creating artwork for a game can be extremely overwhelming unless you develop the right talents and have the right resources.

Creating Artwork for Your Games

The most dramatic change in games over the years has been in the technological advancements in graphics capabilities. Combining quality artists with faster machines and top-notch programming has pushed game art to heights many didn't even think about back in the days of Atari 2600 and Intellivision. Although no game can stand on its artwork alone, eye-catching, intense graphics signify a quality game. Take a look at the popular games. Their graphical abilities are hardly what I'd call lacking.

If you're just beginning your game development career, you're probably asking yourself, "How am I supposed to create killer artwork like the pros?" Well, if your talent is limited to drawing the cat on the back of the matchbook, thank goodness professional game artists are available to bridge the gap from stick figure to menacing, steely-eyed, rock-hard robot monsters.

Throughout this chapter, we'll discuss some useful tips on developing or contracting art for your game. Whether you are...a beginner, a small company with limited resources, or a large company with a barrage of artists on hand, I've tried to put together a total series of art chapters that'll give you some advice, resources, and more advice. You'll soon see that there are many avenues to explore. So let's get out our paint packages, 3D modelers, and step in front of those bluescreens because it's time to put on a graphical feast for the eyes!

Artwork Types—an Overview

We'll start by discussing the two main categories of art and design: two-dimensional and three-dimensional artwork.

Two-Dimensional Artwork and Animation

The bulk of the artwork in the games industry is 2D. Although some 2D images are drawn with a "3D look," the images you see on the screen are simply 2D pictures drawn with perspective. (3D packages are also used. More on this in a moment.) You can create 2D artwork in many different ways, from the old "pushing pixels" method to hand drawing and scanning.

No matter what system of artwork you use, at some point your artist will have to really tweak the image on a pixel-by-pixel level. Products like Deluxe Paint and Photoshop are the tools of the trade for this work. For many sprites and smaller game elements, a single pixel can make all the difference in the final image. Your attention to detail in your artwork can make or break your game.

Hand drawing an image and then scanning the drawing is one of the most basic, yet best ways to create art. This approach works especially well for games needing traditional hand animation imagery, like the Sierra or LucasArts adventure games.

Some artists work on paper and then scan in their art, while others will use a tablet and work directly with their favorite paint program.

With the resurgence of Saturday morning cartoons and movie animation, you will find many skilled illustrators waiting to take a crack at your game art. You needn't look farther than your local animation school. Just be prepared to pay; good animators are in very high demand these days. A recent *Wall Street Journal* article talked about the cutthroat tactics the large animation studios like Disney and Warner Brothers are using to attract top students and seasoned animators to their companies.

In your rush to meet a deadline or cut costs, you may get the urge to use a scanned image without first doing some cleanup work. My advice: Take the extra time and spend the extra money. If you want superior art, you have to put effort into it. Take a look at Figures 9.1 and 9.2. These figures show some examples of color scanned artwork from an upcoming product by Galaxy Software. The artists employed by Galaxy draw and ink by hand (most just scan outline drawings). Then after scanning the images into Adobe Photoshop, the artist spends considerable time cleaning up the image.

Three-Dimensional Artwork and Animation

There are two major forces in 3D graphics and animation in the game industry. As I mentioned briefly when explaining 2D imagery, much of what we call 3D art is simply pre-rendered 3D images. The newest revolution in 3D art is, however, high-end 3D graphics that are drawn on the fly (again, more on this in a moment). While "on-the-fly" 3D graphics have been around for a while, today's technology is so amazing it truly is redefining computer gaming. Both techniques are rooted in creating 3D models, but from that point forward they take decidely different paths to final implementation.

3D Ray-Traced Animation

Best seen in the hit products The 7th Guest and its sequel The 11th Hour, 3D ray-traced animation is the king of pre-rendered 3D animation. Using Autodesk's 3D Studio—or any other good 3D artwork product—the artist creates a model for the image. After all the cameras, textures, and shading have been added, the artist can then animate various objects and move the entire view of the scene. The program renders every frame (this can take a quite a long time, even on high-end systems), creating a "fly-through" sequence. The sequence is then played back during the game.

If you plan to use this type of animation, take some time to evaluate the packages that can help you get started and master your craft. There are two major products for the MS-DOS/Windows platform, about six major Mac packages, and several major packages for the SGI.

Figure 9.1 Raw scanned images.

Figure 9.2 Cleaned-up scanned images.

In Chapter 12, you'll find a full rundown and contact information for the most popular 3D creation products.

On-the-Fly 3D Polygons

You only need to play a game like Virtua Fighter or Virtua Racing from Sega once to understand the term "on-the-fly" 3D graphics. This technique is really quite impressive. Once an image is rendered (I'll get to that in a moment), the wire frame information is provided to the program, which then draws any derived animations from it on-the-fly. No images are pre-rendered; the speed of the computer and the programming code handles all the work.

Using a 3D modeling package the artist will create a typical 3D polygon file. This file is then usually converted from the common 3D format of the construction package to one used by the 3D routines of the program. Many of the 3D API's on the market that help construct on-the-fly 3D games come with conversion programs for this step.

Of course, true on-the-fly animation is limited by the complexity of the image you wish to create. The more points and polygons in an image, the harder it will be to make it fast enough for game-quality animation. Thus, you not only need good artists but ones who can carefully construct cool 3D images without using thousands of polygons in the process.

3D Animation: Is It Worth the Trouble?

Unfortunately, every cloud's silver lining has a bit of tarnish. 3D animation is hot, to be sure, but it is also extremely costly and time-intensive to develop. A common 3D animation development computer has at least 64 megabytes of RAM (usually more), the fastest processor available, and the fastest graphics accelerator imaginable. Are you prepared to make the investment?

In addition, the storage of the animations (both in development and for playback in the actual product) can be a real nightmare. Even if you use CD-ROM you have to make some decisions about how much you can fit. Proper planning is a must to ensure you don't waste money on creating artwork that won't make it into the final project.

3D Animation Techniques

Let's look at the most common applications for 3D animation in games today:

- **Cut scenes** are the non-interactive scenes in a game used as embellishment or as a cinematic-like storytelling device. For example, in Lucas Arts' big hit, X-wing, scenes are used that show the fighter flying in and out of the mother base.

The player doesn't control the action in any way; the animations serve solely to enhance the environment. The downside is that players typically get tired of these embellishments.

- **Canned movement** is simply the use of pre-compiled game sequences. Although players have the ability to choose the direction their character takes (a sure hit), their choices are limited by the number of sequences available. Depending on your game, this technique can be an awesome graphical experience. It is also a ton of work. But when used correctly, canned movement can provide the awesome animation and graphics consumers die for.

Understanding Good Game Art

What is the essence of good game art? In a nutshell, good game art is simply great art—programming and hardware have nothing to do with it. Before all you programming wizards get ready to hang me in effigy, consider any game developed for any platform. I'll bet that the sheer look of the game's art was the first thing that grabbed you—not the underlying programming or the resolution.

Sure, technological advancements create opportunity for even better art, but a *true* artist (I'll tell you where to find true artists later on) can make the most of a program's capabilities, the platform, and any limitations.

Game art breaks down to three fundamental categories: Functional art, realistic art, and artistic art.

Functional art is any element created to communicate a game function. Icons, for instance, are an example of functional art.

Realistic art is an attempt by the artist to depict an actual element. Anything that strives for photo-realism like digital video and scanned images are examples of realistic art.

Finally, **artistic art** is any drawn element that results in an interpreted view of the subject. Artistic art examples include human faces and emotions and alien worlds.

All graphics, animations, and visual elements of your game should adhere to a central theme. A great game will weave the artistic design in closely with the storyline.

Creating a Game Plan

Creating artwork for a game can be extremely overwhelming if you don't take the proper steps to prevent frustration.The steps I generally follow in creating artwork for my games (or any of my other projects) is pretty simple. I've included an outline for you to follow.

I. **The Look**

The first thing is to think about is the result; that is, what look do you want? Take into consideration all elements like palettes, forms of objects, how the animation might look, where things in the interface should be placed, and so on. Most artists will work out these issues in a series of storyboards and conceptual tests.

II. **The Process**

Your next step is to decide how you're going to create all the things you imagined in step I. This process is much more than just saying "I'm going to draw it." For example, lots of game art is made up of repetitive elements. To save space while still creating huge background images, game developers break apart a picture into core components called *tiles*. At this stage you need to think about the approach of creating those tiles. If you're making a 3D image do you draw it by hand, sculpt it in clay, or just use your favorite modelling software?

III. **The Plan**

Once you've thought about the overall processes, you need to come up with a detailed plan for creating the specifics of your art. While the process deals with how you might construct an object, the planning is the who, how much, where, and when of the artwork development cycle. You have to plan the equipment you're going to use, the amount of people you need, timeframes (especially as they correspond to various programming schedules), the palettes you're going to employ, and the types of animations you're going to use, down to the number of frames they are composed of. It's a lot of work, but putting it off will lead to lots of problems.

a. **Match your game design to your art resources and technical capabilities.**

Beginners often plan games with artwork requirements even Sierra would find daunting! It's crucial that you don't attempt to tackle a game that requires art you can't provide. You may need to rearrange a game script to cut out some scenes, or reduce the detail of your textures to enhance the speed of your 3D engine, but do whatever it takes to make sure the artwork is within your limits.

b. **Plan the process to create each piece of artwork.**

At this point, you need to start planning the actual process of constructing the art. I'll be covering some of the many processes by which you can create game art in the remainder of this chapter.

IV. The Tools

At this stage in your game plan, it should be clear to you what tools you're going to need. I think one of the biggest problems many beginners and hobbyists make is trying to do artwork without the proper tools. You need to decide whether you want to purchase the tools necessary to create complex artwork or settle for the tools you have and work with a simpler idea. Stay on top of the tools market. Learn which tools have which features. Always be on the lookout for tools that can speed up your production rate.

V. The Sweat

Once you've made it this far, you're well on your way. Now all that's left is the actual work. Don't sweat. All the effort you put into steps I through IV will pay off here.

Creating an Art Ledger

The best advice I could ever hope to give you is to create an "art ledger" as you develop your game. When you enter your planning phase, this ledger will help you to organize your thoughts in writing. As you progress with your game, the ledger will help you keep on track and focused on your original objective.

The ledger should be set up to help you sketch out your art content plan on paper. For each element you've already designated ahead of time you should include file names for a finished component and any of its sub-components. Even the smallest games have tons of art files associated with them. Experienced developers create extensive naming systems to track their files. The ledger should also include dates and other critical information concerning the availability of artwork. Carefully plan the schedules of the artist and your programmers. You want to make sure that when the programming staff needs specific artwork components, they'll be ready.

Before we move on, I just have to state this one more time: *A little time spent planning will save you many, many headaches down the road.*

Building Up an Artwork Production Stable

Creating a wide ranging art studio in-house is expensive. If you want high-end equipment, you'll pay high-end prices. Because most companies are not able to persuade management to budget thousands of dollars for the ultimate art tools

gaming industry has to offer, they've had to find alternatives. In this section we'll take a look at those alternatives so that you can determine the combination that works best for you and for management.

Outsourcing: The Catch Word of the '90s

One alternative to creating your own art in-house is to outsource it. This alternative provides you with two basic options: Contracting freelance artists or hiring an actual art company that gives you a staff of artists.

Freelance Artists

Many able artists are available who can work on a per project basis. Freelancers work best on small games where they can provide all the art or a single special piece of work. However, heed this warning: Avoid hiring multiple freelancers to work on a single project. Unless you can really coordinate well, you'll have a difficult time getting a consistent look.

When you're evaluating a freelance artist, make sure to spell out *exactly* the sort of service and quality of work you expect. Freelancers generally don't keep the same hours as 9 to 5ers, although most are happy to comply with any schedule you set. You should also ask for a portfolio of work (and references!) to determine if what you want is possible.

Financially speaking, the amount you'll need to pay can vary. You can structure a contract on a per image basis, a flat fee, or an hourly rate. What I do is figure what an artist of their caliber would be worth on salary, then figure out an appropriate hourly translation, and then multiply that by the number of hours I think it will take to construct the art. This can give you an opening bid. The bottom line here is to figure out what your budget is and see what you can get for it. Ask around but certainly be aware you're not going to buy loads of major artwork for $500.

If you are interested in recruiting freelancers, you have several options. Contact the companies whose products you are using to find people with specific skills. Often they have contacts that they can share. Other places you can look are the various headhunting services, local computer artists groups, and art schools.

Check out *http://www.xmission.com/~grue/animate/houses.html* for a listing of animation schools. In Chapter 26, I list many of the major game talent searching firms. Also, be sure to check out the comprehensive listing of the online sites at your disposal in Chapter 26.

Art Companies

More and more conventional animation houses are branching out and doing work for game developers. These are staffs of professional artists who have the ability to satisfy enormous art creation needs. This approach is *not* for the single developer; we're talking big bucks here.

Many art companies are just moving into the game industry. Their experience can revolve around stock/multimedia art or commercial production artwork. Be careful when choosing an art company for outsource work; see if they've done game art work before and if they're familiar with things like 256 color palettes and such.

Trying to find a list of major animation/art companies? Not to worry. Surf on over to the Animation House List Web site—*http://www.xmission.com/~grue/animate/houses.html*

This the best overall resource for recruiting animation and art house companies. The list is regularly updated and includes complete contact information. Not all companies do computer game art, so you'll have to call around and ask.

For even more opportunities, check out the gaming and multimedia resource guides listed in the back of this book.

Game Art Considerations

There are a few important items we haven't discussed yet, but they are essential in game art production.

Resource Files

Typically, all your game art is stored in a *resource file* or files. A resource file is made up of a group of smaller files that, depending on the computer code handling your resources, can be any file type, including graphics, sound, and MIDI. General speaking, the files that fill up a resource file are graphics files.

Resource files serve several functions: The artwork is stored in a format that makes it difficult for all but the most advanced people to modify, and resource files are much easier to handle from a programmer's standpoint by reducing the number of separate files required.

There are many ways to store and organize data into a resource file. You need to discuss with your programmer how he or she prefers the art to be structured for the resource files. Some programmers prefer storing a series of images in one file, while others prefer to use a separate file for each image. However you decide, make sure to

let the artist in on your decision; after all, the artist is the one who will be producing the finished art files for the resource file.

Palettes

Palettes are essential to game art. But the first thing you have to figure out is what the palette restrictions are. These can be of two types: artistic and hardware. Artistic restrictions might be "Everything is very dark and blue" or "All the artwork is quite neon, glowing almost."

Hardware restrictions, on the other hand, involve factors like Windows reserves 20 colors for the system palette, the first and last ten of a palette, meaning that in 256 color mode you now have only 236 colors left.

Consoles and other platforms will have similar distinct situations. Thus it goes without saying that before you begin art production on a new platform, you better be familiar with the graphics features of the machine. If you're working with first time artists, make sure they are aware of everything related to the technicalities of their palettes in the game you are doing.

Perhaps one of the quickest mistakes many beginning developers make as they learn about developing games is about standardizing palettes. I know I learned the hard way. I spent a week doing all sorts of cool graphics for a Windows game. Then I translated all the graphics from Dpaint's .LBM file format to Windows' .BMP format. Overall, I spent about 40 hours on this task. Then I loaded the images into a screen and began to add other imagery to the screen. Well as soon as I added the second picture, which had a slightly different palette, all hell broke loose. The screen flashed as Windows created a common denominator palette for the two images. This was a compromise to say the least; the pictures were remapped to this color scheme and looked pretty bad.

After getting the requisite questions answered I went back to my initial artwork, divided up the imagery that would appear together on the same screen, and then made sure all those files shared the same palette when converted. This solved everything.

Memory Considerations

Another major consideration with your artwork is the memory needed to support it. Complex graphics and animations eat memory. While a CD-ROM can hold over 600 megabytes of information, the memory requirements of high-res animation and

3D canned video can make 600 megabytes look like a tight space. Of course, you can always go to multiple CD-ROMs; some games are regularly shipping on five, six, and seven CD-ROMs now.

The upcoming Digital Versatile Disc (DVD) format, recently agreed to by the Sony consortium and the Toshiba consortium, promises something like 5 gigabytes of space. This new technology, which will be available sooner than you think, promises to increase the amount of high quality artwork and animation in games. Somehow, though, I cringe to think that at some point even *that* much will seem too small. Game developers are notorious for trying desperately to live above their means!

Game Art Components

Now that you have a good understanding of how the world of game art works, let's get a little more specific.

Backgrounds

The largest image on the screen is always going to be your background so it's very important that you give it the consideration it deserves.

Before you begin constructing a background image, you must first determine the exact nature of the background image. Is it a still, or does it have moving elements? Is it a scrolling background? If so, is it a parallax scrolling background? (A parallax scrolling background will be made up of a series of different scrolling planes that move at different rates the further back into the screen they are.) The type of background that you'll be using will affect the way you create the overall image. So get that part clear in your head before you move on.

Working with Tiles

The majority of background images are made up of a group of repeatable elements, which can be broken down into component tiles. The tiles can be put together in any number of ways to create a much more complex background. Figures 9.3 and 9.4 show a set of tiles and then a composite image created from using those tiles.

There are two ways to approach drawing the elements for a tiled background. You can determine ahead of time the exact shape and nature of the background tiles—road, grass, water, walls, brick—and then draw them, or you can create your background image and then use a program commonly called a "tile ripper" to break down the background into the fewest component images possible.

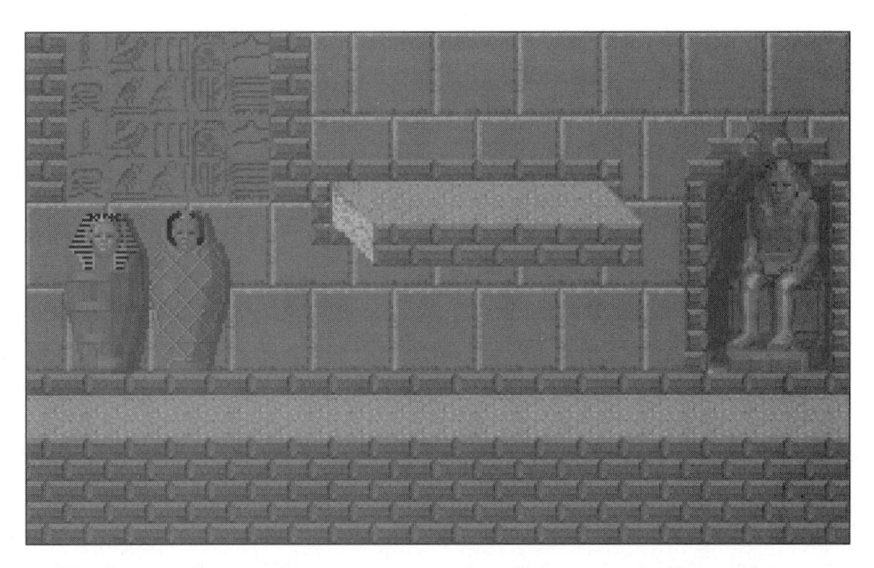

Figure 9.3 This background is composed of the tiles shown in Figure 9.4.

Figure 9.4 These tiles are used to create the background shown in Figure 9.3.

Tile ripping works best for backgrounds that are complex and require a less obvious repetitiveness to the images. Figures 9.5 through 9.8 illustrate that process.

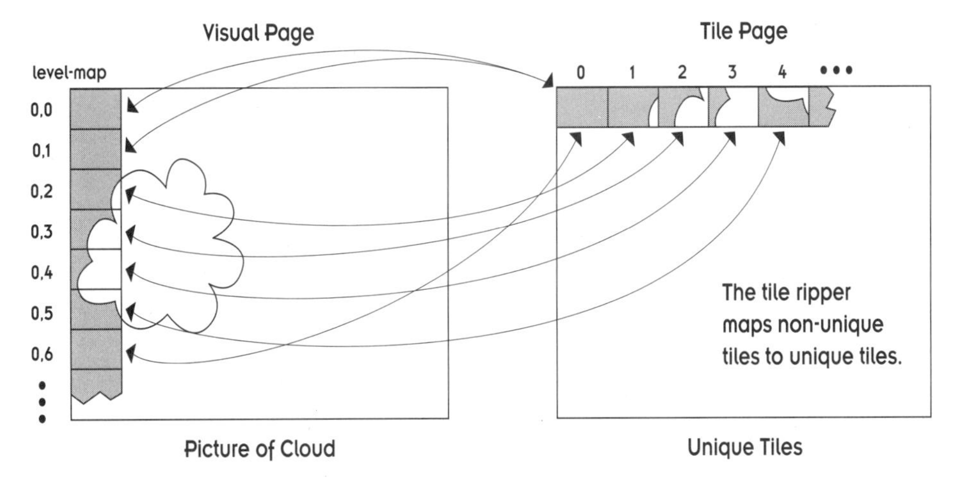

Figure 9.5 The process of ripping and mapping tiles.

Figure 9.6 The complete background before ripping.

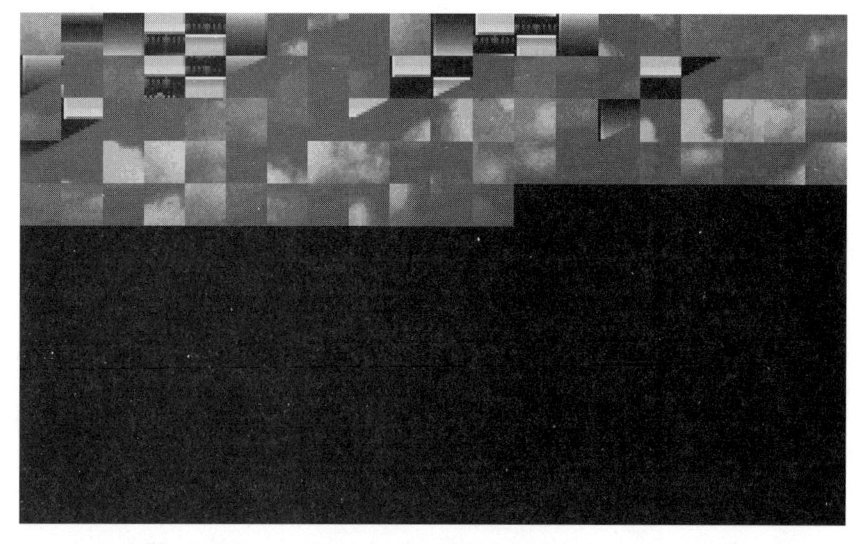

Figure 9.7 The tiles produced after ripping the scene.

Figure 9.8 Building a scene using the tiles.

Tiled Backgrounds Pointers

Here are a few tips on creating tiled backgrounds. While certain tiles can be directly drawn to be perfectly seamless, or you might use a texture generation product like Kai's Power Tools, sometimes you need to do it the old-fashioned

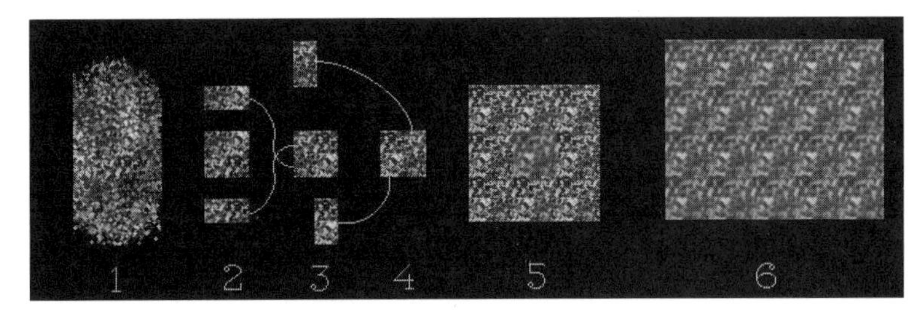

Figure 9.9 How to construct simple seams between files.

way—by hand. Figure 9.9 illustrates an easy technique I use to create seamless textured tiles. The program I use is Deluxe Paint IIe. The process may vary slightly from your favorite program but the middle two steps, which are key, work with every program I know of.

1. Create some sort of pixel-based pattern. I did this by using DeluxePaint's color cycle command and the Spray Can.
2. Here's the key part—Take two halves, the top and bottom, and reverse them as shown in Figure 9.9. (Note: Don't actually flip the images, just reposition them.)
3. Take the two resulting side halves and reverse them. (Note: Don't actually flip the images just reposition them.)
4. Now you can smooth it over like I did or by hand, to work out the internal seams. Be careful not to change the outer edges too much. As long as there are no discernable seams within the image, you should be okay.
5. Test the tile to see if the pattern has any really bad color jumps or seams.

   What we did by repositioning the tile's two sets of halves was automatically arrange the edges to match perfectly. While this can wreak havoc on the inside of the tile once that part is cleaned up (which is much easier than testing the sides constantly), you're set.

Introducing Sprites

Sprites are any moving elements—separate from the other background imagery—in your game. Sometimes sprites are still objects like bullets. They may move from point A to point B, but they don't fundamentally change aside from that. Other sprites are considered animated. This type of sprite also moves from point A to point B but is capable of moving through a series of animations as well. Most sprites fall into the animated category.

Primary Sprites and Secondary Sprites

Sprites, just like actors, have lead and supporting roles. A lead or *primary* sprite is the star, while a supporting or *secondary* sprite lends support to the star. For example, a cowboy firing a gun might be your primary sprite, while the bullets streaming out of the gun are your secondary sprites. The primary sprite or sprites should contain the most detail and should be the focus of your attention. Your primary sprite is the sprite that will bond with the player, so it needs to appeal to the player.

An Expert's Advice on Creating Sprites

Tony Stock, Art Director at The Coriolis Group, has been working on some sprites for an upcoming project and has compiled some advice about creating cool sprites for your games.

Keep Sprite Design Simple

Once you have a basic idea of what your sprite is going to look like, the next step is to execute the actual design. This is a very creative and rewarding process. However, when creating your sprite, it is important to keep the limitations of your resolution in mind. I fell into this trap while spending an afternoon happily sketching a small army of sprites to apply to a side-scrolling game engine that I had agreed to create art for.

My smile turned to disappointment when I saw some of the finer details of my sprite dissolve away as it was converted to a 40×40 pixel image. However, at the same time I was relieved to realize that simplicity was the real key to sprite design. Time that I would normally have spent on the finer details of creating sprites could now be focused on other facets of sprite creation and animation.

Use of Shadows and Highlights

Although simplicity is the key is designing sprites, as an artist I am compelled to make my designs as detailed as possible. An impossible dilemma? No. Using shadows and highlights, you can compensate for the lack of detail in a sprite. Applied properly, shadows and highlights can give a two-dimensional character a three-dimensional effect. Figures 9.10 and 9.11 show a sprite before and after highlights and shadows were applied.

The Character Issue

This is one of my favorite topics in game design. The time comes when the game designer in conjunction with the game artist must work together to create imagina-

Figure 9.10 A sprite before shadows and highlights are added.

Figure 9.11 A sprite after shadows and highlights are added.

tive characters that will appeal to the player, and gain and keep the player's interest in the game itself. One character that comes to mind is the main character in Full Throttle (Figure 9.12) from Lucas Arts. This rough and tumble adventurer rides a motorcycle and has to make his way through some of the toughest characters found in "no mans land."

Figure 9.12 Lucas Arts' Full Throttle main character.

This character obviously has been created with a lot of thought put into detail. I don't mean detail in the images, but detail in the character's actions, words, and deeds. Everything the character does is, well, in-character. He doesn't stop in the middle of the game and pass out flowers at the airport. He is a tough guy and acts that way throughout the game. And he looks the part that he has been designed for—a well-built, tough leather jacket-wearing hooligan with a five o'clock shadow covering his square jaw, and a protruding forehead topped off with jet-black hair. This character has everything you could want in a hero, and because of the excellent execution in his development, it is no wonder this game appeals to its intended audience. Characters—whether heroes or villians—also need to have a personality to be successful. He or she needs to have qualities that the player can relate to and be interested by. If a character is too flat and is without definite qualities, the player may lose interest in that character.

Matching Character Styles

When designing characters, a good game artist will try to create a style and stick closely to it as he or she develops each character, resulting in a continuity throughout the game that contributes to giving the game an identity. Again, I point to Lucas Arts' Full Throttle. As you play the game, you'll notice that all characters contain similar qualities and overall appearances. The men all have square jaws, squinty eyes, and powerful builds. The women have voluptuous builds, full lips, and amazon-type figures. Clearly, the artists were trying to convey that the world of Full Throttle is not for wimps or school kids. The bottom line is this: Emphasize a theme and give the player something to fix his or her imagination on. If there are errors in the storyline, or a character seems out of place, it can ruin the mood that you are trying to create.

Teaching Your Sprite to Move

Animation! If you are a game artist, this topic is unavoidable. Everything we have talked about up to this point—color depth, screen resolution, detail level, character design—affects how we will animate our sprites. It is at this stage that we now need to find ways to take shortcuts. No matter what the other design issues, the faster and more fluid the animation, the better.

If, earlier in your game design, you decided to sacrifice a little game speed for a higher level of detail in your sprites and the speed of the game is at a crucial point, one possibility is to consider using higher-resolution sprites when the characters are still or moving slowly, and less detailed images when the character is moving rapidly. This technique will allow you to keep the fluid motion without dumping your beautiful sprites.

Animation can add character to your sprites. For example, if you made a male and female character in the same game move the same, without any particular style, it would distract from the game play. Likewise, if your main character is machine-gun-wielding rabbit, a good animator will develop movements unique to that character.

Animating your sprites is a tough challenge that will push you creatively but will pay off handsomely when players see your final product.

The Fewer the Better: Keeping Your Frame Rate Low

One thing you must understand is it doesn't take tens of frames to have fluid animation. While 16 frames for each of your key characters animation may indeed be cool, beginners and those on limited resources should concentrate on quality shorter animations. If you're good, you really won't be sacrificing as much as you think. A lot of cool movement can happen in as few as four specific frames of animation. As you design your sprites movements, see how much you can cram into each frame. Really force yourself to get the most out of each image in the animation.

Digital Video Sprites

A few companies are experimenting with digital video sprites. Using products you'll read about in Chapter 10, developers actually create a digital video file that is really a series of frames just like any specific sprites. Then, using a digital video programming API like RAD Software's Smacker, they use that file as their sprite instead of the traditional frame-by-frame drawing process. Digital video sprites are not a replacement for the more traditional method, just an alternative that works.

User Interface Elements

User interface elements are those elements, such as startup screens and option menus, that the user interacts with when preparing to play the game. These screens need to be well rendered because they are the first images that greet the player. I recommend going all out in this area. Pull out all the stops! Create some graphics that reach out, grab the player, and begin to lure him or her into the game. This time is a great place to set the mood for the game by using images and sounds that begin to get the player into the mood of the game. Figures 9.13 and 9.14 are from Epic's Jazz Jackrabbit. I think Epic did an awesome job on their informational and startup screens.

The other type of user interface elements you need to consider are the information windows or controls that are available while the game is being played. My best advice to you in this area is to add a fun twist to your average command GUI items. Make

Figure 9.13 A Jazz Jackrabbit startup screen.

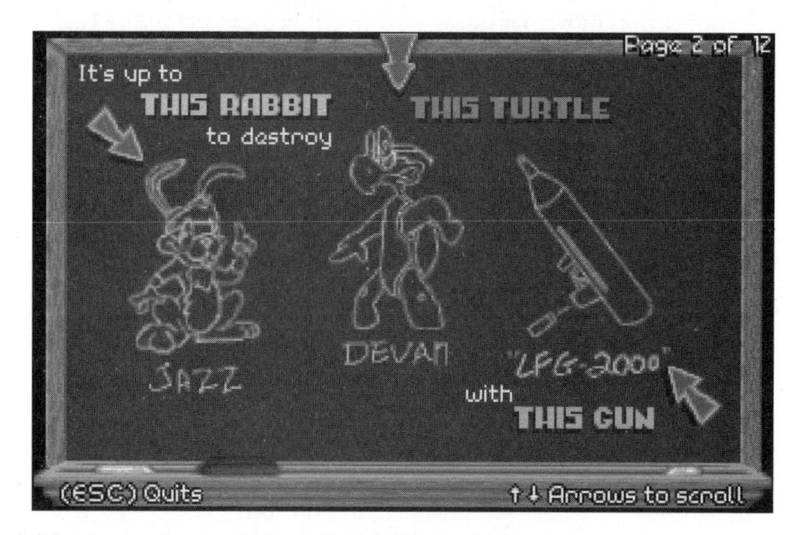

Figure 9.14 A creative approach to interface design.

the buttons cool 3D spheres with funky text. Create cool-looking pointers instead of the typical arrow. The interface is the viewport to your game. Give it the same artistic effort that you give the rest of your artwork.

It's pretty common to see games—especially in the Windows environment—using many features of the interface. I prefer a more creative approach. I create my own cool buttons and boxes.

Art Resources

What I have for you here are not your standard resources. I've received lots of input and did a little digging on my own. If you're not a full-fledged artist and can't really afford one, these places may help you out.

Government Publications

Looking for cool art? Consider browsing publications from the U.S. government. Believe it or not, most of the art, along with maps and other goodies, is not covered by U.S. copyright laws. There is just a wealth of artwork out there. You'll especially find good stuff for military games and geography-oriented art.

Scan from Art Books

Rummage through your closet and drag out those old how-to drawing books. Scan in images and work from there. For me, human figures are tough so I scanned in line-art figures. It made the rest of the drawing a whole lot easier. I've compiled some art book resources in Chapter 12.

Stock Art Archives

If you are not a natural artist, art stock houses may be a profitable stop for you in your artwork endeavors. These places are veritable treasure troves of useful art. Purchasing this imagery can be a lot less expensive than you think, and while I don't use it for artwork in and of itself, I can trace over it in a paint program or use a program like Photoshop to turn it into useful line art. I find stock art to be really useful for things like cars and spaceships where I have trouble with initial concepts and perspective.

There are also a few main 3D model archives (which I list in Chapter 12) that you can purchase from. It may not be the cheapest route, but if you can't draw, you're going to have to spend the cash. In the future, I think 3D and art stock libraries will become an increasingly great resource for developers. Although you have to modify the work you find, the time you save is definitely worth your effort.

Putting It All Together

This chapter has been one of the toughest to write in the entire book. I talked with several artists and drew on my art background to try to come up with a way to "teach" someone how to make cool computer art. The answer as I alluded to in the opening paragraph is simple—you can't. At least not in a book and certainly not in a chapter.

What I hope we've accomplished with this and the next three chapters is to get you at least enough information to send you on the way. There are a lot of tools and ideas that can help you make better art, faster and easier.

CHAPTER 10

If there has ever been a double-edged sword in game development, it's digital video.

Digital Video for Game Development

When used properly in games, digital video is an excellent feature. Unfortunately, it has not always been used in such a way, and has become synonymous with poorly designed linear games that use it as a way to splash lots of eye candy on the computer screen.

The term digital video can represent two distinct things. Most of the time it is used to describe live action that was captured by cameras or from a VCR and then converted to a digital video file for playback by the computer.

Digital video can also more generally describe any animation that is stored in various file formats (more on this later). For example, an artist might create a fully featured 3D animation and render the animation as a "digital video" sequence by storing it in an digital video file.

In this chapter, you'll see digital video from the inside out. We'll discuss the hardware you need to produce digital video and software applications to process it. You'll also find a resource section of books and magazines that will allow you to get even more information on this hot topic.

Digital Video Applications

Linear, full-motion video games are commonly called *interactive movies*. They make up the majority of games featuring digital video. These games are like movies in that they have a single plotline and involve filmed sequences. Games like the Sewer Shark, Night Trap, The 11th Hour, Phantasmagoria, and Blown Away! are just a host of top billing digital video titles.

Other heavily digital video productions use digital video sequences as a filmed version of the animated "cut scene," sometimes even adding a little interactivity to boot. Games such as Wing Commander III and IV as well as Rebel Assault I and II use digital video sequences effectively in this regard.

Still other productions use spot digital video within the game. For example, Electronic Arts' Shockwave, a futuristic space flight shooter, uses some small digital video sequences to embellish a heads-up display in the game; commanders pop up on the video display to offer advice and information. A nice touch.

In my opinion, digital video has worked really well as an embellishment to some games, but when digital video takes center stage (as in Sewer Shark), the quality and technical drawbacks of a total full-motion-video game have not offered really amazing products.

That being said, let's dive in and get a better understanding of how we can sucessfully add digital video aspects to our games.

Money Talks—The Digital Video/Dollar Equation

When it comes right down to it, resources are the biggest factor in producing digital video. Larger companies like EA have set up their own studios or they work with Hollywood production houses to do their video. They hire union talent, bringing in the full stream of makeup, lighting, audio, and other production services. For Wing Commander IV, Origin (an EA subsidiary) decided to build and use actual full sets, a real first. Most companies simply use bluescreening techniques to merge digitized actors with computer generated backgrounds.

For the well-funded companies, production budgets can reach several million dollars. Wing Commander IV's budget is rumored to be over 10 million dollars! But don't count yourself out yet. While EA and others push the production budget to stratospheric levels, some companies are striving to produce digital video on very modest budgets. Void Pirates, by Ian Firth (soon to be released), has a total budget of $25,000, and it uses digital video very effectively.

While producing digital video means spending money, it doesn't necessarily have to mean *millions*. Resourceful developers will find ways to use digital video effectively no matter what their budget.

Codec and Digital Video File Differences

The terms *codec* and *digital video* get tossed around so easily I think a lot of people learning this stuff for the first time get them confused. Simply stated a codec—short for *co*mpression-*dec*ompression—is a format for describing *how* video is stored within a digital video file. And the digital video file is a format that describes how much video is there, what codec it's using, and other higher level information. There are two major types of file formats—Video For Windows (AVI) and Quicktime (MOV)—and several different types of codecs, including Intel Indeo and CinePak. When you create an AVI file, you will choose one of the various codecs to work with the Video For Windows system to deliver your digital video.

Each codec has many different features and abilities and, likewise, pluses and minuses in regard to those features and abilities. Later in the chapter, I'll cover all the major video codecs in detail.

Hardware Neccessities: Breakdowns and Resources

If you're going to capture your own video, the first major decision you'll need to make is exactly what equipment you're going to use. Now, this book isn't going to give you all the specifics about all kinds of video hardware (it would take an entire book to do that!) but I have gathered some good starting points and tips from several developers working with digital video:

- **Consider renting hardware.** Consider this: You have $1,000 budgeted for a camera. While you can get a great Hi-8 camera for $1,000, that same $1,000 could rent some even higher-end equipment for a day. In addition, renting equipment takes the pain out of obsolescence; video equipment technology is changing daily. Whichever way you choose, strive to shoehorn—get the best equipment you can for the project you're doing now!

  One other thing to do is contact the local film office of your state government. Most publish a complete book that has all kinds of vendors and video production help found locally in your state. This is a common service for any state.

  You can find national renters of high-end equipment in *Videography* Magazine, which is included in the *Digital Video Resources* section at the end of this chapter.

- **Every piece in the equipment food chain counts.** You need to understand that equipment goes beyond the camera and a deck. There is a ton of other hardware you can bring in to improve and affect your video in the production phase, including capture boards and bluescreens.

Video Cameras

It's very difficult to recommend a video camera. Technology is just moving so fast, prices are dropping daily. In addition, the digital video setups used by major companies can run into the hundreds of thousands of dollars. If you're looking to spend that kind of cash for a digital studio, that advice is best found elsewhere.

However, this high price tag doesn't mean you can't create good digital video with cameras that fit within your budget. That bit being said, here are some contacts for getting the best digital video setup without sending you to debtor's prison:

Avid Technology
1 Park West
Tewksbury, MA 01876
Phone: 508 640-6789 **Fax:** 508 640-9486
Email: 71333,3020@compuserve.com

Among video mavens, Avid is a major force, leading the way with comprehensive non-linear, digital video editing products. From editing systems to sound editing and scoring products (Avid owns Digidesign) to lower end products like Elastic Reality and Media Suite Pro, Avid is a player in every aspect of digital video production.

If you're looking to build a major in-house digital video studio, Avid should be on your short list of vendors.

B&H Photo
119 West 17th Street
New York, NY 10011
Phone: 212 807-7479 **Fax:** 212 366-3738

There are a number of retailers in this business, and I don't really want to recommend one over the other but, sometimes you need to break your own rules. B&H Photo is one of the largest, most complete, high- to low-end video equipment dealers in the country with an extensive mail-order business. For a mere $9.95, you can purchase their complete (and I mean complete) catalog of equipment—guaranteed to make you drool. Even if you don't order from them, the catalog is worth having as a resource bible of equipment available to solve your needs.

Sony
Business and Professional Products Group
3 Paragon Drive
Montvale, NJ 07645-1735

Sony manufactures systems for both home and full-scale professionals. Their cameras and decks are used worldwide and they have been increasingly integrating their products on the low end for personal computers and digital video.

Panasonic
One Panasonic Way
Secacus, NJ 07094
Phone: 800 528-8601

Sony's "crosstown" rival Panasonic also manufactures low-end and high-end digital video equipment.

JVC
41 Slater Drive
Elmwood Park, NJ 07407
Phone: 800 252-5722

Along with Sony and Panasonic, JVC rounds out the top trio of high-end camera and video equipment manufacturers.

Capture Boards

Most of the major video card manufacturers make a large assortment of "frame grabbing" boards. You might check any of the regular multimedia magazines for the up-to-the-minute rundown of the latest and greatest. Here though, are some of the more popular board manufacturers for PCs and Macs with contact information.

Intel
2200 Mission College Boulevard
Santa Clara, CA 95052
Phone: 408 765-8080

The Intel Smart Video Recorder Pro is a very versatile video capture board that comes with all kinds software, including Asymetrix's Digital Video Producer (though most people upgrade to Adobe Premiere).

This capture board is an excellent choice for small developers with a limited budget.

Radius, Inc.
215 Moffet Park Drive
Sunnyvale, CA 94089
Phone: 408 541-6100

If you're a Mac developer, you're certainly familiar with Radius, the leading maker of Mac-compatible video equipment. Radius offers a complete line of boards and other video equipment from the low to mid-high-end range.

TrueVision
2500 Walsh Avenue
Santa Clara, CA 95051
Phone: 317 841-0332 **Fax:** 317 576-7700

For a higher-end solution consider TrueVision's series of Targa boards, which offer high-quality digital capture. You might also look into the Targa2000N, a top-rate, lower end solution (for both PC and Mac) that includes Adobe Premiere.

Bluescreens

While some people have successfully used blue sheets and blue-painted backgrounds, a professional bluescreen is the way to go if you're looking to achieve top quality.

Professional bluescreeens emit light and don't reflect it as a blue wall would. The difference means that professional bluescreens maintain the consistency of color unlike a wall reflecting light. In addition, a bluescreen uses a shade of blue that is difficult to duplicate. In short, if you've got the budget, use a real bluescreen; the savings in aspirin alone will be worth it.

One disadvantage with bluescreens is that, depending on your use of them, you are limited in the number of simultaneous camera angles you can establish. You probably won't be considering many different angles, but it's an interesting point.

Composing Digital Video Files: Software Considerations

Purchasing the software to compose your digital video files is just one more crucial decision in the world of digital video technology. In this section, I've listed both low- and high-end editing packages for your perusal. Let's take a look now.

Adobe Premiere
P.O. Box 7900
Mountain View, CA 94039-7900
Phone: 415 961-4111 **Fax:** 415 967-9231
WWW: http://www.adobe.com

Premiere is aptly named because it is indeed at the top of the heap of various digital video editing products on the market today.

Premiere is available for both Windows and Mac platforms. Suffice to say, you want to get the most powerful computer and memory setup you can afford to allow the full power of this program to shine through. Of course, that goes for almost any artwork related production package!

Asymetrix Digital Video Producer
Asymetrix Corporation
110 110th Avenue, NE #700
Bellevue, WA 98004
Phone: 206 637-5828

Although Premiere is the benchmark product against which most all other digital video editing products are judged, I would be doing you a disservice to list only that package. Asymmetrix's DVP, a drag and drop video editing product for Windows, is one product worth mentioning.

In:Sync Razor and Speed Razor Pro
In:Sync Corporation
6106 MacArthur Boulevard
Bethesda, MD 20816
Phone: 301 320-0220 **Fax:** 301 320-0335

This digital video editing package is a nice alternative to Adobe Premiere. In:Sync Razor comes in two distinct flavors: The regular Razor is a Windows 3.1/95 application, while Speed Razor is a full blast 32-bit Windows NT video editing application.

As far as I know, it's the only native NT digital video software package around.

What's also cool about the In:Sync folks is their Web site (http://www.in-sync.com/in-sync). Here you'll find a fully capable demo of their lower end product, In:Sync Razor. Unfortunately, the demo works with black and white video only, but for evaluation purposes (or for that film noir game you've been planning!) you'll find it useful.

Higher End Editing Systems

The average game developer doesn't need much more than Adobe Premiere to help capture and edit digital video. However, if you want to move up a step to a more robust process, there are several major systems that you can evaluate. You'd have to have a large block of complex digital video needs to warrant investment in these systems (some are upwards of $20,000), but many companies are making the investment and are building complex digital video studios.

Note that these products are all Mac specific:

Avid Media Suite Pro
Avid Technology
1 Park West
Tewksbury, MA 01876
Phone: 508 640-6789 **Fax:** 508 640-9486
Email: 71333.3020@compuserve.com

Media Suite Pro is one of Avid's lower end, non-linear editing packages. It offers a wealth of features and comes with its own proprietary editing software.

Media 100
Data Translation
100 Locke Drive
Marlboro, MA 01752
Phone: 508 460-1600

Media 100 is Avid's biggest competitor in the mid-range, non-linear editing category. It's a popular system that uses its own proprietary editing software.

Telecast
Radius, Inc.
215 Moffet Park Drive
Sunnyvale, CA 94089
Phone: 408 541-6100

Telecast, one of Radius' top-of-the-line products, uses a special version of Adobe Premiere as its editing software. The specialization is mainly to support some proprietary time coding information, but otherwise, it should be easy to use for all you Premiere junkies out there.

Comparing the Two Major Digital Video Engines: Video for Windows and Apple Quicktime

Apple hit the market first when they debuted Quicktime, a scalable video technology to play back digital video files in a window on the Mac. Quicktime was a software-only solution and with it the age of digital video files was ushered in. Microsoft, not wanting to let Apple have a key edge, and recognizing the importance of digital video, followed with a Windows engine it originally called Audio Video Interleave (the origin of the Video For Windows extension .AVI). This became Video For Windows.

Both engines can display digital video in rapid rates and full scale resoultions, depending on the underlying hardware, and both work with a variety of codecs. The big difference is in cross platform capabilities—unlike Video For Windows, Quicktime has both a Windows and Mac implementation. Some developers decided to use that cross-platform capability to design digital video games using Quicktime. However, as they found out, the Quicktime for Windows implementation was, well, buggy. Supposedly a number of bugs have been fixed in the latest version. I do see more developers using Quicktime for Windows as a result.

Despite the cross-platform pluses of Quicktime, many Windows developers still use Video For Windows. With tighter programming hooks, more documentation for Windows developers, and wider consumer acceptance due to it being directly part of Windows 95, Video For Windows has become the standard.

A Crash Course in Digital Video Codecs

Having put you on the right course for some good equipment information, the next major topic to tackle is the actual meat and bones of capturing and playing back digital video. You must decide which codec or compression scheme you will use. You have two choices here: Spend day and night writing your own routines or use several major digital video engines and codecs.

For many reasons (chief among them the slim chance that you're going to be able to produce a better video codec!), the majority of developers work exclusively with "off-the-shelf" solutions.

As I mentioned earlier, there are several major codecs out there, each with different characteristics. You need to understand these differences in order to make an informed choice. Let's take a look at what's available.

SuperMac CinePak
Radius, Inc.
215 Moffett Park Drive
Sunnyvale, CA 94089-1374
Phone: 408 541-6100
Email: support@Radius.com

SuperMac CinePak is one of the granddaddies of video-compression technology. Microsoft, 3DO, Sega, Atari, and Creative Labs, to name just a few, have all been on the CinePak bandwagon at one point or another. Although CinePak is still often used because of its excellent cross-platform capabilities, age has its disadvantages as well. This is a codec in desperate need of an upgrade; newer products like Indeo Interactive and Truemotion are moving in. Rumor has it that Radius is introducing an update soon; check their CinePak Web site for more information.

Intel Indeo
Intel Corporation
2200 Mission College Boulevard
Santa Clara, CA 95052
Phone: 408 765-8080

Intel Indeo is the dominant video codec on the PC platform. The codec is freely available by Intel, and comes standard with Video For Windows. The codec, while mainly wedded to the Windows platform, is available for Video For Windows, OS/2, and Quicktime (Mac and Windows versions) making it an excellent cross-platform solution.

The latest version release (3.2, V3.24.01.01) continues to build upon the excellent playback performance and image quality Indeo is known for. On a Pentium processor-based PC Indeo can support full-screen digital video.

As you'll read later in the chapter, Intel has introduced another Indeo codec, Indeo Video Interactive. This codec is not a replacement for Intel Indeo; rather, it is an interactive addition to the Intel family of codecs.

MPEG (Motion Pictures Expert Group)
WWW: http://www.om-1.org/

MPEG was formed to draw up a scheme for enabling full-screen motion video with a high compression rate. The system is originally based on JPEG (Joint Photographic Experts Group), which created a uniform standard for the compressing and rendering of still image files.

MPEG can achieve frame rates up to 30 frames a second by storing a full screen at the beginning and every four frames thereafter. Then MPEG works out the differences between each frame of video. A very neat idea, but it has some drawbacks.

First, MPEG can't cut to any frame automatically because you can only look at still full screens in the file (every fourth frame). In addition, MPEG uses such a complicated mathematical process that users must have a really fast Pentium system or special MPEG equipped accelerator boards to handle it. The other codecs we've seen are software-only systems. Finally, to encode MPEG you need specialized hardware, some of which can be quite expensive.

What's great about MPEG is that when combined with the proper hardware, the playback is definitely fluid. And the hardware powers that be are definitely pushing MPEG; several large board manufacturers are sponsoring MPEG versions of game software and building large bundling packages for their boards to entice consumers.

For the most part though, developers will most likely stay away from MPEG and concentrate on the other existing software-only codecs.

TrueMotion S
Duck Corporation
Tribeca Film Center
375 Greenwich Street
New York, NY 10013

TrueMotion S is currently one of the best digital video codecs in the business.

TrueMotion, according to Duck, is "The only video frame-specific, software-only video compression solution available today that provides true television quality across multiple platforms. Content developers can compress video images once and play them back on a variety of computer and gaming platforms."

TrueMotion's licensing system works on a product by product basis, with Duck taking a percentage per unit shipped. As Duck's President Stanley Marder puts it, "We're right in there with you; if you don't make money neither do we; if you do well, we all make money."

Apparently many major game companies agree. Licensees include SEGA, Capcom, Nintendo, Electronic Arts, Crystal Dynamics, GameTek, Magnet Interactive, and many more.

TrueMotion features a compression rate of 20:1 and full-screen playback. Duck Corporation is aiming TrueMotion directly at MPEG. MPEG takes a lot more throughput than TrueMotion to achieve amazing results.

TrueMotion Package Evaluation
Horizons Technology
3990 Ruffin Road
San Diego, CA 9212
Phone: 619 292-8331 **Fax:** 619 292-7321

Getting a handle on TrueMotion's capabilities has been tough. Until recently you had to deal directly with Duck. Now you can bypass the company for evaluation purposes. While game developers shipping a product need to deal with Duck concerning licensing fees, there is a package out on the market for other developers featuring the Truemotion S technology. The product, from Horizons Technology, is aimed at the non-game developer/users that Duck doesn't want to deal with. You can purchase this version for approximately $495. If you like the results, you can contact with Duck to get the full license property and comprending technology (see next entry) to proceed with your game.

The Comprending Engine
Duck Corporation
Tribeca Film Center
375 Greenwich Street
New York, NY 10013

From the same people who brought you TrueMotion comes a great technology specifically useful for game developers. It's called *comprending* and it's a revolutionary way of using digital video in your games.

Comprending is a combination of two common digital video technologies, *compression* and *rendering*. What this product does is allow you to create "video sprites." Essentially, most digital video used in games has been a single file that contains all the foreground and background images. With comprending you can take one or more digital video files and actually overlay that video on top of a background image on the fly.

For example, imagine that you're developing a basketball game and you want to pull out from the action, which is full screen, and overlay a couple of announcers on the background. The comprending engine allows you to decompress and draw a digital video announcer (filmed on, say, a bluescreen) and immediately overlay it on the screen.

Another example might be a football game in which all the players are digital video sprites! This is wild stuff that promises to ensure that digital video will be used in a much less linear way.

Already many game companies have licensed and begun using this technology.

Smacker!
RAD Software
307 West 200 South, Suite 1003
Salt Lake City, UT 84101
Phone: 801 322-4300

If you told really smart game developers to go sit in a room and write a flexible and useful game-oriented digital video codec and playback library, they'd go in the room, pick up the phone, and call RAD Software. They would order Smacker!, hide it in the desk drawer for three months, look busy when you walked by, and spend the time playing games.

Smacker!, written by Jeff Roberts of RAD software, is a cool product, so cool that over 90 games for Christmas 1995 used it, including Mechwarrior from Activision and Wetlands for New World Computing.

Jeff originally developed Smacker! to help with a game he was working on (Access' digital video hit Under A Killing Moon). Most digital video codecs work to please a huge group of developers, some who could care less about making games. Smacker! concentrates on the key aspects of digital video essential for today's game developer:

- **It's optimized for only 256 color files.** Most codecs have to account for 24-bit color and scalability. This means their compression schemes and speeds aren't always optimal for the 256 color images that make up 99 percent of games these days. Smacker! is fully optimized for 256 color mode, which results in better playback speeds and quality, and tighter file compression.
- **It's designed for developers, not end users.** Smacker! includes lots of goodies for developers, including support for FLC and FLI files, AVI files, and sequentially numbered image files. Smacker! also supports Smacker! calls from your code with a full API you can order. In addition, Smacker! provides a script language, which offers a ton of interactive scripting features.
- **It allows you to touch up compressed files with Animator Studio.** Once files are compressed, you can touch them up to improve their quality. Smacker! specifically works well with Animator Studio, a popular animation product from Autodesk.
- **It increases playback speed.** For some codecs and users of them, compression speed is often a major concern. However, for game developers looking for maximum performance on the playback end, Smacker! doesn't let them down.

Smacker! has a number of pricing schemes, and while some might think they're expensive, they're quite cheap considering the overall gains you make from a shipped product. The basic package runs approximately $195. Then if you want your shipped product to have playback of an *anonymous capability* (that is, without any pop-up displays), you need to order a redistribution license. There are a variety of such licenses, all around $1,000. Moving beyond that, they offer C callable APIs for DOS, Windows 3.1x, Windows 95, and Mac that run from $3,000 to $15,000, depending on the number of products you will ship and whether you require source code.

For complete details and updates (they're planning a Sega Saturn playback library, VB OCX, and Windows MCI extensions), you should definitely call them.

Indeo Video Interactive
Intel Corporation
2200 Mission College Boulevard
Santa Clara, CA 95052
Phone: 408 765-8080

Indeo Video Interactive is an entirely new version of Intel's original Indeo codec. This version uses a hybrid wavelet-based software video that enables realtime interaction and control of video and graphics, with emphasis on sprites over video and video on top of other video.

Not only do you get this increased interactive focus, but the new codec features improved image quality, especially at lower data rates (great for animation playback), and a new scalable quality feature that optimizes performance on Pentiums (it is Intel after all, what'd you expect?). Indeo Video Interactive boasts several cool features:

- **Transparency.** This feature allows you to display video or graphics of different shapes on a video or graphics scene, and interactively control the playback on the fly.
- **Local Windows.** This feature allows you to create independent simultaneous video playback windows with a large video playback or a graphics scene. This technique is especially useful for creating panned video. For example, imagine a car chase scene in which you actually pan from right to left during the video feed on the fly!
- **Random Keyframes.** A lot of video codecs place keyframes at specific intervals in the video—not the most flexible or perfect way to provide fresh image quality. Indeo Video Interactive allows placement of keyframes anywhere in a movie.
- **Change Saturation/Contrast/Brightness Controls.** This feature allows you to change all these specificationson the fly. Now you can send brightness up to pure white in a car crash or black out in a steep dive in an airplane!
- **Scalable Quality Feature.** With scaling you no longer have to settle for that common denominator approach.
- **No Costs!** Intel will license Indeo Video Interactive to any software developer for free and on a royalty free basis.

Currently Indeo Video Interactive is only available for Windows, but Intel plans to have a Quicktime version out soon.

WinToon
Microsoft Corporation
1 Microsoft Way
Redmond, WA 98052
Phone: 206 703-2079

WinToon, a frame-based animation tool rather than a sprite-based animation tool, is a system for playing back cartoons like animations. WinToon is a set of Video For Windows extensions that can "bluescreen" the foreground frames from a movie with an arbitrary background image.

To build full-screen cartoons, you use the tools to create a WinToon AVI file that contains "dirty rectangle" information. WinToon tracks the dirty rectangles of each frame and updates the screen. Video For Windows handles audio synchronization.

You can also use the WinToon runtime that comes with this kit to develop a Windows-based application that can play a WinToon AVI file.

Which Codec Is Best?

Each codec offers something the others don't; they're all different. All the codecs are used by at least one game on the market today.

The answer to the question then is to use whatever works best for you. For the PC platform I would use Smacker! with its wide range of features useful for the game developer. Indeo Video Interactive for PCs is also a good option. With its wealth of features it's sure to be used quite a bit. For consoles, TrueMotion seems to have had made some considerable gains, being used for a number of today's top console titles. WinToon, for all it promised, isn't really being used too much, but because it's free you can evaluate it for yourself.

Outsourcing

Now that I've given you the lowdown on system components for digital video, I should note that as with any other process in game development, you have the choice to outsource this work. For many companies, even large ones, outsourcing digital video shoots is the method of choice. For the most part you are still in control, just everything concerning the actual filming and processing, and sometimes direction and other film-oriented work, is taken care of by the company. For outsourcing services, you can contact the local film office of your state government; most publish a complete book that has all kinds of vendors, casting agents, and video production help found locally in your state.

Tips for Making Better Digital Video

Creating quality digital video is a matter of understanding the potential pitfalls. If you're planning on investing in this technology, make sure to read this section for some advice on making your digital video the best.

Creating Smoother Playback

The smoothness of digital video is directly related to the number of frames you see per second. Even though high frame rates produce smoother playback overall, lower frame rates can be smooth enough, depending mostly on the image you're trying to place in a digital video file. Table 10.1 lists the frame rates for several common types of video.

The average compression ratio for video is 20:1. This figure is an average because the exact compression ratio depends on the complexity of the video content and the quality desired in the video playback. If the content of the video is very complex and has a large number of changes between frames, more space will be required to store the needed information. The more complex the content, the more space it requires, and the lower the compression ratio.

Another factor for smooth video is the placement and number of keyframes in the video file. Keyframes are fully digitized frames, not "tween" frames that your codec has made. Of course, there are some tradeoffs. Investigate the possibilities and see for yourself.

Capturing Video

I have a whole list of tips for you in this most crucial area. Consider the following as a kind of checklist that you should review each time you set out to capture video.

Table 10.1 Common Frame Rates

Video Type	Frame Rate
Saturday Morning Cartoons	12-15 frames per second
Standard Film	24 frames per second
PAL TV	25 frames per second
NTSC TV	30 frames per second
Doom II on my Pentium 120	35+ frames per second!

Understanding Your Camcorder

Consumer-grade camcorders provide a good quality signal when shooting live, but some models do not play back from recorded videotape. When digitizing from videotape, it is best to use a high-quality editing deck rather than the camcorder itself.

Use a time-base corrector, which is used to match the video levels from the source to a standard television color bar test pattern. This ensures that black appears as pure black, white is not too bright, and the colors are accurate. Using a time-base corrector can correct some of the video quality errors inherent in some consumer-grade video equipment.

Strive for the Cleanest Video Possible

Clean video is a must. The best compression works best with clean video. If colors bleed and lots of "noise" is visible, not only will you be stuck with poor-quality video, you will be forced to use a less acceptable compression scheme.

Using the Best System Your Budget Allows

We talked about this right up front, but it bears repeating: The idea is to shoehorn your development process, and in digital video that means capturing your video with the rawest digital form. Capturing at a compression level can introduce noise and artifacting. What you ultimately want to do is get a specific setup that has an incredibly fast hard drive and lots of memory. This will allow you to select a really raw form of capture. Once that form is captured, you can use a product like Adobe Premiere to "shoot it down" to compressed levels for playback in your game.

Tweak the PC!

When you capture straight to the hard disk, you might want to consider giving your hard drive a quick tune-up. Optimizing your hard disk can affect the overall quality of the capture. Also keep your eye on the things that slow down the system, like other programs running, TSRs, and such.

Pre-Recording? Bring Extra Tapes!

If you're capturing now and editing and composing later, it's best to overshoot than undershoot. Buy some extra tape and take several shots of the same scene. Trust me, when you bank on perfection the first time through, you're bound to end up a loser.

Dealing with Lighting

Any production person will tell you lighting is one of the key ingredients for all good production. A relative of mine is a theater production student and she has spent more time learning lighting than any other facet of production. It's key not only needed for a good looking video, but stable lighting can help tremendously in producing clean crisp colors, which reduces noise.

I highly recommend, if you've got the money, bringing in a light production person. If you're on a tight budget, truck on down to your local library and get a good book on lighting. It's that important. You should really make lighting a priority in your digital video education.

Adjust for Proper Video Levels

A tip I picked up from the SuperMac Web site was to adjust for proper video levels. Some codecs (like Radius' Cinepak) work best with a signal providing even distribution of luminance and chronimance levels. They suggest capturing a single frame then loading that frame into Adobe Photoshop. Then you can run a histogram to get a perfect roadmap to calibration.

Experiment with Frame Rates

The frame rate determines how much data is compressed as the video is captured. Generally, the lower the frame rate, the lower the quality of the video.

Most multimedia users agree that 15 frames per second (fps) is the minimum acceptable frame rate for digital video. However, some videos (for instance, videos with limited motion) can go as low as 10 or 12 fps with no apparent loss in smoothness. Try capturing at different frame rates to see which one works best for your application.

Avoid Dropping Frames

If possible, you don't want to drop any frames during capture. Video files with dropped frames will appear to stutter during playback because some of the original video frames are missing from the file. If your capture utility reports dropped frames during capture, try capturing several shorter segments and edit them together. Also, don't use disk compression programs like MS DoubleSpace or Stacker. Compressed drives are slower and will affect performance.

Set Up Digital Video Palettes

If you're not careful, digital video can cause huge palette problems for your program. Before you start capturing tons of video, make sure to match your video palette with your program's palette. The trick is making sure that all other onscreen graphics that are present when the video plays adhere to the same palette. I recommend that you use the standard palette many codecs use (especially in the case of Intel Indeo, whose palette optimizes playback as well), or create your own.

Intel maintains a great source of information on digital video palettes on its Web site at: *http://www.intel.com*. I recommend you stop by to browse for awhile.

The Audio Component

Your sound is as important as your video. If your audio isn't up to snuff, you'll be watching your game collect dust on the computer store shelves.

Calibrate Audio Levels

Use the software that came with your sound card to properly calibrate the input audio levels on all of the audio sources that will be used in your project. Set the audio level so that the majority of the sound is close to 0 decibels. Going past 0 decibels is likely to result in distorted audio. See your sound card documentation for more information.

Several wave editing applications allow for the WAV file to be normalized, which digitally boosts the gain.

Use the Lowest Sampling Rates for Audio

One thing to do when capturing video to a file is use a really low audio rate to cut down on the bandwidth and allow for a higher capture rate. Later, using Premiere you can capture and lay down an audio track separately.

Post Processing Options

There are many different products out there to help you enhance your overall digital video file.

Adobe After Affects, which for now is available only for the Mac, is to digital video what Adobe's Photoshop is to photo imaging. Like Photoshop, After Affects offers a plug-in architecture, which means other vendors offer additional new effects to work within the After Affects program.

For PCs there is Autodesk's Animator Studio Pro, which can add a host of animation capabilities. This package offers a nice range of features to enhance your digital video. Don't settle for the capture and compress form of digital video. Raw digital video might as well be stick figures you drew and animated by hand; it looks like garbage. Extensive post production will go a long way toward making cool digital video for your games.

The Next Generation of Digital Video: Quicktime VR

Quicktime VR is an extension of Apple's core Quicktime digital video engine that uses an innovative 360 degree panoramic photography technique that gives VR-like immersive experiences of real-world spaces and items. Users can experience spatial interactions without special VR equipment. All in all it's a novel use of digital video with some surprisingly cool results.

What's neat about Quicktime VR is that you can create scenes by modeling them on a computer or by actually stitching together 360 degrees of photographic stills you take with a camera and a special tripod. Quicktime also supports what it calls Object Movie Elements. These are items that you can move around independently to see all the sides of the item.

Quicktime VR development is possible only on a Macintosh platform, but playback is possible in Windows as well. Apple will license to developers both the Quicktime VR runtime software (for Macintosh and Windows) and the authoring tools (for Macintosh only).

In addition to the costs of the tools, there is a modest royalty arrangement for distributing the Quicktime VR runtime software. Apple has broken it down into two title types, CD-ROM titles and Enhanced Audio CDs. For CD-ROM titles if you ship less than 25,000 units, there is no royalty, and over 25,000 units it is $400 for every 5,000 units shipped. For Enhanced Audio CDs (Like CD+) if you ship less than 50,000 units, there is no royalty, and for over 50,000 units it is $750 for every 25,000 units.

The Quicktime VR Authoring Tools Suite comes with four CD-ROMs containing authoring tools, runtime software, Macintosh and Windows APIs, and tools for Macromedia Director use of Quicktime VR.

Quicktime VR
Apple Computer, Inc.
1 Infinite Loop
Curpertino, CA 95014
Phone: 408 996-1010

Apple also sells an instructional videotape on implementing Quicktime VR scenes, which is sold through Apple's APDA. Implementing a Quicktime VR scene using photographic imaging requires simple equipment, but takes some skill. Tables 10.2 and 10.3 shows the system requirements for using the various versions of Quicktime VR.

Quicktime VR Resources

Now that you know what Quicktime VR can do, I bet you want to run right out and get it! At the very least, you'll want some information on this very cool technology.

Apple Computer, Inc.
P.O. Box 319
Buffalo, NY 14207-0319
Phone: 716 871-6555 **Fax:** 716 871-6511

Table 10.2 System Requirements for Quicktime VR Runtime

Macintosh Systems	**Windows-Based Systems**
Macintosh with 68030, 25 MHz processor	PC with 80386, 33 MHz processor
8-bit, 256 colors (16-bit video is preferred)	8-bit, 256 colors (16-bit video is preferred)
8 MB RAM	8 MB RAM
Double-speed CD-ROM drive	Double-speed CD-ROM drive
Quicktime version 2.0 or later	Quicktime version 2.0 or later
System 7.1 or later	Windows 3.1 or later

Table 10.3 System Requirements for Quicktime VR Authoring

680x0-Based Systems	**PowerPC-Based Systems**
68040 system running at 33 MHz	Any Power Macintosh with floating-point unit (FPU)
16-bit video, thousands of colors	16-bit video, thousands of colors
System 7.0.1 or later	System 7.1.2 or later
At least 40 MB RAM	At least 40 MB RAM
Hard Disk Space: ~10 MB per panorama (if using Photo CD)~5 MB per object	Hard Disk Space: ~10 MB per panorama (if using Photo CD)~5 MB per object
HyperCard version 2.2	HyperCard version 2.2
Quicktime version 2.0 or later	Quicktime version 2.0 or later
ResEdit(TM) version 2.1.1	ResEdit(TM) version 2.1.1
MPW Version 3.2	MPW Version 3.4b2

Following is the ordering information needed when contacting APDA. Please call APDA for shipping fees or to request more information.

- Quicktime VR Authoring Tools Suite v1.0-PAL standalone, R0637Z/B
- Quicktime VR Authoring Tools Suite v1.0-NTSC standalone, R0629Z/B
- Quicktime VR Authoring Tools Suite v1.0-PAL and MPW Pro, B2472LL/B
- Quicktime VR Authoring Tools Suite v1.0-NTSC and MPW Pro, B2473LL/B

As I mentioned earlier, an 18-minute instructional videotape is included with the Quicktime VR Authoring Tools Suite v1.0 that provides an overview of photographing Quicktime VR scenes. This videotape is also sold separately through APDA. Ask for the following:

- Videotape: Photographing QuickTime VR Scenes-PAL, R0645LL/A
- Videotape: Photographing QuickTime VR Scenes-NTSC, R0646LL/A

World Wide Web

Pages with Quicktime VR information are located at: *http://qtvr.quicktime.apple.com*

Surround Video
Microsoft Corporation
1 Microsoft Way
Redmond, WA 98052
Phone: 206 703-2079

I know, I know, this section was supposed to be all about Quicktime VR. Well, when either of these giants makes a move, the other is sure to be breathing heavy in pursuit. Such is the case with Surround Video. Even though I have confirmation that Surround Video exists, there is no hard evidence. Technically, Surround Video is vaporware. However, let's discuss it anyway so you know what it is if you see it.

Surround Video is basically Microsoft's answer to Quicktime VR. One thing MS is promising is that Surround Video will be royalty free (a definite swipe at the royalties Apple is charging for Quicktime VR).

Surround Video has an editor and playback engine for runtime playback. This engine can put together and display 360 degree photographic images as taken with a panoramic camera (just like Quicktime VR), and solves the distortion effect through a remapping algorithm. The editor supports scripts that define hotspots, scene transitions, sounds and overlaid bitmaps.

Until it ships, Quicktime VR has this new video technology to itself. To obtain more information on Surround Video, send email to mmdinfo@microsoft.com.

Performers: Getting the Best for Your Dollar

Many developers might think they can cast their friends or themselves in roles for their games but as the pros have learned, it doesn't always work. Just as demand for faster and better graphics has fueled ever more amazing graphic engines, the same is happening for in game acting talent. The first wave of games seemed to basically forsake real talent and hoped to simply amaze us with the pure spectacle of digital video itself.

Today that just doesn't cut it. Good actors are good actors for a reason! Their non-verbal acting and pure professional delivery can make a big difference. I'm not saying not to cast yourself or your friends; just make sure you all have talent or the roles are small enough that bad acting isn't very visible. The more extensive your digital video is, and the longer the actual individual scenes are, the more you need high-quality talent.

But where do you get that?

Elsewhere in this book, in a section titled *Organizations*, you'll find listings for organizations like the Screen Actors Guild, The Directors Guild, and other performing arts organizations. Now you know why. Many of these organizations have specific contracts covering the use of their members' talent in interactive games.

If you get a contract with a big company to do a title, you might need to work with organized talent because they're obliged to do so. Always check with the publisher to make sure what your specific situation is. Union talent provides a great way for you to get top notch performers. Of course, they do come with a price.

Electronic Arts' subsidiary Origin Systems had a walkout of union talent off the set of Wing Commander IV when some technicians objected to the working policy. While some renogotiation led to a return to work, they did lose some time in the shooting day. The walkout was a symbol of gaming's new era, where working with highly skilled talent can introduce a whole new set of problems that aren't necessarily of a technical nature!

Resources for Digital Video

This wouldn't be a chapter of mine if I didn't include some resources for you to browse, now would it? Take a look at some of the resources listed here. You're bound to find some useful information in most of them.

Magazines and Newsletters

Several magazines offer good help to the digital video enthusiast. These include some I'm hanging on to list later as part of overall graphics resources, such as *Digital Video* Magazine (which despite the title covers more than just digital video), *New Media*, and *Computer Graphics World*. So besides the few really hardcore digital video-specific periodicals listed here, check out the great computer art magazines too; there's lots of good digital video information to be found there as well.

Digital Video Magazine's Full Motion Newsletter

ActiveMedia, Inc., (IDG)
600 Townsend Street, Suite 170
San Francisco, CA 94103
Phone: 415 522-2400 **Fax:** 415 522-2409
Email: letters@dv.com **Subscription Fax:** 603 472-2419
Subscription: $49.95 **Newstand:** N/A **Publishes:** 6/Year **Pages:** 20

Digital Video Magazine

DV Full Motion
120 Bedford Center Road, Suite 4
Bedford, NH 03110

This newsletter comes from the producers of *Digital Video* Magazine and focuses on using Adobe Premiere, After Affects, and other Adobe digital video and related products. I haven't actually read this newsletter, but have heard that it is very helpful.

Videography
Miller Freeman PSNInc.
2 Park Avenue, Suite 1820
NY 10016
Phone: 212 779-1919 **Fax:** 212 213-3484
Email: videography@psn.com
Subscription: $30.00 **Newstand:** $3.95 **Publishes:** 12/Year **Pages:** 170

Videography is the magazine covering high-end video/digital video production. If you're serious about putting together the proper digital video resources, you should be reading this magazine. You'll find information on computer digital video, as well as all the latest and greatest hardware.

***Video* Magazine**
Hachette Filipacchi Magazines
1633 Broadway
New York, NY 10019
Phone: 212 779-1919 **Fax:** 212 213-3484
Email: videography@psn.com
Subscription: $9.97 **Newstand:** $3.95 **Publishes:** 10/Year **Pages:** 110

Video Magazine is decidedly lower end—most useful for that home-theater freak you might know. Even so, they cover a lot of good equipment from the non-broadcast-quality spectrum, which for many hobbyists/shareware/ lower-end developers may be more than adequate. I recommend that you get *Videography* first.

Books on Digital Video

The Digital Videomaker's Guide by Kathryn Shaw Whitver (Michael Wiese Productions; ISBN 0-941188-21-3)

This handy guide starts with an overview of digital video terms, formats, and studio requirements. It also deals with how to get the production process rolling, as well as specifics on marketing, copyright, and distribution. *The Guide* includes a complete bibliography and a resource guide.

Web Sites

I found some really useful information at the various codec-related Web sites. SuperMac and Intel, makers of two of the most often used digital video codecs, have a lot of great information on their sites, and pointers to additional tools and services.

CinePak Information and Digital Video Tips
`http://www.radius.com`

SuperMac invented CinePak but Radius bought SuperMac, so visit Radius for more info. They have a specific page of information and contacts for the CinePak contact.

Indeo Information and Extensive Digital Video Tips
`http://www.intel.com`

Intel has been a key pioneer in interactive digital video. This site has a ton of useful information on capturing, editing, and programming digital video.

MPEG Sites
`http://www.om-1.org/`
`http://www.optibase.com/primer2.html`
`http://www-plateau.cs.berkeley.edu/mpeg/mpegptr.html`

Because MPEG plays a large role in the Web community, you will find tons of MPEG sites on the Internet. I've found that the three listed are among the more useful.

Adobe Premiere and After Effects Information and Tips
`http://www.adobe.com`

Adobe Premiere is the leading digital video editing package for Windows and the Mac. Check here often to see what new products and extensions Adobe is adding to its growing line of digital video applications.

Digital Movie News
`http://spider.lloyd.com/~dmnews/`

This is a really cool site with lots of help for people making full-length movies with only a camera and their PCs. There's lots of good basic information here on almost every aspect of digital video production.

Northwestern University Library
Marjorie I. Mitchell Multimedia Center
`http://www.library.nwu.edu/media/resources/`

This site is a good starting place for links to all kinds of film, video production, and digital video information on the Web.

Digital Video Magazine Web Site
http://www.dv.com

Digital Video Magazine has a ton of useful information for the digital video enthusiast, as well as information on all sorts of graphics products.

The Poor Man's Guide to Digital Video for Game Development by Ian Firth —Diversions Software

I asked Ian Firth to share a few quick notes about his experience working with digital video. Ian is the author of several popular shareware and low-end commercial products. His current project is a major effort called Void Pirates. For this game, Ian wanted to have a bunch of digital video sequences. There was one catch, Ian doesn't work for Electronic Arts; he works for Diversions Software—and is the only employee, I might add. Thus Ian's budget wasn't exactly big (heck, a set for Wing Commander IV probably cost more than Ian's entire budget!).

However, Ian has used some hard work and a few tricks to create some really awesome digital video for his game. He proves that even a low-end developer can use a supposed high-end technique to make a really neat product.

Adding digital video to your CD-ROM game has reached a crossing point of simplicity and price. For an investment of less than $1,500 you can create digital video of quality comparable to outside sourcing. How? What do I need? How much will it cost?

Step 1. Buying a Camera

(If you have a video camera, skip to step 2.)

Start at the local media or camera store and look for a brand name video camera that has Hi-8 output. You will be able to find one between $600 and $5,000 dollars, depending on features. I use a Sony CCD TR400, and the list price has dropped from $1,500 to around $900 since I bought it early in 1995.

Here are a few tips to keep in mind while you're looking:

- Try to get the best camera you can, but be especially vigilant for the camera's lighting specifications; remember, lighting is key!

- If you plan to record first then digitize, consider buying a separate deck for digitizing; many built in camera decks are of a lower quality than standalone decks.

Step 2. Buying a Capture Card

Video capture cards come in a variety of styles. Some offer capture only, while others offer output to tape as well. The Intel ISVR Pro offers exceptional quality at a decent price (around $500). Install the capture card into your system, and set it up according to the installation manual.

Plug your video camera into the capture card, and turn it on. Run the capture software that came with the capture card.

You should now be looking at a live feed of your humble home office. Interesting.

Step 3. Bluescreen Options

Bluescreening, or *chroma keying*, is the practice of removing a color from an image, and making it transparent, allowing another image to show through. All parts of the first image not keyed out are displayed above the underlying image. This process is used daily by local news stations, when the weatherman steps in front of that big weather map.

To create a bluescreen for home use, you have several choices. The first requires a half gallon of paint and a roller. I painted my living room wall blue for the production of Void Pirates. It was easy, and cost about $10. You can also use blue (or green) paper, cloth, or bedsheets to create your bluescreen. Another technique is to hang a screen away from a wall allowing it to be backlighted, which offers a better quality of color.

The key is to achieve a solid color without hotspots or dark areas.

Step 4. Lighting

I use two 600W video lamps, purchased at the local camera shop for $375 a pair. Even though 1200 watts sounds like enough, it still resulted in underexposed images, due to my camera's low light capabilities. Light placement is critical. You want to maintain even color while making the subject apparent. Experimentation is key.

At this point you can begin filming your characters and their dialog to tape, using the capture card as an onscreen monitor. This technique allows you to

save your video on video tape, and dump it to disk as needed, since it consumes large amounts of disk space.

Step 5. Creating Background Art

I created the backgrounds using Caligari Truespace2. It's quite a full-featured package, and costs a lot less than 3D Studio, and it runs in Windows. In order to scale the backgrounds properly for the planned shot, I created a 3D dummy human model in the place I want my actual human subject. The model is then removed before rendering.

Step 6. Final Capture

Capturing the video from tape is outlined in the capture card's documentation, and is a simple affair. I capture all my video at 24 bit. Indeo and CinePak are 24 bit by nature, but include a fixed 256 color palette in the codec itself for playback on 8 bit displays. Keying involves cueing your video and selecting the color to be removed. A background image is then placed behind the character, and they appear in your virtual set.

Once captured, the digital video can be manipulated with video editing software. Adobe Premiere is the choice of professionals, and is my recommendation for quality work. For editing, I use Indeo 3.2. The color palette is nice, if not a bit dark. I also use it because everyone else uses CinePak, and I wanted to be different.

If you're thinking about Indeo Interactive, take your time. This new codec is still an infant, and is yet to be optimized...recommended playback system is a P100 16MB...so it's not yet an option. The Beta and 4.1 release were poor performers, and compression was extremely slow, so for now I'm sticking with the vanilla Indeo.

Using Premiere, I add simple effects like a green tint or a simple transition. When I'm satisfied with the output, the video is then saved to disk, and compressed for CD-ROM playback.

Step 7. Post Production

The overlays were hand drawn, and overlaid one at a time. Needless to say, I won't work this way again. I now use Autodesk Animator Studio and that removes the need to work one frame at a time.

Thanks Ian! I hope this brief list of steps proves to you that attempting digital video isn't as tough as it seems.

After looking over Ian's screen shots (See Figure 10.1), you can see that the quality of the video is impressive. And to think, this was all done in-house by Ian for relatively little money. I will say though that in talking with Ian, it became obvious that he has spent a lot of time working on this game. He's experimented heavily with digital video, and you will too before you get everything perfect for your first real game shoot.

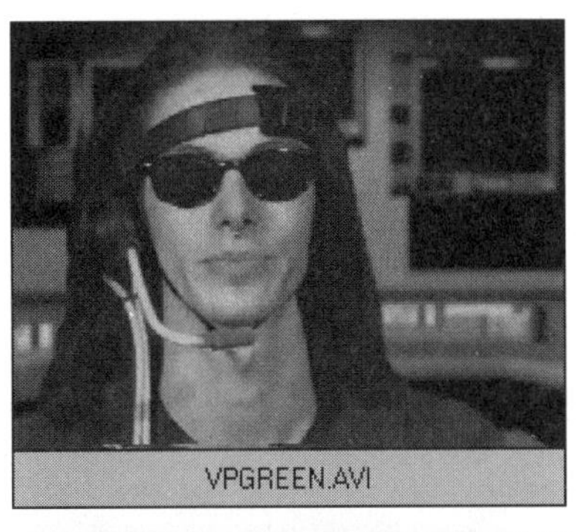

Figure 10.1 Sample video from Ian's game..

CHAPTER 11

Game design is a very deliberative frontloaded process.

Capturing the Moment

The Art of Motion Capture

One of the fastest growing technologies in game development today is motion capture animation, also referred to as *performance animation.* This revolutionary technology combines sophisticated 3D modeling software, special video technology, and live subjects for capturing actual movements for animation purposes. With it, developers are able to create incredibly fluid and lifelike digital actors for games.

There are two applications of motion capture technology: *magnetic* and *optical.* Using either method, subjects are fitted with magnetic or optical transmitters on their limbs and joints. With optical systems, the transmitters are reflective sensors and high-tech cameras record the subject's position as he or she moves. A magnetic system, on the other hand, works with a set of attached sensors to return realtime position and rotation data. The difference (or *advantage* as some might say) with the magnetic system is that instant feedback is provided to the subject, allowing readjustment if necessary.

For either scheme, the basic process is the same: The subject is monitored by the system with spatial and positional coordinates transmitted at a rate of over 100 times per second. The information is then recorded to a database. From this database, the information is translated into a motion file that can be applied to a 3D object—from Wavefront or 3D studio, for example—and animated accordingly. Not only does motion capture eliminate the necessity to animate by hand, but the quality of the motion is much better. And, depending on your game, motion capture techniques can be quite cost effective.

As you have probably guessed, motion capture is perfect for products like fighting games that incorporate realtime animation with polygons.

Magnetic and Optical Solutions

I can't tell you from actual experience (though I wish I could!), but optical systems are considered less accurate than magnetic systems. Because the optical sensors can overlap in a field of view, it's difficult to work out which sensor should be where, which results in more maintenance with the optical systems as you work out those kinks. Still, many companies are employing optical systems because of the freedom they provide and the results are reflected in the games constructed with them. Acclaim Entertainment's in-house system is an optical system, and their motion capture work is very solid. Figure 11.1 shows how performers are outfitted for optical motion capture.

Most motion capture systems available are of the magnetic type. The sensors on the subject's body are connected to the main unit by wires, which sort out positional and orientational data from the varying magnetic fields generated during movement.

Photo courtesy of Motion Analysis Corporation.

Figure 11.1 Optical systems make it quite easy to capture multiple performers since they free you from the wires associated with the current magnetic systems.

One disadvantage of the magnetic system is that distortion can be introduced if you use it in an area that contains a lot of steel. If you can't receive good AM radio signals, chances are a magnetic system might be hampered. Of course, you should *test* it out and work with the manufacturer to be sure.

Another disadvantage with magnetic systems is that movement is often restricted by wires used to track movement. Luckily, most games don't require large movements for their captures. Both of the major manufacturers of magnetic systems, Polhemus and Ascension, say they are expecting to debut wireless versions by the end of 1996.

Motion Capture and Traditional Animation Techniques

Now that you've been introduced to motion capture, let me take a moment to point out why rendering 3D animations with motion capture—when applicable—is superior to traditional animation key framing methods. In key framing, you create two different positionings of an object and then have the computer create animation by rendering the in-between frames based on movement information you give it about the object. This information includes precise details about how the object and other affected parts of it really move from one place to the other. Some programs are

able to do this with a powerful technology called *inverse kinematics*, but even then this technique is not as "pure" as motion capture.

The bottom line is that motion capture supports a more precise form of natural movement because it captures exact information from a live source and it does not interpret a fictional movement.

The Bottom Line: Will Motion Capture Cut Costs?

If money is really tight, motion capture may not be for you yet. The problem with such cutting edge technology is that you have to spend to save. Motion capture can save you money, but not until you've invested a fairly large initial sum of money to get the basic technology you need. If you can just hang on as the technology and your experience improves, the savings will materialize.

Because of the high upfront costs, some companies have decided not to invest, but instead work with motion capture providers or experiment with a growing number of motion capture "clipfiles." Learning with these tools tends to be less costly.

From the Labs to the Consumer

As with most technology, motion capture started out as a primarily proprietary and experimental technology. Today, though, there are several systems you can buy and adapt to your own use, and several services that will work directly with you to generate motion captured animation files. Certainly games like Virtua Fighter, FX Fighter, 3D Baseball, Bioforge, and more show that motion capture is a realistic development technique that has reached the end user product category. Figure 11.2 shows a company actually capturing an Akido fight using an optical system. Motion capture has been used especially well in fighting style games and sports games.

If you're serious about using motion capture techniques, you're going to have to do some homework if you want to get the most for your buck. Evaluate the products currently available (see the *Resources* section at the end of this chapter) and contact some of the major companies that you know have been working with motion capture to get their input.

Some Specifics

Let's get into a real down home discussion about motion capture technology. You should be aware of the issues—cost, outsourcing compared to in-house development, available packages—surrounding this hot new animation technique.

Photo courtesy of Motion Analysis Corporation.

Figure 11.2 Using an optical system to capture an Akido fight scene.

Motion Capture Is Not a Godsend

Motion Capture is an exciting new technology, but it's not the "end all be all" of animation. Try motion capturing a hydra or a dog. A dog may be tough (especially mine), but a hydra? Heck, it doesn't even exist!

Traditional animation will always be necessary; you just can't replace it with motion capture. Some mythical roleplaying games, for example, work best with traditional animation considering the space limitations and number of different motions you might have.

Motion capture solves a ton of animation problems, but it's not a full purpose animation solution, and it brings with it a whole crop of new problems.

In House or Outsource?

So you've decided that motion capture is the solution you need for a particular game. Now you must decide if you're going to do it in house or if you should outsource the project. Your decision will be based on costs, expertise, and the schedule—the usual stuff in a game decision-making process. I suggest that you go out of house for your first attempt, but make sure you take an active role in the process. That way you can bring your next project in house, and apply your experience and expertise.

A number of companies are outsourcing motion capture, most notably game maker, Acclaim Entertainment. A number of providers have begun to spring up and, with the potential of this technology in the future, there will, no doubt, be many more outsourcers putting their hands into the pot.

Wavefront, a division of Silicon Graphics, Inc. that markets high-end animation and game development software, has certified a number of its customers to provide performance animation motion capture services using Wavefront software and SGI hardware. Check with Wavefront for more information on suggested studios. These providers offer expertise with "data stages" and can help on a contract basis anyone who hasn't yet invested in an in-house motion capture system.

There are dozens of companies now offering motion capture services. Aside from the companies I mention in the *Outsource Options* section, you can find other companies by using the World Wide Web and by contacting the four major manufacturers of motion capture hardware listed in the *Hardware Companies* section. Not only will they help you find a good studio, a few of them even have their own studio.

Understanding the Limits

I mentioned a moment ago that there are indeed limits to motion capture. Specifically, many of the systems, both custom and off-the-shelf, magnetic or optical, limit the number of nodes—between 15 and 20—that you can track in one session. This basically limits you to human forms—and never more than one at a time. (Although you may have two subjects interacting, you'll most likely be capturing only one of them at a time.)

In addition, you're dealing with a ton of collected data that needs to be shoehorned into a game, which also limits the size and sophistication of your captures.

Capturing More Than Full Body Motion

You may not have considered this approach, but motion capture works for more than just human body movement. Some systems, like Adoptive Optics Associates' Face-Trax, can capture facial expressions as well. Using the same process as in body motion capture, a subject has reflective stickers placed on his or her face. A head mounted display (as pictured in Figure 11.3) relays the facial movements it reads from those stickers. While most games have concentrated on the full motion capture technology, no doubt the use of this technique for interactive movies and talking 3D graphics will occur in the future!

Photo courtesy of Motion Analysis Corporation.

Figure 11.3 Using a motion capture screen for capturing facial expressions.

Combining with a Bluescreen

For the most part, motion capture is a non-bluescreen event. But when combined with the subject on a bluescreen stage, you are able to show the subjects how their motion capture is being displayed in relation to the background of the sprite they are moving.

The realtime interaction with the background that the bluescreen provides can be invaluable to the final product. It's a unique twist, no doubt, but one worth looking into, depending on the situation you are trying to replicate with motion capture.

Choose Your Motion Capture Studio Closely

Everyone's got their own way of doing things in this business. When you are evaluating companies to do your motion capture work, you need to find what services, besides the actual motion capture, they are willing to provide for you. Services such as editing are crucial to your final product and not all studios offer that. Trust me, captures are *never* clean; additional editing work will need to be done. Make sure you get a studio that is willing to help, and can work with your art or animation staff to make sure you end up with a useful file.

Avoiding Disasters

Steven Speilberg doesn't show up to film a scene without having storyboarded and scripted it. And the actors don't show up unprepared either; they have probably run through the scene several times. While not on the scale of filming a movie like Jurassic Park, motion capture requires procedures similar to storyboarding, scripting, and rehearsals. You must develop a detailed list of the motions you need and, if need be, storyboard them as well. You also need to make sure your subjects completely understand the motions they are to perform and have thoroughly practiced them beforehand.

Understand the Costs

Obviously, costs will vary from center to center but my research seems to indicate that costs range from $2,000 to $3,000 per day for capturing and $1,000 to $2,000 for editing services on those files. A typical day results in 50 to 75 captures, so a game with 300 captures, including editing services, can run you anywhere from $12,000 to $30,000. I realize that there is a huge difference between the high end and the low end of this cost span, but depending on the studio rate and the complexity of your captures, the cost varies heavily. Once you have determined your needs and discussed them with several studios, you will be able to pinpoint a more accurate cost. Remember, this stuff might not be necessary if you can do it using conventional animation techniques or with "puppet-like" animation devices.

Understand Your Modeling Software

Once you have your motion capture files, you're going to manipulate them within 3D animation software. Most of the major packages like Alias, Wavefront, SoftImage, and 3D Studio have various ways of handling the files. Before you spend a lot of time manipulating your files, become thoroughly familiar with how your software will work with the files. Also, a lot of the major motion capture studios have developed some cool in-house tools. I didn't have time to check with them but I suspect that more than a few might license or sell their in-house technology to you for your own use. When you talk to the various studios, check to see what software they're using and if they've got any special tools that you can use to help with the files back at your place.

Motion Capture Resources

We've covered the specifics of motion capture from top to bottom. So let's now take a look at what's out there in the way of resources. As you have seen throughout this chapter, you'll have many choices and decisions to make once you've set your sights on motion capture techniques for your game animation.

Hardware Companies

When you're going to do motion capture, you sure as heck need the right hardware to do the job. I've listed the four major companies that supply the type of hardware you'll need.

Adaptive Optics Associates, Inc. (Division of United Technologies, Inc.)
54 Cambridgepark Drive
Cambridge, MA, 02140

Phone: 617 864-0201 **Fax:** 617 864-5855
Web: http://www.aoainc.com/ **Email:** info@aoainc.com

AOA markets a wide range of hardware and software products designed to do motion capture. Two of the most widely known are:

- **Mutli-Trax** A 2D and 3D realtime motion capture system.
- **Face-Trax** A realtime facial optical expression capture system.

Ascension Technology Corporation
P.O. Box 527
Burlington, VT 05402

Phone: 802 860-6440 **Fax:** 802 860-6439
Web: http://world.std.com:80/~ascen/./ **Email:** ascension@world.std.com

Ascension brings us a sound magnetic field system called Flock of Birds. As I mentioned earlier, steel interferes with the operation of magnetic systems; however, by using a DC magnetic field and AC magnetic field, Flock of Birds claims to be more receptive to steel environments (though not immune to problems).

Polhemus Incorporated
Polhemus Magnetic
POB 560
1 Hercules Drive
Colchester, VT 05446

Phone: 802 655-3159

Polhemus markets Ultra-Trak, a DC magnetic field motion capture system.

Motion Analysis Corporation
3617 Westwind Boulevard
Santa Rosa, CA 95403

Phone: 707 579-6500 **Fax:** 707 526-0629
Web: http://www.crl.com/~macorp/

Motion Analysis Corporation's ExpertVision HiRes System is an optical-based motion capture system, which uses proprietary hardware and software developed by Motion Analysis. They have also developed FaceTracker RT for capturing facial expressions. CAPCOM, SNK, Accolade, and Atari are among the companies that stand behind Motion Analysis' products. I'd also like to thank them for letting us use their photos for this chapter.

SimGraphics
1137 Hunnington Drive
South Pasadena, CA 91030

Phone: 213 255-0900 **Fax:** 213 255-0987

SimGraphics, developers of Vactor Performance offers a wide range of motion capture hardware services.

Outsource Options

I've singled out two companies that have been especially active with game developers; however, these are by no means are the only shops that outsource motion capture.

Acclaim Entertainment Inc.
Optical Advanced Technologies Group
71 Audrey Ave
Oyster Bay, NY 11771

Phone: 516 624-8888

Acclaim is known internationally for its work in electronic games, most notably, Mortal Kombat and NBA Jam. As a side business, it has set up several studios around the country to do motion capture with its custom optical capturing system. This system has been used in many of Acclaim's recent titles like Frank Thomas Baseball.

Bio Vision
Optical
2882 Sand Hill Road, Suite 116
Menlo Park, CA 94025

Phone: 415 233-7906 **Fax:** 415 233-7920

Bio Vision is one of the premeire motion capture studios around. They use an adjusted optical system that they've tweaked with their own software.

Motion Capture "Clipfiles"

Prepackaged motion captures? Why not? Here's a company that is offering clipfiles to allow developers to use motion capture animation without all the hassle that goes along with it.

ViewPoint Datalabs
625 South State Street
Orem, Utah 94058

Phone: 801 229-3000 **Fax:** 801 229-3300
Web: http://www.viewpoint.com

ViewPoint Datalabs is a major vendor of 3D graphic objects. They've recently teamed up with Bio Vision to offer an extensive line of motion capture datafiles. Much of what they offer is available directly through their Web site.

Web Sites Devoted to Motion Capture

OZ WebSite
http://www.oz.is/OZ/Misc/MCapture.html

This Iceland-based outfit has an awesome site for 3D graphics. Their Web page, called the Motion Capture Homepage, is a good site for pointers to other motion capture outsourcing and hardware companies.

Ascension FAQ
`ftp://ftp.std.com/ftp/vendors/Ascension`

Want to read a lot of cool technical stuff about Ascension's Flock of Birds motion capture hardware? Then point your browser here and spend some intimate time with FAQ.TXT.

MOTEK
`http://www.support.nl/motek`

MOTEK, a European-based company, has a very informative and very cool Web site about motion capture. They provide a wide range of motion capture services for people across the pond.

CHAPTER 12

Half of the battle of creating game art is having the right tools.

Game Art Tools

Once you've decided that you want to create artwork for your own games, the next step is to get all the stuff you'll need to do a bang-up job. In this chapter, I'll discuss a wide range of art tools in detail. Of course, some of the more high-tech tools are beyond a small developer's budget, but many are relatively inexpensive and can perform virtual miracles! Well, I might be kidding about the miracles, but you'll soon see that the price tag is not always indicative of the basic capabilities.

The Basics

There are certain tools that every artist needs in his or her electronic tool chest. In this section, I will give you a general rundown of these tools before we get into the specific packages available on the different platforms.

Basic Paint Package

Everyone, even the artistically challenged, needs to have a basic pixel pushing art package. Even if you aren't the one drawing the lifelike human forms, you still need to construct simple icons, change a color, or round an edge. You don't need to pay an artist to do these simple tasks. Fortunately, you'll find plenty of economically priced paint products for both the PC and the Mac. You just need to know what to look for. When evaluating paint packages, you'll want to make sure that you have a super pixel-by-pixel editor. You may also want to get a package that incorporates a lot of artistic tools and imaging tricks for some of the fancier tasks you intend to perform. Either way, make purchasing a good paint package a top priority.

2D Animation Package

Most game animation is accomplished by programming or through digital video engines like Video For Windows, WinToon, or Quicktime. Still, a conventional 2D animation package such as Autodesk Animator Studio is a really useful tool. With it you can develop digital-video animations by hand or create a successive set of frames a programmer can then animate by writing code. While a good paint package could also produce those frames—and I know you have a good paint package—most good 2D animation products feature tools that make such tasks much easier to perform.

3D Rendering and Animation

Today, a 3D rendering package is almost a necessity for every developer. 3D is the name of the game. Of course, 3D rendering doesn't come cheap—Studio 3D is a $2,000+ package. GameWare, which runs on an SGI, will have you buying $15,000 of hardware just to run the $8,000 program. Ouch! My advice: If you've got the money, hook up with one of these packages; they're worth every penny. If you're on a tight budget, there are some killer shareware products you can try. (These products are listed later in the chapter.) With a lot of time and effort, these products can help you to create some nice imagery, so check them out.

3D rendering packages offer many features. Most packages work in a similar way, but the ones I researched worked differently in enough ways that you've got a wide range of choices. Next I'll present some background information to help you get up to speed with the major features, characteristics, and terminology of these tools.

Inverse Kinematics

Remember the song that goes "The knee bone's connected to the thigh bone, the thigh bone's connected to the...." Well, this childhood diddy is the basic theory behind *inverse kinematics* (IK). In a nutshell, IK uses skeletal forms to determine the animated movement of an entire 3D object. By understanding how a limb or body reacts to movements of another portion of the body, animators can create amazing walking and talking images with a lot less work than before IK was around.

Polygon Modeling

Polygon modeling is the most traditional form of modeling, in which images are created entirely out of polygon-based models as shown in Figure 12.1.

Spline Modeling

Spline modeling is much more flexible than polygon modeling, for most objects, especially characters. With splines, you define a line that then is "swept" in a 360 degree transition, turning it into a 3D object as shown in Figure 12.2. This is an

Figure 12.1 Creating images out of polygon-based models.

Figure 12.2 Creating 3D objects by using spline modeling.

awesome technique for creating organic models that don't contain sharp edges. Developers looking to create extensive organic 3D models are going to need the best of spline modeling packages available.

Metaball Modeling

Metaball modeling allows you to construct models by gluing together various spheres. By working with shape primitives that aren't made up of sharp angled edges, modelers can create cool organic objects far easier.

3D Paint Packages

For most 3D work, you'll simply be able to wrap a texture onto a surface to create a 3D shape. However, for many forms, especially organic forms, these textures don't always wrap correctly—you'll often find that the object has inconsistencies, tears, and bleeds. In this case, you can use some really cool paint programs that allow you to paint directly onto the surface of a 3D object. This technique allows you to add a tremendous amount of detail to the 3D objects in your games.

Not all of the major 3D rendering packages offer 3D painting features in a native form (Studio 3D, for example), so you'll need to get a plug-in product.

Textures

Textures are simply graphical images that represent the surface of a 3D object. For example, consider a wooden chair object. Once the chair has been defined in a 3D environment, an artist will add depth to the object by wrapping a 2D wood surface texture around the 3D object. The artist would instruct the modeling program he or she is using that the 2D image is the surface of a particular portion of the 3D model.

Accomplished 3D artists typically develop an extensive library of textures. But we all have to begin somewhere. There are many different texture creation products and stock libraries available, and as you might expect, they are all sufficiently diverse enough that you might want to purchase as many of them as you can afford. I'll present a very comprehensive list of those texture libraries later in the chapter.

Imaging Software

While I haven't seen many games that have been developed with digitized photos, game designers and artists still make use of imaging software to put together their creations. The most popular imaging products are Debabilizer (a Mac-only product) and Adobe Photoshop. Both of these packages are used extensively throughout the industry. Imaging software like these two programs is great for taking 3D art and video files and adding effects to them. They can also be helpful for palette manipulation, fixing up "hand and scanned" artwork, reducing color schemes in high-color artwork, and other important tasks.

Conversion Software

Conversion software is found either as part of imaging software products like Photoshop or as lower-end products. These latter packages—mostly shareware—convert graphics file formats and resize and perform limited photo effects to files, usually in some sort of batch process.

Building Your Tool Suite

Art tools are some of the most expensive programs in the computer software industry. If you're a small developer and you don't have the cash to develop a huge selection of tools, you've got to save up, choose carefully, and make the most of lower-cost shareware products. Often, you can find cool shareware programs to help with tasks like file conversion, simpler image-processing operations, and even 3D modeling. In most cases, the registration fees cost one-sixth to one-third the cost of comparable commercial package.

Another trick is to look for bundling deals. Sometimes tools manufacturers run specials, bundling their products with other companies' products to offer computer users really good deals. This is one important reason you should pay close attention to the various computer art and multimedia magazines. (And yes, I will include a listing of art magazines at the end of this chapter.)

If you're a student, check to see if the company offers a student discount. Many of the major companies do offer such a discount, and you can save hundreds, if not thousands of dollars, by making the most of your student status.

Cool Art Products for Multiple Platforms

Most of the major development platforms have their own tools for creating various art content. However, a few major packages have versions available for multiple hardware platforms. These packages also tend to be among the best products around. First, we'll cover some of the multiple-platform products, then we'll highlight the platform-specific packages.

Paint Packages

We'll begin with a paint package that I feel is really exemplary. Of course, there are many more out there for you to evaluate, but this one is my favorite.

Fractal Design Painter 4.0 (Windows and Macintosh)
Fractal Design Corporation
P.O. Box 2380
Aptos, CA 95001
Phone: 408 688-5300 **Fax:** 408 688-8836
WWW: http://www.fractal.com

Fractal Design Painter was first released in 1991, and since then it's gotten rave reviews and found widespread use among all kinds of artists throughout the computer industry. Figure 12.3 shows a sample screen shot of the latest and greatest Fractal Design Painter 4.0.

The program provides a feature called "Natural-Media" painting, which lets you simulate on the screen processes that many artists perform using traditional art tools and media. For example, you can paint on the screen as if you were using charcoal on a sheet of paper or you can apply oil paints to different types of paper. This is an amazing feature and it helps many non-computer artists transition to the computer.

The newest version improves on all the features and it even brings back a useful feature that was discontinued. Once again you can create shapes by drawing vectors (lines) and then you can perform bitmap editing techniques on the lines drawn to fine tune your images. This is like having the features of Deluxe Paint and Corel Draw combined into one program.

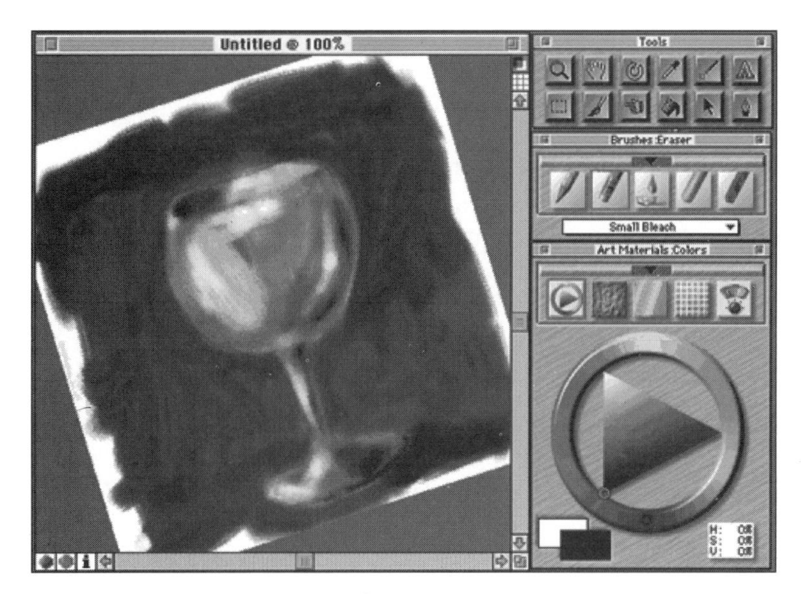

Figure 12.3 Fractal Design Painter.

If you are a Fractal Design Painter user, you'll want to check out the useful newsletter called *Artistry* published by a couple of independent computer artists from New York City. You can get your copy of *Artistry* by visiting Compuserve's GO GRAPHICS forum or by visiting *http://www.delta.com/peter/paint/tools/tools.htm* on the World Wide Web.

Modeling Software

One odd thing about 3D modeling software packages is that there aren't many available for multiple platforms. Lately, I've noticed a couple of packages moving into different platforms, but for the most part, the really great packages only work with a single platform. That said, there are a couple of interesting Mac/PC and SGI/PC packages available.

Poser (Windows and Macintosh)
Fractal Design Corporation
P.O. Box 2380
Aptos, CA 95001
Phone: 408 688-5300 **Fax:** 408 688-8836
WWW: http://www.fractal.com

The company that brought us the incredible Fractal Design Painter has a really neat solution for creating animated figures—a definite need of any game developer. This package, called Poser, is a modeling and rendering application that allows you to create an infinite variety of human figures that can be posed, rendered with surface

textures and multiple lights, and easily incorporated into artwork. Poser works closely with all kinds of products like Photoshop, Director, and, of course, Fractal's own Design Painter.

Both male and female base models—from infants and children to adults to super hero-like characters—are supplied, and each can be moved, modified, and shaped into any pose and viewed from any angle. If you grab the hand of a figure and move it, Poser knows exactly what to do with the rest of the arm. Once you've created the wire frame look you want, you can add light sources, texture and bump maps, and render the image. You can export the models as graphic images or as DXF files for use in other 3D packages.

Poser comes with a slew of libraries featuring lots of examples, body shapes, lighting schemes, and textures. Human figures are a necessity in game art, and creating them is difficult even for experienced artists. Fractal's Poser definitely fills a much needed gap.

LightWave (Amiga, Windows, NT, and SGI)
NewTek, Inc.
1200 SW Executive Drive
Topeka, KS 66615
Phone: 913 228-8000 **Fax:** 913 228-8099
WWW: http://www.newtek.com

Ever since NewTek came into existence as a top-flight creator of Amiga software, they have constantly amazed people with awesome products produced at an extremely low price point. Their modeling package LightWave, which works with Amiga, Windows, NT, and SGI, is no exception. It sells for under $1,000 and it offers excellent modeling capabilities, inverse kinematics for character animation, plug-ins, and simple creation of organic and aerodynamic objects with *metaforms*, which transform rough geometry into organic-looking objects.

LightWave allows you to render full ray tracing graphics and you can output your creations in a number of file formats. It also features key framing animation capabilities. LightWave also comes packed with license-free objects, images, and textures. Figure 12.4 shows an example of LightWave3D. This image came from the Web site at *http://cse.unl.edu/%7Emohrt/lightwave/* (which is a tutorial site that demos the product for you).

Here's a magazine designed to help you get the most out of LightWave. It offers a regular assortment of tips, tricks, news, and companion products for Newtek's LightWave 3D. The magazine comes in two formats: a printed version and a Web version. Contact:

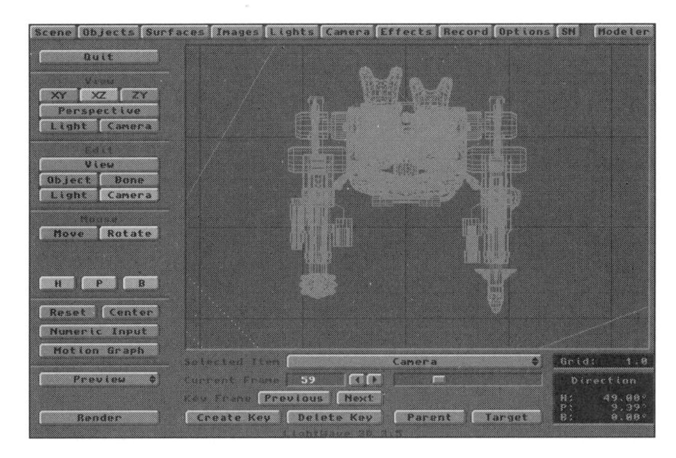

Figure 12.4 LightWave 3D example.

> **LightWave Pro Magazine**
> Avid Media Group
> **Phone:** 408 743-9250
> **WWW:** http://www.portal.com/~amg/

Martin Hash's 3-Dimensional Animation (Windows, Mac, and SGI)
Hash Inc.
2800 East Evergreen Blvd.
Vancouver, WA 98661
Phone: 360 750-0042 **Fax:** 360 750-0451
WWW: http://www.teleport.com/~hashinc/

While Animation Master is Hash's flagship product, they continue to push forward in developing low-cost, 3D animation packages. Martin Hash's 3-Dimensional Animation, which is available for Windows, Mac, and Power Mac platforms for a list price of $199, is just one more example of their objective. For small independent game developers, Hash's 3D experience and downright cheap price tag provide every reason to investigate this package, which rolls modeling, animating, and rendering into one bundle.

Beginners will find this package extremely helpful with its comprehensive online help, a training video, and a CD-ROM full of sample actors, props, scenery, and images. Among its standard features are such major 3D staples as spline-based modeling, character-based motion, inverse kinematics, patch modeling and animation, skin, materials, skeletal morphing and bending, ray tracing, and lip-synch keyframing. Whew! That's a lot of standard features!

Ray Dream Studio (Windows and Mac)
Ray Dream Inc.
1804 N. Shoreline Boulevard
Mountain View, CA 94043
Phone: 415 960-0768 **Fax:** 415 960-1198
WWW: http://www.raydream.com/

Ray Dream Studio is available for both the Mac and Windows platforms. Priced under $500, it seamlessly integrates four components: Ray Dream Designer 4, Ray Dream Animator, Dream Models, and Extensions Portfolio. These four products offer a complete 3D modeling and animation package that is priced just right for small individual developers. The Extensions Portfolio component allows customers, VARs, consultants, and developers to create product extensions and enhancements to the product.

The modeler, Ray Dream Designer 4, offers a full range of features such as perspective, subtle shadows, lighting effects, textures, and reflections. It also incorporates wizards that simplify the process of creating 3D images or scenes. This feature especially makes the package well-suited for beginners. The shader allows users to specify properties in several channels including color, highlight, shininess, bump, reflection, transparency, refraction, and a glow channel that makes objects appear to emit light. Finally, the package includes over 500 textures and 500 models.

The Animation model gives you access to inverse kinematics, rotoscoping, tweeners, object deformation, and object Behaviors. These are all features that are supported in packages costing hundreds, if not thousands, of dollars more.

Ray Dream was just getting their own home page setup as I was finishing this book. This user created site by David Ramirez almost fooled me into thinking it was the official Ray Dream site—it's that good. *http://www.webcom.com/~dram/rdd/welcome.html*

POV-RAY (DOS, MAC) + Associated Modelers (DOS, Windows, and MAC)
Walnut Creek CDROM
4041 Pike Lane, Suite D-www
Concord, CA 94520
Phone: 510 674-0783 **Fax:** 510 674-0821
Email: info@cdrom.com **WWW:** http://www.povray.org

Much of the shareware 3D modeling market revolves around a product called POV-RAY. (POV is short for Persistence Of Vision.) This highly capable rendering program was written for the public domain; the developers even allow you to have access to the program's source code.

The problem with POV-RAY is that it renders scenes but it doesn't construct them. For modeling, you'll have to use another program that works in conjunction with POV-RAY. There are several major POV-RAY-compatible modelers available, as is the latest version of the program itself, at the POV-RAY Web site or CompuServe's GRAPHICS forum (GO GRAPHICS).

You can also visit your local bookstore for one of many books dedicated to teaching you everything there is to know about POV-RAY and its associated modeling programs.

Imaging Products

As you read earlier, imaging software can do some pretty neat things to your art. I've listed two here that you will have plenty of fun with.

Adobe Photoshop (Windows, Macintosh, and SGI)
Adobe Corporation
1585 Charleston Road
P.O. Box 7900
Mountain View, CA 94039-7900
Phone: 415 961-4111 **Fax:** 415 967-9231
WWW: http://www.adobe.com

Perhaps the most well-known and awesome image processing product is Adobe Photoshop (see Figure 12.5). Originally a Mac-only product, it's now available for both Windows and Mac platforms. Photoshop really does so much it's hard to label

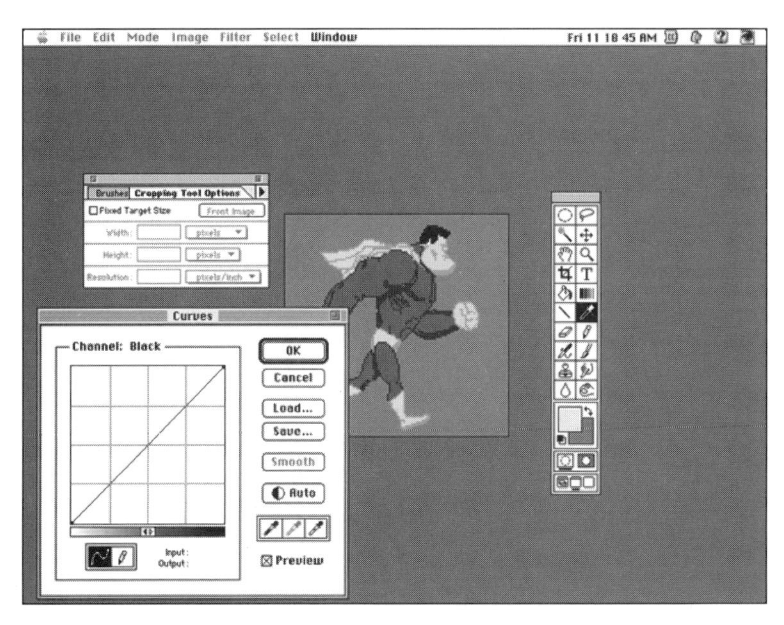

Figure 12.5 Using Photoshop to enhance an image.

it: It's a drawing package, a file conversion product, a digital effects product, and it has extensive photo-imaging capabilities and supports plug-in extensions. If you were able to buy only one product for your game art toolkit, Photoshop should be that product.

JAG II (Windows and Mac)
Ray Dream Inc.
1804 N. Shoreline Boulevard
Mountain View, CA 94043
Phone: 415 960-0768 **Fax:** 415 960-1198
WWW: http://www.raydream.com/

Available for both Macintosh and Windows, this is an interesting utility that automatically smoothes the jagged edges in digital images and animations. Used in post production, JAG can improve the quality of images created in painting, photo-retouching, and video applications after you've done everything you want.

Kai's Power Tools (Windows, Macintosh, and SGI)
MetaTools, Inc.
6303 Carpinteria Avenue
Carpinteria, CA 93013
Phone: 805 566-6200 **Fax:** 805 566-6385
WWW: http://www.metatools.com

Several years ago, Kai Krause, a leading computer artist, began designing a line of computer graphics tools that today is widely known as Kai's Power Tools (KPT). Versions are available for Windows, Macintosh, and Silicon Graphics. KPT is a set of powerful utilities that operate as plug-ins for products like Adobe Photoshop, Fractal Design Painter, Autodesk Animator Studio, and other programs that implement "Adobe's plug-in technology."

KPT is used by artists to expand their ability to work with and manipulate scanned images. The product gives you gradient designing, texture designing, and other graphical assistance.

The latest version of KPT (3.0) is only available for the Mac; however, MetaTools is planning ports to the other platforms.

Here's an additional KPT Website you'll want to check out: Kai's Power Tips and Tricks for Adobe Photoshop, *http://the-tech.mit.edu/KPT/*. (This is a reprint of 23 tips and tricks that were developed by Kai Krause.)

Pyromania (Mac and PC)
Visual Concept Entertainment
Box 921226
Sylmar, CA 91392-1226
Phone: 818 367-9187 **Fax:** 818 362-3490

Do you like to blow up stuff? If so, this is the product for you. Some special effects people got together and created the pyromania CDs, which come with high resolution 640×480 images and animations of elements like explosions, all kinds of fires, flames, smoke, and space explosions. You can use these images royalty free in any product and many game developers have already. This is one of the special products that really is a jewel to find and use because it gives you access to high quality art and special effects for a low price. There are two products: Pyromania 1 for PCs and Mac and Pyromania 2, which so far is Mac format only. Both products sell for $199.

The PC Platform: Dos, Windows, and NT

Believe it or not, the PC is actually a good platform for artwork creation. While I doubt I'm revealing top-secret information by saying that the range of tools available for the Mac is better and easier to deal with, the PC really does have a number of just plain excellent products.

Painting and Imaging Packages

Just take a look at the products I've listed in this section and you will surely be amazed at the number of quality products for the PC. All of the packages have several unique features that will help you to narrow down your choice to a product that really suits your needs.

Autodesk Animator Pro and Animator Studio (Windows)
Autodesk
111 McInnis Parkway
San Rafael, CA 94903
Phone: 800 879-4233 **Fax:** 206 860-2196
WWW: http://www.autodesk.com

Autodesk Animator Pro, which recently was put through a major update, is probably the best PC-based animation package available (see Figure 12.6). Let's take a look at some of its more interesting features.

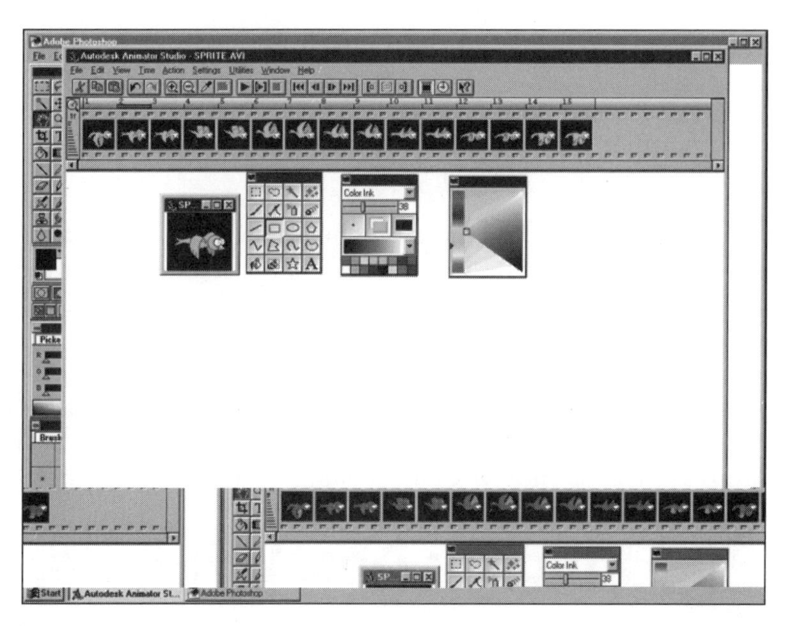

Figure 12.6 Using Autodesk's Animator Pro to create PC animations.

Animator handles 24-bit color with 8-bit alpha-channel transparency, and works with Photoshop-compatible plug-ins like Kai's Power Tools. You can even paint on a multiframe animation using video sprites. For example, suppose you've got one animation running; you can run another animation and create a composite animation from both of them.

Animator's animation features include a full set of graphics functions, including airbrush, lines, fill, and the other usual characters. This program also supports onion skinning to do great line art animation.

With its newest release, Autodesk has added an integrated studio for recording, editing, and synchronizing audio from sources such as CDs, tapes, and external microphones. Sophisticated editing features include the ability to independently modify pitch and tempo to stretch or "squeeze" a sound track to fit an animation without changing its pitch.

Overall, if you're not dealing with a major SGI package and you need animation capabilities, you're going to have to search far and wide to find a better animation package than either Animator Pro or Animator Studio.

Deluxe Animation (DOS)
Electronic Arts
1450 Fashion Island Boulevard
San Mateo, CA 94404
Phone: 415 571-7171 **Fax:** 415 570-5137

Like its sister product Deluxe Paint, Deluxe Animation is a now discontinued product that has found its way into many a game developer's tool box. This product allows developers to create frame-by-frame animations of sprites. It works just like Deluxe Paint except you can edit all kinds of screens and test the playback of them by having the product automatically page flip the screens. It also offers some limited automatic animation tools, as well.

The bad new is that this product supports only 256 colors and only 320×200 resolution. But even when you're working with a product in 640×480 resolution, many of the sprites aren't bigger than 320×200 so the resolution problem, while a drawback, isn't a huge deal.

Despite being discontinued, you'll still find this product around—and it's priced right. So, if you can get your hands on a rare copy, don't let it go!

Deluxe Paint IIe (DOS)
Electronic Arts
1450 Fashion Island Boulevard
San Mateo, CA 94404
Phone: 415 571-7171 **Fax:** 415 570-5137

Deluxe Paint is still considered one of the best pixel-pushing editors around. Its suite of tools and easy-to-use interface, as shown in Figure 12.7, allows artists to get down and dirty and really edit at the pixel level. As of early spring 1995, EA has discontinued production of this product, although you'll still find copies. Pick it up if you see it!

Shareware

Are you on a shoestring budget? No problem! Here's one of several quality shareware paint packages.

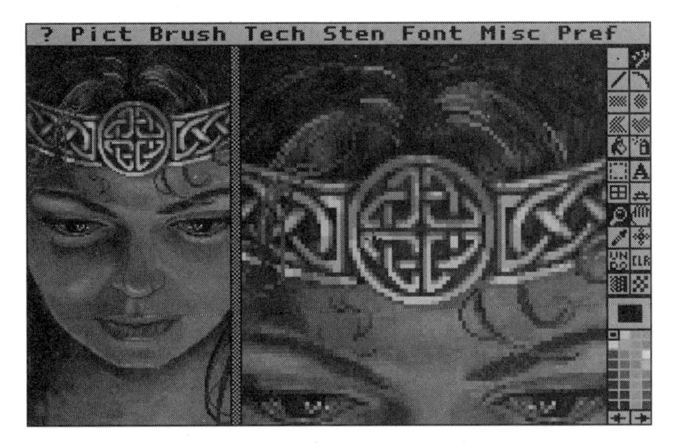

Figure 12.7 Deluxe Paint II.

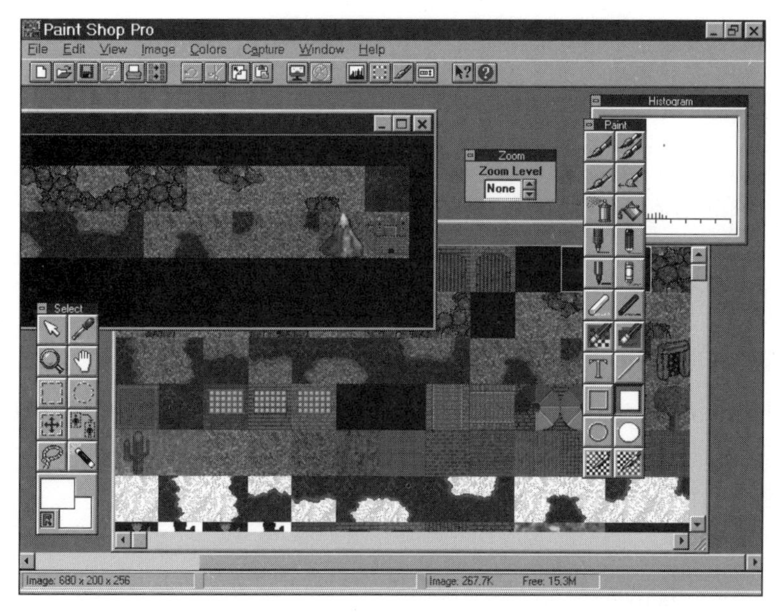

Figure 12.8 The complete shareware painting program, Paint Shop Pro.

Paint Shop Pro (Windows)
JASC, Inc.
PO Box 44997
Eden Prairie, MN 55344
Phone: 612 930-9171 **Fax:** 612 930-9172
WWW: http://www.jasc.com/

For a $69 registration fee, you get one of the best bargains in art tools. Paint Shop Pro is a Windows paint package with a lot of power, as shown in Figure 12.8. It has seen numerous enhancements over the years and no doubt will see more. Currently, this product is a real work horse offering the usual array of drawing options, as well as support for numerous file formats (making it an excellent conversion utility). In addition, it features an array of image-processing options, including plug-in architecture compatibility for Kai's Power Tools. In fact for $99, JASC will send you both Paint Shop Pro *and* a special version of Kai's Power Tools!

Three-Dimensional Artwork and Animation Products

While the PC has never been known as an overall graphics powerhouse, it has been unusually blessed with several top-notch 3D modeling and animation packages. Now with Pentium processors, Windows NT, and 3D graphics cards hitting the market in earnest, a new round of 3D products is emerging that is giving birth to a new round of unbelievable 3D power.

Autodesk 3D Studio (DOS) and 3D Studio Max (Windows NT)
Autodesk
111 McInnis Parkway
San Rafael, CA 94903
Phone: 800 879-4233 **Fax:** 206 860-2196
WWW: http://www.autodesk.com

When the Atari ST and Amiga shipped, each included a major art package: DEGAS on the ST and Deluxe Paint on the Amiga. The two programs' respective creators, Tom Hudson and Dan Silva, went on to play critical roles in the development of one of the best 3D rendering products for IBM/DOS-based systems, 3D Studio.

3D Studio has been in use by a majority of top-notch game development shops for many years. Even with the move by the larger publishers to Silicon Graphics-based workstations, many still use 3D Studio. In fact, Trilobyte, the company behind the 7th Guest and now the 11th Hour, used 3D Studio for both products.

In the life of 3D Studio, 1995 was an important year: the product was split into two distinct product lines. The Yost Group, the actual programmers of 3D Studio, have totally redesigned 3D Studio into a new product called 3D Studio Max. Since 3D Studio Max is for Windows NT only, Autodesk has committed to releasing further upgrades of the current 3D Studio product, which runs in a DOS environment.

How long this strategy lasts is probably based on customer demand. Rest assured, though, that 3D Studio users, while seeing amazing advanced features implemented in 3D Studio Max, will see further work and functionality in 3D Studio, as well. Perhaps they will even move that product into Windows 95 and sell it as a scaled down version of 3D Studio Max. Stranger things have definitely happened.
3D Studio Max represents a complete redesign of the original product. As SGI workstations began moving in on what was basically 3D Studio's turf, the team at Autodesk and The Yost Group sat down and began reworking the entire product. Almost three years later they have ended up with a Intel architecture product that gives a lot of the SGI packages more than a run for their money.

The biggest change resulted in 3D Studio Max being a Windows NT product, not DOS, not Windows 95, just Windows NT. This really isn't a big deal. To get the best performance from 3D Studio previously, many developers were running it on state of the art hardware anyway, so switching to Windows NT for most 3D studio veterans should not be a hardware upgrade headache.

The entire product has been built around object-oriented programming, giving 3D Studio Max exceptional plug-in architecture and allowing for quick updates in addition to the more esoteric abilities like human modeling, various platform support, and facial expressions.

Additional 3D Studio Max features include:

- A developer API document
- A multitasking, multithreaded environment
- Multiple processor and 3D acceleration hardware support
- Advance Time Editing, which allows you to synchronize animation with sound
- A Space Warps plug-in, which allows you to create cool worm holes, explosions, and black hole effects

Speaking of plug-ins, 3D Studio Max has created a really rich environment for plug-ins, which will undoubtedly produce lots of cool accessories—both in-house and third party—some of it specifically for game developers.

In fact, one plug-in, Biped, is such an important tool, it warrants discussion. One of the major problems that the SGI platform addressed was animation. The Biped software combines several technology firsts with very advanced inverse kinematics (IK) and skinning functions to make any two-legged character move at any pace, with corresponding gait, arm swings, and center-of-gravity dynamics.

Biped incorporates lots of awesome flexibility in the way you render animations. Literally by controlling footprints on the screen, you can create fluid walking, running, and jumping characters.

Biped incorporates three major processes to create animations:

- **Step-Driven Animation** Given a sequence of footprints, along with their timing, Biped generates an initial rough sketch of the keyframes for a movement. Changing the positions of these footprints results in a change in the associated creature's motion, as it precisely follows the footprint positions.
- **Free-Form Keyframing** The user may add or alter keyframes of Biped software's initial rough sketch in a free-form manner, changing any motion associated with the target creature. Keyframes and footprints can be modified independently. Biped's flexibility lets the animator adjust footprint locations and timing at any point during the animation development process by adapting the keyframed motions to match the changes made to the footprints.
- **Physics-Based Interpolation** Unlike spline-based schemes employed by other animation systems, Biped's keyframe interpolation specifically takes into account the kinematics and dynamics of a two-legged creature under the influence of gravity (which, by the way, is user definable).

Biped also has a skeletal/skin deformation feature much like the various SGI packages do; this helps render bulging muscles and other skin characteristics easily.

Basically, 3D Studio Max is the cat's meow when it comes to PC based 3D animation packages. And its relatively low price is just going to put it in the hands of even more developers.

Here's a good unofficial Autodesk Products users page: *http://www.opencad.com/Magic_Mirror/.* Check out this site for comprehensive information about using Autodesk products—especially 3D Studio from the pro's that use 'em daily.

Truespace2 (Windows)
Caligari Corporation
1933 Landings Drive
Mountain View, CA 94043
Phone: 415 390-9600 **Fax:** 415 390-9755
Email: sales@caligari.com **WWW:** http://www.caligari.com

Truespace originally started out as a 3D rendering package for the Amiga in the late 80s. While the demise of the Amiga really killed Truespace, the program has had a kind of glorious rebirth as the major competition to 3D Studio from Autodesk.

This package's basic drawing features include drawing spline shapes into 3D objects, constructing a 3D object from any 2D shape, creating 3D beveled text with any TrueType font, rendering up to 24-bits with alpha channel, and the ability to include transparencies and shadow and fog effects.

Truespace also offers powerful animation capabilities, which include field rendering and animated textures, motion blur and depth of field, support for FLC (Autodesk) and AVI (Microsoft Video) video formats, morphing, frame-by-frame animation, and easily definable 3D animation paths for objects.

Truespace is entirely icon driven and works with Photoshop-compatible plug-ins so you can use products like Kai's Power Tools directly in the program. Truespace also uses Intel's 3DR to provide realtime solid rendering. This eliminates the need for mesh frames in edit mode. (The mesh mode is still available if you prefer to use this feature.) Truespace also comes with a CD-ROM of 600 3D clip objects and hundreds of textures and materials like wood, glass, stone, and more.

Of special note is that Caligari Truespace is now available to SONY PSX developers as a native PSX application. So the cross-development capabilities for IBM to Sony Playstation are extremely solid in regards to Truespace!

Animation Master (Windows)
Hash Inc.
2800 East Evergreen Boulevard
Vancouver, WA 98661

Phone: 360 750-0042 **Fax:** 360 750-0451
WWW: http://www.teleport.com/~hashinc/

Animation Master is quite a powerful and inexpensive 3D modeling and animation package. It's specifically designed for character animation, providing a very powerful spline-based modeling system, and including such features as character morphing, facial movements, and direct support for the Polhumus motion capture system.

Animation Master takes a full 3D character animation system—Playmation's 3D—and adds all kinds of major rendering features and several new high-end features like inverse kinematics, motion blur, field rendering, shadow buffers, and depth buffers.

This product is available in versions for Windows and Windows NT workstations (Alpha, MIPs, and Intel), and all object and motion files are completely portable. With the Windows version, you can use a Windows network to increase rendering times and flexibility.

The Macintosh and Power Macintosh Platforms

Even if you're a PC-only developer, having a Mac around might be a good thing. The Mac not only offers a wide range of excellent art creation products, but if you own any dual platform products that were originally released as Mac products, you'll get earlier updates.

Paint Packages

Again, let's start with paint products. We covered Fractal Design Painter and Photoshop earlier but there is one Mac-specific package widely used for painting on the Mac Platform.

Studio 8/32
Electronic Arts
1450 Fashion Island Boulevard
San Mateo, CA 94404
Phone: 415 571-7171 **Fax:** 415 570-5137

This is one of the most popular paint programs for the Mac. While I believe it's been discontinued, you might still find a copy or two sitting around some of the larger mail-order houses.

Three-Dimensional Artwork and Animation Products

Here is where the Mac truly excels. The products I've listed here rival the 3D Studio Maxx package we discussed earlier.

Extreme 3D
Macromedia, Incorporated
600 Townsend Street
San Francisco, CA 94103
Phone: 415 252-2000 **Fax:** 415 626-0554
Email: info@macromedia.com **WWW:** http://www.macromedia.com

Extreme 3D began life as a 3D creation product known as Macromodel. The reborn Extreme 3D uses spline-based modeling and includes some new features (such as surface trim) and user interface improvements. Most notable is that Macromedia has replaced its rendering module, which used to be Pixar's RenderMan, with its own renderer. One other significant improvement is that all object and scene animations are now time-based and frame-based.

Specular Infini-D
Specular International
479 West Street
Amherst, MA 01002
Phone: 413 253-3100 **Fax:** 413 253-0540
WWW: http://www.specular.com

Infini-D is a powerful spline-based modeler with photorealistic rendering. Infini-D features excellent texture flexibility with a built-in texture generator, animated textures, and much more. Another cool feature is the ability to take any Adobe Illustrator or Macromedia FreeHand file and turn it into a 3D object. Also, you can use any Adobe Photoshop file as a texture, lighting gel, or background. Visit their web site and download a working demo copy of the program.

Strata Studio Pro
Strativision, Inc.
2 West George Boulevard
St. George, UT 84770
Phone: 801 628-5218 **Fax:** 801 628-9756
WWW: http://www.strata.com

Strativision has perhaps one of the best advertisements available for its 3D rendering product; it was used by the Miller brothers to create MYST. And any product that created that spectacular display of 3D animation has a lot going for it.

This product offers all of the major 3D animation features, including metaballs, 3D sculpting, extrude along path, photo-realistic ray tracing with atmospheric effects, and much more.

Strativision recently received an equity investment from computer graphics stalwart Evans & Sutherland, which is bound to enhance future upgrades of this package. Rumor also has it that there is a Windows version in the works.

Image Processing Products

Aside from Photoshop, there is one other mainstay among the Mac art community that makes all the rest of us PC people envious.

DeBabelizer Toolbox 1.6 and Debabelizer Lite (MAC)
Equilibrium Technologies
3 Harbor Drive, Ste. 111
Sausalito, CA 94965
Phone: 415 332-4343 **Fax:** 415 332-4433

I hate the fact this tool is only available for the Mac. It is a major image processing and big-time palette manipulation program that for many is just indispensable. This award-winning product includes dozens of essential editing tools for automated image processing while also providing extensive translation for over 60 bit-mapped graphics and animation formats.

Its biggest and most praised feature is its 24-bit to 8-bit color reduction and palette controls. Among them is a feature called SuperPalette, which automatically creates the best palette for a series of images. It can even modify effects over time on a series of QuickTime frames, still images, or other animation files. DeBabelizer runs native on any Power Mac or 680x0 machine.

The DeBabelizer Lite package is less expensive and translates between over 55 different cross platform bit-mapped formats. It does *not* however offer internal scripting, image processing, or palette manipulation as the full version does.

Silicon Graphics Indigo Workstations

On the SGI platform more products and technology have been developed by the companies that produce high-end graphics tools than companies who make lower end products. Currently, some of the higher end products are being purchased by PC companies to bring these tools down to the larger, PC-based markets. For example, SoftImage was purchased by Microsoft and SGI bought the other two graphic product mainstays, Alias and Wavefront.

This is important because the strategic relationships these deals form may decide the product you use, either by its success or because the company you work for or with, say for example Sega, cuts a deal with them. Sega, in fact, has a major deal with Microsoft and SoftImage to make SoftImage the official 3D development product for Sega's Saturn.

Project Maya

With SGI buying Wavefront and Alias they have discovered some overlapping products. To clarify their high-end graphic software situation, SGI announced Project Maya. Project Maya will merge the two product lines into a single line, using new software to produce a smooth, convergent upgrade path for users of the products.

With Project Maya, SGI is trying to focus on the creation of synthetic actors and environments. The goal is to support the key character features like facial movements and motion capture. Already, both Alias and Wavefront have incredible software technology in this area, but Project Maya is meant to symbolize the importance and speed at which SGI is moving in this area. The creation of digital actors is important for both SGI's fast-growing game-development customers, as well as its bread-and-butter Hollywood-studio customers.

Project Maya is to be an open architecture system and will include plug-ins and some sort of scripting language. Overall, it's an exciting time to be doing development with tools like SoftImage and Project Maya. With the weight of SGI and Microsoft now behind SoftImage, Alias, and Wavefront, we can also expect a much more accelerated rate of development. Although you will see some implementation of the Project Maya in the latest round of Alias and WaveFront products, SGI has said that the real implementation of Project Maya won't hit until late 1996.

Paint and Imaging Packages

The SGI platform has some really awesome paint and imaging packages that span the whole range of expected features. Let's take a look.

Amazon Paint/Amazon 3D Paint/Piranha Animator
Interactive Effects, Inc.
102 Nighthawk
Irvine, CA 92714
Phone: 714 551-1448 **Fax:** 714 786-2527
WWW: http://www.webcom.com/~ie/

These three packages offer a complete high-end graphics paint system for SGI workstations. All three packages list for $3,000. Let's look at the features that you get for this steep price tag.

Amazon Paint In development for over four years, Amazon Paint is a leading paint system for Silicon Graphics workstations. This package has over 50 image-processing tools, plug-in architecture support for products like Kai's Power Tools, over 20 special brush effects, advanced texture mapping, as well as support for any Type1 Postscript fonts.

Amazon 3D Paint Using Amazon's 3D paint you can paint directly onto the surface and across the seams of multiple 3D models with all the functionality of the 2D version of Amazon Paint. Support exists for model files created in Wavefront, Alias, and SoftImage.

Piranha Animator Piranha Animator is Amazon Paint with advance scripting and keyframe animation support. Among its features are rotoscoping, advanced editing, matte animation with a range of different composing functions, and compatibility with a number of external rendering and output devices for digital video production.

Some pretty prestigious game developers use these tools, including Acclaim, LucasArts, Capcom, Namco, and Cyan, to name but a few.

GameGen

MultiGen Inc.
550 S. Winchester Blvd., #500
San Jose, CA 95128
Phone: 408 261-4100 **Fax:** 408 261-4101
WWW: http://www.multigen.com

As MultiGen says in their press literature: "GameGen is the realtime interactive 3D game authoring toolset specifically designed to create render-ready databases that run smoothly and economically on the target game platform of your choice."

Basically we're talking about a game-specific 3D modeling and animating system much like Alias|Wavefront's GameWare package. (I'll cover this package in the *Three-Dimensional Modeling and Animation* section.) GameGen features all sorts of 3D modeling perks, including realtime previews, morphing, and multi-platform file support (Nintendo, Ultra 64, Sony Playstation, and PCs with 3D graphics cards).

One thing the folks at MultiGen are pushing hard is the future. Recently they demonstrated a fully immersive 3D construction product called SmartModel. Using a head mounted display and two datagloves, artists can actually interactively model 3D scenes. (I just want to know one thing: Who's going to bother completing games when playing with the modeling software is just as fun?) The software was shown at SIGGRAPH '95 to well-received reviews and is scheduled for release in spring 1996.

Nichimen's Graphics Tools

Nichimen Graphics

12555 W. Jefferson Blvd. #285
Los Angeles, CA 90066
Phone: 310 577-0500 **Fax:** 310 577-0577
WWW: http://www.nichimen.com

Nichimen is yet another company offering cool high-end SGI tools devoted to game developers. This company offers a full suite of tools for rendering, painting, and animating art specifically tailored for games.

N-Paint A 2D paint package loaded with various special effects, rotoscoping abilities, animation functionality, and extensive scripting capabilities to automate repetitive tasks.

N-Geometry This modeling package can output any number of animation formats: rendered frames, SGI movie files, 3D game animation files, skeletal motion capture files, images, objects, scripts, or attribute sets.

N-Dynamics Nichimen's systems animation package.

N-Render Nichimen's rendering package.

Action Editor This special product facilitates using Nichimen's tools to specifically create content for the Sony Playstation.

Three-Dimensional Modeling and Animation

SGI systems really shine when it comes to three-dimensional modeling and animation. After all, SGI machines really have the processor horsepower over their PC and Mac counterparts to perform the complex processing needed to handle 3D. Let's take a look at a few of the more popular 3D packages.

Power Animator and GameWare
Alias|WaveFront
110 Richmond Street East
Toronto, Ontario Canada
M5C 1P1
Phone: 416 362-9181 **Fax:** 416 362-0630
WWW: http://www.aw.sgi.com/

Alias and Wavefront were once major competitors in the high-end 3D graphics software market. That was until Silicon Graphics decided to purchase both the companies and merge them together as Alias|Wavefront. The resulting alliance promises to be an important force, as I described in the brief explanation to SGI's Project Maya endeavor.

For now, though, developers "only" have access to the current incarnations of some mind-boggingly awesome graphics software. Specifically, among the products both companies offer, the two most often used by game developers are Alias' Power Animator and WaveFront's GameWare.

In creating GameWare, Wavefront has combined the traditional artistic creation of art with the technical specs used in games. For example, this product has a powerful 3D graphics rendering engine that takes into account the color and geometry limitations of consoles and various PC platforms. Thus, you can render a really high-resolution person with all kinds of textures, and GameWare will redraw that graphic to work as best as possible for the desired platform by rendering new reduced palettes or creating 2D graphical versions of its 3D renderings.

Additionally, because this is high-end technology, WaveFront offers training and assistance in the entire GameWare process. The trainers and support techs are knowledgeable about game development and the industry, not just 3D rendering and artwork creation.

Overall, this software might be out of your reach—technically and financially—but like everything in this business, you can expect that the features and ideas here will trickle down over time. However, I advise you to be as familiar with this product (and other such products) as possible; if you sign on with a bigger company or publisher, you may find yourself with access to this high-end suite of tools. Of course, when you're interviewing with one of these large companies, it's best to sound knowledgeable on the latest technological trends.

Here's an unofficial Web site you can access to get the latest information and tips on these products: (*http://www.uni-uppertal.de/computer/software/grafik/Alias/welcome.english.html*). This is a cool well-run unofficial Web home page. You'll find lots of links and some software also.

SoftImage 3D and SoftImage Toonz
Microsoft Corporation
1 Microsoft Way
Redmond, WA
Phone: 206 882-8080
WWW: http://www.softimage.com

SoftImage, creators of high-end animation tools, found themselves thrust into the spotlight when Microsoft plunked down a whopping $135 million to buy the company. What's really cool about SoftImage is that it's geared to cel animators and replicates—in software—the traditional, hand-crafted cel animation.

SoftImage, in its role as a supplier to Sega for Saturn Development Tools, is incorporating a set of extensions in SoftImage 3D. This toolkit includes Saturn file output filters, color reduction tools to move down from 24-bit images, and an online viewer to preview images as they would look on a Saturn.

Figure 12.9 A screen shot of SoftImage from the company's Web site.

Version 4.0 of SoftImage, as shown in Figure 12.9 incorporates such cutting-edge features as pencil testing, palette editing, an ink and paint module, and a flip module, and can be further customized by adding separate modules for scanning and rendering.

And if you're disappointed because you don't use an SGI platform, you'll be happy to hear that a Windows NT version of SoftImage's product line is in production.

SoftImage's users page can be accessed at (*http://delphi.beckman.uiuc.edu/softimage/*). Here's where all those SoftImage fanatics are hanging out. Check out this comprehensive Unofficial SoftImage Web page for complete information on the SoftImage community.

Texture Creation Products

In researching this book, I talked to several 3D artists and I heard the same thing from all of them: You can never have enough textures when doing 3D work. With that in mind, I searched out the best texture libraries and texture creation products.

What's amazing is that each of these products offers a different approach or a different set of textures. From wild geometric patterns to alien skin textures to all takes on wood and fabrics and surfaces, you might find yourself in the poorhouse if you invest in all of these products. And believe me, each one is worth the investment.

For 3D artists, textures are a lifelong pursuit. So, if you're serious about doing 3D work, it's high time you got started on that texture library!

Alien Skin Textureshop
Virtus Corporation
118 Mackenan Drive, Suite 250
Cary, NC 27511-3625
Phone: 919 467-9700 **Fax:** 919 460-4530
Email: info@virtus.com **WWW:** http://www.virtus.com

Ohhhh aliens! Everybody loves a good slimy (or scaly, smooth, or metallic for that matter) alien. Alien Skin Textureshop is a neat product that allows you to create cool alien skin for your 2D and 3D products. It runs either as a Photoshop plug-in or as a standalone product.

Adobe TextureMaker
Adobe Systems, Inc.
Mountain View, CA
Phone: 415 961-4400 **Fax:** 415 961-3769
Email: info@adobe.com **WWW:** http://www.adobe.com

This Mac-only package is Adobe's entry into the texture creation business. TextureMaker excels at creating those staple textures like wood, marble, and sandstone. You can also use this product to create different skin surfaces (though not like Alien Skin) and other organic textures. TextureMaker also offers various animation effects.

Xaos Tools' Terrazzo
Xaos Tools, Inc.
600 Townsend Street, 270 East
San Francisco, CA 94103
Phone: 415 487-7000 **Fax:** 415 558-9886

This product uses various mathematical algorithms, many based on symmetrical routines, to create simple but really cool textures.

TextureScape
Specular International
479 West Street
Amherst, MA 01002
Phone: 413 253-3100 **Fax:** 413 253-0540
WWW: http://www.specular.com

Just for starters, TextureScape comes with 750 textures. That number alone is worth the price of admission. This product isn't just a library of textures (of which you can purchase more), but an entire new texture-generation system. *MacUser* wrote about this product "Unsurpassed in the level of control it provides over texture composition."

TextureScape allows you to create all kinds of amazing textures and output them in a variety of graphics formats (PICT, TIFF , EPSF, and Quicktime, among others). You can even create animated textures by choosing keyframes and then letting TextureScape morph them from frame to frame, outputting the result as a Quicktime movie.

Texture Libraries

As more and more 3D games are developed, the demand on 3D artists is growing dramatically. Rapidly building a kick butt texture library should be one of your primary concerns when ramping up for 3D production. The following libraries can serve as excellent foundations for such an endeavor.

Texture Universe
Autodesk
111 McInnis Parkway
San Rafael, CA 94903
Phone: 800 225-6106 **Fax:** 206 860-2196
WWW: http://www.autodesk.com

This CD-ROM contains over 400 ready-to-use textures and backgrounds. The collection is pretty wide-ranging, from wall surfaces to animal skins. A utility is included for browsing and searching the textures in either DOS or Windows.

Fractal Design's Really Cool Textures
The Sensational Surfaces CD-ROM
Fractal Design Corporation
P.O. Box 2380
Aptos, CA 95001
Phone: 408 688-5300 **Fax:** 408 688-8836
WWW: http://www.fractal.com

The makers of Fractal Design Painter have five texture libraries, all modestly priced. One, known more specifically as The Sensational Surfaces CD-ROM, contains five libraries of 20 natural textures each, including wood, paper, stone, stone tiles, and other surfaces. The CD-ROM contains both the Macintosh and Windows versions of the textures.

The CD-ROM is derived from the textures created by Artbeats Software, Inc., a premier supplier of textures for computer art and multimedia. Most of these textures are photographic in origin and bring a further sense of reality to natural-media capabilities.

Artbeats Texture Collections
Artbeats Software, Inc.
2611 South Myrtle Road
Myrtle Creek, OR 97457
Phone: 503 863-4429 **Fax:** 503 863-4547

Artbeats Software, Inc. is a leading developer and publisher of background and digitized images for pre-press and multimedia users. Artbeats' products include Prelude, Seamless Textures Collection Volume I, Marble & Granite, Wood & Paper, and Marbled Paper Textures. The company has also created some specific bundled packages, including Backgrounds for Multimedia Bundle, Volumes 1 and 2, and the Full Page Images EPSF Library.

Wild Tiles!
Cameo Graphics
3400 Jackson Street
Oxnard, CA 93033
Phone: 805 486-5591 **Fax:** 805 486-5591

Wild Tiles! is a collection of over 2,000 300×300 tileable designs rendered in various file formats. None of these textures is your run-of-the-mill photo-realistic types, which makes this collection a great alternative.

Wraptures Volumes 1 & 2 and Page Overtures Volumes 1 & 2
Form and Function
1595 Seventeenth Avenue
San Francisco, CA 94122
Phone: 415 664-4010 **Fax:** 415 664-4030

Wraptures is a collection of 250 seamless tileable photographic textures. Each set costs about $120 and contains over 100 textures. You can request free literature from Form and Function, which gives you a thumbnail of every texture in the collection. Each texture comes in multiple-bit depths and sizes, and all are royalty free.

Page Overtures is another two volume set of textured images. Unlike Wraptures, these textures are not designed for the 3D market. The images are more or less sized, and are at a color depth for page layout and paint products. Still, this is a great-looking collection of photo-realistic textures that any good artist could bring into Photoshop, resize, and drop the bit depth to make use of the texture in 3D work.

Three-Dimensional Libraries

As 3D worlds become constantly more complex, the use of 3D clip art is going to increase. There are many reasons to use 3D art and just as many reasons to not use it. Most notably is that many models are optimized for game development, meaning they've got a large amount of polygons, which isn't exactly good for on-the-fly animation. Others aren't exactly what you want, and still others are just not very good. However, there are some quality 3D libraries and 3D model "brokers" that you can use to cut down on the time and cost associated with in-house 3D model production.

Here are some resources for 3D clip art.

Three-Dimensional Object Stock Libraries

The libraries listed here should provide you with an abundance of images for your projects.

Viewpoint DataLabs International
625 South State Street
Orem, UT 84058
Phone: 801 229-3000 **Fax:** 801 220-3300
WWW: http://www.datalabs.com

Viewpoint Datalabs is best described as a 3D modeling brokerage. This company manages a large database of 3D models, which, when converted, can be used in a wide variety of top programs. Artists can actually submit 3D models for Viewpoint to resell. The whole process works over the Internet. Figure 12.10 shows a screen shot of some of the images available on their Web site.

As this database grows and catches on, it will become an awesome resource for those out-of-the-way models—like spacecraft, human figures, and such—that are so often needed for games.

Viewpoint bought the rights to the Avalon's online 3D database, which was the leading Internet site for public domain 3D models.

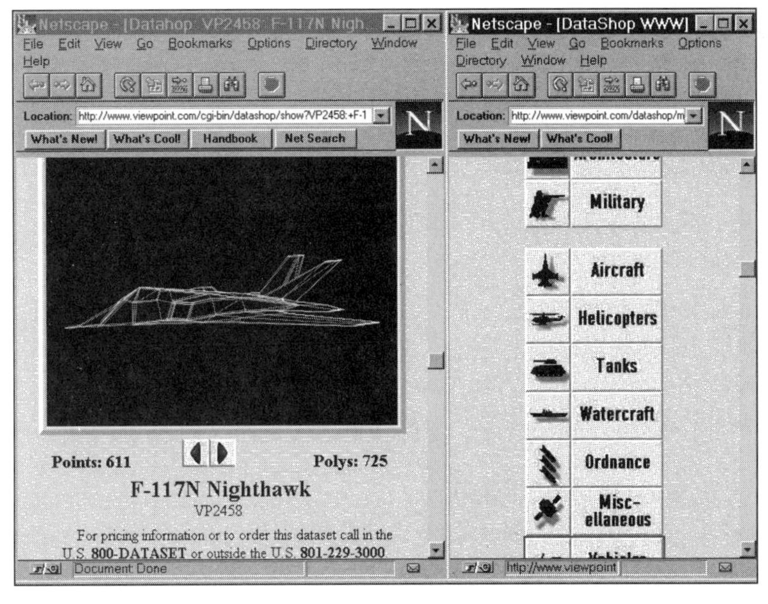

Figure 12.10 Some images from Viewpoint's Datalabs Web site.

Viewpoint took over management of the old China Lake free 3D model archive some time ago. If you go to their Web site, you can fully access all the cool models that were available at China Lake here now—all for free!

The Mesh Mart
WWW: `http://cedar.cic.net/~rtilmann/mm/index.htm`

The Mesh Mart is another online 3D object broker being developed by Richard Tilmann. While Viewpoint is larger, The Mesh Mart will provide a source of 3D mesh object files for the growing number of 3D modeling artists and developers.

The UK-VR Sig 3D Object Archive
WWW: `http://www.dcs.ed.ac.uk/~mxr/objects.html`

Yet another 3D model archive but with a slight twist. It focuses on free models that are optimized for VR applications. Their models are often compact, simpler representations making them also excellent for games. Criterion, maker of the 3D game library Renderware, is a supporter of the site, which is maintained on behalf of the United Kingdom Virtual Reality Special Interest Group (UK VR-SIG).

CD-ROM-Based Libraries

The libraries listed here are all collected on CD-ROM.

3D Props CD-Roms
Autodesk
111 McInnis Parkway
San Rafael, CA 94903
Phone: 800 879-4233 **Fax:** 206 860-2196
WWW: http://www.autodesk.com

Autodesk, which recently entered the 3D model library arena, currently has two CD-ROMs each containing over 300 models.

Replica 3D Libraries
Specular International
479 West Street
Amherst, MA 01002
Phone: 413 253-3100 **Fax:** 413 253-0540
WWW: http://www.specular.com

From the developer of the Macintosh-based modeling software Infini-D, comes 13 volumes of 3D models. Among the various categories are furniture, transportation, dinosaurs, starships, and human forms. You also find several texture volumes to use as well.

Three-Dimensional Conversion Products

Unfortunately, not every developer uses the same packages to produce games. Even some of your own packages might not offer compatible file formats for you to move among products. Here is one piece of conversion software that is sure to help you.

InterChange
Syndesis Corporation
235 South Main Street
Jefferson, WI 53549
Phone: 414 674-5200 **Fax:** 414 674-6363
WWW: http://www.webmaster.com/syndesis/

InterChange, available as a plug-in to 3D Studio or as a standalone for Windows, translates between over 20 different common 3D file formats, including 3D Studio, LightWave Objects & Scenes, Wavefront, Alias polysets, RenderWare, AutoCAD DXF, and POV-RAY 2.0. InterChange preserves geometry, surface information, hierarchy, rotational centers, and more.

Additional Hardware

You can input artwork into a computer using either scanners or digital cameras. Both have their specific uses. Let me wrap up my product reviews with these two pieces of hardware.

Scanners

The best bet for introducing hand-made artwork into a computer is to use a scanner. Three major scanner manufacturers come to mind. Here's all the contact information you need to find out about their latest and greatest models.

Hewlett Packard
3000 Hanover St.
Palo Alto, CA 94304
Phone: 415 857-1501 **Fax:** 415 857-7299
WWW: http://www.dmo.hp.com/peripherals/scanners/main.html

Hewlett Packard makes a complete line of excellent flatbed scanners under its ScanJet brand name.

MicroTek
3300 NW 211th Terrace
Hillsboro, OR 97124
Phone: 503 645-7333 **Fax:** 503 629-8460

If you're looking for one of the best price/power relationships in the scanner business, MicroTek's complete line of hand and flatbed scanners are one of the best values in the business.

Agfa
200 Ballardvale Street
Wilmington, MA 01887
Phone: 508 658-5600 **Fax:** 508 658-8982
WWW: http://www.agfa.com

After Xerox, German-based Agfa is one of the biggest professional printing and graphic arts hardware manufacturers in the world. They make a complete line of awesome scanners. Check out their Web site (which is, by the way, unusually excellent) for more information.

3D Scanners
Cyberware, Inc.
2110 Del Monte Avenue
Monterey, CA 93940
Phone: 408 657-1450 **Fax:** 408 657-1494
WWW: http://www.cyberware.com/

Maybe you have a rich uncle who will die and leave you a ton of cash. Or perhaps your latest game will be a goldmine. Whatever lighting bolt of luck strikes you, if you've got the cash to spend, add this company to your rolodex. Cyberware manufactures a variety of hardware devices to enable 3D scanning.

Using lasers, the hardware scans an object in seconds and from that scan constructs a 3D mesh representation. Cyberware has standard devices that are desktop and full-body size (the full body model retails at over $400,000!). They'll even custom design equipment for you.

Maybe someday costs will come down enough for us average developers. Meanwhile, if you ever needed a device to dream about, here it is.

Digital Cameras

Digital cameras are useful for creating natural-world 3D images for your computer. They're also awesome for capturing real-world textures digitally (a brick right off a wall, for example). Here is the contact information for the three major creators of digital cameras and accompanying software.

Agfa
200 Ballardvale Street
Wilmington, MA 01887

Phone: 508 658-5600 **Fax:** 508 658-8982
WWW: http://www.agfa.com

Agfa has created a line of digital cameras based on Nikon lens technology for highly accurate and detailed digital photography.

Kodak
Eastman Kodak Company
343 State Street
Rochester, NY 14650-0518
Phone: 716 724-4000 **Fax:** 716 722-1178
WWW: http://www.kodak.com

Kodak makes two types of digital cameras. Both are self-contained units and can function as attachments for common SLR cameras.

Apple Computer
1 Infinite Loop
Cupertino, CA 95014
Phone: 408 996-1010 **Fax:** 408 996-0275

Apple markets a sister series to the Kodak's digital cameras called The Apple Quicktake.

Tablets

Many artists prefer to create art by hand, and for them working with many of the cutting-edge graphics programs with a tablet is a necessity. Here is the contact information for the three most common tablet manufacturers.

Kurta
3007 East Chambers
Phoenix, AZ 85040
Phone: 800 445-8782

Summagraphics
8500 Cameron Rd.
Austin, TX 78754-3999
Phone: 512 835-0900 **Fax:** 512 339-1490
WWW: http://www.summagraphics.com

Wacom
501 S.E. Columbia Shores Blvd., Suite 300
Vancouver, WA 98661
Phone: 360 750-8882 **Fax:** 360 750-8924
WWW: http://www.wacom.com

Art Magazines

I have found several really great magazines that I think will help any game developer in the art arena.

3D Design
Miller Freeman, Inc.
600 Harrison Street
San Francisco, CA 94107
Phone: 415 905-2200
Subscription: $29.95 **Newstand:** $3.95 **Publishes:** Monthly **Pages:** 100

3D Design focuses on the issues professional 3D designers face every day. Within a mere 100 pages, you'll find hands-on, how-to feature articles, product news and evaluations, and analysis of design-oriented issues and trends.

Computer Artist
Pennwell Publishing Co.
10 Tara Boulevard 5th Floor
Nashua, NH 03062
Phone: 603 891 0539 **Fax:** 603 891-0539
Subscription: $24.95 **Newstand:** $3.95 **Publishes:** BiMonthly **Pages:** 100

This magazine covers a wide range of computer artwork creation, including illustration and 3D modeling. Games are given nice coverage with a feature or two every so often. You'll also find a lot of news articles about new products and developments.

Computer Graphics World
Pennwell Publishing, Co.
10 Tara Boulevard, 5th Floor
Nashua, NH 03062
Phone: 603 891-0123 **Fax:** 603 891-0539
WWW: http://www.lfw.com/WWW/CGW/cgwhome.htm
Subscription: $50.00 **Newstand:** $4.95 **Publishes:** Monthly **Pages:** 100

Also published by Pennwell, *Computer Graphics World* focuses on a wider range of graphical issues beyond traditional artwork, including digital video, high-end imaging, and more. Of course, you'll still find discussions on SGI-type products, animation packages, and more for the traditional artist.

Digital Video **Magazine**
ActiveMedia, Inc. (IDG)
600 Townsend Street, Suite 170
San Francisco, CA 94103
Phone: 415 522-2400 **Fax:** 415 522-2409
Email: letters@dv.com
Subscription: $24.97 **Newstand:** $3.95 **Publishes:** Monthly **Pages:** 112

You may recall that I mentioned this magazine in Chapter 10 when we discussed digital video in depth. *Digital Video* magazine is the undisputed king of digital video, but this great magazine doesn't stop there. You'll find information on 3D animation and modeling, multimedia authoring, and audio. With lots of tutorial and in-depth coverage on how to produce video and how to make models that you can integrate into multimedia and interactive products, *Digital Video* magazine will surely keep you interested.

***3D Artist* Magazine**
Columbine, Inc.
P.O. Box 4787
Santa Fe, NM 87502-4787
Phone: 505 982-3532 **Fax:** 505 820-6929
Email: info@3dartist.com **WWW:** http://www.3dartist.com/
Subscription: $33.00 **Newstand:** $3.95 **Publishes:** Monthly **Pages:** 100

These guys at Columbine are 3D maniacs; they don't just write about this stuff, they live it night and day. Before Miller Freeman introduced *3D Design*, this was the only major 3D-specific magazine around.

What I really enjoy about this magazine is their extensive Web site, which, among other things, allowed me to sign up to recieve their bi-monthly newsletter *The Tesselation Times*. Every two weeks, on email, I get a complete news breakdown of new products and announcements and general happenings in the world of 3D graphics and design. If you haven't subscribed to *The Tesselation Times,* you should!

Planet Studio
120 Bedford Center Road, Suite 4
Bedford, NH 03110
Phone: 603 924-0100 **Fax:** 603 924-4066
Email: planet_studio@dv.com.
Subscription: $59.95 (Charter) **Newstand:** N/A **Publishes:** 6/yr **Pages:** N/A

From the folks at Digital Video magazine comes this offshoot newsletter. *Planet Studio* is a bimonthly newsletter covering all the multimedia products produced by Autodesk and any affiliated plug-ins. This means you get dedicated high-end coverage of 3D Studio, Animator Pro/Studio, and more.

Books

Here is a description of some of the better books to help you with game art creation tasks.

Siggraph Book Reference

http://www.siggraph.org/artdesign/publications/bookshelf.html

There's some overlap between what I list here and what this page has, but for the most part this is a great source of coverage to find books old and new to help you create cool art and animation.

Computer Art/Painting Books

Fractal Design Painter 3.1 Unleashed by Denise Tyler (Published by SAMS, June 1995; ISBN 0-672-30707-3)

Denise Tyler is a freelance computer and game artist. She wrote the art how-to section for Andre Lamothe's *Tricks of The Game Programming Gurus* book published by SAMS. In her book she features all sorts of cool stuff and shows you the ins and outs of Fractal Design Painter. An accompanying CD-ROM includes all of the samples as well as demo software.

3D Modeling and Animation Books

Animation and Modeling on the Mac by Don and Melora Foley (Published by Peachpit Press; ISBN 0-201-88420-8)

Although this is Mac-focused book, there is a ton of information here relevant to any 3D artist. The book has tips and examples for all sorts of cool Mac graphics products like Premiere, Photoshop, Infini-D, After Effects, Paint Alchemy, Ray Dream Designer, Electric Image, form*Z, DeBabelizer, and more!

Becoming a Computer Animator by Mike Morrison (Published by SAMS; July 1994, ISBN 0-672-30463-5)

This is a book that covers all the basics of computer based animation. It has interviews with industry experts and covers both 2D and 3D animation. The companion CD-ROM (a dual Mac/PC product) comes with several animation program demos. It also covers job information for the most common computer animator jobs including interactive entertainment!

3D Studio Hollywood & Gaming Effects by New Riders Development Group (Published by New Riders Publishing, November 1995; ISBN 1-56205-430-9)

Wow! A 3D Studio book with specific tutorials and ideas targeted for special effects and game artists. A CD-ROM accompanies this book and features tools from professional animators and game designers.

3D Studio IPAS Plug-In Reference by Tim Forcade (Published by New Riders Publishing, 1995; ISBN 1-562-0543-17)

There are over 200 different plug-ins for 3D Studio. How do you figure out which ones might be useful for your special needs? Get this book, that's how. If you're a major 3D Studio user, this book will help you get even more out of it by explaining and showing you the variety of products that extend and supplement an already great product. The accompanying CD-ROM includes more than 100 plug-in demonstration programs, such as Schreiber Instruments' Fractal Bouquet and Positron Publishing's MeshPaint 3D.

Inside 3D Studio Release 4 by Steven D. Elliot, Phillip L. Miller (Published by New Riders Publishing, January 1995; ISBN 1-56205-415-5)

If you want a cover-to-cover tome on 3D Studio, this is a good place to look. The companion CD-ROM contains over 200 megabytes of meshes, utilities, textures, and bump maps.

Adobe Photoshop 3 Filters and Effects by Gary David Bouton (Published by New Riders Publishing, May 1995; ISBN 1-56205-448-1)

This book covers all the various Adobe and third party filters for use with Photoshop. An accompanying CD-ROM includes all demo versions of plug-in filters and several custom design filters as well as sample images.

Adobe Photoshop Creative Techniques by Denise Salles, Gary Poyssick, and Ellen Behoriam (Published by Hayden, December 1995; ISBN 1-56830-132-4)

Basically, this book is a step by step guide that covers Version 3 for Macintosh.

Kai's Power Tools Filters & Effects by Heinz Schuller (New Riders Publishing, September 1995; ISBN 1-56205-480-5)

A step-by-step guide with a CD-ROM containing a demo version of the product. This book covers how to work with KPT within popular products like Fractal Design Painter and Adobe Photoshop.

Scanning: Your Personal Consultant by Jonathan Hornstein (Published by Ziff Davis Press, Febrary 1995; ISBN 1-56276-297-4)

Real World Scanning Halftones by David Blatner and Stephen Roth (Published by Peachpit Press, 1994; ISBN 1-566-0909-38)

Do you need a good book or two to help you get the most out of your scanner? These two books will show you how to get the highest quality reproduction out of your scanner. Both cover halftones, scanner tips, adjusting scans, scanning software, and more.

More Art-Oriented World Wide Web Listings

I've presented some vendor-specific Web sites throughout this chapter to help you locate more information about the products discussed. This section includes some of my favorite Web sites for locating general information, tips, techniques, and resources on game art and animation topics.

General Art and Animation Sites

Brian Leach's Digital Illusions
`http://www.mcs.net/~bcleach/illusions/`

This is one of my favorite sites on the Web. As Figure 12.11 shows, it features a complete self-published online magazine devoted to cutting edge computer animation and art. Check out this Web site as you explore the various art resources available to you on the Web.

Animation Site
`http://www.cam.org/~pawn/ANIMRES.html`

Animation Spots on the World Wide Web
http://laotzu.art.niu.edu/~asifa/animspot.html

Both of these sites are good jumping off points for locating information on computer animation tools, tips, and techniques.

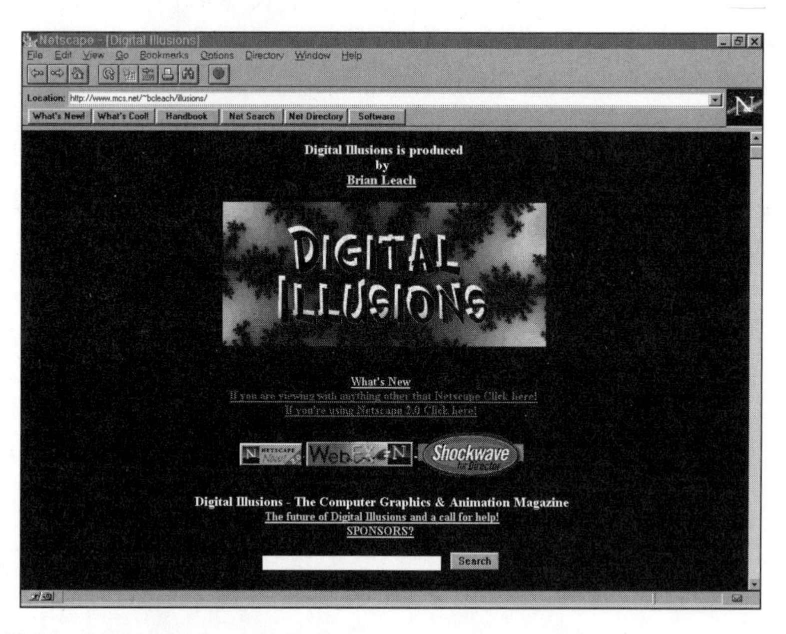

Figure 12.11 Digital Illusions' Web site.

General 3D Art and Animation Sites

3D Site

http://www.3dsite.com/3dsite/

3D Site contains tons of links and information concerning the creation and animation of 3D computer graphics. This is an excellent jumping off point. Here you'll find an unbelievably complete list of links to information about your favorite art programs.

GWeb—An Electronic Trade Journal for Computer Animators

http://www2.cinenet.net/GWEB/index-text.html

GWeb is an informal trade journal for people in the computer animation industry as well as those pursuing a career in computer animation. Some of the main highlights of GWeb include an up-to-date job listing section and insightful, behind the scenes interviews with the people leading this industry.

Organizations

ACM/SIGGRAPH—The ACM Special Interest Group on Graphics

http://www.siggraph.org/

Siggraph is the organization for graphic artists, programmers, engineers, and researchers. Tune into this site to catch up with cutting edge topics and examples concerning computer graphics.

International Animation Association

http://laotzu.art.niu.edu/asifa.html

The ASIFA is a leading organization for professional animators around the world. Check out this web site to find out more about becoming a member and to explore the resources about traditional and computer based animation.

Awesome List of Animation Schools

http://samson.stud.hivolda.no/~asifa/

I presented a list of animation schools earlier in this chapter but this list is absolutely amazing. It features a complete world-wide list with detailed summaries about the courses and resources of every major art/animation school around. You've got to see this to believe it.

Motion Effects Website

http://www.tiac.net/users/motionfx/

This 3D animation and effects house does all sorts of custom work for commercials, television, and such. They provide an informative Web page jam packed with lots of good links to 3D model sources, texture sources, and other graphic information. This is an excellent searching point to find all the Web has to offer you to make cool graphics for your games.

CHAPTER 13

Good music and sound can be as important, if not more important, than great graphics.

Creating Music and Sound

The Power of Music

Music has the power to put people in a certain mood or enhance the mood they are already in. Nobody really knows why, but most experts agree on this fact. It's amazing to me then that sound has not received much emphasis in the gaming industry. Well, maybe not totally amazing. Adding sound to games has been difficult in the past—especially with the PC platform—and it has become known as the incorrigible stepchild of the industry. If you ever hear programmers cursing uncontrollably, it probably is because they are having trouble implementing sound.

Things are looking up, though. Microsoft has released DirectSound, a much improved sound programming development platform for Windows, and the industry has seen four or five major packages—each with a unique set of licensing and programming features—emerge for DOS. On consoles, the switch to CD-ROM and the influx of several amazing musical chipsets has brought better digital and synthesized sound to those systems as well. In the PC hardware realm, cards now supporting full surround-sound stereo 16-bit wavetables are becoming commonplace.

Still, creating awesome music and sound effects for both PCs and consoles is probably one of the more difficult obstacles to overcome. The many programming issues, file formatting concerns, and production issues form a complex web that can be daunting to untangle.

This chapter covers everything—and I mean *everything*—I could find on sound and music. From MIDI setups to redbook audio information to design ideas and sound libraries, I've tried to include everything to help you add high-quality sound and music to your games.

The discussion of sound involves three key categories:

- Sound
- Sound effects
- Music

Although these categories are definitely interrelated (not to mention subjective), each category has its own distinct qualities that sets it apart from the others. Let me take a moment to define these terms as I'll be using them. *Sound* is the general concept of reproducing any sound, be it a sound effect or music—after all, an explosion and Beethovan are both essentially waveforms. *Sound effects* are the little blurbs you hear throughout a game, like the clawing and heavy breathing of aliens, or the sound a laser gun produces when it is fired. *Music* is the melodic rythmic background sound that sets the tone of the game.

The Fundamentals of Sound and Sound Production

We' re going to begin with the absolute fundamentals of sound theory. Sound is simply a series of vibrations in the air, called *soundwaves*. Normally these soundwaves are represented by a 2D graph with the X axis denoting the time the soundwave persists and the Y axis showing the difference in air pressure. If a soundwave is regular and repeating, the sound produced by this wave gets a fixed tonality, just like a music note. If the soundwave is irregular, you get something like a gunshot or static on your TV set. Figure 13.1 shows a basic soundwave.

The number of times a soundwave is repeated is called the *frequency* of sound. Frequency is measured in *Hertz* (Hz)—1 Hz equals one repetition per second, while 1 kHz (or KiloHertz) equals one thousand repetitions per second. You experience frequency every day. The higher the frequency, the higher a note sounds. The *amplitude* of sound is represented on the Y axis. The larger the amplitude, the louder the sound. Multiplying the function that represents the soundwave (f(x)=sin x) is a classic trick for increasing the volume (f(x)=2sin x). Figures 13.2 and 13.3 show how sound increases in volume as you heighten the form of the wave.

An Introduction to FM Synthesis

FM, or *Frequency Modulation*, is the term that indicates that the frequency of a soundwave is being changed. *FM synthesis* was the first real sound technology for

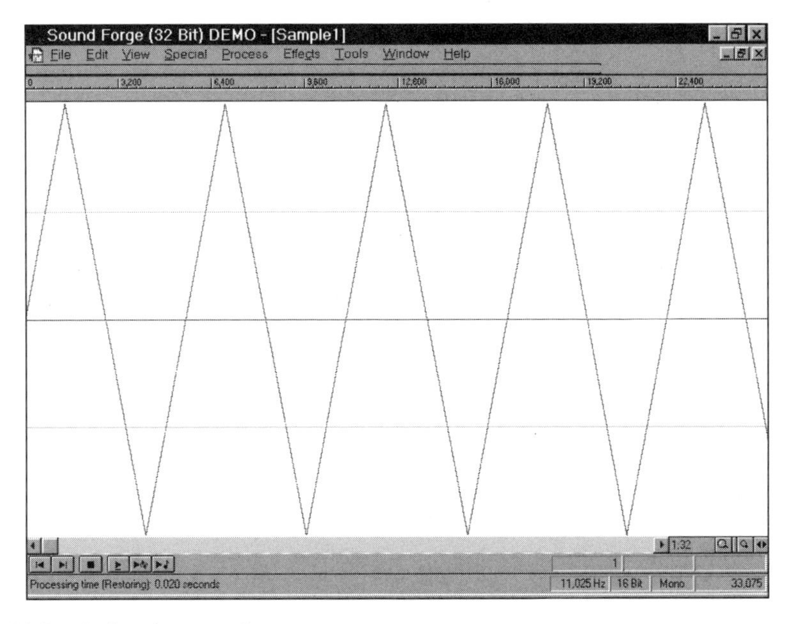

Figure 13.1 A simple soundwave.

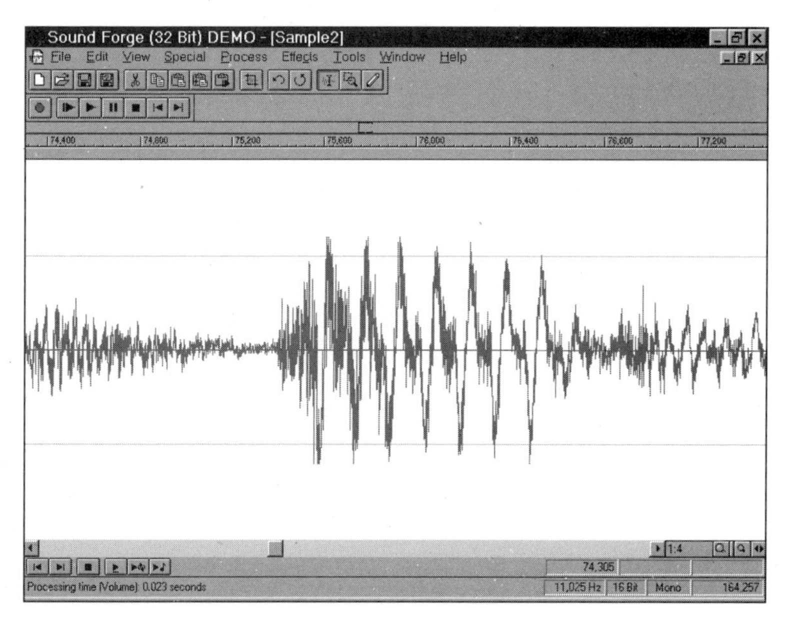

Figure 13.2 Sound represented at a modest volume.

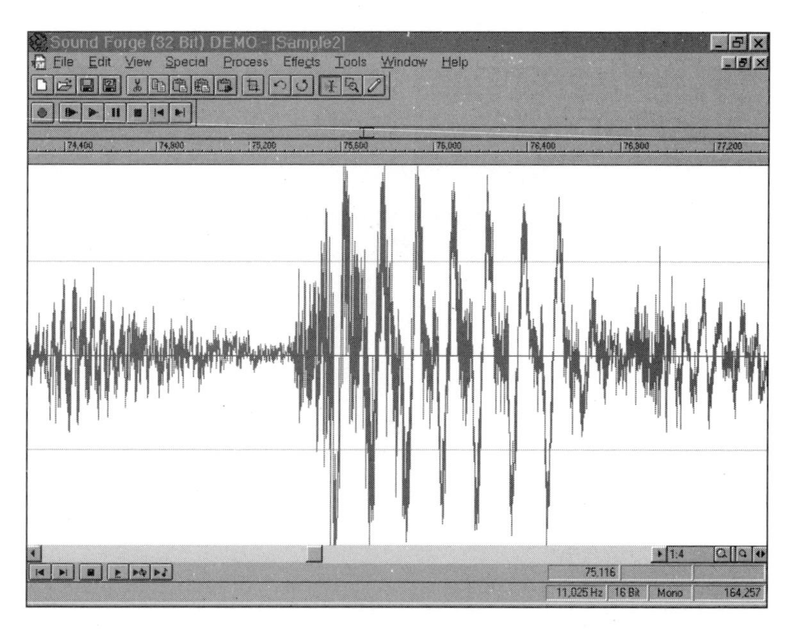

Figure 13.3 Sound represented at a high volume.

computers. It synthesizes sound by using a mathematical simulation—albeit a primitive simulation—of the sound in question. A sound card or chip that uses FM synthesis creates music by applying changes to the frequency of a sound with given

amplitude, soundwave, and tonality. Of course, a number of other parameters are involved, but you don't need to know about those just yet.

FM synthesis works with a simple *sinewave*, or a derivation of it. While this works great for representing a flute or any other simple sound, it's a lousy approach when you want to simulate a string ensemble, and you can forget about doing voice overs! The soundwave of a flute looks like a sinewave. In other words, a sinewave representation of a flute will sound acceptable. The soundwave made by a string ensemble, on the other hand, has little resemblance to a simple sinewave representation and will not sound like the real thing when simulated through an FM synthesis card. Figures 13.4 and 13.5 show the difference between a simple soundwave and a complicated sound effect like captured music.

Digital Audio

Digital audio produces sound by playing soundwaves that have been recorded (or *captured*) and then saved as a file. These files are known as *samples.* When you hear someone talk about a WAV file or an AU file, they are referring to a digital sample. Additionally, while the term *sample* can be used to refer to a sound effect, it tends to be used by people who make musical recordings.

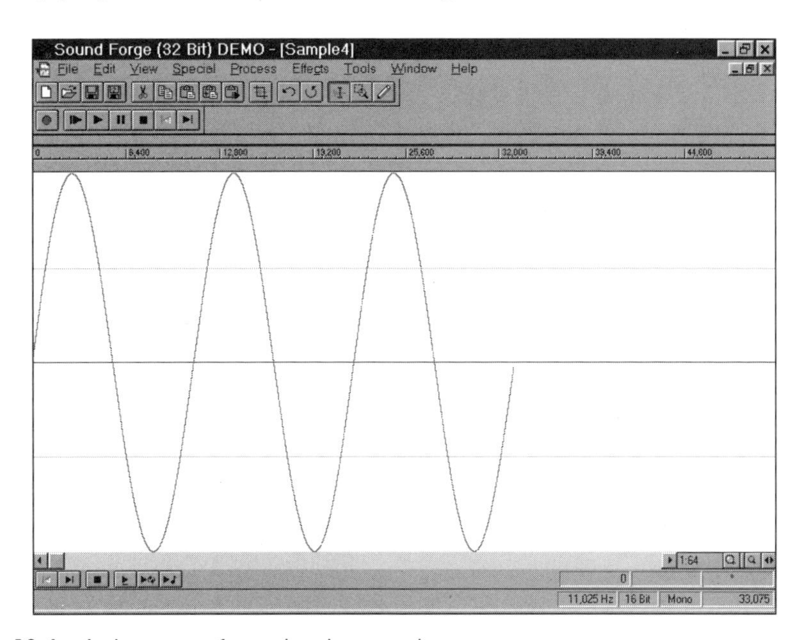

Figure 13.4 A sinewave for a simple sound.

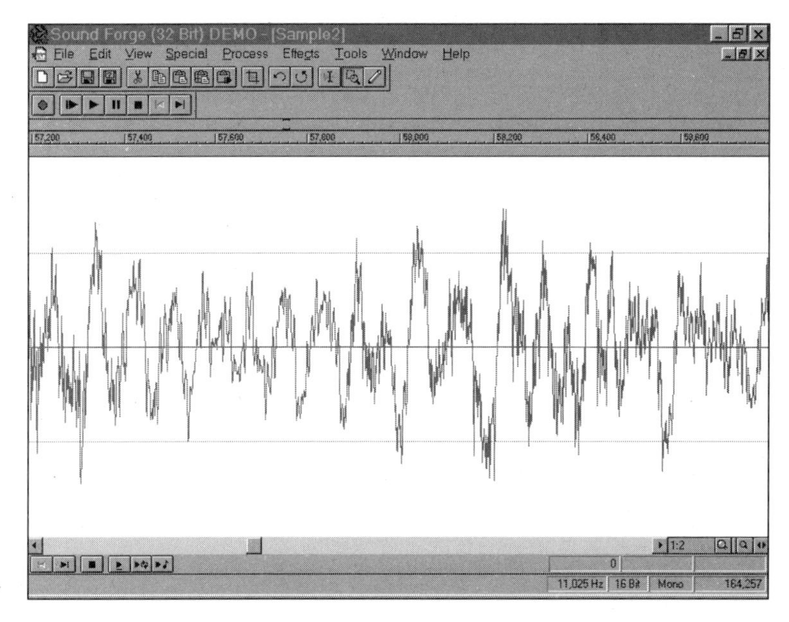

Figure 13.5 A complicated soundwave for a sound effect.

Digital audio has been around in various forms for many years, getting its start on the PC with the SoundBlaster which featured 8-bit, mono digital audio. Today, most cards feature 16-bit or 32-bit full range stereo digital audio.

The quality of samples varies greatly, depending on the frequency of the sample, the range of bits it uses, and so on. It's important to know the standards of the various formats you can use; we'll get into that a little later.

Redbook Audio: The Emerging Standard for Music Tracks

While I said we'd jump into standards a little later, one standard that is important to cover as a fundamental sound reproduction concept is *redbook audio.* Most of you are already familiar with redbook audio—it's the standard used for producing music CDs. The specifications for various CD formats (CD-ROM, CD-I, CD Plus, and so on) come in colored-coded manuals; the one for audio is color-coded red, hence the term *redbook.* Redbook audio is basically a digital audio standard of the highest quality: 16-bit sound at a 44.1 kHz sampling rate stored directly on a CD-ROM.

Games stored on CD-ROM are increasingly utilizing the redbook standard for direct CD audio feeds, so you need to be aware of how it's used. Developers press a CD with both redbook audio tracks and CD-ROM tracks. When the game needs music, it simply plays it back off the CD just like you would in your player. For more information, see *Using Redbook Audio for Your Music Tracks* later in the chapter.

An Introduction to 3D Audio

The game industry has been using 3D graphics for a long time, but 3D sound has always been a thing of the future. Well, the future is upon us now. A host of new software and hardware technologies that will offer truly awesome digital effects and allow developers to create games with realistic 3D sound effects have been produced. We'll cover them later on.

3D audio schemes modify samples to produce a 3D representation of sounds. Let's discuss this method using a car racing game as an example. In this type of game, a 3D audio sound effect would truly give the player the sensation that he or she were in an environment where cars are passing right by.

Sound Formats

At last count, I uncovered 24 different audio file formats. I'm sure you're scratching your head wondering, "If there is only one fundamental set of math concerning the re-creation of a sound, why are there so many formats?" The reason is simple: Everybody likes to show off his or her own standard and proclaim its superiority.

I don't want you to get bogged down in a sea of formatting standards, so here's a basic rundown of the formats you should be most concerned with:

AIFF and AIFC (Apple Interchange File Format and Apple File Format Compressed) This format was created by Apple and it's also commonly found in SGI circles. The AIFC version of the file introduced compression.

Gravis Patch The Gravis Ultrasound, a very popular board (especially in Europe), uses this exclusive format denoted by a .PAT extension. The format allows for multiple samples to be placed in one file. It supports 8-bit and 16-bit sound resolution and multiple sample rates. Gravis Patch is a mono format.

Quicktime Apple's video playback engine also has an accompanying sound format. The format supports an unlimited number of tracks and up to six different compression schemes. Quicktime also supports the AIFF format as well as a more native format to integrate sound and music directly into a movie file.

RIFF (Rich Interchange File Format) This format, invented by Microsoft, is specific to the Windows platform. It supports both 8-bit and 16-bit resolution, multiple sample rates, stereo, embedded text, markers, and playlists.

VOC This format from Creative Labs is the original native format of its SoundBlaster PC sound cards. Two versions are available: Old and New. The main difference is in the resolution of the formats; Old supports only 8-bit resolution while New supports 16-bit resolution.

WAV This is the most common form of a *sample* on a Windows platform. It was designed by Microsoft and supports 8-bit and 16-bit resolution, multiple samples, and stereo and mono playback. WAV files can support a wide variety of audio compression algorithms. Most Windows games use this format.

Zap! Bam! Thhhsssppp! Entering the World of Sound Effects

The trick to remember with sound effects is that you want to generate as high a quality sound effect as you can initially, and then bring it down to a lesser-quality sound format to reduce the memory overhead. Of course, you want to find a workable compromise here—good quality sound and reasonable memory usage. By starting with the most advanced format, you will retain the best quality as you pare the sound down. Unfortunately, this process is not as simple as "record high and reproduce low;" there is a whole lot more to it. If you're not careful, your sound won't be as smooth as intended. This effect is known as *aliasing*. So with that quick lesson in mind, let's learn some more.

Sound Editing Tools

To create great sound effects you'll need good editing software. For the most part, you will be creating sound effects from CD-ROM libraries. Although these libraries provide brilliant sound effects, they rarely include the perfect sound. It will be up to you to edit and experiment with your sound files to get exactly what you're after. This is where the editing packages come in. The trick is to use a package to manipulate existing sounds or design a new sound that will keep your players coming back for more.

All of the packages listed here are top-notch. Personally, I like Sound Forge and Gold Wave (shareware). However, you'll find advocates for every package presented.

Sound Forge (Windows)
Sonic Foundry, Inc.
100 South Baldwin Street, Suite 204
Madison, WI 53703
Phone: 608 256-3133 **Fax:** 608 256-7300
WWW: http://www.sfoundry.com

This is a very useful sound editor. It includes all kinds of effects and makes editing a breeze. You can see for yourself by downloading the demo (saving is disabled) from their Web site. Figure 13.6 shows an example of Sound Forge in action.

Sound Designer II (Mac)
Digidesign
1360 Willow Road
Menlo Park, CA 94025
Phone: 415 688-0600

Sound Designer II is one of the best and most popular sound editors available for the Mac. It features tons of effects and professional editing capabilities. It also supports "plug-in" technology allowing other companies (specifically the 3D sound companies) to create new sound effects packages and use them within Sound Designer II.

Sound Edit 16 (Mac)
Macromedia, Inc.
600 Townsend
San Francisco, CA 94103
Phone: 415 252-2000 **Fax:** 415 442-0200
WWW: http://www.macromedia.com

This long time Macintosh sound-editing package is available as a standalone tool or in one of the multimedia authoring bundles Macromedia offers.

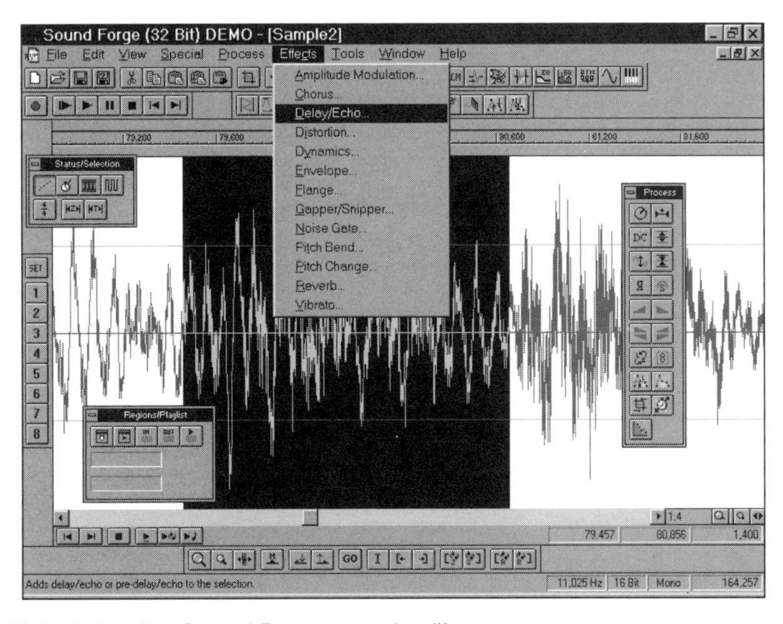

Figure 13.6 Using the Sound Forge sound editor.

Alchemy
Passport Designs
100 Stone Pine Road
Half Moon Bay, CA 94109
Phone: 415 726-0280 **Fax:** 415 726-2254
WWW: http://www.mw3.com/passport/passport.htm

Passport Designs is one of the leading music software companies around. Their high-end sound-editing package, Alchemy, is a great choice no matter what your needs are.

Disc-To-Disk
Optical Media International
51 East Campbell
Campbell, CA 95008
Phone: 408 376-3511

Disc-To-Disk is one of those odd little utilities that just makes you say, "Why didn't I think of that?" Disc-To-Disk captures CD audio digitally right off a CD-ROM, bypassing the need to run it through your sound card's digital-to-analog converter. The results are crystal clear.

You can store the results in several popular sound formats and then go to town with your favorite sound editing program.

Shareware Sound-Editing Packages

In the shareware arena, two products—Gold Wave and Cool Edit—stand head and shoulders above the rest. Both handle a wide range of sound files and offer tons of digital editing effects. I prefer Gold Wave, but I could give you a list of those who swear by Cool Edit, so the choice is yours.

Cool Edit
Syntrillium Software Corporation
P.O. Box 60274
Phoenix, AZ 85082-0274
Phone: 602 941-4327 **Fax:** 602 941-8170
WWW: http://www.netzone.com/syntrillium/

Cool Edit is the most-often used shareware sound editor. With all the features and power it has, I'm not surprised it's so popular. Figure 13.7 shows an example of Cool Edit at work. Three registration schemes are available: $25 (Lite), $50 (Basic), and $100 (Preferred).

Gold Wave
Chris Craig
P.O. Box 51
St. John's, NF

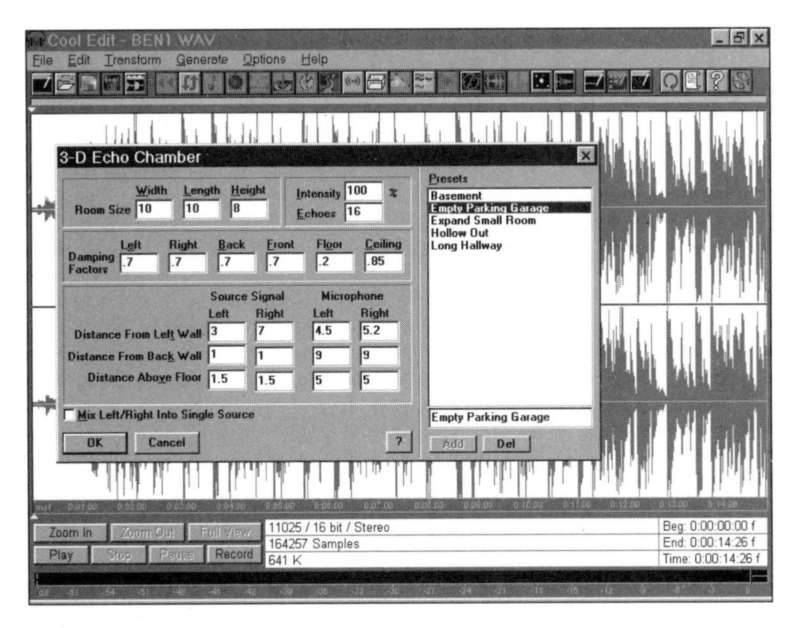

Figure 13.7 Using Cool Edit to edit sounds.

Canada A1C 5H5
Email: chris3@garfield.cs.mun.ca
WWW: http://www.cs.mun.ca/~chris3/goldwave/home.html

Gold Wave is a digital audio editor, player, and recorder. It supports and converts several RIFF, WAV formats such as PCM, MULAW, ADPCM, and other file formats such as VOC, Amiga 8SVX, Sun, and NeXT. It can also display and edit separate channels of stereo sounds. You can register Gold Wave as standard for $30 or as deluxe for $50.

If you're going to do your own digitizing, the first thing you need to do is go to a music store and get a top rate microphone. Unfortunately, most of the microphones provided with regular sound cards are not professional quality.

Recently, I came across the following potential resource for information about microphones:

Allen Sides Microphone Cabinet
Cardinal Business Media
Available from Electronic Musician Magazine
Phone: 800 233-9604

This CD-ROM provides a complete run-through of everything you ever wanted to know about microphones. You'll have to shell out $69.95, but if you're looking for a major resource for purchasing just the right microphone plus recording techniques, this is your source.

If you really want to explore sound, you might want to look into some of the other equipment you can get to improve your sound effects, like portable DAT recorders for field recording. If you want to get the ultimate in audio equipment, check out the various magazines like *Electronic Musician* and *Keyboard* for the complete scoop on major audio gear.

Foley Sound and Offscreen Action

Foley sound, in movie terms, is sound effects that are created by people, called Foley artists. These artists re-create for movies the sounds we take for granted such as horses galloping, people falling, glass breaking, and so on.

In games, the concept of Foley sound is the same, but sound artists take it a step further and redefine sound effects that are not created by objects you see in the scene. In Doom, for example, you don't see the aliens but you hear them, and boy, do you tense up as you hear them. As I said earlier, sound creates mood for a scene. Essentially, all sound effects in a game need not correspond to foreground objects. Just because you can't see it shouldn't mean you can't hear it. This concept is important for developers to remember.

With the rise of 3D sound techniques, placement of sound and the routines to transmit that message need to be further taken into account. Using 3D sound you can actually define mixing techniques that really do sound like they're taking place outside the view area of the screen. In effect, this sound technique widens the field of play "beyond the monitor."

The Fundamentals of Music

We've talked about sound as an all-encompassing theory, sound effects in general, and now let's get into music. If you aren't confused yet, I congratulate you. This section will introduce you to the basics of music production. Music can be accomplished in many different ways, especially with today's CD-ROM formats and larger memory. Digital audio is much more available to developers than it used to be for adding even more options.

Digital Audio Provides Quality Music Capabilitites

Three specific techniques are available for using digital audio to create music tracks for your games. The simple approach is to create an audio sound track by simply recording all of your music to a looping sound file. With this approach, you'll want to keep the sample quite short, but designed in such a way that the looping creates a rhythmic sound rather than just repetitive sound. Apogee's Terminal Velocity used this approach very well. The other two techniques, which we'll cover a little later, involve using MOD files and redbook audio tracks.

Getting the Scoop on MIDI

MIDI is the tried and true standard of most computer game music. Since MIDI is a series of computer bytes that represent notes to be played by the sound card, it's extremely useful for game developers. MIDI songs are quite small, which can really help to limit your memory overhead. In addition, MIDI can be quite interactive; you can change MIDI data on the fly, and quickly and fluidly weave in and out through different soundtracks.

In the past, most musical notes produced by sound cards for MIDI were done with FM synthesis. Today, though, all the major sound cards use a process called *wavetable synthesis.* Wavetables are made up of stored samples of instruments that are used to create sound. Some cards even allow programmers to load their own sample instruments.

Most programmers now use a specific MIDI set called *general MIDI.* General MIDI is a standard set of 128 sounds. If a composer writes a song using the general MIDI setup, he or she would not need to create a custom set of MIDI instruments for the music. This makes working with outside musicians a breeze. Unfortunately, as some have pointed out, general MIDI can be a pain in the butt to convert to dedicated consoles that don't feature built-in general MIDI sounds. In this situation, you would have to supply the instrumental sounds in digital form for consoles, which takes up tons of memory; sometimes you don't have enough to spare.

In addition, general MIDI works against the philosophy of creating customized sound. Because all the instruments are standardized, even different compositions can sound surprisingly alike. Your own tests will decide how canned your music sounds, but be aware that as with anything else in game development you sacrifice one thing for another.

Everything You Need to Know about MIDI

Most MIDI devices—electronic keyboards, modular synthesizers, audio mixers, drum machines, and so on—are external. They talk to each other over a three-wire cable. You might not realize it, but your sound card includes a MIDI compatible synthesizer. This MIDI device lives inside your computer and talks directly to your computer's bus. Most sound cards let you hook up additional MIDI devices through a set of MIDI ports known as *In*, *Out*, and *Through*.

MIDI is actually a real-time interactive network. In theory, any device that includes at least one MIDI In and one MIDI Out port can talk to any other MIDI device. Many MIDI devices also offer a MIDI Through port to pass along data that comes in the MIDI In port. MIDI devices are not limited to three ports, however. In fact, many products provide several ports in various combinations of the three types.

The Musical Connection

When most people hear the term "MIDI," they think of musical applications. After all, the letter "M" in MIDI stands for Musical. But as we explore MIDI's musical features, keep in mind that it has grown far beyond its original specifications.

At the hardware level, MIDI provides a simple asynchronous serial interface that transmits data in ten bit chunks at a rate of 31.25 kilobaud (31,250 bits per second). The ten bits include a start bit, eight data bits, and a stop bit. Although we won't be dealing with many hardware issues in this chapter, you'll want to remember the transmission rate when you create your MIDI apps.

The data that travels through the MIDI cable controls electronic musical instruments—synthesizers. Before MIDI, in the late 1970s, as these instruments began to acquire the sophistication of digital electronics, their manufacturers developed various proprietary systems for interconnecting their products. Their main goal was to create integrated musical workshops so that musicians could compose and play music on several instruments simultaneously. This required at least one synthesizer, along with a device that could record what was played as a *sequence* of control events, or keypresses, just like a player piano roll. With such a system, you could later substitute a different note, change the duration of a note, or eliminate a note entirely without recording the entire passage again. And because you were only recording keystrokes (rather than analog waveforms), you could even change the tempo of the music without changing its pitch, or transpose the pitch without changing the tempo. These recording devices became known as *sequencers*. Once that problem was solved, it didn't take long for most manufacturers to recognize the need for a standard protocol to link sequencers and synthesizers. That's how MIDI was born. Figure 13.8 shows a typical MIDI hardware setup.

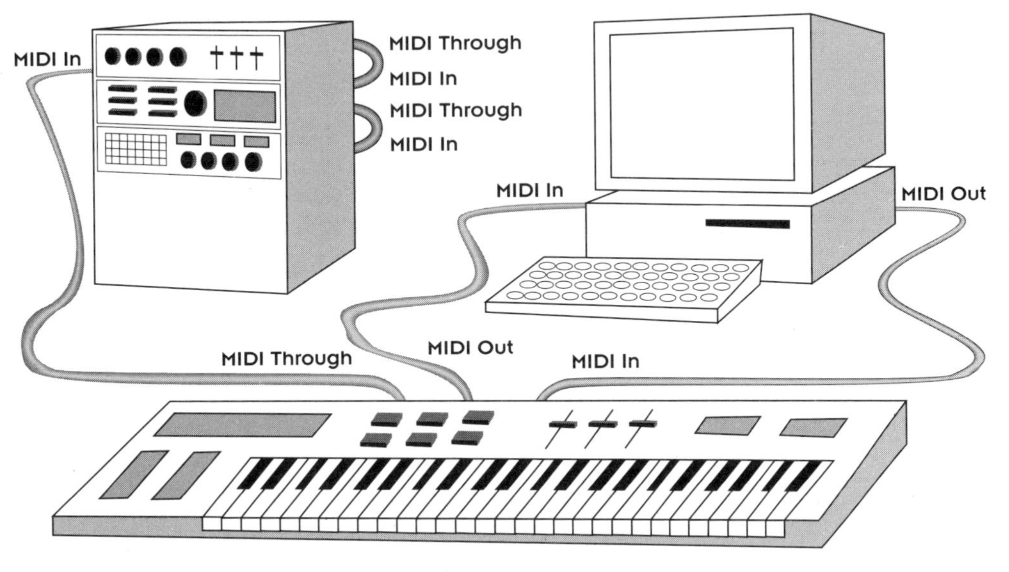

Figure 13.8 A typical MIDI hardware setup.

Once you can make a sequencer talk to a synthesizer, you can make synthesizers talk to each other. If you plug the MIDI Out port of one instrument into the MIDI In port of a second instrument, you can play the second synthesizer from the keyboard of the first. Most manufacturers now offer their major models in two versions, one with a keyboard and one without. Keyboardless versions are usually called *synthesizer modules* and they often come in "rack mount" cabinets. In the pre-MIDI era, keyboard players, like Rick Wakeman and Keith Emerson, often appeared on stage in synthesizer pods, surrounded by walls of keyboards. Like space aliens in their cockpits, they flailed around from instrument to instrument, which made for a flashy performance, but created a setup nightmare. Today, performing keyboardists may play one or two keyboards on stage, while controlling dozens of instruments stacked on racks, neatly out of the way.

A Look at MIDI Messages

MIDI devices communicate by sending each other messages. Messages are divided into two general categories—*channel* and *system*—and into five types—*voice, mode, system common, system real-time,* and *system exclusive.*

The first category, *channel messages,* includes *voice messages* and *mode messages.* These messages are grouped into the channel message category because they are transmitted on individual channels rather than globally to all devices in the MIDI network. To understand how MIDI devices identify channels, let's take some time to review the structure of a MIDI message.

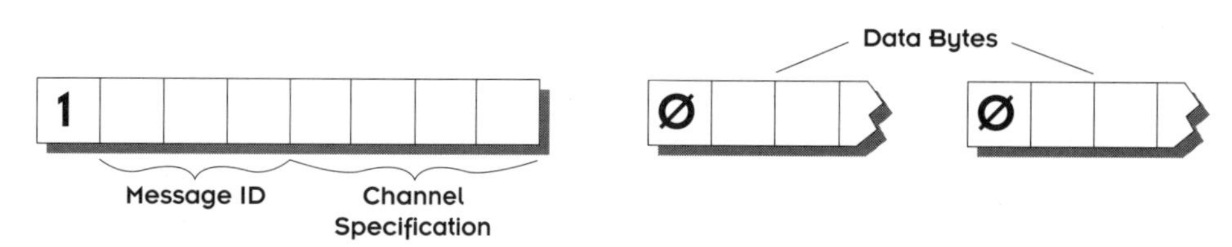

Figure 13.9 How MIDI messages are structured.

As shown in Figure 13.9, a MIDI message includes a *status byte* and up to two *data bytes*. It's easy to identify a status byte because all status bytes have their most significant bit set to 1. Conversely, the most significant bit of any data byte is set to 0. This convention holds for all standard MIDI messages and not just channel messages. Therefore, the data in each byte must be encoded in the seven remaining bits.

MIDI devices transmit all messages on the same cable, regardless of their channel assignments. In the early days of MIDI, musicians and recording engineers were accustomed to 48 track audio mixers, tangled patch panels, and fat umbilical cords stuffed with wire. These folks had a hard time understanding that they didn't need a separate cable for each MIDI channel. The four low-order bits of each status byte identify which channel it belongs to. Four bits produce 16 possible combinations, so MIDI supports 16 channels over a single cable string. (Keep in mind that although MIDI users and vendors number the channels from 1 through 16, internally they are numbered 0 through 15.) The three remaining bits identify the message. Three bits encode eight possible combinations, so channel messages could come in eight flavors, but they don't. A status byte with all four high-order bits set to 1 indicates a system common message—the second general category, which we'll get to after we tackle the channel messages. So, there are only seven channel messages.

Channel Voice Messages

Most of the channel messages are voice messages, as shown in Table 13.1. Voice messages:

- Instruct the receiving instrument to assign particular sounds to its *voices*
- Turn notes on and off
- Send *controller* signals that can alter how the currently active note sounds

A *voice* is the portion of the synthesizer that produces sound. Most modern synthesizers have several voices—that is, they have several circuits that work independently and simultaneously to produce sounds of different *timbre* and *pitch*. Timbre is the sound that the instrument will imitate, such as a flute, cello, or helicopter. Pitch is the musical note that the instrument plays. To play two notes together, the synthesizer uses two voices. Those voices may play two notes with the same timbre, or they may play

Table 13.1 MIDI Channel Voice Messages

Voice Message	Status Byte Hex Value	Number of Data Bytes
Note Off	&H8x	2
Note On	&H9x	2
Polyphonic Aftertouch	&HAx	2
Control Change	&HBx	2
Program Change	&HCx	1
Aftertouch	&HDx	1
Pitch Bend	&HEx	1 or 2

two notes of different timbres. A Control Change message *modulates* the current note by altering its pitch, volume, or timbre to produce various effects, such as vibrato or tremolo.

Voice messages are followed by either one or two data bytes. A Note On message, for example, is followed by two bytes, one to identify the note and one to specify the *velocity*. The velocity specifies how the note should sound. For example, if the synthesizer's voice is set to sound like a piano, the velocity could determine how loudly the note should be played. (In the keyboard world, the faster you strike a piano key, the louder it plays.) To play note number 80 with maximum velocity on channel 13, the MIDI device would send the following three hexadecimal byte values:

```
&H9C &H50 &H7F
```

To turn off the note, it would send either the Note Off message:

```
&H8C &H50 &H00
```

or the Note On message with a velocity of 0:

```
&H9C &H50 &H00
```

Note: *The Note Off channel voice message accepts a velocity because some synthesizers can use the release velocity to determine how a note should decay once it has been shut off. Almost any instrument will accept a Note On message with a velocity of 0 in lieu of a Note Off message.*

Often, you will hear musicians and synthesizer technicians use the term *patches.* Each synthesizer make and model offers unique controls for designing and setting timbres. A patch is the control settings that define a particular timbre. The actual contents of a patch depend on the particular instrument, so rather than sending the whole patch to the instrument through MIDI (although this is also possible), the Program

Change voice message sends a number from 0 to 127, in order to select a patch already stored in the instrument's own *voice bank* memory. For example, to set the instrument on channel 13 to its patch 104, you would send it the MIDI message:

```
&HCC &H68
```

Four of the channel voice messages—Control Change, Polyphonic Aftertouch, Aftertouch, and Pitch Bend—signal a *controller* change. For example, when a saxophone player blows harder, the instrument may sound harsher. By cleverly programming the synthetic saxophone, a keyboard musician can use a slider, foot pedal, or some other device to simulate the breath control of a sax player. Let's take a look at these voice message types.

Pitch Bend was so common on synthesizers when the MIDI specification was created, that it was given its own MIDI message (&HEx). This message signals the synthesizer to raise or lower the pitch of currently active notes on the channel. Pitch Bend messages do not contain note values. The value of the Pitch Bend message bytes reflects the degree to which the pitch bend controller (usually a wheel or lever beside the keyboard) has been moved up or down. The degree to which the pitch changes is up to the instrument itself.

Like Pitch Bend, *Aftertouch* was considered valuable and common enough to be granted its own MIDI message types. The first type of Aftertouch, known as *Polyphonic Aftertouch* (&HAx), transmits a value on a particular channel, for a particular note, that indicates the degree of pressure on the key after it has been struck. Many electronic keyboards now support this feature, which enables keyboard players to get some of the control that other musicians get by changing the pressure on their mouthpieces or bows. The other Aftertouch control message (&HDx) is used when an instrument supports aftertouch, but not on individual notes. In other words, a change in pressure on one key will affect all the notes currently playing on the channel.

The creators of the MIDI specification realized that other types of controllers were found on some instruments, and that more would follow. So, they created one general purpose channel voice message (&HBx) to handle them. The first data byte of the Control Change message selects the controller type, and the second byte specifies its current value. You'll find a complete listing of the pre-defined controller types in the *MIDI 1.0 Detailed Specification* (see the bibliography). Actually, the Control Change message supports only 121 controllers, numbered 0 through 120. The remaining 7 values are reserved for the Channel Mode Messages.

Channel Mode Messages

Mode messages determine how an instrument will process MIDI voice messages. Now that you understand how to send MIDI channel voice messages, you'll have an easier time understanding how to send channel mode messages. Unfortunately, some of the modes themselves have caused more confusion than any other aspect of MIDI.

Channel Mode messages are a special case of the Control Change message. They always begin with a status byte containing the value &HBx, where x is the channel number. The difference between a Control Change message and a Channel Mode message, which share the same status byte value, is in the first data byte. Data byte values 121 through 127 have been reserved in the Control Change message for the channel mode messages. These are listed in Table 13.2.

Of these messages, the least understood—and therefore most creatively interpreted by instrument manufacturers—are Omni Mode On, Omni Mode Off, Mono Mode On, and Poly Mode On. Actually, modes are independent of the mode messages; the messages just change the mode on the fly. The intent of these modes is to determine how an instrument responds to incoming channel voice messages.

Omni Mode means that the instrument responds to messages on all 16 channels. So, if Note On messages are transmitted on all channels, the instrument in Omni Mode will attempt to play them all, up to the maximum number of voices available. Some synthesizers, *monophonic* instruments, can only play one note at a time. Others, known as *polyphonic* instruments, can play 8, 16, 32, or other numbers of simultaneous notes. If a device with only 8 voices receives 15 simultaneous Note On messages, it will play only the first or last 8.

Table 13.2 Channel Mode Messages

First Data Byte Value	Description	Meaning of Second Data Byte
&H79	Reset All Controllers	None; set to 0
&H7A	Local Control	0 = Off; 127 = On
&H7B	All Notes Off	None; set to 0
&H7C	Omni Mode Off	None; set to 0
&H7D	Omni Mode On	None; set to 0
&H7E	Mono Mode On (Poly Mode Off)	0 means that the number of channels used is determined by the receiver; all other values set a specific number of channels, beginning with the current *basic channel*
&H7F	Poly Mode On (Mono Mode Off)	None; set to 0

For most real-world applications, Omni Mode isn't discerning enough. (In fact, it isn't discerning at all.) Most polyphonic instruments can play not only a multitude of simultaneous notes, they can also play them with a variety of patches. So, one synthesizer can sound like a whole band. In Poly Mode, each channel is assigned a patch. All notes on each channel play with the same timbre. For example, you could set channel 1 to play bass, channel 2 to play piano, and channel 3 to play drums. In Mono Mode, only one note can play at a time on each channel. Poly Mode has some powerful capabilities, but we don't have room to discuss them here. For detailed coverage of MIDI modes, order a copy of the *MIDI 1.0 Detailed Specification.*

System Messages

The second general category of MIDI messages are the *system messages,* which include *system common messages, system real-time messages,* and *system exclusive messages.* These messages carry information that is not channel-specific, such as timing signals for synchronization, positioning information in pre-recorded MIDI sequences, and detailed setup information for the destination device.

There are four types of system common messages, as shown in Table 13.3.

The six system real-time messages, listed in Table 13.4, primarily affect sequencer playback and recording. These messages have no data bytes.

The third type of system message, the system exclusive message, is used to transfer data between devices. For example, you may wish to store patch setups for an instrument on a computer using a *patch librarian* program. You can then transfer those patches to the synthesizer by means of a system exclusive message. The name *system exclusive* means that these are messages exclusively for a particular device, or type of device, rather than universal messages that all MIDI compatible products should recognize. A system exclusive message is just a stream of bytes, all with their high bits set to 0, bracketed by a pair of system exclusive start and end messages (&HF0 and &HF7).

The MIDI Offspring

Since the introduction of the MIDI protocol, four other MIDI standards have appeared:

- MIDI Show Control 1.0
- MIDI Machine Control 1.0
- Standard MIDI Files 1.0
- General MIDI System, Level 1

The MIDI Show Control and MIDI Machine Control standards specify a set of system-exclusive messages that can control various types of non-musical equipment.

Table 13.3 MIDI System Common Messages

System Common Message	Status Byte Hex Value	Number of Data Bytes
MIDI Time Code	&HF1	1
Song Position Pointer	&HF2	2
Song Select		
Tune Request	&HF6	None

Table 13.4 MIDI System Real-Time Messages

System Real Time Message	Status Byte Hex Value
Timing Clock	&HF8
Start Sequence	&HFA
Continue Sequence	&HFB
Stop Sequence	&HFC
Active Sensing	&HFE
System Reset	&HFF

The Show Control focuses specifically on stage lighting and sound control systems, although it is designed to control just about any kind of performance system, including mechanical stages. The Machine Control standard specifies system exclusive messages to operate audio and video recorders.

The biggest problem that surfaced after the widespread adoption of the MIDI protocol was in sequencer file formats. Shortly after the introduction of the first MIDI-equipped synthesizers, several sequencer programs appeared. Sequencer programs allow musicians and composers to record and play back MIDI information. With a sequencer, one person can compose and play an entire symphony, using nothing more than a computer and a few synthesizers. All these programs, no matter which platform they supported, adhered to the MIDI communication protocol. They had to, or they wouldn't work. But the files in which they stored their data were another matter. Each software developer created its own proprietary format, which meant that you couldn't create a music sequence with one program and play it back with another. So in 1988, the International MIDI Association published the second component of the MIDI standard, *Standard MIDI Files 1.0.* Standard MIDI files are built from *chunks*, which contain some header information and a series of data bytes. Sound familiar? Although not identical, MIDI standard files and RIFF files have quite a bit in common. In fact, a Windows MIDI file is actually a standard MIDI file embedded in a RIFF chunk.

Standard MIDI files made it possible for musicians to share their files, regardless of hardware and software platforms. But this new standard brought to light another problem. The *tracks* in a MIDI sequencer file may specify a program number, which determines the instrument sound, or patch, with which that track should be played. But every instrument has its own assortment of patches. So, while program number 30 on one synthesizer might be a brass section patch, the same program number on another instrument could be a tympani drum, or a sci-fi phaser gun. Playback of a standard MIDI file might produce all the right notes, however, they may be on all the wrong instruments. The General MIDI System standard attempts to solve this problem by offering a standard program list, consisting of the 128 most common patch types, from pianos to gunshots (literally—General MIDI program 1 is 'Acoustic Grand Piano,' and program 128 is 'Gunshot'). General MIDI also specifies a layout for percussion instruments, called the General MIDI Percussion Map. Percussion is a special case, because non-melodic percussion sounds, such as drums, cymbals, and cowbells, need to occupy only one note position, so you can theoretically fit up to 128 separate percussion sounds in one patch. General MIDI includes 47 percussion sounds, and specifies that percussion should be transmitted on MIDI channel 10.

General MIDI is considered a *system* rather than a *specification,* because not all instruments need to comply. In fact, that would defeat the purpose of programmable synthesizers, which enable artists to continually invent new sounds. Some synthesizer modules are designed specifically for use as General MIDI devices, and come pre-programmed with compliant patches. Other synthesizers support a General MIDI mode, but also provide a separate programmable patch bank. And some instruments don't support General MIDI at all, unless you program and arrange the patches yourself.

The Unique MOD File Format

MOD files could easily be considered a type of digital audio file, but they've got such a peculiar history and structure they really are a format unto themselves.

MOD files got their start on the Amiga and have now migrated to the PC, Mac, and even workstations. They are part sample file and part music file. The files contain samples and playback information, which indicates which sample is played at which time. The approach is kind of like combining both WAV files and MIDI together and coming up with a new format. The samples are called *instruments,* but they don't have to be actual instrument sounds; any sample can be part of a MOD file, which is what makes them so special. You can have voices, sound effects, or even crowd screams!

Let me explain how MOD files work: Most music—in terms of the stuff musical groups produce—is comprised of four distinct tracks: drum, bass, rhythm, and a "lead" track. Programmers applied this concept to the Amiga and utilized all four of the Amiga's "voices" to replay digitized samples of instruments on these tracks. By looping and switching instruments on the tracks, programmers created a software reproduction of some really amazing sounds. In addition, lyrical snippets could be added because the playback technology was all based on digital audio and not FM synthesis.

On the downside, MOD files can have tinny pops, which occur as a result of poor sample quality and the type of sound card used. Since its debut, the MOD format has undergone numerous facelifts resulting in several versions. Unlike MIDI, no one controls the MOD file format so new MOD formats have appeared often. You can find new MOD file formats with up to 32 simultaneous channels, a maximum of 255 instruments, possible sample rates of up to 48 kHz, and 16-bit source samples of (almost) unlimited size. Although these newer formats can be useful, you should investigate their effect on the speed of your game as they can be quite taxing. Unfortunately, MOD files are not covered in game or other programming books even though many PC games still use MODs. See the associated sidebar for more information.

Game Developers' Guide to MOD Files

Modules are digital music files, made up of a set of samples (the instruments) and sequencing information that tells a MOD player when to play a sample on a particular track at a specified pitch. Thus, MODs are different from pure sample files such as WAV or AU, which contain no sequencing information. MODs are also different from MIDI files, which do not include any custom samples or instruments. MODs are extremely popular in the demo world because they offer a way of making music of an acceptable quality rather cheaply. With the advent of high-quality sound hardware, new generations of MODs may even rise to a sound quality nearing that of professional quality sound.

Sequencing information is based on patterns and tracks. A pattern is a group of tracks with a certain length, usually 64 rows. The tracks are independent of each other, meaning that a four track MOD can play four voices or notes simultaneously. The patterns can be sequenced in a playlist, so that repeating the same sequence of patterns doesn't require rewriting them. This makes MODs a hybrid between pure sample data files such as WAV, VOC, or IFF/8SVX and pure sequencing information files like MIDI.

As I've mentioned, the MOD world is riddled with all kinds of different formats, some of which are getting incredibly fancy. There are three main components to the major formats:

- Number of instruments that can be programmed in to the file
- Frequency range of the samples

- Number of channels or digital streams that can be played at one time

Let's take a quick look at each of the popular MOD formats that are in use today:

MOD

This is the main type of MOD file in use today. It was the first standard and it is based on the original Amiga format. There are several slight variations offering more instruments but the basic capabilities of this format support 31 instruments with four playing at any one time at an 8-bit resolution.

S3M and MTM

S3M and MTM are somewhat similar in their format. Both offer 8- and 16-bit samples and both are capable of supporting 32 simultaneous channels of music. S3M can support up to 99 instruments available. To build MOD files, you should use the ScreamTracker formats editor for S3M and the Multitracker editor for MTM. S3M also apparently can mix in some FM instruments—up to 9 on SB and SB PRO cards.

XM

This is the latest and greatest format on the scene. It supports up to 32 tracks, 128 instruments, multi-sampled intruments, an extremely large sample size, and lots of MIDI support. Samples can be 8 or 16 bits. The FastTracker editor can be used to create files of this format.

Creating MOD Files on the PC

Creating a MOD file requires a MOD writing program commonly called a *tracker*. So far, I have heard of only one MOD tracker for Windows and try as a I might I couldn't actually get my hands on it. The other major trackers are all DOS-based. The ones most often used include:

ScreamTracker

This MOD editor created by a member of the European demo team Future Crew is a full featured MOD maker that supports the S3M format as well as many other former MOD formats. You can find this editor at:
`ftp://ftp.cdrom.com/pub/demos/music/programs/trackers/scrmt32.zip`

FastTracker II

This MOD editor supports S3M and all kinds of samples and several other MOD formats. You can find this editor at:
`ftp://ftp.cdrom.com/pub/demos/music/programs/trackers/ft203.zip`

MultiTracker Module Editor 1.01b

Here's yet another MOD editor to play with. It is not as full featured as the previous two but with MOD editors each one is different enough to warrant playing with several to find your favorite. You can find this editor at:
`ftp://ftp.cdrom.com/pub/demos/music/programs/trackers/mtm101b.zip`

MacMod Pro

This is a complete player and tracker for the Mac, capable of creating MODs from 4 to 32 channels. This program can be found at:
`ftp://wuarchive.wustl.edu/systems/mac/info-mac/snd/util/mac-mod-pro-322.hqx`

Conversion Tools

In addition to creating and editing MOD files, you'll need a way to convert your MODs. Unfortunately, converting between different formats and especially to non-MOD formats is a difficult process. Converting from one of the later MOD formats to a earlier format is not for the faint of heart; going from an earlier format to one of the latest incarnations is far easier and there are a couple of products to help you out.

PT-MID 0.3 for the PC

This program converts general MIDI files to a couple of MOD formats. The converted MODs still require some tweaking and re-editing using a MOD editor. You can find this conversion program at:
`ftp://x2ftp.oulu.fi:/pub/msdos/programming/convert/ptmid3.zip`

PT-MID 0.3 for the Mac

This program converts general MIDI files to a couple of MOD formats. The converted MODs still require some tweaking and re-editing using a MOD editor. You can find this conversion program at:
`ftp://ftp.mm.se/playerpro/ptmid_0.3_folder.sit.bin - Mac`

Key Mac MOD resource at Opcode

This page on the Opcode systems site contains a large collection of all the known Mac related MOD programs:
`http://www.opcode.com/omn/mac_mod.html`

More MOD Information

To obtain more information about MODs, check the ever updating MOD FAQ that Matt Behrens maintains on the Web:
`http://www.csis.gvsu.edu/~behrensm/absm-faq/index.html`

Programming

I've only seen a few programming resources for MOD files and let's just say that most of them aren't the most useful. (Mostly because of all the different file types and programming work required to play high powered MOD files.) Here are some of the better resources available:

Midas MCI Mod Driver
Cinematix Studios
63 E. Main #713
Mesa, AZ 85201

This is a Windows driver for traditional MCI multimedia systems. It's based on the DOS version of some MOD playback libraries created by Petteri Kangaslampi and Jarno Pannanen. This Windows MCI version was written by Benjamin Cooley of CINEMATIX. Since it works through the driver system of Windows, any programmer can easily offer MOD playback through commands to the MCI MMSYSTEM.DLL in Windows.

The version I used (1.04) is a little buggy. So be sure to thoroughly test your setup here to insure it works. MIDAS plays both the original MOD and the newer S3M format files.

In short, this tool isn't quite ready for primetime, but check back with them to see if they have a new version.

DigPAK Mod Patch

These are the popular sound libraries from John Ratcliff that have a MOD. You can find this file on CompuServe's Game Developer Forum.

Tiny Play

There are a couple of related Tiny Play items to be had; one is the original version of the product provided. Secondly, I found a 32 bit Watcom C++ implementation that provides more source. The 32 bit Watcom implementation is fairly basic and doesn't support every known MOD format, especially the higher end. You can find this file on CompuServe's Game Developer Forum.

Using Redbook Audio for Your Music Tracks

Redbook audio is the process of actually laying down a music track on a CD-ROM—exactly like the process used to create an audio CD. This is the music format of choice for many programmers because the sound quality can't be beat. However, redbook audio works only as a linear format; you cannot branch to other tracks. Once you tell the program to play a redbook track, you can't ask the CD for additional information. Therefore, you better make sure you've loaded everything you needed off the CD into RAM.

Some programs that use CD audio (and a technique you may want to consider) actually allow players to put in their own CDs and use that for the music—a nice touch, wouldn't you say?

Digital Audio versus MIDI Music

Digital audio is making big headway into the music industry and CD-ROMs helped accelerate the process. But keep in mind that even though the sound quality from digital audio is better than MIDI (depending, of course, on the resolution of the playback device), digital audio is basically a linear format and MIDI is not. For example, when a game is designed to play a track of digital audio off of a CD-ROM and you quickly switch to another track, there will be split second of silence. MIDI, however, can respond instantaneously to interactive events.

Believe it or not, this distinction is important. If you're doing an action arcade game where the tempo and such can change rapidly, using redbook audio streaming from a CD-ROM just isn't going to work. Interactive MIDI however will. On the other hand, if you're creating a racing game and the only pace change occurs during a crash and you can fade out the music, a digital audio stream should work just fine.

Digital audio is definitely a growing and extremely exciting addition to music production; just understand it isn't an all-purpose music production technique or a substitute for MIDI.

Here Comes 3D Sound

The current wave of innovation in music and sound types is the notion of "3D sound." 3D sound is somewhat of a misnomer because it's used to describe everything from simple "beyond-the-speaker" sound to full 3D aural experiences. Let's discuss the more common classifications.

- *Spatial enhancement* is a technique that adds depth and space to existing sounds. Using a spatial sound algorithm a sound can be given a wider field of playback on a speaker system. This technique is known as "going beyond the speakers."
- *Stereo spreading* is basically advanced panning. Using simple techniques and shifting sound playback timing between left and right speakers (and thus the listener's ears), sounds can be "placed" in a 180° space facing the listener. For optimal use of this technology, listeners need to position their speakers (headphones will not work) to find the "sweet spot" that enhances the use of this process.

- *"True" 3D sound* takes a mono input and then attempts to "place" the sound through algorithmic modifications and timing techniques. Unlike the previous two techniques, the object is to make the sound truly 3D with a range of 360° both around as well as above and below the speaker and at any "distance." Listeners will need four speakers or headphones. Again speaker placement is key for optimal performance.

  Microsoft is working on a "True 3D" standard to promote as its Direct3D Sound technology. Products claiming "True 3D" will conform to a spec that offers 360° surround sound.

Pre-Processed Sound or Realtime Mixing?

When you are considering adding 3D sound to your games, you have two issues to contend with: Deciding on the role 3D sound will play in the game, and deciding how to implement it.

If your sound effect will be a consistent sound—always moving left to right in a simple arc, for example—pre-processed sound would be the best to use for your implementation. Using a product like Sound Designer II and a plug-in product from a technology company like QSound, you can take a sample and turn it into a 3D sound. Once you've finished the conversion, simply store the sound as a WAV (or any comparable) file that can be played back in the game.

However, if your sound effect will change depending on game circumstances (mixing in realtime), you'll have to use a 3D sound SDK to implement it. I'll discuss three viable 3D sound technologies in Chapter 14.

Is 3D Sound for You?

3D sound, for all the hoopla, is simply another mixing technology that you can employ to heighten the intensity of your games. Of course, the sound can be unbelievably good. However, until consumers are able to get more advanced sound hardware into their homes—better sound cards, additional top-quality speakers (true surround-sound 3D technology requires more than two speakers)—this technology may have to take a back seat to your other options. In addition, you need to consider the work involved in creating the sound. Just because a game has a 3D Sound label doesn't mean the sound is good.

The Ins and Outs of Sound Cards

Unless you think the PC speaker is a good enough for your audience, then welcome to the wonderful world of sound cards! If you're serious about producing a top-notch game, you will need to go on a sound card shopping spree. And don't be cheap; buy more than two. Unfortunately, not all sound cards are created equally. Because each card has its own idiosyncrasies, which can affect how music and sounds come across to the user, you want to be able to handle as many situations as you can. For example, early sound cards had as few as nine melodic voices, whereas modern sound cards have 32. If your music is created on one of the newer sound cards, you'll definitely have problems converting it to an older card. In addition, some cards also provide stereo, while others still use mono. Some say they provide stereo, but reduce the number of voices by half to provide it.

At the very least, you should understand the differences among the major models out there so you can up the ante to newer sound features as they become widely available to consumers.

The Changing Standard: Wavetable Cards

As you know, sound is a wave that can be captured digitally. Storing those waves onto sound cards for playback was a natural progression in sound card development. Here's how they work: The sound card manufacturer samples the instrument he or she wants to emulate and puts it on the sound card. When you select a particular instrument, the sound card looks up the waveform for that instrument, transforms it to get the requested tonality, and plays the transformed version of the waveform. Most manufacturers allow you to replace the samples with your own custom waveforms, and most instrument sets on wavetable cards conform to a standard. But be forewarned: Some cards do not conform to the standard. Where you might have intended a real impressive distorted guitar bit to play, the user actually hears a harpsichord doing unharpsichord-like things. In this case, your solution would be to create your own instrument bank and load it in at the beginning of your game, or before you start playing your music. This process is actually what happens when you play music through an FM synthesis card. Since the amount of data to define an instrument is quite small, it's no problem to include the instrument data in the music piece itself.

There is one minor drawback: Storing separate instruments with waveform representation takes much more memory than storing them through a kind of mathematical formula, which results in a higher price tag for wavetable cards and memory requirements that can't always be met. However, because wavetable cards provide for realistic sound, they will no doubt become the standard in gaming.

You need to keep a careful eye on things when you or your musician is creating new instrument files, which can easily happen if you're using multiple composers. In this type of situation, you need to lay down the law. Decide how many different custom instrument sounds you want

and then work with your composers to make sure that those don't proliferate. If you manage the "sound palette" early on, you'll thank yourself later.

FM Synthesis versus Wavetable

The difference in sound between an FM and a wavetable card is enormous. Although most music made on an FM card will sound good on a wavetable card (assuming the instrument bank of the FM card conforms to the instrument standard of the wavetable card—the biggest reason many developers use the General Midi standard), the opposite is not true; you cannot count on the fact that music created on a wavetable card will sound good on an FM card. I recommend purchasing both a wavetable card and an FM synthesis card to protect yourself and your composer from embarrassment.

The Progression of Wavetable Technology

Wavetable cards have gone through several progressions. The first generation of wavetable synthesis was actually a digitally controlled analog oscillator where parameters controlling the waveform were kept in memory.

The second generation of wavetable synthesis used a complete digital oscillator, with the waveform held in memory in its basic form (one period usually). Parameters controlling the sound's behavior were also stored in memory. I use the general term "memory" instead of RAM because in some case the memory used is actually ROM, FlashROM, PROM, EPROM, buffers, and so on.

The third generation of wavetable synthesis, which can be found in two flavors (RAM or ROM), is based on the second generation, but uses bigger wavetables to hold the waveforms with more information. This allows for even greater realistic sound reproduction.

Next Stop, Complete DSP

The next major stop for sound cards is the move to fancy Digital Signal Processor chips. DSP chips, which are added to sound cards, are able to control large waveforms that are held in the card's memory. They also can do amazing effects very rapidly to stored waveforms. Do you want to render the same sound file as if it were in a large hall or a small room? DSP chips can do this in realtime! This technology will allow sound designers to implement live mixing techniques to an extent that we haven't heard before in games.

The Logical Conclusion

The bottom line is this: Sound in games is directly related to the available card technology (isn't that just a brilliant thought?). Unfortunately, the various sound cards available—FM synthesis, wavetable, and wavetable with extensive custom sample features—make for some major roadblocks in your programming strategy. What sampling should you use? What instruments should you support? Should you use downloadable samples or just general MIDI? Thankfully, programming packages are available to help you get over the hurdle. These packages are covered in Chapter 14.

In the end it's up to you to stay on top of the sound technologies rapidly debuting. You should also keep track of the installed base of similarly capable cards. Before you begin to produce music, let alone program it, consider the common features you'll support in your sound and music as well as the special features you might add to your music to take advantage of a certain card's capabilities.

Working with a Musician

Considering that music has the ability to put you into a certain mood, you may wonder why so few games have music that you actually like. The answer is twofold: First, no one can create music that everybody likes; and second, music is often overlooked by the game industry. During the past few years, however, music in games has emerged from the backstage to take its place at the podium. Nowadays, much more attention is being given to the music. Some games even feature popular rock groups in their credits.

Unless you have universal talents, it is very unlikely that you'll be able to make a good game and produce good music for that game all by yourself. Both game making and composing are two crafts that take a considerable amount of time to master. In most cases, good music in your game means getting a composer or musician to create the music for you.

This section discusses everything you need to know once you decide to outsource your musical requirements. I'll go over the type of composers and musicians you should be looking for, where you can get them, and, most importantly, what their abilities have to be. This is by no means the definitive guide, but it should give you some valuable insights. Let's begin by discussing the various types of composers you will encounter when you decide to hand the music ball to someone else.

The Professional Interactive Composer

If you're serious about creating quality sound, the only way to go is to hire a professional. Although you will find many fine composers out there scoring for TV and film, you really want to narrow your search to those composers who concentrate on

games and multimedia titles. There are over a dozen major game/interactive composition houses around. They're good, they know the business, and they've done games.

These musicians know MIDI inside out. They've worked with digital audio, and will be familiar with the formats and sound capabilities of all the cards and consoles. You will find this to be a huge advantage when you need to tweak the score to play on the various systems on which your game runs.

Many composers in the industry are independents and contract to other companies as well. Taking this into consideration, you will need to shop around to find composers who are able to meet your time frame.

My advice is to hook up with a large production house rather than dealing directly with a single composer. A production house has a large base of composers working for them. They will be able to find a composer to suit your needs within your specified time frame and within your budget.

The Professional Composer

Notice that the word *interactive* has been omitted from this heading. Professional composers and musicians have this annoying habit of not understanding that the medium on which their work is being performed is limited. This is a setback worthy of its significance. Don't underestimate the need for the experience with interactive formats.

If you can get them to understand these limitations, chances are that they'll see it as a challenge and produce good stuff. If not, don't even bother. The problem, as you might expect, is that you have to be able to get their music on the computer. I discuss this process in detail later in this chapter. But the benefit of using a standard composer is that you draw on unused talent. It's a tradeoff for sure, but if you can find a composer who is willing to give you 100 percent, there's no reason the lack of experience should matter.

Amateur Musicians

You're producing your first game, it's not retail level, it could be nice shareware. You can't afford a professional composer. What options do you have? There's always the guy across town with the MIDI setup. And there are plenty of wannabes aching for a shot at the big time. However, these guys are usually so convinced of their own genius that you can't get anything decent from them. And who knows. If you're lucky you might find an unknown dying to work for peanuts. Wouldn't that be great!

Let me give you a few pointers on dealing with amateurs. You want to find a perfectionist, someone who is willing to go the extra mile to produce quality music. Of

course, some kind of musical background—like being able to write scores—should be mandatory. And finally, you need to find someone who is willing to listen to instructions (and you need to be able to provide explicit instructions).

Finding a Composer

Here are some simple tips to finding musicians or letting them know to find you:

- *Post Want Ads Online*

  The best place to look for composers, aside from the multimedia resource guides, is online. A post on CompuServe's Game Developer forum and the MIDI forum, and some of the top Web sites like Happy Puppy should bring you a considerable list of replies to sift through. Be sure to define what you're looking for and ask for a package of files demonstrating their talents. If you want a particular style, mention that too.

- *Individuals and Companies*

  There are independents who roam around and companies like Sega's music group, Rob Wallace Music, and Team FAT, which represent a trend toward forming companies to offer a broad range of styles.

- *Web Sites*

  Again the best place to look is online. Many of the companies producing sound have Web sites with demo music downloads and contact information plus references to products they've done. In two hours of surfing I came across numerous home pages for qualified, experienced game musicians and sound editors.

  A simple visit to the various Web search engines like Yahoo! and Digital's AltaVista will get you surfing around to pro musician sites in no time.

- *The Computer Game Developers Conference*

  You can also find good musicians at the CGDC. Many of these folks bring demo tapes with them, so be prepared to listen.

Hiring a Composer

Hiring a composer or musician is a major decision but it's not too hard to do; you will need to simply take the time to listen to a lot of demo tapes. It's a good idea to constantly be recruiting musical talent. Musicians are very often individual contractors and can be tied up at any given time, so it pays to build up a stable of reliable musical talent.

When evaluating a demo tape it's a good idea to listen for multiple implementations—for example, a song rendered as digital audio, General MIDI, and perhaps as a wavetable. If the composer also engineers sound effects, be sure to get a sample disk and look for sounds rendered at different rates and such. A good musician will be able to tweak the same song or sound to enhance it individually on the various file formats and specifications.

You'll want to also find out their technical background—just because they know MIDI doesn't mean they're technically astute. Remember, the variance in sound cards can have a tremendous affect on the approach to producing music for games. The more technically astute your composer proves to be, the better he or she will be able to handle those little adjustments or provide you with several variances to their music.

Working with Your Composer

Now that you've gone to the trouble of hiring a composer, weeding out all the riffraff, you want your working relationship to be a productive one. If you've hired a professional interactive musician, you will probably not have to be involved too much after your initial discussion until the "finished" product is at your door. Of course, this depends on what type of composer or musician you have.

You cannot expect the other types of composers and musicians to be fluent with computers, and most likely you or someone on your staff will have to help personally. Spend the time to work out any technical jargon and be precise as to your needs. Bear in mind that you most likely have more experience with computers than the composer, and that you'll have to be patient. Likewise, the composer should realize that your ultimate musical knowledge is limited to "I know what I like."

As developer, though, it's ultimately your responsibility to make sure the composer knows as much about how you plan to use his or her work in your game as you do. Make sure to thoroughly discuss the formats you're going to use, where in the game MIDI is going to be, how you like your files to be formatted, and the associated naming conventions.

Licensing Music and Digital Audio

An alternative to dealing with a musician is to work with a music publisher to obtain licensed music for commercial use. Licensing music isn't as difficult or expensive as you might think, although cost is dependent on the artist, the catalog, the song, and length of what you want.

One great example of using licensed music in a game is Road Rash III by Electronic Arts for the 3DO. In making this title, which is a motorcycle racing game with the added feature of having to knock down your opponents using batons and chains, EA went out and licensed music from grunge rock bands like PAW. The result was awesome sound, complete with lyrics that complemented the title like no other score could.

Wow! I bet you can't wait to start adding Sex Pistols' songs to your newest shoot-em up. Before you get too far ahead of yourself, let's look at the realities. Licensing music is a major research project and is best left to a good lawyer who has multimedia knowledge or a *rights acquisition specialist.* A rights acquisition specialist can get you the music you want much faster than you will. If your time is worth money, give the money to the specialist and save the time.

Of course this isn't the whole story so let me explain some more and give some general advice.

Who Owns the Song?

The first thing to understand is that a performer is not necessarily the owner of a song. For example, I love U2's version of "All Along the Watchtower," but the owner of the song is not U2 or anyone other than the original publisher. In addition, if I get the rights to "All Along the Watchtower," I can't use U2's or any other musician's version of it without their permission. Complicated huh? Welcome to the world of licensing music. Now you understand why it hasn't been used too much. This is why an acquisition specialist is useful; they know the ins and outs of who owns what, and you don't.

Not Every Song Is Available

One funny thing about ownership is that it gives you control. Just because music is licensable doesn't mean every song ever written is available to license. You can be sure that Bobby McFerrin's famous song "Don't Worry, Be Happy" isn't available for your Doom-like slugfest. (Although, you never know. Maybe Bobby is an avid gamer!) And forget organizations like Disney—they have their own multimedia projects and I doubt they're licensing anything to competitors.

When you try to obtain licenses to use music, you'll need to do a little homework. Define a number (the more the better, most don't pan out) of songs, groups, and genres for your rights acquisition specialist to work with. And let him or her do the leg work.

Remember the Audience

If I have said anything of importance in this chapter it is this: Make sure you know what your intended audience is listening to before you spend money on licensing music. Making a wrong move here can be pretty embarrassing. I'm a developer's dream when it comes to musical taste; I listen to everything—Rap, Grunge, Classical, Techno, House, Acid, Jazz, Industrial, Folk, and World Music. Heck, I even have

some sea shanties and chants in my collection. But I am the exception. Consider your choices wisely.

Digitizing Your Song

Once you get the rights to a song, you need to digitize it for use in your game. Before you rush out to Tower Records to buy Soundgarden's latest for your cyber-thriller, check with your rights acquisition specialist (see how important these are?) to see if you can get the masters from the licensing company to send to your sound techie folks.

The Bottom Line

Here is the bottom line: Expect to see more and more music acts being used or even exclusively authoring soundtracks for games. It's not a question of if, but of when. Getting a jump by learning more about the entire process can be a real plus. On that note, here is a list of contacts and resources for licensing music:

The Hollywood Movie Music Directory
Hollywood Creative Directory
3000 W. Olympic Blvd., Suite 2525
Santa Monica, CA 90404-5041
Phone: 310 315-4815 **Fax:** 310 315-4816
WWW: http://www.hollyvision.com

This directory contains contact information for various music-related companies in the music industry, including music clearance agencies. It's an excellent guide to own if you will use major licensed audio in your games.

ASCAP (American Society of Composers, Authors, and Publishers)
One Lincoln Plaza
New York, NY 10023
Phone: 212 621-6000
WWW: http://www.ascap.com/

ASCAP is an organization of over 68,000 composers, songwriters, lyricists, and music publishers. The organization handles collecting and distributing royalty fees for their members. Stop by their Web site, which contains a great resource guide for locating musicians or anyone working with or within the music industry. You'll also find lots of good information on legal issues.

BMI
WWW: http://bmi.com/

BMI, like ASCAP, is an organization of songwriters, composers, and publishers in the music industry. They collect and distribute royalties for public performance and digital copying of their works. Just like the ASCAP folks, they have an awesome Web site with lots of good links and information about working with and within the music industry.

NMPA (National Music Publishers Association)
and
The Harry Fox Agency, Inc.
711 Third Avenue
New York, NY 10017
Phone: 212 370-5330 **Fax:** 212 953-2384
WWW: http://www.nmpa.org

The NMPA, which has been around for more than seventy-five years, is a major legislative, legal, and educational association for music publishers. The association also operates a subsidiary, The Harry Fox Agency, established in 1927, to provide an information source, clearinghouse, and monitoring service for licensing musical copyrights.

I encourage you to visit their Web site; it is an excellent place to get information on musical clearance.

Music Production Resources

You can always count on an industry generating several quality resources for their followers. The music industry is no exception. The following magazines do not necessarily devote their pages to how electronic music fits into the gaming world, but the technology is the same.

***Keyboard* Magazine**
Miller Freeman
600 Harrison Street
San Francisco, CA 94107
Phone: 415 358-9500 **Fax:** 415 358-9527
WWW: http://www.mfi.com/keyboard/
Subscription: N/A **Newsstand:** $3.95 **Publishes:** Monthly **Pages:** 150

This magazine covers everything related to computer and music technology. It's read religiously by professional musicians and audio people, and has feature articles about creating music in the interactive multimedia and games environment. If you're creating music for games or just interested in electronic music as an industry and you aren't reading this magazine, you're absolutely crazy.

Electronic Musician
6400 Hollis Street #12
Emeryville, CA 94608

Phone: 510 653-3307 **Fax:** 510 653-5142
Subscription: N/A **Newsstand:** $3.95 **Publishes:** Monthly **Pages:** 110

Along with *Keyboard* Magazine, *Electronic Musician* is the major magazine covering all the issues of making music using computers. Each edition is jam-packed with information about MIDI, digital sound, and the latest electronic music equipment.

Future Music Magazine
Future Publishing
30 Monmouth Street
Bath BA1 2BW
Phone: +44 1225 822511 **Fax:** +44 1225 446019
Subscription: £87 **Newsstand:** N/A **Publishes:** Monthly **Pages:** 100

From England-based Future Publishing, which publishes a number of major computer, game, and other special interest magazines, comes a wonderful magazine on high-tech music and computer music production. I bet you're wondering how much £87 is, right? Depending on exchange rates it's roughly $130.

A Little More About MIDI

To get into the full array of MIDI-oriented products, it would take me into the next millenium. While it's fairly easy to narrow down the key sound editing packages, sorting out the best MIDI sequencing software and other utilities is an absolute headache. But I want to point out a couple of packages that could be helpful to small developers who plan to generate their own music.

Shareware and Commercial Packages

I use the following shareware and commercial packages to play around with MIDI files:

WinJammer
WinJammer Software Limited
69 Rancliffe Road
Oakville, Ontario
Canada L6H 1B1
Phone: 905 842-3708 **Fax:** 905 842-2732
Email: 72662.3021@compuserve.com

WinJammer is a great MIDI sequencer product that's available as shareware (see Figure 13.10). While you can find other more extensive packages, this is a good program for small developers who need a simple product to rework MIDI files, change instruments, experiment, and so on. The company also offers WinJammer PRO, which is a substanial upgrade for those who need to go to the next level.

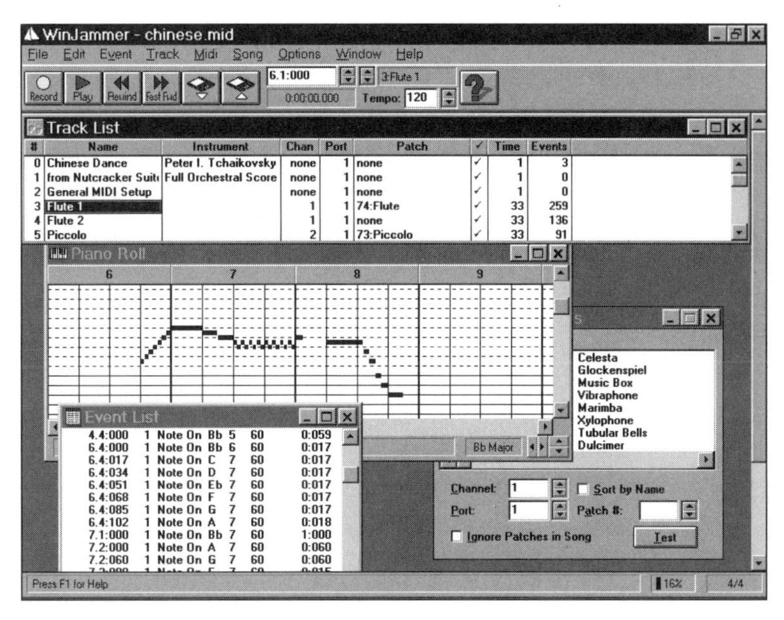

Figure 13.10 WinJammer in action.

You can find WinJammer at http://www.shareware.com or in the MIDI forum on CompuServe.

SuperJam
The Blue Ribbon SoundWorks, Inc.
1605 Chantilly Drive, Suite 200
Atlanta, GA 30324
Phone: 404 315-0212 **Fax:** 404 315-0213

From one of Microsoft's latest acquisitions comes Blue Ribbon Soundworks. Their key product, SuperJam, is the perfect tool for those of us who are less musically inclined but who want to generate some simple tunes. It's available on a wide range of platforms including Windows, Mac, and even Silicon Graphics. This tool is best used to generate music you can use until you can find a professional composer to hire.

SuperJam uses some of Blue Ribbon's automatic composition technology to generate "music on the fly." It comes with over 25 different musical styles such as classical, jazz, reggae, and rock 'n roll.

Autoscore
Wildcat Canyon Software
1563 Solano Avenue #264
Berkeley, CA 94707

Phone: 800 336-0983 **Fax:** 510 527-8425
WWW: http://www.wildcat.com

If you are creating games simply for the fun of it, check out this product. As a hobbyist, you might not be much of a musician, nor do you have money to hire one. This product allows you to literally sing into a microphone and it translates the pitch of your voice to music. If you can hum a tune or a rhythm, you can make music with this product. It also takes input from live musical devices, so if you play a little clarinet or guitar, you'll be well on your way.

Of course, using Autoscore isn't exactly a professional way to generate original music but it does work. (I fully tested it, but I'm not going to let you hear me sing.) A demo copy is available on the company's web site so you too can test it and see if it works for you.

Key MIDI Software

Here is a general listing of the heavyweights in MIDI software. You'll also find a few interesting resources. For the most complete breakdown, subscribe to the magazines listed in this chapter. These magazines will help you get on the road to becoming a MIDI software and hardware expert.

Artic Software
P.O. Box 28
Waterford, WI 53185
Phone: 414 534-4309 **Fax:** 414 534-7809
WWW: http://execpc/com/~artic

Artic Software is a great MIDI software resource for VB programmers. Its founder Arthur Edstrom sells a large range of useful tools for VB programmers including MIDI Cool Tools. In addition, he has a number of useful MIDI utilities for all MIDI mavens including a cool database management product to keep track of MIDI files.

Cakewalk Music Software
P.O. Box 760
Watertown, MA 02272
Phone: 800 234-1171 **Fax:** 617 924-6657

Cakewalk makes a whole range of MIDI and digital audio tools. Its MIDI sequencing product Cakewalk Pro is one of the most used sequencers around.

Mark of the Unicorn, Inc.
1280 Massachusetts Avenue
Cambridge, MA, 02138

Phone: 617 576 2760 **Fax:** 617 576-3609
WWW: http://www.motu.com

Mark of the Unicorn was founded in 1980 and is best known for its Performer product—a long time benchmark MIDI package. Today they have an extensive line of products for Macs and PCs. Their Web site is a very good place to start and features demos and extensive literature on their products.

Opcode Systems
3950 Fabian Way
Suite 100
Palo Alto, CA 94303
Phone: 415 856-3333 **Fax:** 415 856-3332
WWW: http://www.opcode.com

Opcode is one of the oldest and best music software companies around. They have extensive MIDI product lines for both the Mac and PC platforms. Their Web site is quite comprehensive and features downloadable demos of some of their products.

Passport Designs
100 Stone Pine Road
Half Moon Bay, CA 94019
Phone: 415 726-0280 **Fax:** 415 726-2254
WWW: http://www.mw3.com/passport/

Passport not only makes the earlier mentioned Alchemy sound editor but a nice range of MIDI sequencing software. Their most notable lead products for MIDI are MusicTime—a nice entry level package—and MasterTracks Pro (Mac and Windows)—their key sequencing product.

Voyetra Technologies
5 Odell Plaza
Yonkers, NY 10701
Phone: 914 966-0600 **Fax:** 914 966-1102

Chances are if you have bought a sound card in the last 18 months, you're familiar with Voyetra. This company supplies a lot of the simple music utilities that come bundled with PC sound cards these days.

CHAPTER 14

Implementing sound correctly is a matter of knowing what products to use.

Music, Sound, and Audio Programming Packages and Resources

Understanding the Basic Programming Packages

If you were to mention sound to a game programmer, chances are he or she would roll his or her eyes at you and then charge headlong into a discussion of the sorry state of sound development and programming. In this chapter, I'll lead you to the best resources directly available for implementing sound in your games, and then let you do the experimenting.

It's easy enough to talk about sound, sound formats, and sound cards but that doesn't do you any good when you're looking to get down and dirty and add some sound to your games. You need to start at the very beginning. What about programming sound? What are the choices and approaches available to you? How does Windows figure into the picture? These are great questions, and I've got the answers. The bottom line in approaching sound and music programming is simple: You need to find yourself a good programming library and get to know it like a brother. There are a lot of great things you can do with sound, as you'll see later in the chapter, but you need to begin here.

All the solutions focus on different feature sets resulting in different price and licensing structures. You'll have to do some heavy comparison shopping and evaluate the products to find the ones that work best for you.

If you don't have the luxury of a large company bank account and have to spend your pennies carefully, you'll want to take a look at the provided lower end solutions that are appropriate for a smaller budget.

DOS and Windows Solutions

I found several companies that offer sound programming libraries for both DOS and Windows. Although all three were first developed for DOS, the companies have moved their APIs to Windows and have been working to take advantage of Window's unique features, especially the new DirectSound technology.

Unfortunately, none of the companies sell a one-size-fits-all library, but some will allow you to license multiple versions for a price break. Make sure to inquire about the specifics of each package so they can better help to meet your needs.

Miles Sound System (AIL)
RAD Software
307 West 200 South Suite 1003
Salt Lake City, UT 84101
Phone: 801 322-4300 **Fax:** 801 359-6169

Now in its fourth year, Miles Sound System (formerly known as AIL) is one of the leading interactive audio-programming libraries in use today. Trilobyte put their stamp of approval on RAD's system when they used it in their blockbuster The 7th Guest, and Origin Systems used the library when they developed sound for Strike Commander.

The library provides a variety of audio playback resources for sound effects, digital audio, MIDI, and interactive hooks. Previously the product was published by John Miles himself, but he has now teamed up with RAD Software to better support and extend the product into new areas.

Shipped products must pay a license fee, which runs from $3,000 for the right to use it in one product to $7,000 for a full year worth of product releases and tech support, which can be renewed at $1,750 a year. Gaining access to the source code goes for more. As always, contact RAD to confirm current pricing and licensing fees.

Sound Operating System
Human Machine Interfaces, Inc.
30 East Broadway, Suite 180
Eugene, OR 97401
Phone: 503 687-6509 **Fax:** 503 687-6479
Email: hmi@efn.org

HMI's sound system is the other top-of-the-line product for sound implementation for games. Their Sound Operating System has been used by a number of top game companies and features a wide range of musical formats, including MIDI, interactive MIDI, and digital audio.

HMI is a high-end solution costing several thousand or more depending on the licensing and support schemes you need. However, like the Miles System, you get a lot of power for that price. HMI supports many different sound cards and lots of special digital mixing features.

DiamondWare Sound Tool Kit
DiamondWare, Ltd.
2095 N. Alma School Road, Suite 12-288
Chandler, AZ 85224
Phone: 602 917-3474 **Fax:** 602 917-5973

On the low end of the sound implementation spectrum, MidPak and DigPak had the playing field to themselves until DiamondWare came along with their Sound Tool Kit (STK), which sells for under $300.

The current version (DOS only) supports protected-mode DOS products, and its API performs with relative ease in a number of languages, including Pascal, Basic, and C. The downside of the STK is that it only works for Sound Blasters and SB compatible clones. While it supports 95 percent of the installed base of sound cards, STK doesn't allow you to tweak MIDI playback to take advantage of the differences in every sound card. But hey, if you want *that* kind of versatility, you need to shell out the big bucks. Still, DiamondWare's product works great, and for most smaller developers it's combination of ease of use, speed, protected-mode operation, and low-cost licensing agreement is hard to pass up!

DiamondWare is moving their Sound Tool Kit product to Windows and should have the first version out as this book hits the shelves. Low-end developers have had a rough time with WaveMix.DLL, which, until now, was the only option available. The Windows STK provides the same functionality as WaveMix, except it's supported, has planned upgrades, and has a slightly more robust feature set than WaveMix does. DiamondWare expects that the follow up to this release will offer an even more robust feature set while still serving the small developer with its aggressive pricing scheme.

DOS-Only Solutions

If you are developing games for the PC, the APIs just described offer extensive DOS implementations. There is also one other stalwart of DOS sound APIs you should consider:

MidPak-DigPak
The Audio Solution
747 Napa Lane
St. Charles, MO 63304
BBS: 314 939-0200 **Email:** 70253.3237@compuserve.com

This combo of programs was created by John Ratcliff, best known as the programmer behind the EA hits 688 Attack Sub and Seawolf. In his quest for top-quality sound, John created MidPak for MIDI and MOD file playback, and DigPak for sound effects. Both products are available for free, but if you ship a product using them, you have to pay a license fee of $500 per product for your program. If you use both the MidPak and DigPak libraries in your program, you'll need to pay a $1,000 fee.

Both of these programs have been in existence for quite some time, but support is limited. John runs a BBS system to help users answer their questions. Support can also be obtained through email. (What'd you expect for free?) Several books, including *PC Game Programming EXplorer* and *Action Arcade Adventure Set* (Coriolis Group Books) and *Tricks of the Games Programmer Explorer* (has a chapter authored by Ratcliff) provide basic coverage on programming these libraries.

Windows-Specific Solutions

In the past, Windows sound was most often described as "better than what was available in DOS without an API." Not the best description, but for the most part, the sound options in Windows weren't as robust as programmers would have liked. The biggest problems with Windows-based sound turned out to be that Windows sound ate processor time and Windows had difficulty synchronizing sound. The API set for Windows consisted of calls to MMSYSTEM.DLL and provided programmers with low-level MIDI functions, as well as high-level sound and MIDI and CD-audio support.

Later on, due to a need for multiple audio streams in Windows, a programmer at Microsoft wrote what became known as the *WaveMix DLL*. Although this library allowed for far greater control and simultaneous playback and mixing of multiple WAV files in Windows, it was clearly a stop-gap solution. In fact, early on, Microsoft chose not to acknowledge or promote the library because it wasn't developed as a tool for programmers. (It was developed to implement multiple sounds for their Microsoft Arcade Pack.) Support was provided only by the original programmer; however, as more game developers moved to Windows, Microsoft put their weight behind WaveMix. Of course, that is all in the past (or is it?). Let's see what's available today.

The DirectSound API
Microsoft Corporation
1 Microsoft Way
Redmond, WA 98052
Phone: 206 882-8080 **Fax:** 206 883-8101
WWW: http://www.microsoft.com

With Windows 95, Microsoft moved to a new sound platform called the *DirectSound* API, which was first released in a beta version at the 1995 Computer Game Developers Conference. Although DirectSound provides much better low-level functionality and speed, it doesn't give you the higher level or more extensive APIs that programmers have found in the previous DOS sound APIs. Because of these limitations, many programmers will more than likely use Windows versions of their favorite APIs, which will themselves use the lower level DirectSound technology to implement sound in games.

DirectSound is part of the Windows Level II Developers SDK, which you can order directly from Microsoft for $495.

WaveMix
Microsoft Corporation
1 Microsoft Way
Redmond, WA 98052
Phone: 206 882-8080 **Fax:** 206 883-8101
WWW: http://www.microsoft.com

WaveMix, while being displaced by the DirectSound API for Windows 95, still warrants discussion if only for its backward compatibility to Windows 3.1. Originally WaveMix debuted as part of the Microsoft Arcade pack, but then it found its way

into developers' circles and became an official part of Microsoft's early Windows game platform strategy.

Many developers will find WaveMix to be an easy-to-use solution for 3.1/95 multiple WAV file playback. Be forewarned though, WaveMix is extremely buggy, especially under Windows 95. Use with caution, but check it out since it's free.

You can download the WaveMix.DLL from many places; on the Internet try *http:// www.shareware.com* ; on CompuServe head to the Game Developers forum (GO GAMDEV), and on America Online search the software libraries.

AudioActive
The Blue Ribbon SoundWorks, Ltd.
1605 Chantilly Drive, Suite 200
Atlanta, GA 30324
Phone: 404 315-0212 **Fax:** 404 315-0213
Email: 72662.352@compuserve.com

Just as this product hit the market, Microsoft stepped in and purchased the company to improve their below average audio tools offering.

AudioActive is, in essence, a musical expert system. Your program tells the AudioActive engine the type of music it wants, describing the scene, style, and mood, and the engine responds with the appropriate musical score. It draws on a database of work from various composers from which it is able to develop new musical scores on the fly.

Other Solutions

Before the hatemail starts in droves there are other packages available for implementing sound. I based my picks on those I knew were being widely used, had professional full-time companies behind them, and were easily available.

Should you decide that you want to see what else is available, by all means go ahead. With the sound and music programming market in transition from DOS to Windows and new technologies like interactive MIDI and major digitial audio coming, there are lots of opportunities for newer packages to come along.

Additionally there are several "freeware" resources floating around many of the major game programming online sites to use if you've just got no money to put into your effort. Most of these are pretty much "what you see is what you get." If you're going to try and make a substantial effort to create a major shareware or retail game, the previous packages are your best route.

3D Sound Resources

I talked generally about 3D sound in Chapter 13. Here are the leading companies providing products that allow you to implement 3D sound.

QSound
QSound Labs, Inc.
2748 37 Avenue N.E.
Calgary, Alberta, T1Y 5L3 Canada
Phone: 403 291-2492 **Fax:** 403 250-1521

QSound is a longtime developer of 3D sound technology. Their algorithms work primarily to enhance speaker playback of sounds either through pre-processing or realtime mixing. Companies can request evaluation products from QSound directly, but don't you dare ship a product without purchasing the user license. QSound offers the following products:

- **QCreator** is a Windows audio authoring tool for creating pre-processed QSound effects.
- **QXpander** is a plug-in for Sound Designer II, which allows for pre-processing of existing stereo material (for example, a stereo effect off a sound effects CD-ROM) and expanding it "beyond the speakers" using QSound algorithms.
- **Qmixer 32** is a Windows 32-bit DLL used for mixing and realtime playback using the QSound technology. The SDK requires a Pentium delivery platform and operates a lot like WaveMix's API. Here's how it works. A programmer maintains a database of sound object positions relative to the player in realtime. That information is then passed along with the actual sound to the QMixer technology which renders the adjusted sound to achieve a 3D positioning.

For more information surf on over to *http://www.intel.com/pc-supp/multimed/audio/qsound/qsoundpc.html.*

SRS Labs
SRS Labs Worldwide Licensing Program
2909 Daimler Street
Santa Ana, CA 92705
Phone: 714 422-1070 **Fax:** 714 852-1099
WWW: http://www.srslabs.com

Originally developed at the Hughes Aircraft Co. by senior audio scientist Arnold Klayman, SRS, which stands for Sound Retrieval System, produces a fully immersive, three-dimensional sound image from any audio source with two or more standard stereo speakers. Whether the signal is mono, stereo, surround sound, or encoded with any audio enhancement technology, SRS expands the material and creates a realistic,

panoramic sound experience with no "sweet spot" or centered listening position. SRS doesn't artificially manipulate the signal through time delay or phase shift to produce its natural, musical, and true-to-life sound image.

SRS is "single-ended," meaning there is no special encoding/decoding process—files are rendered in familiar file formats like WAV. Game companies using the technology include Interplay and Spectrum HoloByte/MicroProse.

For more information, you can contact SRS directly or visit their Web site (and while you're there, download some sample sounds).

AudioReality RS
Crystal River Engineering
490 California Ave, Suite 200
Palo Alto, CA 94306
Phone: 415 323-8155 **Fax:** 415 323-8157
WWW: http://www.cre.com/cre

AudioReality RS (Room Simulation) 3D sound algorithms not only reproduce 3D sounds, they also re-create sounds in 3D environments based on the calculated acoustical structure of the room. For example, wood, carpet, and other materials can affect sounds in a room. A carpet absorbs sound making it softer, while a metal-walled room makes sound resonate more. One of Crystal River's more interesting products is Protron, which is an AudioReality Pro Tools plug-in that allows audio designers to create fully spatialized three-dimensional audio tracks in the Digidesign Pro Tools dynamic mixing environment.

On the realtime mixing front, Crystal River provides an AudioReality game API that works with Microsoft's DirectSound 3D technology.

Speech Recognition Packages

These days, it's not unusual to find games that use spoken words in addition to text. If you decide to develop such a product, it's important to understand that spoken words carry as much weight as any other portion of your game. Don't settle for your next door neighbor to do the voice overs; professional voice-over artists and actors who are available, are readily employable and the difference is considerable. Unless your neighbor happens to be an accomplished actor, your voice overs might be missing such subtleties as voice pitch, emotion, and proper enunciation. This isn't to say you need to bring in Don Pardo to do every major voice over piece; just give spoken words the same consideration you give to any other "castable" performance in your product.

Spoken words add realism to a product, but they alone are often not enough. In certain situations, you will find it necessary to reinforce the spoken words with a text display:

- Children's products should have a text display to help kids read along as they listen.
- Some adventure and RPG products imbed clues into conversations that players have with non-player characters. In this case, a text version of the talk might be useful to help the player remember everything that was said.
- Closed captioning for hearing-impaired folks should be a consideration when you design a game with spoken words. Don't assume that the introduction of spoken words removes the need for the text.

Let's take a look at some of the resources available to you should you decide to design a game that includes spoken words.

VoiceType Application Factory
IBM Corporation
Old Orchard Road
Armonk, NY 10504
Phone: 914 765-1900
WWW: http://www.ibm.com

This speech recognition toolkit is based on the IBM's Continuous Speech Series products for Windows and OS/2. The toolkit, which sells for less than $400 and recognizes over 30,000 words, comes with several utilities to help manage and use spoken words and phrases in programs. Players use microphones hooked into their favorite sound cards to interact with the game.

The original toolkit works as a set of 14 C function calls, and there are implementations for Borland C++ and Microsoft Visual C. In addition, A&G Graphics Interface has a Visual Basic implementation kit so even VB folks can take advantage of this technology.

The toolkit requires 3 MB of memory and 7.5 MB of hard drive space, so a standard 8 MB system is more than capable of handling the overhead. The technology is also speaker-independent, which gets rid of the annoying training system associated with past voice recognition efforts.

Microsoft Speech API Software
Microsoft Corporation
1 Microsoft Way
Redmond, WA 98052
Phone: 206 882-8080 **Fax:** 206 883-8101
WWW: http://www.microsoft.com

The Microsoft Speech SDK enables software developers to provide native speech recognition and text-to-speech capabilities in their Windows software. The text-to-speech routines synthesize speech from regular ANSI text, which allows your pro-

grams to actually talk to users without the need for using expensive and memory-intensive recorded voices. Text-to-speech won't fit every bill, but for those unique situations, perhaps with a highly variable game conversational system, it might be an ideal addition.

The Microsoft Speech API provides developers with a standard programming interface to speech technology. Microsoft is working with third-party engine developers to enable their engines to work with the Speech API standard.

Microsoft's speech recognition technology is available by ordering their Speech SDK, which may still be in beta as this book comes to press.

Speech recognition technology has come a long way since its initial appearance. Don't avoid it because of poor past experiences. While you might not want to make speech recognition a requirement of game play, it can be a neat feature to offer. However, be cautious. Speech recognition can be drowned out by blaring soundtracks and special effects.

If you want to check out a really cool Web page chock full of information on using speech in games, go to *http://www.well.com/user/earl/gamespeech.html*. Here you'll find a reprint of my article—written for a CGDA newsletter—on using speech in games. You'll find lots of cool stuff and gain insight from my first-hand knowledge.

Music Resources

We've covered a number of resources for music production and implementing music in games. What follows is an explanation of the various sound effect libraries available and further resources to help you find out even more about using sound in games.

Sound Effects Libraries

Most major publishers have extensive archives of professional-quality sound effects libraries. If you have access to one of these, use it.

The rest of us will have to build our own library. Luckily this task is fairly easy. You may have to lay down some money, but if you look hard you can find good sound collections that provide you with all you need to develop lots of new sounds on your own.

You can purchase sound effects in three ways: one at a time, as single CDs, and as sets of CDs. Most of the companies I have listed in this section charge between $50 and $150 for a single CD and up to several hundred dollars for a set of CDs. If that is still too rich for your blood, you can check some of the various Web sites I have listed, which allow you to download single sound effects.

The Hollywood Edge
7060 Hollywood Blvd., Suite 1120
Hollywood, CA 90028
Phone: 213 466-6723 **Fax:** 213 466-5861
WWW: http://magicnet.net/~drport/sdx/net/hwedge.html

This is one of the most famous and most often used sound effects libraries in existence today. The entire library was created by Soundelux, a longtime coalition of recording studios that produce sound effects for major Hollywood films.

To date, Soundelux has compiled some 3,000 hours of sounds (from the original DAT) that it compiles into CDs and online archives you can purchase. The current complete set, which is made up of various packages, spans over some 50 CD-ROMs. The sets are available directly and through many major stock music and sound companies.

Sound Ideas
105 West Beaver Creek Road, Suite #4
Richmond Hill, Ontario, L4B 1C6 Canada
Phone: 905 886-5000 **Fax:** 905 886-6800
WWW: http://www.sound-ideas.com/

Looking for a zillion different sound effects? Look no further. Sound Ideas, which has aggressively promoted itself to the game development community, offers tons of sounds and many well packaged sound libraries.

The company is currently working to set up online distribution, as well as move their libraries from regular audio CDs to CD-ROMs. You can order a free demo and a full catalog by sending email to info@sound-ideas.com.

Network Music, Inc.
15150 Avenue Of Science
San Diego, CA 92128
Phone: 800 854-2075 **Fax:** 619 451-6409
WWW: http://www.networkmusic.com/home.html

This library contains over 5,500 sound effects compiled on 72 CDs. If you want to request a demo CD and browse through the company's extensive catalog, check out their Web site.

Valentino Sound Effects Library
TV Music
500 Executive Blvd
Elmsford, NY 10523

Phone: 800 223-6278
WWW: http://www.tvmusic.com/

The Valentino Sound Effects Library covers 44 CDs and is a complete library pulled from television, radio, and feature film. TV Music provides three ways for you to preview their selections: You can order an audio CD demo and 80-page catalog by sending email to info@tvmusic.com; you can download a complete listing of their files (in Adobe Acrobat format) from their Web site; or you can order a CD-ROM for Windows or Mac that demos every selection with the library.

Sound Tip

Search the Leading Sound Effects Libraries

The Robert Puff Music Site in Seattle, located at *http://www.rpmseattle.com/rpm/efx/efx_the.html*, allows you to search through the leading sound effects libraries to find just the sound you want.

Stock Sound Companies

There are dozens of stock sound companies around that can assemble digital files or tapes of sounds you might need. You may pay dearly for custom stock like this, but sometimes it's the fastest way to find that special sound effect you want. *Interactivity* magazine recently published a long list of such companies.

Major Record Chains

Next time you're in Tower Records or some similar large chain, check out the sound effects sections. You have to be careful to make sure you're buying useful libraries—many of the collections are CDs like the Star Trek sound effects disc, which isn't meant for use in a game. However, if you look often enough, you're bound to find some great stuff. I found an animals CD-ROM once for $9.95 that gave me some good grunts and snorts to use for monsters in an RPG game.

The Web

The Web is a great place to find dealers of CD-ROM libraries to order. Some stock companies are experimenting with downloading files directly from Web sites but unless it's clearly a site designed as such, *do not* download anything without permission.

Major Card Manufacturing Contacts

There are certainly a lot of manufacturers of sound cards out there and to list them all seems ridiculous, as a few key manufacturers seem to be the moving force in Sound card technology. Therefore, here is the listing of the major companies:

Adlib Multimedia Inc.
20020 Grande Allee East, #850

Quebec City, PQ Canada G1R 2J1
Phone: 418 529-9676 **Fax:** 418 656-8742

The Adlib boards were the first major music board to hit the PC market.

Advanced Gravis
101-3750 N. Fraser Way
Burnaby, BC Canada V5J 5E9
Phone: 604 431-5020
WWW: http://www.gravis.com

Advanced Gravis is the maker of the famous Gravis UltraSound (GUS) card, which has become a very popular board—especially in Europe.

Creative Labs Inc.
1901 McCarthy Blvd.
Milpitas, CA 95035
Phone: 408 428-6600
WWW: http://www.creaf.com

Creative Labs is the reigning king of the sound card market. Their SoundBlaster product line is synonymous with sound on the PC. Visit their Web site to sign up for an extensive developer program.

Ensoniq
155 Great Valley Parkway
Malvern, PA 19355
Phone: 215 647-3930
WWW: http//www.ensoniq.com

Ensoniq, a relatively recent entry into the sound card wars with their SoundScape line, has made some impressive gains on the competition with such lucrative contracts as the one they share with Gateway, which uses Ensoniq as their choice sound card provider.

Roland Corp.
7200 Dominion Circle
Los Angeles, CA 90040
Phone: 213 685-5141 **Fax:** 213 722-0911

Roland is considered along with Yamaha to be the top of the line in sound cards. Their Sound Canvas product is one of the best sounding cards available. Unfortunately, Roland still hasn't set up a Web site. If you want information, contact them directly.

Turtle Beach Systems Inc.
1600 Pennsylvania Avenue, Unit 33
York, PA 17404
Phone: 717 843-6916
WWW: http://www.tbeach.com

Turtle Beach makes a complete line of sound cards from lower-end to higher-end wavetable cards.

Yamaha Corp
Consumer Products Division
P.O. Box 6600
Buena Park, CA 90622
Phone: 714 522-9240
WWW: http://www.yamaha.com (consumer site)
WWW: http://www.ysba.com

Along with Roland, this leading synthesizer manufacturer has been producing higher-end MIDI and sound cards. The sound chip in the Saturn was also developed by Yamaha.

Surfing for Sound

I've found a few notable locations for information and resources regarding sound and music. There is a lot of stuff available to you online; you just need to know where to go.

CompuServe

The best place for information about sound programming and MIDI music resources is CompuServe. If you've spent any time on CompuServe, you've probably stumbled onto the infamous Game Developers forum (GO GAMDEV). This place is just loaded with everything related to gaming. Once you've had your fill there, be sure to stop by the MIDI (GO MIDI) and multimedia forums (GO MULTIMEDIA), which give you direct contact with almost all the major players in the computer music scene.

Web Sites

The following Web sites are useful for a variety of purposes. Stop by when you've got a few extra minutes and browse through the goods.

`http://ac.dal.ca/~dong/music.htm`
This is a good site for information on music and sound file formats, as well as shareware tools.

`http://ally.ios.com:80/~midilink/`
This is an excellent site for all sorts of MIDI authoring tools and resources.

`ftp://mitpress.mit.edu:/pub/Computer-Music-Journal/CMJ.html`
This site is home to MIT's *Computer Music Journal*, a leading technical journal on music and sound as it pertains to computers.

`http://www.eeb.ele.tue.nl/midi/index.html`
This is an excellent site for good MIDI links.

`http://www.xraylith.wisc.edu/~ebrodsky/`
This site by Ethan Brodsky is a good site for finding information on programming sound resources.

`http://www.futurenet.co.uk/music/futuremusic.html`
Future Music is a UK-based magazine that covers all sorts of computer and music issues. This Web site contains much of the material found in the magazine's pulp-based version.

`http://interact.uoregon.edu/MediaLit/FC/WFAETechnical`
This is another excellent site for more links to explore the Web's musical resources.

The Future of Sound

The future of sound is pretty clear, although this may be hard to believe especially when you consider the problems encountered implementing sound, the different APIs, and the competiting sound cards and file formats. On the PC programming front it appears that the programming tools are moving toward the DirectSound API and will continue to build upon robust Windows music and sound capabilities. DirectSound-compatible programming APIs will allow developers to leverage their existing familiarity with common DOS APIs, as well as give them easier access to DirectSound's features.

We haven't talked much about the game consoles but expect those game systems to integrate even more complex chip sets to keep pace with what the latest sound cards will offer on the PC.

For MIDI, the future definitely usher in an upgrade to specification 2.0, which will include a number of new hooks for interactivity—especially interactive games. The use of wavetable cards and sound cards with more RAM for downloading patches will also increase the digital audio feel for MIDI.

Music hardware will see a move toward adding 3D sound technology built into the cards, as well as better sound quality through enhanced speaker technology.

PART 5

Game Development Issues

CHAPTER 15

There's no right way to develop a game, but there are hundreds of wrong ways!

A Technical Overview of Game Development

Approaching Game Development

I've been serving as a forum sysop on CompuServe's Game Developers forum for about six months and I'm often asked what language I use to make games. My common reply is that my choice of language depends on the game I'm making.

Game development, especially the actual writing of the final software, is a process of choices. And the only way you can make wise choices is to fully understand what it is you're trying to accomplish. There is no "right way" to develop a game. Your particular situation is dependent on many factors, including the platform you work on, the platform you are designing for, the demands of your target audience, the many products available, the languages you know, and so on.

If there was ever a time for me to get up on a soapbox and proclaim my philosophy for all to hear, this is it (I can see the hate email coming already): *To find success as a game developer, you need to focus on the finished product and not the process.* The process you undertake will be a direct result of the intended product itself.

The idea in this chapter and the next several chapters is to help you build a toolbox of solutions that will allow you to develop games smartly. Successful developers are always looking for ways to expand their development ability to make their game dreams a reality.

The first thing you have to understand is that there has been a shift in approach to developing games. The industry is now focusing on developing products rather than on programming software. The key to developing today is to be able to define a product that will sell, match it up with the correct process, and get it to market.

How you approach this problem will depend on your situation. You can start from the desired end result and work backwards, deciding at each stage what the best approach is. Or you can start from the beginning, assessing your ability and deciding what game best suits your resources.

I want to discuss both methods in more detail because I feel they hold the key to success in games.

Filling a Niche

Many of today's big publishers and developers are able to make any game they desire. They have the programming acumen and art and sound staffs capable of doing almost anything. But if these companies developed games just because they could, they'd be in bankruptcy court sooner than you could say Doom III. What sets these companies apart is that they want to develop products that sell, not create games that make the programmers pat themselves on the shoulders. They look for opportunities to fill a particular area of interest and then draw on the available technology to develop a product that meets those needs. Once they have pinpointed the product, they plan the process that will produce the product they originally envisioned.

Working within Limitations

In the second approach, developers are by some means limited in their ability to construct games. This may be because they work with a particular language, have limited art capacity, or just lack programming strength. A big mistake small developers often make is trying to create games that are beyond their means. While the idea may be great, a product that is not up to snuff will not sell. These developers would be better off working within their limitations to find a end product that will be successful.

For example, suppose arcade games are the new hottest trend. You have a great idea for a game but you only program in Visual Basic, and Visual Basic is not the best language for creating arcade games. Should you force the game to fit into Visual Basic or should you develop a game that is better suited to your programming expertise? It may seem obvious, but every day I encounter developers looking to break into the games market who are developing beyond their abilities.

Remember, the big boys have millions of dollars at their disposal to recruit top programmers, artists, and sound designers. You are probably not in this league, so make the most of your situation and focus on producing games that are the best in their category.

The Sum of It All

In the end these two situations boil down to one thing: *product* versus *process*. Great developers are able to keep their eye on the product and not the process. The process of developing their games evolves from a pre-defined idea of what they think will sell, how much it will sell for, and how quickly it needs to be developed, among other factors.

Today, starting development without having answered such crucial product-oriented questions can kill a developer. Don't let this happen to you. Learn to become as good a product planner as you are a program developer, and learn about all the different approaches to constructing a game. I didn't say it would be easy!

Reshaping the Key Factors in Game Development

Gone are the days when a developer or development team sat down and started creating a game without first considering the entire situation. Gone are the days when you decided to write your own 3D API because you could. Gone are the days when off-the-shelf solutions were second rate to your own designs. A lot has changed

in game development, and as interactive games have become a major force in the industry, we need to look at the new role of product development.

There are many factors to consider when constructing games for today's industry, and these factors play a key role in defining the process that you'll use to construct games. Let's cover some of these topics briefly:

Development Costs and Shipping Dates Time spent in getting a product to market is increasingly becoming a major factor in all of software development. Today, if you miss Christmas, you can write off sales you could have had. Likewise, if you get to market with the first NFL game with updated stats, you gain sales you might not have had. The drive to reduce costs and development schedules means companies are increasingly concentrating on becoming more efficient in their development process.

No More One-Track Minds In years past, programmers did it all themselves. They wrote all the code, and when the game shipped they threw out the old code and started from scratch. Today, though, the idea of a company (or single developer) writing every piece of code themselves is madness. Companies are now focusing on building in-house technologies and game engines in an effort to increase their ability to deliver products quickly while keeping costs low. This push has produced not only internal solutions, but tons of tools and even complete authoring packages, which are getting so sophisticated that they can rival using a low-level language. No longer do you have to roll your own digital video routines or develop in C++. Other options are available to you.

The best developers take the off-the-shelf tools strategy even further, and develop complete suites of tools internally. In fact, companies often form two distinct development units: One unit develops key technologies, such as a general 3D engine or an internal scripting language, and the other unit is left to work up great game ideas and turn those ideas into finished products.

Putting Game Production in the Hands of Designers The goal of many companies now is to move product development away from programmers and into the hands of game designers. For example, a company might create an internal RPG construction kit that is powerful yet easy enough for a designer with little programming experience to use.

Evolutionary, not Revolutionary, Development Developers used to literally start from scratch with each new project. These days, many companies are learning that it's best to construct games one after the other in an evolutionary process—building and enhancing on an existing product.

For example, Microsoft's Flight Simulator is enhanced with new features and cutting-edge technology with each release. The game builds upon itself.

Now, certainly, many developers will insist on starting from scratch every once in a while, but as games become ever more complex and costly to develop, and engines become even more prevalent, the evolutionary development process will be a sure winner.

A Quick Guide to Enhancing Your Development Ability

If you are just starting out as a developer, you might feel that there is so much to do and you can easily become overwhelmed. For example, just as you figure out how to develop a cool 3D raycasting game, others have moved on to developing games based on 3D polygons. Game development is an occupation where you always feel that you've gotten behind the curve without any chance of catching up. Fortunately, there are several key things you can do to put yourself on the competitive edge with everyone else.

Spend Money

The bottom line is that you've got to spend money. Put another way, you aren't in the position to object to spending whatever money you can possibly afford. You need to systematically save up and work to purchase the means to develop correctly. For example, if you have saved up $500, get a hold of Microsoft's Level II Developers SDK for $495. If you're serious about Windows game development, you *need* this kit. Sure, maybe Microsoft should make it cheaper, or maybe they should have released their Windows Games SDK for free, but they didn't. So you've got to shell out the dough. While you're groaning about it, other developers are buying it.

Get in "The Know" and Interact More

One of the other key aspects that separates successful developers from wanna-bes is that they focus on increasing their knowledge of the market, industry, tools, and other key pieces of information. I've outlined too many sources of good information—many of them free or very inexpensive—for you to just ignore them.

Getting in "the know" means taking the time to read the trades, attend conferences, interact with other developers, and work with the key technology companies that shape the game industry. Just knowing how to program doesn't cut it any more.

Get to Know the Evangelists and Attend Developer Programs

A key aspect of game development today is being prepared now to make the games that will ship a year from now. Just because you don't have thousands of dollars to spend on R&D or 20 years of programming experience, doesn't mean that you can't keep pace with the industry. Failure to do so can sink you before you even get started.

One of the best ways to stay on top of the industry hub-bub is to get to know the people who are commonly called *evangelists.* In the high-tech industry, evangelists are special representatives from key hardware and software companies (like Apple or Microsoft) that work within an industry to help keep developers informed about strategic moves that may impact the market. For example, Microsoft evangelists for the game industry worked to help developers learn about Windows 95 technology that would help them. Evangelists also help by getting developers Beta versions of new products, patches for their programs, and more.

Most of the major companies for sound boards, graphic cards, operating systems, and other key technologies have evangelists and also have special programs for developers. Creative Labs, for example, has a program to help developers order hardware at a discount, share technical information, and organize conferences.

If you're serious about developing, don't be hesitant to call these companies, contact the evangelists, and sign up for their developers programs. Sometimes the developers programs can cost money, but other times you need only fill out a questionnaire to get validated.

Get Access to Beta Products

This all leads to perhaps the biggest edge you can get, which is getting access to Beta versions and inside information. Since game development is about computer technology, it's constantly being re-invented by changes in technology. Getting in early on these changes is not only important to help you keep pace, it can actually give you key opportunities to break into the market.

Microsoft provided Activision with access to early versions of Windows 95, which allowed them to develop one of the first major games for Windows 95—just in time for the debut of the product. Activision racked up lots of sales not only for making a great game, but for having one of the first major Windows 95 games.

Getting access to Beta versions is not as hard as it seems; you simply have to be up on the industry and contact the key companies and their evangelists to get the products you want.

Tools and the Game Development Platforms: A General Discussion

One of the few decisions that can have a major effect on how you make a game is the choice of platforms you want to support.

DOS

Just over a year ago DOS was the primary platform for computer gaming. However, it's rapidly losing ground to Windows. (Although with backwards compatibility to DOS games in Windows 95, some developers will continue to stick to developing in DOS.) As more people move to Windows, the progression of new programming tools and libraries for DOS development will begin to dry up.

Windows 95/NT

The new target for many developers is Windows 95. With the full court press by Microsoft on the marketing end, as well as key technology such as the Game SDK, Windows 95 is where all the action for PC-based games is headed. Not all the tools for this platform come from Microsoft. Because game development for Windows requires a lot of work (and Microsoft doesn't have all the answers), a slew of tools has arrived (many from the DOS world). I'll cover these in the next chapter.

OS/2

Believe it or not, there is a group of dedicated people making games specifically for OS/2. There's even an OS/2 games SDK. While OS/2 is pretty much going to be a stepchild to Windows, some people enjoy making dedicated products for it and, as you'll see later, there are some key resources to help with that.

Macintosh

Despite Apple's woes and Microsoft/Intel's superior marketing of the PC, the Macintosh platform is still very much alive. With millions of Macs out there operated by hungry game players, more companies are finding success developing for this platform. While Mac sales will never match the PC, they are still significant enough to present a return on investment for top-selling games. Additionally, many smaller developers found success first on the Mac. Two great examples are Marathon games and Cyan, makers of a little hit called MYST.

As the Mac has quietly risen to more prominence among computer game developers, the industry has seen several major developer tools and products created to help with the construction of Mac-specific games.

Videogame and Console Platforms

Consoles are where the majority of money is made in games and will be for some time (for more on this idea see Chapter 27). In the past, console development was difficult and costly. Fortunately, today's 32-bit console development is more accessible to developers than ever before.

This accessibility is partly because the tools have gotten better and the machines have gotten faster, allowing for PC-knowledgeable developers to port their games to the console platform. In addition, because three of the four console leaders—Sony, Sega, and Panasonic—have gone to CD-based hardware, the costs of producing a game from a publisher's stand point is a lot less (no costly cartridge manufacturing). With this shift, publishers are starting more projects than they normally would have in the past.

Let's take a brief look at the four key platforms in the videogame market.

Sega's Saturn

Sega's Saturn seemed to debut in second place behind Sony's Playstation offering. But with recently improved development tools and Sega's Arcade division pumping out hot software for the Saturn, it won't stay in second place for long. While developers praise the ease of developing for the Playstation, the rumblings about Saturn are that once you become familiar with the machine, there's lots of power under the hood to be tapped.

Sony Playstation

The Sony Playstation is currently winning the race to be the dominant 32-bit game console. With four million players and a programming environment developers are raving about, the Playstation will certainly be a major target of developers for quite a while.

Nintendo Ultra 64

This is the only cartridge-based machine of the next generation. With an April 1996 release, its sales figures are nothing more than pure speculation, but certainly Nintendo has come in late and won major market share before. Based on major Silicon Graphics 3D technology, this player offers developers amazing performance unseen before in consoles. However, with its cartridge-based hardware and Nintendo's infamous control, I doubt that more than a handful of major developers will ever attempt to make products for this machine.

Panasonic/Sega M2

After sitting on the sidelines, 3DO's M2 technology is now in the hands of Panasonic, who have said that they will team with Sega and others to produce a next-generation 64-bit machine. While some the overall specs of the M2 technology are widely known, the ultimate configuration hardware has yet to be determined. The original 3DO technology was ahead of its time and poorly handled, which is why it failed. With both Sega and a more mature Panasonic handling the M2 technology, it could become a major force.

A Quick Primer on Console Development

Almost anyone can develop for most of the major console platforms—but you won't be able to publish your development unless you are an approved publisher or working with an approved publisher.

If you do decide to develop for consoles, you'll need to get a specific development kit for that console and the necessary hardware to run it on. Both Sega and Sony use a PC-based system while Nintendo uses an SGI-based setup. These setups usually consist of a C compiler, an assembler and debugger, tons of libraries for graphics and sound, and specially tailored hardware that mimics the console's operating system on the developer's computer.

In Chapter 19, I've compiled all the information and contacts you need to get on the path for developing games for consoles.

Picking the Language to Do the Job

After deciding on the platforms you're going to develop for, your next major task is to decide what tool you're going to use to author your product. Deciding on which language to use seems easy enough. C/C++ is the choice of 90 percent of the developers working in this business. However, you do have alternatives to consider, and more and more developers are using high-level multimedia authoring systems like mTropolis and Macromedia's Director. Understanding all the options will make a difference in the approach you take to develop the end product you want.

C/C++

As I mentioned a moment ago, the dominant language of game development is C/C++. Originally developed at AT&T Bell Labs as the language for its Unix operating system, C has long been a crucial development tool. Still used in its original form, a newer variant called C++ is rapidly overtaking its older sibling.

C/C++ offers the best combination of product speed and portability, which is tremendously important in today's world of multi-platform games.

Most C compiler packages allow you to program in both flavors of the language, and while C++ may be the newer form of the language, many programmers still use the straight forward C.

The C++ Difference

C++ is an *object-oriented* language. Object-oriented programming, or OOP for short, is best described as taking programming function subroutines to their highest incarnation. In OOP, programmers create self-contained pieces of code referred to as *objects.* The idea is to simplify programming by creating reusuable objects that are essentially "foundation code" for other objects. For example, you might have a sprite object, which essentially is a piece of code that defines all the common basic attributes of a sprite. Then by defining some specifics such as the height and width and perhaps direction of the sprite, the program can render and draw that sprite on the screen. The reusability of objects and how that can simplify programming is what makes C++ an incredibly powerful language.

C Compilers

One of the great or not so great things about the C language is that there are many different choices for the C compiler you can use. None of them varies in any drastic ways, but the subtleties, such as final speed of the resulting code, some syntax, and editor functions, are enough to have people constantly taking sides in declaring the best compiler.

Assembly

Assembly language used to be the dominant language of game design back when slower processors and simpler design made it a necessity to elicit the tight code needed to produce games on the older 8-bit computers and consoles. As computers increased in performance and C compilers became widely available, Assembly took a back seat in the game industry. However, because it still produces the fastest code around, some Assembly language is still used in games today. Programmers mainly use it to create subroutines, which are called from C/C++, for sections requiring intensive speed, such as certain graphical functions.

Assembly language is the most difficult to understand. The general law of computer languages states: The lower level the language, the faster it is, and the harder it is to program in it. Don't be discouraged. You can learn this language and it will prove to be a great asset to you as you develop games.

Visual Basic

You mean I can create great Windows products and actually get some sleep too? You can if you use Visual Basic (VB). VB, from Microsoft, is a hybrid form of Basic written especially for Windows. VB works in the Windows environment and allows you to create neat interfaces, development tools for level editing, conversation editors, and other professional-looking products rapidly. And it's pretty easy to learn. In addition, by learning how to access the Windows API, a special slew of calls to the Windows operating system, you can do some nifty animation and sound effects!

One big advantage to VB is the enormous amount of third-party add-on products—called OCXs—that extend VB's features. OCXs are self-contained routines that you can modify with VB and reuse in your program. For example, a sound OCX might allow you to load, play, and do all sorts of other things with sound in your VB project.

For beginners looking for a place to start learning programming—especially Windows programming—VB is your tool. Some of the skills you'll learn can eventually be brought to use in more sophisticated languages like C/C++. Using VB to learn how to use the Windows API calls is a good example of a skill that can be transferred to more robust game languages.

However, you should know that VB has its drawbacks. C/C++ is much faster, and speed in games can be crucial. I don't think you'll see Doom being created with VB any time soon.

VB also does not create standalone executables like C/C++. VB is what we call an *interpretive* language, meaning that it doesn't actually compile. While you can create executable standalone versions of your VB programs (royalty free), your user must also have the runtime file in order to use the program, which is an extra burden for VB.

I am truly amazed at the programming capabilities of VB. I wholeheartedly recommend it to beginners, and even to pros, to create games. For pros who are using C/C++ for a speedy arcade game consider using VB as the main backoffice tool to develop level editors and such. Some of the best third party Doom editors were created in VB.

Delphi

The newest language on the scene is none other than Delphi, a hybrid Windows programming language from Borland. Delphi is basically a specialized Windows version of Pascal. It allows you to create full EXE files, unlike VB, and it's just slightly slower than C/C++. Delphi can also work with OCXs.

The Programming Alternative: Multimedia Authoring Packages

In the past several years, there have been a number of retail games created in what are commonly referred to as *multimedia authoring packages*, which include such products as Macromedia's Director or Asymetrix's Toolbook.

While most programmers would prefer to use a regular full-fledged programming language, many are finding exactly what they need in authoring packages. With their rapid development process and much easier learning curve, they are achieving quick results.

It should also be noted that many of the products offer amazing cross-platform development schemes. Director, for instance, offers immediate cross-platform compatibility to Mac, Windows, and 3DO, and now with World Wide Web extensions, I wouldn't be surprised to see Sega's Saturn and Sony's Playstation added to complete the total 32-bit cross-platform product availability.

Of course, there are tradeoffs. You'll have to contend with speed issues and runtime modules that have to be properly distributed with your product.

It Pays to Be Multilingual

While you may have chosen one language to become proficient in, take the time to learn about some of the other languages I've mentioned. Even if you don't plan on programming in C or Assembly, having a basic knowledge can help you to understand code examples and gain ideas for whatever language you're using. I'm drawing on my rudimentary knowledge of C to read books about Windows programming to learn more about controlling Windows from Visual Basic. While I can't write a program in C, I can dissect code, so I can learn from it.

Guidelines for Choosing the Right Language

Now that you know a bit about the various languages available, how do you go about choosing the best language for the job at hand. Personal preference? Skill? Time? An educated choice is going to include all of these factors. But to help you along, consider the following guidelines:

- Most games today should be constructed with C/C++ in order to be rapidly portable and fast enough to accomplish proper animation and player feedback. However, if the desired end result is possible using a multimedia authoring package or a language other than C/C++, you should seriously consider the alternatives.

- Assembly should be used to fulfill crucial speed issues in games requiring immense realtime graphical feedback. You should use this technique only as a last resort because Assembly can slow the ability to port games.
- VB and Delphi are excellent PC-based tools that can be used to build prototypes and editors for full blown C/C++ applications.
- Delphi is a great language for programmers familiar with Pascal or for VB programmers looking to step up their performance level without moving to C/C++.
- Multimedia authoring packages, such as Macromedia's Director, offer alluring cross-platform development, ease of use, and rapid development environments, but can limit your ability to construct certain game types. They can also be quite slow.
- Delphi or Visual Basic cannot be considered for projects requiring porting to a non-Windows-based platform.
- If you focus on the product, not the language, you will apply the best authoring tool to develop your game in the fastest, least costly way.

Many times I meet programmers who insist on doing everything with one language. However, as more higher-level languages and other hybrid authoring tools evolve, the ability to craft a product with multiple languages and tools will increasingly become a major skill.

Jeff Duntemann, Editor-in-Chief of *Visual Developer Magazine* and co-founder of The Coriolis Group, said it best in an editorial he wrote in early 1995. He predicted that programmers of the future who will be most in demand are those who will be able to move with ease among all the major languages, using the best features of each to craft the products required by the market place.

I agree with this sentiment wholeheartedly. For the game industry, the same holds true. The development groups with expertise over a wide range of authoring tools and environments will be the ones with the flexibility and speed needed to produce tomorrow's games under tomorrow's pressures.

Multimedia/Game Authoring Systems

When big-gun developers like Oracle saw the potential role of multimedia authoring packages in the game development process, they jumped on the bandwagon and began producing some of the hottest authoring packages around. These products are increasingly being used, so I want to take the time to detail the major offerings available. (See Table 15.1 at the end of this chapter for a detailed product comparison.)

MacroMedia Director
Macromedia, Inc.
600 Townsend Street
San Francisco, CA 94103
Phone: 415 252-2000 **Fax:** 415 626-0554
WWW: http://www.macromedia.com

Director from Macromedia, the most well-known and most often used multimedia package, is the benchmark program competitors compare their own packages to.

Director can animate text and graphics, create hotspots, and perform all of the other standard multimedia functions. The package includes an integrated scripting language, called Lingo, which offers extensive interactive coding. Director programs can also interact with outside extensions written in other languages, such as C.

What makes Director the current heavyweight in the authoring package market is that it's been around for quite a while and has built a loyal following. In addition, Macromedia has been incredibly successful in porting Director player technology to a multitude of different platforms, including Mac, Windows, SGI, 3DO, and now with the Shockwave player Director files can be played directly off the Internet with a compatible browser.

Macromedia will be shipping the next version of Director, Director 5, in late 1996.

mTropolis
mFactory
1440 Chapin Avenue
Burlingame, CA 94010
Phone: 415 548-0600 **Fax:** 415 548-9249
WWW: http://www.mfactory.com

If Director is the old pro, mTropolis is the zippy new rookie on the block. mTropolis is only available in an authoring form for Macintosh as I write this, but a Windows 95 version is currently in the works. You can, however, ship finished product for playback on a Windows platform.

Many major game developers have taken quite an interest in mFactory's product, including Rocket Science, Cyan, Viacom New Media, and Inscape.

The core technology behind mTropolis is called mFusion, and it's billed as a scalable core technology that delivers true object orientation. The cool thing about the object-oriented environment is that it's tailored to take advantage of reusable components. For example, you could create a clock object that could be placed in any program with a simple drag and drop procedure.

mTropolis is quite fast, as well; hundreds of objects can be responding to events and messages while animation and sound are also being processed. In fact mTropolis features a multi-threaded kernel designed specifically for synchronous multimedia, which improves playback performance. A 486 25 MHz is considered the low end of the platform for acceptable performance, which is pretty good.

The extensibility of a development system is defined by the degree to which it can seamlessly acquire new capabilities, both for the authoring environment and for titles that will be executed by the player. mTropolis, through mFusion, allows developers to easily introduce their own objects and other programs they've written in C/C++.

mFactory recommends that you use a Power Mac with 24-bit color and 12 MB RAM as your authoring platform. Platform requirements for Windows 95 authoring will most likely will be a Pentium with 24-bit color and 16 MB RAM.

Oracle Media Objects
Oracle Corporation
500 Oracle Parkway
Redwood Shores, CA 94065
Phone: 415 506-7000
WWW: http://www.oracle.com

Oracle has tabled their database development in hopes of becoming a major force in interactive television and the Internet. The Media Objects multimedia authoring package is a part of that plan.

At the time of this writing, Oracle is only available as an authoring package for the Mac, but they are planning on shipping a Windows version in the first half of 1996. As far as playback platforms go, Oracle is promising to give runtime support for a dizzying array of devices from Mac and PCs to set-top boxes and videogame consoles.

An Oracle Media Objects application consists of one or more distinct screens that a user interacts with. Each screen contains its own graphical layer, as well as various objects that are linked and controlled by a rich, high-level scripting language called Oracle Media Talk.

Through the Custom Extensions Software Development Kit (SDK), Oracle Media Objects provides a number of mechanisms to extend and customize its capabilities. Developers can implement reusable utilities in libraries, extend the programming language by integrating new commands and functions into the language, and create new, custom object classes to add to Oracle Media Objects' existing set of objects.

Oracle Media Objects has some pretty fierce competition from mTropolis and Director, but with such a powerful package—which is being offered for free on their Web site—they're certainly not going down without a fight.

MediaForge
Strata Inc.
2 West Street
St. George, UT 84770
Phone: 801 628-5218 **Fax:** 801 628-9756
WWW: http://www.strata3d.com

MediaForge from Strata is a Windows 95/NT-based authoring package, just itching to make its debut. The product is currently in development and is expected to ship sometime in 1996.

Strata says MediaForge is a full 32-bit authoring, event driven, multi-threaded multimedia authoring environment. It comes with over 100 special effects and an embedded Visual Basic editor, and, with support for OLE controls, it's highly extendible.

MediaForge will also offer built-in sprite controls, smooth animation, and MIDI, WAV, and CD sound.

QuarkXPress
Quark, Inc.
1800 Grant Street.
Denver, CO 80203
Phone: 303 894-8888
WWW: http://www.quark.com

If it seems like everyone is getting into the multimedia authoring market, it's because they are. Quark, however, is offering a unique approach to the myriad of products positioning themselves as retail-quality multimedia development tools.

Quark's latest offering is QuarkImmedia, an authoring tool that sits on top of QuarkXPress, which provides QuarkImmedia with lots of excellent layout and graphical capabilities. QuarkImmedia supports digital video, sound, animation, hotspots, and includes a comprehensive scripting language, database connectivity, online functions, and an XTension technology, which allows you to add your own features to it.

Although QuarkImmedia products can only be authored from a Macintosh system running QuarkXPress version 3.2, they can be used by using a viewer program that runs on Macintosh and Windows, and works with the Internet as well. Quark is considering porting their playback technology to other platforms.

Reading Resources

If you're still eager to continue on your quest to develop the ultimate game, I suggest you pick up some reading material on the overall subject of good software construction. When it comes to good resources on the overall software programming process (and especially the management of it), these four books are constantly recommended, and all are bibles to software developers everywhere.

Writing Solid Code by Steve Maguire (Microsoft Press, 1993; ISBN 1-55615-551-4)

This book, written by a former Microsoft developer, is an excellent book about writing good computer code. It explains Microsoft's debugging techniques and provides a solid discussion on the fundamentals of programming. Steve offers practical advice garnered from years of experience coding software and working at Microsoft.

Code Complete by Steve McConnell (Microsoft Press, 1993; ISBN 1-55615-484-4)

This book is another excellent source for software development techniques. It covers implementation planning, design, construction, and quality control with examples in both C and Pascal.

Debugging the Development Process by Steve Maguire (Microsoft Press, 1994; ISBN 1-55615-650-2)

The third in a series of excellent books from Microsoft Press about developing computer software. This particular text focuses on the management and teamwork aspects of software development, and provides exceptional real world advice.

Dynamics of Software Development by Jim McCarthy (Microsoft Press, 1995; ISBN 1-55615-823-8)

This latest in the series of books from Microsoft Press focuses on the development manager's role in the software development process. You'll find lots of information on developing, planning, finishing, and even marketing your products.

Selecting Your Language

The table listed on the following pages is designed to provide you with useful comparison data so that you can better choose a language for your programming projects.

Table 15.1 Comparison of Programmer Languages for Game Development

Product	Speed	Portability	Authoring Platform
C/C++	Well written C code can be extremely fast.	C is highly portable but you still need to do lots of work to rewrite a program for a new platform.	There is at least one if not ten different versions of C for virtually every platform.
Assembler	The fastest of languages.	Due to its low level processor specific focus, Assembler isn't as portable to other platforms as other products.	There is an Assembler for every major platform.
Delphi	Since it compiles to stand-alone execut-able, Delphi is quite speedy, although it is slightly slower than C/C++.	Delphi can only develop Windows products.	Delphi is only available for authoring for and in Windows.
Visual Basic	Visual Basic is situationally slow. In areas such as graphics it can be quite slow. OCXs and Windows Calls can speed things up. Overall though this is not a program for creating cutting edge 3D Arcade games.	VB is not portable to any non-Windows based environment.	VB is a Windows only development system.
Director	Director is also situationally slow. Depending on your needs it can be fast enough or too slow.	Director is very portable. Authors can write one product for many platforms: Win-dows, Mac, SGI, consoles, and the Internet.	Versions of Director exist for Windows and Mac.

Table 15.1 Comparison of Programmer Languages for Game Development

Ease of Use	Cost	Future?
C has a much higher learning curve compared to other authoring products but that's a factor of its excellent speed and portability.	The entire gauntlet of costs from freeware versions to versions that cost $1,000.	C will continue its dominance as the primary development tool but will over time lose some share to other higher level tools.
Assembler is the most difficult to learn and use — most programmers avoid it except for the most needed of situations.	Most C programs include an Assembler package.	Assembler was once in the position C is in, but today it has taken a position as a strong benchplayer.
Delphi is easier to use than C but still not easier than Visual Basic. Derived from Pascal, Delphi is an excellent choice for people familiar with that language.	Delphi runs roughly around $500 to start.	Delphi's future seems solid for now and it is gaining acceptance. The only question remains the health of its creator Borland.
VB is quite easy to learn at first but more difficult to master to a point of being able to create a quality title. Still it's perhaps the easiest of languages to grasp.	Depending on the version and vendor it can run from $200 to $1000.	Microsoft is backing VB big time and rumors are VB will receive increased ability in key areas for games and multimedia where it's increasingly being used.
Director is a very easy product to use. However, like VB, it takes time to master it enough to do quality work.	Director costs about $1,000. Macromedia from time to time bundles it with other key products, which can bring its price down some.	Director is the current authoring package leader and currently a hot item with its Internet technology. Version 5 is due soon and there's no reason it won't have a long life and play an increasingly important role in the games industry.

Table 15.1 Comparison of Programmer Languages for Game Development

Product	Speed	Portability	Authoring Platform
mTropolis	mTropolis is perhaps the fastest of the authoring product.	mTropolis is quite portable and the product is designed to make components created with it highly reusable. Programs created with it can be played on Mac, and PC platforms are planned.	For now there is only a Mac authoring environment. Windows 95/NT is planned sometime for release in 1996.
Oracle Media Objects	OMO is situationally slow. Depending on your needs it can be fast enough or too slow.	OMO is highly portable. Oracle is offering players for Windows and the Mac as well as planned versions for set-top box products and possibly consoles as well.	For now (until a Windows 95 version ships) authoring is Mac-based only.
Strata MediaForge	Strat MediaForge is also slow for certain applications. Depending on your needs, it may be fast enough, however. Calls to external OCXs can help speed bottlenecks by farming them out.	MediaForge is very much a Windows tailored package. However it's a major Mac product developer, so who knows?	Authoring requires Windows 95/NT.
QuarkImmedia	QuarkImmedia isn't meant for Arcade quality speed and therefore doesn't offer such.	Players exist for the Mac and PC; there's talk about consoles but only if Quark receives enough demand from its users for such.	Authoring is so far only available to Mac users who must already have QuarkXPress.

Table 15.1 Comparison of Programmer Languages for Game Development

Ease of Use	Cost	Future?
mTropolis is a complex product but only because of the power it offers. Its GUI base interface and drag and drop authoring help make things easier than programming for sure but there's a lot under the hood to master.	mTropolis is far more expensive than other authoring packages so far. Prices run close to $5000 and more depending on your specific situation.	It's new, it's powerful and it's just getting around. mTropolis has a bright future but only if the company can make money. Great products have come and gone; mTropolis looks like it has staying power—but in the technology world you really don't know until a couple of years pass.
Like all other authoring packages, this is meant to be far simpler than a traditional programming language, but in doing so one spends time learning to work with it to properly learn how to get the most out of it.	OMO is actually free for now—whether that remains or it goes for $1000 some day is yet to be seen.	One would think with Oracle backing it, there could be a long future and many new versions. However only they know and Oracle could easily go another route, not needing the revenue of this product one bit. Only time will tell—good thing it's free for now.
Visual Basic users will love the embedded VB scripting language, and overall it's a slick user interface. To master it and work with the OCX controls will require some work.	Strata MediaForge runs around $1,500.	Strata is a good company with strong backing and this is becoming a key product for them. With support for OCXs and other extensions coupled with Strata's enthusiasm the future seems good if the sales come through.
It's quite a simple environment to those already familiar with QuarkXPress. For others it may take much more time to master.	It can cost several thousands to work with, being that you need QuarkXPress as well as QuarkImmedia to author.	Quark has high hopes for this environment and it's a novel idea. However as to what level of interactivity they'll take it to in the future, it's hard to see it reaching the levels of some of the above mentioned products.

CHAPTER 16

If the future of PC games is the Windows platform, you'll need the best resources you can get your hands on to make the transition from DOS to Windows.

Windows Game Programming: Up Close and Personal

Microsoft has generally been viewed as a bit player in the games market, but in 1995 this situation changed. Single-handedly—like only Microsoft could—they swept in with a suite of announcements, software, and joint ventures that have created a stir among game developers. Although developers everywhere were thrilled about the possibility that the PC games market might finally take the lead as the game platform of choice, they were also keenly aware of the issues that surround a titan like Microsoft taking its place in the industry.

As Windows 95 becomes the key operating system for millions of the world's PCs, game developers will have access to a powerful, game-friendly operating system with an extensive suite of tools for creating incredible games. At the forefront of these tools is Microsoft's Windows 95 Game SDK, which is, perhaps, the single most important development toolkit for the Windows gaming platform. Having said that, I think the Windows 95 Game SDK is a good starting point for covering the assortment of resources available to you for developing Windows games.

Introducing the Windows 95 Game SDK

The Windows 95 Game SDK is a suite of APIs and products that makes developing games for Windows as it should have been all along: powerful *and* straightforward. For years, Windows was too slow for many speed-intensive games, but now with the Game SDK this limitation is beginning to disappear.

Why is the new SDK powerful and important? *It gives developers direct access to the PC's hardware.* Although game developers working in DOS have long had this luxury, they've had to contend with DOS' inability to directly manage display drivers and sound drivers. Microsoft removes this headache with what it calls the *Game Subsystem.*

The Game Subsystem is comprised of four major components:

- DirectDraw
- DirectSound
- DirectInput
- DirectPlay

These subsystems, which are all 32-bit APIs, allow developers to directly control video display memory and audio buffers with digital mixing and 3D audio. They also provide easier access to networking and various fancy input devices like Microsoft's Sidewinder 3D Pro joystick.

Before moving on to other components, let's go over the main APIs that make up the Windows Game SDK.

DirectDraw

DirectDraw is a low-level object layer that gives Windows programmers direct access to video cards, while maintaining high-level functionality. Essentially, DirectDraw provides you with device dependent access to video memory in a device independent setting. In Microsoft's own words, "DirectDraw is a memory manager for video memory."

DirectDraw is only available for Windows 95 and Windows NT. It currently exists as a standalone library, but eventually it will be folded directly into the Windows operating system with future revisions.

DirectDraw works with most graphics display hardware with the exception of older cards with VGA chipsets that don't support linear access to the card's frame buffer. I suggest that you monitor updates from Microsoft and other developers as more extensive use and testing yields specific video card problems.

Among DirectDraw's most useful features are its support for double-buffered page flipping (a must for smooth animation), access and control of the on-board graphic card's blitter chips, support for 3D Z buffers, improved image stretching routines (a major plague in previous GDI/WinG systems), and, of course, much higher frame rates.

How It Works

DirectDraw isn't really a complete replacement for the traditional GDI; it's a separate solution aimed at high-performance programming. The traditional GDI still exists for programs or routines that don't require the functionality provided by DirectDraw. In addition, as far as Video for Windows is concerned, DirectDraw includes a layer of code—called *DirectVideo*—that works as a buffer between the Video for Windows engine and DirectDraw, resulting in faster displays and tighter integration to DirectDraw.

DirectVideo replaces the Universal Draw Handler of the original Video for Windows DCI architecture, allowing MSVIDEO to talk to DirectDraw without Microsoft having to rewrite and replace all the existing MSVIDEO.DLLs in use. So far, Microsoft has not indicated whether or not DirectVideo will be folded into MSVIDEO.DLL, but I suspect this will happen.

DirectDraw is mostly contained in DDRAW.DLL, a 32-bit DLL. This DLL performs all of the various DirectDraw API calls and then passes them through what's called the DirectDraw *HAL*, or *hardware application layer*. This layer is basically a fancy driver that is supplied by the hardware companies who intend to make boards that are Windows 95 compatible. It is here that the various hardware-independent commands are translated into hardware-dependent routines.

DirectSound

DirectSound is similar to DirectDraw in that it's aimed at game and multimedia developers. It also bypasses traditional Windows components (in this case, the MMSYSTEM.DLL) and increases speed and functionality in doing so. Like DirectDraw, DirectSound is an entirely separate component that at some future time will be folded in with existing Windows functionality to provide better overall consistency to the Windows API. Unlike DirectDraw though, DirectSound is not yet available for Windows NT. DirectSound was designed in conjunction with John Miles, the veteran sound guru who is also the author of his own DOS-oriented sound system API.

DirectSound's features include the ability to communicate with the sound hardware to determine exactly what functionality it has (great for scaling your app's sound routines), on-the-fly WAV mixing, the ability to play multiple WAV files, and much more.

DirectSound was originally slated to include a complete section of API calls dedicated to 3D sound effects. However, Microsoft has pulled out the actual software implementation of 3D sound, promising it for a later date. Much of the documentation still exists to provide you with an idea of what they're going to be implementing in the future.

Just like DirectDraw, DirectSound accesses dedicated hardware through a HAL, which in turn tells DirectSound what the hardware can and can't do. If a specific feature is not available or the HAL driver is missing, DirectSound uses conventional techniques to deal with sound, implementing all the audio changes in software and not providing the hardware acceleration that might otherwise be possible.

DirectSound promises a number of low-level features, especially in the use of 3D sound. It won't be long before most of the major sound toolkits from DOS will migrate to Windows and incorporate DirectSound into their APIs. In addition, these packages will offer other features, such as familiar APIs to their DOS counterparts, special effects, and in some cases, backwards compatibility to Windows 3.1. Already, HMI, Diamondware, and Miles Sound are working to move toward this model of sound API programming. (See Chapter 14 for more information on these products.)

Jeff Roberts, a RAD Software designer and author of Smacker!, has written some nice code that helps you implement various sound routines with Microsoft's DirectSound API. These routines are included on the accompanying CD-ROM.

How It Works

DirectSound is a low-level digital audio mixing technology. It creates all of its effects on the fly in software, but is able to pass functionality to the hardware, when applicable, for increased performance. Consequently, DirectSound can work with a wide range of hardware. It provides for increased hardware functionality without revisions in the software.

DirectSound also allows you to mix digital audio streams in realtime. You simply set up all kinds of base sounds in memory and then send derived versions of them to the sound hardware for playback. You can also change pitch or stereo effects on the fly! This technology, as I'm sure you can see, creates excellent interactive audio capabilities.

DirectInput

One common complaint of PC-based games was their lack of digital joystick support. I can hear you now, "But didn't the Gravis UltraPad offer digital support?" Well, yes. But this was only one vendor and they used a specialized driver. The DirectInput API provides all kinds of cool joystick and other input control functionality, including digital support and a slew of other interesting features like support for more firing buttons.

Microsoft recently announced that it would start selling a high-quality joystick called the Sidewinder 3D Pro that contains a number of new features, including six buttons. The strategy is to give Windows the needed features so that it can compete with consoles having fast digital joysticks with lots of different buttons.

DirectPlay

DirectPlay is a total game-specific communications protocol. It supports local area network games and serves as a protocol for online client/server games, as well. You send commands to the API, which are then translated into the various low-level protocols and are read and interpreted by a DirectPlay client on the other end of the network.

Direct3D and Reality Lab

Although Direct3D is not technically a main component of the Windows Game SDK, I feel it deserves a closer examination. In February 1995, Microsoft acquired RenderMorphics Ltd. and announced its intention to incorporate the popular Reality Lab realtime 3D rendering engine into future versions of Windows. In addition, it also announced Direct3D, which will work as a go-between for 3D accelerator cards, 3D APIs, or your own 3D code and specialized 3D graphics hardware.

As I mentioned earlier, Direct3D is a low-level library that optimizes playback of 3D objects, depending on the associated code library and hardware in the machine in which it is running. If, for example, the graphics hardware in the your machine can accelerate 3D polygons, Direct3D can step in and help the 3D library take advantage of the graphics card's ability to do so. Likewise, if the graphics hardware in your machine can't do anything special to render 3D graphics, Direct3D will toss the command back to the 3D API and ask it to perform the task at hand. Either way, the

graphics get placed on the screen, allowing programmers to concentrate more on supplying kick butt 3D games.

Direct3D will work with any library or 3D hardware card that chooses to support it. Microsoft purchased RenderMorphics and its Reality Lab product to ensure at least one of three emerging major 3D libraries (the others being BRender and Criterion's Renderware) would offer support. Because Direct3D will offer developers advanced 3D features, a royalty-free development environment for all of Microsoft operating systems, and cross-platform capabilities, BRender and Renderware would be silly to pass this one by.

Check out Chapter 21 for a closer examination of all of the activity taking place in the 3D games movement.

I covered Surround Video earlier in the digital Video section. It has yet to be released by Microsoft and is being positioned as a competitor to Apple's Quicktime VR product. While some believe it won't ever ship, I think it's being delayed as Microsoft reworks a lot of its digital video engine to solve some conflicts it has with DirectSound and DirectDraw. Of course, this is only my guess but there's a lot Microsoft needs to do to bring Video for Windows up to speed with newer technologies, and I think we can expect that to happen and for Surround Video to make its debut then as well.

If you're serious about building major Windows applications and working with the Microsoft Game SDK, you should subscribe to the Microsoft's Developer Network Level II program.

For a $495 fee, Microsoft sends out every three months a slew of code, SDKs, operating systems, and more, all on CD-ROM, directly to developers. Also included on the Level II CD-ROMs are the Game SDK, Windows 95, device drivers, sample code, and the Microsoft Knowledge Base—a giant database of common developer question and answers.

You also get discounts on Microsoft Press books, a subscription to their developer newsletter, and information about events and new technology coming from Microsoft.

Microsoft Developers Network (MSDN) Level II Subscription

One Microsoft Way
Microsoft Corp.
Redmond, WA, 98052

Phone: 206 882-8080
WWW: http://www.microsoft.com/MSDN

The Future for the Windows Game SDK and Windows 95/NT

In a January 8, 1996 article, *Electronic Engineering Times* (EET) wrote about a project Microsoft has going that could very well become the future of the Game SDK API.

The project, called the "Simply Interactive PC," is a streamlined version of Windows that has been optimized for entertainment and Internet access. The article quoted a Microsoft executive as saying that the Simply Interactive PC is the focus of Microsoft's move to deliver more interactivity to Windows. While the article speculated that it might just be an attempt from Microsoft to throw up a smokescreen to downplay the current hype about the $500 PC (some people actually think they can deliver a usuable PC with all sorts of multimedia stuff for around $500), Microsoft says it's not.

It appears that Microsoft has finally recognized that home PCs, aside from those being used as part of a home office, are primarily bought for games, multimedia reference, and Internet access. Windows 95 has a ton of features that are virtually useless to these users. If Microsoft strips the operating system down to a few core components (including removing all 16-bit code) and focuses on meeting the needs of these users by adding Internet hooks, a built-in 3D API, and better video, they could have a highly optimized home version of Windows.

The article indicates that the Simply Interactive PC will be "a collection of open specifications—including a new family of 32-bit Windows drivers—bringing advanced multimedia capabilities to an X86-based system." Clearly, Microsoft is working to overthrow the console market—working even harder than it already has with Windows 95.

Two crucial technologies will drive the Simply Interactive PC. The first, *low-latency audio*, is essentially a collection of interfaces that facilitate access to fast, kernel-mode services in the Windows operating system. These interfaces would enable software to be written for the emerging generation of DSVD (digital simultaneous voice and data) modems, which Microsoft views as a driver of future online entertainment and PC-based videoconferencing applications. Low-latency audio will also support a MIDI (musical instrument digital interface) connection, easing the generation of CD-ROM-style audio.

EET goes on to say that the other technology employed by the Simply Interactive PC is a new driver model called the "Win32 driver model (WDM)," which, according to the article, makes it easier for developers to tweak different hardware setups for optimized performance. Also according to *EET*'s report,

Microsoft will converge all versions of Windows NT, Windows 95, and future versions around this new driver model to unify Windows as a whole.

Microsoft is already promoting a major component of their Game/Simply Interactive PC development SDK. They have been actively plugging their low-latency audio technology, and have indicated that they will be merging the low-latency work into their DirectSound API. It's apparent that Microsoft intends to push new Games-oriented technology until Windows becomes both a powerful and successful gaming platform.

Don't miss out on the opportunity to be in on this technology. Stay in touch with Microsoft and make sure to attend the key developers conferences.

CMP's TechWeb *(http://www.techweb.com)* has a complete archive of *Electronic Engineering Times.* Visit this Web site and download a copy of the article about Microsoft's Simply Interactive PC development.

Game SDK Resources

Already there are several books and online resources to help you get up to speed on the Windows Game SDK. Of course, keep checking the shelves of your local book store because many more are on the way.

Books

Let's take a look at the books first.

Direct Draw Programming by Bret Timmins (M&T Books, New York, NY, 1996; ISBN 1-55851-460-0)

Looking for dedicated DirectDraw text? Look no further. This book is a comprehensive guide to the most important of all the segments of the Game SDK.

Visual Basic 4 Network Gaming Adventure Set by David Allen (The Coriolis Group, Scottsdale, AZ, 1996; ISBN 1-883577-32-2)

Although this book focuses on Visual Basic 4, its coverage is distinctly angled at a key component of the Game SDK—the DirectPlay interface. (For more information on using Visual Basic to program Windows games, see the *Delphi- and Visual Basic-Specific Tools and OCXs* section later in the chapter.) It is the only book out that shows you how to use DirectPlay with Visual Basic, or any language for that matter. David Allen is quite an expert on creating multiplayer, network games and he is in fine form in this book as he takes on OLE game servers, Network DDE, and techniques for building 32-bit high level communications libraries around DirectPlay.

Windows Game SDK Developer's Guide by Martyn Deobald (The Coriolis Group, Scottsdale, AZ, 1996; ISBN 1-883577-84-5)

This book provides everything you need to learn to create stunning high-resolution games under Windows. The big strength of the book is that it is much more than just a "tour" of DirectDraw, which is what you'll find in many of the other books that claim to cover the Windows Game SDK. Martyn tackles the entire Game SDK, including DirectDraw, DirectPlay, and DirectSound.

Windows 95 Game Developer's Guide Using the Game SDK by Michael Morrison and Randy Weems (SAMS, 1996; ISBN 0-672-30661-1)

This book and CD-ROM combo covers some of the basics of creating games for Windows 95 with the Microsoft Windows 95 Game SDK. Topics include game programming basics, Animation, DirectSound, Network Gaming, and more. Don't expect a lot of detail in this book.

Windows 95 Games Programming by Al Stevens and Stan Trujillo (M&T Books, 1996; ISBN 1-55851-448-1)

With four full-featured games, a complete game builder's toolkit, and a C++ games engine, this book on Windows 95 game programming tries to cover a lot of territory. A CD-ROM with the book includes all the code and examples contained in the book.

The Windows 95 Game SDK Strategy Guide by Clayton Walnum (QUE, 1996; ISBN 07-8970-661-X)

Long time programmer and author Clayton Walnum has done a "port" of his game Aztec Adventure (which he used to show how to use WinG in an earlier book) to DirectDraw and implemented other Game SDK features to give you a real life set of examples for using the Windows 95 game technology. The big weakness of this book is that it doesn't go into much depth about the Windows Game SDK—you'll only find limited coverage of DirectDraw. I think the publisher (or author) got a little carried away with the title, which is misleading to say the least.

Online Resources

Next time you're surfing, stop on by one of the sites listed here.

Microsoft's FTP Site

`ftp://ftp.microsoft.com/developr/`

For those of you who haven't gotten around to ordering an MSDN Level II CD-ROM, you can find a bunch of interesting material, including early documentation for the Windows 95 Game SDK on Microsoft's FTP site.

Microsoft's Developers News Site (Article about their COM Architecture)
http://www.microsoft.com/DEVNEWS/ARCHIVE/COMODEL.HTM

The *COM*, or *Component Object Model*, is the underlying technology behind the Windows 95 Game SDK. Read all about it here.

Microsoft's Windows 95 Games Launch Page
http://www.microsoft.com/windows/games/

When Microsoft launched Windows 95, they turned the roll-out into a huge event and they created a site dedicated to that event in an online "Cybercast." Check out all the hype here.

Watcom Web Site
http://www.watcom.on.ca/q_and_a/win95gdk.txt

Watcom has published this document to help you work with the Windows 95 Game SDK and their Watcom C compiler.

Additional Windows Tools and APIs

In addition to the Direct*X* APIs from the Windows 95 Game SDK, programmers still have access to these veteran solutions: the WinG graphics API, the WaveMix sound API, AutoPlay, and WinToon—an extension to the Video for Windows format. Let's take a look at these APIs in more detail.

WinG.DLL

Knowing that Windows' GDI graphic routines couldn't give it the speed increase it really needed, most game programmers not only chose to stay out of Windows, they *had* to stay out if they were looking to implement fast, animated, arcade-like graphics in their games. Instead they stayed in DOS because they could get optimized graphic routines and draw directly to the video memory, which gave them the best speed.

To combat this problem, Microsoft invented WinG, which enabled higher performance graphics in Windows. WinG allowed programmers far more flexibility and provided direct interaction to bitmaps stored in memory and their associated palettes. Using WinG, programmers could speed performance considerably, depending on the situation, over previous Windows routines.

Although WinG has been more or less folded into the Windows 95 32-bit GDI API, it's important to familiarize yourself with this library, especially if you plan for backward compatibility to Windows 3.1. WinG is available for free online at CompuServe's WinMM forum. You don't need WinG for Windows 95.

WaveMix.DLL

WaveMix.DLL got its start in the Windows Arcade Pack. It was later promoted online in the Windows MM forum. WaveMix.DLL allows for the playback of multiple WAV files, which isn't possible under the normal MMSystem.DLL in Windows or Windows 95.

Microsoft didn't really support this library in its humble beginnings, but as more and more programmers started discovering WaveMix, Microsoft realized it could play a crucial role in their own emerging games strategy, and adopted it as a sound solution.

As Microsoft moves into DirectSound, WaveMix will maintain its relevancy as a free solution for programmers, and as a backward compatibility solution for Windows 3.1.

AutoPlay

One thing all game developers—heck, all software programmers—understand is that one of the biggest problems consumers have is getting software to start up on a PC. AutoPlay, which is a CD-ROM solution for startup problems, is key to solving startup and installation problems associated with software, especially game software.

Using AutoPlay, you can have a user's system launch quick title screens or jump straight to the proper install scheme when the user inserts a CD-ROM into his or her drive. With proper AutoPlay drivers and code in place, the user will never have to deal with any menus or file managers to run a product from a CD-ROM.

AutoPlay is one of those little features that can make a huge difference. Using AutoPlay will help you to make PC games as easy to use—from a startup standpoint—as those developed for the dedicated gaming consoles, which hopefully will cut down on returns based on the startup and setup problems that plague the PC games industry.

Non-Microsoft Software Solutions

Not every Windows programming tool comes from Microsoft. Increasingly, you'll find programming libraries and tools coming from third-party vendors. Some products actually interact with the Windows 95 Game SDK's Direct technology, making it easier to use, while others are actual replacements.

Many of the products have DOS roots, which make it much easier to migrate your DOS programming skills to Windows. Let's take a look at what's available.

Animation for Windows Developer Kit
Autodesk, Inc.
2320 Marinship Way
Sausalito, CA 94965

Phone: 415 332-2344 **Fax:** 415 491-8308
WWW: http://www.autodesk.com

Autodesk's Animation for Windows Developer Kit lets you add FLI or FLC support or animation to your applications. The kit comes with a DLL, VBX, and an MCI driver.

Media!Lab
Metagraphics Software Corporation
200 Clock Tower Place, 201E
P. O. Box 222235
Carmel, CA 93922-2235

Phone: 408 622-8950 **Fax:** 408 622-8955
WWW: http://www.metagraphics.com

Media!Lab is a multimedia animation programming tool for Microsoft Windows. It features imaging, animation, video, and sound wrapped up neatly in a C/C++ programming toolkit.

Check out their Web site for a complete suite of demos showing off the results and code behind the library.

WinDirect 2.0
SciTech Software
5 Governors Lane, Suite D
Chico, CA 95926

Phone: 916 894-8400 **Fax:** 510 208-8026
WWW: http://www.scitechsoft.com

WinDirect allows you to shut down the traditional Windows GDI and take over the entire graphics display hardware within Windows. Once the GDI is out of the picture and you have direct access to video memory, things speed up considerably (much like they do with DirectDraw). WinDirect applications can program any standard VGA video mode, such as 640×480×4 or 320×200×8, or they can run standard VGA ModeX style graphics, and even call the standard VESA BIOS routines to run high-resolution SuperVGA graphics.

The WinDirect product comes with a Windows version of SciTech's PM/Pro library, which provides services for calling real mode code, for directly accessing linear frame buffer memory on SuperVGA devices, and for providing a virtualized frame buffer for SuperVGA devices that do not have a hardware linear frame buffer.

WinDirect doesn't get in the way of any of the other standard Windows multimedia fuctionality, such as the MMSystem.DLL that handles sound, CD-ROM interaction, and more.

WinDirect is a licensable product: $99.95 allows you to ship up to 20,000 copies of a single product and $599.95 allows you to ship an unlimited quantity of a single product. You can find demos and evaluation code for WinDirect on SciTech's Web site.

FastGraph for Windows
Ted Gruber Software
P.O. Box 13408
Las Vegas, NV 89112

Phone: 702 735-1980 **Fax:** 702 735-4603
WWW: http://www.accessnv.com/fastgraph/

From the makers of one of the leading DOS graphics libraries comes FastGraph for Windows. FastGraph replaces the Windows GDI and increases graphics performance significantly. FastGraph gives you a set of fast, intuitive low-level functions to write to the frame buffer. It is intuitive because it closely resembles the direct screen writes many DOS programmers are used to.

FastGraph for Windows provides all the "moves" and "draws," the bitmap manipulations, the palette management, the double buffering, and other capabilities that game programmers are accustomed to using. In addition, it maintains much of the API from the original DOS version of the product, making for an easier transition.

FastGraph for Windows supports Windows 3.1 (both Win16 and Win32s), Windows 95, WinG, DirectDraw, and Windows GDI blitting. While WinG and DirectDraw are recommended for fast program execution, they are not required. FastGraph will autodetect the optimal blitting mechanism and use whatever it finds on the system.

FastGraph for Windows supports a number of compilers, including most C/C++ compilers, Borland's Object Pascal, and Delphi. FastGraph will only set you back $249; source code is available at an additional cost. There is no royalty for shipping products made with FastGraph.

Delphi- and Visual Basic-Specific Tools and OCXs

If you've read Chapter 15, you already know that I consider both Delphi and Visual Basic (VB) to be excellent programming languages for making Windows games. Delphi is especially speedy as it compiles to standalone executable files, while VB, now in version 4, is a bit slower and has the drawback of needing run-time files to assist it. Either way though both offer interesting alternatives to C/C++ programming in Windows. In this section, I've listed several interesting products and resources that you can employ if you use one of these two products to develop your games.

Windows' OCX and VBX Controls

OCX and VBX controls are among the more interesting resources for programming Windows games. These controls can be used by products like Delphi and VB to enable the multimedia functionality needed for computer games. I've listed the three major controls worth checking out—especially if you're a VB programmer.

MediaDeveloper OCX
Lead Technologies
900 Baxter Street
Charlotte, NC 28280
Phone: 704 332-5532 **Fax:** 704 372-8161

MediaDeveloper provides developers with a strong base of multimedia routines to play with. Among its features is support for all kinds of digital video formats, audio formats, and animation. It also has a built-in database, which helps you control all the different multimedia files you might use in your game.

MediaKnife
Media Architects Inc.
7320 SW Hunziker Road, Suite 305
Portland, OR 97223
Phone: 503 620-5372 **Fax:** 503 620-5451

MediaKnife is one of the best known VBX controls among Visual Basic multimedia/game developers. MediaKnife comes with six custom controls that help you to create hotspots, animate sprites, implement sound, incorporate palette effects, and more.

MediaShop
Motion Tool Works
330 Townsend St, Suite 123
San Francisco, CA 94107
Phone: 415 541-9333 **Fax:** 415 541-0555

MediaShop is a full-tilt multimedia programming tool. Not only does it help programmers to implement and integrate multimedia content into their programs, it comes with integrated tools like a WAV editor and several animation creation tools (for integrated creation of CEL animation).

Delphi Books and Magazines

For you Delphi programmers, take a look at the magazine listed here to help you along with all things Delphi.

Delphi Informant Magazine
Informant Communications Group, Inc.
10519 E. Stockton Boulevard, Suite 142
Elk Grove, CA 95624-9704

Phone: 916 686-6610 **Fax:** 916 686-8497
Subscription: $49.95 **Newsstand:** $4.95 **Publishes:** Monthly **Pages:**100

Delphi Informant provides in-depth articles on this newest of Borland languages. If you're looking for a complete monthly fix of reviews of Delphi components, code examples, book reviews and more, you need to subscribe to this magazine.

Visual Basic Books and Magazines

Because Visual Basic is such a popular programming language, you can find a lot of written material to help you along as you learn. I've listed but a few of the more pertinent books and magazines. These should keep you busy for a while.

Black Art of Visual Basic Game Programming by Mark Pruett (Waite Group Press, Corte Madera, CA, 1995; ISBN 1-878739)

This book contains an assortment of projects to show you how you can create different types of games with VB.

Build Your Own PC Game in Seven Easy Steps by Scott Palmer (Addision-Wesley, Reading, MA, 1995; ISBN 0-201-48911-2)

This book about programming games with Visual Basic covers game design, algorithms, graphics, animation, sound effects, and everything else that goes into making a game for Windows with Visual Basic. The CD with the book includes images, backgrounds, sprites, buttons, and other multimedia content you need for a game. In addition, the book contains the code and other sample games constructed by the author.

The Visual Basic Guide to the Windows API by Daniel Appleman (Ziff Davis Press)

Another must-have for VB users. This extensive book covers how to call the Windows API with VB code. VB is a little different in the way it handles calls to the Windows API, and no other book will show you better how to do it. The accompanying disk includes code samples and other useful information.

Programming Games for Beginners: Visual Basic for Fun and Profit by Chris Howard (SAMS, 1993; ISBN: 0-672-30313-2)

This book provides a nice introduction to VB and VB game programming. It includes source code for many different types of games.

Visual Basic 4 Multimedia Adventure Set by Scott Jarol and Anthony Potts (The Coriolis Group, Scottsdale, AZ, 1995; ISBN 1-883577-01)

For those of you using VB in your game development process, this book is a must-have. It covers many VB programming techniques useful for game development like sprite animation, WaveMix, Video for Windows, Hypertext, MIDI, and more! The CD-ROM contains a suite of interesting tools and code samples.

Windows 95 Multimedia Programming by Mitch Gould and Van Thurston, Jr. (M&T Books, New York, NY, 1995; ISBN 1-555851-413-9)

Yet another Windows multimedia book. Although not focused on games, it does cover some of the basic multimedia functionality you need to know to create games with Windows 95. It covers sprites, sounds, graphics zooms, pans, and hotspots.

Visual Basic Programmer's Journal
Fawcette Technical Publications
280 Second Street, Suite 200
Los Altos, CA 94022

Phone: 415 917-7650 **Fax:** 415 948-7332
WWW: http://www.windx.com
Subscription: $22.95 **Newsstand:** $3.95 **Publishes:** Bimonthly **Pages:** 150

For those game developers employing Visual Basic either as a primary development language or as a support product for building editors and such, this is the magazine for you. Although VBPJ takes on a more business-oriented edge, many of the articles are applicable to game development projects. However, there have not been any specific columns or articles devoted to game development with Visual Basic.

Of special note is their Web site, which is an incredibly comprehensive site for everything that comprises VB development.

Online Resources

Don't forget to log onto the Web to find a wealth of information on both Delphi and Visual Basic. Here's a few of the sites I found:

Omnisoft VB Multimedia Site
`http://www.omnisoft.com/~omnisoft/mmrs.html`

Omnisoft, makers of the Powermedia control for VB, have put together this nice Web site with pointers to tools and resources for VB multimedia and games programmers. You can also check out issues of their VB multimedia magazine, which they produce on the site.

Silicon Commander's Delphi Turbo Sprite Toolkit Page
`http://www.silicmdr.com/delph.htm`

From shareware developer Silicon Commander, comes the Delphi Turbo Sprite Toolkit, a really cool set of source code for implementing neat sprites in your Delphi games.

General Windows Programming Resources

We've talked about the specifics; now here are a few more general Windows-related programming resources.

Install Programs

Every good program for Windows must have a good install program. Currently the two following programs are among the best around for building excellent installation programs for your Windows products.

InstallShield
Stirling Software
1100 Woodfield Road, Suite 108
Schaumburg, IL 60173-9946

Phone: 708 240-9111 **Fax:** 708 240-9120
WWW: http://www.stirling.com

According to the makers of InstallShield, nearly 75 percent of all Windows applications use InstallShield to install their applications. Part of the reason for this install program's success is that a version of InstallShield, InstallShield SDK, was distributed with various Microsoft developers tools. InstallShield Express is a soon to be offered product that will give developers a visual system for building their install applications.

InstallShield now has a one-size-fits-all license for $395; it allows the developer to use InstallShield for an unlimited number of installation systems. Check out their Web site for more information and to download demonstrations of the product.

PC-Install
20/20 Software, Inc.
8196 SW Hall Boulevard, Suite 200
Beaverton, OR 97008

Phone: 503 520-0504 **Fax:** 503 520-9118
WWW: http://www.twenty.com/~twenty

PC-Install is an award-winning, professional installation program. The product includes a royalty-free license allowing for the distribution of an unlimited number of copies and use with an unlimited number of applications.

Complete installations can be created in minutes using PC-Install's English-like commands. According to the company, with PC-Install, you can create a professional installation in less than 30 minutes.

PC-Install can install to Windows 95, Windows NT, Windows 3.x, Windows for Workgroups, and even DOS. It can even create a single set of diskettes that will install to all three operating systems.

A downloadable demo of their product is available on their Web site as well.

Books and Magazines

I pulled out the Windows 95 Game SDK-oriented books and the VB- and Delphi-oriented books earlier for organizational purposes. Listed here is a slew of other titles to help you with all your other Windows game-oriented programming needs. While some of these books concentrate on the WinG.DLL, a lot of what they offer is still quite applicable with or without using the Game SDK routines.

Amazing 3D Adventure Set by Lary Myers (The Coriolis Group, Scottsdale, AZ, 1995; ISBN 1-883577-15-2)

This book, offers the latest and greatest version—both DOS and WinG versions—of Lary Myer's ACK 3D raycasting engine including graphics, source code, and map editors. If you want to implement a lightening-fast 3D raycasting game in Windows, check out the code in this book. The provided CD-ROM contains a wealth of programming tools, source code, artwork, and other goodies for creating 3D games.

Black Art of Windows Game Programming by Eric Lyons (Waite Group Press, Corte Madera, CA, 1995; ISBN 1-878739-95-6)

This book is designed to show you how to program a number of simple game projects using WinG.

Dungeons of Discovery: Writing Dazzling Windows Games with WinG by Clayton Walnum (Macmillan Computer Publications, 1995; ISBN 078-970-0603)

This useful book covers the WinG programming extension for Windows. Walnum, who has been writing for years (some may remember him from the old Atari magazine *ANALOG*), does a great job explaining WinG and shows it in a C++ MFC format. Not only does the CD-ROM come with complete source code and the WinG library, but it also includes a complete 3D dungeon (not a raycaster!) program to dissect and rebuild.

Visual C++ Multimedia Adventure Set by Peter Aiken and Scott Jarol (The Coriolis Group, Scottsdale, AZ, 1995; ISBN 1-883577-19-5)

This new book covers WinG, WinToon, and other Windows programming tenets for gamers and multimedia developers. Topics covered include full-motion video, animation, music, image manipulation, and special effects. All of the source code and resources are included on an accompanying CD-ROM.

Microsoft Interactive Developer
Fawcette Technical Publications
280 Second Street, Suite 200
Los Altos, CA 94022

Phone: 415 917-7650 **Fax:** 415 948-7332
WWW: http://www.windx.com
Subscription: $N/A **Newsstand:** $3.95 **Publishes:** Bimonthly **Pages:** 100

Here is a new offering from the people who bring you *Visual Basic Programmer's Journal*. This magazine, which is hitting the press for the first time as I write this chapter, is geared toward Windows 95/NT interactive development. I assume this means they will focus on products like VB, Visual C++, Internet Studio, and more. I guess we'll have to wait and see. Be sure to get the first issue; it's bound to be a collector's item.

Microsoft Systems Journal
Miller-Freeman Publishing
600 Harrison Street
San Francisco, CA 94107

Phone: 800 666-1084
WWW: http://www.mfi.com
Subscription: $50.00 **Newsstand:** $4.95 **Publishes:** Monthly **Pages:**100

Microsoft Systems Journal is totally devoted to hardcore Windows development issues. While this journal is sanctioned by Microsoft and includes some articles written by Microsoft employees, it is published by Miller-Freeman, who is best known as the publisher of *Dr. Dobb's Journal*.

Visual Developer
The Coriolis Group
7339 E. Acoma, Suite 7
Scottsdale, AZ 85260

Phone: 602 483-0192 **Fax:** 602 483-0193
WWW: http://www.coriolis.com
Subscription: $21.95 **Newsstand:** $4.95 **Publishes:** Bimonthly **Pages:** 100

The folks who have brought you the leading magazine for PC developers—*PC TECHNIQUES*—for years have started a new publication titled *Visual Developer Magazine.* The first issue is planned for April/May '96. As its name indicates, the new magazine will cover the hot area of visual development with languages like Visual Basic, Delphi, Visual C++, Java, JavaScript, VRML, and so on. Judging by their award-winning Web site, The Coriolis Group has some incredible content lined up for the coming year. Expect to see features of special interest to game programmers on topics like game development with Java, high-performance programming with DirectSound, developing network game servers, and creating Web-based multimedia and games. *Visual Developer Magazine* promises to feature some of the best writers in the technical press including Michael Abrash, Peter Aitken, Diana Gruber, Jeff Duntemann, Tom Swan, Al Williams, and many more.

Online Resources

And finally, get online to find a few more general Windows resources.

CompuServe Windows Multimedia Forum
`GO MMWIN`

The Windows Multimedia forum hosts a specific section on games programming for Windows. The libraries there contain lots of interesting downloads of new Windows source code, including games done with the Game SDK and more.

Microsoft Developer Web Forum
`http://www.microsoft.com/devonly/`

I hope you don't need me to tell you to check in with Microsoft's comprehensive site on programming resources for its products, but just in case you did....

CHAPTER 17

The WinTel (Windows and Intel) platform isn't the only outlet for games or game development—you have other choices.

Developing Games the Non-Windows Way

With the advent of Windows 95, Microsoft elbowed their way into the game development arena with quite a fanfare. And they probably will corner the market with such major offerings like the Windows 95 Game SDK. But that doesn't mean that other options don't exist. With such alternatives as DOS, OS/2, NeXTStep, and BeBox (I bet you're really wondering about those last two!), you shouldn't limit yourself to a single platform until you've explored what's out there.

In my attempt to be as complete as possible, I've gathered several resources that cover these alternative development platforms. You may not like what they have to offer, but you can't make an intelligent decision unless you've educated yourself on the alternatives. So let's jump right in.

Working with the DOS Platform

I must admit, once Microsoft came through with their Windows 95 Game SDK, DOS-based game programming lost a lot of its appeal. And I'm not the only one who thinks this.

Already a number of major companies like Activision have pronounced that they have shelved development of DOS platform games. Still, despite what appears to be the death of DOS platform games (Microsoft even held a "DOS is Dead" party on Halloween), some developers continue to develop games for this platform. It's the Old Faithful of game development. And with a large, worldwide base of machines that can't run Windows, a very mature toolset, and the control it offers developers, I think DOS is still a viable option. Although you probably won't see many more retail DOS games in the future, shareware developers and hobbyists will make sure that DOS development is around for a long time to come.

Graphics Libraries

There are numerous resources for DOS game developers. Here are the major packages not already covered (for Sound APIs see Chapter 14).

FastGraph for DOS
Ted Gruber Software
P.O. Box 13408
Las Vegas, NV 89112
Phone: 702 735-1980 **Fax:** 702 735-4603
WWW: http://www.accessnv.com/fastgraph/

In the DOS games world, FastGraph is one of the most popular graphics libraries. FastGraph gives you a set of fast, intuitive, low-level functions to write to the frame buffer.

FastGraph provides all the "moves" and "draws," the bitmap manipulations, the palette management, the double buffering, and other capabilities that game programmers are accustomed to using. In addition, it offers such other needed game resources as joystick and mouse control.

FastGraph will only set you back $249; source code, however, is available at an additional cost. There is no royalty for shipping products made with FastGraph.

There is also a shareware version of FastGraph, FastGraph Lite, which is available on both CompuServe and the Ted Gruber Web site. In addition, senior programmer Ted Gruber, and game developer Diana Gruber, in her book *Action Arcade Adventure Set*, discusses techniques for creating games with FastGraph. The book, which is described in detail later in this chapter, is a complete guide to creating arcade games with Fastgraph and C. It also includes a disk containing FastGraph Lite and its source code.

GX Graphics
Genus Microprogramming
1155 Dairy Ashford, Suite 200
Houston, TX 77079
Phone: 713 870-0737 **Fax:** 713 870-0288

Genus' GX Graphics is yet another graphics library to help you quickly develop speedy graphics for your DOS-based games.

WordUp Graphics Toolkit
Egeter Software
94 Andover Drive
London, Ontario N6J 3X2
Canada
Phone: 519 641-7542 **Fax:** 519 641-7542
WWW: http://kosmic.wit.com/~kosmic/gooroo/main.html

Egeter Software produces a wide range of graphics packages known collectively as the WordUp Graphics Toolkit. The main package is the WGT 5.0 Commercial Graphics Library and it supports all kinds of features, including serial/modem communications, joystick, 8-way scrolling, SVGA, drop-down menus, sprites, FLI/FLC, basic 3D rotations, file selector, and 3D rendering. The package also includes tons of source code.

The cost of this toolkit runs from as little as $40 to $1,000 and more, depending on your needs and licensing requirements.

Egeter's Web site has lots of source code examples, tutorials, and more for you to browse through. Many of the demos cover some current interests such as polygon graphics and a "magic carpet"-style engine. You can also find WGT resources at *ftp://x2ftp.oulu.fi/pub/msdos/programming/wgt/00index.html* and on CompuServe's Game Developers forum.

UniVBE
SciTech Software
5 Governors Lane, Suite D
Chico, CA 95926
Phone: 916 894-8400 **Fax:** 510 208-8026
WWW: http://www.scitechsoft.com

UniVBE, short for Universal VESA BIOS Extension, is a popular product for DOS game developers everywhere. The UniVBE driver, which supports over 160 different SVGA chipsets, makes super VGA cards compatible with VESA BIOS Extension (VBE 2.0) programming standards so that games, CD-ROMs, utilities, and other applications will work properly (and faster) in high resolution modes. This package includes chip detection, power management, monitor centering, and compatibility and performance testing utilities.

Lots of programmers work with UniVBE and the VBE 2.0 standard to ensure a wide compatibility with all the various cards out there. In addition, because it supports the new VBE 2.0 standard, UniVBE can make applications written to take advantage of VBE 2.0, significantly faster by using protected mode access to the graphics card. UniVBE is the first product that will let you take advantage of the power of VBE 2.0.

MegaGraph Graphics Library (MGL) **2.0**
5 Governors Lane, Suite D
Chico, CA 95926
Phone: 916 894-8400 **Fax:** 510 208-8026
WWW: http://www.scitechsoft.com

Also from SciTech is the MegaGraph Graphics Library (MGL), a full-featured 32-bit graphics library for PC compatibles. It provides fast, low-level 2D and 3D primitives that can be used for realtime graphics applications. The MGL fully supports all graphics resolutions from 320×200 right up to 1600×1200, with pixel depths ranging from 4 bits per pixel to 32 bits per pixel.

You can download the evaluation versions of the MGL directly from their Web site; the full version will run around $200 should you find it worth your money.

SciTech also sells a $99 plus pack for the product that contains a set of utility libraries for MGL that implements both 2D and 3D rendering techniques, including rotations, scales, vector math, transformations, wireframe, flat shaded and smooth polygons, and a GUI library.

All libraries are provided pre-built for all supported compilers, but SciTech doesn't support the plus pack—it was simply built by an in-house SciTech programmer as an add-on to support the MGL library.

MetaWINDOW
MetaGraphics Software Corporation
200 Clock Tower Place, 201E
P. O. Box 222235
Carmel, CA 93922-2235
Phone: 408 622-8950 **Fax:** 408 622-8955
WWW: http://www.metagraphics.com

MetaGraphics' MetaWINDOW is a high-performance graphics programming toolkit designed for PC programmers developing DOS real-mode or protected-mode applications. MetaWINDOW provides a full set of graphics primitives that includes points, lines, squares, rectangles, circles, ovals, arcs, wedges, polygons, bitmap text, and seed and boundary fills. Enhanced features include rounded-corner rectangles, advanced object detection, scaleable text, dynamic font facing, image scaling, fill rules, dash styles, line cap styles, full standard and transparent raster operations, plus user-definable, multi-colored patterns up to 32×32 pixels in size.

MetaWINDOW fully supports drawing to virtual bitmaps in either conventional, EMS, XMS, or virtual disk-cached memory. You'll also find support for multiple independent windows, as well as mouse and keyboard events. MetaWINDOW supports over 80 graphics modes from HGA to SVGA and VESA up to 1280×1024 resolution.

Two add-on libraries, MetACCEL and MetHICOLOR, are also available. MetACCEL speeds up MetaWINDOW by a factor of ten on certain VGA accelerator cards, such as the ATI Graphics Ultra series. MetHICOLOR allows you to support HICOLOR graphics, as well.

Among companies MetaGraphics claims as customers for MetaWINDOW are Davidson, Sony, and Maxis.

MetaWINDOW, which is royalty free, is packaged in several levels—from $399 to $899—to accommodate your needs, and the add-ons range from $399 to $599 each. You can also obtain source code versions from MetaGraphics.

DOS-Based Resources

If the beginning of this chapter didn't convince you that DOS is still a viable game-development platform, the amazing number of resources available should.

Online Resources

As expected, the majority of free hacks and source code on the Internet and the commercial online services is DOS-based. I sifted through a lot of them and the majority are of use only to the hobbyist and learning developers—what did you expect for free?

The two best places to go DOS resource hunting are CompuServe's Game Developers forum (GO GAMDEV), which has a full library of DOS hacks, source code, and demos; and the ×2 FTP site in Finland (*ftp://x2ftp.oulu.fi*), which is perhaps the largest FTP site for game developers. Chapter 24 provides a complete list of all the key online sites for all game developers, many of which have pointers to DOS resources.

The following sites, though, are specific to the DOS game platform.

rec.games.programmer FAQ
`http://www.eleceng.ucl.ac.uk/~phart/game/FAQ/rgp_FAQ.html`

Most of the information here pertains to DOS programming even though the overall newsgroup covers a wide variety of topics.

rec.games.programmer IBM PC FAQ
`http://www.eleceng.ucl.ac.uk/~phart/game/FAQ/rgp_FAQ_ibmpc.html`

This file contains pointers to and specific information on a lot of fundamental DOS game programming issues.

PC Game Programming Encylopedia (PCGPE):
`ftp://x2ftp.oulu.fi/pub/msdos/programming/gpe/pcgpe10.zip`

Put together by the people from rec.games.programmers, this extensive file covers a ton of programming issues, most which focus on DOS game programming.

Mode X FAQ
`http://www.eleceng.ucl.ac.uk/~phart/game/FAQ/modex.html`

The infamous mode X is a key way to achieve speedy game graphics. This FAQ details the programming of this undocumented VGA graphics mode.

Books

Of course, reading materials on DOS are everywhere. Here are the cream of the crop.

Action Arcade Adventure Set by Diana Gruber (Coriolis Group Books, 1994; ISBN 1-883577-06-3)

This book covers how to create various side-scrolling games, like the infamous platform game Jazz JackRabbit, using C and the FastGraph graphics library. The book covers everything from artwork creation to side-scrolling game design to programming to advice on how to sell your creations. The book comes with everything you need including a copy of FastGraph Lite—the shareware version of the FastGraph graphics library.

PC Game Programming Explorer by Dave Roberts (Coriolis Group Books, 1994; ISBN 1-883577-07-1)

If you're testing the waters with your first DOS game, this book is an excellent read. It covers all the fundamentals of VGA game programming in C. It then moves on to cover the MidPak/DigPak sound libraries and other DOS gaming staples. Part of the book is a complete breakdown of Alien Alley, a DOS-based shooting game with scrolling graphics, sprites, full collision detection, and sound.

The book includes a disk packed with source code from the book, and the full version of Alien Alley. Dave Roberts explains concepts in a simple, easy-to-read manner. For the novice, it's hard to find a better place to get your feet wet.

Teach Yourself Game Programming in 21 Days by Andre LaMothe (SAMS Publishing, 1994; ISBN 0-671-30562-3)

This game programming version of the venerable "21 Days" series from SAMS is written by the author of *Tricks of the Game Programming Gurus.* While *Tricks* concentrated on 3D raycasting principles, this book focuses on a broad-based range of fundamental procedures, code, and tools that helps beginners develop a solid background in a number of areas. The book includes a CD-ROM full of shareware and code from the book.

Creating Turbo C++ Games by Clayton Walnum (Que Publishing, 1994)

This book, which is tailored to the inexpensive Borland C++ compiler (but which isn't exclusively in need of it), contains over 400 pages of fundamental information on topics like 256 color VGA graphics, object-oriented programming, and class creation. Included with the book are simple complete games such as a dungeon program, a card game, and a life simulator. A definite must for beginning DOS developers.

Programming Games In C by Robert B. Marmelstein (M&T Books, 1994)

This book covers simple game construction in C. In fact, it's so simple that nothing concerning VGA graphics is even included! The book includes a disk of source code.

Graphics Programming and Animation—Ultra Fast Assembly Routines for EGA/VGA Graphics Animation by Peter Jungck (R&D Technical Books)

This book and disk combination covers how to directly access VGA hardware for fast graphical routines and includes over 170 programs and sample game. An added bonus is Jungck's ProGraphx Toolbox, which the author has used to develop various shareware products. The main languages used are Assembly and C, but some examples of Pascal are also included.

Programmer's Guide to the EGA, VGA, and Super VGA Cards (3rd Ed.) by Richer F. Ferraro (Addison-Wesley, 1993; ISBN 0-201-62490-7)

Looking for an excellent general reference on the VGA card? Check out computer graphics maven Richard Ferraro's guide to programming VGA.

Turbo C++ Games by Que (Que Publishing, 1993; ISBN 1-5652-947-26)

This is a basic book about creating simple games with Borland's Turbo C++. I found it to be a good source for beginning C and game programmers.

C++ Games Programming by Al Stevens and Stan Trujill (M&T Books, 1995; ISBN 1-55851-449-X)

Another "basics" book, but one that covers C++ not plain C. More intermediate-level developers may be looking for something more expansive, but for the beginner looking to learn, it offers a few good chapters.

Developing for OS/2

If you didn't think I was nuts before, you definitely do now. However, I committed myself to covering all kinds of resources and tools, and the fact is there are a lot of cool OS/2 tools to play with. OS/2 may be the stepchild of operating systems, but those who do use it are enthusiastic proponents of it, IBM notwithstanding.

While I doubt many retail-oriented publishers will pursue OS/2 game development, it could be a good outlet for shareware developers or developers creating Internet front ends or just plain hobbyists and OS/2 enthusiasts. Therefore, in an effort not to leave any stone unturned, here is a run-down of resources for OS/2-oriented development.

OS/2 Development Tools

The Developer's Toolkit/ Game and Entertainment Toolkit
IBM Corporation
Worldwide Developer Assistance Program (DAP)
WWW: http://www.austin.ibm.com/os2games/devnews/dapapp.html

IBM's main OS/2 SDK, the Developer's Toolkit, and their specific toolkit for games, the Game and Entertainment Toolkit, are an absolute must if you're going to do any level of OS/2 game development.

The Game and Entertainment Toolkit contains a Games Class library, which eases OS/2 game development. The library is object-oriented and provides, among other things, tools for rapid development of networking (both local and Internet) games for the OS/2 platform. Let's cover a few of the key components of the Game and Entertainment Toolkit:

Direct Interface Video Extensions (DIVE)

DIVE is an API that is currently found in OS/2 Warp. DIVE gives OS/2 Warp applications direct access to the PC video hardware, while providing a high level of performance. Sounds similar to DirectDraw, doesn't it?

The DIVE engine works in much the same way as DirectDraw. You write to the DIVE API, which automatically takes care of the idiosyncrasies between cards and optimizes performance based upon the strength of the underlying hardware. This means that if DIVE detects graphics display hardware acceleration capabilities in the user's machine, the game may actually run faster through the display engine than it would with direct video buffer access.

DIVE is a DLL which, much like DirectDraw for Windows 95, optimizes blitting operations by interacting directly with video memory. Using DIVE, programmers can write directly to video memory or to a DIVE blitter for more high-level functionality.

DIVE provides image scaling, color space conversion, and bank-switch display support, among other features.

Direct Audio Interface

Windows 95 has DirectSound and OS/2 has Direct Audio Interface. With this toolkit, programmers can do all sorts of low-level mixing work with WAV files by communicating directly with the audio device.

Joystick Support

The OS/2 Game and Entertainment Toolkit also includes a joystick device driver. This driver works to help optimize joystick support for DOS games working under OS/2. Stop by *http:\\www.austin.ibm.com.os2game* to download the driver.

3D Graphics with BRender

IBM plans to distribute Argonaut's 3D graphics API (BRender) as part of their Game and Entertainment Toolkit. BRender will be distributed under Argonaut's end-user license. This is a limited license permitting the user to evaluate the product. Should you wish to include BRender in your game, you need to contact Argonaut for a commercial license. For more information on BRender, check out Chapter 21.

Here are a few more notes about sound and music development with OS/2. OS/2 has an MCI (Media Control Interface) which, much like the Windows MCI, lets you play digital audio files, control CDs, or play MIDI files with simple API calls. By using OS/2's multithreading capabilities, developers can more easily synchronize different multimedia segments with each other.

For example, OS/2 includes a feature called playlists that help increase the speed and flexibility of playing back multimedia content in OS/2. With playlists you can play MIDI or WAV files directly from memory. In addition, there is an associated Basic-like language that tells the OS/2 Multimedia engine exactly how to play a given file.

This language can perform loops, synchronization hooks, and automatically shift memory. For example, you might script several WAV files in a playlist including a screeching sound, then a scream, and finally a crash to create a car crash effect. In this case, each WAV file can be independent and the playlist will handle the exact instance of each during playback without any further help from the programmer.

Ultimotion
IBM Worldwide Industry Hardware Support
Phone: 800 426-4579 ext. 200 **Fax:** 708 635-3620
WWW: ftp://software.watson.ibm.com (in the \PUBS\OS2\MISC directory)

OS/2 offers a full 32-bit video engine with support for MPEG, Indeo, and Ultimotion video codecs. Ultimotion, IBM's video format, claims to have 15 frames per second playback at 320×240 resolution on 486 systems and 30 frames per second on faster Pentium-equipped systems.

To work with Ultimotion, you have to order the Ultimotion Development Kit from IBM. The kit includes all the documentation and sample files you need for either Windows or OS/2 playback, and a license for Ultimotion products.

The kit is available at no charge to qualified developers.

Porting Games

SMART (Source Migration Analysis Reporting Toolset), which was licensed by IBM from One Up Corporation for its Developer Toolkit, helps developers move their software from Windows to OS/2 and is part of the OS/2 Developers Connection. IBM claims SMART can convert as much as 70 percent or more of Windows API message code to 32-bit OS/2 code.

OS/2 Game-Oriented Web Sites

It seems the OS/2 forces have created an excellent set of sites on the Internet from where they can network and promote their OS/2 specific games.

OS/2 Games Home Page
`http://www.austin.ibm.com/os2games`

As a game developer, be sure to ask about having your application listed here. Also ask about how you can supply demo code for users to download.

OS/2 Game Development News
`http://www.austin.ibm.com/os2games/devnews/gdevnews.html`

This is the main IBM site for dissemination of OS/2 game development information.

The Ultimate OS/2 Gaming Page
`http://www.cc.gatech.edu/people/home/buie/os2games.html`

Want the scoop on everything having to do with OS/2 gaming? Then check out this site.

OS/2 Game Development Info
`http://naftalab.bus.utexas.edu/os2games/devcon/`

This is the best overall site to get all the information and tips on development tools and practices for OS/2 games.

OS/2 Game Review!
`http://hamton.eng.ua.edu/college/home/ee/ungrad/gjones/www/os2/ogr.html`

This is the site to read Alex Brady's OS/2 gaming newsletter.

NeXTStep

NeXTStep
NeXT Software, Inc.
900 Chesapeake Drive
Redwood City, CA 94063
Phone: 415 366-0900 **Fax:** 415 780-3929
WWW: http://www.next.com

NeXTStep? Now before you get all hot under the collar, understand that I am including the NeXTStep solely as a development platform. Originally designed to be the operating system for the NeXT computer system, NeXTStep is a totally object-oriented version of the Unix operating system. Several developers, notably Id Software, are using the NeXTStep operating software to develop key in-house tools, like map, level, and game object editors for their games.

NeXTStep is an excellent environment for this because it allows for rapid development of GUI components and provides the C++ application framework that some editors need to be speedy enough.

NeXTStep costs about $4,995 and is available directly from NeXT. College students and others may qualify for deep discounts, so check with NeXT before you discount (excuse the pun) calling them altogether. Figure 17.1 shows a picture of an early Quake editor running in the NeXTStep environment.

BeBox

BeBox
Be, Inc.
800 El Camino Real, Suite 300

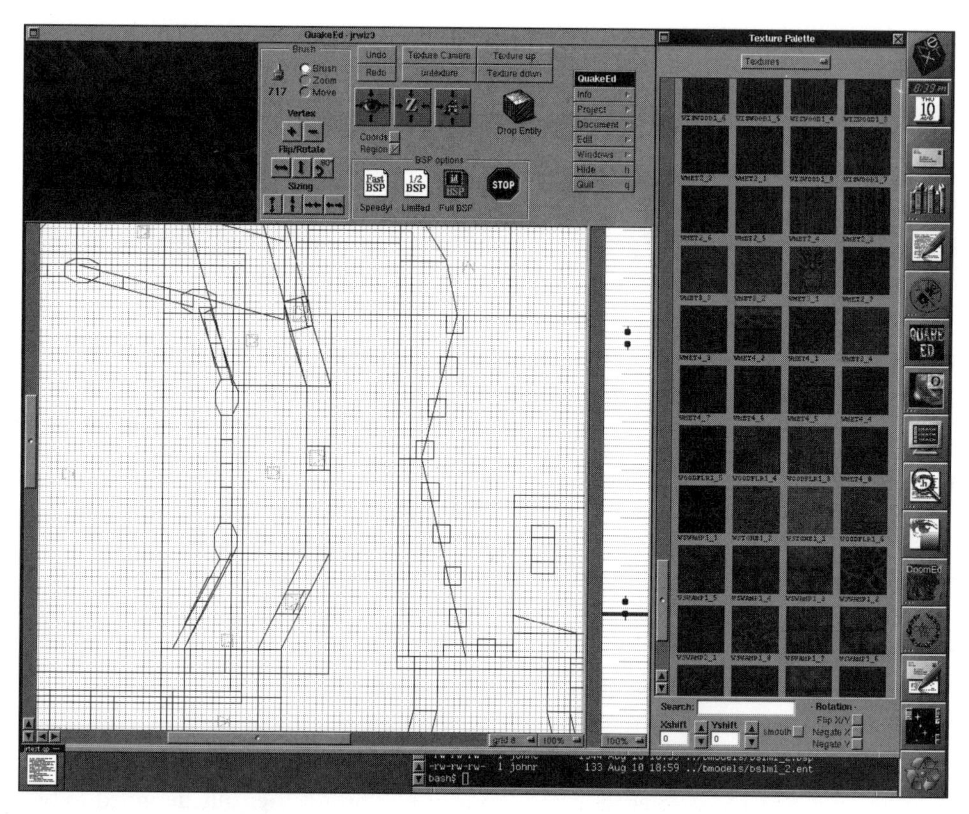

Figure 17.1 Quake editor running in the NeXTStep environment.

Menlo Park, CA 94025
Phone: 415 462-4141 **Fax:** 415 462-4129
WWW: http://www.be.com

I can hear you now, "BeBox?! First OS/2, then NeXTStep, now an entirely different computer system?" Well, using BeBox follows the same logic as using NeXTStep. You're not going to write games *for* it but you might write games *with* it.

The BeBox is a new machine that's getting a lot of attention from developers as it may evolve into an excellent back-end development platform.

The Be computer company was founded by former Apple executive and engineer Jean-Louis Gasee. The BeBox is being positioned not as a replacement for Macs or Windows-based PCs, but as a supplemental machine aimed at special-purpose applications, such as MIDI/music production, digital video production, special-purpose multimedia, and more.

The BeBox, which utilizes the ultra-cool PowerPC chip known to provide excellent speed and parallel processing, is hoping to become a successor to the aging Amiga and Atari ST computer systems, which, despite not cracking the mass market, found extensive use in key niche markets. Currently, many hardcore developers are looking at the BeBox to serve as an excellent development platform and provide a cheap alternative to expensive SGI and Alpha-based workstation solutions.

Take the time to explore and digest all the information on the BeBox. Their Web site is an excellent stop with lots of information about the system. Full production is just getting underway, and many who've evaluated the machine up close have come away impressed with the multitasking, multithreading operating system. Besides, how can you not like a computer that comes with a specialized port called the "GeekPort!"

CHAPTER 18

Don't discount the Mac—this platform really offers a lot for game players and developers.

Developing Mac Games

The Power of the Mac

The Mac has been quite a stepchild in the business world of PC clones. But it has been an even bigger one when it comes to game playing and game development. This situation is unfortunate because Macs really excel at many of the graphical and multimedia types of development tasks that are important to game developers. Fortunately, there is still hope for the Mac because more and more game developers are turning to this platforms in hopes of finding better ways to develop games.

In my talks with a number of tool developers, I discovered that many more companies were asking for Mac game-related development tools. Part of this demand is being created because some multimedia developers are turning to game development to seek out new markets. And in the past, the Mac has been one of the leading platforms for multimedia development. The Mac turns out to be a slightly better platform for doing graphics-intensive development, which is such an important part of game and multimedia development. Although there are far fewer Macs in use than PCs running DOS or Windows, there are still millions of Mac owners who are potential customers for great games—enough to keep Mac game developers busy for quite some time!

In this chapter, we'll explore some of the better resources available specifically to help developers create Mac games. Although this is one of the smaller chapters in the book, don't be fooled into thinking there aren't a number of game development tools and resources available for the Mac. Since we've already covered products and tools like Quicktime VR, Quickdraw 3D, sound programming resources, and art tools in other chapters, our goal now is to focus on the specific Mac programming and development resources we haven't already covered.

Developer Programs

One thing about Apple is that they offer an extensive set of developer programs and support items. If you're even thinking of being a commercial or shareware developer, chances are you'll benefit tremendously from one of the major Apple developer programs available. Here is the key information about those programs.

Developer Services and Products
Apple Computer, Inc.
1 Infinite Loop, M/S 303-2T
Cupertino, CA 95014-6299

Phone: 408 974-4897
Email: devsupport@applelink.apple.com

Apple offers several actual developer programs but when you join any one program, you automatically get access to a number of key resources that can be helpful, such as development hardware purchasing privileges, online services, resource and referral pointers, marketing help, and conference information.

The available programs of interest to game developers include:

- Macintosh Associates Program
- Macintosh Associates Plus Program
- Macintosh Partners Program
- Apple Multimedia Program

The key components of Apple's developer programs are informational mailings, developer CDs, and technical support calls.

Mailings and Developer CDs

An Apple developer mailing includes information about the latest Apple news, strategies, products, and technical information, as well as marketing help. These mailings also include *Apple Directs*, which covers business and technical issues for Mac developers. In addition, Apple provides the Developer CD, which is a series of CDs totaling over 1.8 gigabytes of information including system software, development tools, code examples, and technical documentation.

Most importantly, the developer programs also include key access to new pre-release documentation and technology to keep you on the cutting edge.

Technical Support

Apple provides its developers technical phone support, which gives you direct access to R&D Engineers who can help you get the most out of Apple technology in your games.

This category is where most of the difference resides for the major development programs. The Macintosh Associates Program ($250 per year) gives you the key components described earlier but no phone support. With the Macintosh Associates Plus Program ($500 per year) you get up to ten support questions per year, and the top-of-the-line Macintosh Partners Program ($1,500 per year) will give you unlimited calls.

The Apple Multimedia Program

This is a great program for both multimedia developers and game developers. Program members receive a comprehensive array of multimedia marketing resources and technical and business resources. These are updated quarterly and include:

- Co-marketing opportunities
- Promotional and networking opportunities
- Direct-mail program
- AMP developers showcase
- Invitations to tradeshows and events of specific interest to multimedia developers
- Special access to key multimedia development/production survival guides, developer CDs, informational whitepapers, tools, and tips

Apple knows multimedia developers need lots of marketing help, thus the Apple Multimedia Program includes market research reports, multimedia guidebooks, and videos.

Joining the Program

The cost to join the Apple Multimedia Program is $300 per year. Applications are available by calling Apple at 408 974-4897. You can also get application information by visiting their Web site at *http://dev.info.apple.com/app.html.*

APDA
Apple Computer Inc.
P.O. Box 319
Buffalo, NY 14207-0319

Phone: 716 871-6555 **Fax:** 716 871-6511
WWW: http://dev.info.apple.com/apda.html

The APDA is an Apple service that offers one-stop shopping for over 300 development tools, resources, and information. You can call the above number and order a catalog and development program. Members receive discounts.

Programming Tools and Code Resources

A number of resources are available, including Web sites, books, and magazines for locating the better Mac programming development tools and libraries. The list of resources isn't as big as you might find for other development platforms, such as PCs; however, the selection is still quite good.

HyperArchive at the MIT Laboratory for Computer Science

`http://hyperarchive.lcs.mit.edu/HyperArchive/HyperArchive.html`

This is the primary reference point for most of the source code and game relevant libraries I am about to mention. Most of the resources here are freeware/shareware libraries but surprisingly these are excellent resources. While the PC world's resources are far more skewed toward professional code libraries and examples, the homebrew Mac resources featured are almost entirely skewed toward the home brew attitude most developers love.

In each case I'll reference the specific link page at this site that directly lists the mentioned resource. Be sure to scroll through the links on the referenced page to find the specific download link. Also, plan to spend more time searching through this thorough and well organized site!

Tesla Game Kit & Stuff

`http://hyperarchive.lcs.mit.edu/HyperArchive/Abstracts/dev/src/HyperArchive.html`

The Tesla Game Kit by Chris K. Thomas is a demo game creation source code kit. It provides many useful key game components such as an optimize sidescrolling sprite toolkit, a simple sound engine, a sprite collision engine, and a full sample game using C++.

Ingemar Ragnemalm's Sprite Animation Toolkit (SAT)

`http://hyperarchive.lcs.mit.edu/HyperArchive/Abstracts/dev/lib/HyperArchive.html`

SAT is a library for programmers who want to make arcade games or other programs involving animation. It is distributed as a compiled library, together with numerous sample programs.

Among its features are direct-to-screen animation in black and white, 4-bit color and 8-bit color, optimized assembly language source code, and so on. The toolkit also can re-configure itself after screen depth changes and it supports several screen depths including switching between color and black and white graphics.

SAT also includes utilities for menu bar hiding, setting mouse positions, asynchronous sound, and so on. In addition, the entire download also features six demo programs with source going from simple examples to a complete arcade game called HeartQuest.

SAT was developed by an experienced shareware game programmer. The library has already been used to make four arcade games that have been released—Slime Invaders, Bachman, HeartQuest, ISG, and Bert—and more are coming.

Glypha III v.1.0.2 Complete Source Code

`http://hyperarchive.lcs.mit.edu/HyperArchive/Abstracts/dev/src/HyperArchive.html`

Glypha is a clone of the great arcade game Joust. Better still for game developers is that John Calhoun, the author of Glypha, released all the source code to the public domain so people could learn how to program games on the Mac!

As Calhoun says, "I've never felt that there was any advantage in hoarding programming secrets from others. I don't even have any problem with releasing source code to my commercial games…."

3D Game Machine
`http://hyperarchive.lcs.mit.edu/HyperArchive/Abstracts/dev/src/HyperArchive.html`

This is an API toolbox for 3D arcade game development. It includes a realtime 3D rendering library as well as routines for manipulating 3D virtual environments. 3D Game Machine is optimized for games with free-form shaded texture mapping and up to 15 frames per second at 640×480 resolution.

Animation Class Library
`http://hyperarchive.lcs.mit.edu/HyperArchive/Abstracts/dev/src/HyperArchive.html`

ACL is an object-oriented animation framework that allows programmers to create powerful interactive animations. ACL classes provide enough features for creating applications with fast interactive 2D animations. The features are too numerous to fully mention but the library handles collision detection, sprite movements and effects, scrolling, double buffering, and much more.

The entire library includes documentation libraries for Symantec C and Codewarrior as well as fully commented headers and demo examples.

Tetris Clone Source Code
`http://hyperarchive.lcs.mit.edu/HyperArchive/Abstracts/dev/src/HyperArchive.html`

The site features a Compact Pro archive containing the Think C 5.0 sources for "Tetris Light." This is a lightweight Tetris program with source code freely available under the GNU General Public License.

Flight-Simulator Source Code by Chris Moll
http://hyperarchive.lcs.mit.edu/HyperArchive/Abstracts/dev/src/HyperArchive.html

This site features the source code for a program to demonstrate how to do 3D perspective drawing and clipping. It's written as a sort of crude flight simulator—you "fly" through a rather simple world. It also shows you how to do simple animation. All of the math used is fixed-point to make the speed tolerable on lower-powered Macs. With an FPU, the speed would be roughly the same using floating point.

The package contains the source code, a ThinkC (version 5.0.3) project, and an executable version compiled for any Mac.

VR Flight Simulation Source code
`http://hyperarchive.lcs.mit.edu/HyperArchive/Abstracts/dev/src/HyperArchive.html`

This demo of a VR flight through clouds comes complete with the source code to the project. The demo and source cover several 3D rendering techniques.

Books and Publications

You won't get very far in the Mac development world without an ample supply of good programming books. Fortunately, a few publishers, such as Addision-Wesley, have made a real commitment to publishing useful, high-quality technical titles.

Addision-Wesley
`http://www.aw.com/`

Rather than list all of AW's Mac development books, it's better to point you to their Web site so that you can get the most up-to-date details of their publishing program. Addision-Wesley is the official publisher of Apple Computer and thus has a large catalog of Mac books and technical guides from Apple and non-Apple affiliated writers.

Tricks of the Mac Game Programming Gurus by Jamie McCornack, Ingemar Ragnemalm, et al. (Hayden Books, 1995; ISBN 1-56830-183-9)

Tricks of the Mac Game Programming Gurus is a Mac edition of what has become a popular series of "Guru" books. This book contains information, source code, and how-to's on a number of key Mac game programming techniques. Topics include QuickDraw 3D, Power Mac optimization, sprites, sound, and more.

Throughout the book, you'll find special interviews with some Mac game programmers who share some of their secrets on how they developed their games. The CD-ROM includes all the source from the book, a "lite" version of the popular Metroworks C/C++ compiler, demo of tools, and tons of Mac shareware games and demos of some major Mac retail games.

Sex, Lies, and Video Games: How to Write a Macintosh Arcade Game by Bill Hensler (Addision-Wesley, 1995; ISBN 0-201-40757-4)

This book covers all sorts of topics to make a game for the Mac. Topics include sprite animation, off-screen and on-screen animation, sound programming, game theory, and interaction techniques. The book culminates by putting together a full-blown arcade game and comes with a disk that has all the source code for it.

The Macintosh Solutions and Multimedia Developers Guide

JointSolutions Marketing
Phone: 408 338-6471

The Macintosh Solutions and Multimedia Developers Guide, a compilation of the latest Macintosh solutions-based products and multimedia tools, is published twice a year in both printed and electronic form. A companion piece, *The Macintosh Application and Part Developers Guide*, was published in October 1995.

Magazines

***develop* Magazine**
c/o APDA
Apple Computer Inc.
P.O. Box 319
Buffalo, NY 14207-0319

Phone: 716 871-6555 **Fax:** 716 871-6511
WWW: http://dev.info.apple.com/develop/developtoc.html
Subscription: $39.95 **Newsstand:** N/A **Publishes:** Quarterly

develop is Apple's quarterly technical journal, which is included on its Developer CD-ROMs. If you don't get the Developer CDs, you can still subscribe to just the magazine. Each issue also comes with a Bookmark CD, which contains the source code for that issue of *develop*, plus all the back issues, technical notes, sample code, and other software and documentation.

Note: The develop *magazine site also has selected articles and stuff from current and back issues.*

***MacTech* Magazine**
Xplain Corporation
P.O. Box 5200
Westlake Village, CA 91359-5200

Phone: 805 494-9797 **Fax:** 805 494-9798
WWW: http://www.mactech.com
Subscription: $39.95 **Newsstand:** $4.95 **Publishes:** Monthly **Pages:** 100

MacTech Magazine (formerly *MacTutor*) was established in 1984 to provide a forum for programmers and developers. The aim was (and still is) to provide a place where the latest developments and technologies can be shared within the Macintosh community, independently of Apple's developer programs. Each issue comes with an accompanying disk that contains source code and other information from the current issue.

In addition, their Web site is a major archive of information and you can also order tools, back issues, and the infamous MacTech CD-ROM that contains tons of development information and much more!

Online Sites

eWorld

`http://www.eworld.com/`

eWorld is an Apple-specific online service that they constructed in 1994. While it's now being moved to the Web, it's still a major focus of Apple. Their main goal is to have a large online area devoted to the Mac. While I haven't been on eWorld myself for quite some time, it's sure to have a number of good programming and game and multimedia development resources.

You can sign for eWorld on the Web by surfing to:
`http://eweb03.online.apple.com/webcity/eworld/join.html`

AOL - Mac Development Forum

`http://www.aol.com`

To be honest, CompuServe's offerings are weak in the area of Mac game development. AOL, on the other hand, has a healthier assortment of Mac resources. On AOL, use the keyword MDV to access the Mac Development forum.

Apple Computer

`http://www.apple.com`

Where else should Mac programmers start looking for online resources than on Apples own Internet site? I've included some more specific Web pages to visit for locating resources more suited to game developers.

Apple's Quickdraw Archive

`http://www.info.apple.com/gx/gx.html`

Here you can check out Apple's information about its core graphics technology.

Apple Tech Info Search Engine

`http://til.info.apple.com/til/til.html`

Here you can search Apple's Tech Info archives to find software and development tools.

Land O'Mac Geeks

`http://dev.info.apple.com/geeks.html`

This page provides more links than you can follow in a week of surfing. It is the best place to go if you want to search Apple's technical issues database.

Mac Programmers FAQ

`http://www.smartpages.com/faqs/macintosh/programmer-faq/top.html`

This area is filled with tons of basic information, books, contacts, and other cool Mac programming information. Surf over to here and read up on many of the hot and current Mac programming issues.

Comp.Sys.Mac.Game.Programming.Book
`http://www.best.com/~mxmora/c.s.m.g.p.b.0.html`

This is perhaps the single best online resource of direct interest to budding Mac game developers. This site explores a number of Mac game programming topics with all sorts of code examples and pointers.

Robert Lentz's Mac Programming Resources
`http://www.astro.nwu.edu/lentz/mac/programming/home-prog.html`

Honestly, after, if not before you surf through the key parts of Apple's Web site, this should be your key URL for learning about all sorts of major resources for Mac programmers.

QuickDraw Fanclub
`http://www.ixmedia.com/quickgx/`

This is an entire site filled with information about Apple's QuickDraw graphics format.

MacWeek Magazine Entertainment Site
`http://zcias3.ziff.com/%7Emacweek/entertainment.html`

You can subscribe to *MacWEEK* and spend time reading about everything going on in the Macintosh world, or you can just link to this site with your browser and read just the part about Mac entertainment from this leading Mac news source.

Mac Games Central
`http://qltec.com/QL/GameCentral.html`

The Hovel of Mirth Macintosh Game Site
`http://www.princeton.edu/~pjcreath/macgames/`

The Entertaining Macintosh
`http://www.princeton.edu/~pjcreath/tem/welcome.html`

Much of the native Mac game development revolves around the shareware game scene. These sites are among the best to check in on to see what's hot and new in the Mac shareware/retail demo scene.

The Future of Mac Game Development

In early 1996, Apple had by all accounts a rough time. It was courted by Sun after announcing key reduction in profits in its quarterly profits. On top of that, a series of management shakeups resulted in a new CEO and management team. Despite these moves many industry pundits have far more questions than answers about the future of the Mac and Apple.

While no one is playing the death march just yet, all of Apple's recent troubles don't make for happy users, executives, or developers. None the less, the Mac and key Apple technologies, such as Quickdraw 3D, still promise to be major players in the game development scene.

As long as Mac game sales are profitable enough for larger companies to keep developing for the Mac and porting their top-selling PC games, opportunities will be strong. In the last two years a number of innovative small companies have broken out of the pack by offering fun Mac developed games. Some of these companies are then finding themselves crossing over in the opposite direction and porting their hit Mac games to the PC! So while the world may have some doubts about the Mac market—there are more than enough success stories to focus on to give you inspiration as a Mac developer.

To top it all off is the unknown impact of Apple's Pippin device, which I describe in the next chapter (Chapter 19) on game consoles. Should Pippin take off (which isn't out of the question), it could provide an unparalleled new outlet for Mac games. No one's promising anything, but Apple has risen from the bottom more than once; they could easily come back once again!

CHAPTER 19

You may never get the chance to develop for one of these machines, but never assume.

Developing for the Consoles

Developing games for one of the platforms I described in earlier chapters is certainly not to be taken lightly, but console development is a real challenge. Console development is tricky because you must first figure out with whom you need to connect so that you can learn how to become an approved developer. You must also consider a number of other issues in your endeavor to develop games for the Sega Saturn, Sony PSX, Nintendo Ultra 64, M2, or any other console. This chapter will sort out some of the obstacles and put you on your way to becoming a hotshot console developer.

For the most part, developing for consoles requires a developer's best friend: cold hard cash. While computer games can also involve large development funds, a console product absolutely *requires* a major financial commitment. To develop for a console, you will need clearance from the company controlling the console hardware or from a publisher evaluating your company or your product. These folks aren't looking for games created on a shoestring budget; they are looking for major talent who can turn great ideas into big money making games.

Only experienced developers with track records in the games market—especially with consoles—will find the road an easy one to walk. This isn't to say an upstart couldn't break in, but roadblocks are specifically set up to sort out only those with the best potential and desire to develop the awesome games that will sell.

Understanding the Particulars of Console Development

The first step you need to take is to evaluate the various consoles in use. You'll need to get realistic and decide if you have a chance of being accepted by the manufacturer you're targeting or by an established game publisher that has development deals. If you take on a console project as a result of working with a publisher, for the most part, that publisher will help you get set up with the appropriate development platform.

However, if you're dealing directly with a manufacturer—either by choice or necessity—you'll need to begin by calling and inquiring about official developer status. This task can be somewhat time-consuming and frustrating. Not only do you have to reach the right person, but you'll have to spend some time answering that person's questions and concerns regarding your interest in developing for their platform. Chances are that this process will involve some sort of application questionnaire.

Consoles, being proprietary in nature, require a number of special tools for game development. Once you are accepted by the manufacturer (or in conjunction with your application), you will need to purchase these tools, which come in the form of cross-development kits. You can purchase a kit from the console manufacturer or through another manufacturer, such as Cross Development System in England. The typical cross-development kit runs anywhere from $8,000 to $10,000. As you will see, not all cross-development systems work on PCs. 3DO, for example, used a Mac-based system. A cross-development kit from any of these companies is not going to involve the computer hardware you'll need. That equipment can run in the thousands of dollars. Remember though, this is nothing compared to what you will make on a good game for any of the hot console systems.

I doubt that the majority of developers reading this book will be able to or be interested in developing console-based products directly on their own. Still, these consoles represent a majority of the revenue related to game development, and you may find yourself in a situation where you could be developing for one of these systems. This chapter provides you with enough information to get you started on your own with development console software.

System Breakdowns

In the interest of getting you up to speed with the systems in use, I have prepared a section detailing the specs on each of the console systems. This coverage includes brief overviews of the developer programs and kits the parent company makes available. I also have listed the major companies (though not all) doing work for the key console manufacturers.

What is interesting is that all of the major consoles have taken different approaches and align themselves with different strategic partners. This introduces a number of headaches in trying to decide how and where to make money in the console market. For example, Atari's Jaguar isn't the hottest selling machine (in fact it's dead in the water right now), but that doesn't mean you can't make money on it. And Atari might have a lower entry threshold, which might make it appealing. On the other hand, the Ultra 64—Nintendo's new machine—seems poised to both sell well and provide a wealth of power, yet its reliance on cartridges, Nintendo's strict third-party rules, and expensive development systems based on SGI technology, can be insurmountable obstacles.

This means that you have to look at the total picture when deciding on console development. Start by selecting the types of games you want to produce and review the budget you have (including promotional funds if you plan on publishing your product yourself or as an affiliated label), and see which machine fits best. By concentrating on the software you want to sell and the hardware platform that best supports your creations, you'll be able to make an educated decision based on the product that generates revenue for you.

Sony Playstation

Sony Corporation of America
9 W. 57th St., 43rd Fl.
New York, NY 10019-2791
Phone: 212 833-6849 **Fax:** 212 833-6923
WWW: http://www.sony.com

While Sony's Playstation (see Figure 19.1) represents the consumer electronics and entertainment giant's first foray into the console market, Sony has been developing computer and videogame software for years. Known also as the PSX, the Playstation brought Sony into entirely new ground as this company reached for a large share of the overall gaming pie.

While other companies, both past (Mattel) and present (Hasbro and 3DO), have had difficulty entering the console market after successful leaders have been established, Sony has held their own. They've created an elegant system with a lot of horsepower and they offer it at a low price. Many industry experts thought the console gaming market belonged to Nintendo and Sega, but Sony has come along to prove this notion incorrect.

Ironically, the Playstation was initially designed in conjunction with Nintendo, but at some point Nintendo closed a deal with SGI and ditched Sony for the high-flying workstation maker. Not satisfied to be left at the altar, Sony pursued the development of the console substantially—the Playstation is the fruit of Sony's efforts. Will Sony get sweet revenge against the groom? This will be hard to tell until the Ultra 64 ships, but so far the Playstation has seen excellent success.

Sony successfully launched the Playstation in Japan to sales of over 1 million units in its first six months. As of fall '95, Sony had what critics can only call a quite successful U.S. launch as well. Recent sales figures put Sony well on the way to passing the 4 million unit mark worldwide.

Figure 19.1 Sony's Playstation (PSX).

Sony has also garnered significant third-party support with more than 120 licensees in the U.S. and another 350 in Japan and Europe. Many former PC-only developers, like Bullfrog, have gone on record as saying the PSX (and to some extent the Sega Saturn and Nintendo Ultra 64), is the first console they will support. In the past, these companies might have licensed their products to another company to develop the console version; today, they'll be developing the console version themselves. With all that fanfare and some impressive hardware, Sony's PSX should definitely be on your evaluation list if you're considering developing for consoles, and must be on your list if you already are developing for consoles.

Sony is in a great position. They have great distribution muscles—after all they are one of the world's most recognizable and favored brands. In addition, their movie and TV studio and music publishing expertise (Columbia Pictures and Sony Music), and their software development expertise (Sony Entertainment and subsidiary Psygnosis), put them near the top of the electronic entertainment industries. You can bet they will not be accepting a back seat to anyone.

The PSX Specs

The Playstation is a product of the Japanese arm of Sony, and is manufactured through their multitude of plants throughout Japan and the Pacific. Here's a brief rundown of the PSX specs.

CPU

The Sony CPU is an R3000A made by MIPS, a Silicon Graphics chip division. The R3000A is a 32-bit RISC chip running at 33.8 MHz, providing 30 MIPS (Millions of Instructions per Second) of power with a bus bandwith of 132 MB/second.

The overall operating system, which takes up 512K ROM and 64K of RAM, is a multi-threaded operating system. Sony has created an extensive set of C libraries to allow programmers to access all of the key APIs for the machine.

Graphics Processing

At the heart of Sony's graphical processing power are two special graphical co-processing chips. First is the GTE or Geometry Transfer Engine, which handles a ton of 3D polygon specific tasks. The PSX also provides the DVP or Digital Video Processor, a specific chip for processing digital video. The GTE, which runs at 66 MIPS, is capable of approximately 1.5 million shaded or 500,000 texture-mapped and light-sourced polygons per second. The DVP supports JPEG and MPEG1 compression, among other schemes, and helps to easily stream data directly off CD-ROMs to the system.

Sony definitely targeted the two major next-generation graphics properties with its custom silicon and it shows in the games. Overall, the entire graphics system provides for 16.7 million colors, resolutions from 256×224 to 740×480 (though

higher resolutions may have a lower color scheme), and thousands of sprites, which puts it in strong competition with other consoles.

Sound

Would you expect the company that invented the CD, the Mini-Disc, and the Walkman to skimp on sound? Hardly. The Playstation features a full DSP, with 24 channels of sound, and full CD-quality audio. The Playstation supports MIDI instruments and allows you to load up to 512K of sampled waveforms. Digital effects like looping, digital reverb, and pitch modulation are also available.

Memory

Like most consoles, the Playstation has several types of RAM including the main RAM (16 Mbits), VRAM (8 Mbits), sound (4 Mbits), and a buffer for streaming data off the CD-ROM. The machine also supports RAM cards (128K) to store saved game information.

CD-ROM Drive

The Sony Playstation includes a double-speed CD-ROM drive with a 300K/second data transfer rate and a maximum capacity of 660 MB of information.

Peripherals

Sony has said they are going to make a Playstation mouse, a "combat cable" to play head-to-head against a friend using two TV monitors, a four controller unit for sport games, and an analog joystick for flight simulations.

Entering the Sony Development System

To become a Sony developer, you need to secure developer status from Sony, which costs $18,000 and buys you one Sony development kit. The Sony development system, developed by SC Systems in England, is PC-based. It comes with two ISA cards which basically make up the Playstation hardware; a separate CD-ROM drive connects to the cards. The system uses the hard drive to simulate CD-ROM throughput.

The software includes a GNU C compiler, an assembler, numerous libraries, and various other tools. A development system is also available from PSY-Q, which will be described later in the *Key Console Development Tools* section.

Sony-Oriented Web Sites

I've found a number of valuable Web sites for you to peruse during your next online fact-gathering mission.

Unofficial Sony Home Page
`http://www.vidgames.com/`

Some of the Web's unofficial pages are better than the official pages—this one fits that bill.

Another Unofficial Playstation Page
`http://www.pitt.edu/~aaronr/newps.html`

Another excellent page for Playstation devotees.

***Game Zero* Magazine's Sony Links Page**
`http://www.primenet.com/team-0/links/sony.html`

Do you want to find the rest of the Sony Playstation enthusiast pages? Check this specific-links page by *Game Zero* Magazine.

Sega Saturn

Sega of America
255 Shoreline Dr., Ste. 200
Redwood City, CA 94065
Phone: 415 508-2800 **Fax:** 415 802-3063
WWW: http://www.segoa.com

In the first round of the second coming of consoles, Sega was just an ugly stepchild to Nintendo. But when the hardware shifted to 16-bit, Sega broke through. It launched the Sega Genesis System before Nintendo released a comparable system, and learning from past mistakes, Sega captured major market share, transforming themselves into a major player in home videogames.

Knowing that getting out in front of a new generation of consoles is key to success, Sega has brought forth the Saturn (see Figure 19.2) as its leading entry in the 32-bit/ CD-ROM console wars.

Figure 19.2 Sega's Saturn—the leading 32-bit offering.

Sega also is using its leadership position as perhaps the premier developer of video arcade game machines. Its arcade division has pumped out groundbreaking games like Virtua Fighter, Out Run, Hangon, Sega Rally, Virtua Cop, and more. These divisions are now making sure that they move those hit products to the Saturn, which should help Saturn succeed.

Despite being a solid machine and having key Sega software, the Saturn has not been as successful as Sony's Playstation. Perhaps Sega's recent software from its arcade division, namely Sega Rally and Virtua Fighter 2, may give it a boost in 1996. But don't rule out this platform; the Saturn has the right stuff to become a leading console for quite some time.

The Saturn Specs

The key thing about the Saturn is that this machine has a lot of silicon. Programmers I've talked with who are working with the Saturn claim that it's tougher to program than the Sony, but that's because there are so many chips with so many features to unlock. This is the quintessential double-chip machine; most of the key components have two chips working in parallel. Let's take a closer look.

CPU

The Saturn contains two Hitachi SH2 RISC CPUs, both running at 28.6 MHz and 25 MIPS. Both CPUs are connected to the RAM, so both can exchange data with memory, directly increasing the overall speed. The CPU contains a 4K data cache, and it has the ability to execute complex mathematical functions—a must for 3D graphics.

The Saturn boasts two types of buses: One is used to extract data from the CD-ROM and cartridge expansion to the central controller, and a second bus, which is 16-bit and runs at 28 MHz, connects directly to the video and sound subsystems from the central controller unit.

Graphics Processing

The Saturn has two major graphics chips: VDP 1 and VDP 2, with VDP being an acronym for Video Digital Processor (sounds powerful, huh?).

The first VDP is the sprite and geometry engine for the Saturn. The chip has two 256K frame buffers to handle rotation, and can pull data from a 512K "texture RAM cache" for special texture effects. The VDP1 handles both 2D and 3D sprite draws, and can map sprites into the geometry engine.

The second VDP chip concentrates on background graphics. This chip can generate up to five simultaneously active backgrounds, and can rotate two playfields at once. It is also possible to have three normal scrolls at the same time as a field of rotation. These two chips definitely pack a solid one-two combination.

Sega claims the Saturn can handle up to 200,000 texture-mapped polygons per second and 60 frames per second animation. Resolution runs from 320×224 to 720×576 with 24-bit true color graphics giving 16.8 million available colors.

Sound

The Saturn is equipped with two incredible sound chips—a 16-bit Motorola 68EC000 sound processor running at 11.3 MHz, and a Yamaha FH1 processor running at 22.58 MHz. You get eight FM channels, 32 PCM channels, FM synthesis, PCM synthesis, 44.1 kHz CD-quality sampling rate, and two CPUs.

Other features include Direct Memory Access (DMA) for file transfer, a 16 channel digital mixer, and a 128-step digital signal processor. There's more power here than ever seen in a console or personal computer before.

Memory

The Saturn has 2 MB of RAM, 1.54 MB of VRAM, 512K of audio RAM, and a 512K CD-ROM cache.

CD-ROM Drive

The Saturn is equipped with a double-speed CD-ROM drive, providing for 320K of transfer throughput.

Peripherals

Aside from the normal joypads and joysticks, the Saturn's most interesting peripheral is the steering wheel setup it produced for its driving games. Sega has always been a major creator of driving games (Outrun, Virtua Racing, Sega Rally, and so on) and this is a neat peripheral.

Entering the Sega Development System

Contact Sega to become a registered developer. Development kits for the Saturn are provided by Sega subsidiary Cross Development System, a UK-based developer of major console development products. (See the *Key Console Development Tools* section for a breakdown of Cross Development's SNASM2 development system for the Sega Saturn.) PSY-Q also markets a set of development tools for the Saturn.

Saturn-Oriented Web Sites

I found two really great sites for you to search for information on Sega's Saturn.

Unofficial Sega Home Page

`http://www.primenet.com/team-0/gmezero/saturnhome/`

This is a really nice site done by the team at *Game Zero* Magazine.

Game Zero Magazine's Sega Links Page
`http://www.primenet.com/team-0/links/SEGA.html`

If you're looking for all the best Sega-related Web sites, set your browser to this URL and you'll hit them all.

Nintendo Ultra 64

Nintendo of America
4820 150th Ave. NE
Redmond, WA 98052-9733
Phone: 206 882-2040 **Fax:** 206 882-3585
WWW: http://www.nintendo.com

Nintendo. The name is synonymous with the resurgence of consoles, having single-handedly re-created the market back in the late 80s. While Nintendo lost market share in the 16-bit console arena because of hardware holdups, they are coming back with a vengeance with their next-generation Ultra 64 (see Figure 19.3). Nintendo is banking on a system so superior in quality that it will redefine consoles and blow away the market.

Although Nintendo hasn't released one spec on Ultra 64 (long known by its code name Project Reality), they sent hearts racing when they announced the developer of the Ultra 64 would be graphics chip and workstation leader, Silicon Graphics, Inc. The teaming of the leader in console hardware with the leader in graphical workstations was exciting news to say the least. In addition, Nintendo's announcement of an entry price of under $300 was considered unbelievable since SGI workstations can cost over $25,000 dollars on the low end.

Recently, though, as high-tech analysts and others have taken a closer look at the new system and specifications have leaked out, including a picture supplied by Nintendo, Project Reality seems to be just that: reality.

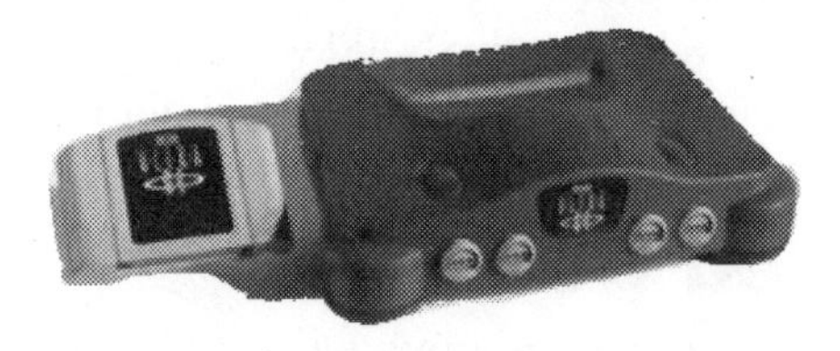

Figure 19.3 Nintendo's killer Ultra 64.

The Project Reality Specs

The Ultra 64 is perhaps the most interesting of all the consoles. Technologically, it can be summarized in three letters: S G I. When word broke that SGI and Nintendo were working together, many skeptics wondered how Nintendo would be able to cram SGI technology into a box that would cost less than the circuit board work for an SGI workstation. Here are the amazing specs:

CPU

The Ultra 64 is powered by a custom-designed R4200 MIPS chip from Silicon Graphics and it runs at over 500 MHz. The specs say it can hit 100+ MIPS and 100+ MFLOPS (Millions of Floating Points per Second).

Graphics Processing

The graphics on the Ultra 64 are powered by SGI technology scaled down (or better yet, shoehorned) to fit this system. Using a custom graphics processor SGI calls the "Reality Immersion" chip, the Ultra 64 is capable of 320×224 to 1,024×768 resolution with a 16-bit color depth. Initial reports claim a performance of 100,000+ realtime, texture-mapped polygons per second, with all kinds of incredible realtime graphics effects like texture mapping, morphing, scaling and rotation, shading, transparency, anti-aliasing, and more. With SGI behind this system, how can it be anything less than amazing? Wouldn't you like to find one of these machines under your Christmas tree?

I suspect that the majority of these graphical features are handled through a comprehensive set of graphical APIs built into the operating system software.

Sound

The Ultra 64 features a full 24-bit sound capable (CD-quality) DSP, running at over 50 MHz, providing 64 channels of FM synthesis sound. A full one megabyte of RAM is said to be reserved specifically for sound data within the system itself, serving, I assume, as a cache from the cartridge to the actual chip set.

Memory

The Ultra 64 has 2 MB RAM, 1 MB of VRAM, and 1 MB of RAM devoted to sound. The cartridges will store quite a bit of information, retrievable at near-RAM speeds.

Cartridges

The Ultra 64 at the time of this writing is going to use cartridges and not CD-ROMs like its competitors. In addition, it will be using a large-scale compression scheme to pack those cartridges with massive amounts of data in an effort to compete with CD-based systems. (Note: I still believe that when the system debuts it will ditch the cartridge and go with a CD-ROM system—though I have no way of knowing this officially.)

Peripherals

The joystick for the Ultra 64 is almost as revolutionary as the machine itself. What Nintendo did was meld a digital gamepad (good for arcade-style response) with an analog joystick device (great for flight simulation-style games) on the same controller.

On top of that, controllers have ports for SRAM cartridges, which allows players to save game information. This is a neat feature for fighting games and RPGs.

Entering the Nintendo Development System

Nintendo is the most exclusive of all the console companies. Unless you're among the cream of the developer crop, your chances of publishing an Ultra 64 game are pretty slim. In addition, the hardware costs are pretty steep since the development environment centers around SGI technology (what'd you expect? a Timex Sinclair?). Perhaps, if you sign a hot game to a major company like EA, you might get a shot. But unless Nintendo changes its strict policy (one that for them has been incredibly successful), your best bet is with Sony, Sega, or the other consoles.

Ultra 64-Oriented Web Sites

The Ultra 64 is very hot, and the Web has several awesome sites for you to find out all there is to know about this soon-to-be premier system.

Cap Scott's Nintendo Ultra 64 Web Page

`http://www.pitt.edu/~szm/nu64-cap.htm`

Captain Scott is a major Nintendo maniac and this page shows you just how much time this guy has on his hands.

Ian Mapleson's Ultra 64 Page

`http://www.cee.hw.ac.uk/~mapleson/sgistuff/ultra64/ultra64.html`

This is an excellent fan page. What would we do without videogame fanatics who somehow find time to run a Web site, too?

The Nintendo Ultra 64 Unofficial Home Page

`http://www4.ncsu.edu/eos/users/s/sgbooth/www/u64page.html`

It may be unofficial but don't let that designation fool you. This is a great page with lots of cool information on a system that hasn't even shipped yet!

Game Zero Magazine's Nintendo Links Page

`http://www.primenet.com/team-0/links/nintendo.html`

If you're looking for all the rest of the Nintendo nuts out there spreading the gospel, surf to *Game Zero*'s Nintendo Links Page to find the preachers.

M2

3DO
600 Galveston Dr.
Redwood City, CA 94063-1140
Phone: 415 261-3000 **Fax:** 415 261-3231
WWW: http://www.3do.com
and
Matsushita Electric Corporation of America
One Panasonic Way
Secaucus, NJ 07094-2917
Phone: 201 348-7000 **Fax:** 201 348-8378
WWW: http://www.interscape.net/jvc

It's kind of hard to detail exactly what M2 is. The original plan was to release it as an add-on product to boost the original 3DO's power in the wake of the hot new systems being launched by Sega, Sony, and Nintendo.

However, as the M2 technology progressed, the overall direction of 3DO has taken some dramatic turns. In late 1995, 3DO sold the M2 technology to Panasonic, who was their partner in the first 3DO project. In doing so, 3DO signaled that they were getting out of the console hardware business and concentrating instead on software for many platforms (especially M2), developers tools (like their MPEG encoder), and the Internet.

Matsushita/Panasonic meanwhile announced—soon after acquiring the M2 technology—that it was getting together with Sega to produce a next-generation 64-bit platform (see Figure 19.4), which will probably be a derivative of the original M2 spec. This merger has benefits for both parties involved: Sega will have a backup plan should Saturn ultimately stumble (which remains to be seen), and Panasonic will be bursting in on the console market. The new system spec, like its 3DO console predecessor, is intended to be manufactured by several companies at once.

Figure 19.4 The mysterious M2 platform.

The M2 Specs

The M2 is really more of a next-generation specification than a true product line at the moment. Still, it's an impressive array of technology and certainly will warrant serious development investigation once products based on the spec actually hit the store shelves.

CPU

The M2 is built around a custom designed RISC-based PowerPC 602 CPU running at 66 MHz. In case you aren't familiar with the PowerPC technology, this is the chip (which is a collaborative design between IBM, Apple, and Motorola) that the Power Mac is based on.

Graphics Processing

The M2 is a full 64-bit system with potential rendering speed of 100 million pixels per second and 1 million polygons per second. I stress the word potential; final specs and system software will definitely change performance. The M2 hardware features such graphics routines as hardware MPEG-1 video, texture mapping, MIP mapping, Gouraud shading, filtering, and 3D perspective correction (the perspective correction feature has to be seen to be believed!). Figures 19.5 through 19.7 show off some screenshots from the 3DO Web site hyping the graphics of the M2.

Figure 19.5 Science fiction scenes from 3DO.

Figure 19.6 3DO is great for fast action animation.

Figure 19.7 3DO can also do dinosaurs!

Sound

The M2 features a 66 MHz DSP chip providing 32 channels of digital sound with hardware MPEG audio decompression and 44.1kHz CD-quality sound.

Memory

The neat thing about M2 memory is that, unlike other consoles, it has one big memory chunk (4 MB to 6 MB) that is applicable to graphics/video, sound, and any other general systems. This approach makes it much easier on programmers because they don't have to deal with multiple separate units of RAM.

CD-ROM Drive

Chances are that M2 products will use either a quad-speed CD-ROM drive or, if costs permit, a DVD (Digital Verstile Disc), which would provide an amazing amount of storage capacity.

Peripherals

The M2 is powerful enough to provide Web surfing capabilities, so aside from the usual array of joysticks (both digital and analog), I suspect that a mouse and a keyboard will also see the light of day. In addition, the 3D graphics certainly can provide an amazing VR experience. If sales are high enough, we might even see some of the major PC-VR vendors, such as Virtual I/O or CyberMaxx, move their gear to this platform. Again, everything is speculation.

Entering the M2 Development System

Based on past 3DO specs, I am guessing that the development environment for the M2 will be Mac-based. Despite its ties of hardware and software specs to the Power Mac, the fact remains that the M2 is a Macintosh system. Until final specs ship, the up-front developer cost isn't currently available.

Pippin

Apple Computer
One Infinite Loop, M/S 38E
Cupertino, CA 95014
Phone: 408 996-1010 **Fax:** 408 974-2113
WWW: http://www.apple.com
and
Bandai America
Bandai America, Inc.
12851 E. 166th Street
Cerritos, CA 90703
Phone: 310 926-0947
WWW: http://www.dir.co.jp/cib/7967/welcome.html

This latest fruit from Apple, the Pippin, is a most intriguing addition to the console wars. Pippin is essentially a Power Mac trimmed down and sold console style for under $500. With the Apple name, Power Mac specs, and overall PC-oriented heritage, the Pippin could be a dark horse candidate for the console race.

Apple is currently signing up licensees for the Pippin. The first licensee is Bandai Co., a major Japanese toy giant best known for their Power Ranger dolls. Figure 19.8 shows the Bandai Pippin System. Don't let the kiddie-toy-oriented Bandai fool you. Distributing those products world wide requires major merchandising power—the kind of power that is needed to make Pippin a success.

Apple expects manufacturers from the consumer electronics, toy, computer, publishing, telephone network, and cable TV industries to create their own versions of Pippin tailored for their specific markets and like games, interactive TV, or surfing the Internet.

If successful, Apple could create a product that expands the overall Mac product line. Mac-oriented developers would have a huge new outlet for their games, and in addition, with Pippin's computer orientation, writing Internet applications and other similar products would be a snap for developers.

The Pippin Specs

Apple has always had products that somehow seem ahead of their time, the Apple II, Mac, Newton, and perhaps now the Pippin. It's a Mac in a $500 box. Some snickered when Apple announced the project—but late in the year as a number of industry heavyweights like Scott McNealy of Sun Microsystems and Larry Elison of Oracle began talking about a $500 PC like device, a lot of people began seeing that Apple had a product that may be ahead of its time.

Figure 19.8 The Bandai Pippin System.

CPU

The Pippin is built around a 66 MHz PowerPC 603 RISC CPU. It features an 8K data cache and 8K instruction cache. The Pippin also features an expansion PCI port for future upgrades.

The Pippin runs a Mac OS derivative, specialized for such console features as low-overhead, TV monitor viewing, and multimedia capabilities. Specifically, the Pippin has a PowerPC native version of QuickDraw with the Macintosh Toolbox intact; the computer-specific features have been removed, and key system software boots up directly from the CD-ROMs used in the machine.

Graphics Processing

The Pippin supports 8-bit and 16-bit video and has the same graphics-processing capabilities as that of a typical 66 MHz PowerMac—pretty substantial. Although you can hook up the Pippin to a TV set, you can also use a VGA monitor for crystal-clear graphics viewing.

Sound

The Pippin has both input and output abilities for stereo, 16-bit, 44.1 kHz sampled sounds.

Memory

The Pippin has 6 MB combined system and video memory. Memory expansion cards in 2, 4, and 8 MB increments can boost the system PC-level RAM specifications. There is also a 128K SRAM for storing/restoring backup memory, which is useful for saving games and such.

CD-ROM Drive

While most consoles feature a double-speed CD-ROM drive, the Pippin clocks in with a quad-speed CD-ROM drive. After all I've told you about this curious console, did you expect anything else?

Peripherals

The Pippin features joypads. Using an apple ADP port, a mouse and keyboard can be connected.

Entering the Pippin Development System

Check out the Web page referenced in the Apple contact information at the beginning of this section to find out more information about Pippin development. Much of Pippin development simply involves making adjustments to Mac programs to run in the more limited environment (for example no hard drive, no keyboard, a joypad, and so on).

So go back to Chapter 18 and reread about Mac development resources with the Pippin in mind. These resources should set you on your way to being a knowledgeable Pippin developer.

Key Console Development Tools

Too bad that when you program for a console you don't just fire up your favorite PC or Mac C compiler, make the game for that machine, and then hit the "Sega" button for a new console version. What is good, however, is that with these newer PC-like 32-bit consoles, the tools available to actually program console games are very strong.

Two major companies develop the software and hardware interfaces that allow you to program for consoles. If you're truly interested in developing for the console market, I suggest that you get on the phone to one or both of these companies.

SN Systems PSY-Q
SN Systems Limited
Quayside
40 Hotwell Road
Bristol ENGLAND BS8 4UQ
Phone: +44 (0)117 929 9733 **Fax:** +44 (0)117 929 9251
WWW: http://www.snsys.com

PSY-Q is a subsidiary of Psygnosis, a major game developer and subsidiary of Sony. They sell the main suite of products for developing for the Sony Playstation, including C compilers, assemblers, and debuggers. PSY-Q has also recently moved into the Saturn development market. I recommend that you stop by their Web sit, which has a ton of information about their development products.

Cross Development Products
23 The Calls, Leeds
West Yorkshire LS2 7EH
United Kingdom
Phone: +44 (0) 113 242 9814 **Fax:** +44 (0) 113 242 6163
Email: enquiry@crossprod.co.uk

This company has been a leading developer of console development products for quite a while, having shipped development kits for Atari's Jaguar, Sega's 32x and Genesis, and the Super Nintendo Entertainment System. Recently, Cross was acquired by Sega and has concentrated on a Saturn version of their SNASM2 development system. Unfortunately, they haven't yet put up a Web site. To get information about all of their development products, you'll need to send them email.

Consoles Today, Consoles Tomorrow

While some PC developers have wished that consoles would just go away, it's not going to happen. Just looking at some of the market analysis material presented in Chapter 27 will convince you of that. What has made some developers biased against consoles is that the earlier consoles were tough to program, the markets were tightly controlled, and cartridges were costly to manufacture and ship.

In one generation that has all changed. Today, consoles can be programmed in C instead of Assembly. In addition, most consoles use CD-ROMs instead of cartridges, which provides for tremendous storage capacity and cheaper production costs. Consoles also have amazing graphical features and power, state-of-the-art sound chips, and much less rigid development rules. It's no wonder that many previous PC-only developers, such as Bullfrog, Origin, and Spectrum Holybyte, are actively producing console games. In an interview with *Next Generation* magazine, Peter Molyneux of Bullfrog stated that Sony Playstation programming was like programming for the PC.

In addition, as we've seen with the PowerPC-equipped M2 and especially with Apple's Pippin, there is a growing convergence of actual computer technology and operating systems and consoles. At some point in the near future, perhaps all consoles will be stripped-down PCs with added features for gaming. If that change does come about, anyone who can program and develop for a PC will be able to develop for the console market, too.

Console-Related Web Sites and Resources

Earlier, I highlighted a few console-specific Web sites. Here are few more sites of interest to any console developer.

Silicon Graphics
`http://www.sgi.com`

The brains behind the coolest workstations in the biz are also the driving force behind Nintendo's Ultra 64 console. SGI workstations and software are also used by many other console developers, including Sony, M2, and Sega, for development of graphics and sound. SGI's Web site has lots of information about their involvement in the console business.

MIPS Technologies
`http://www.mips.com`

R4300i Background Information
`http://www.mips.com/HTMLs/R4300i_B.html`

R4300i Tech
`http://www.mips.com/HTMLs/r4300i_docs/R4300i_Pr_Ov/Prod_Overview.book.html`

These three Web sites point you directly to information about the company that produced the CPUs for both the Sony Playstation and the Nintendo Ultra 64. You will also find some fundamental information about the actual chips the consoles are using.

GO!'s Videogame Page
`http://www.anime.net/~gurupub/games.html`

This is a great site for information about all the consoles and the console scene. There are also lots of good links for you to follow.

Tronix Multimedia
Phone: 212 447-5980
WWW: http://www.calyx.net/~tronix/

Tronix Multimedia is a cool company for console developers and gaming enthusiasts to know about. Tronix caters to developers and die-hard gamers who just can't wait to have all the latest and greatest stuff. Many times, console hardware and software are released in Japan months earlier than in the U.S. and Europe. Sometimes you might need to get your hands on a product released there before it ships in the U.S. Or perhaps you're just checking out the competition, or evaluating products for conversion efforts. Whatever the reason, Tronix is your saving grace. This company specializes in two things: Getting products imported from Japan and getting products that ship in the U.S. and out to you the day they are available.

Their Web site features all the news about what's shipping here and there, as well as Tronix's founder Joe Catuadella's great reviews of the games. If you need to get an import or even a key domestic game, call Tronix.

PART 6

Other Development Issues

CHAPTER 20

AI for games involves hacking out your own way of adding intelligent-like features to your products.

Artificial Intelligence for Games: A Practical Overview

First, I want to thank Keith Weiner of DiamondWare for helping me with this chapter. Keith was particularly helpful in identifying Artificial Intelligence (AI) resources and providing explanations of some of the more fundamental AI technology used by game developers. However, don't blame him for my possible miscues.

For the most part, I'm not an AI expert. Whenever I want to learn more about a complex technology like AI, I track down someone who has spent a significant amount of time working with the technology. So to get a handle on the world of AL, I contacted Phil Steinmeyer who at the time had just finished programming New World Computing's Heroes of Might and Magic. His game uses quite a number of AI features. When I asked Phil how he implemented his AI techniques, he said "I sort of thought about how I would make decisions, then I hardcoded my ideas into the game. And it only took 7,000 lines of C code!"

The moral here is that there is no AI magic bullet. Most of what's been written about AI has focused on decision-making games like chess. Games like Heroes of Might and Magic, however, don't exactly have hundreds of years of chess history to draw upon. So in most cases, AI for games comes down to hacking out your own way of adding intelligent-like features to your products. But the more you understand some of the fundamental AI techniques, the better you can apply them (and change them) to come up with your own creative applications.

This chapter is designed to give you an overview of AI. It features some practical AI advice that you can use in your next games. My approach is to distill much of the field of AI into what I think is useful (or interesting) to game programmers.

AI Meets the World of Games

My experience has shown that it's hard to obtain a practical overview of AI. Numerous journals, books, and articles have been published but they usually cover topics that are of interest to academia. (Or at least you'll need a doctorate degree just to read them.) For example, you will find little of specific relevance to game programming in a magazine like *AI Expert*—although you might learn some new technology buzzwords or catch up on the latest AI fad.

The problem is that most people who write or speak about AI are more interested in research than they are in creating products for the masses. They tend to focus on topics that seem to have little relevance to the concerns and interests of working programmers. If an AI topic has practical applications, it has far less appeal to them than one that only has a place in the research labs. Unfortunately, many AI researchers are now moving into areas where the goals are so broad and ambitious as to be virtually unreal. (Pick up an AI journal and you're bound to come across an article like "Using Neural-Nets to Add Complete Human Memory to Pocket Calculators.")

Game programmers, on the other hand, are just learning to use some of the technologies AI researchers and academics have come up with in the past. Some of these technologies include expert systems, intelligent searching engines, decision-making algorithms, natural language processing, and cognitive reasoning. While the pioneering research being done in academic AI circles may someday give game developers tools they can use and exploit, let's return to earth and explore how the available tools and technologies can be used to make today's crop of games a little more intelligent and exciting.

What Game Developers Want

Game developers are much more interested in figuring out how the monsters in *Doom* decide what to do (and how they could have been made much smarter) than they are in discussing the latest AI trends. They want to know how to program believable characters with which the player can interact, or they want to know how to create smart opponents for wargames.

They strive to simulate systems and societies such as in Populous or SimCity. So, whether you are creating a racing game with good opposing drivers or an RPG with tough battles with monsters, you'll want to come up with ways of using real AI techniques to create realistic interaction, unique challenges, and smarter interfaces.

Is It Artificial or Intelligent?

As you might have gathered, Artificial Intelligence is a misnomer to begin with, especially when it is applied to games. The real goal is to use technology to add "human" or intelligent-like qualities to games. The more clever and natural the techniques are, the more convincing they will be to players. I think a better name for this technology would be "simulative intelligence," which in the end is the goal every game should strive to achieve.

Every now and then a game might use leading technology like neural-nets but most don't require such leading-edge technology. (The ones I have seen using this approach are exactly the same types of games most researchers are concentrating on, backgammon, chess, checkers, and Go. You probably won't find a copy of Attack of the Midget Mutant Zombies at your local software store that uses neural-nets.)

For purposes of this chapter, let me define what I think artificial intelligence represents in a game:

A non-player controlled object acts in a manner that makes it appear as if it has made a decision *similar to the way a real person would have made the decision using* multiple factors. *This is achieved using a decision-making algorithm that processes information provided by the program based upon the* rules *laid out by the designer that govern what the decision-making algorithm knows or doesn't know.*

In my definition I've used three terms that I think need further explanation:

Decision An "intelligent" object makes a choice instead of acting at random. While you might use random numbers to add in a simulative sort of range or add weight to a particular decision, the ultimate decision is made by choosing between at least two possible outcomes. The better an object can anticipate the player's reactions (and even more so the further repercussions or "depth of reaction") to the possible choices, the more intelligent the object will appear to the player. Just as important, the decision must take root in an initial stimuli. This stimuli typically consists of observed information such as the number of tanks surrounding a base or some internal stimuli like "gee I'm hungry," which itself may be a factor of the time of day.

Multiple Factors Being human, you know that few decisions are ever cut and dried. For example, just trying to decide where to go for dinner can involve numerous factors, some of which overlap. Do you want to drive the car to get there? Do you want to go with a friend? What type of food do you want? How much money do you want to spend? If your time is limited, do you want to go somewhere that has fast service? Do you need to make reservations? You get the idea ....

To make an object intelligent it also must be able to consider multiple factors and make quick decisions. Such factors will contribute to how it reacts to different situations. The more factors your algorithms can support (or process), the better your chances will be for creating a realistic environment. As an example, consider a wargame where you're working on rules that define the behavior of the opposing generals. You might simply have them consider how many tanks, planes, and boats the other side has and then have them make production decisions to keep pace on a one-to-one basis.

On the other hand, you might bring in other factors. For example, they might take into account the number of island bases they need to defend, which in turn would make them decide to create more planes and boats instead of tanks. They could also decide if the position they need to take should be offensive or defensive. In addition you might get creative and add in emotional factors like aggressiveness, meaning even in bleak times they still make more planes to keep up the offense despite the fact that they should make tanks. Remember, an "intelligent" decision does not necessarily have to be the best or most rational.

So as you attempt to simulate intelligence, first try to determine the information (multiple factors) that will be used to make decisions. Also, think about the characteristics the decision makers will use to evaluate the information.

Rules You also need to determine under what circumstances and rules will an object have access to the information it needs to make a decision. For example, in a wargame will the computer see the entire field or will it only see the portion of the field its forces occupy? If the computer can see the entire battlefield, it should be able to make better decisions, but if the player can't, the computer is "cheating." Of course, this might be the only way to even out the game because the computer needs more information to make up for the player's obvious better intelligence.

The Appearance to the Player Is What Counts

Of course, the goal of AI is not to create systems that are good at "cheating." But in a game, "cheating" may turn out to be the best way for you to make an opponent challenging enough. But be careful, because if a player can detect the computer is cheating, you can bet he or she will get mad and probably give up on the game. Additionally, for most AI developers, the goal is to create the best computer opponent possible and sometimes this results in an opponent that is too good.

This leads to two contradictions in computer game design. First, the majority of players must be able to beat the game at some point. Do you remember the notion of achievement we covered in the design section of this book? AI researchers might strive to create a program that can beat Gary Kasporov, but as a game designer and player I don't want that. I just want a computer challenging enough that can beat me if I don't watch my every move and one I can beat when I'm playing well.

Secondly, striving to create a game that is too intelligent, complex, or sophisticated can make the game seem quite artificial. For example, consider a basic wargame. An AI proponent would insist on making the computer the greatest general in the world. Well, that truly would be artificial because a game may want to create an opponent that simulated things such as a general making a mistake or maybe making the game simulate the tactics of a certain general. The point here is that AI theory tends to emphasize creating optimal situations, not realistic simulations.

Thus, what you should be trying to construct is the overall realistic appearance of your opponents and characters to the player. Don't try to turn your non-player characters into the world's most intelligent optimal opponents, but rather try to meld traditional coding and AI techniques together into some routine that presents the depth, challenge, and simulative presence of other worlds to players.

Whatever techniques you use are not as important as the end result. But understand that when someone says "put some AI in your game," they probably aren't suggesting that you try to program a complete and complex neural nets system or implement massive tree searches. They probably just want to see you add more realistic scenes and characters to your games.

Examples of AI Used in Games

Let's look at some specific examples of AI technologies that are used in games. Hopefully, they will give you some ideas of how you can apply AI to your own projects.

Intelligent Opponents

The most common form of AI in games is to create computer controlled opponents. Since most games are played by a single player, this involves designing and developing the opponents the player will have to overcome in the game. To achieve this, you could use some simple AI algorithm like an A* search to help an opponent navigate its way through a maze toward an attacking player. You could also use a simple technique of making moves by first anticipating how the player might react.

Keep in mind, however, that you don't need to create the world's greatest opponents. Your opponents only need to be challenging enough to the people who play your game. Also keep in mind the context of your game. For example, a chess game is all about strategy and making the very best decisions. In an RPG, the elements of storytelling and character development may be more important. Thus, don't bog the player down in challenges that are too complex because the computer is so darn smart.

Additionally, you can incorporate other design ideas to give your players realistic and interesting challenges. If you don't have the time or inclination to add sophisticated AI algorithms, you might give an opponent more tools or resources to work with to even out the game. For example, you might create tanks that have extra armor so that the player needs to compensate for that, and perhaps with the added armor the "dumber" computer may actually score a little more. The overriding goal is to create opponents that appear "intelligent" and offer the player a sense that he or she is operating in as realistic an environment as possible. Whenever you can, use clever algorithms that represent thought processes instead of just brute-force techniques. Don't forget that your players want challenging opponents and AI is just one component in your arsenal of design ideas to apply.

Intelligent Non-Player Characters

Often, AI techniques are thrown around in the game development world in such a way as to become synonymous with opponents. This happens because most early games like chess were designed for one-on-one play. However, as any good adventure or RPG game developer knows, AI can cover non-opposition characters as well.

For example, if you are building an RPG and you want your towns to come alive—that is to have characters in the game move about in an intelligent manner—you can use some algorithms to determine where the characters should be during the course of a day. You can use an AI-like algorithm such as A* that can help you move an object from one place to the other and avoid obstacles.

Intelligent Systems and Worlds

This instance of AI in games is the most simulative in nature, but basically it can rely on some AI elements too. Here you're trying to meld all the different decision-making objects in your game into a cohesive whole. For example, you may have armies in a wargame and they all could make their own little AI-like decisions based on their immediate surroundings.

With this approach, you concentrate on the inter-relationships of separate decision-makers in your game and how those interrelationships can be organized to present a cohesive whole. By having a higher-up decision making scheme that works to coordinate the decisions of groups, or by having objects literally say to everyone else "I'm going here!" the other objects can make a different decision. A great example of this can be found in a wargame. You could have ten tanks and they all think basically the same way and so they all decide to go after the player's weakest tank. Now if tank one says "He's mine," the rest of the tanks can adjust their strategy to go after other tanks.

So as you build multitudes of intelligent objects, you have to take in account how they all act within an intelligent system.

How to Approach AI in Games

As I mentioned previously, many programmers approach AI development by simply thinking up the actions they themselves would do and then they try to find a way to make the computer think like they would.

But there are some areas of AI research where you could benefit by reading up on the available AI textbooks, papers, and resources. Let's quickly run through some fundamental AI topics that you may want to get up to speed on.

Searches

Many AI algorithms involve searching through possible options. For games, this is obviously a major concern. For example, a well known A* algorithm has been developed by AI researchers that helps you search through a map for the shortest path between two points given the beginning and ending points and any known obstacles.

To employ such a search in a game, you first have your program compile a list of options, such as all of the available moves for a chess piece. Then, you use various AI techniques such as pruning, breadth first, and so on to find an optimal choice.

Many different techniques have been developed for traversing through information and many of the basic techniques are derived from AI work, which you can find in the numerous texts and papers published. Later I'll list some of these resources.

Sorting

Sorting and searching are sort of the same thing but basically you might want to explore AI techniques for determining the best order for making decisions. For example, you might want to have a strategy game where the computer opponent is constantly reshuffling priorities based upon the currently observed circumstances.

Several AI techniques like the traveling salesman problem or airline booking cases are presented in general textbooks, which can help you learn how to implement AI-like sorting algorithms for your games.

Expert Systems

Expert system are perhaps the most useful AI technology developed to date. In an expert system you compile all sorts of basic rules in an "if then" logic structure. Then, the computer would use the rules to make intelligent decisions.

Take for example a football game. A company like EA interviews an expert like John Madden for hours and hours, recording all his unbelievable knowledge about football. He might say, "If I'm on my one yard line, I'll probably run the ball 90 percent of the time to not risk a sack and thus a safety." EA takes this information and sets up a rule-driven database filled with all of Madden's advice. This allows the computer to make decisions like Madden would by looking for rules and outcomes that match situations that occur during the course of the game.

This technique works really well when you can bring in an expert and reduce his or her expertise to some effective rules of thumb. Sports games are particularly well-suited to the expert system approach. For other types of games, such as a wargame, you might first program the game without using any AI techniques. Then, play it yourself over and over. As you become an expert at playing against yourself, you can develop your own rules to create an expert system.

Machine Learning

Machine learning involves having the computer generate the expert system rules from its own experience. Sometimes it's possible to have the computer play itself over and over, basically making random decisions and then recording the results. As it plays itself, it can draw upon its previous experience and appear to get smarter and smarter.

This approach works especially well for games that are based on very strict rules, such as card games. They are better suited for machine learning because they offer a discernible fixed amount of situations. That's not to say machine learning can't be used with other less structured games. Of course, machine learning is tricky stuff to pull off, so I suggest you experiment with simple, structured games first.

If you are looking for more information on this topic, Diana Gruber of Ted Gruber software wrote a great article with code in a recent issue of *PC TECHNIQUES* Magazine (Volume 5, Issue 6; Dec/Jan 1996). This article is a well-written tutorial that discuses how to create computer opponents for games.

Neural Nets

Neural nets are at the cutting edge of AI and basically are the natural progression of expert systems and machine learning. The idea of a neural net is to try mimic the way the human brain works (hence the name). I'm not going to fry my brain trying to explain what exactly that means, but for the most part neural nets are AI systems that adapt and learn by constantly analyzing continued stimuli, much like you or I would learn about anything we encounter in life.

The best thing about neural nets is that lots of AI research, such as the TD-Gammon project presented in the sidebar that follows, is being done specifically using games. Thus as you explore neural nets in your AI research you'll be pleasantly surprised by the direct examples of it being applied to games.

TD-Gammon—A Major Game-Related AI Project

TD-Gammon, a world-class backgammon computer program, was the product of years of research by IBM's Dr. Gerald Tesauro. In July 1995, it was commercialized for OS/2 Warp by Tesauro and Keith Weiner.

TD stands for "temporal difference," a technique used to train neural nets to learn complex non-linear functions, such as positional values in board games. An explanation of it is beyond the scope of this chapter, but Tesauro has published papers about it.

Tesauro used a neural net as the evaluation function in the game of backgammon. What's unique is that he encoded no human expertise into the function, letting it "learn" as it played hundreds of thousands of games itself for more than a month on an RS-6000 workstation. According to former world-cham-

pion Bill Robertie, TD-Gammon plays better than all but a handful of players in the world today; in the grueling format of the world championship tournament, it might even be a favorite to win because it does not lose its ability to concentrate like humans do.

Note that most other attempts to get neural nets to play games have not met with this kind of success. One theory for this is that backgammon has a significant random component: the dice. This random input insures that an otherwise deterministic system explores a representative sample of the entire state space. In chess, any computer-run learning session would likely play endless variants of similar games, changing as each losing side learned from its worst mistake.

On the surface, backgammon is harder for computers to play well. The dice ensure that the game tree branches far more numerously than in chess. This only furthered the incentive to find a technique that did not require deep tree searches.

TD-Gammon's evaluation function is so strong that its searches are two-ply. The evaluation function won't be able to tell you that a given state is sure to win, unless it has an opportunity to evaluate that state. Therefore, it's critically important for it to prune the option tree it generates for a given move. This way it wastes as little time as possible evaluating unpromising nodes, and evaluates as many really good ones as possible.

Instead of generating a node for all legal moves, it generates only those that are plausible. By implementing this idea, it's possible to reduce the average number of branches in chess from 30 to 10 per node. This reduces the number of nodes in a 6-ply search from 729 million to just 1 million.

For more about TD Gammon, the game you can play, surf on over to:

`http://www.austin.ibm.com/pspinfo/funtdgammon.html`

and

`http://forum.swarthmore.edu/~jay/learn-game/systems/td-gammon.html`

AI Resources

More than any other technical topic (except game programming), AI is something that you can probably never read enough about. Peter Molyneux of Bullfrog Productions, makers of Populous, constantly talks about the number of AI books and articles he has read and the topics he has researched over the years. The next time you play a Bullfrog game, you can easily see the fruits of his labor. To help you build your own reading list, I've included some of the better online resources that feature AI topics.

Books

AI Book Database

http://www.blackwell.co.uk/cgi-bin/bb_catsel?09_IN3

Enter this Web site and you'll begin searching Blackwells, a British bookstore that has an extensive listing of AI books including a synopsis of the topics covered in each book! After you decide what types of AI you need to implement, go here to find an amazing amount of content to start digesting.

Magazines and Journals

List of Major Journals and Magazines

http://ai.iit.nrc.ca/ai_journals.html

There are over a dozen AI journals and publications worth exploring and possibly subscribing to. The trick is deciding which one meets your specific needs. Rather than list them all, I'm going to take the easy way out and point you to the above Web site, which provides a more complete, up-to-date listing than I could have put together on my own.

AI Publication Database

http://donkey.CS.Arizona.EDU:1994/bib/Ai/

This site features a large database of books, papers, and articles published about AI. Surf on over here and search until your heart is content.

Other Online Web Sites

Artificial Intelligence Resources

http://www.comlab.ox.ac.uk/archive/comp/ai.html

Are you ready to start learning more about AI? This site features dozens of links to top AI resources available on the Web. If you only have time to check out one site, this one should be it.

AI links at the Knowledge System Lab in Canada

http://ai.iit.nrc.ca/ai_point.html

Aside from the previous listed site, this is my other favorite massive link site for AI resources. I especially like this specific page on the site, which lists all the major AI journals in publication.

Machine Learning in Games Home Page

http://forum.swarthmore.edu/~jay/learn-game/

This is a great site that serves as a jumping off point for a ton of resources about AI in games. But before you expect to find dissertations on AI for arcade games, understand that the games this site features are the ones AI researchers have been working with for years including chess, checkers, backgammon, and so on.

comp.ai.games FAQ

http://www.cs.pdx.edu/~idr/game/comp.ai.games.html

comp.ai.games is the main Usenet newsgroup to check. Point your Web browser to the above URL to view the FAQ produced from this group.

CHAPTER 21

3D "on the fly" games have been around for a while but today they've become the norm and not the exception!

3D Game Engines and Resources

Although 3D games have been around for quite some time, you'd think from all the hype that we'd been working in two dimensions until yesterday. I'm not talking about games like SimCity, which *appear* 3D. (The graphics used in these games are merely drawn to look 3D.) I'm talking about games like Starglider, Elite, Flight Simulator, Mercenary, and others—all true 3D games—that existed long before Doom or Virtua Fighter. However, because hardware has made such leaps and bounds in the last two years, *realtime* 3D graphics have quickly become commonplace. By realtime, I mean a program that is able to render a complete 3D scene on-the-fly at runtime using 3D graphics algorithms.

As cool as it is, realtime 3D graphics have produced a serious dilemma for the industry. Demand for breakthrough 3D games is at an all time high. Normally, such high demand is met by equally high supply. 3D games, however, require an enormous amount of time and expense. Not only do you need cutting edge programming talent, but such games require expensive 3D modeling systems and skilled artists as well. In addition, as the "eye candy" factor of these games wears off, players are now demanding better gameplay to go along.

In this chapter, I'll provide you with descriptions of the best resources and advice to get you started on your way to creating hot 3D games. I'll describe the ins and outs of the latest 3D technology—from raycasting and polygon game engines to 3D chipsets and graphics cards—and provide you with an extensive list of resources to help you find more information.

3D Game Types

There are two common forms of 3D graphics seen in gaming today: 3D raycasting, which is the technique employed by Id Software's Doom, and 3D Polygon games, which include flight simulators or products like Sega's Virtua Fighter.

Raycasting is the technique employed to create 3D first person point-of-view games. With raycasting, a game engine will place a player in a 2D wall-filled world and then project out rays from the player's position that basically represent the player's viewpoint to the world. Once the program calculates which walls and objects the viewer's eye catches, it is able to draw walls and other parts of a scene from a library of object textures and graphics. In addition, the program can calculate other features such as lighting effects.

Polygon games on the other hand work by geometrically describing a total 3D image made up of hundreds, if not thousands, of primitive triangles or polygon objects. The game engine is not only able to render any view of these objects but can map smooth textures and lighting effects to create sensational looking 3D games.

In some cases you can combine the two methods. For example, a first person raycasting engine can be used for all the background, walls, and scenery and a 3D polygon engine can be used to render the objects and creatures.

Raycasting/First Person Point-of-View

Ever since Castle, Wolfenstein 3D, and Doom burst onto the gaming scene, raycasters and first person point-of-view games have become household topics—at least to those within the gaming community. Many programmers and companies have created their own 3D raycasting engines. Some of these engines—like Lary Myers' ACK-3D—have been documented for the public, while others—like Id's Doom engine—are made available to license. Licensing can be tough, though. Id has only licensed the Doom engine twice and that was to companies that operate more or less as sisters of Id themselves.

While some programmers might consider them passé, 3D raycasters still have a lot of life left in them. Here are some of the key 3D raycasting resources out there for you to cut your teeth on.

ACK-3D
The Coriolis Group
7339 East Acoma Drive, Suite 7
Scottsdale, AZ 85260
Phone: 602 483-0192 **Fax:** 602 483-0193
WWW: http://www.coriolis.com

Early in 1993, Lary Myers, a regular on CompuServe's Game Developer's forum, started posting code that allowed developers to create their own raycasting games like Wolfenstein 3D or Doom. Since then, Lary has worked for over a year to redo the entire package and prepare a book version of it to explain all of the code and the technology behind it.

The result is ACK-3D, which comes complete with source code for DOS and Windows versions of the engine. The book version, *Amazing 3D Games Adventure Set*, also includes a companion CD-ROM that comes with editors, graphics, and full-fledged demos of the product. Contact The Coriolis Group for ordering information. To see ACK-3D in action, check out H.U.R.L. from Deep River Publishing, which was based on the ACK-3D engine.

Although ACK-3D is hardly cutting edge technology, access to the source code and a complete book on its inner workings, make it perhaps the best system to learn about raycasting programming. Figure 21.1 shows an example of the types of games you can create with the ACK-3D engine.

Figure 21.1 Sample game created with the ACK-3D engine.

ACKNex
Conitec Datensysteme GmbH
Dieselstr. 11c
D-64807 Dieburg
Germany
Phone: 49 6071 92520 **Fax:** 49 6071 925233
Email: 100042.1745@compuserve.com

ACKNex is the work of a German software developer who took the original work of Lary Myers' ACK-3D engine and moved it up to a whole new level. This DOS package now includes sound, MIDI, joystick support, level editors, six degrees of movement and tilt, motion dynamics, and resolution up to 320×400 in 256 colors. According to Conitec, the engine renders at 15 frames per second on a 486DX-66 and 33 frames per second on a Pentium 90 (only 320×400 degrades this by 40 percent).

ACKNex also includes a scripting language called the World Definition Language, which helps you describe wall characteristics and more. Pricing consists of some upfront fees, as well as a royalty for shipped products. Contact Conitec for more information.

You can find demos of the ACKNex system on CompuServe's Game Developer's forum or at ftp://x2ftp.oulu.fi. Figure 21.2 shows an example of this engine at work.

Atlantis
Digital Dialect
13451 Cheltenham Dr.
Sherman Oaks, CA 91423
Phone: 818 905-5410 **Fax:** 818 905-1243
WWW: http://www.digitald.com
http://www.primenet.com/~mcase/

Figure 21.2 A scene from the AckNex demo.

Atlantis is a major 3D development engine for building first person point-of-view games. Unlike most of the first two generations of 3D engines, this engine features floors over floors, which allows you to have a room over a room—a feature that is not possible in Doom. The program can also render texture-mapped polygon objects within the environment. Figures 21.3 and 21.4 show some examples of the Atlantis engine.

The Atlantis engine consists of two parts: a runtime engine library, which can be linked with your host application, and a World Builder, which allows for complete editing of all aspects of the game engine, including rendered previews. The engine runs under DOS, Windows 95, and Windows NT, and can render into any window size as well.

Atlantis allows you to create wall textures that are transparent, translucent, and scaled to any size, and source textures that can be 64×64, 64×128, 128×128, 128×256, or 256×256 pixels in size before being scaled. As far as specific 3D raycaster game items supported by Atlantis, there are doors, elevators, projectiles, sprites, conveyor floors, pits, water, and more.

Before you run out and contact Digital Dialect, understand that their package is for *major game developers* and requires a substantial license fee. Don't waste your time or theirs if you're not ready to step up to the plate with proper funding here. A demo of the system is available at the Digital Dialect Web site.

Figure 21.3 Sample output from the Atlantis engine.

Figure 21.4 Sample water scene created with the Atlantis engine.

Pie 3D Game Creation System
Pie in the Sky Software
1596 Ayrault Road
Fairport, NY 14450
Phone: 800 537-3344
WWW: http://catalog.com/psky/

Pie 3D is an all-in-one package aimed at non-programmers who want to create a Doom-like game. With this DOS-based package, which uses lots of pull-down menus and a windowing-like interface, you can edit maps and paint graphics to create a 3D shooting environment. Figure 21.5 shows an example of the tool at work.

This is not really a professional-level product. Perhaps you can make some fun freeware/shareware with it and practice your design and development skills, but if you're a developer looking to create a comprehensive retail product, look elsewhere.

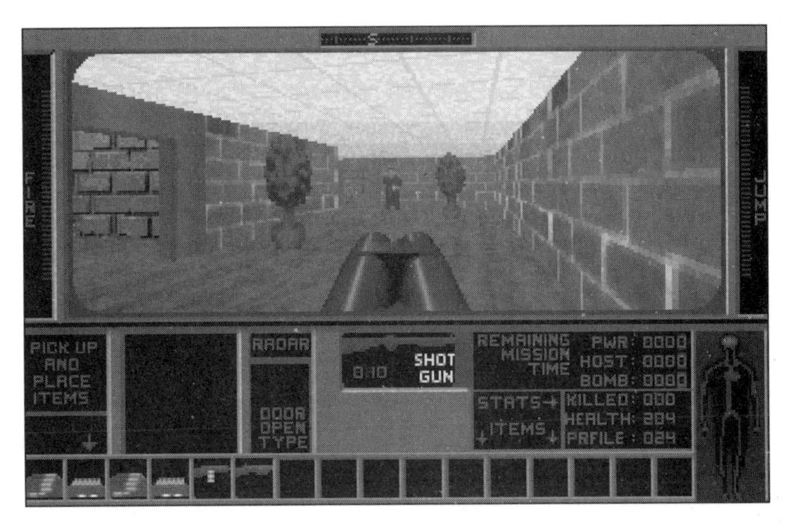

Figure 21.5 The Pie in the Sky game creation system.

Raycasting Resources

Raycasting and 3D raycasting engines have been hot topics with game developers online and in print for some time. People can't seem to get enough of this stuff. Here are all the resources—reading materials and Web sites—I located to help you get your fix of the raycasting scene.

Tricks of the Game Programming Gurus by Andre Lamothe, Densie Tyler, and John Ratcliff (SAMS, 1994; ISBN 0-672-30507-0)

This was the first of four major books published on raycasting engines. Not only does it contain code examples and explanations about creating a DOS-based raycasting engine, but you'll also find tips on creating wall textures and other artwork, as well as tips on implementing sound and music using the MidPak and DigPak libraries.

Gardens of Imagination by Christopher Lampton (Waite Group Press, 1995; ISBN 1-878739-59-X)

From the man who brought you *Flights of Fantasy*, comes this book about 3D raycasting. One thing about Lampton's books is that he explains things so well. *Gardens* covers all the basics about raycasting and VGA programming, and comes with a complete 3D engine.

Amazing 3D Games Adventure Set by Lary Myers (Coriolis Group Books, 1995; ISBN 1-883577-15-2)

Perhaps the most complete and advanced book on raycastig is this book by Lary Myers. The code presented is the latest version of his ACK-3D engine, and, unlike the original version found on CompuServe and the Internet, is not publicly available.

This book covers both DOS and Windows implementations (using WinG).

Netwarriors in C++ by Joe Gradecki (John Wiley & Sons, 1995; ISBN 047-1110-64-7)

This book is the weakest of the four available, but it attempts to make up for that by explaining the networking code behind some of the popular 3D games. By taking this track and including a CD-ROM packed with all sorts of stuff about games from the x2ftp.oulu.fi site on the Internet, this book may be worth looking at. For its graphics engine, it uses an old "unauthorized" version of Lary Myers' ACK-3D engine.

3D Engine Links
`http://www.bushnet.qld.edu.au/~guy/graphics/engines.html`

Maintained by Karsten Isakovic, this Web site features the most up to date and comprehensive collection of 3D engines—including raycasters—available. If you're looking for the latest and greatest in freeware/shareware or commercially available engines, check here fist.

Id Software Home Page and Wolfenstein Source
`http://www.idsoftware.com`

Id made raycasting and Doom household words. Now you can watch the progress of Quake, their latest offering. Also look for the Wolfenstein 3D source code. While Id doesn't support the code, you can still read through it and learn from the pros!

Polygon Games

When programmers talk about polygon-based games, they are referring to any game—be it a fighting game or baseball game—that uses a polygon graphical engine. The key ingredient is a graphical system that relies on realtime animated characters to provide a heightened realism.

The most important aspect to constructing a polygon-based game is how you approach the programming of the actual graphics engine. You have two major choices here: Go it alone and construct a set of graphical routines from scratch or use an existing 3D API.

The APIs, which I'll cover in detail in a moment, can cost you anywhere from $1,000 to over $10,000 plus royalty arrangements. Don't let the price tags shock you. The APIs offer an extensive set of functionality that your own routines would be hard-pressed to duplicate. Still, while these APIs claim excellent speeds, some games may be better off not using them.

As always, the key to finding out if these packages will meet your needs is through evaluation. The next section covers the more general issues of the various 3D APIs. Although you may have the resources to build a 3D polygon game straight from code, to do so without first evaluating the API options available to you is foolish.

3D Polygon APIs

At the heart of any 3D polygon-based product is either a proprietary drawing engine or, increasingly, a third party 3D API. As 3D games have exploded, several major 3D libraries have been developed that not only help with the 3D drawing but offer extensive cross-platform capabilities and speed in developing these types of products. All of the APIs listed here use their own set of polygon file formats for storing objects and all of them come with some sort of conversion product for moving between the major 3D packages to their format. Because most of these packages are either inexpensive or feature a free trial phase, testing all of them is not really an expensive venture.

BRender
Argonaut Software Ltd.
Rich Seidner
Head of U.S. Operations
1040 Noel Drive, Suite 209
Menlo Park, CA 94025
Phone: 415 328-7841 **Fax:** 415 328-7842
WWW: http://www.argonaut.com

BRender from Argonaut Software is an outgrowth of Argonaut's extensive work with 3D graphics. Argonaut was founded by Jez San, a longtime game developer known for his 3D Nintendo-based games like Starglider and StarFox. Argonaut also developed the FX chip that Nintendo uses to provide extra 3D polygon power to its SNES system. You can see a nice showcase of BRender's power in the Argonaut-produced game FX Fighter, a Virtua Fighter-like product for the PC, developed in conjunction with GTE Interactive. Figure 21.6 shows an example of this fun game.

The product supports all color depths, 16- and 32-bit Z-buffering, texture mapping with perspective, and object penetration. It's available for DOS, Windows, and various console platforms, and is considered by many to be the fastest of the current 3D APIs (not that the others are slouches).

Evaluation copies are free, but there is a time limit which when reached requires you to return or pay for the product. BRender can be licensed with a flat rate or a royalty structure.

RenderWare
Criterion Software Limited
1030 East El Camino Real, #309
Sunnyvale, CA 94087
Phone: 408 489-5103
Fax: 408 245-2135

Criterion Software Limited
20 Alan Turing Road
Guildford, GU2 5YK, UK
Phone: 011 44 483 448800
Fax: 011 44 483 448811

WWW: http://www.canon.co.uk/csl/cslhome.html

Figure 21.6 An example from FX Fighter—a game created with the BRender system.

Criterion is actually a division of Canon, the Japanese computer and consumer electronics giant. Its 3D library, called Renderware, is perhaps the most mature of the major 3D APIs with over 400 functions, support for major modeling file formats, and platform support for Windows, DOS, and the various consoles. RenderWare has been used by several major game companies, including virtual reality pioneer Zombie Interactive.

Rendermorphics
Microsoft Corporation
One Microsoft Way
Microsoft Corporation
Redmond, WA, 98052
Phone: 206 882-8080
WWW: http://www.microsoft.com

Rendermorphics was a standalone company until early 1995 when it was acquired in a rash of buying sprees by software giant Microsoft Corporation. Microsoft has recently made a large-scale push to establish Windows as the preeminent platform for games and the Rendermorphics 3D library is part of that process.

As of this writing, Rendermorphics is still in the Beta stage of development. I encourage you to get in on the Beta testing cycle by calling Microsoft. Microsoft hopes to ship the full version by mid-1996.

QuickDraw 3D
Apple Computer, Inc.
1 Infinite Loop
Cupertino, CA 95014
Phone: 408 996-1010
WWW: http://product.info.apple.com/qd3d/QD3D.HTML

Not wanting to be left out of the emerging 3D computer world, Apple has laid down its gauntlet with Quickdraw 3D and 3D Metafile technology. QuickDraw 3D is a cross-platform application program interface for creating and rendering realtime graphics. It consists of human interface guidelines and a toolkit, a high-level modeling toolkit, a shading and rendering architecture, a cross-platform file format, and a device and acceleration manager for plug-and-play hardware acceleration.

QuickDaw supports a new file format called the 3D Metafile file format. It's especially developed for cross-platform 3D graphics applications. Apple is proposing this format as a standard for 3D graphics files (which could really use one!). QuickDraw 3D and supporting applications can easily work with this format and in making it a proposed standard others may follow suit. QuickDraw 3D demos and information for the Mac is available on Apple's Web site.

Apple has said it will be porting the Quickdraw 3D API to the Windows platform later in 1996, which will offer major cross platform development help for computer game developers.

Aside from the documentation that comes with QuickDraw 3D, Addision-Wesley and Apple Computer have created a new book, which describes itself as "the definitive" book on QuickDraw 3D:

3D Graphics Programming with QuickDraw 3D by Apple Computer, Inc. (Addison-Wesley, 1995; ISBN 0-201-48926-0)

3DR
Intel Corporation
RN6-18
2200 Mission College Blvd.
Santa Clara, CA 95052
Phone: 408 765-8795 **Fax:** 408 765-5165
WWW: http://www.intel.com

3DR is not a game toolkit like the previous APIs I've described. It's a basic, yet powerful, package that Intel offers at no cost to establish basic support for 3D graphics on the Pentium platform. 3DR features a simple API, texture mapping, bitmapping, real perspective correction, smooth shading, Z-buffering, and anti-aliasing.

Intel created 3DR technology to push the software community to create powerful applications that will utilize Intel's processors to their fullest potential. In addition, Intel's 3DR establishes a benchmark for all other 3D APIs to match.

Overall, 3DR is an interesting package. It's not very fast compared to products like BRender or RenderWare, but it offers beginning developers a chance to easily work with 3D functionality. In addition, I found the accompanying documentation to be quite helpful in understanding a lot of the basic math associated with 3D graphics.

Polygon Resources

Here are the more helpful sources of information on 3D polygon graphics programming. I've included both books and Web sites.

Black Art of 3D Game Programming by Andre Lamothe (Waite Group Press, 1995; ISBN 1-57169-004-2)

From the man who brought you *Teach Yourself Game Programming in 21 Days* and *Tricks of the Game Programming Gurus*, comes this book/CD combination, which covers tons of information regarding creating 3D polygon games using C.

It also goes on to cover other game programming techniques, such as artificial intelligence, modem communications, sound, and music.

Learn 3D Graphics Programming on the PC by Richard F. Ferraro (Addision-Wesley, 1995; ISBN 0-201-48332-7)

This is an awesome book weighing in with 1000+ pages. Ferraro covers a wealth of topics about 3D graphics programming and uses Criterion's RenderWare which amazingly is on the CD-ROM that comes with the book! The book covers information on using cameras, polygons, lighting, materials, textures, and splines, and advanced 3D topics including object creation, application management, rendering tips, palette optimization, call backs, and much more.

Building a 3D Game Engine in C++ by Brian Hook (John Wiley & Sons, 1995; ISBN 047-1123-26-9)

From a self-confessed 3D graphics addict comes this book on building 3D game engines in C++ for the PC. This book covers the basics in a very direct and clear manner.

Computational Geometry FAQ
`http://www.cs.berkeley.edu/~jeffe/compgeom.html`

3D polygon graphics is more about math than it is about programming. Check in here for all sorts of help with the computational geometry that goes into doing realtime 3D polygon programming.

I_COLLIDE

`http://www.cs.unc.edu/~cohenj/I_COLLIDE.html`

This is a 3D polygon collision detect library created by a group of Computer Science students at the University of North Carolina. While it's been used primarily for architectural walk-throughs and such, the entire source code is available at the above address. While you might find it hard to implement in a gaming environment, the tutorial applications can be very helpful.

3D Hardware Companies

Both consoles and high-end workstations have had 3D hardware standards in place to help developers with 3D game programming. The PC, however, has been left out of the loop. As with sound, the problem is that there isn't a standard until consumers and the marketplace ordain one. But unlike the sound situation, there is much more initial competition among 3D hardware manufacturers.

Some of this dilemma is solved by the use of generic APIs that take your commands and optimize them for the detected 3D chipset. Additionally, some of the hardware companies are looking to work with developers to optimize that developer's games for use on their specific cards. If you have a major 3D game, they may provide help and marketing or development funds to help market card specific versions of your game. Typically, though, this offer is made to the cream of the crop.

Chip Makers and Board Makers

There are really two types of companies we're going to discuss in this section: the underlying chip developer and the associated board manufacturers. As a developer, you will be more concerned with contacting and working with the board makers.

What you'll discover as you read this section is that the major board makers like Creative or Diamond stand behind different chip makers (it is the computer business afterall, what did you expect, a standard?), so competition is fierce. It's not clear right now who will emerge as the winner in the field when the dust settles, but my guess is that more than one will still be around. Luckily for developers, the APIs existed before the boards, which has allowed for a smooth integration between common programming standards (using the APIs) and the different hardware specifications (of the boards). This is welcome news for the many developers who are still trying to get a handle on 2D graphics.

Unless you're really looking to tweak performance with each board, working through products like DirectDraw or a major 3D API should shield developers from the underlying graphics hardware in the user's machine. This, of course, requires the API manufacturer to keep up with and provide support for 3D hardware.

Nonetheless, I suggest that you get in touch with the various hardware companies so that you can keep abreast of developments and marketing plans. Let's take a look at the major players in this portion of the gaming field.

The Glint Chipset and Glint-Derived Boards

The Glint Chipset
3D Labs Inc.
2010 N First Street, Suite 403
San Jose, CA 95131
Phone: 408 436-3455 **Fax:** 408 436-3458
WWW: http://www.3Dlabs.com/3Dlabs
http://www.webmaster.com/3dlabs

The Glint family of 3D processors includes chips aimed at the professional user of 3D graphics on the desktop, and at game players looking for the ultimate 3D experience.

The main chip of the Glint family is the Glint 300SX, which is geared toward the 3D graphics creation and animation markets, and has support for CAD, OpenGL, and similar products.

The game version of the Glint chip provides realtime, true-perspective, texture-mapped graphics, Gouraud shading, optional Z-buffering, fogging, blending, translucency, overlays, and stencils. It accelerates polygonal graphics and titles coded in any of the industry-standard APIs, including the upcoming 3D game API for Windows 95. Criterion Software, the makers of RenderWare, have an alliance with Creative Labs to provide game developers with RenderWare Tools.

3D Blaster
Creative Labs
1901 McCarthy Boulevard
Milpitas, CA 95035
Phone: 408 428-2345 **Fax:** 408 432-6717
WWW: http://www.creative.com

Creative's boards that use the Glint architecture are being marketed under a series called the 3D Blaster board. This is clearly a move to lure the millions of Sound Blaster owners to this board. As noted above, the actual game version of the Glint chip was co-developed by both Creative Labs and 3D Labs.

The 3D games chip used on 3D Blaster has been developed exclusively for use by Creative, and provides highly interactive, texture-mapped 3D graphics at a price-point suitable for consumer products.

Creative Labs licensed Criterion's RenderWare device driver for the 3D Blaster graphics accelerator and will make this driver available to the game developer community. That driver will allow any game developed with RenderWare to be accelerated by Creative's 3D Blaster.

Creative also runs a special developers' program that will keep you up to date on their APIs and their Soundblaster and 3D Blaster products. Membership provides you with discounts on Creative products. To apply for registered status, complete the Developer Application form available on Creative's Web site or call Creative's FaxBack system at 408 428-2389 and request document # 4500.

The NVidia Chipset and NVidia-Derived Boards

NVidia Chipset
NVidia Corporation
1226 Tiros Way
Sunnyvale, CA 94086
Phone: 408 720-6100 **Fax:** 408 720-6111
WWW: http://www.nvidia.com

While the Creative/Glint approach focuses solely on pushing the overall graphical and 3D graphical performance, NVidia has focused on providing a total multimedia chip that offers enhanced graphical performance coupled with sound capabilities.

This chip and the derived boards (being primarily pushed by Diamond) are of importance and interest to game developers because Sega recently selected the NVidia chip as the hardware required for its cartridge games ported to the PC platform. Certainly a company that warrants that kind of specific interest from Sega deserves attention.

Their main chip, NV1/STG2000, which was co-developed by NVidia and French electronics giant, Thomson, combines multimedia, video acceleration, and 3D graphics functionality. The chip offers realtime photorealistic 3D graphics, full-motion video with special effects, and concurrent wavetable audio, GUI acceleration, and enhanced game port performance. A whole lot of performance! Let's take a closer look.

The chip can accelerate 2D and 3D graphics at 1,280×1,024 with 65,000 colors. It also accelerates video formats, including MPEG CinePak, using hardware scaling, horizontal and vertical interpolation, and interframing. Video texture mapping at up to 30 frames per second is also supported.

From a 3D perspective, the chip is great with curved surfaces and provides perspective correction, many surface and lighting effects, and good overall polygon support.

The wavetable audio is 16-bit and uses a full 350 Mips audio engine supporting 32 panned mono voices and 50 stereo channels. Samples are stored inside RAM, not ROM, a nice touch.

Sega's endorsement shows this is a full-fledged multimedia solution. Developers writing specifically for this chip will find a complete system to work within and take advantage of. Those applications using DirectDraw and other standard APIs should also be able to give consumers of the NVidia boards enhanced performance without too much work.

The main boards featuring the NVidia chip will be coming from Diamond Multimedia Systems, a longtime graphic board and multimedia upgrade kit manufacturer.

Diamond Edge 3D
Diamond Multimedia Systems, Inc.
2880 Junction Avenue
San Jose, CA 95134
Phone: 408 325-7000 **Fax:** 408 325-7070
WWW: http://www.diamondmm.com

The Diamond Edge 3D comes in two major flavors: One is based on Thomson's STG2000 version of the NVidia architecture and is sold in 1 MB and 2 MB versions; the other is based on the NV1 model and is available in 2 MB and 4 MB VRAM versions.

Diamond has lined up over 200 developers to make products for and compatible with their boards. Sega's deal is with NVidia directly, but I suspect that means Sega's products will work with *all* compatible boards.

The board's capabilities are identical to those of the chip, but of special note is an 8-channel digital game port with 13-bit sampling resolution. Sega is making its joysticks and other peripherals compatible with this port, which is driven by the built-in support within the NVidia chipset.

Diamond says the board is optimized for Windows 95, with complete support for all of Microsoft's Direct APIs, including DirectDraw, 3D-DDI/Direct3D, DirectSound, DirectInput, and SurroundVideo.

Diamond offers three developer support programs: Solitaire, Marquis, and Clarity. Solitaire is aimed at hobbyists and enthusiasts and has no annual fee. You receive quarterly developer news, forum assistance, SDKs at a discount, and evaluation units (at a discount) of Diamond products.

Marquis costs $950 annually and is good for smaller developers. It provides free SDKs, cheap evaluation units, developer hardware discounts, 35 percent off their developer conference registration, and developer telephone assistance.

The top of the line program, Clarity, will set you back $1850 each year. This program is aimed at hardcore developers (those doing NVidea development). In addition to the items mentioned previously, you also get free admission to their developer conference as well as free access to two special support suites, including developer intensive groups, priority technical support, confidential FTP sites, and more.

The MPACT Chipset

MPACT Chipset
Chromatic Research
Phone: 415 254-1600
WWW: http://www.mpact.com

This product was released as I finished up this section. (Although major cooperatives like the Diamond/NVidea or Creative Labs/3D Labs alliances have popped up, you can certainly expect as much in the future.)

This chipset is much like the NVidia chipset because it combines many multimedia functions on one chip. This is truly an all-in-one solution as it provides integrated video, 2D and 3D graphics acceleration, plus audio, fax/modem, and much more.

The chip supports Windows 95 APIs and once boards start showing up, you can expect this chipset to go head to head with the NVidea chip.

The Apple Solution

Apple QuickDraw 3D Accelerator Card
Apple Computer, Inc.
1 Infinite Loop
Cupertino, CA 95014
Phone: 408 996-1010
WWW: http://product.info.apple.com/qd3d/QD3D.HTML

Apple has its own 3D API which has its own 3D accelerator card. The Apple QuickDraw 3D accelerator card is a PCI card that can accelerate QuickDraw 3D graphics up to twelve times normal rates. In fact, you can actually use multiple cards to increase the performance—in this case, two cards are better than one!

General 3D Game Resources

I have found a load of excellent resources—both reading materials and Web sites—that will let you in on everything 3D game programming has to offer.

Computer Graphics: Principles and Practice, 2nd Edition by J.D. Foley, A. van Dam, S.K. Feinder, J.F. Hughes (Addison-Wesley 1990; ISBN 0-201-12110-7)

This is considered the bible of 3D graphics by almost every programmer in existence. It's a huge textbook of everything and anything that has to do with 3D graphics programming. It's perhaps the most-often-cited book in all of 3D graphics.

Zen of Graphics Programming by Michael Abrash (Coriolis Group Books, 1995; ISBN 1-883-57708-X)

Michael Abrash is one of the most popular writers and graphics expert, covering topics on graphics, assembly language, and code optimization. Although he previously worked for Microsoft, he was lured away by Id Software to work on their upcoming release Quake. This book is a compilation of much of his work to-date on realtime graphics, and contains a complete version of his X-Sharp 3D graphics library.

The code is very clear and Abrash explains things in a manner that all technical writers should aspire to. A new edition of this classic work is scheduled to be published in the Spring of 1996.

Taking Flight by Christopher D. Watkins and Stephen Marenka (M&T Books, 1994; ISBN 1-55851-384-1)

This book covers a lot of the basics that go into creating a very simple 3D flight simulator. If you're an absolute beginner, this book offers a good starting place.

Flights of Fantasy by Christopher Lampton (Waite Group Press, 1993; ISBN 1-878739-18-2)

This was the first of what became a slew of game programming books. This basic text covers DOS VGA programming and 3D graphics, culminating in the creation of a simple 3D flight simulator. Much has been printed since then and the book is now dated, but it's a wonderful read, especially for its excellent explanations of the basic math behind basic 3D graphics.

Brian Hook's 3D Graphics Book List
`http://cadserv.cadlab.vt.edu/bohn/text_files/3D_books.4.21`

Brian Hook has probably read every book there is about 3D graphics. And he has something to say about every one of them. If you're looking for the Leonard Maltin of 3D graphic book reviews, look no further.

BSP Tree Sites
`http://www.dcs.qmw.ac.uk/~mel/BSP.html`
`http://www.qualia.com/bspfaq/`
`http://www.ddj.com/ddj/1995/1995.07/dwyer.htm`
`ftp://ftp.mv.com/pub/ddj/1995/1995.cpp/asc.zip`

BSP trees are an essential component to 3D graphics to help speed up the drawing of complex 3D images. They were used in Doom and are being used in products like the upcoming Quake. The above referenced Web sites are excellent resources for finding out more about this 3D graphics technology.

3D Graphics FAQ
`file://ftp.csh.rit.edu/pub/3dfaq/`

Take a look at this comprehensive Internet FAQ, which covers a lot of ground on 3D graphics.

3D Graphic Accelerators FAQ

http://www.cs.columbia.edu/~bm/3dcards/3d-cards1.html
http://www.cs.columbia.edu/~bm/3dcards/3d-cards2.html

Maintained by Blair MacIntyre this site is an excellent source of information on everything in the 3D graphics card scene. While it focuses on high-end boards of less significance to game developers, its coverage is very complete and does include the lower-end consumer boards like NVidea.

Siggraph

http://www.siggraph.org/

Siggraph is the ACM (Association of Computing Machinery) special interest group on 3D graphics. This organization, which also sponsors the Siggraph conference and publishes the various Siggraph journals, is a key outlet for major work on realtime 3D graphics. Topics cover the cutting edge of university and corporate research into 3D graphics.

Their Web site serves as a comprehensive resource to find out about the organization, its publications, and the Siggraph conference, and allows you access to their archives.

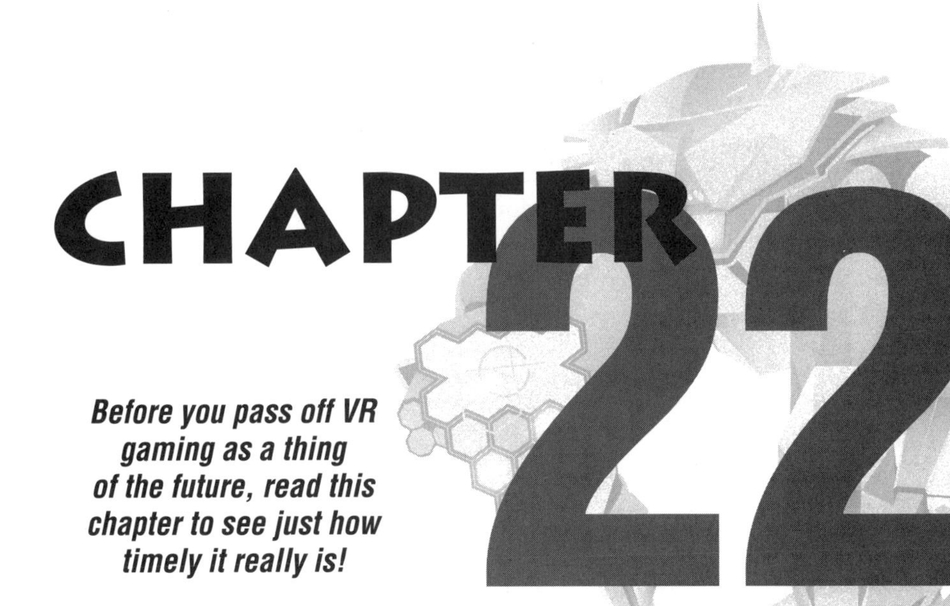

Before you pass off VR gaming as a thing of the future, read this chapter to see just how timely it really is!

Virtual Reality Games: An Overview

Virtual reality (VR) has finally come of age, and game developers are finally starting to take this "futuristic" form of gaming seriously. Although developers have known all along that virtual reality can bring exciting features to games, they have been more focused on creating technology that can sell to consumers. As you're probably aware, the hardware costs and processing technology for immersive VR have been prohibitive until recently.

But now a lot of VR technology is nearing consumer price points, and consumers are eating up this fun and exciting technology. Already, one major startup, Zombie Interactive, is leading the charge to be the first major PC-oriented VR software development house.

While the push to put VR technology into homes is just beginning, VR is already quite established in other parts of the gaming industry. Immersive VR theme parks, such as Mech Warrior, Sega's VR Center at the Luxor Hotel in Las Vegas, and Disney's Aladdin Flying Carpet VR ride are becoming big businesses. By spreading out the costs, these centers can actually afford the large hardware capital required to build state-of-the art immersive VR. In addition, this business is only a precursor of some of the amazing technology and entertainment that will someday grace our homes.

Let's look at the entire realm of VR game technology and examine the opportunities that currently exist and those that are paving the VR path of the future.

Developing PC-VR Games Software

Creating PC VR games isn't radically that different from creating other types of 3D graphics games. Of course if you plan to go all the way and create a full body suit game or a major location-based VR center, you will have your work cut out for you.

But developing a title to run on a PC and work with the current set of 3D HMDs (*Head Mounted Displays*) or 3D glasses (or perhaps a glove) shouldn't be as difficult as you might think. Programming 3D graphics is getting easier by the day, and specialty hardware companies are working furiously to provide good development tools and support.

This isn't to say that you can create a cutting edge VR title by taking your basic 3D game and reworking a few things. While a few first wave VR titles will be little more than basic 3D games, eventually companies will create games that really are unique to the genre.

A Few Key Design Issues

The most radical development problems often arise in the design stage. Display hardware and VR input hardware alone provide for some definite design challenges. For example, if a user wears a VR HMD, how does he or she use the keyboard? And what about Joysticks; do you only support regular joysticks or perhaps some sort of 3D joystick like the Spaceball Avenger?

In addition, the display capabilities of HMDs, while amazing, are not as crystal clear as a 17-inch Sony Trintron VGA monitor. Especially with fast graphics, head panning can cause motion blur, which in turn causes problems like VR sicknesses.

VR Sickness and Dismal VR Hardware Failures

VR opens up a whole can of worms when it comes to the physiological and even psychological effects games can have on people. Unlike other passive mediums, game violence, or any action for that matter, are initiated by the decisions, actions, emotions, and so on of the player. The more we immerse players in realistic-like environments, the more we blur the lines between real life and virtual life, and problems are bound to occur.

Sega, who is very involved in the location-based VR scene, was developing a home based HMD VR system. The system never materialized despite the efforts of developers at Sega. Sega reportedly did tests and commissioned a study on the long-term effects of HMD-VR on people. They found that many players were getting very disoriented and sick.

Hasbro, the venerable toy giant, was working with key developers at the David Sarnoff research center to create a major VR console device that went down in flames in 1995 and cost them $39 million. One of the major problems was due to sickness and health effects caused by the VR device. Companies like these are especially worried that some 12-year-old will fall and hurt him or herself after playing a VR game. Imagine what this sort of hysteria would do for a company's stock prices.

Programming PC-VR

For the most part, PC-VR is first about programming cutting edge 3D graphics. Mostly this involves working with the types of 3D APIs I profiled in Chapter 21. Additionally, you might want to work with the 3D sound APIs and technologies that were profiled in Chapter 14.

For the VR component, you'll need to contact the major VR hardware vendors and say the magic phrase—"Tell me about your development kit." Many of the hardware developers who create 3D glasses and input devices offer help to developers who are

writing VR software. They especially like game companies because best-selling games can really give their hardware sales a shot in the arm.

The first thing to do if you're either thinking about making an existing game compliant with VR hardware or developing a completely new idea is to call one of the companies listed in this chapter and find out:

What assistance they can offer you. (Most of the companies, if not all of them have some sort of developer program.) This can include full-fledged development kits and programs with tons of technical help and customized drivers, or it may be as little as some helpful lines of C code.

What special software drivers or support code they have. Not all VR HMDs or input devices are created equal and some may have special features you'll want to support.

What development partnerships they support. Many of the HMD companies have teamed up with other 3D API companies to offer discounts and complete packages. Check to see what other game companies the VR hardware companies are working with.

Keep Experimenting

Unless you are simply adapting an existing title to support VR features, you'll probably need to allocate a bit of time for experimenting. Zombie, the only major startup in the PC-VR game scene, is staffed by developers who've been working on the cutting edge of VR application development for years. Thus, they've been doing the work you need to begin doing now.

Trying to plunge full force into VR can be a big mistake. You'll need to really get up to speed with the products offered by different companies and you'll need to learn about all of the product's features and limitations. Now is a good time to get started and when this technology really goes mainstream, you'll be ready to capitalize on it.

Hardware Visuals: HMDs

The heart and sole of VR is the *Head Mounted Display* or HMD. Two main types of HMDs are available: those with motion tracking and those without. Obviously, the more glamorous development for HMDs involves motion tracking, but motion tracking hardware is more expensive and can cause problems like motion sickness. We will discuss some of those issues later.

All HMDs incorporate LCD displays to present a field of view directly to the player. The screens are the same as those used in small LCD televisions or camcorders. The average resolution of these displays is around 320×240, or just better than low-resolution VGA graphics, and color on most hardware is limited to 256 or 8 bits. In addition, the resolution or dot pitch of the viewing hardware—the LCD screens themselves—isn't very good, so rendered art will lose detail; in fact, text is somewhat unreadable. Although close-ups can produce pixelating effects on graphics, which is intensified by the LCD hardware employed, the specs conform somewhat nicely to that of many low-resolution VGA games like Doom or Descent. Game developers should easily be able to overcome these graphical constraints.

Several major PC- and console-based VR HMDs are currently available. You should note, however, that while most HMDs are built using the same technology—and, in many cases, the same components—there is a discernible image quality difference among all the units. I suggest that you inspect the systems, and see what you can do to optimize your product's appearance on each system.

Seventh Sense
Virtual Entertainment Systems, Inc.
555 White Plains Road
Tarytown, NY 10591
Phone: 914 631-9400 **Fax:** 914 631-9487

This system works specifically with PCs and has a single screen setup. The unit is capable of displaying 100,000 pixels and can form a 70 degree field of vision. It incorporates stereo sound and connects graphically via its own card. It sells for approximately $499.

Virtual i*glasses
Virtual i-O
1000 Lenora Street, Suite 600
Seattle, WA 98121
Phone: 800 646-3759
WWW: http://www.vio.com/

i*glasses look like a pair of sunshades for the year 2040 after the ozone has been depleted. The glasses are sold in two styles: one with head tracking and one without. They are even available in a tortoise shell variety.

The image quality is top-notch and is optimized for NTSC video display, which, while producing nice pictures, reduces the field of vision to 30 degrees. The display is made up of two active matrix LCDs and can display 138,000 pixels. Stereo sound is also incorporated. The non-head tracking unit costs $599 and the head tracking unit costs $799.

CyberMaxx
VictorMaxx
501 Lake Cook Road, Suite 100
Deerfield, IL, 60015
Phone: 708 267-0007

This is VictorMaxx's second HMD entry for the home-PC virtual reality market. It's relatively inexpensive at $599. The Cybermaxx features two displays each with 120,000 color pixel active matrix LCD capabilities, and has a 60 degree field of view.

VFX1 Head Mounted System
Forte Technologies, Inc.
1057 East Henrietta Road
Rochester, NY 14623
Phone: 716 427-8595 **Fax:** 716 427-8595
WWW: http://www.fortech.com

The VFX1 Head Mounted System (HMS) brings the next generation of PC virtual reality to the market today. It is a true integrated VR headset with 3D color imaging, 3D stereo sound, and 3 axis head tracking. The VFX1 HMS, which has the widest field of vision at 80 degrees, sets a standard design for head mounted systems by providing an integration of technology and comfort in an affordable, cost-effective package.

Although this system is the most expensive, with an SRP of $899, it offers more than all the other systems currently available. You get what you pay for! Figure 22.1 shows the VFX1 HMD.

Figure 22.1 The VFX1 HMD display.

Polarized Glasses 3D Solutions

A cheaper alternative to 3D immersive head mounted displays consists of a fairly simple technology of 3D shutter glasses that produce a 3D depth effect into monitors when worn. The advantage of this type of 3D display technology is primarily cost. Shutter glasses can run for around $200 or even less and thus are far more mass market than their full HMD counterparts. Shutter glasses can also be combined with an outside head tracking device to enable that capability as well.

Right now a number of companies, such as Logitech, Reveal, and others, are releasing 3D glasses for the market. They're also working with developers like Id, Apogee, Trisoft, and others to bring out versions of popular 3D games that work with the glasses. The glasses offer some cool effects for the price and could become a nice mass market item.

Here are some manufacturer contacts for 3D shutter glasses. Reveal was especially helpful in responding to my inquires.

Reveal Computer Products
6045 Variel Avenue
Woodland Hills, CA 91367
Phone: 818 702-6564 **Fax:** 818 340-2379
WWW: http://www.reveal.com

Reveal is launching a pair of shutter glasses soon. Their Web site is a good place to check out their developments. They offer a developer program for obtaining a set of glasses, demos, and code examples to help you put their product to use.

Logitech
Moulin Du Choc
CH-1122 Romanel-sur-Morges
Switzerland
Phone: +41-(21)-863-51-11 **Fax:**+41-(21)-863-53-11

Logitech makes a set of 3D glasses. I saw them in use (it was hard not to) at the huge party they threw at last year's CGDC. Contact Logitech for more information.

StereoGraphics
2171 East Francisco Boulevard
San Rafael, CA 94901
Phone: 415 459-4500 **Fax:** 415 459-3020

StereoGraphics is perhaps the leading supplier of 3D shutter graphics. They make both glasses and a monitor mounted tracking device. Their main products are the CrystalEyes and SimulEyes VR stereo-viewing systems. StereoGraphics is also teaming up as an OEM for some other companies.

Figure 22.2 Stereographics 3D Shutter Glasses without the monitor mounted head tracking system.

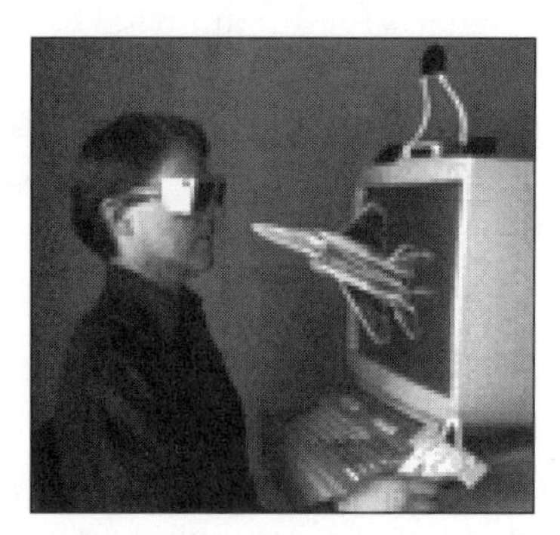

Figure 22.3 Stereographics 3D Shutter Glasses with the monitor mounted head tracking system.

StereoGraphics produces versions of their products for every computer imaginable from PCs to SGI workstations. Figure 22.2 and 22.3 show Stereographics 3D Shutter Glasses with and without the monitor mounted head tracking system.

VR Input Devices

VR hardware doesn't end with the viewing component. Indeed, perhaps some of the most innovative hardware involved in VR is in the input and feedback devices.

VR Data Gloves

Perhaps the most famous of VR input devices is the data glove. There are two good sources of gloves and certainly more will become available soon. I'm especially enthused about the looming debut of the PC Powerglove, which will provide PC users with really cool but inexpensive data glove technology.

PC Powerglove
Abrams/Gentile Entertainment
WWW: http: //www.usa.net/age/PC.html
Email: pcpglove@ageinc.com

Remember the Mattel Powerglove for the Nintendo? It was an amazing (not to mention inexpensive) implementation of expensive VR glove technology. Unfortunately, with poor support from Mattel and limited specific games, the Mattel Powerglove didn't exactly break out of its niche existence (despite doing $80 million in business). However, as PC-based VR has grown, the designers at Abrams/Gentile Entertainment went back to the drawing board and have produced the PC Powerglove. This data glove offers six degrees of tracking, finger bend sensing, feedback sensors, and sweat sensors.

Abrams/Gentile plans to ship in the first quarter of 1996; however, you can contact the manufacturer now via the Web or email to get development kit details.

3Space Glove
3Space
1131 Steeles Ave. W., Suite 1406
Toronto, Ontario M2R 3W8 Canada
Phone: 416 661-8425
WWW: http://www.io.org/~3space/glove.htm

This company makes a couple of 3D VR data glove products, including a modification of the original Mattel Powerglove. You supply the Mattel Powerglove and they'll send you a conversion kit to make it work with the PC.

A Survey of Glove-Based Input

Next time you're surfing, jump over to *http://www.cs.monash.edu.au/~dcron/glove/glove.html* to get an overview of VR glove technologies. You'll find an extensive bibliography that points you to major papers and articles on glove-based technologies.

VR Joysticks and Other Inputs

Data gloves are not the only input devices available to VR gamers. This section details everything from the "joystickesque" spaceball to the VR vest.

Spaceball Avenger
Spacetec IMC Corp.
600 Suffolk St.
Lowell, MA 01854
Phone: 508 970-0330 **Fax:** 508 970-0199

When computer workstations first started giving desktop access to really cool 3D graphic creations, users needed a quick way to move objects around in a 3D space (six-way movement). Designers came up with the "spaceball" input device, which has become the "joystick" of the 3D age. The spaceball allows users to pull and push it in any direction, including up and down.

As consumer VR emerges, games with intricate 3D worlds will require uninhibited six-way movement. Spacetec has jumped on the opportunity to bring the spaceball concept into the game world, creating an actual 3D joystick (see Figure 22.4).

Batter Up! and PC Golf
Sports Sciences
Phone: 216 963-0660
WWW: http://www.sport-sci.com

This company makes two impressive sport-oriented VR devices. Batter Up! is a VR baseball bat that measures the force and direction of your swing, and can translate the calculations into a set of numbers that allow it to interface with many major baseball games.

PC Golf uses a 26 inch VR golf club. As with the VR bat, the club measures the force and direction of your swing and then translates the calculations for use in games like PGA Tour from Electronic Arts.

Aura Interactor — VR Vest
Aura Systems Inc.
2335 Alaska Avenue
El Segundo, CA 90245
Phone: 800 909-2872

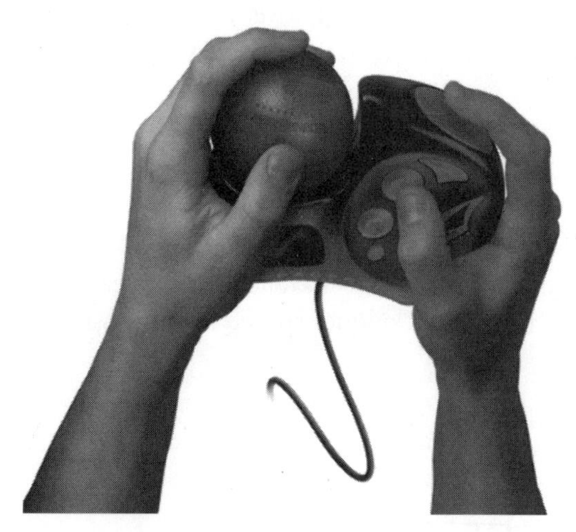

Figure 22.4 Spacetec's 3D joystick.

This vest is a simple idea, but one with cool implications (although reviews are not too good). This vest plugs into your sound card and when an explosion-like sound is played, the whole vest vibrates and the explosion erupts from an encased speaker on the vest. Warning, do not play Terminal Velocity or Doom with this vest! <grin>

ThunderSeat — VR Seat
ThunderSeat Technologies
6330 Arizona Circle
Los Angeles, CA 90045
Phone: 800 884-8633

I used to think flight simulator fans who bought flight sticks were a bit on the nutty side. I'm not sure what I'll think when they buy this wild contraption. ThunderSeat is a complete flight seat with all the fixings, and built-in speakers and sub-woofers.

For true immersive VR games to emerge in the homes, much of the appealing cabinetry and "control" design that makes location-based games so great will need to be designed for home use. The ThunderSeat is, perhaps, only the beginning of more immersive game control environments.

Total Control Joystick
Total Control
WWW: http://198.30.134.10/virtual/

Total Control is a special VR joystick device that allows for six-way movement.

VR Resources

As I mentioned earlier, VR is not just a wacky futuristic idea of B movies any more. It is a reality. I've found a multitude of resources available to help you understand this new gaming field.

VR Locations and Rides

Despite the great emergence of home based PC-VR technology, the real action is still in the arcades, VR location centers, and theme parks implementing cool state of the art VR games. Just as it was important (and still is important) to look at the arcades for VR implementation ideas, VR developers should also check out the location based VR centers to see where the home based products will be headed.

In addition, location based VR entertainment is becoming a big multibillion dollar business. Thus, it may provide some great opportunities for you more readily than you think. Just looking at the investments made by Sega, Disney, Dreamworks, SGI, and dozens of smaller companies as well as looking at the rate at which cybercafe's, arcades, VR centers, and other outlets are opening up, you'll see that VR games are exploding.

Atlantis VR Centers

http://vr-atlantis.com/~atlantis/index.html

This is by far the single most amazing site for VR games. It covers an immense amount of information on location based entertainment. I thought of writing a ton of information about LBE centers and such but once I saw this Web site I realized I could write a whole book about it.

Books and Magazines

Here are some of the better general-interest titles available. Most of the VR books I've seen, however, don't provide good coverage on game development or offer great practical advice.

The Official VR World VR Explorer Edited by Sandra K. Helsel (Meckler Media, 1996; ISBN 1-56884-704-1)

From the editor of *VR World* Magazine comes this soon-to-be released book that will explore the applications of VR as it exists today.

Virtual Reality Systems by John Vince (Addison-Wesley, 1995; ISBN 0-201-87687-6)

This book covers a lot of fundamental VR components, including the math/algorithms behind it, emerging technologies, and VR graphics.

VR Bibliographies
http://www.cms.dmu.ac.uk/~cph/VRbib.html
http://www.hitl.washington.edu/projects/knowledge_base/elec.html
These two locations offer links or abstracts on a ton of written information about the VR scene. If you're looking to catch up on a lot of the research done on VR in the academic or private home brew scene, check in here.

***VR World* Magazine**
Meckler Media, Inc.
20 Ketchum Street
Westport, CT, 06880
Phone: 203 226-6967
WWW: http://www.mecklerweb.com/mags/vr/vrhome.htm
Subscription: $29.00/yr **Newsstand:** $4.95 **Publishes:** Bimonthly **Pages:** 100

VR World Magazine is the leading general-interest publication for the VR scene. You'll find a lot of excellent resources and articles that focus on VR games. Mark Long and Joanna Alexander of Zombie Interactive also write a regular column on VR games. Each year, they publish an issue that provides a complete wrap-up of VR resources.

CyberEdge Journal
1 Gate Six Road, Suite G
Sausalito, CA 94965
Phone: 415 331-3343 **Fax:** 415 331-3643
WWW: http://pomo.nbn.com/home/www/6.html
Subscription: $129.00/yr* **Newsstand:** N/A **Publishes:** Bimonthly

CyberEdge Journal like *VR World* covers cutting-edge consumer- and business-oriented VR news, articles, and reviews. (* $249 if ordering as a business)

VR NEWS
P.O. Box 2515
London N4 4JW, UK
Phone: +44 181-292-1498 **Fax:** +44 181-292-1346

I couldn't track down all the information on this London-based newsletter/magazine. I did find out, however, that it was launched in 1991 and has an average monthly readership of around 10,000 in some 40 countries.

More Online Sites

Take a look at these sites next time you find yourself on the Web. There's a lot of information for you to ingest on this emerging technology.

Virtual Reality Entertainment Corp.
`http://ns1.win.net/~vre/`

Created by the maker of VR arcade games, stop by this site and see the latest and greatest Virtual Reality Entertainment Corp. has to offer.

Gravity Corp.
`http://www.gravity.com/`

This company, which concentrates on VR games and other applications, was formed from the remnants of the breakup of VPL Research of the original pioneering companies in the VR scene.

Antares Virtual Reality Systems
`http://www.dnai.com/~antares/antares/edu.html`

Antares has a couple of unique VR hardware devices you might find interesting. All of their offerings are detailed here.

Aladdin VR Ride Article
`http://vr-atlantis.com/~atlantis/vr_systems_html/aladdin_article1.html`

Disney's Aladdin ride is a wild VR system that utilizes state-of-the-art SGI graphics hardware, awesome Disney artwork, and a cool interface mechanism. While you have

to go to Disney World to actually experience this marvel, you can read about it here and avoid the crowds.

Virtual Reality Resources
http://ruby.ils.unc.edu/houseman/commercial.html

This is a very nice site that lists all kinds of links and resources for VR developers.

Zombie Games

Located in Seattle, Washington, Zombie Inc. is a new virtual reality (VR) entertainment company founded in 1994 by Joanna Alexander and Mark Long—both pioneers in the field of virtual reality. They formed Zombie to apply their VR research and development expertise to the design of VR games for the next generation 32-bit/64-bit systems.

Zombie is a next generation game designer developing some of the first commercially available virtual reality games for home use. Last fall they released Locus and Ice and Fire, two PC-VR games featuring 3D graphics, VR headset compatibility, 3D audio, and multi-player networking. One of their cooler VR games, Locus is a VR sports game sort of like hockey/soccer. Figure 22.5 shows an example of Lotus in action. The game features network support for up to nine players (three teams of three) and fast game play. You can find a demo of the game at the company's Web site.

Zombie, Inc.
114 1/2 First Avenue, South Studio 3
Seattle, WA 98104
Phone: 206 623-9655 **Fax:** 206 623-9714
WWW: http://www.zombie.com/

CHAPTER 23

Multiplayer games are the future and the infrastructure for these games is rapidly coming into place.

Network, Multiplayer, and Online Game Development

Among all the trends out there today none is probably hotter than network, multiplayer, and online games. Almost every major game now comes with some sort of multiplayer option and the entire online industry is rushing to offer major multiplayer games.

In this chapter, I'll provide you with a basic rundown of the types of multiplayer games that you can create and discuss their implementations through modem hookups or by using the Internet/Web or commercial online services. I'll also provide you with a discussion of the resources—tools, books, Web sites, and others—to help you master the development of one of these game types.

Modem-to-Modem Games

With two machines and two modems, players can directly hook up long distance to play the same game. The modems send information back and forth and the game is able to display the actions of both players as if they were sitting right next to each other. The ability to use a modem opened the door wide for the field of multiplayer games.

For the most part, developers creating these types of games hard-code the interface and protocols themselves without the use of a toolkit. Sound tough? Don't worry, writing a modem routine is pretty standard fare. Take a look at some of the books that I have listed in this chapter.

Software and Reading Resources

As I just mentioned, there are a couple of great books on serial communications programming. I've also found a really cool package from Sirius Software that allows you to access hundreds of multiplayer games. Let's take a look at that package first.

Game Connection
Sirius Publishing
7320 East Butherus Dr., Suite 100
Scottsdale, AZ 85260
Phone: 602 951-3288 **Fax:** 602 951-3884

Game Connection is a neat product that allows BBS operators to offer multiplayer games using a modem on their BBSs. Essentially it allows for normal modem-to-modem games to be played via an intermediary server—in this case, the BBS. If you are interested in uploading your own game to a BBS using this service, check Sirius' BBS to see if it's compatible with their Game Connection package.

Game Connection runs as a major BBS/Worldgroup DLL with *no additional* hardware required. Game Connection allows an unlimited number of concurrent games to be played and the number of players in any one game is limited only by the game itself and the number of incoming BBS lines. Game Connection has a built-in teleconference feature that allows users to chat before they start a game or while they are waiting for another user to enter or exit.

Serial Protocols by Tim Kientzle (Coriolis Group Books, 1995; ISBN 1-883577-20-9)

This book provides a thorough treatment of major serial protocols and it shows you how to create your own hybrid protocols (great for games). A disk, complete with source code, is included.

C Programmer's Guide to Serial Communcations by Joe Campbell (SAMS, 1995)

Now in its second edition, this all-in-one handbook is a complete guide to serial communications programming in C.

Network Games

A network game is a product that operates as a multiplayer game over a Local Area Network (LAN). Several types of LAN protocols exist, so you'll need to choose a couple of popular ones to support. Novell Netware IPX, Microsoft's NetBios, and now their Exchange Client networking are the most commonly found.

Software and Reading Resources

Here are some of the better resources available to help you add network capabilities to your games. I've also included information on a great book devoted to network gaming.

NetNOW!
Human Machines Interfaces, Inc.
30 East Broadway, Suite 180
Eugene, OR 97401
Phone: 503 687-6509 **Fax:** 503 687-6479

From the folks who bring you the Sound Operating System comes this multiplayer library that provides IPX and NetBIOS support for adding network gaming abilities to your products.

Features include 32-bit protected mode support, players limited only by the network itself, lots of sample code, complete C source code, and royalty-free distribution. What more could you ask for?

DirectPlay
One Microsoft Way
Microsoft Corp.
Redmond, WA, 98052
Phone: 206 882-8080
WWW: http://www.microsoft.com/MSDN

DirectPlay is part of the Microsoft Windows 95 Game SDK, which itself is part of the Microsoft Developers Network Level II CD-ROM (see Chapter 16). DirectPlay is essentially a universal networking game protocol for Windows 95.

DirectPlay will help you handle local area network game programming as well as online remote server game programming.

Visual Basic 4 Network Gaming Adventure Set by David Allen (Coriolis Group Books, 1996; ISBN 1-883577-32-3)

I highly recommend that you check out this excellent book. While it primarily explores VB4 programming, you will also find some excellent help in programming and designing Windows-networked games using Microsoft's DirectPlay technology. But the book is more than just a guide to DirectPlay. In 750 jam-packed pages it covers an amazing amount of technical network programming issues for game developers including LANs, WANs, OLE game servers, remote-access servers, Network DDE, and more. This is the most in-depth book on network game programming by far.

Remote-Access Server Games

A remote-access server game has two components: a server product and a client product. These can be configured as a local area network setup or as a dial-in wide area network (WAN). The client is built to interface with specific server software. Users download or purchase at retail the client software and then dial in direct or via an Internet connection to a specific server that runs the server software.

The server takes in all the client information and sends out responses such as other player locations. A good example of this type of multiplayer game is Id's forthcoming Quake.

With Quake, Id is also including an entire offline game system in their client software. Using this setup, users can play the game offline against the computer or dial up various servers to play against human opponents.

What's unique about Quake is that Id will be licensing (or distributing freely) the server software to independent server operators, which gives the operators the ability to really customize their Quake worlds (much like many do with their own Doom levels). With this approach, users might find an entirely different customized Quake world to play in each time they dial up—a dynamically changing community concept.

TCP/IP and Winsock Programming

Most remote-access server games work over the Internet, which uses the TCP/IP protocol. The TCP/IP protocol is the main low-level communications "language" of the Internet, and while it was invented years ago it has held up well among all the advancements of the Internet. With Windows and other programs, you run a program called a sockets layer, which helps you work commands from your programs into TCP/IP for transmission over the Internet. As far as socket programs go, the most major one to know about is the Windows version called Winsock.

Here are a few resources worth looking into.

Developing for the Internet with Winsock **by Dave Roberts** (Coriolis Group, 1995; ISBN 1-883577-42-X)

Dave Roberts, author of *PC Game Programming EXplorer*, has written another informative book. This book covers everything you need to know about how to create Windows applications that communicate over the Internet. In this book you'll find numerous pages of source code examples written in C and C++. Dave Roberts has an immense talent for explaining highly technical topics so that they can be readily understood.

Distinct TCP/IP
Distinct Software
Phone: 408 366-2101 **Fax:** 408 366-0153
WWW: http://www.distinct.com

This company sells a line of powerful Internet programming tools for everything from Visual Basic to Pascal to C/C++. The products include large manuals, tons of sample code, small, fast DLLs, and Visual Basic-compatible OCXs, and much more.

Custom APIs and the Emerging Game-Optimized Networks

A little later on I'll talk briefly about what is looking to be the major forums for online remote-access gaming. There are several companies, including DWango and the ImagiNation Network, that are emerging as providers of these services and of the telecommunications networks needed for developers to publish online games. Each of these companies is building a special game-optimized national network, as well as the custom APIs that developers will use to make their games work on those networks.

These companies will also be providing the network support, and take care of billing and other infrastructure items you definitely don't want to deal with. (Just imagine trying to talk little Billy out of suicide because someone just killed his 30th level fighter in your RPG title—you laugh, but it's happened.)

If you think you'd like to develop games using this approach, see the *Gaming-Specific Networks* section later in this chapter for more details.

Native Web Games

As the Web has grown not only in users but in the ability to deliver rich graphical, audio, and video content, its ability to be a platform for games is quickly becoming a reality.

Certainly we won't see games like Doom running as a native Web application in the near future, but already I've seen crossword games, trivia games, an adventure game, and other less-intensive projects done as native Web apps. The Web offers some very lucrative possibilities.

For example, companies looking to draw customers to their Web site may hire game developers to create cool games to run on their sites as a bonus for their visitors. So let's take a look at some of the major Web languages and technologies that over the next two years will be used to produce interactive games on the Web.

The Web Browsers

While Internet-based games using interactive Web browsers are in their infancy, this area is growing fast. The ability to access a game on demand and interact with dynamically changing content, not to mention potential multiplayer situations, makes even the rudimentary Web-based games an intriguing development (and one this author is investigating substantially).

Surprisingly, when I first started this book there really wasn't much to speak of in the world of Web-based games. This was due partially to my own ignorance about what was available, but mostly because Web-based technology is an ever-evolving process. Today, as this book goes to print, there is a lot to report on.

Both Microsoft and Netscape are releasing incredible new tools and browsers with significant power to enable a lot of cool interactive content, especially in the area of game development. The key components of these tools are the browsers themselves. What was once a war of many different browsers has boiled down to the Netscape 2.0 browser and Microsoft's Internet Explorer. Everyone else is just a bit player as far as I'm concerned.

Of the two, Netscape's 2.0 browser is the more advanced, having implemented extensive plug-in architecture, including MacroMedia's Shockwave player, JavaScript, and Java, Sun's dynamic Web language. Microsoft says it will catch up quickly, and that is a pledge no one takes lightly. Expect a lot of leap frogging from both browsers.

Development Tools and Languages

In the early days of the Web, the only two real "languages" associated with it were HyperText Markup Language (HTML), which defined how pages looked, and CGI scripts, which were simple "backoffice" programs used for limited processing of Web interactions. In 1995, and now in 1996, an explosion of technology has lead to the availability or near availability of several major "Web/Internet" languages. Let's quickly explore each one and look at its potential as a Web-game authoring tool.

BlackBird (Internet Studio)
Microsoft Corporation
One Microsoft Way
Microsoft Corp.
Redmond, WA, 98052
Phone: 206 882-8080
WWW: http://www.microsoft.com

The original code name for this product was BlackBird. Recently, the name has been changed to Internet Studio. Unfortunately, no one knows one day to the next exactly what Microsoft is doing with this technology—not even Microsoft. Currently, Internet Studio is an authoring tool that Microsoft was originally developing to enable significant interactive content to be delivered on the Microsoft Network (MSN), Microsoft's own commercial online service. However, Microsoft has redeployed BlackBird as an Internet-based platform. Normally such a major change in logistics would cause serious headaches to the developers, but because MSN is based very closely on the TCP/IP network architecture that the Web itself is based on, the switch should be a piece of cake.

Internet Studio is a Windows 95-only product, and works using Microsoft's OLE object technology. Essentially, it treats OLE programs as distributed applets much like with Java (more information on Java in a moment). Internet Studio is also a page layout interface for designing forms and laying out objects and controls, much like Visual Basic.

Internet Studio isn't really a product I see being used for major arcade games, but for the odd Web-based game or non-intensive program, it might fit the bill.

Scribble
Microsoft Corporation
One Microsoft Way
Microsoft Corp.
Redmond, WA, 98052
Phone: 206 882-8080
WWW: http://www.microsoft.com

Scribble is an interesting product. Microsoft is, at the time I write this, still developing the full product, but basically Scribble is a next-generation MUD development product. MUDs, as we've already talked about, are text-based adventure games that

are played over the Internet. Scribble adds graphical abilities and other multimedia functions to what has traditionally been a text-based world.

Shockwave
MacroMedia Inc.
`http://www.macromedia.com`

Director has more lives than a cat. In this incarnation, MacroMedia has convinced Netscape and other browser makers to embed the Director playback engine directly into their browser software.

Now authors can embed Director programs into their Web sites and construct interactive games and other media for direct access by Web browsers.

Java
Sun Microsystems
`WWW: http://www.sun.com`

Of all the emerging Web development technologies, Sun Microsystems' Java promises to be the most exciting of all. Java is a complex language similar to C++ and is platform independent. Programs written in Java can run on any machine that has a Java interpreter layer available, which includes many machines at this point. Although Java, for obvious security reasons, does not give the programmer any direct access to any machine's hardware, it includes extensive programming flexibility and graphical capabilities. In the short time that Java has been available I've seen several dynamic apps, including a really well done crossword game, complete with nice graphics display and great interface.

The Web-Based Game Developer: DownTown Digital

One company to check out is New York's DownTown Digital (*http://www.dtd.com*). This startup, using AT&T for backing, has been creating native Web games for a while. Although they're a long way from Doom, I found their offerings to be pretty cool.

Right now they have several trivia games including my favorite, Two Minute Warning. Each game is completely Web based, includes cute but simple graphics (for fast loading of course!), and uses extensive CGI scripts to update the screen, track scores and high scores, as well as present questions to players and process responses.

DownTown Digital is interesting because they're working (quite well, I'd say) within the Web's limitations. Until giant fiber optic lines and cable modems become commonplace, the key to developing a successful native Web game will be in finding a way to make a fun game without pushing the Web to its breaking point.

Commercial Network Multiplayer Games

Commercial network games are similar to remote-server access games. The big difference here is that these games are sponsored by an online service. With an online service at the helm, the amount of multiple players is increased significantly (based on the service's higher bandwidth), and the hardware choices and programming practice is defined by the service and not by you as a developer.

What's strange about the online services is that for all their subscribers and all their money, they haven't exactly rolled out a major number of online games. Part of this probably has to do with the underlying network protocols they use (many of the older, more established networks aren't based on the easy-to-program TCP/IP protocol). Another reason is probably that is hasn't, until recently, been an especially worthwhile venture. For example, even though GE's Genie online service has had some of the most interesting and extensive online gaming offerings, they haven't been all that successful. Only in the past year or so have these services seen a surge in the number of game-playing members.

If you'd like to see further game development in the commercial online arena, I suggest that you contact the individual services. A word of caution: Each of the services listed in this section is now being deluged with requests and proposals about network games. Make sure you approach them in a professional manner; otherwise, you'll be wasting your time.

What It Means to Run a Major Multiplayer Game

One thing to understand is that multiplayer games take a lot more work to create and support than single player games. In fact, after a multiplayer game is released the work just starts. This is why the big commercial services and special gaming networks are stepping in. Running a major multiplayer game or gaming service requires:

- A billing structure and customer service operation
- A constant team of designers to update material
- Online moderators to help keep things from going out of hand (and they will—especially if you don't have moderators)
- A constant barrage of marketing and PR efforts to pull in new layers

- A technical telecommunications network across the country that holds together

Now you may be great at designing games, programming them, and maybe even updating them, but as you move into multiplayer technology, you'll need to decide who will moderate your networks, do the online billing and support, as well as develop the telecomunications network to support it all. And that's why you may need to think about hooking up with a company like CompuServe, Mpath, and TEN.

These companies also aren't just major service organizations. They're consultants and experts with the technical and design skills needed to make a successful multiplayer game work. Take the time at your next gaming conference to go to a few sessions that are sure to be held around the topic of large scale multiplayer gaming and you'll learn that multiplayer gaming is a universe all unto itself. Taking the time to team up with the companies that are leaders in the business will probably be the second most important thing you can do (besides developing your game itself).

CompuServe

WWW: http://www.compuserve.com

CompuServe is the oldest of the four big networks, and has had some great games available, most notably Sniper!, written by Steve Estvanik. (Steve frequents the Game Developer's Forum when he's not off on some exotic adventure in a far-off corner of the Earth.) Although CompuServe has been slow in jumping on the game bandwagon, don't expect that to last long. They've been working overtime to make sure they catch the other online services off guard in this arena.

Check out their Worlds Away (GO AWAY) forum, which finally debuted this fall. This is a project that originally started at LucasArts, then found its way to Fujitsu and now is on CompuServe. Customers download a full client front-end that runs over the CompuServe network. Users assume graphical personas (called Avatars) and they can walk around, play games, and interact graphically. This system doesn't offer any innovations in the way of gameplay, but the graphical presentation and some of the additions they are planning show that CompuServe is working hard to offer cutting-edge technology.

America Online

WWW: http://www.aol.com

At one conference I attended, word was that America Online (a billion dollar company) earns 50 percent of their revenue from chat groups. AOL won't confirm this, but they don't discount it either. The bottom line is that this network knows what online interaction means to their bottom line. In fact, AOL executives have gone on record saying they see games as the next major killer app for online services.

Toward those ends, AOL is expected to be a major developer—in conjunction with partner companies—of online games played both over the Internet and their service.

AOL also has set up a program specifically for new developers, called the "Greenhouse Project." This program is designed to help AOL recruit bright new talent to the online industry. While AOL works with major companies like Stormfront Studios (who did their Neverwinter Nights AD&D game), the Greenhouse Project is focused on discovering startups and new developers. Getting in is not going to be easy. Contact AOL for complete Greenhouse information (Keyword Greenhouse).

Prodigy

`WWW: http://www.prodigy.com`

Prodigy may have the appearance of its stodgy parent companies IBM and Sears, but this service is a large player with lots of accounts and has a good service infrastructure. They are also moving into online gaming. Unfortunately, the company is on the sales block, which has slowed development of the network. I expect that once a buyer is found, Prodigy will expand itself aggressively to keep up with AOL and CompuServe.

The Microsoft Network

Microsoft Corp.
One Microsoft Way
Redmond, WA, 98052
Phone: 206 882-8080
WWW: http://www.msn.com

The Microsoft Network (MSN) has been pretty slow in getting up and running, partly because Microsoft is shifting MSN toward the Internet rather than building it into a huge commercial online service. In the games area, Microsoft hasn't accomplished much more than signing a deal with TEN (Total Entertainment Network) to make that service available to MSN subscribers. Of course, that doesn't mean Microsoft is ignoring online games; this company has the unique reputation of entering a market at the last second and succeeding.

Gaming-Specific Networks

Although some of the companies listed in this section have been around for a while, the astounding growth of online gaming has launched these old-timers to newfound

success. So who are these networks and how can I find out what's going on with them? Well, I'm glad you asked....

The ImagiNation Network
The ImagiNation Network, Inc.
577 Airport Blvd., Suite 300
Burlingame, CA 94010
Phone: 800 462-4461 **Fax:** 415 548-0211
WWW: http://www.inngames.com/

The ImagiNation Network was an ambitious plan by Sierra On-Line to break into the online network business. Sierra reasoned that it could leverage its awesome game design and development skills and create a lucrative game network.

The plan, while solid, didn't exactly work out as planned. Sierra poured millions into the network, but the returns didn't materialize, despite the cool stuff they put together. In 1994, they sold the service to AT&T, who at the time was working to put together an online strategy (one could say they still are!).

DWango
Technology Solutions, Inc.
475 Park Ave. South
New York, NY 10016-6901
Phone: 212 696-2000, ext. 240
WWW: http://www.dwango.com

DWango is a nationwide server set up for multiplayer gaming. Already the company, which has some 30,000 users, offers online remote-server gaming for Doom, Heretic, Terminal Velocity, and Hexan, among others. Players download the DWango client software from Technology Solution's BBS or the Web. Then they can log on to a local server.

If you think you have a game that would be great for DWango (just look at the quality of their offerings already), contact them to learn how you can make your game compatible with their network.

Total Entertainment Network
`WWW: http://www.ten.net`

The Total Entertainment Network (TEN) was formed by the merger of online game developers Outland, Optigon Software, and the Software Creations BBS. TEN isn't up and running yet, but will be soon. (Perhaps TEN will be active by the time this book is published.) TEN has a complete API for developers and they have lined up an impressive array of game developer partners, including SSI, Spectrum Holybyte, Apogee, and Maxis.

Contact TEN to order a complete developers kit. The developers kit has everything you need to begin reworking your titles for multiplayer games on the TEN network.

MPath
Mpath Interactive, Inc.
2465 Latham Street, Suite 101
Mountain View, CA 94040
Phone: 415 528-4000 **Fax:** 415 528-4029
WWW: http://www.mpath.com

Mpath is competing head to head with TEN in the race to create an Internet network optimized for playing games. Mpath has its own network API and other services to support online gaming, and they are also setting up shop as a consultant and partner with a number of leading game companies to help them build online Internet games.

Kesmai Corporation
609 East Market #303
Charlottesville, VA 22902
Phone: 804 979-0111

Kesmai is one of the leading independent developers of major online games. They have programmed a number of online multiplayer gaming hits, including perhaps one of the most successful multiplayer realtime games of all time—the infamous Air Warrior on Genie.

Origin Systems
12940 Research Boulevard
Austin TX, 78750
WWW: http://www.ea.com/origin.html

I only mention Origin because they're about to launch what may be the most successful online game released to date. Origin is developing a multiplayer Internet version of Ultima. Code named Mulitima, this product is still in Beta as I write this. Because the Ultima series is one of the most popular series of all time, having spawned over a dozen games, I believe that Multima will be absolutely incredible (and successful).

CHAPTER 24

Here are some last minute resources every developer should have.

Final Development Wrap-Up

We've covered a lot of general ground on developing games. I've featured developer programs, development kits, commercial libraries, books, magazines, and more for all of the game areas in the game development field. What's left? Well, a few things actually.

In this chapter you'll find descriptions of some of the more general programming and game programming resources that were left out of the previous development chapters. I thought it would be better to cover them here because they are more applicable to a wider range of development tasks. Here you'll find everything from general programming resources to additional Web sites that can help you expand your knowledge of software development.

Magazines

While all of these publications do not just focus on game development, you'll find them to be especially valuable. After all, every good developer needs to keep current on topics like object-oriented programming, Web development with Java, code optimization, user interface design, searching and sorting algorithms, file I/O techniques, database management, and more. The magazines included in this section are the meat and potatoes for the software development community as a whole. As game development has grown in stature in the software industry, many of these publication are increasingly devoting pages to specific areas of interest to people developing games.

Game Developer **Magazine**
Miller Freeman, Inc.
411 Borel Avenue, #100
San Mateo, CA 94402
Phone: 415 358-9500 **Fax:** 415 358-9749
WWW: http://www.mfi.com
Subscription: $29.97 **Newsstand:** $3.95 **Publishes:** Monthly **Pages:** 80

This is the only development magazine devoted entirely to game development. It features articles on programming topics like polygon graphics, 3D animation, sound programming, interface development, low-level graphics support, and so on. You'll also find articles on game business topics as well as key production issues, such as graphic creation, writing, and game packaging and marketing. Some issues also feature interviews with noted game developers and designers.

Dr. Dobb's Journal
Miller Freeman, Inc.
411 Borel Avenue, #100
San Mateo, CA 94402
Phone: 415 358-9500 **Fax:** 415 358-9749
WWW: http://www.mfi.com
Subscription: $29.97 **Newsstand:** $3.95 **Publishes:** Monthly **Pages:** 140

Dr. Dobb's Journal is the granddaddy of computer software development magazines. It provides great coverage of a number of advanced topics of interest to leading-edge developers including programming language design, algorithms and data structures, code optimization, 3D graphics, and much more. Also featured among its pages are articles by Michael Abrash. (Michael is a leading game developer who works for Id Software.)

Software Development
Miller Freeman, Inc.
411 Borel Avenue, #100
San Mateo, CA 94402
Phone: 415 358-9500 **Fax:** 415 358-9749
WWW: http://www.mfi.com
Subscription: $29.97 **Newsstand:** $3.95 **Publishes:** Monthly **Pages:** 120

Software Development is similar to *Dr. Dobb's Journal* and *Visual Developer*, in that its coverage tends to be general programming issues.

***Visual Developer* Magazine (VIZ)**
7339 East Acoma Drive, Suite 7
Scottsdale, AZ 85260
Phone: 602 483-0192 **Fax:** 602 483-0193
WWW: http://www.coriolis.com
Subscription: $21.95 **Newsstand:** $4.95 **Publishes:** Bimonthly **Pages:** 110

Published by The Coriolis Group, this new publication is a spin-off of their highly successful *PC TECHNIQUES* which featured programming and technical articles covering a wide range of topics and languages. In the past, *PC TECHNIQUES* has devoted quite a bit of space to covering technical topics of interest to game programmers. In fact, last year the publisher devoted an entire issue to game development.

The new magazine, called *Visual Developer Magazine*, will feature the latest trend in software development—creating software the "visual way." You can expect to see a number of articles on game, multimedia, and Web development.

Microsoft Systems Journal
Miller Freeman, Inc.
411 Borel Avenue, #100
San Mateo, CA 94402
Phone: 415 358-9500 **Fax:** 415 358-9749
WWW: http://www.mfi.com
Subscription: $36.95 **Newsstand:** $4.95 **Publishes:** Monthly **Pages:** 100

Microsoft Systems Journal is totally devoted to hard-core Windows development issues. While many Microsoft people write for it, and it is sanctioned by Microsoft, the

journal is published by Miller-Freeman, the publisher of *Dr. Dobb's Journal.* Articles on the Windows Game SDK, Wavemix, and other key Windows multimedia/game technologies have been published.

New Media
901 Mariner's Island Boulevard, Suite 365
San Mateo, CA 94404
Phone: 415 573-5170 **Fax:** 415 573-7446
Subscription: $19.95 **Newsstand:** $3.95 **Publishes:** 13/Year **Pages:** 128

New Media is a publication that covers the much broader spectrum of multimedia in general. Of course, games are a part of that. Most of the articles focus on the multimedia creation process and tools for multimedia, with the majority of that devoted toward non-game interactive forms.

Don't let that mislead you though; *New Media* has a lot of relevant articles for game developers and its coverage of new products and tools is top-notch.

Interactivity
411 Borel Avenue Suite 100
San Mateo, CA 94402
Phone: 415 358-9500 **Fax:** 415 358-9527
WWW: http://www.mfi.com
Subscription: $29.95 **Newsstand:** $3.95 **Publishes:** BiMonthly **Pages:**100

Interactivity is a sister publication to *Game Developer* and focuses on a wider field of interactive development that includes games, online publishing, education, and traditional multimedia. Don't expect to find much programming code here, but there are lots of technical articles on developing art, animation, and sound.

This is definitely a magazine to be on any game developer's subscription list. In the premiere issue, I found articles about MYST's development, 3D Studio Power Tools, a look at CD-ROM production basics, and lots more.

Books

Encyclopedia of Graphic File Formats by James D. Murray and William VanRyper (O'Reily and Associates, 1994; ISBN 1-56592-058-9)

This is the ultimate guide to graphics file formats. All others pale in comparison. Some of the formats included are BMP, TIFF, GIF, Kodak Photo CD, Dore raster file, Pixar, and Rayshade, to name a few. The CD-ROM includes all kinds of source code and vendor technical documents.

Digital Image Warping by George Wolberg (IEEE Computer Society Press Monograph; ISBN 0-8186-8944-7)

This book covers a wide range of advanced digital algorithms and code. It's definitely not for the novice programmer, but if you want the goods on texture mapping, morphing, and other realtime 3D graphics, this book, along with Foley and Van Damns text, is a must have.

Multimedia Demystified: A Guide to the World of Multimedia from Apple Computer, Inc. (Random House; ISBN 0-679-75603-5)

This is simply an amazing resource. While it's produced by Apple Computer, it doesn't just concentrate on Mac multimedia, but multimedia in general including games. You'll find a wealth of information here about financing, art production, sound production, and much more. It includes information for both pros and beginners.

CD-ROM Buyer's Guide & Handbook by Paul T. Nicholls, Ph. D. (Pemberton Press Inc., 1994)

From the publisher of *CD-ROM Professional* Magazine comes this useful book on CD-ROM production issues, such as mastering, duplication, indexes, and much more.

Mathematical Elements for Computer Graphics, 2nd ed. by David F. Rogers and J. Alan Adams (McGraw Hill 1990; ISBN 0-07-053530-2)

This is a good second book after getting the Foley and Van Dam tome. It's got a lot of mathematical theory as it pertains to computer graphics. The book is known for its very straightforward and clear explanations of all the topics covered including transformations, curves, splines, and 3D transformations.

Graphics Gems edited by Andrew Glassner (Academic Press, 1990; ISBN 0-12-286165-5)

Graphics Gems II edited by James Arvo (Academic Press 1991; ISBN 0-12-64480-0)

Graphics Gems III edited by David Kirk (Academic Press, 1992; ISBN 0-12-409670-0)

Graphics Gems IV edited by Paul S. Heckbert (Academic Press 1994; ISBN 0-12-336155-9)

The *Graphics Gems* series is a large volume of books packed with all sorts of graphical advice, source code, and hacks that cover an enormous array of items. It's been a staple for many developers for years and almost every year AP has brought out a new edition.

Zen of Code Optimization by Michael Abrash (Coriolis Group Books, 1994; ISBN 1-883577-03-9)

This book by Michael Abrash (who is now working on Quake at Id Software) shows you a ton of code optimization techniques and tips for C/C++ and assembly language.

Advanced Graphics Programming Using C/C++ by Loren Heiny (John Wiley & Sons, 1993; ISBN 0-471-57159-8)

This book, written in conjunction with The Coriolis Group, covers many graphics processing items such as morphing, image processing, ray tracing, light modeling, and animation.

General Web and Online Sites

`rec.games.programmer`

The major newsgroup on the Usenet that game developers, recruiters, hobbyists, and enthusiasts hang out on. Fire up your favorite newsreader and take part in what are sometimes lively discussions.

x2ftp Games Programming Archive
`ftp://x2ftp.oulu.fi`

This should be one of the top destinations for any game developer cruising the Internet. It's a large and constantly growing archive of all kinds of programming resources. The site is huge and includes FAQs, source code, demos, tool libraries, and more. If you haven't been here, you haven't been on the Net.

CompuServe's Game Developers Forum
CompuServe Information Service
(After you log on, GO GAMDEV)

The Game Developers Forum on CompuServe is a great resource not only for its awesome library of information but the message boards that are filled with tons of information from beginners and major developers alike. Aside from rec.games.programmers, this is the major message board and daily interaction site for game developers around the world. This is a place I often hang out (when I'm not updating this book).

The Nexus
`http://www.gamesdomain.co.uk/gamedev/gprog.html`

The Nexus is a major gaming site out of England that also features a game programming and development section with a lot of interesting resources and links.

Game Programming Page
`http://www.asti.dost.gov.ph/~jay/gameprog.htm`

I love it when authors post their own creations and try to create cool tutorials on their own Web sites like this one. Too bad the site was still incomplete when I visited. However, this site is still worth a stop and could be a great beginners' site in the future.

The Game Programming Page
http://www.cs.umu.se/~christer/GR/game_programming_page.html

One of my top destinations. It features numerous links to game book sites, which in itself makes this a great site. You'll also find a number of awesome game development related links.

Sunir Shah's Game Site
http://intranet.on.ca/~sshah/booklist.html#Game

An amazing site, and one I contributed a list of book resources to when I came across the site. Sunir provides an extensive list of game related programming and development books as well as Web sites. The site contains numerous links and it seems to get updated every now and then. A great bookmark for your Web browser.

Games Programming Homepage—UCL
http://www.ee.ucl.ac.uk/~phart/game/

This site is still under development but it shows promise. The author is trying to compile a lot of tutorial-like information to help game programmers. Keep a close eye on this site.

Denthor of Asphyxia
http://goth.vironix.co.za/~denthor/

This well known demo programmer has posted a number of his tutorials and sample software on his own home page. Well worth a visit.

Knut's Home Page
http://www.oslonett.no/home/oruud/prgrming.htm

The usual links are fine but this site also features Knut's own Watcom C tutorials, which you may find to be a helpful resource. (The tutorial only consists of one article at the moment but the author is planning to expand it.)

Game Developer's Page (GDP)
http://falcon.jmu.edu/~schutzmd/gdp.html

This page shows a lot of promise. It includes a good diverse set of links and resources, including Mac, Windows, as well as DOS resources. The best part is that the content is increasing. You'll find excellent links to demos and source code, too.

Happy Puppy Game Developers Page
http://www.happypuppy.com/games/devel/

Not only is Happy Puppy perhaps the number one game enthusiast site on the Web, it also has a specific game developers area worth checking in on.

Game Programming Home Page by Emre Kitchen
http://www.ocf.berkeley.edu/~emrek/gp/gameprog.html

This is an average site with good links to newsgroups and key topics for developers.

Daniel Gottliebsen's Game and Demo Programming Links

http://www.formlink.com.au/gamedemo.html

This site isn't extensive but it does offer some pointers to unique sites that aren't referenced in other places.

PART 7

Business, Marketing, and Legal

CHAPTER 25

The game business is an industry with tons of technical innovations and financial surprises occurring every day.

The Business of Games

What's This Business All About?

The business of games is about two things: having fun and making money. Of course, you can have fun making great games, but you *need* to also make money to buy toys and oatmeal for the kids. The obvious solution to this dilemma is to make money by making games. Sounds simple, doesn't it? Well, it's not quite so easy. Making a great game is only the first 50 percent of your journey. The second 50 percent is wrapped up in publishers, distributors, retailers, advertising outlets, venture capitalists, and consumers.

It doesn't take much research to see that the best game companies are headed by wizard developers who are also well versed in the business of games. Once you have a deeper understanding of the business of games, you will be better prepared to work in the industry, and the quality of your games will improve.

The Structure of the Game Business

Understanding the business of games means knowing how software is distributed, how games and game companies are funded, how shareware works, and what promotional tools publishers and developers use to get their games accepted and appreciated by customers. We'll be covering all these topics in this and the next several chapters. Let's begin now with Figure 25.1, which illustrates the basic key relationships in the game development business.

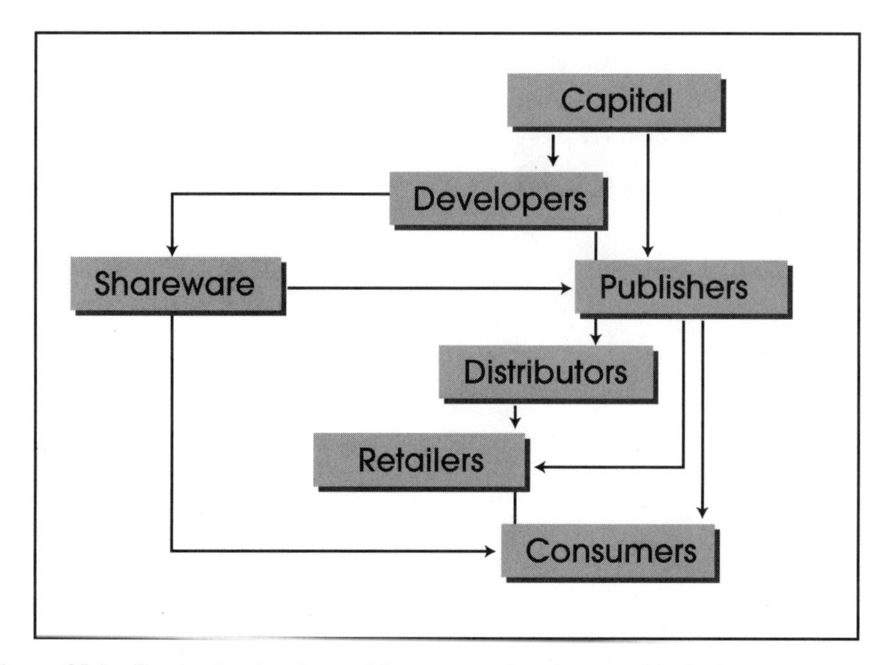

Figure 25.1 The basic structure of the game development industry.

As you can see, this figure is basically a flow chart. Let's break the process down into its components:

- Financial capital flows to developers and publishers to help produce a product. In return, the capital seeks a "piece of the action," usually some sort of ownership either of the product or the company.
- Developers and publishers interact with each other to create the product.
- The product is offered to consumers through one of several channels: direct retail orders, distributors, direct consumer orders, and shareware.

Note: Shareware is shown here as a means of bypassing the traditional distribution and retail process of selling software.

Why This Stuff Is Important

You're probably scratching your head and wondering why on Earth you need to concern yourself with all this business garbage. All you want to do is make great games, right? Well, for one thing, I'll bet you want your games to make money. And secondly, you probably want to build a successful company that allows you to keep making great games without landing in the poorhouse.

I have met many developers who work hard and program amazingly cool stuff, but they don't have a clue how they can get published, build a business, attract customers, and master other business issues. So, please spend some time keeping up on the entire industry. (By the time you finish with all the reading sources I'll present over the next few chapters, you'll be an expert!) While tackling the business portion of the industry may not be as immediately beneficial as learning the latest texture-mapping scheme, in the end it could prove to help you achieve success.

Understanding the Natural Developer Progression

The folks at Looking Glass Technologies, the makers of Flight Unlimited, represent an excellent example of what I call the *natural developer progression*—the various stages a game development company goes through in making the transition from a small design team to a full-blown publisher. While not every publisher goes through every stage (some cash out or go out of business), the set of stages gives you some excellent insight on how to reach for success in the game development field:

Stage 1: Develop the First Product A team of developers bands together to produce their first project.

Stage 2: The Signing The team signs with a publisher, or they self publish their project using shareware channels.

Stage 3: Broaden the Scope Building on past success, the team begins to develop a strong company with development and industry expertise enabling growth. The goal here is to build more and better products.

Stage 4: Build a Track Record With a suite of products produced, the team establishes a brand name among consumers and industry players.

Stage 5: Widen Profiles The team, either through an affiliated label or an exclusive publishing agreement, locks down a long-term distribution arrangement. Spin-off products are typically developed and published to allow the developer to have more income streams.

Stage 6: Full Publisher Once a development team reaches affiliated label status, they are one step from becoming their own publisher. At this stage, the developers must incorporate a sales force and make their own key distribution contacts. In addition, the developers now begin to solicit other developers to distribute or publish their products as well.

There are two key points missing from this progression that shouldn't be overlooked. First is the raising of capital. At some point in this cycle, a developer needs to secure a significant amount of capital. This can take the form of a small seed fund from a publisher or benefactor for producing a specific product, or it can be major funding from venture capital financing or even a public offering.

Second, there is the potential for cashing in. Many developers—especially today—never reach the stage where they become full publishers. Not only does this stage take a lot of work and capital, there isn't as much room for full publishers as there used to be. Many developers cash out either after creating a company capable of producing several quality games a year or once they reach the higher profile of affiliated label status.

Deciding Where You Fit In

One of the biggest tricks to finding success in the game development world (or in any part of the software world) is deciding where you fit into the scheme of things within the industry. You don't want to be too far-fetched in this respect, but you also don't want to sell yourself short.

Both of these extremes come about from a lack of focus and understanding of how companies create games and make money from them. Once you have a clear idea of where you stand within the industry, your journey from where you are to where you want to be will be much easier to navigate.

For many of you, understanding your position is relatively simple. Here's a possible scenario: You're a small group of developers, perhaps no more than one or two people. You want to develop a game, perhaps distribute it as shareware or demo it around to various publishers looking for assistance and a deal. You have a little bit of money—enough to pursue aggressive part-time (25 hours or more a week) development or take a gamble on full-time development, relying on saved income or raised capital.

It is at this point that you need to evaluate your place in the industry. The obvious result is to produce a game that makes money. Much of that has to do with making a great game, but a lot of it has to do with deciding what kind of developer you are, what kind of business model you'll be using, what partners you'll need to attract to make it happen, and how to target your consumers. Once you've got all that figured out, you'll soon find yourself skipping to the bank. Let's get you on your way.

Choosing Your Business Model

One thing that's quite different in the game business today as compared to three or four years ago is that there are many different ways to make money. Not all approaches work as well as others, and some of the newer ideas are somewhat esoteric. Becoming familiar with the different business models is important because it can affect the games you decide to make.

For example, if you decide to build on a model that simultaneously develops games that work on multiple platforms, you can't design games that take advantage of many platform-specific features. Or, if you decide to make money with shareware, you need to design games that work well as shareware—these tend to be well-executed arcade products, so developing an RPG wouldn't be as good a choice.

Let's define some of the business models in use today.

Shrink Wrapped Models

The bread and butter of the game industry are games that are sold in finished form at retail outlets throughout the world. Ninety percent or more of the game industry's total revenue comes from retail products. In my opinion, there are two emerging business models for creating shrink-wrapped retail games.

High-End

The software business as a whole is becoming a two-tiered business when it comes to pricing. You either pull out all the stops and marketing efforts to create a blockbuster high-end game or you go for a more value-conscious approach.

High-end strategies are built around two basic philosophies: You can create a product that features well-known performers in high-quality digital video and uses a sophisticated 3D game engine, or you simply sell a product for a lot of money to make up for expected small sales figures (even good games may sell as few as 30,000 copies).

Low-End

For a long time, the majority of new software simply cost big bucks. Sure, there were some value-conscious software packages (anyone remember the British-based Mastertronic?), and companies like EA reissued games that had been out a year or more with budget-friendly price tags, but this wasn't exactly what I'd call quality low-end products.

Today, though, companies like SoftKey, Corel, and Microsoft (yes, Microsoft) are cutting prices to provide new games at prices more appealing to customers.

The developers of these products are learning to make games with lower development time and costs. They're taking advantage of overseas programmers, and using time-saving programming libraries and art tools. While all developers seek to lower development costs, many companies are specifically designing their products so that they don't need tons of multimedia features that cost a lot to produce.

With the retail business model, you have to decide which road you want to take and stick with it. If you want to sell games for $19.95, you can't create games that cost $12 million to produce. (Unless you plan on selling six million plus copies to just break even.) Likewise, if you plan on regularly asking consumers to fork out $79.95 for a game, it had better be amazing.

Shareware/Freeware Models

We'll discuss much more about the shareware model later, but let's list the business models it's spawned.

Direct Sales/LCR (Low Cost Retailing)

A once niche business model that has become a driving force in the industry is the sale of full versions of released shareware. Companies like Apogee, Epic, and MVP have launched themselves solely on the backs of shareware products, while larger publishers such as Interplay and Virgin have also embraced shareware models.

In this model, the developer/publisher of the software releases a game as shareware. The shareware version is a fully playable version of the game, offering a complete playing experience. Then, customers are solicited to order the enhanced version of the product. Enhancements often include the ability to play user-defined levels, more levels of play, modem play, higher quality graphics and sound, more exotic "power ups," and other game features.

In addition, posting the shareware version on public computer networks allows developers/publishers to cut low-cost retail (LCR) publishing deals, which provides them with royalties. (These are deals where a company sells your shareware version at retail and you receive a royalty, say $.30 a copy on a $5.00 game. I'll cover LCR in much more detail in Chapter 31.) Some shareware developers, such as Id and Apogee, have taken this model a step further and instead of cutting multiple LCR deals (many LCR deals are non-exclusive), they distribute their LCR games on their own or give exclusive license to a specific publisher for their retail sales. This allows them to have more control over the retail distribution of their shareware.

Critical Mass

The critical mass approach is just a further progression of the direct sales business model. With this approach, developers use shareware not only to make money through direct sales of the full version of the product as well as LCR sales, they use the critical mass from a successful shareware version to catapult a revised version into success in the retail sector. Id Software and Interplay used this model to successfully market Doom and Descent.

Razor and Blades

This approach is a newer, emerging derivative of the shareware concept. With the razor and blades model, a company publishes a game as shareware and then sells a series of new modules over time. These enhancements might be quarterly CDs packed with new levels of play. Unlike the traditional shareware model, the idea here is to promote a game engine.

One company using this approach in an interesting way is Crack Dot Com. This startup has produced a game called Abuse, a fun-to-play platform game. After the initial release, the company began to solicit new levels from customers, which they can create with a built-in editor. Customers submit their levels to the company. If Crack Dot Com likes the level, they place it on a CD of levels that they then sell. For their work, the level designers receive some small royalty.

This model came about after developers saw the huge after-market companies created by packaging CDs full of new levels for games.

Sponsored Games

While it's only been a fringe business, advertising in games is sure to take off. As more and more people begin spending time away from TV to play games, advertisers are going to have to shift funds to this medium.

In this business model, a game developer creates a game that revolves around a specific advertiser. The advertiser would provide funding and would package and promote the game, giving the developer a flat fee or a royalty based on the number of downloads.

For example, Jeep might pay a developer to create an off-road racing game that allows players to drive all the different Jeep models in a cross-country, off-road race. Users

could send in registration cards for the full version or visit a local dealership for it. And you know what car dealers say, "Just get'em in the door, the sales staff will do the rest."

Online Models

The newest business model in the game industry revolves around the growing online universe. Currently, many major industry players are developing products that combine the fun and money-making potential of the Internet with games. Let's look at the more common emerging business models.

Timed/Subscription-Based Online Game Provider

The online universe has found revenue success primarily through selling time or subscriptions to their services. Thus, most online gaming business models work the same way. Developers or publishers receive money from people who pay to go online and play the games. Sometimes the games will be based directly on the Web or on an online service; other times, a network will be used to simply route messages to and from different machines running locally-based game software.

Retail Shrink Wrapped Client

Using this model, companies sell the program used to play the online game as a retail product. Customers get all the online time they want (or they pay a fee), but need to purchase the product to play the online game.

Licensed Server

This isn't an obvious business model yet, but it could be a potential money maker in some situations. In this setup, developers create their own server product that handles the client package they also produce. The package or the rights to sell client packages and run local servers on the Internet is then licensed to various parties with those parties paying into a franchise-like royalty scheme.

Sponsored Online Approach

The online advertising business has been much slower to develop than many had originally thought. Unlike retail sponsored products, online games can offer advertisers a chance to more readily tailor their ads to demographics. In addition, they can attract multiple sponsors continuously. Sponsored retail products are limited in their flexibility for advertising.

Already, several Web-based game developers like The Riddler Project and AT&T Web Shop Downtown Digital (*http://www.dtd.com*) have been creating Web-based games that depend on advertiser fees for revenue.

Development Business Models

In the previous section I discussed many of the overall models you can use to structure your business ideas. This should give you a good start, but they won't help when you decide to actually begin development on your game. In this section, I'm going to show you the models you can use to develop your game. Whether you choose to develop a game for multiple platforms simulataneously (not really an option for smaller developers) or plan to incorporate licensed property into your game, you need to decide what you want to do before you begin development.

Simultaneous Release Model

This approach is quickly becoming a major practice in the game industry. Using well-managed cross-platform development techniques (including simply waiting for the last version to be completed), developers work to ship the same game title across multiple platforms simultaneously. These products include not only the various computer and console platforms, but also the various language and cultural versions.

As I hinted at earlier, only larger publishers who can afford parallel development teams and to wait for the lagging versions to get finished are really able to pull off this development scheme.

If you can swing it, simultaneous releases make excellent business sense. All the advertising costs can be concentrated at one time, paid for from the profits of multiple product sales. EA, for example, uses this scheme particularly well for its EA Sports label. By simultaneously releasing EA Sports games for PCs and other platforms, they can spread the benefits of the costs of their TV advertising across the sales of all the different versions of the software.

Another issue that comes into play with language translations is the problem of piracy. Although many games are playable no matter what language appears on the screen, you wouldn't market a game with Japanese translation in India. Software pirates, however, aren't concerned with that issue, and actively resell various translations to any market that can use them. By releasing all translations at one time, companies are able to maximize their efforts against pirated versions.

In the multi-platformed, global market that is the game business, companies are increasingly turning to world-wide, simultaneous platform releases as the development and business model of choice. And until the entire world agrees on one hardware platform and one language, this model will continue to be the most pursued model of business by the larger developers in the future.

Platform Specificity Model

Some game development companies have found that they can earn revenue or find development capital from hardware companies by pledging to create software that really takes advantage of the underlying technology. The disadvantage to this approach, however, is that a game so closely knit to the hardware is difficult to port to other platforms. Portability is a valid concern; however, to say that platform specificity closes the book on simultaneous releases is shortsighted. The issue boils down to lag time. If you can create a game that really takes advantage of the features of different hardware, and the lag time between the first version being completed and the next version is short enough (it depends on the company obviously), you could pursue both development schemes. Many smaller developers—especially PC-focused developers—work more toward platform specificity because they see no potential in other platforms. Perhaps the game in development is fundamentally different from one platform to the next (trying to port a digital video driven game to a cartridge base console, for example), or the developer doesn't have the funds or experience in-house to move a game to multiple platforms, or the developer feels the consumer responds better to a product that pushes the capabilities of the hardware they already own. Whatever the reason, creating a game for a single platform has been extremely lucrative for many developers.

Licensed Property Development

Using licensed property in a game has proven to be extremely popular and profitable for game developers. Whether you choose to make a game based on Marvel's X-Men, Disney's latest animated film, or an NBA team and player, you will surely find success with consumers. Companies like Acclaim, 7th Level, Electronic Arts, and Virgin have all aggressively pursued licenses of various types to either drive their design ideas or enhance already developed products.

There's also a very postive flipside to the licensed property business model—creating original characters and game worlds that themselves generate licensable products. For example, a developer might create a series of children's games based on a cool-looking alien, then earn revenue from licensing the alien for children's clothes, books, television, you name it.

If you don't believe it, take a look at Table 25.1 to see a list of games and the products their creators have licensed.

Next time you sit down to develop your game, put a little bit of thought into the characters and worlds you design. You might just find your original ideas plastered on the silver screen!

Table 25.1 Licensed Products Generated from Original Games

Game	Developer	Licensed Products
Carmen Sandiego	Broderbund	PBS game show, Fox Television cartoon, backpacks, and more
Wing Commander	Origin/EA	Series of books
Mario Brothers	Nintendo	Cartoon, movie rights, and everything else you can think of
Myst	Cyan	Novell produced and movie rights
Doom	Id Software	Movie rights

Whatever You Choose, Write It Down!

In just a few short pages we've talked about the structure of the game industry, the progression of a standard development effort, the various business models companies employ to make money from their ideas, the types of development schemes and how those affect revenue, and several examples of companies and products that use innovative distribution and business models to find success.

What all of these companies share in common, despite the emerging variations in their business and development philosophies, is a focused and determined approach to creating and marketing their products. You too will have to develop this approach if you wish to grow your company into one of the blockbusters making headlines today. Chapter 28 provides all the information you need on creating and implementing a business plan to attract the kind of capital required to make it in the game industry.

Forecasting the Future

One theme that I've touched upon again and again in this book is that the game development industry is still very much in its infancy. Part of the game business, just as in any business, is focused on trying to predict the future. Some people use statistics and current trends, while others put their buinesses in the hands of psychics. I recommend that you stay away from the pyschics!

From my work as a market watcher, and in my discussions with numerous industry people, the following future picture emerges concerning the overall industry.

Distribution Changes

The game business is maturing and that means distribution is consolidating. In 1995 alone, many companies were acquired by larger players or were merged with other

companies (Papyrus was acquired by Sierra, Nintendo bought 20 percent of British based Rare, and The Learning Company merged with MECC and SoftKey.) The reason is simple; there are simply too many publishers. In order to secure better distribution and marketing muscle, companies are bulking up by selling out to larger publishers or merging.

This consolidation also means that over time fewer and fewer companies will actually control the access to retail distribution. Although boon to big business, that doesn't mean that smaller developers are going to be left out in the cold. Small companies and other publishers are turning to the growing online publishing model. Once the wrinkles are ironed out concerning credit card security and high-speed connections, there is no doubt that the World Wide Web will become a major component of retail software distribution. With the Web, developers can more easily bypass publishers, distributors, and retailers, and market directly to consumers, increasing their profits and decreasing their headaches.

Combining Forces

While the Web will enable more smaller companies to survive and grow, it will still be available to the larger market leaders. Although the Web will be useful in selling products directly to consumers, there will still be a need for direct retail sales for quite a while. And new directions in this arena have proven to be quite successful. Some of the larger companies have found it to their advantage to combine forces with other companies in distributing their products. For example, Epic Megagames recently released Extreme Pinball. Epic has Electronic Arts handling the full retail version, while Epic themselves are handling the shareware version. This arrangement is easily reversed; MVP Games handles the shareware distribution of some Virgin Interactive games.

New Game Outlets

Perhaps the biggest shift in the overall structure of the games business is the emergence of online platforms and publishers. Companies like Mpath Interactive, Ten, Total Entertainment Network, and America Online are seeking to become significant new entities in the gaming industry.

Additionally, there is a resurgence in the arcade outlet mostly centered around the emerging high-end VR entertainment sites being set up around the world by companies like Sega, Virtuality, and Dreamworks SKG. While arcade gaming continues to be a big business (though not as big as it used to be), these VR centers are more like family entertainment centers and will become a much bigger game software outlet than many people now realize. Perhaps at some point the hardware will become less proprietary and developers will be able to create new software packages to be used in those centers on a regular basis.

Innovators and Market Makers

The structure of the game business is quietly aligning itself in a much clearer picture of what I call *innovators* and *market makers.* Innovators are the actual developers and companies that create the next cool game or new business or development model. Market makers are those companies that move those innovations into wide-scale sales and business success.

While in the past companies wore the hats of both the innovator and the market maker, the business has become so big and dynamic that companies are being forced to commit to one or the other. Id Software and Zombie Interactive, forever the innovators, have taken the plunge and turned over the marketing and distribution of their endeavors to GT Interactive.

On the other side of the equation, companies that aren't exactly development powerhouses, have invested their time in creating lower-cost versions of successfully launched software in hopes of broadening the units sold and making money that way.

In between are a few stalwarts, like Acclaim, Electronic Arts, and Broderbund, who have been around the block enough times to successfully pursue both avenues. However, these giants still find themselves turning to smaller companies for new ideas: EA turned to Bullfrog and Origin for innovative new ideas to market, Broderbund turned to Cyan (infamous for their blockbuster Myst), and Acclaim gobbled up developers Iguana and Probe.

It is clear to me that the future of the games business will shift from a bunch of companies trying to do it all to an equally large if not larger group of companies defining their paths as either innovators or market makers. The result will be a more focused set of companies that can deliver great products to a wider group of consumers, using more innovative techniques for development, distribution, and business alignments. And that means a growing list of awesome games.

It's Up to You

Game development is one of the most exciting industries going. It's an industry with tons of technical innovations and financial surprises occurring every day. In addition, it sits at the intersection of many emerging technologies, such as interactive television, the World Wide Web, virtual reality, and more.

But also remember that amidst all of this excitement are a slew of failures, big and small. Many of those failures can be attributed mostly to a real lack of understanding about the business side of the industry. The business of games is really about creating your own economic and marketing models that allow you to turn your technological experience into successful money-making products. How you choose to make money with games and how you execute that choice will determine your success.

In this chapter, I've outlined the general trends for you. In the next several chapters, I'll concentrate on the real nuts and bolts of turning your ambitions of building a successful game development enterprise into a reality.

CHAPTER 26

Getting your dream job is not as tough as people make it sound, but it's not easy either....

Getting a Job in the Game Development Industry

Getting Your Dream Job

Politics is one of my hobbies (and also one of my past professions!). Right now, you're probably wondering what politics have to do with game development. Well, hold on. I started out in the business of politics by working as a volunteer for a political campaign. I knew very little about campaigning, but figured if I got lucky, I could learn quickly and move on to more interesting work. In time I figured I would learn enough to get hired as a full time professional staff member for an election. For better or worse, my plan worked. I proved myself as a volunteer and I was lucky enough to have a couple of managers teach me a few things, which I applied to help bootstrap myself, and eventually I got to help manage a Congressional election.

Getting a job in any industry, especially the game development industry, can be approached in the same manner. At some point you need to prove yourself and then you can capitalize on the education and reputation you develop. There are quite a few myths about working in the game industry. The reason most people, especially rookies, don't land their dream job is that they aren't aware of the actual intangibles that companies look for.

Fortunately, getting a job in the game development industry is not as tough as people make it sound. But it's not easy either. On the plus side, the game industry is growing rapidly, which means that companies are aggressively hiring people who have many different backgrounds. This means that you don't need to be an expert game programmer just to get a job. On the down side, companies are looking for talented people who represent the cream of the crop. The top tier companies are quite selective; after all they are used to having their pick because many programmers, designers, and technical talent are dying to work for them. Competition is fierce—many people are waiting in line for the same precious job. But if you follow some of the suggestions and tips presented in this chapter, you'll be one step ahead of the pack.

On the Road to Success

To start, we need to clear up a common misconception: Getting a game you have been working on published is not the same as getting a job with a game development company. Getting a job involves going through the process of finding a job: checking advertisements, sending in resumes, going to interviews, and so on. Getting a title published, on the other hand, involves the process of constructing a game, submitting it, and negotiating with a game publisher. In this chapter, we'll only discuss the techniques of getting a great job (or hiring people if you already have a job and you need more talent). We'll start by looking at some of the specific skills and talents needed.

Develop a Love for Games

If you talk to any person in charge of hiring talent for a game company, they'll tell you that they primarily look for people who love games. In other words, the more obsessed you are the better. If your main reason for getting a job in the games industry is to just make a lot of money or hang out with interesting people, forget it. If deep down you're not a game player at heart, you probably should look for another profession. Game companies want people who are experienced playing all types of games: RPGs, fighting games, simulations, wargames—the more the better. I'm constantly surprised at the number of people I meet at conferences or online who have good technical skills and are looking for employment in the game industry but don't play games. If you aren't interested in playing games, look for employment in another area such as writing device drivers or designing banking software applications.

Get Your Portfolio Together

If you want to get a job in one of the creative areas of game development, such as programming, music, design, or art, you need to create a portfolio of your work. This portfolio should be as professional and as unique as you can make it. You don't have to make it too extensive, but it should present samples of your best stuff.

Visit the big demo FTP site (*ftp.cdrom.com and ftp.mpoli.fi*) where people put up somc absolutely wild demos. These examples might give you some cool inspiration for your own demos. Many are written by whiz-kid European programmers. More than a few of the demo authors have been offered employment by leading game development houses. If you create your own demos and you upload them on the Internet or another online service, make sure that you include information about yourself and indicate that you are looking for a position with a game company. I'm amazed at the number of demos I come across that don't include any information about the author.

If you are a programmer and you want to demonstrate your development talents, create demos of your more interesting or technical creations. If you have written a complete game, even if it's outdated in terms of technology, show it off because a completed project demonstrates that you have what it takes to complete a game. From my conversations with various human resources people in the game industry, I've discovered that they particularly look for people who have finished projects. The game industry is crowded with people who are full of great ideas but short on implementation.

Don't Forget Your College Experience

While it is very common in creative fields to come across people who have never finished school, this isn't a good excuse for not going to school. Programming games is a talent, but the intangibles that come with higher education, such as written and spoken communication skills, organization skills, and so on, are very important. Marta Daglow, a recruiter from Stormfront Studios (a growing company that employs 60+ people), stresses that they only try to recruit people with degrees and medium to high GPAs. Perhaps school is important after all.

I have met many young people who think programming games is a way to avoid school; they're dead wrong. Chances are that you're going to need more than programming skills to get to the top, and that's where college comes in.

Get the Work Experience You Need

While you are sending out resumes and waiting by the phone for someone to call you in for an interview, there are some things you can do to develop you marketable skills and make yourself visible. The more you interact with others in the game development community, the better your chances will be for making key contacts and landing the job you want.

Shareware

Shareware is a low cost way for you to focus on the creation, completion, and publication of a game. You can demonstrate your success to a potential employer by showing off your registrations (even if you only collect a 100 or so). Having a shareware game in the market proves that you have some experience in creating and shipping a product. A shareware game can also serve as your cyberspace calling card to demonstrate your talents to others in the profession.

Professional Groups

In the resource section featured in Appendix C of this book, you'll find a listing of several worthwhile groups that support game and interactive multimedia developers, the Computer Game Developers Association (CGDA) being the most notable one. Many have local chapters and annual meetings. These groups provide the best opportunities to find out more about getting a job or moving to a new company if you already have a job.

Shows

You'll also find several major shows listed in Appendix C. These shows are ideal for meeting major players in the game development industry. Attending one of them can be a major boost. The Computer Game Developers Conference (CGDC) runs a jobs fair where you can get a chance to hand out demo disks and schmooze with the people responsible for judging new talent.

If you attend a conference like this, I suggest you go to some of the roundtable discussions where you can get a chance to speak up and show you know a thing or two. This is a great opportunity to lightly engage people in the industry and get a conversation started. Just be careful not to talk *too* much.

Cultivate and Communicate Your Other Related Interests

Recruiter Marta Daglow recommends that you list and briefly describe your other personal interests on your resume or in your cover letter. "Traditionally, you're told not to mention your interests but I think this is a mistake. From our standpoint, game development is a creative industry unlike any other field. We want to know about all of your talents and interests. For example, if you love sports and actively play sports, you might end up being a good candidate for one of our groups developing sports games. If you left this information out of your resume or cover letter, we may overlook you and the job would go to someone else."

Team Work

Whether you just graduated from college or you have work experience, you'll need to convince potential employers that you are a team player. Almost every single game requires a massive team development effort. To deal with so many different talents—artists, musicians, programmers, producers and so on—you'll need special "team worker" skills. Excellent communication skills are not a plus; they're a requirement.

Looking for or Placing Job Listings

Believe it or not, game companies are in such need of talent that they actually advertise in magazines, other publications, and online services to fill important positions. Not only are these sources good for helping you find a job, they can also help you figure out what the hiring profiles look like. This can help you develop the right skills and work them into your resume. Let's look at some of the better outlets for finding a job.

Commercial Online Services

The best place online to track down job postings is the Game Development Forum on Compuserve (GO GAMDEV). This forum features a section for posting game development notices and it also provides an area for uploading and downloading files

that contain more extensive postings. If you are looking for an artist position, you might also check out the Graphics forum (GO GRAPHICS).

Internet/World Wide Web

The Usenet group rec.games.programmers is the place to go on the Internet for openings for programming positions. On the World Wide Web, you'll find many options to work with. Here's a summary:

Game Magazine Sites Make sure you check out the various Web sites that magazines run. Many of the magazines referenced in this book have dedicated Web sites and commercial online sections (CompuServe, AOL, and so on) that feature job listings. The complete set of these magazines is listed in Part VII. Figure 26.1 shows a help wanted listing from a game magazine Web site.

Dedicated Game Sites Some of the more popular dedicated game sites, which I'll list extensively in Part VII, maintain job listings. These listings should be especially useful to you if you want to start with a smaller company or you are an independent developer and you are looking for partners.

Game Company Sites Almost every game company site I've visited has posted job listings. These sites also accept resumes. By far the best way to look for jobs is to constantly roam the Web sites of your favorite game companies and review the updated postings. Many game companies with Web sites post openings on their Web sites on a regular basis. Figure 26.2 shows a sample posting of available openings from a leading game company.

Figure 26.1 Help wanted listings from a game magazine site.

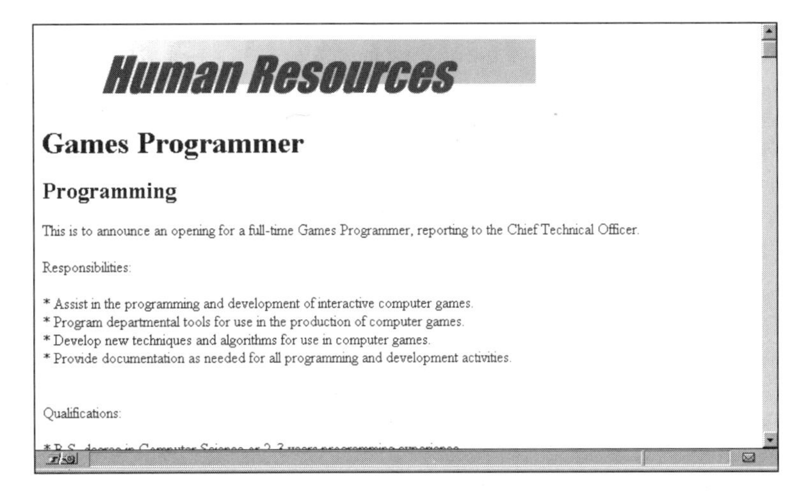

Human Resources

Games Programmer

Programming

This is to announce an opening for a full-time Games Programmer, reporting to the Chief Technical Officer.

Responsibilities:

* Assist in the programming and development of interactive computer games.
* Program departmental tools for use in the production of computer games.
* Develop new techniques and algorithms for use in computer games.
* Provide documentation as needed for all programming and development activities.

Qualifications:

Figure 26.2 A sample of job postings placed on a game company's Web site.

Art Sites In the art development sections of this book I referenced several major art Web sites. Many of them maintain job listings as well as an area for placing work wanted postings.

I think the World Wide Web is one of the best resources available for finding a job in the game development industry. You can easily browse new postings and you can even submit your resume and demos online and receive valuable feedback from potential employers. This can greatly speed up the process of getting a job.

Magazines/Publications

The six best magazines/publications for game developer job postings include:

- Computer Game Developers Association newsletter
- *Computer Gaming World*
- *Game Developer*
- *Interactivity*
- *Next Generation/Edge*
- *Wired*

Conferences

The best conference to attend is the Computer Game Developers Conference (CGDC), which runs a complete job fair. Other trade shows that you might want to attend include the ECTS (European Computer Trade Show) and E3.

Working with Talent Agencies and Headhunters

Because the talent pool of game developers has lagged behind those willing to invest money for creating and publishing games, firms have emerged to help companies find talent. Talent agencies and headhunters provide a valuable service. As more talent, such as actors, artists, and writers, who have traditionally worked through agencies become aligned with the game development industry, talent agencies have stepped in to bridge the gap. Here is a list with brief descriptions for each of the better known agencies.

Michael Katz and Associates
1 San Rafael Avenue
Tiburon, CA 94920
Phone: 415 435-0265 **Fax:** 415 435-9025

Michael Katz, the managing partner of this firm, has worked as President of Sega, Atari, and Epyx. He has also worked at Coleco and Mattel. Today he runs a consulting firm that also operates as a recruitment agency. His firm helps to fill all levels of staffing right up to senior management. They also have permanent talent search agreements with a number of firms. You can fax your resume to them and they will keep it on file.

Mr. Katz recommends that all applicants have a good cover letter explaining their strengths and special skills. Because people in creative fields have so many varied backgrounds, it is often difficult to determine exactly what they have to offer just by reviewing their resume.

id (Interactive Development)
153 S. La Brea
Los Angeles, CA 90036
Phone: 213 935-9723 **Fax:** 213 935-9722

Interactive Media Agency
1950 Sawtell Boulevard, Suite 350
Los Angeles, CA 90025
Phone: 310 477-9923 **Fax:** 310 478-2194

Interactive Media Agency specializes in representing companies looking for programmers and companies to localize U.S. content for the Japanese market. As the Japanese PC market explodes, the need to cross develop products from the U.S. to Japan will grow tremendously.

Korn/Ferry International
600 Montgomery, 31st Floor
San Francisco, CA 94111
Phone: 415 956-1834 **Fax:** 415 956-1988

This recruitment agency has done work for most of the major console-oriented companies. They specialize in executive and management recruitment.

Mason Concepts
6380 Wilshire Boulevard, Suite 1000
Los Angeles, CA 90048
Phone: 213 655-7555 **Fax:** 213 658-1547

This firm concentrates in finding technical people for a number of software and hardware projects. They help companies find staff for projects ranging from graphics and production to hardware development. They have placed people at Electronic Arts, Macromedia, and other companies.

Writers House
21 West 26th Street
New York, NY 10010
Phone: 212 685-2400 **Fax:** 212 685-1781

This is a good place to go to find authors who have multimedia story and script writing skills. This group has placed writers on projects like The 7th Guest and other major multimedia projects.

Game Development Job Descriptions

For the remainder of this chapter, I'll present a number of job descriptions along with their associated salary ranges. The actual positions may vary from company to company. But overall, you'll find that these descriptions will define the basics skills, education, professional backgrounds, and years of experience required.

Special Note: Keep in mind that the salary ranges listed take into account years of experience, geographical location, benefits package, potential royalties or bonuses for hitting sales targets, size of company, and so on. For example, a large game company located in New York that sells millions of dollars of games is likely to pay a producer more money than a small game company located in Iowa. Don't walk into your next job interview and tell the personnel department that you expect to make $100,000 for the producer position because you read that producers make $100,000 per year! Conversely, understand that the top salary for some positions may be low given your specific skills; if you really are worth over $100,000 a year, you may be able to

negotiate such a salary even though you may be outside of the scale for the position for which you are applying.

Producers

Salary Range: $40,000 to $100,000

Producers are basically product managers; they serve as the go-between for management/marketing and the creative people who actually construct a product. But keep in mind that most companies define the producer's role a little differently. In some situations, the producer serves as the overall designer, working to ensure that a product's many disparate parts are designed properly and come together to create the complete, successful game. At other companies, the producer serves more as a project manager who looks after the programming team and keeps things on track. (The producer may even run errands such as getting the programming staff pizza or coffee during a late night of stressful debugging!)

As the salary range indicates, producers take on different levels of responsibilities. You should expect that producers at the top end of the pay scale are required to manage more people and resources, whereas producers at the lower end may only be required to manage a small team. Typically, many companies fill the producer position by promoting from within. Companies look for individuals who are very dedicated (like to work long hours), have managerial talent, are team players, and have good people skills. Most postings you see for producer positions indicate that only candidates who already have experience working as a producer should apply. If your goal is to become a producer, the best strategy is to get another position within a game company, develop management skills, and prove that you have the right stuff to lead people and coordinate major projects.

Summary of professional skills needed:

- A real knowledge of the game industry. Recruiter Marta Daglow offers these words of advice, "If you ask a producer what top five titles are similar to the product they are managing, the producer would know this cold."
- Knowledge and experience with the tools and resources available for game development.
- All of the skills associated with software project management including scheduling, tracking, coding, and testing.
- Software licensing. Many producers play active roles in helping the development staff license software, artwork, and other intellectual properties for constructing games.

- Business management experience including hiring and firing staff, performing reviews, recruiting, and so on.
- Thick skin. The best producers know how to manage projects without letting their egos get in the way. They know how to survive in a world with enormous egos and they are able to do whatever it takes to make their creative staff work as best possible.
- A college degree is typically required by most of the larger game development companies, although in some cases experience can be a substitute. Many producers have degrees in computer science, business, or art.

Programmers

Salary Range: $30,000 to $100,000

Programmers are the people who really drive the technical innovations in game development. Typically, game companies organize their programming teams into subgroups where each group will have a particular expertise and assignment. For example, one group may be involved in programming graphics engines and another group may work on editors or other development tools. Each group is often directed by a lead programmer, typically someone who has more than a few years under his or her belt writing games. There are about three to four main programming job titles used by companies, but for the most part they seem to fit into the three job descriptions I'll present in this section. But before we look at each of these more specific job descriptions, let's discuss some of the basic skills and requirements that professional game companies look for in hiring programming staff.

Professional Programming Experience Is a Must

Game companies aren't interested in hiring game programming wannabes; they want the most experienced coders and professional-quality software designers. The technical demands placed on programmers in game development companies are probably much higher than the demands placed in other industries. Advancements in game technology move at the speed of light, and many programmers find that they have to work as hard as they can just to keep up.

First and foremost, a good professional understanding of C programming is usually necessary (although some companies use other languages and thus won't be as concerned if you are a C expert or not). You should also know as much as you can about graphics, animation, algorithms, data structures, code optimization, and methodologies such as object-oriented programming.

If you are just graduating from college with a computer programming background, you may qualify for a lower-level programming position but you'll really need to have

some solid coding skills. The more projects you get involved with in college, the better. If you get an interview with a game company, make sure that you bring up your school-related experience. If you have some demos, don't be afraid to show them off.

Some companies may hire inexperienced programmers for entry-level software testing positions. But in order to move up the ladder and get more into programming, you'll typically need to take the initiative and develop the needed skills on your own.

Knowledge of Multiple Languages Is a Plus

More and more development companies are starting to use products and tools like Director, mTropolis, in-house programming languages, Visual Basic, Delphi, and Java to make games. Even big companies like Electronic Arts have on-staff programmers who have extensive Director experience. C/C++ may be the primary language in the industry today but if you are the type of programmer who can easily move from one language to another, you'll be much better off. In the future, many more games will be developed using multiple languages and tools.

Experience Outside of the Game Industry Is Okay

Many recruiters try to find programmers in other industries who have a love for games. As Marta Daglow confirms, "We've recruited programmers from HP who we found, interviewed, and discovered that they really loved games. Some of them have become our best programmers."

Don't Neglect Your Communication Skills

Programming is a talent that sometimes is learned to the deprivation of other essential skills, especially communication skills. So, don't expect your pure programming talent to be your only calling card. One company head told me about a programmer they turned down despite some good demo code because the applicant was terrible at communicating his skills and interest in the job.

Junior Programmers

Salary Range: $30,000 to $50,000

To be a junior-level programmer for a game development company, you need a good education with specialized programming skills such as graphics, animation, video, sound, code optimization, and so on. Programmers will start at the junior level position and stay there until they move up to project leader or senior programmer. Junior programmers often work directly under a lead programmer and they often specialize in a particular area such as coding game editors or engines. Many major companies recruit entry-level programmers directly out of school and they train them "on the job." An increasing number of junior-level programmers work with in-house languages. Many companies create sophisticated game engines that provide extensive programming features such as scripting languages. Junior programmers often learn the craft of game programming by using these in-house languages and tools.

Specialized programmers typically have expertise in the non-traditional languages and development platforms such as Director, Visual Basic, Delphi, or Java.

Summary of professional skills needed:

- You must be good at working with others and taking orders and criticism from the top-level programmers. (That is, you must be willing to accept the fact that you are the low person on the totem pole.) The quickest way *not* to get hired for a junior-level position is to act like you just programmed Doom IV and you think you're better than everyone else. If you have this kind of attitude, you're better off trying to start your own game company.
- You must be willing to stick around for a while. Most companies don't want to invest their time training you to become a top-notch game programmer only to have you leave in a year or so. Of course they can't make you stay, but you can bet they will be cautiously looking for the most dedicated and reliable programmers they can find. (If you get an interview and someone asks you what your long term goals are, don't say, "I hope to start up my own game company next year and compete with you." Instead try something like, "I hope to work with a company that is on the leading edge like your company for the next ten years.")
- If you want to get a position programming more creative applications and tools—video, animation, music, and so on, you need to clearly demonstrate you have the specialized skills required. For example, if you want to get a position programming the sound and music libraries, make sure that you tell the company all about the music courses you took in school as well as the programming courses.
- Having experience with alternate languages and development platforms can be a real plus, especially if you plan to get hired for a more creative programming position. At the same time you should have some experience programming in C/C++. Most alternate languages are used in conjunction with C/C++. Therefore, companies want their creative programmers to be versed in C/C++.
- A college degree is not always required; however usually companies will look for those programmers who have some type of training in computer programming.

Technology Programmers

Salary Range: $40,000 to $70,000

Technology programmers don't specifically participate in actually writing a game. Instead, they work behind the scenes to create all sorts of important proprietary code

such as game engines, development tools, and libraries that other project teams use to construct games. Many companies actively look for programmers who have excellent "tool building" skills. In the future, you can expect that more and more game companies will embrace this approach because of the escalating costs of game development.

Summary of professional skills needed:

- You must have two to three years or more of programming experience in one or more areas such as graphical systems, user interface design, video compression techniques, and real time rendering techniques using C/C++ and assembler.
- Both low-level programming experience and good math skills are required. Typically, the technology programmers are the "rocket science" programmers in a game company.
- You must demonstrate the ability to work with multiple architectures. Often, game console hardware and software experience is a must.
- Games industry experience isn't essential but is definitely a plus.
- A college degree is typically required by most of the larger game development companies, although in some cases experience it can be a substitute. Many technology programmers have advanced degrees in computer science or engineering.

Lead Programmers/Senior Programmers

Salary Range: $50,000 to $100,000

Qualified candidates should have three or more years of professional programming experience in C/C++ or another popular high-level programming language. Assembly programming skills are also required in some cases. The lead programmer must also have a good working knowledge of computer architecture in general, and specific hardware-level experience with the equipment that is in use at the company. For example, if you are applying for a position at a company that develops games for the PowerMac and you only have PC programming and hardware experience, you probably are not going to get hired for the job. Because a lot of game development is done on PCs these days, most lead programmers are very experienced with this platform. Experience with RISC systems and any specialized consoles is also especially in demand. Lead programmers with solid industry experience typically command salaries that are at the top end of the programmer salary range.

Summary of professional skills needed:

- Specific programming skills needed include 2D or 3D graphics, animation programming, low-level hardware programming, and very strong optimization skills. Any work experience with other major programming technologies such as sound, video, artificial intelligence, object-oriented programming, and tool development is a real plus. Many game companies are currently scrambling to develop multiplayer games that can be played across networks like the Internet. Thus, experience with Internet programming, protocols, and languages like Java could be important in the near future.

- Strong writing and communication skills as well as math skills are required. The lead programmer often needs to update management about the progress of the development team.
- Good software management skills. Managing programmers is a real art, and good lead programmers know the tricks for pulling together all the parts of a team effort and keeping a project on schedule. Usually, the staff programmers who are promoted to the position of lead programmer are not the ones with the superior programming skills, but the ones who demonstrate leadership ability and understand the critical development cycles from design to coding to testing.
- A college degree is typically required by most of the larger game development companies, although in some cases, experience can be a substitute. Many lead programmers have advanced degrees in computer science or engineering.

Designers

Salary Range: $30,000 to $75,000

Game designers may or may not have a computer programming background. Typically, they come from some sort of creative field such as film, music, or even theater. Designing a computer game is not like anything else, as we've discussed earlier in this book. Thus, you can't really go to school to learn how to become an effective game designer.

Many companies use two or three designers to develop a game. This staff might include writers, programmers, artists, producers, and so on, but usually one person overall is in charge of the "design" of the game. Most companies tend to develop designers in-house. Often, a key member of the project team doubles as the designer. On the other hand, some companies contract out the design work to professional writers or designers.

Summary of professional skills needed:

- You should have professional writing experience (usually in areas like TV, film, publishing, or theater) and professional game design experience.
- Knowledge of the design issues covered in the design section of this book. You should also be familiar with the game business as a whole.
- Programming skills, theater, or video experience is also a plus.

Software Testers

Salary Range: $25,000 to $40,000

Once a game enters a beta test phase, three things are important: All of the bugs or playability problems must get detected, the problems must be fixed, and the game must not stay in the beta testing stage for too long. This requires expert planning, so much so that many companies employ professional testers.

Of course, this may seem like a simple enough job: Play games until you find and make sure all of the problems have been fixed. However, professional game testing requires extensive planning, aggressive analysis, and thoroughness. In addition, testing doesn't necessarily involve play testing or design testing; it often involves grueling debugging sessions where you spend all day trying to recreate errors found by other so that you can ensure that the product will ship bug-free.

Testing is commonly an entry level position at many game companies. Many companies use this job as a proving ground. Many of today's programmers, marketing people, and producers started in testing. If you're looking to get your foot in the door, testing is a common way. Some companies look for programming knowledge while others hire players of their games.

Summary of professional skills needed:

- Serious testing positions are not just for game players. While a true love of games is certainly a requirement, many pro-testers have a technical background. (Many might be junior-level programmers hoping to move up in the company soon.)
- Good communication skills (verbal and written) are required to report bugs and suggest improvements.
- At large companies, testers may be called upon to put together comprehensive testing plans and documentation.
- Don't approach this job thinking you only need your joystick; you'll need a critical eye and a lot of patience to do the job well.

Writers

Salary Range: $30,000 to $50,000

Interactive fiction products are becoming very detailed and complex. For the most part, game companies hire writers on a contract basis but with scripts like that of Wing Commander III, which was about 300 pages, more companies are bringing writers on board full time.

Some games can require a lot of scripting. And writing a script for a game often requires much more work than writing another type of script. While many game companies employ writers specifically for scripting, quite a few writers have developed their specialized skills to become full designers. This is a common career path for ambitious writers.

Summary of professional skills needed:

- You must have a professional portfolio of your writing work. Companies are most interested in seeing any work you've done for television, theater, and film. You need to demonstrate that you can write well and develop scenes having a high degree of interactivity.
- You must demonstrate a good working knowledge of the differences and adjustments needed to write and adapt scripts for games and other forms of interactive entertainment. Don't go to a job interview with the attitude that writing scripts for games is the same as writing scripts for film.
- Obviously, previous game experience helps tremendously.

Artists

Salary Range: $30,000 to $80,000

Although programmers tend to get much of the glory for the successes in game development, artists are just as important. After all, what would Doom or Myst be without the awesome art.

Just like their programmer counterparts at large companies, artists tend to work in groups. Often, a lead artist or art director serves at the top and specialized artists work underneath the lead, hoping to move up the ladder and take charge some day.

Most companies look to hire artists who have specific skills, such as 3D modeling or 2D animation. Rarely do companies demand that an artist have all skills. Another myth is that companies don't look for top-notch fine arts background such as illustration or sculpting skills. While self-trained computer artists are in demand, many top companies look for artists with traditional training. Some companies even require that you take illustration tests. So make sure you bring your #2 pencil to the interview!

If you're a self-trained computer artist or a trained artist without good computer skills, there are many community colleges around the country that offer art classes and classes in computer art programs. I know for example, here in Portland we have a local school of art that offers courses to the public. If you find yourself lacking formal training in some aspect of art creation, you might investigate this opportunity to develop your skill set.

Summary of professional skills needed:

- You must demonstrate a portfolio of work. Many companies also expect to see actual pen and paper illustration experience as part of your portfolio.

- For 3D artists, companies look for people who have experience with modeling, animating, and creating texture maps and lighting.
- Experience in the industry is a big plus (although it's not required). Companies typically look for artists who have skills with the following programs:

  Studio 3D

  Animator Pro

  Alias/Wavefront or comparable high-end modeling software

  Photoshop

  Fractal Design Painter

  Deluxe Paint IIe and Deluxe Paint Animation

Musicians

Salary Range: N/A

Even among large development companies, it's rare to find an in-house musician. Instead, many companies contract out the musical work, although they usually tend to work with the same musician (once they find a musician they like).

You can also find musical companies like Rob Wallace Music that will hire musicians for contracts that they set up with game development companies. A company like this performs the work of getting projects and making sure that everyone gets paid. This can free you to work more on the musical side.

Most musicians charge flat fee rates based on the size and depth of the work required. See the music section of this book for an extensive discussion of producing music for games.

Summary of professional skills needed:

- As with artists, a "portfolio" of work on a demo tape should be submitted.
- Experience in the game and multimedia industry is almost a must these days.
- Complete knowledge of MIDI, FM synthesis, and digital audio production and sequencing is required.
- Capable knowledge of the different console musical and sound systems is often required.
- Skills with interactive music engines are a plus. These engines apply scoring techniques with algorithms to create on-the-fly, dynamically changing music scores based on the gaming situation.

Marketing and Sales

Salary Range: $30,000 to $75,000

Once a game is completed, the job of selling it becomes *the* major focus. (Of course, the marketing and sales staff are always working to position and sell the game, even during development.) The complexity of marketing and selling games has increased tenfold over the past few years because of the many distribution possibilities that have emerged. There are tons of niche markets and each game platform requires a different tactic. This means that marketing is a very important need at many companies.

The game industry is at a mature enough level today that many companies look for marketing people with game industry experience. In a business where shelf space and distribution avenues are at a high premium, good marketing people are highly sought after. If you don't know the difference between a rack jobber, shareware, affiliated label, and bundling deal, don't bother applying.

Summary of professional skills needed:

- A solid college degree. An MBA may be required for high-level marketing positions.
- Previous sales experience within the game or computer industry is a must these days. Most applicants have a minimum of two or three years experience.
- Thorough understanding of distribution and consumer markets as they relate to selling game software.
- Any technical background you can bring is a plus. A good understanding of the computer, online industries, and games in general are all important.

Variants and Hybrids

I've outlined the broad categories for many of the typical jobs in the game development industry. But remember that every company is different. For example, some companies might treat a designer as a producer and others may have as many as four different types of producers (just like in the movie biz). Some companies employ directors and other hybrid positions. Many of these "offshoot" positions aren't advertised. (When was the last time you saw an advertisement for an assistant producer?) This means that these other positions are usually filled by promoting people who are already employed within the company or by using recruiting agents.

You should also keep in mind that the titles used to describe positions are not that important. In fact, they can often be very misleading. To get a clear picture of what a job is all about, take a close look at the skills the position requires. Also consider the company offering the position. For example, a highly technical company might advertise for a producer position. Because of the way the company operates, they may really be looking for programmers with production experience.

Additionally, note that at many companies, the above job lines may be further specified or blurred. On a large project such as Wing Commander, you might have a associate producers and dozens of programmers with leads and associates. At smaller companies and on smaller projects, the designer/producer/lead programmer might all be the same person. Still, in each instance the responsibilities of the title or titles you hold will be roughly the same.

Understand as well that the job descriptions presented in this chapter only covers people specifically involved in producing actual games. There are, as in any company, jobs concerning sales, management, and such. One need not be interested in doing any of the above positions to find work, yet I suspect you wouldn't be reading any of this book if you weren't interested in the above job descriptions, would you?

CHAPTER 27

We all want to make a great game that sells like hotcakes, so we need to keep a close eye on the market and take a few calculated risks.

Game Market Analysis and Resources

Research—The Key to Success

Successful game companies like EA and Acclaim have a secret weapon. They spend tons of money analyzing everything related to the entire game industry—everything from people's hobbies and interests to market trends and driving technology factors including hardware sales, software sales, and so on. They turn over every rock they can, and they use the information they gather to get a better understanding of the people who play games. Their success is based on what they know about their potential customers—what platforms their customers use, what games they're buying, what features they want in their games, and more. For example, when snowboarding became a very popular sport, EA did their homework, spotted the trend early, and delivered Shredfest while the trend was still hot.

To be competitive, you'll need to develop your own techniques and systems for performing market research. Fortunately, there are ways to do market research without spending as much as EA and Acclaim do. You'll find that market research is well worth the money spent, especially when you consider that the ideas you'll glean from it could become a key factor in the success of your game and company. One of the things that separates the big companies like EA from the small developers is not so much their ability to spend money on market research, but their willingness to do so.

Looking at Hardware, the Market, and the Future

The single most important decision you can make as a developer is to select which systems to write games for or port existing games to. Even though you might realize that computer games are most profitable in the IBM/clone market, within this market there are several different "platforms" based on installed configurations. So when you develop a game for the PC market, you need to consider the options: 4 MB machines, 8 MB machines, CD-ROM availability, 32-bit Windows, and so on.

In addition to designing games that work on a large installed base, developers also want to know how installed bases will change by the time their games ship. For example, if you are planning a great state-of-the-art flight simulator, do you design for today's millions of 486s or do you design exclusively to take advantage of a large installed base of Pentiums expected in the future?

To fully understand how market tracking works, let's step back and discuss the three fundamental factors involved in studying the interactive entertainment industry as a whole. They are Moore's Law, the growing demographic of "exposed interactive consumers," and the overall world growth of entertainment spending. These factors are fundamental to the current and future growth of game development.

Moore's Law

You might not have heard of Gordon Moore but you have definitely heard of the company he helped found, Intel. Moore's law goes something like this:

Every two years processing power doubles and the cost for this processing power decreases by a factor of two.

In lay terms, the money you paid to buy a machine today would buy you a machine twice as powerful two years from now. And the machine you buy today, will then be available for half the price you just paid. Now, aren't you glad the real estate market doesn't work this way?

When Moore first made this statement, many people in the computer industry laughed; they figured at some point that computing power would hit a wall. As it turns out, he hasn't been wrong yet. As more powerful technology has decreased in price and become affordable for mass market consumption, developers are pressed more than ever to take advantage of that power to make newer and cooler games.

Exposed Interactive Consumers

Another major factor to consider is Lee Isgur's exposed interactive consumers trend. This trend is perhaps the driving force behind the game business. It shows us that the amount of people who acquire an appetite for interactive entertainment is going to grow some tenfold by the year 2010. Consider these facts. The video game business is roughly 20 years old. Everyone who is over 20 was born at a time when interactive products weren't available. In addition, most major interactive gaming products weren't widely available in homes until 1980. And if you think that the mass-market of interactive gaming didn't really start until Nintendo was introduced, the market is only about ten years old!

This means that the industry is still in its infancy; it will continue to soar as we move into a world where the entire population will have been born at a time when computers and video games are common forms of acceptable entertainment.

Growth of International Entertainment Spending

Recently I was reading an article about Toshiba and Time Warner in *Forbes* magazine. This article described a joint venture to open 450 movie theaters in Japan. The two companies also are getting ready to wire Japan's cable market, which is very poor. The fact is that despite its economic success, many Japanese do not spend a huge amount of money on electronic forms of entertainment. The U.S. leads all countries on per-capita-based spending on entertainment. We *do* like our leisure time!

The rest of the world is quickly catching up, though. Many new economies are growing to the point where a sizable portion of their population has the means to afford such luxuries as movies, a TV set, or even a $200 Nintendo or $2,000 computer. As the rest of the world enters the realm of high-tech entertainment, more opportunities will exist for developers of interactive products. Now is the time to start planning for these expanding global markets.

From Fundamentals to a Foundation for Analysis: The Household Approach

When it comes to statistics, I like to keep things simple. Trying to gather tons of statistics and demographics seems to me to be a waste of time. To lay the groundwork for an analysis of the games market, let's look at a very simple breakdown of the consumer categories that make up the universe of potential game players.

Our breakdown will focus on the average household. A *household* is a common unit used in many marketing/survey/polling situations, especially those concerning products that are purchased and used by an entire family or portion of a family. Table 27.1 shows a household unit breakdown from a survey done by New York-based Alexander & Associates during August, 1995. Although it's a little dated now (none of the Christmas sales show up!), it will serve as an excellent example to illustrate our point.

Table 27.1 The Average Computerized Household

	All HH	PC and VGS	PC Only	VGS Only	None
Millions of Households	92.9	9.6	13.2	17.3	52.9
Mean Household Size	2.73	3.75	2.69	3.46	2.35
Mean Age	45.6	35.9	40.4	33.9	49.9
Mean Household Income	$36,830	$52,803	$54,951	$34,811	$29,207
% Married	55.8	68.3	64.1	59.6	49.8
% Children Present	37.4	68.4	32.6	69.3	21.9
% College Graduate	24.9	36.7	50.3	15.5	19.4
% With PC	24.4	100	100	0	0
% With CD-ROM	7.6	40	32.6	0	0
% With VGS	28.8	100	0	100	0

For the latest survey (which includes far more information than the above numbers), contact Alexander & Associates about their *Video Games and PC Benchmark Study.*

As shown in Table 27.1, four types of households are researched in the game industry:

- PC Only Households
- PC and Videogame Households
- Videogame Only Households
- No System Households

Note: We can could go one step further and determine which computer households have Internet/online access, but for now we'll concentrate on the task at hand and get to Internet/online statistics a little later.

Let's discuss each household structure to give you an idea of what each comprises:

PC Only Households These households are the bread and butter of the computer game industry. They number over 13 million and tend to be middle to upper income families.

PC and Videogame Households This group doesn't vary much from PC only households, although they tend to have more children. They also tend to have younger children overall (which explains the videogame unit). They are also less educated. While their income is the same, because they have more kids, these families have less disposable income. The majority of these families simply view consoles as better for their kids, and use them in addition to the conventional PC they also own. The other part of this group are hard-core game fanatics who want anything and everything concerning games.

VGS Only The console-only crowd shows a dramatic drop in income from the first two households we discussed, which explains the lack of PCs in the household. A $150 game system is far more affordable than a $2,000 computer. Additionally, education levels of these households drop dramatically as well. This group represents the middle- to lower-income household. They enjoy games, but can't afford large computer systems to play on (and as the data shows, they don't like expensive consoles either!).

No System The poorest and oldest of the bunch. A large part of this segment is senior citizens who have fixed incomes and minimal interest in video games. The rest are simply an assortment of people who don't want or can't afford any game platform.

Over time this segment will steadily shrink as the population changes to include more and more people who are quite familiar with interactive games, computers, and gaming platforms. I doubt we will ever see a time when this group no longer exists; there will always be those that choose to sit on the sidelines of the technological revolution.

From Households to Trends: A Brief Market Outlook

Now that you have a basic understanding of the four basic "food" groups of the game market, let's look at where the market is heading.

The Battleground for PC Households

The biggest shift in 1995-1996 has been and will continue to be influenced by the maneuvers of Intel and Microsoft to establish the PC as a major game platform. What, you ask, isn't it already? Absolutely not, I don't care how biased you are; numbers don't lie. Console games outsell PC games close to four to one. However, there is a shift happening in the industry and Microsoft is leading the charge.

The growth for PC gaming is happening in those households that previously identified themselves as owning a PC. This is a two tiered move: The households that currently own only a PC are increasing their purchases of interactive entertainment, and the households that own both a PC and a console are increasingly turning to PCs for their gaming needs.

Losing the Battle

Let me take a moment to separate fact from fiction and desire: *There is no data to suggest that VGS households will move to the PC platform.* Unless computers become available for drastically reduced prices (less than $500) or as I like to say, "buying a PC becomes as easy as buying a car" with complete "MSAC" (Microsoft Assistance Corporation) financing, this group will continue to purchase console-only systems. In addition, those households without any system suffer from a sharp drop in income and have more in mouths to feed. These families will definitely not be putting a $1,000 to $3,000 multimedia PC on their list of needs.

PC Hardware: Moving Toward High-Tech Gaming Capability

The current trend in PC hardware is moving toward establishing the PC as the bona-fide game platform, complete with high-speed network/modem connections, sophisticated 3D graphics boards, VR headgear, and symphonic-quality sound capabilities.

While it's great that PC manufacturers and owners are adding all this cool hardware, the additional computing standards and more hardware features mean more for developers to keep track of. For the savvy developer, this means watching sales of 3D graphics cards, VR gear, modems, and more. Some of this data will be available from the manufacturers themselves, but many developers will need to subscribe to hardware sales figures to get a more exact idea of whether or not they should create a game that embraces the new technology.

For example, developers need only take a quick glance at Table 27.1 to see that roughly four out of ten PC-equipped households currently have a CD-ROM drive. This past year has proved to be somewhat upgrade-friendly, so developers are able to gauge their designs on such current trends. We all want to make a great game that sells like hotcakes, so we need to keep a close eye on the market and take a few calculated risks.

Consoles: The Rock of Gibraltar in Gaming Systems

If you're thinking about developing for a console (or you already are a console developer), you certainly haven't had an easy time picking a path to success. Which console do you develop for? The first three generations (Atari 2600, 8-bit systems, and 16-bit systems) had very long lives. Unfortunately, the current era of consoles has a much shorter life expectancy. Just as 32-bit systems are getting started, 64-bit consoles are starting to move in. The various next-generation 64-bit hardware components like Digital Versatile Disc (DVD) and the amazing 3D chipsets are almost ready to become components of tomorrow's game consoles today. This technology is moving ahead far faster than many companies originally anticipated.

Consoles aren't ready to give up the race to the PC . If you don't believe me, consider the following factors:

- *There is a large definable VG segment that isn't going away.* The companies playing or getting ready to play in this arena understand this fact and don't need to hold back.
- *New players want in.* The very fact that there is a basis for the long-term existence of the console market coupled with the past success of manufacturers in the market has drawn in new players. This is one of the primary reasons we're seeing a higher turnover rate. With more companies trying to establish a foothold in defining the market, there is more of a tendency to debut new hardware faster in an attempt to gain a prominent position. And that's not all. PCs are catching up fast in the game race, forcing consoles to leap-frog even faster. Today's 32-bit players are almost outdated as far as the capabilities needed to deliver the killer 3D graphics that developers are looking for. The market is wide open for new developments.
- *The battle has far larger stakes than you think.* Looming over everything is the fact that many of the new players—particularly Matshusita and Sony—think that these next-generation consoles will eventually emerge to be the "set top box" of

the future. With the advent of Digital Versatile Disc and HDTV (High Definition Television), there will need to be a full-service "set top box" to handle the emerging TV-based services.

Many console developers will feel that the game console will turn into the key delivery platform for these next-generation TV services. Thus, the stakes are high. A market could emerge that would dwarf anything seen so far. Deep-pocketed companies like Sony and Matsushita will sink millions into this emerging market. After all, they want to be the ring leaders when the market matures ten years from now.

- *The market hasn't moved—yet.* With all the confusion about which consoles are good, the bulk of the market has not yet upgraded to new hardware. This means two things for developers: First, the manufacturers aren't locked into their current designs. (As I write this, there are signs that Sega might abandon the Saturn and quickly move to a 64-bit machine before the Saturn base gets so high that they can't afford to offer some sort of trade-in.) Second, new players with new technology, such as Nintendo's Ultra 64 or the Matshushita/3DO M2 player, could easily become the true upgrade path over the whole range of current 32/64-bit players once they debut their systems.

It's easy to see that consoles are going to be a major force for some time. And if you decide to pursue console development, you should closely follow the market. Many console developers are setting up their development processes on high-end workstation equipment and creating tools that allow them to develop above the console fray. If you are part of a large firm, this may be an approach you want to get familiar with.

If, however, you are an independent or smaller developer, there are many multimedia authoring environments—Macromedia's Director and mFactory's Mtropolis, for example—that provide smaller developers who are mainly PC fluent with the ability to break into the console market. These tools also allow developers to write one program and deliver that product to multiple platforms, including consoles. Macromedia, for example, has a player for 3DO already available and is planning other console players, as well.

Building the House on the Foundation: The Hardware Outlook

Having explained the fundamentals and trends of the interactive game market, it's time to translate that into something a little more relevant. Table 27.2 presents a simple "platform outlook" that describes what should be happening hardware-wise in the two key platform categories.

Table 27.2 The Hardware Future of the PC and Console Game Platforms

Years	PC	Console
1996-1997	Pentium PCs with multimedia fixings are the norm. While some developers will reach back to 486 systems, others will press ahead with games that require Pentium performance. Memory requirements should hold at 8 MB, but with most systems shipping in the latter part of 1996 with 16 MB standard, expect some games to break the 8 MB barrier. The key items to look for beyond memory are the rapid rise of specialized peripherals and telecommunications gear. 1996-1997 will see PCs add 3D graphic boards like 3D Blaster. In addition, 28.8/36.6 modems and ISDN modems will spur massive growth in online gaming. Finally, specialized interaction devices like 3D glasses (HMDs and polarized glasses), as well as sophisticated joysticks, steering wheels, and VR devices will begin to ship in larger numbers.	The 3.5 consoles duke it out big time: Sega's Saturn, Sony's PlayStation, Nintendo's Ultra 64, and Panasonic/3DO's M2 technology. It is too difficult to predict a winner right now. What is clear are the losers of the console world—Atari's Jaguar and the first incarnation of the 3DO player seem doomed. The biggest question is the distribution of these future giants. Some people have predicted that each console may dominate a different market, Sony in the U.S., Sega in Europe, and Nintendo in Japan. While all three will have significant market share, each major market will require a different console development strategy.
1998-2000	Pentiums and Pentium Pros will be it. 3D graphics boards and 3D sound cards will become the defacto multimedia standard. Digital Video Disc, the next generation of CD-ROM, will begin to take over. And Internet gaming, via ISDN and cable modem-equipped PCs, should be in full swing with every PC being equipped for massive multiplayer gaming.	Consoles will adapt to the Internet age; multiplayer options will be prevalent (though significant, not like what the PC arena will boast). The console companies will be shifting to even greater next-generation systems. What those specs are is highly speculative, although Digital Video Disc and even more awesome 3D graphics are sure bets. Many console manufacturers at this point may be looking to integrate themselves into the home as universal

Table 27.2 The Hardware Future of the PC and Console Game Platforms (Continued)

Years	PC	Console
		set top cable box providers. Perhaps we may even see a real push by a coalition of companies to debut a "standard" console. Along those lines, Sega and Matshushita recently announced they're combining efforts to push a new platform as a standard.

Finding Out More about the Games Market: From Questions to Solutions

Many questions must still be answered concerning the game market. In this section, I pose the questions developers are asking about the future of the game industry. I'll provide some answers by offering the current research channels available.

Which platforms are doing well?

To check out the console arena, you can simply order a standard market share report. (Check the resources I've listed in the *Numbers, People, and Reports* section later in the chapter.) You can also consult with the actual hardware companies to find out what's hot. Heck, I get this sort of simple data from various company press releases all the time. Be careful, though; the real key is not in the number of consoles in the market, but how the software for that console is selling. Find out how the average title sells on the platform you're considering developing for, and also find out how many titles per console are sold in a year.

Which PC platform should I support?

For tracking the PC platform, you'll have to turn to the major market research firms like IDC or Dataquest to get an accurate gauge of the machines available with a given feature set. Another way is to track sales of hot games that require a certain hardware level. For example, if a Pentium 150-only game sold 1 million units, you can safely assume that there is an ample market for good games needing that sort of horsepower. The catch is that you have to wait to see the sales first before you move.

Which types of game categories are selling well?

PC Data (listed in the *Numbers, People, and Reports* section of this chapter) will, for $2,500 a year, send you monthly sales reports on PC game software. Aside from your own knowledge of the market, this sales data will help you determine average sales for successful games in various categories.

Which international markets are developing and which platforms are being used in those countries?

This is definitely a job for the major market research firms—they don't just track sales of PCs and consoles here. IDC and Dataquest, for example, are worldwide firms that follow many major international markets.

How can I find out what price points are working?

PC Data and NPD's SofTrends, listed in the *Numbers, People, and Reports* section of the chapter, offer market share listings of games by pricing. This information will give you a very good idea what price-points are the best for moving the most merchandise. It will also help you determine what products similar to yours are selling for.

Who are the leading publishers and what's their market share?

To find the key retailers, the best thing to do is read the three major retailing trade publications: *Computer Reseller News, Computer Retail Week,* and *SMART:Computer & Software Retailing.* To find the hottest publishers, check with PC Data (see the *Numbers, People, and Reports* section later in the chapter), which publishes a monthly listing of publishers by market share.

What types of people are buying games? What types of games are people looking for?

Most developers answer these more qualitative questions by looking at their player response cards, which help them to glean information about their customers from questions like "What magazines do you read?" or "What's your favorite sport?" Some companies will bring in market consultants who track trends.

You can also explore answers to these questions using phone surveys or focus groups. The NPD Group (listed in the *Numbers, People, and Reports* section later in the chapter) performs semi-annual surveys about who's buying what in the software world—it's part of their SofTrends marketing report. Electronic Arts takes a more creative approach by inviting local school kids to come by and play games and then they interview them. Where was EA when I was goofing off in school?

I must stress however, that whether you are part of a huge corporation or are an independent sort, the best source for information is going to be your publisher. If you are working with a company that has been publishing games for a while, they should have an exhaustive database of customer profiles for different games. This is what they're there for—take advantage of it.

The Online Outlook

If I were writing this book a year ago I probably wouldn't have included this section. Today, however, many game developers are taking a close look at the market demographics and numbers concerning the Internet and online services.

Online gaming is quickly becoming a big money-making opportunity, and gaming is considered by many major players to be one of the three killer apps of the online world. Therefore, let's examine the outlook for online services in general and gaming in particular for the near future.

Demographic Reports

Three major studies have been produced about the market demographics of the Internet. **O'Reily and Associates,** a major book publisher and Internet developer, did a major survey; **Nielson Media Research** and **Yankelovich Partners** combined forces to publish the infamous CyberCitzen report; and **Jupiter Communications** and **Web directory service Yahoo!** combined resources to do a comprehensive online survey.

While none of the surveys I've seen has been considered to be completely accurate, I'd like to share some of the publicly released statistics from the Jupiter/Yahoo! survey that may interest you and highlight some key issues for online game developers:

- 55 percent of 70,000 respondents said they were accessing the Web from home.

  The Net is definitely becoming a mass market channel; a total of 85 percent reported having some access to the Net from home.

- Net users are highly educated with an income of between $35,000 and $49,999.

  This isn't much of a secret; just look how this demographic correlates with people who own PCs.

- 45 percent of the respondents were dual computer owners.

  For at least the next few years, expect the majority of Net gamers to be hardcore computer owners and gamers. While the CD-ROM market is quickly finding itself awash in a growing non-hardcore audience, the Net is the next domain for hardcore gamers.

Getting to the Nitty Gritty

Aside from a detailed demographic analysis, there are three key elements to tracking the online revolution. Developers want to know:

- How many people own modems and what the speed breakdowns are
- How much time (and that translates to money in access fees) users are spending online each month
- How users are accessing the online services

The Networks

If you find yourself in a publishing deal with one of the big online services, say for example with AOL's greenhouse project, they should provide you with the basic answers to these questions. Although these services would never publicly discuss their customer's profiles, they will supply you with ample information for your joint venture.

Modems and Speeds

To track modems installed and the speeds being used, you'll need to turn to a PC hardware report like The NPD Group's *Hardware Survey* or Alexander & Associates *Video Game and PC Benchmark Survey.* Another route you might take is to track the installation of high speed connections through phone companies—and cable modems once they get off the ground. In addition, consoles will be sporting modem capability too. The company heading up this endeavor is Catapult (*http://www.xband.com*), makers of the Xband console modem device. Serious developers should contact Catapult to get a breakdown of their installed base.

As expected, the bulk of modems currently installed are of the 14.400 variety, with the 28.800 variety coming up a close second. However, developers can expect ISDN and cable modems to be the next rapid ascent in online gaming hardware.

Money and Minutes

The studies mentioned in a previous section (see *Demographics Reports*) have produced detailed analysis of time spent online and should answer most of your questions in detail. However, time spent online playing games is harder to gauge.

I've compiled several interesting statistics here that make some key points about the market:

- *Hardcore Internet users spend a lot of time online.*

  From the Jupiter/Yahoo! reports publicly released statistics we know that the average user's online session lasts more than an hour, and the average user's weekly online time is approximately 20 hours.

  This indicates that Net users are a hardcore crowd—people with the online habits for games, which will require longer average stays and more hours overall.

- *Much of that time is spent looking for interaction.*

  AOL is rumored to derive half of its online revenue through people participating in chat groups. With a statistic like that, many developers are certain that interactive entertainment is really what people are seeking online. What that entertainment is exactly and how much they're willing to pay for it is a whole other can of worms!

- *Users balk at spending much money for "additional services."*

Also from the Jupiter/Yahoo! report is the statistic that only one-third of the respondents polled said they were willing to spend extra money for access to Web sites—and only $1 to $4 a month at that.

The Net has built a ton of its base on lots of free stuff—free browsers, free Web sites, and low access fees. (In fact free access is provided for many of the huge colleges and organizations that make up a large component of the Web.) And everybody likes *free*. Developers will find resistance to collecting money for site access.

Still, for game developers, online games hold the key to potential profits—though the success of games at this point hasn't been great. Another approach might be to sell client software that would contain the cost of supporting the actual online infrastructure. There's plenty of time to make these decisions. Along with the game industry, the online universe is still in its infancy.

Access Providers

How people access the online universe is almost more important than the time they spend online. The means by which people access the Web is a major concern to game developers—browser differences, latency questions (a special type of modem speed issue), and caching issues (discussed in detail in Chapter 23), all affect game design.

In addition, some providers use different backbones—MSN uses UUNET, a major new Internet backbone provider that is building high-speed/low-latency networks. And some are aggressively upgrading their speeds and rolling out ISDN and cable modems. You need to get you hands on as much information as you can if you want to develop online games successfully.

You also can't ignore commercial online services. Even though you might be building for direct Internet presence, these large commercial services are becoming national access providers. For example, I do the majority of my Web surfing through a TCP/IP connection provided by CompuServe.

I'm not giving away any company secrets by saying that tracking provider numbers is tough. My best advice is to subscribe to one of the Net surveys listed in the *Numbers, People, and Reports* section of the chapter. Despite their flaws, they do provide you with some fairly accurate information.

Seidman's Online Insider

A great way to keep your eye on online developments is this free newsletter written by IBM staffer Robert Seidman (*http://www.clark.net/pub/robert*). Topics such as press releases on new Internet studies or online subscriber figures from one of the big services are covered here. You can even find back issues at the Web site.

Send an email message to: *LISTSERV@PEACH.EASE.LSOFT.COM.* In the body of the message type: Subscribe Online-L Firstname Lastname
For example: Subscribe Online-L Robert Seidman.

Online Statistics: How Accurate Are They?

Market researchers have certainly met their match when it comes to researching Web demographics. The three major studies we discussed earlier have been criticized heavily. Most of the criticisms are valid, but the problems have to do with the nature of the online universe rather than mistakes made by the companies doing the research.

For example, many online providers report the number of accounts on their service, yet many accounts are inactive or have been suspended. And some people have multiple accounts. Another problem is that many reports consider AOL subscribers to be Web surfers because AOL offers a browser—but not all AOL people use the browser option.

Also a lot of respondents are so dumbfounded by the technology that they answer questions incorrectly. For example, some people indicated they have access to the Net when they really didn't. In addition, consider that the Jupiter/Yahoo! survey was actually conducted on the Web itself and was voluntary. While I find most of the trends they supported to be true, the final numbers are open for debate.

At some point, the results of such studies will get better, but the overall rule of thumb among Web and online developers is that all the numbers floating around should be taken with a grain of salt.

A Poor Developer's Guide to Market Forecasting

If spending $2,500 is out of your budget but you still want to collect some information that gives you a good idea of platform and software markets, here are some inexpensive tips you should follow.

Keep Your Eye on the Big Publishers

If you want the latest scoop on the viability of a new platform, pay close attention to what some of the largest companies are doing. For example, if EA moves to 32-bit platforms with ISDN modems, they've obviously done the research to tell them this is a potentially viable market. Let their R&D dollars work for you.

Be careful, though, sometimes these companies are simply taking chances. For example, EA backed 3DO not only because of its market potential, but because

EA founder Trip Hawkin was the driving force behind the 3DO company. Although you may want to watch these big boys to see what's hot, you may not want to follow in their footsteps when they choose to abandon a platform. Some companies like to push the edge and they abandon older platforms even though they still have plenty of life.

The Web and Press Releases

When many of these market research firms do a new study, they often release some of the general results to promote their services to large publishers. While you may only find a few very small morsels, keeping your eye on them can help you get a general picture on things out there. You'll want to frequently check the Web sites of the companies listed in the *Numbers, People, and Reports* section in this chapter to keep on top of the latest trends in industry research.

Public Companies and Industry Financial Analysts

The annual reports of public game companies can also offer useful market clues. For example, in Electronic Arts' annual reports they present data on various world regions, game platform software sales, and more.

You can also tap into the various brokerage houses across the country that make their forecasts public. If you invest at all, you might consider asking your broker or financial representative what information they can get for you concerning the computer industry and electronic entertainment.

Finally, Lee Isgur of Jeffries Securities is the dean of interactive entertainment analysts and presents his forecasts each year at the Computer Games Developers Conference (CGDC). If you go to the CGDC, you'll get a copy of his predictions and have the chance to hear his latest thoughts.

The Trade Magazines

There are tons of trade newsletters and magazines out there and rather than cover them all here, I just want to highlight a few of them that offer explicit coverage of marketing numbers and such. For each of these you'll find very detailed information in Chapter 34 later on.

Retail Trades

Most of the major retail trades such as *Computer Reseller News, Computer Retail Week,* and *Smart* offer several pages each issue showing different statistics such as top ten lists, top retailers, and more.

Computer Gaming World

CGW publishes all its reader-response card surveys in the back page. Although they are hardly scientific in their approach, these surveys still provide a clear idea

of what the hardcore gamers are playing and liking. *CGW* has also been doing more structured surveys recently. What it called a comprehensive survey of the gaming public—they announced one last year but in all my research I wasn't able to get my hands on it, nor did I see the full survey offered publicly—I suspect they offered it for sale. Contact *CGW* for more information.

Numbers, People, and Reports: Game Market Data Resources

Before I present you with a listing of sources for research on the game market, I want to share some information to help you understand the types of research you will encounter.

There are three major ways a market research firm can collect data concerning the games industry. They can look at sales data of stores or reports from publishers, or they can survey actual consumers. Your needs will determine the type of research you want to look at.

For example, if you want to see how big the PC platform is, you could look at sales from stores. If you want to see who bought those PCs and what they really used them for, a customer survey would be a better approach.

For surveys, some market researchers use phone interviews and some use mail surveys—there is a big difference between the two. When done properly, a phone survey can be far more precise in its collection and results. A mail survey requires the participant to return the survey; if, for example, only women returned the survey, you'd have incredibly skewed results. However, to even things up, mail surveys tend to be much larger than phone surveys and they readjust the results using mathematical weighting techniques.

So when you plan to buy some market research data, remember first to ask your researcher how the data was collected. Understanding the fundamentals of how the research is conducted can help you understand the collected data much better.

That being said, here are some of the best sources for market analysis relevant to the interactive games industry.

Alexander & Associates
38 East 29th Street, 10th Floor
New York, NY 10016
Phone: 212 684-2333 **Fax:** 212 684-0291
WWW: http://www.alexassoc.com

For the sake of disclosure, I work for this company as a consultant. Alexander & Associates produces a yearly survey called the *Video Game and PC Benchmark Survey.* It is a end-user phone study that calculates the state of the entertainment platform installed base. By making it an end-user study, Alexander & Associates can truly gauge who bought what and how often it's being used. This survey is especially critical for tracking PC game usage because tracking PC sales can be quite misleading. How many people do you know that buy high-end machines and use them to write letters?

For more information about the survey, visit their Web site.

Dataquest Incorporated
251 River Oaks Parkway
San Jose, CA 95134-1913
Phone: 408 468-8000 **Fax:** 408 954-1780
WWW: http://www.dataquest.com

Dataquest is a full-service research organization that produces dozens of reports about the PC industry. Whether you need sales projections for network operating systems or you need to determine the worldwide population of computers that have sound boards, Dataquest is sure to have a report for you.

International Data Corporation
Five Speen Street
Framingham, MA 01701
Phone: 508 872-8200 **Fax:** 508 935-4015
Email: idcinfo@idcresearch.com **WWW:** http://www.idcresearch.com/idc.htm

A subsidiary of International Data Group (the folks who bring you all those Dummies books and *MacWorld* Magazine), International Data Corporation (IDC) is a complete worldwide research firm, focusing on all aspects of the computer industry.

IDC has many products, surveys, market forecasts, and other data for your perusal. Examples of relevant reports they've published of interest to game developers are audio board market penetration, the games industry in general, multimedia PCs, and game consoles.

Jupiter Communications
627 Broadway
New York, NY 10012
Phone: 212 780-6060
Email: jupiter@jup.com **WWW:** http://www.jup.com

Jupiter Communications is a long-time publisher of market analysis information pertaining to the Internet and online services. They have several publications (which I'll cover in a later chapter), but they also produce market reports such as the comprehensive online survey they completed in conjunction with Internet directory maven Yahoo! Check their Web site for more information.

O'Reily and Associates
103A Morris Street
Sebastopol, CA 95472
Phone: 707 829-0515
Email: nuts@ora.com **WWW:** http://www.ora.com

O'Reily and Associates is a leading book publisher and Internet developer. They also do research about the demographics of the Web. If you're interested in their studies of the Internet market, drop by their Web site.

PC Data
11260 Roger Bacon Drive, Suite 204
Reston, VA 22090
Phone: 703 435-1025

PC Data is a computer market research firm that offers some excellent data with pricing geared toward smaller developers. PC Data offers two standard reports that game developers can use to get a firm idea about what's going on out there concerning the game market:

The Game and Education Software Retail Report This report compiles monthly sales data from most of the top national resellers of game and education software. Their coverage is roughly 50 percent of the market (so you can extrapolate from there) and is quite detailed.

After presenting summary data about top publisher shares (LucasArts, Electronic Arts, Broderbund), the report tells you top-selling platforms (Mac, PC) and the top-selling game categories (Adventure, Sports, Simulation). Finally, the report provides you with top-selling price points in share and dollar figures ($19.99, $29.99, $39.99).

That's just the leadoff summaries! What follows is a top 400 list that shows you which games are selling, how many have sold (monthly and total to date), what the average price was, and more.

What's great about this data is that it's very accurate and quite relevant. I especially like the information about price points. Unfortunately, they don't follow consoles; to date their software reports are only Mac- and PC-based.

The Hardware Sales Report Available for the first time as this book goes to press, tracks sales of PC hardware and peripherals around the U.S. The report should give a very accurate idea of what 3D boards are selling well, how many multimedia equipped PCs have sold, and so on.

Developers can contact PC Data for a sample set of reports. Subscriptions start at $2,400 and go up as you ask for more complex and customized data. The $2,400 base subscription gives you a year's worth of reports.

The NPD Group
900 West Shore Road
Port Washington, NY 11050
Phone: 516 625-0700 **Fax:** 516 625-2347
Email: info@npd.com **WWW:** http://www.npd.com

The NPD Group is a subsidiary of Neilson Research. They are also the official software sales tracker for the Software Publishing Administration.

NPD has several key reports it has designed that are of interest to game developers:

National Survey of Hardware Ownership In January 1995, NPD did a mail survey of 15,000 households that they will continue to monitor. This hardware survey looks at what types of PCs are out there and provides information on the consumers that own them. You'll also find useful information on modem and online ownership.

SofTrends Sales Tracking SofTrends is similar to PC Data's sales tracking reports. These reports are compiled from information provided by over 7,500 stores and they include sales, pricing, and inventory data on thousands of software SKUs. Software reports are issued monthly, within four weeks of the close of the month, and contain sales tracked in the various common categories, which includes games and educational games.

Unlike PC Data's reports, SofTrends also tracks software sales as categorized by Targeted Age Range and Content ratings (RSAC). You can receive your information on diskette or by hard copy.

SofTrends Consumer Demographics Twice each year, NPD also captures purchase transactions, demographics, and product satisfaction data from 10,000 PC owners nationwide. SofTrends reports the compiled results in August and February. The 10,000 responses are drawn from NPD's national sample of 300,000 households who participate in market research projects for a wide range of industries.

According to NPD, this study looks at the following elements:

- What was bought—software title
- Date of purchase and the price paid (regular or promotional)
- Percent of households purchasing (penetration)
- Projected unit sales/share and projected dollar sales/share
- Where an item was bought (type of channel and name)
- Distribution of sales volume by type of channel
- Planned purchase information and reason for purchase (Christmas, birthday, and so on)

- Age and gender of buyer and recipient
- Relationship between buyer and recipient
- Satisfaction index

The Yankee Group
200 Portland Street
Boston, MA 02114
Phone: 617 367-1000 **Fax:** 617 367-5760
Email: info@yankeegroup.com **WWW:** http://www.yankeegroup.com

Along with IDC and Dataquest, Boston-based The Yankee Group is perhaps the third of a trio of major PC market researchers commonly used by the entire industry. Of interest to game developers is their unique TAF (The Technologically Advanced Family) survey, which is an annual appraisal of the consumer market in the telecommunications, entertainment, information, computing, and wireless areas.

The Yankee Group surveys a group of households that are made up of what are commonly referred to as "early adopters"—those people who are the first on the block to own the latest cool piece of technology. In surveying this select group, they seek to figure out what the rest of the market will do once they catch up.

In theory, if TAF families start buying Sega Saturns in droves, perhaps that signals that the rest of the market will follow. Early adopters often influence their less early adopting friends.

The TAF survey has been completed each year for the last decade. The most recent survey was completed in September 1994; it covers ownership, adoption, attitudes, usage, and interests of U.S. and Canadian consumers. For more information, stop by The Yankee Group's Web site.

Additional Market Analysis and Research Resources

After you visit the home pages of the previously listed companies, your next stop should be at the following three Web sites:

MMWire By The Numbers
`http://www.mmwire.com:80/buy.html`

MMWire is a leading industry news service that offers a really cool page that archives articles concerning different market research, statistical studies, and reports. Check here every once in a while for a good collection of information.

Software Publishing Association Research Page
`http://www.spa.org/research/research.htm`

The Software Publishing Association is a major conductor of market research and information collection. Visit their research home page for a slew of good basic information about the entire software market.

Red Herring Market Researchers List
`http://www.herring.com/direct.html#mark`

Red Herring Magazine is the leading magazine of the software/new media industry as it pertains to business and venture capital. Their Web site is nothing short of awesome. For links to additional market research sources, check the researchers list. (For complete information about *Red Herring* Magazine, see the business resources list, which is part of Chapter 33.)

CHAPTER 28

Creating great games is expensive, so you'll need lots of money. Here are some tips to help you get the financial resources you need.

By Dean M. Gloster

Game Company Startups: Finding the Critical Mass

Venture Capital and Other Financing Alternatives

Let's assume that you're both a brilliant and well informed game developer. (After all, you did buy this book.) You have a stable of terrific programmers and artists, and the world's greatest ideas for an entire line of compelling computer games. You lack only one major ingredient: money.

Creating great computer games is expensive. Some high-end games—Electronic Arts' Wing Commander III, Sierra's Phantasmagoria, and Interplay's Stonekeep, for example—cost a reported $3 to $5 million to produce. Although many developers have produced outstanding titles for far less than $500,000, consumer expectations and production values have steadily increased. To meet these demands, developers need to employ some top-notch people. Unfortunately, the most highly talented people don't work cheaply. In addition, many game developers have learned (the hard way) that developing games simply on advances from software publishers is a low-profit business: As we'll discuss in Chapter 29, under that business model, software publishers get the lion's share of net revenue from the title, in return for funding development, manufacturing, and marketing expenses, and assuming product return risks. For developers who want a better economic model, substantial capital is necessary to fund their own title development with the staff of their choice, to cover manufacturing and packaging costs, and to create an effective marketing and publicity campaign.

That's where this chapter comes in. It's not easy, but developers with a great team, technology, ideas, growth potential, and a strategy that differentiates their game company from the rest of the pack *can* get outside funding. That funding is available from a wide variety of venture capitalists, private investors, strategic investors, and even (some) debt financing sources.

Project Financing and Company Financing

As a game developer, the first question you must ask yourself is whether you are seeking *project* financing or long-term *company* financing. There are two different universes of potential funding sources. The first option deals with software publishers and other companies or individuals who finance specific titles or projects. We'll cover that issue in detail in Chapter 29. The second option for potential funding sources, which we cover in this chapter, is not really interested in your current title. These investors are more interested in your company and your plans to grow that business in the future. They're banking that your vision will reap huge gains on their investment when your company is sold or goes public.

Company Financing Alternatives

At the initial phase of company financing, a game developer is commonly "bootstrapped;" that is, the company is funded with the founders' own pockets and current operating profits (and maybe even Visa cards). Keeping a low overhead at this stage is crucial. Some companies find creative alternatives to financial concerns; using interns, offering royalty participations, and giving people on-screen credit in lieu of larger payments help to keep the overhead at a minimum. An extreme example of a developer making creative use of limited resources to bootstrap a company is Verin Lewis of Ashland, Oregon's Cyber-ROM Technologies. He worked on Trilobyte's original title The 7th Guest and has branched out since that time to form his own development company. While bootstrapping development of a couple of titles, he shares a house with some of his co-developers rent-free in an artist's community. He supplements his income as an authorized dealer of Autodesk's 3D Studio, and he has free access to thousands of dollars of hardware and software every year because of his local cable access TV show, in which he reviews new hardware and software tools.

But for many developers, the bootstrapping process is far too limiting. Rapidly growing developers require substantial additional capital to position themselves for anticipated future markets. At some point, they seek outside funding, often from venture capitalists, strategic investors, and private investors.

As venture capitalist Mark Gorenberg, a partner with Emeryville, California's Hummer, Windblad Venture Partners puts it, getting substantial outside funding also allows developers to avoid what he calls "unnatural acts" just to pay the bills. Outside funding, he explains, means that you can "concentrate on efforts to build your business strategically, instead of working on projects that create some current cash flow, but do not help you realize your long-term vision." Great. But what steps do you take to get that outside funding?

An Overview of the Funding Process and the Business Plan

The search for funding starts with drafting a business plan that establishes an overall vision and long-term focus. Key points include:

- The market for your games
- How your company will compete effectively in that market
- What differentiates your products from others in the market
- What is particularly exciting about your approach

Begin with a short (but compelling) executive summary that describes your company and what is particularly exciting about it. And leave the gushy adjectives in the thesaurus where they belong. Follow that summary with specifics: the key team, competitive advantages like proprietary technology, and the competition. Your plan should also include financial projections that show how the money raised will be used and the obligatory "hockey stick" projections of future revenue and income, which show explosive growth after the infusion of new capital. How long should a business plan be? If it's used to attract investors, make it as short as possible, and certainly not over 20 pages.

Before you grab pen and paper to begin your business plan, take a look at Michael Colby Orsak's (slightly) tongue-in-cheek list the "top ten reasons developers' business plans get tossed in the trash" sidebar. I'm sure you'll find it quite enlightening.

To understand how to draft a business plan, you need to understand how the plan will be read. In my experience, most venture-type investors read (or at least skim) the executive summary, then quickly flip to the section describing the key management or team members, then flip to the back of the business plan to see the sources and uses of funds and when the company projects that it will break even on the basis of operating income. If the investor is still interested, he or she will then read the rest of the business plan, as long as it's not too lengthy. You can always provide additional information later.

The common complaint venture capitalists and other investors have about most business plans is the "lack of focus." A related complaint is that the entrepreneur seeking funding for his or her company has never clearly articulated how this company is different from the others in the industry (or the slush pile of unread business plans piling up in someone's reception area).

What Investors Really Care About

Interested private investors, venture capitalists, or strategic investors will say "send me a copy of your business plan" when they want to talk with you further. But the truth is, to effectively raise capital, you need a much sharper focus than even a well-written three-page executive summary and 20-page business plan can provide. You need to reduce what is unique, interesting, and worthy of investment about your company to

The Top Ten Reasons Game Developers' Business Plans Get Tossed In the Trash

With tongue only partly in cheek, Michael Colby Orsak of San Francisco's JAFCO Ventures lists (with apologies to the "David Letterman Show") the top ten reasons game developers' business plans get tossed in the trash by venture capitalists:

10. Projecting $1 billion in revenue in year three.
9. Valuations based on 3DO (or Netscape).
8. No free game software included (or the software that is included won't install correctly).
7. More than three Al Gore "information superhighway" quotes in the executive summary.
6. The business plan depends on a platform to be released "real soon, we're sure."
5. Oh, boy! Another fighting game. (Building your company around a me-too idea is exactly the *opposite* of what you need to show a venture capitalist: what makes this company different and exciting.)
4. Trust us—*all* of our titles will be hits. (And the related assertion that we'll do *everything*: games, education, reference, edutainment....)
3. Five words: "Online, realtime, 3D interactive movies."
2. The business plan depends on an extensive network of vapor alliances.

[And the number one reason venture capitalists toss developers' business plans in the trash...]

1. Business plan dismisses large, aggressive companies that will compete for market share.

a short spiel—sales pitch, if you will—that you could write on the back of a business card or tell someone in a short elevator ride. CEO Steve Blank of Rocket Science Games calls this the "back of the business card or elevator test." Whatever you think of Rocket Science Games, Mr. Blank was successful in raising over $10 million for a startup game company in a very crowded market.

And what are examples of successful pitches? In the case of Rocket Science Games, it was something like, "We will take the storytelling and backstory skills of Hollywood, combine them with the eye-catching production values of Industrial Light & Magic, and bring them to the industry of computer gaming, which is larger than the feature film business." That got them over $10 million from half a dozen strategic and venture capital investors. In another case Ed Bernstein, founder of Palladium Interactive and former director of development at Broderbund and Vice President of edutainment products at Mindscape, offered his potential investors a line of products aimed at the children and family niches, coupled with a new business model for dealing with outside developers that emphasized collaborative publishing and shared risks and rewards. That got his startup company over $6 million from two venture funds. In another approach, AnimaTek president George Noceti boasted that his team, which included the creators of Tetris and a team of sixty programmers and computer artists in Russia, could produce games for far less than games of equal quality in development in the United States. That got AnimaTek funding from Spectrum Holobyte.

If your pitch is simply that you're going to "create really cool games," take a number. If, however, your pitch is something like, "We are creating a whole new line of compelling adventure games with themes that will appeal not only to the audience of gamers in the West but also to the growing Asian market," you are much more likely to get a receptive audience.

If it's the concise, exciting, investment pitch that attracts investors, why go through the trouble of drafting a business plan? Any interested investor is going to ask you probing questions about your business and its prospects. If you haven't done the analysis and critical thinking to put together your business plan, you won't be able to answer those questions, and you won't be cashing the investor's check. And even if you aren't seeking outside funding, you still need to do the critical thinking to put together a business plan. Bill Wright, the founder of Wright Financial Solutions, a Berkeley, CA company, advises numerous developers and high-tech companies on strategic planning and financial and accounting systems. He explains, "trying to build a business without a business plan is like trying to build a house without a blueprint. Sure, it's been done, but it's not very practical."

OK—now you have a business plan. Where do you take it?

Venture Capitalists

Venture capitalists are often the initial target source of financing for game developers because they are easy to find; there are several published directories of venture capitalists. An excellent one is *Pratt's Guide to Venture Capital Sources,* Securities Data Corp., 1995, ISBN 0-914470-74-4. For an even more helpful resource, take a look at the resources presented in Chapter 33, which lists over 100 venture capitalists who have made recent computer game or multimedia-related investments. In addition to being easy to find, venture capitalists' avowed purpose is to make minority investments in emerging growth companies. Venture capitalists also have *lots* of money to invest. Most venture funds have between $30 million and $800 million to manage, and they need to put that money to work on a regular basis in order to generate the kinds of returns that their investors expect. Finally, a number of venture capital firms have specifically targeted the area of entertainment software to make further investments: Gabelli Multimedia Partners was formed specifically to make multimedia software investments; Hummer, Windblad Venture Partners invest exclusively in software companies; NHL Partners is a recently formed $30 million dollar venture fund organized by New Line Cinema and the French Media conglomerate Havas to invest in "the development and production of interactive video game software and the distribution and marketing of all multimedia software, including interactive games on a worldwide basis;" and the new Technologies for Information and Entertainment Fund (there's a mouthful) also specifically targets the entertainment software industry.

Who Are These Investors?

Venture capital funds are pools of substantial cash generally put up by institutional investors. The managers of the fund are experienced investors who have a track record of running, advising, or helping prior successful early-stage ventures. Most venture capitalists see thousands of business plans a year and invest in only a handful of companies. (A commonly cited figure is that venture capitalists invest in fewer than one percent of the companies they review.)

Venture capitalists do not typically involve themselves in the day-to-day management of companies they invest in (unless something is going very wrong), but they do generally sit on the board of directors. Often venture capitalists bring, in addition to cash, extensive industry contacts and strategic advice. They are generally bright, knowledgeable, and broadly experienced in dealing with the kinds of strategic issues that rapidly growing businesses encounter. They often act as a sounding board for entrepreneurs and as a resource in helping to find strategic partners or key management personnel that need to be hired as the business expands. Often, venture capitalists will make several "rounds" of investment, putting in an initial amount, and then as the company continues to meet projections, investing a larger, subsequent milestone. Typical dollar amounts in venture capital financing rounds are $1 to $10 million, although a number of so-called "seed funds" like Draper Associates, Wasatch Venture Corp., and Mayfield Software Partners invest in early-stage businesses in the $100,000 to $1 million range.

It is not unusual for several venture capital funds to participate in the same financing round. Although venture capitalists typically put up large amounts of money, they often acquire only a minority interest in the company.

What's the Catch?

For many, this sounds almost too good to be true: There are groups of venture capital investors with millions of dollars to put into early-stage businesses, and all they want is a minority interest. The catch, of course, is that the overwhelming majority of computer game developers (and other early-stage businesses) will never qualify for serious consideration for a venture capital investment. Venture capitalists can afford to be (and must be) extremely selective about the companies they invest in, and they have specific investment criteria that most companies don't meet: Any realistic target for venture capital financing must have *huge* growth potential. Venture capitalists target rates of return that, in less capitalistically enlightened times were routinely referred to as "obscene." How obscene? Venture capitalists routinely look for compound annual return rates of 40 percent or more, or four to ten times their money back in a three to five year period. Venture capitalists need to target these kinds of aggressive returns because *about half of venture capital investments end up as almost complete write-offs.* Many others turn out to be only moderately successful. In order to meet their own investor's expectations, venture capitalists need "home run" returns on a regular basis. That means that most companies that are even quite successful, but merely generate a nice living for the founders and key employees (so-called "lifestyle businesses") are ineligible for venture capital.

Venture capitalists also require that the company have an effective *exit strategy*: Venture capitalists expect that the companies they invest in will either be sold to a bigger company or go through an initial public offering in the stock market within three to five years, liquidating the venture capitalists' risky investment and rewarding them with enormous returns. Unless your projections realistically show the necessary growth potential and unless you are prepared to sell your company or go public (which, for a software company requires growth to over $10 million in annual revenues), you are not a candidate for venture capital financing.

In addition, there are a couple of factors that make computer-game developers a particularly hard sell with many venture firms: First, the unpleasant fact is that most developers are not making much money. There are numerous example of developers who are phenomenally successful (like Id and Cyan), and many other developers who, like Maxis, have grown from an initial title to become publicly traded companies. Still, these tend to be the exceptions. A 1994 Gistix survey of multimedia companies found that 94 percent of developers were not profitable. (I'm not as alarmed about that statistics as some other people; multimedia is a young industry.)

"These statistics, though," says Garrett Gruener of San Francisco venture capital firm Burr, Egan, DeLeage & Co., "do make venture capitalists take a hard look at investments in this area." He adds, "The other problem with game development is that it's a hits-driven business." Unlike many other industries, in which venture capitalists can analyze barriers to entry, competitive features of a product, and niche market preferences, computer games are a consumer product, and any prediction about what consumers will like is something of a guess. "Even in the movie industry," Gruener explains, "where they have decades of experience, knowledgeable people make mistakes all the time about what will be a hit." In the much younger industry of computer gaming, he notes, it is even harder to know with confidence what titles (and what companies) will be winners. Even with these difficulties, Burr, Egan, DeLeage & Co. *has* invested in companies like Broderbund and Berkeley Systems.

What Do Venture Capitalists Want?

To a greater or lesser extent, venture capitalists and other venture-type investors typically look at the underlying team, the technology, and the idea. Of these factors, which is the most important? As one venture capitalist recently explained, "If the three most important factors in real estate are location, location, and location, then the three most important factors in investing in an early-stage company are the people, the people, and the people." (Or, as another puts it, "I'd rather invest in a great entrepreneur with a good idea, than a good entrepreneur with a great idea.")

And what do venture capitalists look for in this team of people? Talent, vision, enthusiasm, energy, a track record of prior success, honesty, integrity, some sophistication about what is required to run a business, and—most important—effective management skills. Mark Gorenberg of Hummer, Windblad Venture Partners, however, explains his firm's analysis of management: "We're not interested in 'boat anchors'—white-haired former executives from another industry just dragged to the meeting to demonstrate 'management experience,' even though they know nothing about this company. We like to see *appropriate* management skills for the kind of business the company is in. If you are a software developer, that may be experience in project management." As his partner Ann Windblad puts it, "How much experience did Bill Gates have when he founded Microsoft?" She prefers to see someone with vision.

What else do you need to attract venture capital? A great team is nice, but they leave the building and go home every night. "You have to have a track record of prior success," concedes Ed Bernstein, who recently founded Sausalito, California-based developer and publisher Palladium Interactive, with over $6 million of venture funding from Canaan Partners and U.S. Venture Partners. "But you also need to show them a unique product, product line, or proprietary technology. *And* you need a significant piece of the distribution pie." That means, at a minimum, you have to be planning to distribute your titles through an affiliate label distribution arrangement, with a long-term goal of growing into a publisher yourself.

Hummer, Winblad's Mark Gorenberg explains, "We want to see companies that can capture an area of market real estate and expand that real estate and defend it against competitors." Other venture capitalists hold similar positions, and are particularly interested in companies like Id and Maxis (with its Sim titles) that can create and grow market niches for entire game product lines.

Successfully Approaching Venture Capitalists

To recap, the first step is to determine whether your company is actually appropriate for venture capital financing. Is your business going to grow hugely with the addition of venture capital, and is your goal to sell your business or go public within three to five years? Do you really have a *company* that you are trying to finance, not simply a game? I have said it before, but it is worth saying one more time: Venture capitalists fund *companies*; they do not fund *title* development.

Your second step is to do your homework on your own company. Analyze your strategy and market, create and revise your business plan, and develop your short investment pitch.

Your third step is to do some homework on potential venture capital funding sources. Concentrate on firms that have at least some potential of funding software developers. It's also helpful to approach firms with offices in your geographic area. Although most venture capitalists firms invest nationally, some limit themselves to the area where their offices are located, and it certainly makes the logistics of meeting, due diligence, and monitoring their investment easier. The list of venture capital funds at the end of Part VII is a nice starting place for your research. For an updated list of this database, check out my firm's (Farella, Braun, and Martel) Web site (*http://www.fbm.com/multimedia*). Another good online resource that lists recent venture capital investment deals is the Price Waterhouse LLP National Venture Capital Survey (*http://www.sjmercury.com:80/features/venture/menu.htm*).

After you have identified potential venture capitalists, do everything possible to get a personal introduction. Again, because of the cascade of unsolicited business plans, an introduction provides you with more credibility and allows your business plan to get more attention than it would get if skimmed by a summer intern or receptionist. Your attorney or accountant may have substantial contacts in the venture capital industry (particularly if located in the Silicon Valley, San Francisco, or Boston areas), and you may be able to get an introduction through other developers you know who have venture backing. There are also panels of entertainment software-friendly venture capitalists at many industry conferences, including Intermedia, Milia, the Computer Game Developers' Conference, Multimedia Expo, Multimedia Live!,

Seybold, Digital Hollywood, and the annual Fall Multimedia Venture Financing Conference hosted by my firm in San Francisco. These panels are an excellent opportunity to meet a group of venture capitalists, to introduce yourself, to give them a business card, and to give them your one-minute elevator investment pitch. Then, when you follow up with your polite cover letter and business plan, you can start your letter with, "When we met recently at the Intermedia conference, you suggested I send you our business plan. As you may remember, a particularly exciting aspect of our business from an investor's point of view is...." When you're looking to find out what's what on the game developer's conference circuit, check out my firm's Web sit, or browse through one of many industry publications that provide this service, including *Red Herring, The Multimedia Monitor, The MDG Bulletin,* and occasionally, *Computer Entertainment News.*

If you find yourself surfing the Web, stop in at Accel Partners Web site (*http://www.accel.com*) for a great resource on dealing with venture capitalists.

Strategic Investors

Although less understood, strategic investors may be, in many ways, even better than venture capitalists as a funding source. Numerous established companies have targeted the entertainment software industry for acquisitions, joint ventures, or strategic investments. Why? Well, particularly in the CD-ROM area, many companies have seen the eye-popping growth numbers in entertainment software sales. But there is more to it than that. Entertainment, media, print, and software companies seek to create synergy with their existing distribution channels or seek to grow rapidly through investments in complementary businesses. Sometimes these strategic investors have different agendas than medium-range profit, ranging from gaining expertise to obtaining access to technology, to locking up a developer from working for competitors, to becoming an instant distribution channel.

What are the advantages of dealing with a strategic investor, instead of a venture capitalist? First, typically you don't have to part with as much of the stock in your company for the same amount of money. Dean Frost is a founding partner of Frost Capital Partners, an investment banking firm in San Francisco that specializes in merger and acquisition work for entertainment and education software companies. He has concluded, after an extensive study of financing deals, that developers' valuations tend to be significantly higher in strategic investment deals, rather than in venture capital investments. In addition, strategic investors usually have something else to offer along with money and business experience. They can often provide branded content, additional channels of distribution, access to foreign markets, access to proprietary technology, co-marketing opportunities, or other strategic benefits. Finally, strategic investors tend to be less concerned about an exit strategy three to

five years down the road from their initial investment because *they* may be an exit strategy. That is, if they are happy with the performance you have given them as a minority investor, they may want to pay a lot more money for the rest of your company three years down the road.

Who Are These Investors?

As long as the computer game industry (or at least the CD-ROM and online end of it) continues to grow rapidly, the world will be full of potentially interested strategic investors. There are three characteristics to look for (other than a large pile of money) in a potential strategic investor, to quickly get to the check writing state.

First, there should be some synergy for *you* in pairing up with this partner. Legend Entertainment, a Virginia-based science fiction computer game developer, received a large investment from Random House. In addition to money, in that investment Legend obtained several things, including access to much of the existing content library of Del Rey Books, Random House's science fiction imprint. Legend also got the opportunity to work on original titles with Del Rey authors and to have those authors available to do novelizations of its original games. Finally, Legend got an additional distribution channel, as Random House is trying hard to broaden the consumer software retail channel by selling entertainment software in traditional bookstores.

Second, there should be some synergy for your investor in partnering with you. Sticking with the Random House/Legend Entertainment example, Random House became an instant channel of distribution for game software, and got an increased opportunity to turn its existing science fiction books into computer games. Similarly, by investing in developer AnimaTek, game publisher Spectrum Holobyte recently obtained more content to distribute and got access to the skills of another outside developer. If your strategic investor gets some independent benefit from the relationship, this improves your chances of getting the financing in a reasonable period of time.

Finally, the *ideal* strategic investor, in my slightly cynical world view, is a potential dinosaur of a company just two steps away from your software development business. They may be facing obsolescence or be threatened by technological advancements and can only risk investing in a company that is a close cousin to the entertainment software industry. If you can find a related company that is nervously eyeing the future and sees the computer game industry as a way to hedge its bets, you have excellent prospects for a successful strategic investment deal. An example of a strategic investment in a game developer that met all three of these criteria was the investment by Blockbuster Video in San Francisco start-up game developer company CAPS, founded by Judy Lange, who had earlier co-founded Crystal Dynamics. At the time of its initial investment, Blockbuster was in the video rental business, facing rising concern over potential future online or interactive TV delivery of video on demand. In addition, through an innovative pilot program, Blockbuster was then experimenting with rental of computer games in its stores, providing a new distribution channel. Obviously, there were advantages to Blockbuster in investing in a computer game developer and potential advantages to CAPS in having a company like Blockbuster Entertainment as a strategic investor. Finally, at the time of the investment (before Blockbuster's purchase by Viacom, which itself has more new media tentacles than an octopus) Blockbuster Entertainment fit my model of a strategic investor who might reasonably be nervous about the effect of technology on its own market niche.

At the end of Part VII you'll find a directory of a few of the many strategic investors who have made computer game or other online and multimedia-related investments. You can find an updated database of investors at my firm's Web site (again, *http://www.fbm.com/multimedia*).

Private Investors

For companies not far enough along to attract venture capitalists and strategic investors, there is still the alternative of private investors. Private investors are commonly known as "angel" financiers, and they can be an outstanding source of capital—if you can find one. The book *Demystifying Multimedia* defines an "angel" as someone "who shares the project vision and wants to bring it into existence." Well, maybe. Typically, the angel shares the *money* he or she has, and occasionally some of his or her accumulated business wisdom. It is difficult to locate angel financiers unless they have a pre-existing connection with the company principals or they have a substantial interest in, or sophistication about, the industry in which they are investing.

Who Are These Angels?

Although the venture capital community is far more visible, historically private investors provide far more capital to startup ventures. But where do you find these investors? The most successful place for obtaining first-stage investments is through friends and family. These people have a pre-existing connection to you, and they have more trust in you than a stranger would. Unfortunately, for most of us who are not related by blood (or by being college roommates) to Bill Gates, Larry Ellison, and the Saudi royal family, the amount of money that can be raised from friends and family is limited. So how do you attract investments from people outside your immediate circle of friends and relatives? There have been extensive studies of the profile of typical private investors in startup businesses. A substantial portion of so-called angel investors have a high net worth, of over $1,000,000. The majority of angel investors, however, are not millionaires, although they have above-average income. Most of them are business owners or middle managers who are generally about twenty years

older than the entrepreneurs that they finance. Typically, private investors can make investment decisions far faster than can venture capitalists or strategic investors. They are particularly willing to invest in startups, and they invest much smaller amounts of money; individual private investors generally lay down $50,000 or less.

One effective strategy for locating private investors is to network through other professionals that you know. Contact your attorney, your accountant, the people on your board of advisors, and various financial advisors, and supply them with a copy of your business plan with a request that they give you leads. Sometimes you can find investors in your own backyard. How about the owner of that production company who is doing the digitized video for your title? Would he or she be interested in investing in you?

Another category of potential investors is highly compensated professionals: Doctors, lawyers, and airline pilots are the traditional short list of target investors. (This approach may be particularly helpful if the kinds of games that your company is creating have some special appeal to your investor audience. For example, if you were doing a flight simulation game, your company might have a particular appeal to airline pilots, many of whom are former military jet pilots.) Along this same line, another source of private investors for startup companies is executives, middle managers, and highly compensated technical people who are leaving much larger companies with golden parachutes, vested stock options, and the like: They often have substantial capital along with relevant business or technical expertise to help make a startup company successful.

Various cities also have venture capital clubs, which provide a forum for venture investors and intermediaries. For a list of venture clubs around the country, contact:

Jim Jensen Association of Venture Clubs
265 E. 100 South, Suite 300
Salt Lake City, UT 84110-3358
801 364-1100

There are even specific networks to put companies together with interested investors. For example, the Silicon Valley Capital Network is located in San Jose, California. (For more information, contact Dennis Laudermilch at 408 541-7627). For a list of the nearest venture capital groups to you, contact:

Venture Capital Network
Box 882
Durham, NH 03824
603 862-3558

You can also try to approach intermediaries (finders, business brokers, and loan brokers) who might be able to find private investors for you. In return, those middlemen would get a portion of the money they find for you. Get references on any finder or broker, and be extremely careful when someone asks for a substantial fee up front whether or not he can deliver investor money.

Computer game developers are in a particularly good business for attracting private investment. In addition to offering the potential of substantial returns if your company is successful, you are in an interesting, glitzy business (even if it doesn't seem that way at two o'clock in the morning when you are trying to fix a software bug). The computer gaming business gives private investors a substantial amount of "psychic income;" they can tell their friends that they are an investor in a company that develops the world's coolest entertainment software.

You should carefully check out the background and motivations, however, of potential private investors. While it is important to do some research about venture capitalists and strategic investors, by talking to the companies they have invested in previously, it is even *more* important to do this with private investors. Venture capitalists have a fairly standard set of expectations: They do not want to run your company, and they do not need their money back until the end of the target investment period. Private investors, however, can have wildly different expectations and goals. Some of them may need their money back on short notice or may harbor the notion that if they are putting money into your company, they ought to actually start running your company, especially since it looks like so much fun.

Finally, an additional note of caution in dealing with private investors: Liability is less of an issue with venture capitalists, who are extraordinarily savvy, experienced, and unlikely to sue over an investment gone bad. But if you are using a business plan to solicit investments from private investors in the United States, you are subject to the federal securities laws. These include the rule that allows investors to demand their money back if they can establish that the investment was solicited on the basis of a "materially misleading" misrepresentation or material omission. In plain English, if you left some information out that would have caused them to rethink their investment, they may have the ability to sue to get their money back. As a result, circulars sent to private investors commonly contain an extensive discussion of the "risk factors" that investors should be aware of before making an investment. (Sophisticated investors understand that this recital of risk factors is necessary under the securities laws and tend not to be unduly frightened by them. Anyone investing in a startup venture is undertaking a highly speculative leap of faith, and should be aware of that.)

Even more important: Whenever you are dealing with private investors in the United States, you need to take steps to ensure that you are not an "underwriter" of an unregistered public offering. There are numerous very specific exemptions from the U.S. securities laws (small offerings, intra-state offerings) that allow you to raise money from small numbers of investors without violating the securities laws that

otherwise require registration. These exemptions, however, are quite narrow. This is, however, only general information, and the law constantly changes. Painful (or expensive) as it may be, if you are raising money from a group of private investors, you should consult with an attorney in structuring and documenting the investment and solicitation materials.

Debt Financing Alternatives

A sometimes overlooked funding source is debt, which allows entrepreneurs to grow rapidly without sacrificing a substantial equity stake. Many small startup companies are funded (at least initially) on the credit cards of the founders. Unfortunately, debt usually requires current interest payments, creating potential cash flow difficulties.

For most computer game developers there is an even more daunting problem about obtaining traditional bank debt financing: It's impossible. I was amused by an article I saw a year ago in a magazine called *Morph's Outpost on the Digital Frontier*, targeted at developers, which described how to impress a banker. But the truth is, the only way most startup computer game developers would get money from a bank is with a handgun. Banks obtain no upside in connection with their loans, and in traditional loan underwriting, they demand both a substantial prior operating history generating positive cash flow *and* assets with a substantial liquidation value as collateral to assure repayment. Most computer game developers do not meet these criteria. Still, there are options for debt financing other than standard bank financing.

For companies with a substantial operating history that still do not qualify for traditional bank loans, there are commercial finance companies and other similar lenders that may offer slightly less conservative working capital loans and other financing. Unfortunately, these loans typically impose substantially higher terms.

Many equipment vendors have arrangements with leasing companies to finance the lease of necessary equipment. Several companies, including Menlo Capital, specialize in providing debt financing to companies with venture capital funding. Some lenders, like Silicon Valley Bank and Imperial Bank, have venture-lending groups. Many banks have special programs for women-owned and minority-owned companies, and there are special programs in *many* cities for making loans to small local businesses, targeted at job creation.

Mezzanine Financing

For larger developers and publishers with a substantial operating history, current cash flow and some assets (even if it's a future receivable, such as the world's greatest bundling deal), there is also an aggressive category of lenders, commonly referred to as "mezzanine financing." Mezzanine financing describes a kind of capital that is somewhere between more traditional senior-debt financing and common stock. In some cases, it takes the form of redeemable preferred stock. In most cases, however, it is some kind of subordinated debt (behind bank financing) with an equity component, such as a warrant to purchase additional stock cheaply or a feature that allows the debt to be converted into common stock. Typically, mezzanine lenders target internal rates of return of about 25 percent, and a portion of that return is the interest rate payable currently out of cash flow. For larger companies, investment bankers (discussed in the next section) are a good source of mezzanine lenders. For smaller companies, loan brokers may have some leads.

Small Business Administration Loans

Small Business Administration (SBA) loans can also be an excellent financing source for loans between $50,000 and $3 million, depending on the type of loan you are applying for. SBA loans are made by private lenders, such as banks, but they are partially guaranteed by the SBA, a federal agency. Because they are partially guaranteed, private lenders are often willing to make these loans even if there is a greater risk of non-repayment. The two main categories of SBA loans are the Section 7(a) Program and the Section 504 Program. The Section 7(a) Program is the most flexible and allows for working capital and equipment loans ranging from $50,000 to $1 million (although individual lenders' limits may be less than this). The paperwork is typically substantial, but in many areas there are qualified SBA packagers who can assist you in putting together all the documentation. For a recommendation of an SBA packager in your area, contact your local SBA office, found in the white pages of your phone book under "United States Federal Government," or contact the SBA directly at 202 653-6570. In addition, some private lenders have special SBA programs for smaller loans. Eric Houser of Citibank in San Francisco explains "with our Capital Access Program, we offer faster loans, with no requirement of a security interest in the personal assets of the owners or the borrower or any personal guarantee." Although one traditional complaint about SBA loans is the length of time it takes to have them approved, Mr. Houser explains that with his bank's Capital Access Program, "we commit to a decision within five days, and usually complete funding in twenty-one to thirty days."

The Section 504 Program, targeted more toward real estate and heavy equipment, permits loans of up to $3 million and more.

Typically, non-real estate SBA loans are 7- to10-year term loans (which is longer than standard bank term loans), and interest rates (which are negotiable) range generally from prime rate plus 2 percent to prime rate plus 2 3/4 percent. There may also be an initial guarantee fee of up to 2 percent of the SBA-guaranteed portion of the loan.

SBA loans are generally secured by all of the assets of the borrower, and some SBA loan programs require personal guarantees from the principals of the borrower, and sometimes a second deed of trust or mortgage on the principals' house.

Throughout the United States, tens of thousands of banks and other financial institutions are authorized SBA lenders. The individual lenders' SBA lending criteria vary greatly in how aggressive they may be. Even if you have been turned down by one lender for an SBA loan, another lender may be willing to provide financing. SBA loans usually carry far lower interest rates than you could pay for similar debt financing and there are no prepayment penalties. While other bank loans permit a debt-to-equity ratio of only 2:1 ($2 of debt for every $1 of capital you put into the business), SBA lenders commonly permit a much higher ratio, allowing you to increase the leverage on your money.

So what do you need to show an SBA lender to get one of these loans? It varies greatly from lender to lender. Eric Houser explains the requirements of Citibank in San Francisco, which is aggressively marketing its SBA loan program to software developers and other perceived high-tech companies. "You should have twelve months of profitability with at least adequate cash flow to service the debt."

Investment Bankers and Underwriters

Another group of professionals exists to help companies with financing transactions, mergers and acquisitions, private placements, and initial public offerings. "Investment bankers" are somewhat misnamed, since they usually don't make investments, and they are not bankers. Traditionally, investment bankers are advisors, go-betweens, and underwriters who assist companies either in making acquisitions and investments or in selling equity or obtaining financing. They help with valuation analysis, due diligence, and deal structures (all of which we will discuss later in this chapter), and are generally well connected with institutional and other financing sources. Speaking generally, *underwriters* are banking firms that assist with the distribution and sale of public offerings (initial public offerings and follow on offerings), and *placement agents* are investment bankers who assist with private placements of large debt or equity investments. A given investment banking firm might do all these things and also manage a venture capital or bridge financing fund.

Investment bankers are essential in public offerings of securities and in large private placements. If well-connected, they can also be helpful in lining up large strategic investors. However, they are generally much less helpful in obtaining venture financing. In addition, most sizable investment banking firms concentrate on transactions of $5 million and more, and prefer to deal with transactions that are *much* larger.

There are, however, a few one- or two-person boutique investment banking firms in various regions that may help with smaller transactions.

Investment bankers are expensive, and they often receive compensation both in the form of initial consultation fees and a portion of financing they obtain. Examples of Investment bankers with game company experience are Frost Capital Partners, an investment banking firm in San Francisco, California that specializes in entertainment and educational software companies. Another is D.H. Blair Investment Banking Co., a New York-based investment banking firm that specializes in private placements and other capital raising for rapidly growing companies with some "sizzle." (A complete list of these companies is available on our CD-ROM.)

The Funding Process and Beyond

You've read this chapter, drafted your great business plan, developed your investment pitch, identified your potential funding sources, and networked to get personal introductions. Now what? First, be aware that it takes a *long* time to obtain to financing. Typically, only private investors are capable of making a decision relatively quickly. But the process of approaching venture capitalists and strategic investors, meeting with them, allowing them to do due diligence on your company, and negotiating the final deal terms can take six months or a year, even if the process is successful. So don't wait until you are almost out of money to go looking for more. (Besides, investors are often more cautious about putting money into a company that is almost completely out of cash, and in your desperation, you won't have much leverage to obtain the best terms with your financing source.)

Here's a rundown of the typical funding cycle for an entrepreneurial company (including game developers):

1. The company is initially funded by the founders and some "seed" money private investors, who are often friends and family.
2. As the company gets bigger or further along, it has more to show to outside investors and a better ability to generate attractive valuation numbers.
3. The company then approaches venture capitalists and strategic investors. Sometimes, strategic partners are found first, and this network of strategic relationships is part of what makes the company attractive to venture capitalists. Other times, venture capitalists put money into the company first, and then assist the company in lining up strategic partners. Jim Breyer of Accel Partners recommends this approach: "First raise venture capital and insanely focus on developing rich products. Then, your company can be positioned to attract partnerships with major media players such as Disney, TCI and Microsoft."

4. Finally, a few years later, after spectacular success, the company goes through an initial public offering, selling a portion of its stock to the public and making the original founders and early round investors fabulously wealthy (at least on paper) overnight. Or, the company is sold to a much larger software company, and the founders continue to toil away, but as wealthy heads of a division of a much larger company.

Due Diligence: Finding Your Worst Nightmare before Someone Else Does

Before writing you a check, any sophisticated investor will insist that your company is properly organized, that it has the rights to use its technology, that it has appropriate arrangements in writing with employees and intellectual property licensors, and that it does not have huge lurking tax problems. (For a more detailed discussion of the legal issues you need to address in forming your company and making sure that your company owns the necessary rights to its games, see Chapter 32.)

To avoid awkward pauses after questions from your potential investors, it is smart to take care of these problems—or at least to develop a strategy to solve them—before going out to get funding. Above all, however, do not lie to or mislead the investors about these issues: This is not only fraud, but definitely is fatal to the long-term process of getting along with your investors. People contemplating giving you hundreds of thousands or millions of dollars are placing enormous trust in you. And if you lead them astray once, they will not give you their money.

Valuation: How Much Am I Bid for This Piece of Blue Sky?

The issue of valuation (how much your company is actually worth, which can be decided many different ways), particularly with a startup enterprise, is difficult. Still, there are some guidelines. One approach is to look at how Wall Street values companies that currently look like what you plan to grow into. Then discount that future valuation for the time it will take to get there and the substantial risk that you won't make it. If this general analysis sounds like an estimate compounded by a guess, that's because it is. Although business schools teach several different formulas for valuing mature companies, none of them is particularly useful for startups or early-stage businesses that everyone hopes will grow rapidly.

"I *wish* we could simply use a discounted present value analysis," says Dean Frost of Frost Capital Partners. "It would make things a lot simpler." His firm maintains a database of recent venture capital and other deals involving entertainment software developers to give them data points for establishing valuation. Mark Gorenberg of

Hummer, Winblad explains that his firm is willing to sit down with the entrepreneur and disclose the terms of their other investments to establish a comfort level that the final figures are within a reasonable range. But essentially the process of valuation is a negotiation between a willing seller (you) who wants to sell part of the equity in a company to a willing buyer (the investor).

Deal Structures

The subject of how to structure investments in early-stage companies could be the subject of an entire book. Several broad themes, however, characterize investments in growing early stage companies. First, investments typically come in the form of equity. The investor expects to share in the huge appreciation of your company as it grows larger. Second, the initial round of investments are typically for only a *minority* ownership interest in the company. The investors understand that the founders need to have a substantial incentive for toiling night and day to create the value for everyone, and they also understand that the founders' equity stake may be further diluted by later rounds of investment as the growing company needs still more capital to expand. Third, initial round investors often insist on the right to participate in later financing rounds at some favorable stock price, in order to prevent extreme dilution of their equity ownership stake and to reward them for making the most risky first-stage investment.

As an entrepreneur, you should be somewhat careful about how your deal is structured; you want to preserve maximum flexibility for later investments. More importantly, if your first round investors are private individuals in the United States who are not "accredited investors" under the securities laws, they may not be able to participate in later financing rounds without enormous legal complications. Typically, there is a broad array of minority investor protections in negotiated deals, like prohibitions against distributing all of the money made by the company in the form of inflated salaries, and in venture deals there are often provisions that allow the investors to replace management or to take over control of the company if the company falls radically short of projections. Investors also often insist on some kind of downside protection, so that if the company is only modestly successful and is sold after a couple of years, they will get their investment back, before the entrepreneurial founders (who have been receiving a salary this entire time) see any upside. Common ways to arrange this deal include structuring part of the investment as a note convertible into stock or giving the investors preferred stock (convertible into common) with a priority right to payment upon liquidation or sale of the company.

After You Cash the Check

You buy this book, create the world's coolest computer game development company, come up with a focused strategy and brilliant business plan, talk to investors and get to the point where you now have a check for several million dollars in your hands.

What next? Well, you will find that a lot of things change once you get substantial outside funding. For example, your first voice mail message may be from your programmer, asking for a raise. It is remarkably easy to go through a huge amount of money in a short period of time, once you have it. Tim Draper, founding partner of Draper Associates, a venture capital fund that specializes in smaller "seed" investments in startup companies, explains that he likes to make investments in the range of $100,000 instead of $1 million, because entrepreneurs always spend exactly as much money as they have, and the corporate culture on overhead and focus on profitability is set at a very early stage in the company. A critique of many startups that received huge initial funding was that they never figured out how to keep overhead low and focus the corporate mission on becoming profitable.

How do you avoid this "venture bloat?" Probably the best rule is to hire only great people. This rule will limit your growth (there are only so many great people around), but it will often pay off in the long run.

Another important rule after you get funding is to continually provide your investors with regular information, even (or especially) if you are starting to miss the projections in your business plan. Almost everyone who invests in startups and early-stage companies understands that the projections may not be met, but *no one* likes to be surprised by bad news that should have been apparent (and revealed) months before.

Finally, the best advice for any developer who has received funding is to make great games and sell them in huge numbers to consumers. The results will make consumers happy, your distributors happy, your investors happy, and you happy.

And they say money doesn't buy happiness.

CHAPTER 29

How you publish your games involves a set of complex trade-offs.

By Dean M. Gloster

Dealing with Software Publishers

It's difficult enough to develop great games with brilliant designs, terrific graphics, slick programming, and compelling play. But it may be even harder to do the *rest* of what it takes to sell a great game: Provide packaging design, game manufacturing, money for development expenses, product fulfillment, relationships with distributors and retailers, effective marketing and public relations campaigns, retail shelf space, and technical support.

Fortunately, there are companies willing to do all this (and more) for developers who can make great games. These companies are *software publishers*. In theory, software publishers are well-funded companies with excellent distribution and marketing, who can fund your development costs and then do a great job positioning, launching, and marketing your title to create huge sales and generate royalties. In reality, of course, your mileage may vary.

Software publishers, however, don't provide this development funding, distribution, and marketing just as a public service for the developer community. Generally, the more services a software publisher provides, the greater the percentage of net sales revenue it will retain, instead of paying to the developer. To illustrate the general economics, let's take a look at four alternative types of development and distribution deals.

Alternative Publishing and Distribution Arrangements

In the world of entertainment software distribution there are many hybrid arrangements, but to simplify somewhat, we will examine four different approaches:

- *The "standard" publishing deal.* Here the software publisher funds development costs through milestone advances to the developer as various parts are completed. The publisher takes care of all aspects of packaging, manufacturing, marketing, and distribution.
- *Variation of the standard publishing deal.* This is a similar arrangement to the first, but in this case the *developer* self-funds the development costs.
- *Affiliate label distribution.* Here the developer not only funds development costs, but also generally pays for manufacturing, and takes on the consumer marketing campaign. In this arrangement, the affiliate label distributor provides order taking, warehousing, and shipping. The distributor also takes care of getting shelf space in the retail stores.
- *Self-publishing.* Here the developer takes on *all* of the above responsibilities.

The "Standard" Publishing Arrangement: Developing on Milestone Advances

The game development business is unique. Almost nowhere else can a talented team with an idea for a compelling product go to an established company and get $500,000 or more to develop it and then turn over the results to that company, which will handle every detail of package design, manufacturing, marketing, distribution, and technical support. Unfortunately, in this arrangement the publisher takes on substantial economic risks: The developer's creative team may split up or be unable to finish the title. (An almost-finished alpha version of a game isn't worth much.) The publisher also faces a substantial marketing risk—what if a better but similar product is released first by someone else? The publisher bears substantial inventory risks, since consumer software retailers can usually return unsold inventory. To promote and market the product, the publisher may have to spend hundreds of thousands of dollars (or perhaps even millions) in publicity, advertising, and marketing support.

The publisher's high risk in the traditional publishing deal, coupled with the golden rule (those who have the gold get to make the rules), results in a meager "standard" royalty for developers. Royalty rates vary, but standard base royalties are 10 to 18 percent of the publisher's net revenues after deductions for shipping, taxes, insurance, and returns. First-time developers typically get royalty rates on the lower side. Even worse, in a "standard" publishing deal, the milestone payments made by the publisher to fund development costs are usually treated as an advance against royalties, and are recouped out of the royalties otherwise payable to the developer.

Later in this chapter I'll provide some suggestions on how to negotiate a more attractive royalty and recoupment arrangement, but unless a developer is prepared to fund a substantial portion of the development costs or has other interested publishers, the publisher usually has almost all the negotiating leverage. To many developers, even a royalty of 15 or 18 percent seems outrageously low, given that the developer often came up with the idea for the game, and created a compelling game using its own cutting-edge technology. Unfortunately, however, this *is* the standard business model, and it is a tough one for developers: A 1994 GISTIX survey of 912 multimedia software developers, for example, found that 96 percent of them reported that their CD-ROM titles were unprofitable. Developers can, however, increase their share of royalty income by taking on some of the risks and responsibilities of a publisher in the standard publishing deal.

Shared-Risk Publishing Arrangement

Developers can improve the economics by self-funding half or all the development expenses. A rule of thumb is that by self-funding the development costs (instead of using the publisher's money), a developer should approximately double the otherwise

applicable royalty. Thus, a base royalty of 10 to 15 percent should increase to 20 to 30 percent. Most game developers, however, do not have the resources to fund the entire cost of the title development, especially if it's going to be an outstanding one, with great graphics. (And in a hits-driven business, you should definitely try to make hits, not also-rans.) Often, however, developers can approach outside investors (generally friends and family, but not always) to fund title development costs in return for a share of the royalties. Other game developers have approached outside companies, like Samsung, to fund single-title development costs (and to provide regional, overseas distribution).

Even if the developer can raise only part of the funds necessary to finance title development, the developer has dramatically improved the negotiating position with publishers. As we'll cover in a few pages, the further along you are in completing your title (assuming you are on the right track), the more likely you will get a publishing deal, and the better the economics of that deal. Many, if not most, software publishers who deal with outside developers are enthusiastic if the developer is willing to fund a part of the title development cost: It reduces the publisher's economic risk if the title is not completed and released, and (in the publisher's view) a developer is more likely to finish the project on time and on budget if the developer's own money (not just time) is at risk.

But for many developers, the only attraction of the standard publishing deal *is* the fact that the publisher will fund the entire development cost. If the developer is going to pay for creating the game, why not go one step further and agree to pay for the modest manufacturing costs and take on some of the marketing responsibilities, ending up with an affiliate distribution deal?

Affiliate Distribution Arrangement

In an affiliate distribution deal, the developer not only funds the entire development cost; in addition, a developer usually pays for manufacturing costs and takes responsibility for the public relations campaign and other "pull through" marketing efforts to create consumer demand. The distributor partner typically provides manufacturing services, product fulfillment (order taking, warehousing, and shipping), and "push through" marketing—effective efforts to get the game into retail stores, through its network of distributors and its relationships with retailers. What does the developer get from the distributor? "One check, one channel service," says Maura Sparks, co-founder of game developer Pop Rocket, whose title *Total Distortion* is being distributed by Electronic Arts as part of EA's affiliate label program.

For developers with substantial resources, affiliate label distribution provides *far better* economic return than the traditional publishing deal. Under a typical affiliate label distribution deal, about 70 percent of the distributor's net revenue is paid to the developer, with some holdback (typically in the neighborhood of 6 percent) for a marketing development fund to pay for co-op advertising and other marketing expenses. This 70 percent of net revenues is, of course, much more lucrative than the 15 percent standard publishing royalty. Many large software publishers, as well as many newcomers, have affiliate distribution programs, including Brøderbund Software, Electronic Arts, Spectrum Holobyte, Davidson & Associates, Maxis, Sega of America, Activision, Acclaim, RandomSoft, nu.millenia, and others.

For developers, an affiliate distribution deal is not only more attractive economically than the standard publishing arrangement, it is also a good intermediate step as your company grows into a full-fledged publisher. Often, you are more effective in creating a public relations and marketing campaign for your game than a major software publisher. After all, who would the editors of *Computer Gaming World* rather talk to—the people who made the latest cool game, or some PR flack from a publisher?

From the distributor's perspective, an affiliate distribution program is often a way to get additional revenue for little additional risk. Major publishers already have manufacturing capacity, space at trade shows, and representatives who call on distributors and buyers, so the addition of some well-produced affiliate label games to the product mix means additional revenue with little additional cost (especially since the larger company charges the developer for the manufacturing and for the proportional marketing expenses, and the developer typically assumes the economic risk of returned inventory). Of course, this approach is not *entirely* risk-free. As Brian Nieder, director of Electronic Arts' affiliate label program explains, "Our name is on the box, and retailers look to EA to pay for the cost of returns," whether or not the developer can repay these costs.

Unfortunately, there are some typical problems that reduce the success of affiliate label deals. First, how committed is the distributor to getting retail shelf space for its affiliate label games (where it only gets 30 percent of net revenues) compared with its own published titles, where its take is more than 80 percent? Brian Nieder dismisses this concern. "Our representatives get paid the same whether they sell one of our titles or one of the titles in our affiliate distribution program." Still, many developers worry that the economic incentives are not ideal.

An even greater problem is that developers often spend every dime that they have completing the title and paying for manufacturing costs. They have no resources left for an effective end-user marketing campaign. Particularly with high-end games (especially on the console side) where other companies are spending millions of dollars for marketing campaigns, the lack of money (and perhaps even marketing skills) reduces sales.

Finally, affiliate distribution arrangements are viewed as only temporary. A successful developer often outgrows affiliate distribution rapidly, becoming its own publisher

once it gains enough market share. This means the distributor's investment of time and resources just creates a competing software publisher.

A couple of recent variations on the traditional affiliate distribution deal, however, have reduced these drawbacks. Many affiliate label distributors are now willing to discuss arrangements that include an advance to fund the developer's marketing costs (and perhaps even manufacturing costs). In addition, Electronic Arts, Spectrum Holobyte, Acclaim, and other affiliate label distributors have made equity investments in some developers in their affiliate programs. This gives them an additional financial incentive to help the developer prosper. It also gives them a continuing share in the developer's success even if the success outgrows the affiliate distribution programs and the developer moves on to become a full-fledged publisher.

Self-Publishing

The final option is to take over *all* aspects of making, marketing, and distributing your game. One word describes this approach: It's *hard.* The digital landscape is littered with dozens of large entertainment and other media companies that thought it would be easy, with all of their resources and pre-existing branded content, to sell computer games. Many other highly focused companies that *only* concentrate on publishing games, which have created and distributed numerous hits, like Crystal Dynamics and Spectrum Holobyte, *have still never turned a substantial profit.*

Publishers have to perform lots of tasks, and most of them aren't as much fun as making games. If you decide to become a publisher, you will learn more than you ever wanted to know about computer codes that have to go on the boxes of your software and the brutal realities of dealing with the retail shelf-space squeeze (particularly on the PC CD-ROM side). You'll quickly learn that you have to practically "rent" shelf space, by paying for co-op advertising and other marketing incentives. On the other hand, several companies with marketing expertise *have* been founded as successful software publishers. With new competing hardware platforms on the console game side, giants like Sega and Sony are encouraging numerous developers to become authorized publishers. (They know that great games are what will sell their hardware.) But don't say I didn't warn you—it's difficult.

Approaching Software Publishers

Let's assume you decide to approach a software publisher with effective distribution (and the money necessary to fund your game development). How do you go about it? At the end of this chapter you'll find a listing of over 100 software publishers. Most of them publish games and consider submissions from outside developers. It is a good starting place. Of course, this industry being what it is, the database was partly obsolete even before it was finished. For an updated version, check out my firm's Web site at *http://www.fbm.com/multimedia.* If you have updates or additions, I would also appreciate you sending me an email at *glosterd@hooked.net* or *glosterd@fbm.com.*

Rules for Approaching Software Publishers

To be frank, the submission process varies depending upon who you are. If your name is Rand Miller and your last title was *MYST,* a simple phone call and description of what you're interested in doing next might suffice. If you are Trilobyte and your current release is *The Eleventh Hour,* you may have success in pitching publishers on the basis of only the sketchiest information about your next title: A publisher already knows what you can do because they have seen it and seen it sell well.

On the other hand, if you have little or no prior track record, you will have to show an interested publisher far more in the way of an impressive proposal, design document, sample art, and a demo in order to strike a deal.

Rule 1: Get as Far as You Can

Before you approach a publisher, you need to put together something that will show well. Why? Because that's the best way to get a good publishing deal. This year, Jason Everett, who screens submissions at Broderbund Software, will receive over 1,200 submissions, but Broderbund will only publish three entertainment titles. These numbers are less daunting at most other publishers, but the point is, what you submit has to stand out. "The farther along a developer is," confirms Scott Lahman, Director of Development at Activision, "the more likely you are to get a deal." He adds, "You can also almost always command a *better* deal." The further along the developer is, he explains, the less risk there is for Activision in funding the remainder of the development.

Rule 2: Have an Original Idea, Not a "Me Too" Title

Gail Williams, manager of the Corel home product line, says, in a comment echoed by almost every software publisher, "We want to see new and interesting ideas, rather than second generation 'me too' titles." Scott Lahman adds, "You have to explain why this product is different and better than something [similar] already out on the market."

Rule 3: Assemble an Impressive Team

Unfortunately, in this industry, ideas by themselves are a-dime-a-dozen: Almost everyone who has ever played a computer game thinks he or she has a great idea for an even better one. But (with the exception of game designers who have had a prior hit) few people are being paid for great *ideas.* What publishers want are developers with a demonstrated capacity to take a great idea, turn it into a compelling game, and finish that game. C. J. Welch, director of licensing and acquisitions at Time Warner Interactive, the arcade and "twitch" game division of the media conglomerate,

explains that only *once* in the last three years of receiving hundreds of submissions has he been tempted to pay for a game design that did not come with a team attached. "The most common weakness of rejected submissions" at Activision, adds Scott Lahman, is "not having a complete team, or having a team that won't match our standards."

Rule 4: Be Persistent and Develop a Thick Skin

Without being obnoxious, you have to be persistent. The director of development or products submissions at a major software publisher is a busy person. Often, you have to be persistent (while being professional) to get your phone calls returned, or to get your submission reviewed. *It is helpful to network for a personal introduction.* Contact everyone you know in the industry to see if they can get you an introduction somewhere. Go out of your way to introduce yourself to potentially interested publishers at the few industry conferences and tradeshows that include developer relations people (not just the marketing flaks). E3 in Los Angeles and especially the annual Computer Game Developers' Conference in Santa Clara are good places to go.

And do not personalize rejection: There are literally hundreds of software publishers, and your submission can be rejected for many reasons that have nothing to do with its merits. The publisher may have a similar game already under development, may have decided to move away from genre titles, or may have made a financial decision not to work with outside developers for a while. Even if you receive several rejections (or a *lot* of rejections), it only takes one yes.

The process of submitting proposals to software publishers is a substantial effort. Contacting the publishers, obtaining their submission agreements, assembling your submission materials, sending it to them, and following up requires a lot of time and enthusiasm. Your enthusiasm for your title is sometimes your best selling point with publishers. "You have to have persistence and passion for your title," says Rachel Bernstein of Frog City Software, a San Francisco-based startup developer that recently closed a deal with SSI to fund development of its original strategy game. Before signing with SSI, Rachel Bernstein had approached about a dozen publishers and entered into preliminary discussions with several.

Rule 5: Have Great Production Values

Whatever you are providing to a software publisher—sample screenshots, character designs, sample art, audio, or a demo—you should aim for outstanding quality. Howard Saroka, director of product development at Phillips Media Games, which has now branched out from CD-I titles to other formats, explains that with an entertainment title, "You have to have *excellent* art." Some publishers will *tell* you that they understand your demo will simply be a mockup, and that it doesn't have to be spectacular. Still, unless you have a great track record or demo reel, you should strive for excellence in everything you send the publisher, even if what you send is quite limited (for example, character designs, rather than a demo). You often only get one shot with a publisher, so you should strive to stand out with great production values. (A videotape with a rambling narration by your lead programmer is not the ideal way to persuade a publisher that you can create fast-paced entertainment.)

Rule 6: Concentrate on (and Communicate) What's Fun About Your Title

This, after all, is the test of what makes a great game: Will it be fun to play? "Great game play is what we're looking for," says Gary Rosenfeld, Vice President of Acquisitions and Business Affairs at Trimark Interactive, which published *The Hive*. This rule ought to be self-evident, but is violated with remarkable frequency.

Rule 7: Do Not Submit Wildly Unrealistic Budgets and Timetables

There are two components to this rule: First, if you are a first-time developer, it is unrealistic to expect that a software publisher will give you $1.5 million in advances to develop your first title. Perhaps you should scale back your expectations and start with a smaller project where a publisher can work with you without the same financial risk.

Second, in their enthusiasm (or desperation to get a deal), developers often propose unrealistically small budgets and time frames for completing a game. This is a mistake: Knowledgeable publishers are generally aware of the actual cost and time to create compelling games. A remarkably unrealistic budget or time frame signals that you may have poor project management skills. "It's definitely a litmus test," explains Jason Everett of Broderbund Software. "If the budget is not realistic, it's a sign that the developer has not been down that track before."

In addition, a developer who has promised a title for an unrealistic budget and delivery date and comes back to the publisher after reality sets in will have trouble getting more money, and may end up going broke, having the title axed, or losing most of the pre-negotiated royalties as part of the workout deal under which the publisher funds title completion.

Realistically, the only two ways to know how much a title will actually cost with any kind of certainty are to have developed a similar game in the past, or to break down the title into each component part and actually create or pay for some of the items in each category. To do this budgeting, however, you have to have a clear idea of everything involved in the title, and you must be fairly far along in developing the game. Usually, you do *not* have all of this information when you first approach a publisher. One alternative is to set an early milestone in your development agreement (after completion of a complete technical design document) as reaching agreement between the developer and the publisher on the complete scope of the title and the final budget.

The Process

After you have identified a list of potentially interested publishers, contact the publishers to obtain their product submission form, non-disclosure agreement, or similar product submission kit. To make their decision making process easier, many publishers (like Mindscape and Broderbund) have a specific form or series of questions that they would like the developer to fill out as part of the product submission process. Before considering your idea, however, most publishers do require a signed submission agreement. Software publishers do this because they are legitimately concerned about being sued. They review hundreds of submissions every year, and a title they create in the future may be superficially similar to a past developer's submission.

On the developer-friendly side, submission agreements from publishers like Maxis, Compaq Software, and Living Books simply provide in plain English that (1) The publisher will preserve the submission as a trade secret, (2) The publisher is free to consider other similar submissions from others in the future and the developer is free to submit the idea elsewhere, (3) The publisher is not liable for losing the submission materials, and (4) The publisher promises not to steal any legally protected intellectual property, and if the developer believes the publisher has done that, the parties agree to submit the dispute to binding arbitration, where the arbitrator has the ability to award the developer the reasonable value for the portion of the work that was misappropriated. Submission agreements can range on the other extreme (for example, Viacom's) to overreaching documents basically providing that if the publisher steals any portion of the work submitted, the developer has no remedy.

Developers are often nervous that their idea will be stolen by some big company. This is unlikely because the hard part of creating great games is not the idea, it is the execution: A rational software publisher is better off striking a deal with a talented developer than trying to steal ideas. But developers who are queasy about the prospect can choose to deal with only (or at least deal first with) the companies that have reasonable submission agreements and a decent representation in the developer community.

The Proposal

Once you have obtained the submission agreement and signed it, you typically send the software publisher a 10 to 20 page proposal. The proposal usually contains:

- A brief description of the game
- A summary of key features and product advantages explaining how these will help the publisher sell lots of copies. (Think *marketing*: What would the publisher put on a sell sheet in order to persuade retailers to stock the game and reviewers to review it?)
- A more extended discussion of each of the different levels, modules, or other portions of the game (perhaps with sample puzzles, and so on)

- A description of the development team and their qualifications
- An analysis of competing products and the market for the product

A well-done proposal for a game title should also contain sample art or story boards (interface design, sample screenshots, character designs, and so on). For developers who do not have an extensive track record, it is also helpful to send in a demo prototype. "A prototype is a *lot* more useful than just sample art or story boards," says Gary Rosenfeld of Trimark Interactive. Again, while publishers do understand that demos are *not* finished titles, what you do show on the demo should have good production values and should install successfully.

The goal of the developers is often to get a meeting with the decision makers to demonstrate what they have on hard disk and to communicate their enthusiasm and creative vision for the game. But don't expect to get a meeting without first sending something in writing. Jason Everett of Brøderbund explains "we are more able to have good questions and a useful discussion, if we have something in advance."

And what do publishers really want? Along with submissions that follow all of the rules I suggested earlier, it helps to have a title proposal for which there is a market, and which can be marketed effectively. Publishers like new and original ideas, but not necessarily whole new categories that they have to explain to retailers. Publishers in general are interested in cutting-edge technology, or at least appropriate use of current technology. Finally, they would like to see submissions from people who have *previously completed* a game title. In publishers' realistic world view, starting a project is easy, but finishing one (especially on time, on budget, and with the features operational as promised) is difficult. It's a lot less risky if your developer has a successful track record (and perhaps even proprietary tools that make the second title easier).

If you do not have any track record, one approach is to assemble a "virtual team" while you are pitching the title: Hook up with other programmers, artists, 3D animators, or whoever, who are willing to commit to work on the title if you get publisher financing, and then use those people (and their prior credits) in pitching the publisher. In the alternative, explain your prior relevant experience (film, video, board game design, productivity software titles) to demonstrate capability, expertise, and the ability to manage and finish a project. Finally, if you have no track record, create the world's most compelling demo that demonstrates all of the necessary skills.

Choosing a Software Publisher

You should approach several different software publishers. First, it will increase your chance of having your title published. Second, if you have several interested publishers for your title, you will have leverage to obtain a better deal. And how do you choose among publishers? First, pick a publisher that has demonstrated the ability to sell huge numbers of similar games. Publishers vary in track record, effective distribu-

tion, and marketing commitment. Second, choose a publisher where you believe you can work effectively with the inside producer. Third, pick a publisher that has worked successfully with other outside developers.

Prototype Funding Agreements

Often, a publisher isn't ready to enter into a publishing deal, but does want to see more—an improved demo, proof of concept, technical design document, or sample first level. If the publisher strongly believes in the developer, the publisher may even be willing to pay for this step. If so, the parties sign a simple letter agreement, where the publisher agrees to advance a small amount of money (typically, $10,000 to $40,000) in return for a deliverable. What does the publisher get out of this? First, the developer does a *lot* more work than just the amount the publisher pays for. Second, the agreement provides that until an exclusive negotiation period expires (typically 30 days after the deliverable is turned in), the developer can't take the project to any other publishers—effectively, for a small amount of cash, the publisher gets an exclusive option for a limited period of time. Finally, there is somewhat limited risk: These agreements usually provide that if the parties *cannot* agree on the terms of an ultimate publishing deal or if the publisher loses interest, the developer must pay back the advances, as soon as the developer strikes a publishing deal with someone else.

And what's in it for the developer? First, you get the necessary cash to get further along with your title. Second, even if the publisher providing this interim funding takes a pass, you then have something even more impressive to show other publishers. Finally, there is another advantage to taking a publisher's money. As Howard Saroka of Phillips Media Games explains, "once a publisher has paid you something, you get a lot more attention" than the pile of other proposals sitting around.

Negotiating a Publishing Deal

After you have impressed the software publisher enough to get to yes, it is time to negotiate the specifics of your publishing deal. Before you propose specific business terms to your publisher, talk to an experienced lawyer familiar with negotiating game development and publishing agreements or *at least* talk to everyone you know in the industry about what's reasonable and what you ought to expect. Then, send a term sheet or outline of the specific business points you would like to see addressed in the final agreement to your publisher to start the negotiations. It is *not* a good idea to wait for the publisher to generate the contract and then to negotiate from their standard language; reach a business agreement on the main deal points first, and then insure that the final agreement reflects that basic business deal. How aggressive should you be on your initial term sheet? Pretty aggressive—it *is* your starting position for negotiation. (But not so aggressive that you brand yourself as patently unrealistic and unreasonable.)

Key Deal Points

Once you finally get a publisher interested in your work (and they are ready to write you an advance check), there are a number of key issues you'll need to know about to negotiate a good deal. Of course, at the top of this list is the royalty rate, but you'll also need to know how royalties are calculated and who has which rights.

Royalty Rates

Numerous publishers claim that they will not pay a base royalty of more than 10 percent in a standard publishing deal to a first-time developer. Often, smaller publishers with less effective distribution will promise higher royalty rates. Developers are often better off going with an established, large software publisher, even at a lower royalty rate, because of more effective distribution and marketing. In addition, games are a hits-driven business. A developer's track record in creating a hit may be more valuable in the long run than a slightly higher royalty rate with a less-effective publisher. Still, to many developers, even a 15 percent "standard" publishing deal royalty seems outrageously low.

Developers can address the meager royalty issue three ways in negotiations with publishers. First, developers argue, with some justification, that the "typical" industry royalty rates should be modified, because they are based at least in part on outmoded business models from the 16-bit cartridge game industry (and, to a lesser extent, on software sold on floppy diskettes). With CD-ROM-based games (and platforms like the Sony PlayStation or Sega Saturn), the publisher's risk from unsold inventory is substantially less than the old 16-bit cartridges, because of the lower cost of goods sold, and the royalty should arguably be adjusted to reflect this.

Second, well-advised developers try to ensure that the milestone advances from the publisher are sufficient to cover *all* the developer's costs, including the salary of the principals, plus some amount to cover inevitable cost overruns, delays, and a little money to last the developer until the start of the next project. Often, developers assume that a larger budget will kill a project. Within limits, this is often not the case. A product manager for one software publisher recently explained that "when developers propose budgets of much less than $500,000 these days, we assume either that they don't know what they're doing or they aren't going to produce the high-quality product we need." Budgeting and planning are absolutely critical. If there are costs that the developer cannot pin down at the time the development agreement is signed (cost of required content, name vocal talent, and so on), the milestone advances should be a specified amount plus the unknown costs of these additional items, which are to be jointly determined later.

Finally, even where the publisher will not budge on the base royalty, a developer can often obtain a "step-up" royalty after a certain number of units are sold. Thus, the 15

percent royalty might increase to 18 percent after 50,000 units sold; increase to 20 percent after 100,000 units, and increase again after 200,000. Given that software publishers' gross margins are typically 60 percent or more, they often agree to a higher step-up royalty.

Royalty Calculation

As important as the royalty percentage is the formula used for calculating that royalty. Typically, royalties are payable on some sort of "net sales revenue," "adjusted gross income," or other similar formulation, based on the publisher's actual receipts less certain expenses or reserves. Typical deductions include sales taxes, duties, shipping and insurance charges actually paid to third parties, replacements, refunds (including reasonable price protection refunds paid by the publisher to its retailers or distributors), and often a reasonable reserve for returns. Some publishers add the cost of goods sold as a deduction.

From the publisher's perspective, it is important not to pay royalties on items that are not ultimately receipts (where, for example, there are massive returns). From the developer's perspective, the deductions from gross income should be narrowly defined to ensure that they do not:

- Swallow the obligation to pay royalties
- Reflect the publisher's general overhead costs

A publisher who pays royalties on sales revenue, but not on "shipping and handling," has every economic incentive to charge $26 per unit, plus $5 shipping and handling, instead of $30 per unit and $1 shipping and handling.

A deduction for "shipping and handling" might be replaced by "actual shipping costs paid to unaffiliated third parties" or "reasonable shipping and handling costs not in excess of $3 per unit," and a reserve for returns might become a "reasonable reserve for returns for six months, not to exceed 10 percent of the units shipped." While these provisions are reasonably negotiable, there are limits on a publisher's flexibility: A publisher with numerous titles on the market is not going to completely reinvent its royalty accounting system for a single developer.

Royalty Recoupment

In a standard publishing deal, the milestone development payments are usually treated as an advance against royalties, and are "recouped" out of the royalties otherwise payable to the developer. The way these royalties are recouped, however, makes a *huge* difference to the developer. In a standard recoupment arrangement as proposed by a publisher, where the milestone advances to finance development were $500,000, and the developer's royalty is 15 percent, the developer would not see any royalty income until 15 percent of the publisher's net sales revenue equaled the $500,000 advance. By that time, the publisher would have received a total of $3.33 million in net sales revenue, and (with most game titles) would have enjoyed substantial profit.

An ideal alternative approach is to negotiate for payment of royalties shortly after the publisher breaks even. There are several ways to accomplish this, including a higher deemed or "shadow" royalty rate on the first 30,000 units sold, or an agreement that after a certain number of units are sold or the publisher's net sales revenue exceeds a certain dollar figure, the milestone advances will be deemed to have been recouped.

A different approach is for the developer to demand a smaller portion of the royalties to be excluded from paying off the advance. Thus, for example, two-thirds of the developer's royalty otherwise payable could be applied to recoup the milestone advances, but the remaining one-third of the royalty rate would be paid to the developer. Unlike the royalty after publisher's break-even formulas, this does not increase the ultimate amount of royalties paid to the developer, but it does accelerate the payment of royalties to help with the developer's cash flow.

Sequels, Ports, and Derivative Works

To profit from a potential hit, publishers need the right to create upgrades, sequels, and foreign localized versions, and want the right to port the title to other platforms or to license the right to do the port. Typically, publishers also want the right to license derivative works like novelizations, and to license the characters for merchandising, television, and movies. Often, the publisher may even want the explicit right to create follow-on products using the same interface and underlying software engine. In addition, a publisher interested in working with a talented developer again often gets a right of first negotiation or right of first refusal on the developer's next title.

On the other side, if appropriate, developers should demand either to retain certain rights or to receive a royalty from these ancillary uses. A typical negotiated agreement might result in the developer having a first right of refusal to do ports, sequels, and derivative software works for a specified (or unspecified) royalty; in any event, even if the port, sequel, or derivative work is created by someone else, the original developer gets a smaller, passive royalty. Developers should try to retain some back end or upside, and occasionally even negotiate for a reversion of rights if (for example) the publisher has not developed a sequel or ported the title to a specific platform within a specified time. Developers are commonly successful in negotiating sharply higher royalties on certain categories of licensing revenue (bundling, foreign localization republishing) where the software publisher is not exposed to inventory return and other typical publishing risks.

Ownership of the Code and Tools

Publishers that have paid for the entire cost of creating a title generally insist that they own the code and have at least a license to the software tools to permit them to modify or enhance the title. But developers often need to have the right to reuse tools, the underlying software engine, or even portions of the code and the basic interface for later products. The agreement should clearly spell out the rights of the parties. Developers who retain ownership of their tools often define the bulk of what they need to create their next title in the list of "tools" in the agreement.

Termination

Publishers generally reserve the right to reject any milestone deliverable and to terminate the developer if the identified deficiencies are not cured within a specified time. In addition, publishers usually reserve the right to cancel a project "at publisher's absolute discretion, for any or no reason." Given rapid change in the marketplace, and the lengthy timeline for developing a great game, this provision is critical for publishers. They want the right to cancel a project if it no longer makes marketing sense.

On the developers' side, there are several important termination issues. First, if the contract is terminated at an early stage, the developer of an original title often insists on the right to take the project elsewhere, and in return must often refund all or a portion of the original publisher's advances upon striking a new publishing deal. If the milestone schedule is set up so that the bulk of payments are at the end of the project, the developer should negotiate either to change this milestone schedule or require a "kill fee" from the publisher that cancels the project simply at its discretion.

A kill fee both makes project cancellation less likely, and insures that the developer is paid for all the work performed to date. For the protection of the developer, the agreement should specify the publisher's producer or project manager who is authorized to speak for the publisher. If the developer does not hear back with acceptance or rejection of a milestone deliverable within a specific period of time, the agreement can provide that two business days after an additional notice from the developer, the milestone is deemed accepted. Any rejection of a milestone deliverable should specify the problems that need to be corrected, and the agreement should provide a reasonable period of time for the developer to correct any deficiencies.

Miscellaneous Provisions

Publishers need explicit representations and warranties that the developer has obtained all necessary rights in the title and the publisher's use will not infringe any rights of any third parties, together with a broad agreement to indemnify, defend, and hold harmless the publisher if the representation and warranties are not true. A developer will want a reciprocal provision covering any materials or licensed content provided by the publisher. Publishers will want a continuing obligation of the developer to cure identified errors and may want some additional consulting services in connection with ports or foreign localizations.

The developer will want a time limit on these provisions, particularly if they require the developer to provide additional services for free. A developer should have the continuing right to audit the books of the publisher to verify the accuracy of the royalty payments, and if the audit reveals a significant underpayment, the cost of the audit should be borne by the publisher. If any confidential information (proprietary tools and the like) is being disclosed, there should be a confidentiality/non-disclosure provision. Finally, developers—who often have far less money for resolving legal disputes—typically want a quick and relatively inexpensive dispute resolution mechanism like arbitration. The arbitration paragraph can provide that the arbitrator must be knowledgeable about the consumer software industry.

This is just an overview of some of the deal points parties should be aware of in negotiating standard publishing agreements. The critical issue, though, for developers, is that their agreements are carefully drafted to address their needs and to reflect a fair and mutual understanding of their business deal. And after you've created one hit game, you have more leverage to get an even better deal the next time around.

Publishers Resource

The remainder of this chapter provides a list of publishers who actively produce, publish, or market games, multimedia, and CD-ROM products.

3DO Company
600 Galveston Drive
Redwood City, CA 94063
415 261-3354

3M Learning Software
Dave Iverson, Program Manager
3M Center
Building 220-2W-04
St. Paul, MN 55144-1000
612 737-3249

7th Level
Richard Merrick, Vice President R&D
1771 International Parkway
Richardson, TX 75081
214 437-4858

Acclaim Entertainment, Inc.
1 Acclaim Plaza
Glen Cove, N.Y, 11542-2708
516 656-5000

Accolade
Sandy Jackson
5300 Stevens Creek Blvd., Suite 500
San Jose, CA 95129
408 985 1700

Activision
Scott Lahman, Director of Development
11601 Wilshire Blvd., Suite 1000
Los Angeles, CA 90025
310 473-9200 x2546

Addison Wesley Publishing
Dan Caton
Vice President for Development
2725 Sand Hill Road
Menlo Park, CA 94025
415 854-0300

American Laser Games
Robert Grebe, President
4801 Lincoln Rd. NE
Albuquerque, NM 87109
505 880-1718

Atari Corporation
Bill Rehbock
VP-Software Business Development
Greg LaBrec
Director of Creative Services
1196 Borregas Ave.
P.O. Box 3427
Sunnyvale, CA 94089-1302
408 745-2000

Atlantic Records
Sandy Smallens, Senior Multimedia Director
75 Rockefeller Plaza, 2nd Floor
New York, NY 10019
212 275-2075

Avalon Hill Game Company
Phyllis Opolko, Marketing Manager
4517 Harford Road
Baltimore, MD 21214
410 254-9200

FormGen, Inc.
Jess Bansal
5655 Lindero Canyon Road, #121
Westlake, CA 91362
818 879-8572

Berkeley Systems
Kevin Hunt, Director - Retail Sales
2095 Rose Street
Berkeley, CA 94709
510 540-5535

Bethesda Softworks
Chris Weaver, President
1370 Piccard Drive, Suite 120
Rockville, MD 20850-4304
310 926-8300

Big Top Productions
548 Fourth Street
San Francisco, CA 94107
415 978-5363

Blasterware
Michael House, Publisher
Sharon Ow, Developer Relations
1901 McCarthy Boulevard
Milpitas, CA 95035
408 428-6600 x6429
Software Label of Creative Labs, currently concentrating on 3D games supporting its 3D Blaster hardware

BMG Entertainment North America
Christian Joerg, Vice President
1540 Broadway
New York, NY 10036
212 930-4342

Broderbund Software
Jason Everett, Product Submissions
P.O. Box 6121
Novato, CA 94948-6121
415 382-4667

Bungee Software
Eric Klein
1935 S. Halstead St., Suite 204
Chicago, IL 60608

Byron Preiss Multimedia
Jeremy Ross, Senior Producer
24 West 25th Street, 11th Floor
New York, NY 10010
212 989-6252

Capcom USA, Inc.
475 Oakwood Parkway
Sunnyvale, CA 94086
408 774-3877

Capitol Multimedia, Inc.
Doug Price
7315 Wisconsin Avenue, Suite 800 East
Bethesda, MD 20814
301 907-7000

CAPS
Rob Sears
Exec. V.P., Product Development
650 Mission Street
San Francisco, CA 94105
415 284-1570

Claris
5201 Patrick Henry Drive
P.O. Box 58168
Santa Clara, CA 95054
408 987-7000

Compaq Software
Mark Wozniak, Developer Relations
Julie Williams, Publishing Program Manager
1111 Bayhill Drive, Suite 475
San Bruno, CA 94066
415 742-5200
415 742-8718

Compton's New Media, Inc.
A Tribune New Media Company
Steven E. Marder, Director Entertainment Business Development
2320 Camino Vida Roble
Carlsbad, CA 92009-1504
619 929-5945

Computer Curriculum Corp.
1287 Lawrence Station Rd.
Sunnyvale, CA 94089
408 745-6270
A unit of Viacom's Simon & Schuster

Corbis Media
15395 South East 30th Place, Suite 300
Bellevue, WA 98007
206 641-4505

Corel
Gail Williams
Corel Home Product Manager
1600 Carling Avenue
Ottawa, ON K1Z 8R7
CANADA
613 728-8200

Creative Multimedia Corporation
514 N.W. 11th Avenue, Suite 203
Portland, OR 97209
503 241-4351

Creative Programming and Technology Ventures
Dr. Stephen Kirkpatrick
7900 East Union Avenue, Suite 1100
Denver, CO 80237
303 694-5324

Creative Wonders
Product Submissions
1450 Fashion Island Blvd.
San Mateo, CA 94404
415 571-7171

Crystal Dynamics
Madclinc Cancpa
Director - Marketing and Development
87 Encina Ave.
Palo Alto, CA 94301
415 473-3400
mad@crystal.com

Davidson & Associates
Mike Albanese
Director of Development
19840 Pioneer Avenue
Torrance, CA 90503
310 793-0600

Diamond Multimedia Systems
Bundling
Paul Nahi
Director of Product Marketing
2880 Junction Avenue
San Jose, CA 95134
408 325-7000

Digital Pictures
Tyler Johnson
1825 South Grant Street, Suite 900
San Mateo, CA 94402
415 655-5369

Discis Knowledge Research, Inc.
Richard Wah Kan, Vice President
Licensing & Acquisitions
90 Sheppard Avenue East, 7th Floor
Toronto, ON M2N 3A1
CANADA
416 250-6537

Discovery Multimedia
Thomas Porter
Publisher and General Manager
7700 Wisconsin Avenue
Bethesda, MD 20814-3579
301 986-0444

Disney Interactive
Steve McBeth, Division Head
500 So. Buena Vista Street
Burbank, CA 91521-6677
818 560-1572

DK Multimedia
Alan Buckingham
Director of Multimedia
16 E. 46th Street, 5th Floor
New York, NY 10016
212 213-4800

Domark Software
1900 South Norfold Street, Suite 110
San Mateo, CA 94403
415 513-8929

Dreamworks Interactive
100 Universal Plaza, Bldg. 601
Universal City, CA 91608
818 733-7070

Edge Interactive Productions
Tim Langdell, CEO
906 Granite Drive
Pasadena, CA 91101
818 790-4334

EdMark Software
Amy Gutman
6727 185th Ave. NE
Redmond, WA 98073-3218
206 556-8825

Educational Insights Interactive
Stan Resnicoff
New Media Group
310 884-1931

Electronic Arts, Inc.
Product Submissions
1450 Fashion Island Blvd.
San Mateo, CA 94404
415 571-7171 x1670

Elite of America
1190 Saratoga Avenue, Suite 210
San Jose, CA 95129
408 236-3266

Empire Interactive
Chris Mate, President
13220 Wisteria Drive, Bay N-2
Germantown, MD 20874
301 916-9302

Enteractive, Inc.
110 West 40th St., Suite 2100
New York, NY 10018
212 221-6559

EMI
8730 Sunset Blvd., 5th Floor
West Hollywood, CA 90069
310 289-6471

Expert Software
Ken Currier, CEO
800 Douglas Road
Executive Tower, Suite 750
Coral Gables, FL 33134
305 567-9990

Fox Interactive
Scott Marcus, Director of Development
2121 Avenue of the Stars,
Suite 527
Los Angeles, CA 90067

GameTek
Tom Reuterdahl, V.P. Development
2999 Northeast 191st, Suite 500
Aventura, FL 33180
305 935-3995

GEnie
Todd Lefkowitz
Director of Games and Entertainment
GEnie HQ
401 North Washington Street
Rockville, MD 20955
800 638-9636

Graphix Zone, Inc.
Glenn Freeman, Production Dir.
38 Corporate Park, Suite 100
Irvine, CA 92714
714 833-3838

Grolier Electronic Publishing
3-Prong Plug Games Unit
Sherman Turnpike
Danbury, CT 06816
203 797-3500

GT Interactive
Ed Thomas, Product Submissions
16 East 40th Street
New York, NY 10016
212 726-6528

GTE Interactive Media
J. Michael Birch
Director of Development
2385 Camino Vida Roble
Carlsbad, CA 92009
619 431-8801

Harper Collins Interactive
10 East 53rd Street
New York, NY 10022
212 207-7000

Headbone Interactive
1520 Bellevue Avenue
Seattle, WA 98122
206 323-0073

Houghton Mifflin Interactive
Connally Ryan, Director Multimedia
Erica Kohnke, Product Submissions
222 Berkeley Street
Boston, MA 02116
617 351-5028

Humongous Entertainment
16932 Woodenville-Redmond Rd.
Suite 104
Woodenville, WA 98072
206 486-9258

IBM
Jim Mediate, Developer Relations
1500 River Edge Parkway
Atlanta, GA 30328
404 644-4881

Impressions Software, Inc.
222 3rd Street, Suite 0234
Cambridge, MA 02142
617 225-0500

IMSI
Amin Mufti, Director of Multimedia
1895 East Francisco Boulevard
San Rafael, CA 94901
415 454-7101

Inscape
Michael Nash, President
1933 Pontius Avenue
Los Angeles, CA 90025
310 312-5705

Interactive Magic
Bob Pickens, President
Bill Stealy, CEO
Debbie Blair
P.O. Box 1349
Research Triangle Park, NC 27709
919 461-0722

Interplay
17922 Fitch Ave.
Irvine, CA 92714
714 553-6655

IVI Publishing
John McIlvaine
Vice President of Sales and Marketing
1380 Corporate Center Curve
Eagan, MN 55121
612 996-6000

Jasmine Multimedia
Jay Samit, President
6746 Valjean Ave., Suite 100
Van Nuys, CA 91406
818 780-3344

Jostens Home Learning
Harriett Perry, V.P.
9920 Pacific Heights Blvd., #100
San Diego, CA 92121-4430
619 587-0087

Knowledge Adventure
4502 Dyer Street
La Crescenta, CA 91214
818 246-4400

Knowledge Experience
Gordon Freedman
Vice President - Multimedia
1299 Ocean Avenue, Suite 250
Santa Monica, CA 90401
310 394-5995 x26

Koei Corporation
1 Bay Plaza, Suite 540
1350 Bayshore Highway
Burlingame, CA 94010
415 348-0500

Konami America, Inc.
Mike Gallo
900 Deerfield Parkway
Buffalo Grove, IL 60089-4510
708 215-5100 x109

The Learning Company
Stacy Pena
6493 Kaiser Drive
Fremont, CA 94555
510 792-9628

Legend Entertainment
14200 Park Meadow Drive
Chantilly, VA 22021
703 222-8500

L. G. Software
Formerly Gold Star USA
1000 Sylvan Avenue
Englewood Cliffs, NJ 07632

Lee, Charlie C.N.
International Business Development Team
LG Building
891, Daechi-dong, Kangnam-gu
Seoul 135-280, Korea
011-822-3459-5768
Fax: 011-822-3459-5706

Living Books
Mark Schlichting, Creative Director
160 Pacific Avenue Mall
San Francisco, CA 94111
415 352-5200

Lucas Arts Entertainment Co.
Steven Dauterman
Director of Development
P.O. Box 10307
San Rafael, CA 94912
415 472-3400

MacMillan Digital USA
Kevin Howat, Publisher
866 3rd Avenue
New York, NY 10022
212 702-2000

Maxis
Doug Litke, Director of Development
2 Theatre Square, Suite 230
Orinda, CA 94563
510 254-9700

McGraw Hill Home Software
Brian Waters
2555 Shoreline Drive, #650
Redwood City, CA 94065
415 802-9010

MECC
Susan Schilling
V. P. Software Development
6160 Summit Drive North
Minneapolis, MN 55430
612 569-1500

MGM Interactive
Ron Frankel, General Manager
Fred Skoler
2500 Broadway Street
Santa Monica, CA 90404-3061
310 449-3000

Microprose Entertainment Software
Doug Kaufman
Producer for External Development
180 Lakefront Drive
Hunt Valley, MD 21030-2245
410 771-0440

Microsoft Corporation
Anthony Garcia, Games Division
206 936-4127
Charlotte Guyman
Family & Home Products
206 882-8080
One Microsoft Way
Redmond, WA 98052-6399

Midisoft Corporation
Raymond Bily, CEO
15263 NE 90th St.
Bldg. 9-10
Redmond, WA 98052
206 391-3610

Mindscape
Darla Donovan
Software Submissions Coordinator
88 Rowland Way
Novato, CA 94945
415 897-9900 x589

Modern Media Ventures
300 Brannan Street, Suite 302
San Francisco, CA 94107
415 546-1515

Morgan Interactive
160 Pine St., Suite 509
San Francisco, CA 94111
415 693-9596

Motown Records
Eddie Ford Brown
Business Development Director
5750 Wilshire Blvd., Suite 300
Los Angeles, CA 90036
213 634-3500

Multicom Publishing
1100 Olive Way, Suite 1250
Seattle, WA 98101
206 622-5530

MVP Software
David C. Snyder
1035 Dallas SE
Grand Rapids. MI 49507
606 245-8376

New World Computing, Inc.
Deane Rettig, Manager
Product Development
29800 Agoura Road, Suite 200
Agoura Hills, CA 91301
818 889-5600

Nintendo Of America, Inc.
Peter Main, Vice President of Marketing
4820 150th Ave. NE
Redmond, WA 98052
206 882-2040

Novell
Jessica Kersey
2180 Fortune Drive
San Jose, CA 95131
408 577-8739

nu.millenia/inc.
Affiliate Distribution Program
16868 Via Del Campo Court, Suite 200
San Diego, CA 92127
619 676-3620
numill@surfnet.com

Origin Systems
5918 West Courtyard Drive
Austin, TX 78730
512 434-4263

Packard Bell Electronics, Inc.
Mal Ransom, Marketing V.P.
5701 Lindero Canyon Road
Westlake Village, CA 91362
818 865-1555

Distributing children's titles from its Active Imagination subsidiary and applications from its Ark Interface subsidiary.

Palladium Interactive
Ed Bernstein, President
Steven Horowitz, v.p. of R & D
3 Harbor Drive, Suite 301
Sausalito, CA 94965
415 289-4000
Fax: 415 289-4090

Panasonic Software Co.
Bill Gardner, Vice President
Makoto Morse, Assoc. Producer
4701 Patrick Henry Drive, Suite 1101
Santa Clara, CA 95054
408 653-1888

Paramount Interactive
700 Hanson Way
Palo Alto, CA 94304
800 821-1177

P.F. Magic, Inc.
Rob Fulop, Director of Development
501 Second Street, Suite 400
San Francisco, CA 94107
415 495-0400

Philips Media Games
Howard Soroka
Director of Product Development
10960 Wilshire Blvd., 8th Floor
Los Angeles, CA 90024
310 444-6500

Playmates Interactive Entertainment
David Luehmann, Executive Producer
16200 Trojan Way
La Mirada, CA 90638
714 562-1743

Playskool
Software division of Hasbro
514 High Street
Palo Alto, CA 94301
415 617-8500

Powerhouse Entertainment
Dominic Vitris, V. P. Marketing
14850 Quorum Drive, Suite 200
Dallas, TX 75240
214 233-5400 x203

Positronic Software
Timothy Bowes
1318 Main Street
Dartmouth, Nova Scotia
Canada B2Z 1B2

PPI Entertainment Group
Karen Richard
Director of Business Affairs
88 St. Francis Street
Newark, NJ 07105
201 344-4214

Psygnosis
675 Massachusetts Avenue
Cambridge, MA 02139
617 497-7794

Quantum Quality Productions
Bruce Williams, President
495 Highway 202
Flemington, NJ 08822

Random House New Media
Wendy Elman, Acquisitions Manager
201 East 50th Street
New York, NY 10022
212 751-2691

Rocket Science Games
Bill Davis, Vice President of Product Development
139 Townsend St., Suite 100
San Francisco, CA 94107
415 328-8181
billd@rocketsci.com

S3, Inc.
bundling
P.O. Box 58058
2770 San Tomas Expressway
Santa Clara, CA 95052-8058
408 980-5400

Sanctuary Woods
Montgomery Woods
1825 South Grant Street
San Mateo, CA 94402
415 286-6000

Sega of America
Joe Miller, Product Development
150 Shoreline Drive, Suite 200
Redwood City, CA 94065
415 508-2800

Sigma Designs, Inc.
46501 Landing Parkway
Fremont, CA 94538
510 770-2661

Simon & Schuster Interactive
Walter Walker
1230 at Avenue of the Americas
New York, NY 10020
212 698-7000

SoftKey International, Inc.
David Patrick
Executive Vice President
Sales and Marketing
201 Broadway
Cambridge, MA 02139
617 494-1200

Some Interactive
Jeff Cretcher, President
539 Bryant, Suite 303
San Francisco, CA 94107
415 284-6464

Sony Electronic Publishing
Mark Hart
National Manager, Publishing
1 Lower Ragsdale Drive, Suite 160
Monterey, CA 93940
800 654-8802

Sony Music Entertainment, Inc.
Fred Ehrlich
Senior VP/General Manager
Emerging Technologies Unit
9 West 57th Street
New York, NY 10019
212 833-8000

Spectrum Holobyte, Inc.
2490 Mariner Square Loop
Alameda, CA 94501
510 814-6368

StarHill Productions
Studio of Rocket Science Games
Dan Irish, Manager
139 Townsend Street
San Francisco, CA 94107
415 442-5000
dirish@rocketsci.com

StarPress Multimedia, Inc.
Mark Williams
Director of Product Development
303 Sacramento Street, 2nd Floor
San Francisco, CA 94111
415 274-8383

Strategic Simulations, Inc.
Lee Crawford
675 Almanor Avenue, Suite 201
Sunnyvale, CA 94086-2901
408 737-6800

Synergy Interactive
444 De Haro Street, Suite 123
San Francisco, CA 94107
415 437-2000
Fax: 415 431-3684

TecMagik, Inc.
Manlio Allegra
3 Lagoon Drive, Suite 155
Redwood City, CA 94065
415 637-1350

Theatrix Interactive, Inc.
fka Berkeley Learning Technologies
Robert Wall, CEO
1250 45th Street
Emeryville, CA 94608
510 658-2800

Three-Sixty Pacific, Inc.
Doug Mogica, Director of Development
2105 S. Bascom Ave., Suite 165
Campbell, CA 95008
408 879-9144

T-HQ
5016 North Parkway Calabasas, Suite 100
Calabasas, CA 91302
818 591-1310

Time Warner Electronic Publishing
Andrew Lerner
Director of Development
Time & Life Building
1271 Avenue of the Americas
New York, NY 10020
212 522-5158

Time Warner Interactive
C. J. Welch
Director Licensing & Acquisitions
675 Sycamore Drive
Milpitas, CA 95035
408 473-9417

Trimark Interactive
Gary Rosenfeld, Vice President
Acquisitions and Business Affairs
2644 - 30th Street
Santa Monica, CA 90405-3009
310 314-2000

Twentieth Century Fox
Home Entertainment
Karen V. Edwards
Director - Interactive International
P.O. Box 900
Beverly Hills, CA 90213-0900
310 369-3383

Ubi Soft
1000 Bridgeway
Sausalito, CA 94965
415 464-4440

Universal Interactive Studios
Mark Cerny, Vice President - Technology
100 Universal City Plaza
Universal City, CA 91608
818 777-5400

Viacom New Media
1515 Broadway
New York, NY 10028
212 258-6000

US Gold
303 Sacramento Street
San Francisco, CA 94111
415 693-0297

Varcon Systems, Inc.
Susan Filippone
10509 San Diego Mission Rd., Suite K
San Diego, CA 92108
619 563-6700

Virgin Interactive Entertainment
Christina Camerota
Product Acquisitions Coordinator
18061 Fitch Avenue
Irvine, CA 92714
714 833-8710

Voyager
Editorial Review Board
578 Broadway, Suite 406
New York, NY 10012
212 431-5199

Walnut Creek CD-ROM
4041 Pike Lane, Suite D-386
Concord, CA 94520
800 786-9907

Warner Active
See also Inscape
Stewart Kosoy, Director of Development
3400 Riverside Drive
Suite 730
Burbank, CA 91505
818 569-0592

Westwood Studios
Brett W. Sperry
5333 S. Arville, Suite 104
Las Vegas, NV 89118
702 368-4850

WMS Games, Inc.
Williams, Bally & Midway Games
3401 N. Chicago Avenue
Chicago, IL 60618-5899
312 961-1687

Xiphias
Helms Hall
8758 Venice Boulevard
Los Angeles, Ca 90034
310 841-2790

Zelos
535 Pacific Avenue
San Francisco, CA 94133
415 788-0566

CHAPTER 30

The strategies for publishing, distributing, and selling game software have changed about as rapidly as the software itself.

The Art of Computer Game Publishing, Selling, and Promotion

Reaching Your Customers

Game packaging and distribution have come a long way from the days when products were placed in Ziplock bags and dumped on the shelves or bins of independently owned stores scattered around the country. Today, many more sophisticated ways to distribute and earn money from games are available.

For most of you, publishing a game is not going to be a major concern—you'll develop a game and hand it off to a publisher in hopes that they know what they're doing. However, just because a publisher can get you into a software chain like Egghead or Software Etc. doesn't exactly mean you're destined to make a lot of money or end up in the game hall of fame. There are literally dozens of different retail outlets and an array of promotional responsibilities that you or your publisher must take into consideration to ensure a successful venture.

In the game business, the term *publisher* often refers to a person or company who performs a number of activities from coming up with ideas, funding the development, creating the packaging, and developing or managing the processes required to take a finished product to market. Of course, not all publishers perform every one of these tasks. The purpose of this chapter is to get you up to speed on the different publishing activities to help you become an expert on how games go from your hands to consumers. You'll learn about techniques like packaging and promotion, and you'll learn how to successfully deal with retailers, distributors, and customers.

How Game Software Is Sold

The first thing you need to learn is that software—especially consumer software like games—gets sold in many different ways. The second thing you need to learn is that each selling outlet handles your product in very different ways.

As a game developer, you'll need to deal with four specific categories of outlets:

- Distributors
- Retail outlets
- Mail order outlets
- Direct consumer outlets

Let's take a look at each of these categories.

Distributors

Although you can directly work with large retailers, you'll need to work with distributors to ensure your products get in the hands of as many national and international independent stores as you can. (Always remember that if your product isn't on the shelf, it won't sell.) There are two major types of distributors: national ones like Merisel and American Software (although Merisel also distributes worldwide) and regional distributors like Abco (although anyone can order from these distributors). You need to decide how to best approach distribution to ensure good coverage. Reading the trade publications and talking with retailers will help you gauge which distributors will be able to fill your needs.

Another type of distributor is the *rack jobber*. Rack jobbers are distributors that physically manage the retail stocking of a particular alternative retail outlet. For example, Kmart and Sears use a rack jobber named Handleman to order stock and to restock products in its stores nationwide. Some publishers can sell directly to such alternative outlets, but usually only the largest publishers like Maxis with the best selling products like SimCity are able to go direct. The rest of us need to deal with the rack jobbers.

Retail Outlets

The retail environment for computers has changed as rapidly as the technology sold in the retail outlets. Both industries have seen rapid growth, shakeouts, success, and fierce competition.

Originally, software—especially entertainment-oriented software—moved through independent chains. Cartridge game products received mass distribution through traditional electronics chains and toy stores. Today, though, the retail environment is much more complex. The days of "Ziplock distribution" are long gone, and the number of traditional computer and console retailers (not to mention the not-so-traditional outlets) has grown exponentially.

Many different types of retail software outlets are available, especially outlets that are selling interactive entertainment products. While you may need to make a specific stop to pick up the latest business application, you'll find games like Doom II everywhere you look. Let's take a look at the retail outlets that are currently distributing game software.

Software and Computer Chains

The first major group are the big computer software chains like Egghead Software, Software Etc., and CompUSA. When dealing with national giants like these, you'll be working directly with buyers from the company. Although these chains still are a great place to sell your games, you have other options now that the gaming industry has become a major source of revenue for retailers.

Bookstores

Bookstores are rapidly becoming major outlets for software. In fact, a growing group of super bookstores like Borders and Barnes & Noble have entire software stores within their bookstores. Some of the bigger superstores like Borders buy direct from publishers; others use rack jobbers. Most of the smaller shops and chains will use a distributor.

Consumer Electronics Stores

Stores like Circuit City and East coast-based Nobody Beats The Wiz are longtime video game retailers that are increasingly becoming PC software distributors. These outlets generally stock only the top 50 or so titles, and many use rack jobbers to get their merchandise.

Major National Retailers

For a long time Sears has been a major retail outlet for software. However, joining them now are massive nationwide retailers like Toys 'Я' Us, Kmart, WAL-MART, Caldor, Staples, and Office Depot, among others. All of these outlets carry a large stock of both video and PC games (again, only the top releases), and most use rack jobbers to fill their shelves.

Regional Heavyweights

Regional stores, like their nationwide counterparts, carry large stocks of the best selling releases, but in a particular area of the country. Here in New England we have a chain of stores called Lechmere, which is as popular as WAL-MART. You should try to learn as much as you can about the regional players in your area; getting your product sold in these stores can be very important.

The Dispublisher Dilemma

Dispublisher is an industry slang word for software companies—like EA and Davidson—that also manage the distribution for other companies in the industry. In some cases, they also serve as the rack jobber for a particular chain. For example, GT Interactive works with WAL-MART This approach allows these companies to manage their own product lines (and gives them premiere status) *and* control over other product lines. This doesn't sound too fair, does it?

While no one has gone to court over this practice and some companies seem unbothered by it at all—dispublishers definitely cause some friction in the industry. My advice is to realize that dispublishers can create some tough situations for smaller developers. Many larger publishers don't practice this approach and have the means to get around the roadblocks built by dispublishers to ensure excellent distribution. These more ethical publishers are the companies you want to do business with.

The Retail Lesson

Most retailers, with the exception of software and computer-only chains, carry only a handful of titles. The game business is increasingly becoming a "hits-based business." Because most consumers don't search out the local computer store and end up buying much of their software in places like WAL-MART, it's getting very tough to crack the stranglehold of distribution. If you want to stay in this business, you've got to persevere. Avoid becoming your own publisher and instead try to sign with an established player. Also make use of alternative channels of distribution (such as shareware) to get your games where they belong—in the hands of consumers.

Mail Order Outlets

You'll find several major mail order companies available in the U.S. and in Europe. Typically, these outfits do large catalog mailings or take out large ads in major trade publications. Many of these companies also sell advertising space in their catalogs, which allows you to be featured prominently in their mailings.

The three types of major mail order outlets include:

- *Major mail order software catalogs* These are massive organizations such as PC Warehouse, MacConnection, and Insight that sell tons of ad space in their catalog and mail hundred of thousands of catalogs to consumers. The advertising placed by vendors help pay for the high costs of printing and mailing the catalogs.
- *Special catalogs* These catalogs tend to be a hodgepodge of different computer, software, and electronics items. Although they lack a particular focus, they can be effective at reaching consumers.
- *Retail specific mailings* Many of the major computer chains like Electronics Boutique and CompUSA also have mail order divisions. Sears and other non-electronic chains also send out catalogs. But just because you're on a store's shelf doesn't mean you'll be in their catalog—usually you need to pay extra money.

The Mail Order Paradox

Mail order can be one of the trickiest propositions for publishers. Let me tell you how it works. You call up a major mail order catalog company and ask to be featured. They say sure! Then, they hit you with a $6,000 advertising fee to include a small listing of your product in their current mailing. (If you expected to get the listing for free, forget it!) The company then uses that money, which is basically profit, to really cut prices—often below what you're selling your product for at retail. If you're not careful, you'll end up competing with yourself by cutting the price of your product in the retail store to keep your client happy. On top of it all, if the product doesn't sell, you'll be out both the cost of manufacturing the product and the few thousand dollars you spent to get in the catalog.

To protect their business, most companies carefully plan how they use major mail order catalogs. Here are some of the guidelines to follow. Try to avoid large costly ads, unless you get a special deal. The goal is to be carried in a catalog for increased access, and not to break the bank. Leave the product marketing to reviews and other promotional efforts. Don't add to your advertising budget just to be included in a catalog. (In fact being in the catalog should be one of the last items on your spending list.) Overall, consider timing the catalog placement to hit four or five weeks after your product has been on retail shelves. This will give your retail customers a jump start to spread the word around about how great the game is. Keep in mind that mail order tends to be a bigger deal with Mac-based products; PC software tends to sell more aggressively in retail channels. Console products sold as mail order tend to reach customers looking for exported titles instead of games they can find on the shelves.

One way you can reduce your exposure with direct mail catalog companies is to trade product for catalog space. With this approach, you run an advertisement in the catalog, and you pay for the advertisement by supplying the catalog company with suggested stocking units of your product. If your product sells well, you can break even quickly and the additional products that are sold will help you make a profit. Again, be careful to not over commit. Start small, and work your way up to larger ads.

Direct Consumer Outlets

Game players are scattered throughout the globe. Customers for your products can be in such remote areas as the north woods of Maine (my home state) or as far away as places like Riyadh, Saudi Arabia.

You don't want these customers to have any excuse—such as not having access to software stores or mail order—to not buy your game. You need to provide them with direct access to your products. Many of the most successful publishers run incredibly successful direct sales divisions. EA, for instance, garners several million from their direct sales.

Most companies get their direct sales by using an 800 number staffed with operators to process credit card orders and shipping people to send out products. Today, however, direct sales also means developing an active Web site and commercial online presence. Companies can also enhance their direct consumer sales with shareware marketing, as well as direct mail efforts. My favorite example of a targeted direct mailing is the card I get from Electronic Arts on my birthday offering me a discount if I purchase one of their products directly from them.

Be careful though; the key to setting up a successful direct sales division is not to go into competition with your retailers and mail order outlets. Keep everything on the up and up and *never* undercut your retailers.

Direct Sales Opportunities

Many companies are experimenting with direct consumer sales of specialized products. For example, Origin offers special limited editions of two of their popular series: Wing Commander and Ultima. These products are specially packaged collectors editions, sometimes complete with signed boxes and more. Of course, a premium price is often attached. This approach can generate a great source of money and it appeals to your hardcore fans, especially if a popular product has a sequel.

I've even heard of Broderbund constructing customized versions of its popular Carmen Sandiego series.

Bundling

Welcome to the wonderful world known as bundling—please fasten your seat belt and move your tray into the upright position, note the exits on either side, and prepare for a bumpy ride.

Bundling is big business in the PC arena. The basic scheme is to bundle a bunch of software for one low price or as a suite of software to go along with some hardware product like a CD-ROM drive. Depending on who you talk to, bundling is the greatest publishing and distribution device ever created or it represents the dark side of the industry.

The three types of bundling practices used in the game business include:

- *CPU Add-On Bundling* Many of the direct mail manufacturers like Gateway 2000 bundle multimedia packages and software with their systems. This is an inexpensive way to edge out the competitors and offer the customer more value. Oddly enough, not many game manufacturers have been aggressive in this area. I think they have held back because hardware vendors were originally pushing "one size fits all" systems instead of specific systems for home consumers.
- *Peripheral Bundling* Again, as a way of creating some small advantage over their competitors, many CD-ROM/multimedia upgrade kits offer games as incentives to get consumers to buy their kits.
- *Retail Bundling* Retail bundling simply involves bundling a bunch of games together for one low price. Some companies do it themselves, while others enter into agreements with bundlers like Sirus, famous for their 5-foot packs of CD-ROMs.

Carve Out Your Own Niche

Look for manufacturers not currently employing a bundling scheme. For example, modem manufacturers might be interested in a cool online game you have. Often the developer must take the initiative in the beginning of a bundling relationship.

The Perils of Bundling

Bundling has taken on a life of its own because of a glut of games and a booming hardware business made up of companies constantly searching for a marketing edge. (Remember the multitude of multimedia upgrades and CD-ROM players?) Couple this with a market full of budget-minded consumers, and voila, you have bundling schemes!

Bundling has been a double-edged sword for the industry. It allows for massive distribution and quick profits for the producers whose software is bundled. (Developers usually receive a small royalty that compounds by the sheer volume of the product distributed.) However, earlier bundling deals flooded the market with mostly older and, at times, inferior products. As a result, many companies have become turned off to this approach.

Today, though, bundling is making a comeback. Many bundling deals now feature new software or new versions of older software. In addition, while the first wave of bundling was accelerated by multimedia upgrade kits, today's bundling is being pushed by 3D graphics cards, 3D glasses, new input devices, and next-generation modems whose manufacturers are looking for more than just the obligatory throw away game. For example, for Diamond's nVidea-equipped 3D Edge graphics card, the bundled game is Segas Virtua Fighter Remix, a far cry from some of the stuff usually seen in bundle deals.

As you can see, bundling is re-emerging in a more mature form. Many of the top-tier developers are working to get bundling deals. They're being more deliberate on the details of the deal, and many have set up specific sales people to secure and manage bundling opportunities.

Hold Your Horses!

More often than not, bundling deals are acquired by companies with products already completed and on the market. While it happens, it's rare for a company to be approached to bundle a game before or during its development. So before you run off to secure your first big bundling deal, finish a product and get it in distribution.

Bundling schemes usually work for developers who take initiative and understand the dynamics of the process. This often involves taking the time to produce specialized versions for bundlers (many times this means customizing your games to the hardware manufacturer's specifications), searching out key bundling contacts, and in general accepting a far lower than average royalty rate.

Sponsored Products and Giveaways

One of the fastest growing business opportunities pertaining to games is *sponsored products.* A sponsored product is one in which a company seeking advertising exposure will fund the development with the expressed interest of attaching or integrating an advertising message to the product. The advantage runs two ways: The game brings glory to the developer and sales (hopefully) to the advertiser.

I am surprised that more sponsored products haven't been developed so far. Although this idea is in its infancy, I think it will become a major segment soon. The demographics of game players, the ferocious competition for consumer dollars, the growing trend among advertisers to employ unconventional marketing methods, and the desire (and need) for development houses to find new ways to earn money will ultimately lead to more sponsored products.

A sponsored product might be given away or sold for a small fee, but my guess is that large advertisers will fund a shareware version of a product, allowing for high-quality shareware titles. The development houses could then sell an upgraded version that would bring in a profit above and beyond the money earned constructing the game in the first place. In the meantime, the advertiser guarantees a nice outlet of the millions of people who will experience the shareware version.

This business model is not too different from that of network television in which a studio shares development costs of a network series (usually at a loss) in return for hopes of success in syndication. (Until recently, the networks didn't get a piece of syndication profits.) Meanwhile, the advertising revenue from the show is made by the network. Pretty spiffy deal.

Next Wave Distribution Outlets

Several distribution outlets now coming into play could change the face of game software distribution. While these upstarts won't replace the old standbys, they certainly provide new ideas to solve several key problems with game distribution.

Kiosk Setups

Some newer distribution companies are experimenting with kiosk systems, which distribute CD-ROMs that are made to order on premises. Working with a large database of games, the system actually uses a CD-ROM writer to create the CD on the

fly. This setup greatly reduces shelf space problems and can integrate product demos as well. Documentation can be provided for products requiring a great deal of instruction.

The tests I've heard about mainly involve placing the kiosks in retail outlets such as bookstores and even supermarkets not currently selling much software. One of these days, you'll be getting ready to leave work and you'll get a phone call from home asking you, "Please bring home bread, milk, eggs, and Doom IV."

High-Speed Telephone Lines, Cable Networks, and Interactive Television

As the software industry and games industry enter the wired world, new distribution opportunities are heating up. Already, Sega is pioneering the whole idea of network distribution. Using a special cable network and cable modems, subscribers can receive up to 50 games per month to play on their Sega Genesis. Currently, Sega subscribers pay $14.95 a month for access to the Sega channel.

@Home, a cable modem startup venture of cable giant TCI and venture capitalist Kleiner, Perkins should be rolling out in 1996. @Home will be offering people Ethernet speeds for Internet access, which would allow for rapid downloading of games to PCs.

While there'll still be a need for CD-ROMs (or, in the future, DVDs), the direct purchasing and downloading of software either on a program-by-program basis or subscription fee will certainly rise to prominence over the next five to ten years.

CD-ROM Superstores

Do you ever ask yourself why game retailing isn't more like the large music superstores such as Tower Records or HMV? Well, they're on the way. Several companies, notably Virgin Stores (no affiliation with Virgin Games) is debuting WOW!, a joint venture of the Good Guys electronics chain and Tower Records. The venture, which opened in 1995 in Las Vegas, builds stores that are a whopping 60,000 square feet and stock everything from music CDs to CD-ROMs and a full line of consumer electronics and computers.

The Future

The key issue to the future is solving the shelf space problem. Because the game industry is currently a "hits-based business," the majority of retail outlets for games are small and only stock the top 10 to 15 percent of available titles. However, at some point this distribution approach is going to change. As the business becomes more mass market and average sales per game goes up, expect more superstores to hit the market and expand the retail space available for games. In addition, expect prices to fall because volume will increase.

Following all of this will be the rise in distribution methods like the Internet, and an increase in direct sales of games. With the Internet and the Web comes the *virtual shelf,* where the developer gets to determine how long a product remains available to the general consumer.

Still, the retail customer is going to make up the bulk of sales in this industry for the time being, and even as newer distribution outlets increase, the ability for a product to be successful at retail will be a major factor in overall revenue for developers.

Interview with a Sales Guru

During the research work for this book I interviewed Ken Tannebaum. Ken had been a top sales representative with Electronic Arts and, at the time of this interview, was settling into his new job as National Sales Director for Virgin Interactive Entertainment.

Q: WAL-MART/Kmart/Toys 'Я' Us/Barnes & Noble. These major chains are now selling tons of software. What sort of advice do you give to companies trying to reach this channel? Do you rely on distributors, do you go direct?

A: It varies. Good Times (GT Interactive) has an exclusive with WAL-MART; they act much like a rack jobber. Kmart and Sears use the Handleman company, also a rack jobber. Barnes & Noble is buying from a distributor. We try to sell direct as often as possible.

Q: How important are the major software chains, and what sort of smaller regional chains are the major software retailers? How do you deal with these chains and how is that different from working with a distributor account?

A: As the PC becomes more of a mainstream market, the mass merchants will become more important. The lion-share of PC entertainment software is sold by Best Buy, CompUSA, Computer City, Electronics Boutique, and Neostar. These accounts are sold directly. The account list is different for the console business. The smaller regional chains are important because they offer more places to sell products (for example, Fred Meyer, Lechmere and so on).

Q: Which catalogs do you see as useful for selling games? Do they sell space?

A: Retailer catalogs are best (for example, Electronics Boutique Direct Mail). The other successful venues are MacWarehouse, PC Warehouse, PC Connection, and so on. They do sell space; they have full-time people whose only job is selling space in the mail order catalogs. It usually is not cheap.

Q: There seems to be about a dozen to two dozen major distributors for game/consumer software. (These don't include companies like Egghead.) Can you describe in general terms how a company would deal with these distributors on new product distribution and day-to-day relations.

A: There is an inherent problem with the way people view distributors in this industry. Most of them are order takers, not sales people. To work effectively with a distributor you need to call on the account (that is, visit them) and give them an order to accept. Thus, the distributor is purely a physical distribution system, not a sales force for you.

To succeed, you either need to have your own sales force or work with a publisher as an affiliated label. But until you have the critical mass to hire your own sales people, you'll have to settle for using publishers and relying on their efforts to sell the product.

Q: Are there any major differences in distributing console products versus PC products?

A: The console products are usually sold on a one-way sale—no returns. (This is a misnomer because you have to mark down dud or dead titles.) PC products are sold with returns. If a PC title does not sell at retail in the first three weeks of release, you can count on taking it back; the retail shelf space is so tight that the retailers will not accept a mark-down and will request a return.

Q: Do you have any warnings that a "go-it-aloner" should be aware of in distributing products?

A: If you are a small publisher, most of the retailers and distributors will not pay the bill until the next title is released. They might pay for what has sold but they usually hold payment to protect the inventory that they own.

Q: What sort of things do you think work well in selling a game to the consumer? What sort of promotions work well to pull game software through the channel? Do rebates work (buy 2 get 1 free)?

A: Whether you choose rebates, sample disks, buy 2's, buy a product and get a free T-shirt or other item, you need to pre-sell your product (using promotion and advertising) to be most successful.

Q: Any tips on how to maintain shelf space over time with a product?

A: The product quality will dictate a long term shelf space (for example, SimCity, 7th Guest, Nascar Racing, all stay on the shelf a very long time because game players love these products).

Q: Do you have any thoughts or information about distributing overseas?

A: Selling overseas yourself is tough. It's best to sign up with an established publisher like Virgin.

Software Packaging

Whoever coined the phrase "don't judge a book by its cover" never worked in the game business. Most software sells because of good packaging. I offer several reasons to account for my statement:

- **Game buyers are often not the people who play games.** Go into any Software Etc. three weeks before Christmas (or any time for that matter) and you'll witness the "blind gamer." This is an adult, most often buying for a child, who wanders around looking for a game to purchase. They'll browse the sections soaking in the information from the packaging looking for something that will satisfy the person they are buying the game for. This is especially the case with educational games.

  What's important is that the buyer doesn't play games, and wouldn't know a name of a hit game. They rely either on the marginally more informed sales staff or many times the box itself.

  Lesson: Boxes need to be informative; you're targeting uniformed buyers, not the intended recipient.

- **There are more uninformed purchasers of games than other media.** This is sort of a variation of the previous point. In this case, the purchaser is the recipient but is equally as uninformed about games as the purchaser we just discussed. Many times, these purchasers are first-time buyers or occasional gamers. They don't read the game magazines and they're not on the Internet praising their favorite games. In many cases, they're often impulse shopping, dropping into the game store or section looking to buy *something*. Packaging for them is key to how they make their buying decisions.

  Lesson: Not all gamers are created equal and the more mass-market consumers do not read up and plan their purchases. They shop on impulse. Your packaging needs to get them to understand why your game is so much better than the other choices. Review quotes and screenshots work well, and you might even consider placing comparison charts on the package between rival products to help make the case.

- **Screen shots still sell games.** If PT Barnum were a game developer, his entire box would be plastered with screenshots. While it might make many developers cringe, the fact is *graphics sell*. Sexy screenshots showing awesome graphics can be a major factor in creating a package that sells itself. While even avid gamers know that awesome eye-candy can mean low interactivity, everyone has succumbed to the allure of screenshots once in their life.

  Lesson: Many consumers are apprehensive to purchase a package without screenshots. Be careful though—screenshots are often the most misleading

information on a box. Don't be deceptive and use phony screenshots; make sure the shots shown depict key gameplay features.

Common Game Packaging Practices

As I mentioned, the first game packages were Ziplock bags. Then, simple cardboard or plastic packaging was introduced. With the launch of Electronic Arts, which followed the record industry's model, came an entirely new approach. EA created album-style packaging with lush graphics and "liner" notes.

Other companies followed EA and packages became fancy very quickly. For their Ultima series, Origin created awesome manuals that were printed on parchment-like paper. Origin also included cloth maps of their game world and a small "trinket"—such as fake coins of the realm—to further enhance the overall package. One company actually packaged its tennis game in tennis ball canisters.

But times have changed. Today there are too many products taking up limited shelf space and packaging has had to change to meet the demands of the retail shelf.

Aside from the switch to CD-ROMs from floppies, the biggest change in packaging is not in the innards but in the box itself. Most software now is placed on its side on the shelf, so spin space has increased. Some packages have as much as a 1 3/4 inch thick box to properly show the title of the product when viewed from the side.

Fortunately, game companies still believe in providing documentation and other embellishments. Developers want consumers to know that a game is more than just the CD-ROM it's stamped on. One thing that separates games from other types of software are the additional features such as maps, posters, and other aids. Some games even include background novellas or comic books. It's important to think about the packaging and required documentation as you develop your game. If you have the budget to include extras, don't be afraid to let your creativity run wild.

Preparing, Pricing, and Assembling Game Packaging

Only a few years ago, CD-ROMs were relatively expensive to duplicate, especially in lower volumes. Today, CDs are rapidly replacing disks as the primary distribution media and you can bet costs will continue to decrease. Many large and small duplication companies have emerged, offering you a selection of services.

Creating a CD-ROM is a two-step process. First, you need to make a master CD. This is often called a *gold master*. Then, the master CD is used to duplicate CDs. If you don't have the equipment to make your own gold masters, don't worry. Most of the professional CD duplication companies will make a master for you for a small charge (less than $500). All you need to provide is a backup tape or SyQuest cartridge, or some other type of media. Although most duplication companies work with a variety of media, make sure you check with them before you go to the trouble of creating media to submit to them.

In addition to manufacturing a CD-ROM for your product, you'll need to produce and manufacture other materials for your product including a box, manual, and so on. You'll also need to have all of the materials assembled to create a finished shrink-wrapped product. Table 30.1 lists some of the components that are often included with game products. Notice that I've included a cost for each component or task and an estimated time for completion. Keep in mind that the costs listed are just estimates. You'll find that prices will vary depending on which vendors you use. Make sure that you shop around and get multiple estimates for any manufacturing tasks.

SPA Packaging Guidelines

Recently, the Software Publishers Association (SPA) issued some guidelines on "Desktop Software Publishing." These guidelines were distributed to help publishers understand how to properly package software so consumers wouldn't be confused by it. Here are some of the more helpful points they suggest:

- Include the product title on all sides of the box: front, back, and all spines.
- Place the platform and media specifications on the front and the left spine. The recommended descriptions to use are: DOS, Mac, Windows, MPC3, Unix, OS/2. (For media type, use 3.5" disk or CD-ROM. Other media identification is at the publisher's discretion.)
- Place the stock keeping unit (SKU) on the bottom spine with the second choice being the back lower-right corner. This is the UPC/ISBN/EAN label and is usually scanned at the checkout counter.

Table 30.1 Components and Tasks Used for Game Packaging

Component/Task	Time to Complete	Cost < 3,000	Cost 3,000 to 10,000	Cost Over 10,000
Create master CD	5 working days	$500 fee	$500 fee	No charge
Duplicate CD-ROM	6-10 working days	$.85/unit	$.75/unit	$.70/unit
Print box	10 working days	$1+/unit	$.70 to $1/unit	< $.70/unit
Print manual	10 working days	$1+/unit	$.70 to $1/unit	< $.70/unit
Assemble components	2-3 working days	$.50/unit	$.50/unit	< $.50/unit

- Place ratings logos on the front of the package. Check with the council from whom you get your product rated for specific information. The SPA and the Computer Game Developers Association (CGDA) strongly recommend use of the Recreational Software Advisory Council's (RSAC) content-based ratings system.
- System requirements should be on the front corner and on an adjacent side spine. The other option is to place them on a lower-back corner and adjacent side spine. At a minimum, the following needs to be identified and specified:
  - Operating system version/platform version number (for example, Mac OS7 or Windows 3.0)
  - Memory/physical RAM requirements and recommendations clearly specified, to include total memory required, including OS overhead
  - Video board support, which includes number of Mac bits or DOS/Windows video memory
  - VGA or SVGA graphics/video resolution/color depth stated as number of pixels horizontal by number of pixels vertical by number of colors (for example, requires 640×480 256 Color Graphics)
  - CD-ROM drive speed (single, double, quad, 6X)
  - Hard disk required (footprint) and available hard disk space (for example, 40 MB free HD space required)
  - Audio sound board support (for example, Requires 16-Bit Soundblaster Compatible)
- Use the smallest size package you can for each product to enhance shelf space and address environmental concerns.
- Check with your channels of distribution to find out their packaging requirements. The following are general guidelines:
  - Make sure the box is at least a minimum of 18 pt SBS or equivalent strength and puncture resistant. If the spine is greater than 1 1/2 inches and the principal front display panel (the front of the box) is greater than 7×9 inches, you should consider a higher caliber stock, an insert for internal support, or both. Goods damaged in shipment that never make it to the shelf represent between 5 and 10 percent of the product that is returned.
  - Make product as "theft proof" as possible. Retail is experiencing a theft problem. Shrink wrap and stickers are being slit and CDs are being removed from the larger package. Secure the CD in an insert away from the top or bottom of package.

- Make sure to place an emphasis on environmental considerations and recyclability in your packaging.

Packaging Standards

Depending on your market, you'll need to have at least one of the following symbols or numbers placed on your products.

Uniform Product Code (UPC)
Uniform Code Council
Phone: 513 435-3870

A UPC symbol is required for retail sales. It is used for product identification and inventory, and is a price point bar code.

International Standard Book Number (ISBN)
ISBN Agency
Phone: 908 665-2895 **Fax:** 908 464-6800

An ISBN number is required by bookstores and libraries to identify the title and publisher for inventory and for a listing of books in print.

European Article Number (EAN)
Phone: 516 487-6370

To sell a product in stores overseas, you'll need a European Article Number. Call the number listed here for more information.

All About Game Ratings

The idea of labeling or rating content in games has been around for a while. Several companies began placing labels (for example, Mature Audiences) on their products some time ago. Sega even instituted its own rating system in the early '90s.

Then along came Congress in 1994. Congressional hearings sponsored by Senator Joseph Lieberman (D-CT) and Senator Herb Kohl (D-WI) responded to growing public outcry over violence in games, especially in fighting games such as Mortal Kombat. The hearings and threat of Congressional intervention accelerated a drive to create a voluntary rating system that would inform parents about potential objectionable subject matter in games.

Two groups were formed out of this movement and both offer processes to rate games. You will probably find use for at least one if not both organizations and their programs. To publish a game and sell it in almost any major retail outlet, you'll be required to include some sort of content labeling or rating label on the product box.

Here are the two ratings organizations and their associated details:

The Entertainment Software Ratings Board (ESRB)
Part of The IDSA (Interactive Digital Software Association)
845 Third Avenue, 14th Floor
New York, NY 10022
Phone: 212 759-0700

In September 1994, the ESRB was started by the IDSA, a major organization in the gaming community made up of the biggest names in the games industry. The ESRB was set up to rate interactive software much like the MPAA (Motion Picture Association of America) rates movies. Games are submitted to the ESRB with an application for rating. The process, which can take several weeks, returns a rating and content "descriptors" (short phrases that give more information about the content of the product) if necessary.

Recreational Software Advisory Council
2067 Massachusetts Avenue, Fourth Floor
Cambridge, MA 02140
Phone: 617 864-5612 **Fax:** 202 293-3055
Email: info@rsac.org **WWW:** http://www.rsac.org

The RSAC was formed in 1994 and is a non-profit organization created in response to the growing Congressional action in regard to entertainment software. While the RSAC concentrates now on game software, its mission covers all forms of entertainment software, and they have also worked in cooperation with the various groups trying to help with World Wide Web content issues as well. All of this is especially focused on children's use and exposure to this medium.

The actual group that formed the RSAC's mission and system of operation was called the *Computer Game Ratings Working Group*, which includes the following organizations:

- Software Publishers Association
- Association of Shareware Professionals
- Shareware Trade Association and Resources
- Computer Game Developers Association
- Educational Software Cooperative
- Software Entrepreneurs Forum

The RSAC rating process was formulated to be an objective content-labeling system. It was designed by a panel of industry people, parents, educators, and experts, including Dr. Donald F. Roberts of Stanford University who has studied the effects of media on children for nearly 20 years. The board of the RSAC is made up of a wide-ranging group of psychologists, educators, publishers, media researchers, and pediatric specialists, ensuring a very well rounded approach to an issue affecting a lot of groups. The RSAC has projected it will have rated over 500 software tiles by the end of 1995.

Details of RSAC Ratings and Process

The basis of the RSAC system is a disclosure format based on answers given in an electronic questionnaire. The questionnaire was designed and distributed by RSAC, and is completed by the software publisher. The form is created by running a custom-created computer program that leads the publisher through an entire set of questions, then completes the review process and prints out a complete review of the product. This approach is really great because a publisher can quickly see during development what kind of rating they can expect and make adjustments on the spot without spending a tremendous amount of time and money going through redevelopment.

The program starts with a general question in three major areas of content (violence, nudity/sex, and language) to see with a quick yes or no if such content exists. Those three categories, and the RSAC procedures for identifying them specifically, have been reviewed by numerous professional groups, including Media Scope and the American Academy of Pediatrics. If these three general questions are answered "no," the program returns a pre-confirmed rating of ALL (suitable for all audiences). If one or more of the questions is initially answered "yes," the program launches into a series of questions to determine exactly what the nature of potentially objectionable content actually is. The questions answered "yes" at this next stage launch even more specific questions until the ultimate rating of the content is determined, removing the subjectivity inherent in a scale system.

For example, the RSAC asks: "Does the software title depict blood and gore of sentient beings?" It's basically a yes or no situation, so you can see there is no room for confusion or interpretation.

All the ratings are tentative; the publisher must submit the form for approval. The ratings determined by the program are based on some published algorithmic approaches to content, as devised by researchers. The cool thing about this is that the approach is pretty consistent for all titles; the rating is the same given to anyone creating a similar product. They are not judged by a panel and are not open to subjective feelings (as the sample RSAC question indicated). However, the ratings you receive can be appealed (there is an extra cost to handle to the work) just in case you don't agree with the outcome.

Also because of its algorithmic approach and software program updates, new ideas and refinements can be rapidly incorporated into the entire RSAC process.

The RSAC used a lot of variables to determine the specific ratings in its system. Here is an example of the variables used to determine a violence score for a given product. For the language and nudity/sex categories a similar extensive set is also used.

- **Types of Violence:** Aggressive Violence, Natural/Accidental Violence, Benign Immobilization, Sports Violence, Strategic Aggression
- **Portrayal of Target Or Victim:** Human, Non-Human Sentient Being, Realistic Non-Sentient Object, Realistic Non-Sentient Object with Implied Social Presence, or Symbolic Non-Sentient Object
- **Level of Damage to Target or Victim:** No Apparent Damage, Minor Damage, Damage, Death or Destruction
- **Victim's Stance:** Threatening or Non-Threatening
- **Consequences to Player:** Reward for Aggression or No Reward For Aggression

The ratings in the categories apply a score from 1 to 4. Using violence as an example, the RSAC would give a Level 4 rating to a product that "contains gratuitous or extreme violence."

The RSAC accounts for various inconsistencies that may result. For example, a wargame might be considered pretty violent, but because of built-in exemptions for things like "strategic aggression" or sports games (like boxing), the rating program adjusts the rating. Again this is done through the explicit questioning of the program.

The questionnaire and definitions in the system are designed to force a higher rather than lower rating in cases of doubt. Publishers may request that the RSAC rating panel make a ruling on any specific point within the context of the disclosure application, and they may appeal the final rating if they feel the methodology was not able to account adequately for the context in which the questionable content appeared.

Filing the Disclosure Statement and Assignment of the Rating

When the game and its accompanying rating form have been completed, the next step is the filing process. An officer of the publishing company must sign the Statement of Compliance that comes with the review forms. The entire package is then sent to the RSAC where it is reviewed to confirm that the process was completed correctly by the publisher and the subsequent rating is consistent (old rating software, for example, might cause incorrect ratings).

Once this review is approved, the publisher will be notified that the rating has been registered by the RSAC, and the rating and RSAC trademark can then be used in ads and packaging.

Appealing a Rating

Ratings given by the program can be appealed to the RSAC directly. The fact that it is a program and sometimes the rules can be misleading are always taken into account. Appeals will be decided by a ratings review panel comprised of volunteer parents and educators. Successful appeals provide feedback and information useful in improving and refining the rating application methodology.

Consumer Use of the RSAC Rating System

The graphic depiction of the rating conveys the rating result at a glance. If there is no potentially objectionable content, the title will display an ALL rating. If one or more subject areas register a rating above ALL, the title will show the rating received in the three variable subject areas on a scale of 1 to 4. In addition, a short description of the potentially objectionable content is included for each subject area.

The RSAC also distributes a chart that explains the rating levels in more detail to assist consumers in making fully informed decisions. This information is provided to the editorial press, supplied to retailers for display in stores, enclosed in recreational software packages, and posted on numerous bulletin boards and online services. In addition, the complete details of the rating methodology will be provided upon request to consumers.

RSAC Pricing Structure

The pricing for the RSAC rating process is very inexpensive and is geared toward the RSAC's support for small developers:

- Companies with over $1 million in revenue pay $400.
- Companies with $100,000 to under $1 million in revenue pay $250.
- Companies with under $100,000 in revenue pay only $50.

The payments are based on the latest fiscal year revenues.

Recently the RSAC also announced that a company can negotiate reduced rates for bulk submissions (say for a previously unrated back catalog of titles). The reduced rate is handled by the RSAC's executive director. Hardship (probably meaning you're broke or a small developer with tons of old titles to rerate) is also considered for reduced rates.

A Boost for the RSAC Process

If you haven't been on CompuServe's Game Developers forum, you might not know that the CGDA endorsed the RSAC ratings process for software. The RSAC

was started as an alternative source from the Nintendo and Sega-backed ESRB. The RSAC is a more PC-based and independent-based rating process, which costs much less than the ESRB. However, so far Toys 'Я' Us has said it will only carry ESRB rated software. Of course, this favorite toy store didn't even carry PC-based software until recently.

In making the endorsement, the CGDA was hoping to persuade large merchants like Toys 'Я' Us to adopt the standard. In a post on CompuServe's Game Developer forum, Ernest Adams, CGDA president, summed up the endorsement this way, "The CGDA does not oppose ESRB, nor do we wish to discourage its use. We encourage the use of RSAC labels, and we hope all parties concerned (Congress, the publishers, the retailers, the developers, and the consumers) will give RSAC at least as much credit as they do to ESRB."

Ratings Don't Guarantee a Spot on the Shelf

In the fall of 1995, Sierra On-Line released their long awaited new product called Phantasmagoria. While Sierra thought they had covered their bases by rating the game and placing mature content labels on the box, retailing giant CompUSA felt differently.

They banned the game for sale at all CompUSA stores and this cost Sierra a major retail outlet. While the resulting publicity from the move may actually have helped Sierra sell more copies, the message the action raised was simple: Ratings are not a guarantee of access to the retail channel. Just because you rate or label the content in your game does not bind any retailer to selling your game. Therefore, if you have a potentially controversial game (Phantasmagoria had several instances of questionable content), you might even go the extra step and talk with your key retail accounts and make sure they don't object. Otherwise, the surprise on shipping day may be for you, not your customers.

Ratings Wrap-Up

Certainly the ratings issue will not go away. As more and more people play games there is both expanded demand for more mature content and the entrance of consumers who may object to content previously taken for granted by gamers. Additionally, in the U.S. and the world as a whole, there has been increased concern over exposing people to especially violent content. Combine those two trends with the special consideration that many games are *interactive*, and you can see the increased demand for ratings that alert consumers (and especially parents) to the content of games.

On top of this, game developers (who may or may not object to the entire idea of ratings) have to become vigilant about the implications of developing with ratings in play.

All About Game Press Reviews

With shelf space so tight and the number of titles growing, game reviews are becoming incredibly important. Game reviews can be divided into two categories: those that reach core gamers and those that reach sources outside this group to the casual gamer and mass markets. You'll want to reach the core group first, because they influence other consumers who look to them for advice.

Keep in mind that most game reviews that get published outside of the trade are written by people who are hardcore gamers (even though their audience isn't). And because the reviewers are often given limited space (as opposed to a magazine chock full of game reviews), they review only games they like. That means successful previews or early reviews can catapult into great reviews outside the normal publications and get you known to a more mass market consumer.

Types of Reviews

First, when I use the term *review* I'm not necessarily talking about a thumbs up or thumbs down assessment of your game. I'm being far more general. A review in my opinion is any press description of your game. Specifically, I have in mind three types of reviews, which I'll discuss in the following sections.

The Preview

You can occassionally get a publication to preview your game by sharing it with them before the game is completed. In most cases, a magazine's editorial board will preview only those games it considers to be ground breaking or tremendously innovative.

When you're sure you have a product that fits the bill, send a demo along with a non-disclosure agreement and some background information—probably after calling them first.

Right now previews are very big—they help sell magazines and more publishers want to use them to build interest. Many companies are giving exclusives to certain magazines to secure a preview article.

One thing I have to stress here: Don't go soliciting a preview until you clearly see the light at the end of the development tunnel. There's nothing worse than showing off a preview, getting that coveted article, and then not shipping for months. Several products, most notably Lucas Arts' recent release The Dig, have had problems concerning early previews and late ship dates.

A preview should be the beginning of a series of steps taken to build demand for a product. Starting too early can kill the entire timing of such efforts.

The "It's Shipping" Announcement

An announcement review is nothing more than a press release. At this stage, you're hoping to get a nice blurb—explaining that the game is available and what it's all about—in the new product release or news section of a magazine.

Getting That Review Secured

The actual review is, of course, the biggest and best thing you can do to promote your game. As with any review, once you clinch it, you want to do everything you can to make it a positive review. Aside from making a good game, the other crucial component of getting a good game review is the actual handling of the review logistics.

Reviewers are not playing games just because they like them; it's their job and they expect some professionalism from you to help them with their work. Essential to all of this is a good press review kit.

The first step in getting your game reviewed is to get past the hundreds of other products getting in front of editors. The best way to do that is by creating a really cool press review kit. A press review kit is a total package of information and accessories to help reviewers quickly experience as much of the game as possible and help them prepare a review. Your kit might include all kinds of press- and company-related information, the full game package, and a reviewer's guide. Some companies also pack in goodies like T-shirts or some cool game-oriented trinkets. For example, if your game is about snowboarding, you could include a fake ski pass or some funky ski glasses.) While these trinkets won't win the reviewers' praise, it's a nice gesture and probably psyches them up to boot up the product..

Perhaps the most essential component after the game itself is the reviewer's guide. A reviewer may have only two to three days, or even less, to evaluate and write a review of your game, so you want your reviewer's guide to be top notch. The idea is to provide them the means to accelerate their experience of the game. For example, assume you've developed great adventure game with 50 different scenes and three distinct paths. Your reviewer's guide would show the reviewer step-by-step ways to experience the game. Basically it's a cheat guide—but the purpose is to make sure that the reviewer sees all the cool stuff in the game.

Because the reviewer's guide is so important, let me take a minute to discuss some of the other elements you should include:

- Make sure that you have a complete list of all the specifications of the game, especially if you have multiple shipping copies. The reviewer may only be playing with the IBM version and never experience the specs needed for the Mac version, so make sure it's right there for them. Don't forget the price, ship dates, publisher, and other essential facts. This information should be included on the first page of your reviewer's guide.

- Embellish your guide with facts and information about who and how the product was developed. If you feature some amazing technology like video sprites, explain that in the review kit. Production elements help the reviewer to realize how much work went into the project and may also help them to embellish their review.
- Include cheat codes. Anything you can show the reviewer to provide a total game experience will help. You needn't share everything, but remember not every reviewer will have the patience to see everything in a game based on his or her skill alone. You might even want to make a special review copy that has different cheat codes to prevent your real codes from getting into the hands of the general public—just make sure the reviewer knows what you're up to.
- If your game allows the user to save sessions, save various games in progress for reviewers to load and play from.
- Let the reviewer know about planned add-ons, give them contact information for development team members.
- Include a disk packed with the best screenshots for their layout people.

Of Special Note: "Other Reviewers"

Once you've created an awesome press review kit, don't just sit on it. Let the world see what you've created in your laboratory! Think about all the other types of reviewers out there who can be of some importance to you: industry analysts, people at other game companies, reviewers at industry magazines, online forum sysops and Web site editors, and most of all distributors and retail buyers.

All of these people might not review your game in a written consumer magazine but an early good opinion can be equally important. You never know when a producer at a major company might happen upon an excellent review and offer you a big-time publishing deal. Hey, it can happen!

Blindly mailing out hundreds of press review kits can get mighty expensive, so when you're designing your budget, take time to think beyond the circle of major magazine reviewers. Oh, and send me one too while you're at it! <grin>

Making a Good Impression

There are two basic ideas I need to stress here—your game is your ultimate calling card, so get it out there, and dress it up when you send it out the door for review. Most of this stuff will be handled by a publisher but even then, the more familiar you are with the entire process the better you can work with the publisher to help them get your game reviewed.

I can't stress enough how important it is to get involved personally in the promotion of your product. Just because you're hooked in with, say, Electronic Arts doesn't mean you can kick your feet up. EA is definitely a juggernaut promotional machine, but developers who go the extra mile will make the most of what EA has to offer.

Resources

Promoting your game is major undertaking; getting it reviewed is simply one of the more important elements. If you're just starting out, I suggest you invest some time in picking up a few sample reviewer's kits. I was able to get several just by making a few phone calls to a couple of the major publishers who regularly do reviewer's guides. Everyone's got an idea on how to create the ideal kit, so take it all in with a grain of salt.

Another important resource is a listing of press contacts that will receive your reviewer's kit. In this book, I've provided about as comprehensive a list of game magazines as found anywhere; however, for specific contacts, you're going to have to do some homework. You should begin considering alternatives to the mainstream trades: Local papers, non-traditional games magazines, and even television shows are great places to start. Game magazines hit the core of the gaming market, but an entrepreneurial developer will cultivate other sources as well.

Game Promotion and Advertising

When it comes to promotion and advertising, games are somewhat akin to any other packaged good—you buy ads and do promotions to create demand. But games are unique and require special attention. Let's talk about a few specific things you can do to create a frenzy for your products.

The Game Specific Advertising and Promotion Model

Advertising in the interactive entertainment field has really paralleled the maturation of the industry. What started as small black and white ads for mail order games in the back of arcane computer hobbyist magazines has grown to include multi-million dollar marketing budgets, including trade shows, traveling caravans, television ad buys, tons of in-store promotions, and, of course, splashy four-color ads in dozens of special interest magazines.

Nothing speaks more of the maturity of an industry than advertising. Any marketing textbook will tell you that as products find less ground to compete based on features and technology, more advertising is employed to distinguish a product from the competition. Certainly games still find ample room to compete on features, but that difference isn't as much as it used to be. Just look at the top-tier golf games: Links, Microsoft Golf, and PGA Pro Tour. Because they all seem similar to a blind consumer's eye, the ground now shifts to marketing, promotion, and advertising to establish higher volume sales.

Advertising is incredibly important and understanding how games are advertised can give you a better idea of how the industry operates as a whole.

Understanding Advertising Costs

The first aspect of advertising you need to understand are costs and how they're determined. Advertising costs are typically evaluated in terms of Cost Per Thousand (CPM; M being the Roman numeral signifying 1,000). CPM defines a given medium's cost basis to reach 1,000 people. So if a magazine rates its CPM at $100, and it has 100,000 subscribers, you're looking at a cost of $10,000 to place a full page ad. The CPM varies in price depending on how the magazine and its advertisers view the reader mix.

Next, demographics come into play. For example, *GamePro* is a major magazine with over 300,000 subscribers, but its average reader is considerably younger than the average *Computer Gaming World*'s reader. *CGW* also has a smaller subscriber base. Although *CGW* might have a higher CPM because advertisers are willing to pay more to reach the older and probably richer demographic, a single page in *GamePro* would probably be more expensive because of the larger circulation.

Print Advertising and Beyond

Advertising games has primarily been a print medium enterprise. I've listed many magazines that accept ads to promote games. But while print is the primary way to advertise your game, there are many other forms of advertising being used in today's increasingly mature market . Let's look at all of them and see how they've been used to advertise games.

Print Advertising and Promotion

I've provided a comprehensive list of all the major gaming magazines I could find. (They're in the back of the book.) The magazines are important because, among other reasons, advertising in these magazines is the *number 1 way* to promote a game.

Beware though, publications like *Computer Gaming World* are not the only place to run ads. Increasingly I've found two consumers of games: People who are hardcore game players and people who play games occasionally. These two groups find their information from completely different sources. Game players are your hardcore

audience. These people enjoy many types of games and purchase games on a regular if not habitual basis. They're the bread and butter types who read publications like *Computer Gaming World*, *Next Generation*, and other trade publications.

People who play games, on the other hand, are consumers who purchase a game every once in a while. The key here is that the games these folks purchase parallel an interest they have in their actual life. For example, take the bank executive who plays golf. Does he find out about Links Golf from Access by reading *Computer Gaming World*? I don't think so. For this market, an ad in *Golf Digest* might be just as good, if not better in promoting the game. A combination of both is most likely the best scenario.

Exploring alternative advertising outlets that aren't game oriented but reach the same target market—especially among special interests like sports, driving, military, and so on should be your first advertising target outside of game industry media. Game developers need to broaden their previous practices to anticipate the market beyond consumers who spend the majority of their time at the mall in Software Etc. to people who might be spending most of their time in Macy's.

Beyond that, just pay attention to mainstream publications like *Rolling Stone*, your local paper, and *Newsweek*. The most successful game publishers are looking to break past the obvious market to a more casual consumer.

In-Store Promotion

Two types of promotions are used at the retail level: Co-op and simple in-store promotional campaigns. Co-op, which is used much more by hardware manufacturers, is basically an agreement between a retailer and the distributor/publisher or developer of the product to jointly purchase advertising. This is a useful tool to use in areas of the country such as New York City or San Francisco where you might need to purchase local media to make an extra sales push.

Most publishers, however, can usually get by with simple in-store promotions for their store-specific marketing campaigns. These include offerings like in-store rebates, free sampler discs, in-store demos, or video tape reels of upcoming titles.

Remember, many game purchases are decided in the store on the spur of the moment. Once you've generated enough interest with your fabulous campaign to get consumers into the store because they've heard of the product, you can then try various ideas to make the consumer really want to buy your product as they're browsing. This technique is especially useful after the game has been out for a while.

Online Promotion

Online services are growing so fast that no one can keep up. The amount of new users and new content providers coming onboard everyday is simply amazing. The low cost of establishing an online presence provides developers with the ability to directly talk to consumers—one of the most desirable forms of marketing today.

Here are a few tips for those of you using online outlets to promote your products:

- **Don't count on or wait for your publisher.** Sure, your publisher wants to sell your game as much as you do but that doesn't mean they're going to promote your games online as aggressively as you will. Many developers do their own promotional Web sites that work in conjunction with their publisher's site. Always discuss something like this with your publisher first, but be sure to think about taking the initiative and building your own online presence.
- **Don't limit yourself to one service or just the World Wide Web.** One thing you've got to understand about the online world is that it's extremely segmented. Users on eWorld don't often have accounts on CompuServe. And not everyone on America Online uses the Web. To have a complete online presence you need to cover all the bases—establish outlets in many of these self-contained online areas and set up a Web site, too.

  Certainly costs are a factor, but a lot of the services offer different levels of presence, from a full forum to being part of a group forum like the Game Publishers Sections on CompuServe. Either way it's an excellent way to potentially reach millions of consumers.
- **Promote the online sites as much as anything else.** If you're placing ads or doing any sort of promotion on your own, make sure the online site or Web site is prominently displayed.
- **Don't be static.** One of the biggest problems about operating a promotional venture online is keeping it fresh. Make sure you spend the time to update and upgrade, and introduce new content to your online forums. For example, start an electronic mail newsletter that talks about the site and new events or products debuting. You can use a typical mailing list server to get subscribers.

  Other ideas would be to schedule contests and monthly chats with the people who made the game (building up name recognition for your programmers can be a plus). Whatever approach you take, make sure you do something. It's such a waste to see companies spend the time to build an online presence only to let it become stagnant.
- **Be creative with your online promotions.** The best online forums, especially Web sites, are the ones in which the company really takes a creative approach. Spend some time browsing other publisher's sites to get your creative juices flowing. Sierra OnLine recently debuted a Web site that allows users to customize the site to their liking. By allowing users to control the site, Sierra has gained insight into users' tastes in games!

Advertising on the Boob Tube

Console hardware companies have made their mark in the world of TV advertising by promoting both their consoles and software. Surely you've seen the wild "SE—GA!" spots, which propelled Sega into market leadership as the advertising established them as the "hip" hardware for kids to own. If the power of advertising had never been seen before in the game market, it certainly was evident with Sega's campaign.

Still, as companies and products have grown, other companies have gotten into the act and established their credentials in the use of television advertising. The most notable of these has been EA with its EA SPORTS ads featuring a deep-voiced announcer who proclaims "If it's in the game it's in the game!"

Unfortunately, TV advertising is not a suitable promotional strategy for most developers, but as I pointed out in Chapter 25, in order to justify the cost of TV advertising publishers are working to simultaneously release multiple games of similar style (for example a line of sport games) on multiple platforms. That means tighter coordination between subdevelopers, tighter deadlines, and different programming and art development processes. So even though only one percent of publishers can consider TV advertising, it really does have that "trickle down" effect.

The trick to television advertising is simple, focus your media where it can best reach your target demographic (cable's ESPN is one good example) and build brand image. While certainly announcing a new product is good (and that's an important aspect of advertising), good TV advertising concentrates on creating brand recognition.

For example, look at EA's ads. While they may specifically talk about a certain product, say John Madden Football, they spend a considerable amount of time just letting the viewer know a basic message "BUY EA SPORTS GAMES." EA is looking to cement the EA Sports brand as *the* sports game. In situations that force consumers to make a choice between similar products, advertising is the medium that gives the edge. Sports games are perhaps one of the more mature gaming markets, and so it's no wonder that TV advertising here has been especially active.

A common misconception is that TV advertising is prohibitively expensive, but when used correctly, you can achieve an amazing amount of exposure for a relatively smaller amount of money than you might think.

What's Your Role?

Most developers think that once their game is in the marketing department's or publisher's hands they can sit back and wait for the royalty checks to roll in. That is *not* the approach I'd recommend. Even if you have the powerhouse marketing machine of Acclaim or EA on your side (and most of us don't), you should constantly ask yourself what you can do to get more people to buy your game.

Royalties are not based on how cool your game is or how many polygons you're moving per second; the success of your game is based on the number of copies that are sold. And that should be pretty important to you. Fortunately, there are many things you can do to get your game better advertised, reviewed, and promoted. I've put together a set of them in the form of rules, which, with a little luck, will help you obtain more successful sales.

Rule #1: Get to know the marketing and sales departments and kiss their butts. If you are not on a first name basis with the people who are marketing and selling your product you're already in trouble. Come royalty-check time you might find that being obnoxious or just plain ignorant of them might cost you big time. If the marketing folks like you they just might work a little harder and sell a few more copies of your game. They might even allocate more of their precious ad budget on your game.

Rule #2: Educate the sales and marketing people. The point of Rule #1 is to become marketing's best friend; Rule #2 tells us to become their mentor. The one thing you can count on is that the sales and marketing guys aren't technical and they're not always avid game players—even if they love games. They are very busy folks, handling up to 40 products at one time. Thus, you need to do everything you can to make them knowledgeable about your game. The more they know about it, the better they'll be able to be position it and the more the retail buyers will be excited about it.

Most companies have standard techniques for taking information from developers and getting it to the marketing and sales staffs. This information is the absolute minimum they need to do a good job—you should try and be more pro-active and ask what else you can provide.

Rule #3: Make yourself available. Game developers are more often becoming stars. This newfound stardom translates into potential interviews and features with top magazines and other media like *Wired* or NPR radio. Make it known to your new friends in marketing (see Rule #1) that if they can get your game covered by giving an interview, you will do it.

You can also go online and mingle with the gaming masses, or have people who worked on the project hit the newsgroups and the various online sites and talk about the game. There is nothing hardcore gamers (whom you're trying to make your national sales force) like better than to interact online with their favorite developers. You can inform them about tricks and tips, how you programmed it, and more. Don't expect any marketing department to do this sort of thing for you—they're busy enough as it is.

Rule #4: Promote your company as well. Imagine you're a lead developer and part owner of Great Games, Inc.—a small development house that just published a

game through Monster Games, Inc. While Monster Games will focus on promoting that game, you need to focus on promoting your company.

First, you want people to associate the new game with your company, making them want *any* game you produce in the future. Second, you want other developers, publishers, investors, and such to take notice. This is where interviews and online presence can really be the most helpful.

But don't just blast out of the gate talking about your company and how great it is. You have to be careful not to make the publisher or the marketing crew mad (see Rule #1). Coordinate with them; they may want to cultivate your company name as well. Let them know what you're doing to get your name out there. Your priorities may be different, but be careful not to turn differences into disputes.

Rule #5: Don't assume your marketing and sales people know anything about marketing or sales. Over the years, publishers have really excelled at selling games. Today at a medium size publishing company, the marketing people tend to be veterans of the industry with college degrees. In short, they know what they're doing. However, you know as well as I do that not all publishers are created equal. In fact, some score some pretty low marks when it comes to marketing. Their idea of marketing might be buying a few ads in a couple of game magazines and getting two or three of the big chains to carry the game. They're not pushing for the big reviews, posting marketing information on the newsgroups, working hard to get demos to the store sales people, and so on.

Again you have a role here; learn more about marketing in the games industry and coordinate with the sales and marketing staff to make sure they're doing all the stuff you think should be done. But please be tactful; you don't like someone telling you how to program, and they're not going to like someone telling them how to market. If they aren't pushing your game out to all the magazines you know about, exchange press lists with them. If they don't do reviewer's guides, do it yourself. If they're not buying ads in major trades and you think they should, try a nice letter asking them why.

But don't whine and moan and make nasty phone calls, which will come back to haunt you (again, see Rule #1). The bottom line is if the PR and marketing machines aren't as amazing as you'd like, you'll probably have to pick up the slack. But do it with a smile. After all, the money goes in your pockets also!

Just because the game has been completed doesn't mean your work is done. You have a huge role to play, no matter what sort of developer you are. By simply being more vigilant and aggressive about the marketing and sales of your game, you might just help sell several thousand, if not tens of thousands, more copies. That could mean thousands of dollars more for you.

CHAPTER 31

For the small developer, shareware is the publishing model of choice. Avoid the pitfalls and you'll find the secrets to success.

Finding Success with Shareware

Understanding the Basics of Shareware

Shareware is one of the fastest growing distribution and business models in the games industry, especially among smaller developers. For this reason, I decided to devote an entire chapter to helping you understand the role shareware plays in the game business.

Shareware is a distribution concept that a developer uses to directly market a game. Typically, a game is broken into two parts: one that is distributed freely (called the shareware version) and an upgrade, which is distributed for a price. The goal is to entice players with your freebie so that that they bang down your door to purchase the upgrade, which is bound to be even *more* amazing.

Many companies now use shareware as both a direct marketing tool and as a process to promote a game that will eventually wind up as a retail product. Id Software successfully took that route when they released Doom as shareware, offering an upgraded version with additional features and 20 new levels of play. Id experienced phenomenal success with Doom. This success, in fact, created such a stir over future versions that Id had to ship 500,000 copies of Doom II to meet the demand.

Of course, Id Software, aside from developing an awesome game, had spent a lot of time learning the peculiarities of shareware. From earlier efforts like Wolfenstein and Commander Keen, they learned how to make the shareware concept work to their advantage.

So in the interest of accelerating your knowledge of how shareware fits into a developer's toolbox (and sending you on your way to becoming the next success story), let's start with a discussion of the pros and cons of shareware.

Pro: Shareware Offers Higher Per Unit Margins

Perhaps the biggest advantage shareware offers is the money that gets placed directly in the hands of the developer. Because shareware is a direct selling method, there are no middlemen to take away the profits. Let's look at an example: Product X sells for $35. A variable cost to cover simple packaging must be included. We'll use $5.

In a retail environment, here is the breakdown for Product X:

Retail Price	$35.00
Retailer Cost	$17.50
Author Royalty @ 15%	$ 2.40 (This is your slice if you're the author.)
Variable Cost Per Unit	$ 5.00
Leftover	$10.10 (Here's your slice if you're the publisher.)

Now let's look at the same package when it is distributed as shareware:

Price	$35.00
Variable Cost Per Unit	$ 5.00
Shipping	$ 2.50
Leftover	$27.50 (A developer royalty of 15 percent or more depending on the shareware publisher, which works out to about $4.25 a game is also typically included.)

Using the first method, you can see that the publisher needs to sell three to four times the number of copies just to equal one sale through shareware channel. As a developer working on royalties, you would have to sell over ten times the number of copies if you weren't using a publisher and double or more if you went through a shareware publisher. And remember, retailers may want to see you launch a good ad campaign before they consider stocking the product!

Of course, actual situations may vary, but you get the point: Shareware is a powerful development and distribution model that can possibly even up the revenue through much larger profit margins. It's one every developer should consider.

Pro: Increased Distribution and Longer Shelf Life

Shareware titles will continue to make you money as long as people want to register them (a good reason to make sure your game is top-notch). Since the "shelf space" here is made up of thousands of potential server archives, products can be available to consumers long after they're gone in retail. In fact Apogee was receiving orders for some of its first text adventures five years after those titles made their debut.

Cyberspace—the main outlet for shareware—spans far more of the world than do retailers. I mean, do you really think that there's a Software Etc. on Madagascar? (Let me know if there is!) So unless your product is amazing and you hook up with a major international publisher such as Electronic Arts, shareware on the Internet may be your only hope to reach international markets or out of the way places (like Saudi Arabia or Eastport, Maine). Translations might be a problem, but shooting the bad guys is a fairly universal concept.

Pro: Extremely Low Entry Cost

If you are a small or part-time developer, shareware publishing offers you a really cheap way to get your software "in the channel" and potentially make money—you need only consider distribution costs and the time you put into your project. Trying to create your own retail distribution, however, can cost thousands and thousands of dollars.

Con: Shareware Registrations Are Very Low

Unless you have an awesome hit, your total registrations are not going to make you fabulously rich. I know, I just told you about Id's big hit with Doom, but trust me, Id is the exception to most of the rules in the games industry. There has never been a real study of the registration rate for shareware, but many figure it at 1 to 2 percent or less of people who acquire the shareware version. That means even if one thousand people have the shareware version of your game stored in their hard drives, the total amount of upgrades might be 1,000 to 2,000 people.

Con: The Money Is in Retail

Shareware distribution of a game is often used as only one of many distribution schemes. While Doom, Terminal Velocity, and Epic Pinball certainly made some money from direct registrations, the bulk of their profits came from low cost retail (LCR) deals (which pay some tidy royalties) and publishing of the full version at retail. The only time a game makes the bulk of money on shareware upgrades is if it never makes it to retail. We'll talk more about distributing your product as a retail game later on.

Con: Protecting Yourself and Your Product

While shareware can be quite successful for developers, it can also be extremely vicious. Many authors report seeing retail copies of their shareware being distributed by unauthorized publishers. Some developers don't understand all that is involved in uploading their game (for more information see *Preparing Your Shareware for Distribution* later in the chapter) and then wonder why people didn't register. Others get burned by signing bad LCR agreements. These things happen mostly because developers don't take the proper precautions or initiatives to make shareware work for them.

I've listed several resources that can help you learn as much as possible about shareware. Check them out and make good use of them.

Developing a Good Shareware Game

Remember, shareware is a system to distribute your product; it's not a product in and of itself. The trick to developing good shareware is to make a game that is designed to work well with the shareware concept.

Here are the three key things that make for a good shareware game:

- **Shareware versions should be compressed for quick download time.** A majority of shareware is distributed over online services and the Internet, which means that short download times are key to getting large amounts of downloads. You can do this easily by omitting the large graphics and sound files.

Shareware games need to hook players quickly. Because your consumers haven't spent a lot of money to get your product, they have nothing to lose if they find it boring or difficult to play. It's essential that you capture your audience quickly and keep them interested. Games with familiar rules work well as do games that can be played for short intervals during the day. Card games have been among the more successful shareware games because many people know the rules, and they can play a few rounds of Solitaire before the boss makes it down the hall!

- **Keep 'em coming back for more.** The object of shareware is to provide a full gaming experience without providing a game that leaves customers completely satisfied. It's a difficult balancing act but one you need to find.

  Most successful shareware games are structured in stages or levels, which is why you haven't seen many RPGs or interactive stories done as shareware.

Upgrade Schemes

The most important detail decision to make in designing a game for shareware is deciding what will go into the shareware version and what will go into the full version. Creativity in upgrades is the key to making your shareware product a success. Features (or limitations) like time-outs (play my really cool game but not for more than five minutes at a time!) or thirty day trials (if you don't buy my game in thirty days, I'll explode!) don't really work well. The main reason is that they don't provide a complete gaming experience and then offer the player the chance to experience more and enhanced versions of the same. With that in mind, let's discuss some common schemes used by shareware authors.

1/3-2/3 Rule

Scott Miller from Apogee software pioneered the idea now commonly referred to as the "Apogee Method." He thought that a game should be divided into thirds, where the first third of the game would be the shareware version and the remaining two thirds (called episodes) could be purchased directly from Apogee. This is a scheme that has worked tremendously well.

Enhanced Play and Features

A big trend in shareware recently has been to include both enhanced play and hot features in the full version of the game. For example, Apogee's upgrade to its shareware game Terminal Velocity provided users with more episodes to play, access

to higher graphical resolutions, more powerful weapons, and other game play enhancements. Be careful not to hold back features that make the game enjoyable. For instance, offering an upgrade from 22 kHz sound to 44 kHz sound in the full version is fine, but omitting sound in the shareware version is not.

User-Defined Levels

Perhaps the one feature that made the full version of Doom most desirable was the chance to play user-defined levels. The shareware version of Doom didn't offer the ability to play the thousands of new levels that were designed by fans of the game. If you wanted to play those levels, you had to have a registered version of the product. And looking back, one of the reasons for the commercial success of Doom was due to the fact that everyone wanted to play those additional levels.

Understanding the Nuances of Distribution

There are two facets to distribution you'll need to concentrate on: Free distribution, which means getting the game out to the public using many different techniques, including the many locales that make up the online community; and paid distribution, which is basically LCR royalties on shareware versions of your game.

Let's discuss the various distribution outlets for demos and shareware first. Then, I'll more specifically talk about LCR distribution.

The Online Community

The more places your software is available for downloading, the more downloads you'll get. Because the registration rate—even for amazing games—is low, you need maximum exposure to generate the amount of downloads that will translate into profits. I realize that it's difficult to find the time to upload your games to every BBS, online forum, and FTP site in cyberspace. Heck, I barely have enough time to check my watch to find out I don't have any time! I suggest contacting the Association of Shareware Professionals (ASP) to help you find the best locations to spread your shareware game.

Web Sites

Today, Web sites are quickly becoming the leading distribution system for shareware games. Many shareware companies are setting up their own inexpensive Web sites and offering complete downloading and ordering services. But that's not all. I've found many sites on the Web where gamers are encouraged to congregate and check out the latest and greatest in game demos and game shareware. Here's a top ten list of where to get your game uploaded:

Perhaps the leading game site today is Happy Puppy's Games OnRamp:
`http://www.happypuppy.com`

The Games Domain in England is a major game site:
`http://www.gamesdomain.co.uk/`

Walnut Creek's CD-ROM site is very active:
`http://www.cdrom.com/`

Ziff Davis' Web site is a key shareware site:
`http://www.zdnet.com`

Exec PC is a major BBS/Web site:
`http://www.execpc.com`

The Oakland FTP site is one of the top archives:
`ftp://oak.oakland.edu/`

Simtel is also a major Archive:
`http://www.coast.net/SimTel/`

Here is a large shareware source:
`http://www.softsite.com/`

Shareware Central:
`http://www.q-d.com/catalog.htm`

This shareware distributor has a large active Web site:
`http://jcsm.com/`

Commercial Online Services

The major online services, namely America Online, Prodigy, CompuServe, and Microsoft Network are huge download sites. The trick to getting your game out on these services is to visit each one and learn the ins and outs of the many forums within these services where gamers congregate. For example, on CompuServe you'll find at least a half dozen forums where major shareware games are uploaded.

BBSs

BBSs used to be the backbone of shareware distribution. Many BBSs are quickly changing from local area boards to sites on the Internet, but there are still thousands of regular BBSs that pull in the best shareware consumers. Because there are so many BBSs, you'll need to investigate some of the services available to assist you in uploading your games to them.

Catalog Disk Vendors

There are several shareware catalog vendors and authors report they do earn registrations from shareware versions ordered from these catalogs. (The catalogs are also

good promotional tools as well.) The catalog customers are used to ordering by mail (and you, the shareware author, *are* essentially a mail order business). Thus, catalog buyers are likely to order from you.

CD-ROM Sales

The concept with this distribution technique is to bundle shareware games onto a single CD-ROM. Sounds great, right? Unfortunately, unless you take the proper precautions, this approach can be disastrous.

Many times CD-ROMs include games that are acquired illegally or have so many games included that users don't bother registering for any products. Why would anyone pay you $20 or $30 for two additional episodes of your game if they still have 2,999 of the 3,000 games on their CD unplayed? Here are a few tips to help you make the best of your CD-ROM distribution opportunities:

- Always make sure you'll be getting a royalty for placing your game on a CD-ROM.
- Ask what other programs will be featured on the CD-ROM. You don't want to be one of thousands (unless it's meant to go to a BBS or Internet Servers). Larger shareware companies such as Id, Apogee, and Epic restrict the number of games that can be on a CD or even insist on exclusivity.

The bottom line is that you need to keep control of your CD-ROM distribution and use it to help you. Refuse to let sleazy CD publishers make a buck off you without giving you the opportunity to make money for yourself.

Shareware of the Month Clubs

These companies run boiler room telemarketing operations. I have heard numerous complaints that some do not disclose the nature of shareware to the customer. The salespeople simply offer to send the customer monthly disks in exchange for a monthly fee. Although my investigations show that authors have gotten registrations from these organizations—probably because the subscribers are past registers of shareware and thus are more apt to do it again—I don't recommend using this distribution method.

Retail Sales

Shareware games that are sold in retail outlets run the gamut from disks in sleeves sitting in a cardboard box on some store counters to beautifully packaged games indistinguishable from ordinary retail games. Contrary to popular belief, many shareware authors report that retail sales are a poor source of registrations. Here's why. Retail customers are used to walking into a store, paying their money, and then *owning* the merchandise. Telling them that they must register for the full version of a game when they think that they already own the game just doesn't work. Don't completely discount this source of income, however. The sheer mass of distribution will surely bring in a registration or two.

But retail does offer another approach: If you receive royalties on these sales, they become a source of income that can bring in hundreds or even thousands of dollars per month. Again I'll point out that some LCR games make more in retail than they do in shareware registrations. LCR is so important to the success of shareware developers that I'd like to examine it in detail.

A Look at LCR Distribution

Once shareware proved itself to be a viable and profitable method of distribution, a lot of small companies hopped on the bandwagon and got into the retail shareware distribution business.

Here's how it worked: A vendor would download shareware games, put them on disks, and sell them at user group meetings, to local retailers, and through mail order. This shareware became known as Low Cost Retail because typically the products sold for $5.00 to $15.00. What a deal! The only person who got the shaft was the developer! These LCR vendors didn't pay royalties on those sales. At first, it was felt they were doing a service getting the product out to the user community, enhancing the chance for a full registration. Well, for many developers—especially game developers—that argument got old. As shareware products became more sophisticated, it was clear that the selling of shareware was a lucrative business and some companies were cleaning up. As a result, developers began enforcing their rights to the distribution, and began banning the rights to reproduce copies of the shareware for distribution on disks or CD-ROMs.

At this point, the larger shareware houses had no choice but to offer royalties or flat fees to developers or go out of business.

Today, LCR is the lifeblood of shareware developers. While there are still disreputable vendors out there illegally reproducing shareware, savvy developers are now aggressively developing and enforcing LCR publishing agreements.

Non-Exclusive and Exclusive Distribution Deals

The majority of non-shareware games are published through contracts that name one publisher as the exclusive publisher of the product. Many times this is because the publisher puts up the money to develop the product, and is technically

the owner or part owner of the product. In the shareware world, the money to create such a product is usually from the developer's own pockets so ownership of the product rests with them. Thus, the majority of publishing deals in the shareware world are non-exclusive.

Shareware publishers usually sign multiple publishing deals with vendors in order to maximize profit and distribution. Sometimes to accommodate a specific deal, the developer might agree to make some slight modifications to the products. These modifications usually involve removing the word shareware from the product, making language changes for international distributors, or even making a special version of the product. When you sign an LCR deal that requires you to make such changes to the product, consider adding a development cost. Asking for a fee can sometimes weed out less serious distributors as well.

Make sure you are clear as to who handles the technical support for a shareware product once you turn it over to a shareware publisher for distribution. If the publisher will be handling technical support, you'll want to be sure the game has been modified to direct calls to the publisher. The last thing you want is to get hoards of people calling you about something you have no responsibility for.

Some companies—notably the larger shareware companies like Id, Epic, and Apogee—have gone to exclusive publishing agreements in order to better control the distribution of their software. In addition, some of their offerings have reached a level equal to that of retail offerings. Thus, exclusive deals with distributors that have national distribution networks are really a necessity.

Royalties and Flat Fees

Before you negotiate a royalty agreement or a flat fee payment with a shareware vendor, do some investigating on the vendor in question. As I've pointed out, there are many reputable shareware vendors, but there are a few out there who would just as soon scam you. If you think that a vendor who approaches you with a potential publishing deal is a fly-by-night or disreputable operator (contacting other prominent shareware developers quickly can get you this information), the flat fee option tends to work best. In addition, most shareware developers use flat fee contracts for dealing with international publishers.

In the case of a reputable, well-known publisher with a good distribution track record (again easily corroborated by other developers), a royalty agreement works best.

Working with Shareware Publishers

Up until now, we've been basically talking about doing the entire shareware process yourself. Before I go any further, I want to talk about using a shareware publisher as an alternative.

Success in shareware is found by getting wide distribution on the various online services and the World Wide Web, as well as in cutting all sorts of LCR publishing deals. If you're not the type interested in doing the substantial work required to accomplish that, you're going to have to get a shareware publisher interested in your product. A shareware publisher can help you to maximize the return on your development investment by paying you royalties gained from their expert distribution schemes. Many of the major shareware publishers are very good at wringing the most from the shareware system.

Unlike many traditional publishers, shareware publishers rarely offer financial support. Instead, they tend to provide you with access to artists and musicians who they hire to work on your project. This type of support is crucial to helping you make the most of your game. A publisher can also serve as a guiding force, a critic, a cheerleader, and all around support network.

Shareware is very much a marketing-driven process, and a successful publishing house makes the most of marketing. That's why they exist and that's why you use them.

Becoming Your Own Publisher

The spirit of shareware is very much an entrepreneurial one; therefore, it's no surprise that many would-be authors (this one included) have dreams about doing it all themselves. Going it alone can be a very rewarding experience, but it can also be a disaster. Self-publishing takes a lot of hard work and determination to keep on top of things. By self-publishing, you'll be responsible for marketing, packaging, shipping, processing checks, tech support, and taxes just to name a few. (Are you thinking this over again?) Let's discuss the top issues you'll need to address to act as your own shareware publisher.

Preparing Your Shareware for Distribution

Before you post the shareware version of your game, you need to do more than just create the program and installation process. For shareware, there are several files you will want to include in your zipped online version to allow your users to use your shareware products properly.

Note: Examples of all these files are on the CD-ROM.

- VENDOR.DOC This file extensively states your terms for distribution. This document covers you if you need to take legal action in a situation.
- FILEID.DIZ This small document is used by BBS people to explain what your game is about.
- FOREIGN DISTRIBUTORS LIST This document lists your foreign distributors. As your software moves around the world, this list helps people in other countries obtain your software from a local source.
- ORDER.DOC This text file is basically a form that allows your users to mail in their order. Order forms are helpful for your international customers.
- CATALOG.DOC/EXE Any good shareware developer is continually writing new products. Use this document (or program) to shamelessly promote yourself. If you don't, who will?

Receiving and Processing Orders

Shareware is a form of direct marketing and people will actually directly order the product from you. Thus, you need to be prepared to take orders by mail, phone, fax, and online.

How successful your product is or is expected to be will dictate what processes you use to accept orders. Let's discuss all of the possible options you have to process orders for shareware.

Mail

Accepting checks and cash through the mail is an easy way for people to order your product. Remember, though, that shareware, especially for games, is often a gut decision. If you only accept mail orders, you might be losing revenue from the impulse buyer.

If you work from home, I suggest that you use a P.O. box for your return mail address. If you're successful in your shareware endeavors, you'll have the whole world knowing your address if you don't. A P.O. box is also a business expense that you can write off.

Installing an 800 Line

Installing a toll-free 800 number certainly increases your ability to land more sales. Of course, cost is always an issue, and these things aren't really cheap. However, if your business is thriving, contact your phone company and see what they have to offer.

Note: Remember also to publish a non-800 number for international callers and in-city orders.

Credit Card Orders

Now that you have that nifty 800 line, you'll probably want to process credit card orders you receive by phone. To use this technique (which can only elevate your sales), you need to get a merchant account from a bank. This is a major process and warrants some discussion.

Merchant accounts can be difficult to obtain if you work from home. Many banks insist on an away-from-home base of operations, and often require a storefront. They'll want to see a sample of your product too, so bring along *packaged* versions (that means in a box with artwork, folks) of the product to show off.

In addition, you must also have a spotless credit history for the bank to take a risk on you. If you have tried everything and are still having difficulty, I suggest that you contact the Association of Shareware Professionals. They have contacts with banks that are educated about shareware and are more experienced and open to setting up merchant accounts with shareware companies.

Order Services

Many shareware authors are turning to order services to process credit card orders. This could be a good approach for you, especially if you are having trouble getting a merchant account. One of the best and biggest is PSL (Public Software Library), a Dallas-based company that processes credit card orders for shareware authors. They charge a small fee per transaction ($5 per transaction and 4 percent of the total amount charged to the credit card), but there is no charge if you do not get a registration. PSL will either ship the product directly or will relay the order information to you or your designated agent by CIS email or telephone within one business day. Statements and checks are computer prepared and mailed promptly following the end of each month.

Building Online Distribution

America Online and CompuServe both offer the chance to set up company forums that can be used for order processing services. Once you've got several products going, set up your own private forum and allow visitors to check out your products and news there. Not only will you receive revenue from the downloads, but from online time spent in your forum. To set up a forum like this you need to contact the services directly. In the online resource appendix in the back of the book I list contact information for the major online services.

CompuServe's SWREG

For authors who wish to exploit the power of online services but aren't looking to go as far as creating a specific forum, CompuServe offers a great service called SWREG, which allows people to register their shareware versions and pay for the upgraded

version through their CompuServe account. By using certain code numbers, users tell CompuServe whose product they want. CompuServe then takes their customer information and charges their account, taking 15 percent for itself and passing the rest on to the author along with the address information they need to fulfill orders. It seems to be a wonderful enterprise, and authors I've talked to think it works especially well in getting foreign registrations.

For more information, log onto CompuServe and use the keyword function: GO SWREG.

Tying up the Loose Ends: Packaging, Customer Records, and Tech Support

Besides figuring out where to put your product and how to get money from people, there are a few other things you'll need to do if you're going to be a full-service operation.

- **Packaging Your Orders** Because your first shareware product will probably not be your last, take the time to create a professional package worthy of your good name and your customer's good money. Make sure you provide written instructions for the product as well. You want to give every reason for this customer to register your future products.
- **Keep Customer Records** Good customer records are essential if you want to provide professional service to your customers, including direct mailings to your registered uses with updates and new products that may appeal to their interests. You'll also find the records helpful in distinguishing between registered and unregistered customers.
- **Provide Quality Tech Support** Most shareware companies provide very little tech support to unregistered users. With the exception of getting the shareware version running on a computer, tech support is reserved for registered users. Make sure you provide the quality support expected from a professional.

You might want to consider using a publisher for your first shareware effort. Once you've had a little guidance, earned a little bit of money, and gained name recognition, your footing for your own venture might be much better. This is the approach Id Software took and so far you can't argue with their success, can you?

Promoting Your Shareware

A key aspect to shareware is promoting it. The first fact of shareware is that in order to get a registration, your game must be downloaded and played. In other words, people have to know it's there. And that comes down to one thing: promotion.

We talked a little about traditional game software promotion in the previous chapter. Shareware, however, is a special case and definitely warrants discussion. Many of the popular game magazines like *Computer Gaming World* and *PC Gamer* now have regular columns devoted specifically to shareware. And, interestingly enough, some major daily newspapers are also featuring online and shareware columns. Both of these resources can be seriously exploited to your advantage. When contacting game magazines as a shareware author, ask specifically to have your package forwarded to their shareware columnist—or directly contact that columnist through email. (Many writers provide their online address as part of their column.)

Hard Work Is the Key

What you get out of using the shareware concept is exactly what you put into it. If you're smart and use shareware to its fullest potential and aggressively get those LCR contracts, you'll do well. If you develop a traditional game, label it as shareware, and post it on CompuServe and sip lemonade in the sunshine, you probably will still be driving that Pinto for a few more years. Making a success of the shareware publishing and development model is tough work. Don't think for a minute that it's not.

The opportunity is there for the taking; it's up to you to make it work.

The Future Is Shareware

I don't think I'll be going out on a limb by saying that the future of almost all game publishing will be modeled after today's shareware games. Shareware, once dismissed as amateur hour, is now the rule of thumb for many developers and the industry as a whole. The thing holding back shareware growth is not the concept but the emergence of key technologies that will let the concept flourish.

Once the next generation of ISDN lines and secure Internet transaction technologies cement themselves in the world (which is happening far faster than anyone ever imagined!), many software companies will sell shareware through the Internet.

This is how I see it: Authors/publishers will create a Web site for their products. Users will log on and download a quick demo/shareware version of the software and play it to get a good idea of whether or not they like it. Later, they'll log back into that Web site and use their credit card to purchase the full version of the software, which would then be downloaded on their machine—or if the product is stored on a DVD, it would be overnighted directly to them. It's only a matter of time.

Shareware Resources

To help you get into and maximize the shareware business, I've listed a number of resources including organizations, magazines, books, and online services.

Organizations

Association of Shareware Professionals (ASP)
545 Grover Road
Muskegon, MI 49442-9427

Phone: 616 788-5131 **Fax:** 616 788-2765.
WWW: http://www.asp-shareware.org/
CompuServe: Go Shareware*

The ASP is the leading organization for shareware authors, vendors, and publishers. Its members and publications offer lots of good advice for budding shareware companies. Most of ASPs member's software is not of the game variety but much of their knowledge about distribution, running a business, and the shareware software industry in general can be invaluable. Originally, the ASP had a set of bylaws that made it impossible for the way games were marketed as shareware for those products to be recognized as ASP sanctioned shareware. Recently, however, the ASP changed many of its rules to accommodate the changes in strategy many authors were using.

** Aside from their Web site, I strongly recommended that you check out the ASP's forum on CompuServe. The message threads alone are worth the price of admission.*

Educational Software Cooperative (ESC)
11846 Balboa Blvd. #226
Granada Hills, CA 91346

WWW: http://execpc.com/~esc/

The ESC is a non-profit organization of developers, educators, publishers, and distributors of educational software. While it's not specifically a shareware organization, it plays such an active role in the shareware community (many of its members use shareware) that I thought I'd include it here.

They publish a bi-monthly newsletter with reviews, help for marketing, and discussions of educational issues.

STAR (Shareware Trade and Resources)
3315 E. Russell Road, Suite H-272
Las Vegas, NV 89120

CompuServe: GO UKSHARE

Star was originally started as an alternative to the ASP in the days when the ASP had a much more strict set of guidelines for its definition of shareware. Now that the ASP has changed its bylaws there has been talk about STAR merging with the ASP, but so far it's been talk. Star publishes an excellent newsletter called STARGAZER and runs an excellent Web site.

Conferences

Shareware Industry Conference (SIC)

The Shareware Industry Conference is a annual gathering of shareware publishers, vendors, and developers. It's a great place to go to learn from people who are successfully using shareware to earn a living (some part-time, some with full blast companies). Previously it used to be held in Indianapolis but in 1995 they moved it to the more temperate climate of Scottsdale, AZ. Check in with the ASP home page to keep abreast of the next scheduled conference.

Books/Publications/Newsletters

A Programmers Guide To Shareware by Nelson Ford and George Abbott (Found on ASP Web Site)

This is an excellent free file to download that contains tons of resources for shareware developers. It answers a lot of the basic questions you need to answer especially if you're going to go it alone and publish a product yourself.

How to Sell Your Software by Bob Schenot (John Wiley & Sons; ISBN 0-471-06399-1)

This book from the author of the online document "The Shareware Book" covers a wide range of issues about selling software including shareware, catalogs, retail channels, and bundling.

The Shareware Book by Bob Schenot

This is another tell-all book about shareware marketing and resources for it. It was published as a book and as an online document that you can register. I got my copy from the ASP forum on CompuServe.

Making Money Selling Your Shareware by Steven C. Hudgik (Windcrest/McGraw Hill; ISBN 0-07-030865-9)

***Zshare* (Ziff Davis Shareware Newsletter)**
`http://www.zdnet.com/~ziffnet/cis/sw_cs.html`

Zshare is an online zine from Ziff-Davis publishing that is devoted to shareware coverage. It is "published" monthly and is distributed in a Windows Help File format. It provides an excellent source of reviews, author interviews, and shareware industry coverage.

I especially like the well written interviews with successful shareware authors, and the nice screenshots of the latest shareware games and programs. I would advise you to download several months worth of issues. You can find ZShare at the Web site I have listed.

Ziffnet Threads (Ziffnet's Magazine and Shareware Catalog)
Available to CompuServe's Ziffnet Subscribers

Ziffnet is a special section of CompuServe that costs an additional $2.95 per month. However, it is a worthy addition for shareware authors because it opens up additional marketing (by giving you access to some very good forums on CompuServe) and resource opportunities.

In addition, subscribers to Ziffnet receive in the mail the Ziffnet Threads reports, which are filled with shareware listings and excellent coverage of shareware products, especially games. GO Ziffnet on CompuServe for more information.

Online Resources

RamIsle Software Web Site
`http://delta.com/ramsisle/ramsisle.htm`

RamIsle Software is the maker of VendInfo, a key program to use in distributing shareware. They have built a great Web site that is an excellent resource for shareware authors.

Jim Knoph's home page
`http://www.halcyon.com/knopf/jim`

Jim Knoph a.k.a. Jim Button is known as the father of shareware and is a legend to shareware authors around the world. His company Buttonware was built into a multi-million dollar company on his pioneering shareware marketing effort. His Web site is a wonderful sort of "museum" to shareware and his early efforts. Good links and a wonderful story make this a nice visit.

Major Game Shareware Publishers

Believe it or not, there are entire multi-million dollar companies built around producing successful shareware products. Not every company is a major money maker but some are. Visit their online sites to download good examples of successful shareware products and examine how they structure their games to work well as shareware.

Also, many of the principles of these companies can be contacted by email and are quite helpful at giving you tips and advice about shareware in general.

Apogee Software
P.O. Box 496389
Garland, TX 75049

Phone: 214 278-5655 **Fax:** 214 278-4670
WWW: http://www.apogee1.com/

Apogee was one of the first shareware companies. Founded by Scott Miller and George Broussard, Apogee pioneered the 1/3 2/3 rule many shareware authors now follow. Today Apogee is one of the biggest shareware companies, with such huge hits as Duke Nuk'em, Wolfenstein, Blake Stone, Terminal Velocity, and Rise of the Triad, among others.

MVP Software
1035 Dallas SE
Grand Rapids, MI 49507

Phone: 616 245-8376
WWW: http://mvpsoft.com/mvp_home.htm

MVP Software was started by Dave Snyder. It has published such memorable hits as Karen Crowther's Pickle Wars, MVP Bridge, and Strike Force. MVP just published the shareware version of Virgin Interactive's Cannon Fodder.

Epic MegaGames, Inc.
3204 Tower Oaks Blvd. #410
Rockville, MD 20852

Phone: 301 983-9771 **Fax:** 301 299-3841
WWW: http://www.epicgames.com/

Epic MegaGames got their start with the shareware hit Jill of the Jungle. Founded by Tim Sweeny, Epic has published several successful Shareware titles such as Epic Pinball, One Must Fall, Jazz Jackrabbit, and the new Extreme Pinball. One of their first hits was the adventure construction kit program ZZT.

Id Software
Mesquite, TX
Phone: 214 613-3589
WWW: http://www.idsoftware.com

Id Software got their shareware start writing the early shareware hits for Apogee including the big hit Wolfenstein 3D. Then in 1994 came the shareware hit of all time, Doom. Id has since gone retail with its sequel Doom II but returned to shareware with the release of Heretic, a fantasy based spin-off of Doom by Raven software. Id's widely anticipated next product is Quake.

CHAPTER 32

Before getting too far into the work of developing games, you'll need to learn the basic legal ropes so that you can help your company prosper and protect the legal rights to your great games.

By Dean M. Gloster and Kat H. McCabe

Game Development Legal Issues

Let's say you have great skills, game ideas, team members, and the goal of developing games as an independent. But with independence, comes responsibility: You will have to deal with legal issues in running your game company and making your games.

Fortunately, you do have a guide—this chapter, which will cover issues in forming a game development company, an overview of what game developers should know about intellectual property, key issues in dealing with employees and independent contractors, and consideration in licensing other people's intellectual property to make your game.

Issues in Forming Your Game Development Company

There are four issues you should address early in forming your game company:

- Who will own your company and what is the business deal between the principals?
- What is your vision of what your game company will do?
- What form of business entity are you going to operate (for example, partnership, corporation, or sole proprietorship)?
- How will you handle the departure—voluntarily or otherwise—of any of the original founders?

Who Owns What?

The days of the "lone wolf" game developer, where one person could write the code, produce the art, design the game, and even make the funny background noises are just about gone. Creating great games requires a talented *team* of designers, programmers, and artists. Typically, game development companies are now founded by a group with complementary skills, who are willing to risk a substantial amount of their time (and forego more stable and lucrative opportunities elsewhere) to participate as original founders of a new company. Sometimes several of these founders continue to work at their day jobs somewhere else during the startup phase, until the new company is well established.

But haggling over business points among friends may be less pleasant than figuring out how to make the world's coolest adventure game. In the rush to create a great game and manage a startup business, it is easy to neglect the little step of getting an agreement in writing among the participants: Exactly who owns what? Unfortunately, it's also often difficult to get a fair agreement in writing at the outset of a venture, when individuals' roles and commitments are still subject to change. But even though it's difficult, you should come to *some* agreement. The consequences of not agreeing can otherwise come back to haunt everyone involved later: Even wonderfully well-intentioned people operate differently and have remarkably selective memories.

There are three rules in addressing the relationship among founders, initial employees, and initial independent contractors of a game development company:

1. Get the ownership deal in writing.
2. Provide some mechanism for preserving flexibility, because people's roles change.
3. Ensure that any agreement gives ownership of the intellectual property rights in the game to the new game development company, so that no one individual has veto power over going forward to create the title.

Here are several alternatives that preserve flexibility, while still getting a basic deal in writing:

- The co-founders could agree on a letter agreement stating their intent to divide ownership of the company, but stating that its allocation of ownership is a non-binding statement of intent, and that they intend to enter into a definitive mutually negotiated written agreement six months later. The agreement should clearly provide for what happens to all of the intellectual property rights in the game they are developing if the parties *do not* ultimately reach agreement. For example, if someone doesn't reach agreement with the company, he or she can be paid a specific amount for the work done to date. Finally, when the roles are clear, the founders should enter into a final, written agreement.
- A second alternative is to create an arrangement so that the founders' ownership rights "vest" over time. This ensures that anyone who leaves or is forced out by the others has a much smaller ownership share. Perhaps more useful is an arrangement that allows the founders to each receive a vested ownership interest to begin with. Of course, this ownership interest could be subject to a buyout right of the other partners (at a modest sum, which increases over time) of the departing founder's interest.

Often key team members may end up volunteering huge chunks of time as a title is developed before there is any money from investors or a software publisher to pay them. One approach with these project members is to enter into an agreement like the *Work for Hire Agreement* in Appendix B. An agreement like this specifies that the key team member offers a specified amount of time or specific services such as writing the code for a running demo, doing character design, drafting the proposal, creating the interface, or doing the game design. In return for this work, the individual will then be hired for a fee to be mutually agreed upon (including perhaps a share in eventual royalties) if the game developer gets funding to complete the title. The critical element of the agreement is that if the individual and the game developer

cannot later agree on terms for going forward, the game developer still has the right to use the code, art, or other deliverables in the final title *upon paying a specific fee set forth in the agreement.* An arrangement like this protects both parties' expectations, preserves flexibility going forward, and still gives the fledgling game development company the comfort of knowing that for the set fee it can use the deliverables created by the independent contractor.

Your Vision or Mission Statement

If you are going to devote long hours to creating a game development company and making great games, you should start by devoting some attention to your long-term goal. A clearly articulated goal of what you plan to do over the next few years will help your future strategic planning, build a shared vision among the founders, and even assist you with future recruiting. Spend the time to brainstorm and refine your long-term goals. (It will also prevent enormous grief if you discovery early that the founders have radically different long-term goals that must—or cannot possible be—accommodated.)

The Form of Your Game Development Company

A business can be organized in one of several different forms. For example, you can set it up as a sole proprietorship (one individual "doing business as" a game development company), a general partnership, a limited partnership (where limited partners do not put their own assets at risk), or a corporation. Tax, personal liability, overhead costs, and the need to raise money from outside investors are considerations that guide your choice of entity.

We could go on for many pages about the advantages and disadvantages of each form, but let's face it: That discussion would be only a little more interesting than a Web site featuring random pages from the tax code. Instead, a brief discussion will be presented in Appendix B of the alternative entities most often used in the U.S. I'll also present some of the important considerations you'll want to think over before deciding among those entities. For most fledging game development companies, the issue of choosing the form is *not* enormously time critical: For example, you can initially form a partnership or sole proprietorship, and then later incorporate when other founders join the company, you raise funds from outsiders, or you actually get that publishing deal and then need to enter into a lease for space and equipment. As discussed in Appendix B, many start-up game development companies in the U.S. are organized as "Subchapter S" corporations with limited liability (the shareholders/owners are not responsible for the obligations of the company) and no requirement that the corporation pay separate corporate income taxes.

What Happens When a Founder Leaves?

You should also have a written agreement among co-founders about what happens when one leaves: The remaining founders don't want a partner or shareholder's ownership interest sold to a stranger, and they don't want to reward someone who is no longer contributing to the business with a continuing share in the growth of the game development company.

There are two difficulties in structuring any fair arrangement: First, with any closely held game development company, the value of a partial ownership share is a huge question mark. Second, any buy-out arrangement of a departing owner shouldn't require so much cash that the game development company can't continue: The system you set up shouldn't reward the first person to leave if the business runs into trouble.

There are no easy answers, and no one solution suits all companies. Here are, however, some common, workable variations. The important thing is to have *some* arrangement in writing. Even if this arrangement has to be later revised (again, in writing) as the company's situation changes, it will provide guidance in the event of a breakup. It is much easier to agree, in advance and in abstract, before individuals' perception of what is fair crystallizes around their own personal self interest.

Death or disability are easy to handle: Once your game company is generating substantial revenue, you can cover the risk that one of the key owners will die or become disabled by funding a buy-out with term insurance, bought by the company (which should be relatively inexpensive, especially if all of the founders are relatively young).

If there are only two owners of the business, a common buy-sell provision is the standard negotiating technique of letting one party cut the cake and the other party determine which half to take. Either owner may announce to the other that he or she wants out by selling ownership interest for a certain sum *or* by buying the other owner's interest *for the same amount.* The other owner, then, will have the choice of whether to buy or sell, though he or she will have to do one or the other. It is generally a fair arrangement, although it does not take into account that one party may have far more money to fund a buyout.

Another common alternative is for the owners to collectively value the business every year. Any departing owner's value would be paid out over some specified period of time. If the parties cannot agree on a valuation, they could submit the issue to binding arbitration, and the arbitrator would decide how much the value changed from the last-agreed valuation. A variation on this approach is to use "baseball-style" arbitration, where each side proposes a fair valuation to the arbitrator, who only has the ability to pick the best of the two numbers. This has the effect of encouraging

each party to pick a number closer to the middle. Finally, some established companies use specific formulas based on a percentage of revenue of a specific period, and so on.

Whatever your buy-sell arrangement is, it should also provide for what happens to the intellectual property of the company: Most often, since the departing partner or shareholder is being paid for his or her share of the value of the company (including its intellectual property) all rights remain with the company. But partners or shareholders might also agree that each of them has the right to reuse the software tools and underlying game engine, for example.

What Every Game Developer Needs to Know About Intellectual Property

Almost everything a game developer creates or relies on to make a living involves intellectual property. Games, licensable characters, and software tools can be protected by copyright. Proprietary technology and know-how are protected as trade secrets. A name, goodwill, and reputation are protected by trademark law. And often game developers license intellectual property from others (propriciary tools, code, art, characters, and just about everything else that could go into a compelling game).

What follows is a *brief* overview of relevant intellectual property considerations, how they matter to you as a game developer, and (where relevant) how to protect your intellectual property rights.

Trademark Rights

Trademark rights (including service marks) allow you to protect a name and the associated name recognition with consumers, and give you the right to prevent others from using confusingly similar names to promote similar products. Is this important? Absolutely. First, it allows you to build value in your company through name recognition. (Retailers and consumers who bought vast quantities of the last games from *Id* and *Cyan* will also buy their next ones.) In addition, failing to secure proper rights to your marks means that after you have spent enormous efforts promoting your name and putting it on boxes, another developer or publisher with rights to a similar name might go to court to prevent you from distributing the games.

How do you obtain trademark protection? It's easy. As long as no one else has registered it first, in the U.S., protection is established by your use of the mark "in commerce." You come up with a great name for your game development company ("WizardWarez") and then use it in connection with your goods or services. The mark doesn't have to be registered, but if the mark is *not* registered, the mark is only protected in the geographical area in which it's being used. For example, if you are using your name for 3D modeling and rendering in the San Francisco Bay Area, someone else can use that name for similar services or goods in and around Austin, Texas.

You can expand the geographic area where you have exclusive rights to your mark by registering it with either the state government (generally a waste of time) or with the United States Patent and Trademark Office. Registering your mark with the state government allows you to stop other subsequent uses of a similar mark state-wide. Registering with the federal government allows you to stop subsequent users of a mark similar to yours for similar goods or services throughout the U.S. Finally, you can also register your mark in other countries to obtain exclusive rights to the name in those countries.

Your first step is to run a computerized database search to check to see if anyone else has already registered your proposed mark (or applied to do so) for your category of goods or services. An inexpensive and thorough database is TrademarkScan, available through the Dialog Information Service. If this database search shows that no one has previously registered the same mark for your category of goods or services, you can then take the next step and have a trademark search firm such as Thomson & Thomson do an expanded search, which will also pick up companies using the name in commerce that have *not* registered the mark. At the time of this writing, the cost of an expanded Thomson & Thomson search for a single mark in any one category is $330 U.S. Thomson & Thomson's address is:

Thomson & Thomson
500 Victory Road
North Quincy, MA 02171
Phone: 617 479-1600 **Fax:** 617 786-8273

If no one else is using your proposed mark, a trademark attorney can file a simple application for registration of the mark with the Patent and Trademark Office. Trademark registration is *not* something you should put off. The rights of different users of the same name are tied to:

- The entity who registered the mark first
- Whether someone registered the mark before someone else began using it

Copyright

Almost everything a game developer creates is potentially protected by copyright law—the code, art, game design, user manual, and the finished game. Copyright at first protected original "literary and artistic" works in any tangible media. The law has since been clarified to specify that copyright extends to protect software code (avoiding messy disputes over whether a set of ones and zeros is actually "literary" or

"artistic"). Copyright, however, only protects the *expression* of ideas, not abstract ideas themselves. (You can't, therefore, copyright "boy meets girl," but you can copyright a film or book based on this premise; you can't copyright the idea "player shoots monsters" but *Id* could copyright *Doom.*) *Copyright* is not just one right, it is an entire bundle of legally protected rights:

- The right to make copies of a work
- The right to distribute the work
- The right to publicly perform or display the work
- The right to create derivative works (such as sequels, ports to other platforms, Saturday morning cartoon shows, or comic books)

The "author" of a work (art, code, or game design) owns the copyright in it as soon as it is created in a tangible medium, whether or not the copyright is registered. If the work is created by an employee within the scope of that person's employment, the owner of the copyright is the employer. But if the person creating the work is an independent contractor with some substantial discretion over performing his or her duties, the independent contractor owns the copyright *unless* there is a written, signed agreement making the results "work for hire." These issues are discussed a little later in this chapter, under the heading, *Dealing with Employees and Independent Contractors.*

In the U.S., a copyright does not have to be registered for the author of the work to be entitled to copyright protection. But registration does provide some advantages, including the right to sue for statutory damages if someone else infringes your copyright.

The process for registering a copyright in the U.S. is simple: Obtain the correct form from the U.S. Copyright Office, fill it out according to the instructions, and return it to the Register of Copyrights with a filing fee of $20.00 and a deposit (copy) of the work that you're seeking to register. For a computer game or demo, use Form PA. If you are simply registering text, use Form TX. The copyright office is remarkably easy to deal with. You can request up to ten copies of the form together with the applicable circular (R55 - "Copyright Registrations for Multimedia Works" for a computer game), and you can obtain these forms and circulars by calling the copyright office at 202 707-9100. While you're at it, ask for Circular 1, Copyright Basics. If you need more help about the specific form, the copyright office's general information number is 202 707-3000, or deal with an intellectual property lawyer.

Right of Publicity

Individuals also have a protectable interest in their name and likeness, that allows them (and in some states, allows their heirs) to prevent the commercial use of their identities without compensation. Most often, the right of publicity is invoked by celebrities to protect their rights to receive compensation whenever their name or likeness is used to promote a product.

The protection of "name" and "likeness" are interpreted pretty broadly: Professional obnoxious person/radio talk show jockey Howard Stern sued over the online use of a photograph of his, er, posterior, and former Tonight Show host Johnny Carson successfully sued to prevent a portable toilet manufacturer from promoting its product as the "Here's Johnny."

The right of publicity is created by a patchwork of various state statutes and court decisions. It has been expanded to cover "look alike" and "sound alike" actors impersonating celebrities. (Little known legal fact: While you can carry a concealed handgun in Texas without a license from the state, you cannot perform as an Elvis Presley impersonator without a license from *his* estate.) If you are going to use the name and likeness of anyone (particularly a celebrity) in your game or in promoting your game, you need to obtain permission from that individual. (And more than likely, you'll need to fork out some cash!)

"Moral" Rights

In some obscure jurisdictions like France (and, to some extent, California), authors may have certain "moral" rights, including the right to have their name associated with their work and the right to prevent others from later modifying that work. Typically, intellectual property agreements require authors to waive their moral rights.

Patents

If you invent a "new and useful process, machine or improvement" which has utility, is novel, and is non-obvious (that is, something well beyond an extension of current state of the art), your invention may be patentable. Certain categories are not patentable subject matter, including abstract ideas or principles, laws of nature, scientific truth, and mathematical algorithms. Nevertheless, concrete inventions, including processes, may be patented even if they *use* underlying algorithms and laws of nature. After some dispute over the matter, courts and the Patent and Trademark Office now accept that software-based processes and inventions (not just mechanical ones) can be patented. The Patent and Trademark Office, however, has more difficulty researching prior art with software patents.

There are current efforts underway to change U.S. patent law, but at the time of this writing, patents are available only to the first inventor of a specific invention. To qualify as the first inventor, the invention must be both conceived first and reduced to practice with diligence. If you believe that you are the first inventor of a novel invention (a unique new 3D rendering engine, motion capture technology, way of digitizing video, and so on), should you file an application for a patent? It depends. Unlike copyright—where even if you don't register, your creation of certain intellectual property gives you rights—a patent is a *legally-granted monopoly* from the government.

The holder of a patent has the right to exclude all others from making, using, or selling the invention throughout the U.S. for a period of seventeen years, even if they later develop the same technology independently. (Patent rights, however, are subject to being lost in court upon proof that the patent was not properly granted.) If you intend to build your company around a core proprietary technology (or intend to later derive huge revenues from licensing it to the rest of the industry), it may make sense to seek patent protection. Further, patents (and even patent applications) may create value in your company in the eyes of potential investors and acquirers. But there are disadvantages to applying for a patent as well:

* In order to obtain a patent, the inventor must disclose the invention in great detail, so that another person could reproduce the invention in accordance with the claim of the patent. This is not as great of a problem as it may seem, because under current law, patent applications are not a matter of public record until a patent is actually granted or denied.

Aa patent application is a much more involved process than simply applying for a trademark or registering your copyright, and there are substantial costs involved (such as paying the patent lawyer).

Trade Secrets

A final category of legally-protected intellectual property is "trade secrets," which may include many of the ideas, processes, techniques, and know-how that somehow does not fit into the other categories. Trade secrets of a game developer might include game ideas, techniques for processes for digitizing video, special methods of collision detection, or even lists of potential investors. Trade secret protection is generally governed by state law, and varies substantially among states. Generally, though, a trade secret is proprietary information that gives your company a competitive advantage and which you maintain as a trade secret. And, how do you maintain information as a trade secret? First, it has to be the kind of information that is not generally known in the industry. Second, the information must be treated as confidential and kept secret.

Trade secret law is unusual in that it is always applied *retroactively*: If there is a dispute over whether someone has misappropriated one of your trade secrets, the question is, did you undertake reasonable steps to maintain it as a trade secret? These steps would include limiting access to the information to those with need to know, by having employees and independent contractors sign confidentiality agreements, and disclosing the information to the outside world *only* in connection with signed confidentiality and non-disclosure agreements. A sample short-form non-disclosure agreement is set out in Appendix B.

Dealing with Employees and Independent Contractors

When you hire people to help you with your title, key issues that come up include making sure that the company owns and protects *all* of the work done for the project and giving the people helping you the incentive to produce great work.

Owning the Rights

Your company creates the coolest new game. The game was your idea. You assembled and led the team. You might reasonably assume that your company owns all of the rights in that title. But it may not. If the people who worked on the title were *employees* of your company whose work was within the scope of their employment, your company *does* own all of the rights of the title. But the general rule is that if *independent contractors* (not employees) create something, *they* own the copyright to the resulting work, not the company that hired them, unless there is a signed agreement in writing. Of course, if an independent contractor does do work for you that is going into a computer game, you certainly have at least an implied license to use that work in your computer game. But there is a huge question over the scope of that license, and whether you can resuse the work in ports to other platforms, sequels, or whether you can you can use it at all if there is some kind of payment dispute.

There is also a highly technical argument that anyone making a contribution to a computer game is contributing to an "audio visual work" and you own the rights to their contributions even if there is no written work for hire agreement. To be on the safe side, though, you should always obtain a written "work for hire" or assignment of copyright agreement from your independent contractors (and from anybody that a court may later decide was an independent contractor). The Sample Employment Agreement and sample Independent Contractor Agreement in Appendix B both contain extensive work for hire and assignment of rights provisions.

Protecting the Rights—Trade Secrets and Non-Compete Agreements

In addition to owning the copyright in the works your company creates, it's important to protect your company's proprietary technology and other trade secrets.

The people you hire are going to know the most about your project; you have to make clear to them that certain information is secret and that they have an obligation not to disclose it to people outside the company. Again, getting a signature on a written agreement (see the Non-Disclosure Employment and Independent Contractor Agreement in Appendix B) is the best way to show a court that you kept your confidential information secret.

Incentives and Profit Sharing

Start-up ventures often make the mistake of handing out equity in the company too freely and too quickly. This is tempting when there's little money to offer as incentive to join the company. But having a large number of shareholders with voting and other legal rights in the company can make life difficult. If, down the road, the company wants outside investment, diluting the Company equity detracts from the image of strong management and business skills that you must project.

Key *project* employees may not be key to the company's long-term issues. Very often, the better form of incentive is profit-sharing, such as a royalty bonus pool. Instead of handing out ownership of the company, you can give key project employees a share of the royalties from the *title* they are working on. For example, the developer agrees to contribute to the bonus pool a percentage of the royalties received from the game after payment of specific loans from the founders to finish the titles. The definitions should be precise—you don't want to fight about the amount of money in the pool. The bonus pool is then shared by all of those employees and independent contractors who are part of the bonus pool program. One "golden handcuffs" approach is to require employees to still be around to share in any royalties (which discourages turnover). A different alternative is to have each recipient's shares in the bonus pool to "vest," meaning they become effective after certain milestones are reached. For example, if programmers leave after six months, they get only part of their share in the pool, while if they stay through the beta-testing, they get their whole share.

Tax Requirements

If you hire employees, there are certain tax obligations to deal with. In the U.S., every employer must withhold income from employees' paychecks for both income tax and social security taxes, and those amounts must be paid to the government. If no income is withheld, the employer, including both the company and the individuals responsible for payroll, may be liable to the government for the full amount that should have been withheld. In addition, the employer pays its share of social security taxes, federal and state unemployment tax, plus worker's compensation insurance. Even if you call someone an "independent contractor," the IRS can come back and later insist that they be treated as an employee, under a multi-factor test. (If, for example, someone is working full-time for you for two years, using only your equipment, they'll be an "employee" for tax purposes, *whatever* you call them.)

As your company grows, you may want to reward long-term key employees with stock that vests over time, to give them an incentive to stay with the company and to build its long-term value. You can set up a "qualified" incentive stock option plan with certain favorable tax treatments.

Licensing Intellectual Property from Others

As a game developer, you may end up having to license a wide variety of intellectual property from others to make your games (or to make them as compelling and marketable as possible). In addition to software tools, you may license a game engine, art, and music. In addition, your game may be based upon third parties' intellectual property: Numerous games are based on licensed characters, science fiction books, or celebrities (particularly in the case of sports titles).

Key content that you license from other people may be valuable in two different ways. First, great content (compelling design, art, well written code, and great production values) makes a great title. Second, certain key content may have some *brand* or "marquis" value, creating the all-important marketing hook. Particularly in the world of PC/CD-ROM, where there is a brutal retail shelf-space squeeze (more titles out than there is shelf space for them) and an almost complete lack of an effective preview mechanism, a marketing hook is increasing critical. Software retailers (and publishers) are increasingly looking for an angle that will make a particular title catch consumer attention and achieve huge sell-through numbers. For example, with the launch of the game title *The Daedalus Encounter* the presence of "Wayne's World" actress Tia Carrere was almost endlessly hyped. Particularly with sports titles, licensing is a substantial sales factor.

Game developers have to understand the multiple layers of "markets" they have to sell to. First, a developer seeking outside funding for a proposed title has to convince the publisher of the title's appeal. Second, the publisher or its distributor has to convince the retailers that the title will sell enough units to justify shelf space. Third, based largely on what is on the box, consumers must be persuaded to buy the game.

Rules for Licensing Content

In case it has not been obvious from the rest of this chapter, reduced to one word, intellectual property rights in computers games are: *complicated.* The following rules, however, may save you from substantial grief in this area.

1. *Acquire or license content from the right owner.*

   This commandment is violated with remarkable frequency. Let's say that (for whatever reason) you want to license a film clip as part of your computer game, and you know that Turner Broadcasting "owns" the film. For an outrageous fee they are willing to license a short clip to you, but as you sign the papers you are puzzled when your contact at Turner innocently asks "and how much did you pay everybody *else* for this clip?" Your use of that film clip, it turns out, might also infringe upon the copyright owner of the music playing in the background, the publicity rights of the actors who appear in the film, the copyright owner of the underlying book that the film was based on, and a nearly limitless number of other rights holders (and professional guilds) that will either demand payment or threaten to sue.

2. *Get representations, warranties, and indemnities.*

   Any time you license intellectual property from a third party, you should have them "represent and warrant" (that is, promise) that they have all necessary rights to the materials, that they haven't assigned any of those rights to anyone else, that they have the power to enter into this agreement, and—most important—that your use of the intellectual property in your game will not infringe upon any rights of any third party, including patent, trademark, copyright, and trademark rights. You should also have them agree to "indemnify, defend and hold harmless" your game development company from any liabilities or expenses if their representation and warranties are breached. These are fancy legal words meaning that they agree they will not seek any recovery from you of any cost or expenses in connection with third party claims of infringement, that they will pay you back for any settlements or legal judgments that you have to pay, and they will pay the cost of your attorney's fees in dealing with third party claims. Of course, an agreement like this doesn't do you much good if the person giving you an indemnity doesn't have assets, but it does force them to at least consider whether they have clear title for all the rights they are licensing to you.

3. *Get all the rights you need.*

   If appropriate, when you are negotiating for rights in connection with your game, insure that you get the rights for sequels, ports to other platforms, future platforms, interactive TV or online distribution, a waiver of moral rights, and a public display rights so that you may show the material on your demo reel or at trade shows. If you have an agreement that some material is provided to as "work for hire," insure that you also have license of all copyright rights in the material from the author: Some countries outside the U.S. do not recognize "works made for hire." The agreements I draft typically say not only that materials provided are a work made for hire, but also that the author:

- Assigns copyright in the work
- Grants worldwide, perpetual license to use the work
- Covenants not to sue over your use of the work

The business deal, of course, may be that you are receiving only narrow rights, and that the party licensing those rights to you is free to exploit the work in other media, but do make certain that you have all of the rights that you may need, or that you have pre-negotiated a price if you do want to acquire rights for ports, sequels, and other derivative works.

Acquiring Rights Cheaply

In addition to those general rules about licensing intellectual property for your game, here are some suggestions on how to license intellectual property without going broke in the process:

- *License key content, not everything under the sun.*

  Because there are often multiple rights holders, it is critical to identify the truly *key* content and to avoid paying large royalties (or up-front payments) for content that is not critical. If, for example you are creating a baseball game, you might license one celebrity, for the use of his name and appearance on the title ("Cal Ripkin's Endurance Baseball — So Compelling You'll Be Playing It For The Next Forty Years"). If, instead, you want to use the rosters of all the professional baseball teams, you might instead negotiate an agreement with the Professional Baseball Players Association. Finally, if you want to use the teams and their logos, you may have to negotiate with Major League Baseball. Licensing all three would probably cost so much that the licensing fees would make it impossible to make a profit on the game. Similarly, one recognizable celebrity doing voices for your title (or appearing in your video-based title) may give you a substantial marketing hook. But hiring the whole host of name acting talent would provide rapidly diminishing returns (and rapidly increasing costs).

- *Non-exclusive rights are less expensive than exclusive rights.*

  Let's say you want to license particular music for your game or the computer game rights to William Gibson's latest science fiction book: In either case, if you simply get *non*-exclusive rights, the owner of the intellectual property will generally charge you less, because he or she has the right to license the same property again to someone else. You can get most of the benefits from an exclu-

sive license by simply negotiating for a headstart: a blackout period of, say, eighteen months, when they can't license the same rights to anyone else.

- *Pay in something other than money.*

  Credit (someone's name on a splash screen) is often helpful in closing a deal, and increasingly, game developers and publishers have been able to do tradeouts or provide publicity value as a way to reduce key content acquisition costs. For example, if you, large record company, license this intellectual property for our CD-ROM title, we will include hot links to your web site. In theory, you might even get payment from someone else for putting their name or product in your title. Motion picture producers *routinely* receive hundreds of thousands for "product placement," for putting products in their films.

- *Pay fees or royalties, but not both.*

  You can reduce up-front payment costs by giving people a share of your royalties. If at all possible, however, avoid *both* having to pay a substantial up-front license fee *and* giving the same person a substantial share of your royalties.

- *Pay royalties only out of your "net."*

  When you agree to pay royalties, be sure that you only pay licensing fees based on a percentage of what *you* actually receive, not your publisher's gross. It can be a huge mistake to agree upfront to additional payments based on certain sales figures, only to later find that because development advances from the publisher are recouped out of royalty payments to you, you are still not receiving income from your game at the time you are obligated to pay licensing fees.

- *Use an option to tie up content cheaply.*

  One way to minimize your costs in acquiring content (especially at a time when you have very little money) is to simply acquire an *option* to use the content, in return for a small payment and an agreement to pay more later *if* you use the content. For example, you could negotiate with the author of a science fiction book (and perhaps that author's publisher, depending on what the publishing agreement says) to get an exclusive *option* for two years to create a computer game based upon the book. If you exercise the option and actually go forward to create the game, the agreement could provide that you would be required to make additional minimum payments (and perhaps royalties). In the meantime, you have the legal ability to cut a deal with a software publisher, and you know that you won't be wasting your efforts in designing a game around intellectual property that you will not be able to acquire.

  Similarly, if the artists, programmers, or other independent contractors you deal with are unwilling to grant you broad rights (other platforms, sequels, foreign language adaptations) without substantial additional payments, you might negotiate with them to at least fix the price in advance when you do wish to acquire those rights later. (Otherwise, once your game is a hit, they would have enormous leverage to extract much more money out of you.)

This chapter is not a substitute for specific legal advice on your situation, and many of these areas raise complicated legal issues. But with this brief overview of some of the basic legal issues that you face, you should have the background to help your game development company prosper and to help you protect the legal rights to the great games you plan to make.

CHAPTER 33

A future moving at the speed of light....

By Dean M. Gloster

Business Resources for Game Developers

Now that you have your business plan in place, you're probably anxious to send it out and get some response. Perhaps some big investment company is waiting in the wings to offer you everything you need to get your company off the ground. To help you take that next step, this chapter presents a set of resources including venture capital firms and investment bankers and underwriters.

Venture Capital Sources

This section lists over 100 venture capitalists who have made recent computer game or multimedia-related investments. As you use these resources, keep in mind that they are highly selective and busy people. So the rule of thumb is, don't waste their time. Before you contact any of these companies, make sure that you have your business plan together and that you have a solid well-thought-out plan to sell. Although venture capitalists are dedicated to making minority investments in emerging growth companies, they turn down many more proposals than they approve.

ACCEL PARTNERS

One Embarcadero Center, Suite 3820
San Francisco, CA 94111
415 989-5656

Contact: Jim Breyer or Don Gooding
Typical Size of Investment: $300,000-$6M
Industry Preferences: Software, health care, telecommunications
Sample Investments: Mpath Interactive, Books that Work, Jostens Learning, Macromedia, UUNET, Santa Cruz Operations, Spectrum Holobyte, Starlight Networks, Mediashare, Remedy, Tenth Plant Explorations, First Virtual, Lightspan Partnership, Net Wise, Progressive Networks

ADOBE VENTURES, L.P.

P.O. Box 7900
Mountain View, CA 94039-7900
415 962-4812

Contact: Fred Mitchell
Typical Size of Investment: Large investments
Industry Preferences: Software (They are a joint venture of Adobe Software and Hambrecht & Quist.)
Sample Investments: Cascade Systems International, Electronic Submission Publishing Systems, Inc., Netscape, mFactory

ADVANCED TECHNOLOGY VENTURES

2884 Sand Hill Road, Suite 100
Menlo Park, CA 94025
415 321-8601

Contact: Jos C. Henkens
Typical Size of Investment: $500,000-$1M
Sample Investments: Media Vision, Accel Graphics

ADVENT INTERNATIONAL CORPORATION

1875 S. Grant St., Suite 310E
San Mateo, CA 94402
415 358-0525

Contact: Ph Chi Wu, Vice President
Typical Size of Investment: $1M-$15M
Industry Preferences: Varies
Sample Investments: Versant Object Technology

APPLIED TECHNOLOGY

One Cranberry Hill
Lexington, MA 02173
617 862-8622

Contact: Frederick Bamber, Thomas Grant
Typical Size of Investment: $500,000-$1M
Industry Preferences: High technology, multimedia, video
Sample Investments: Digital F/X, Fluent, Kub Systems, Human Code, Inc.

ASPEN VENTURE PARTNERS, LP

10898 Mora Drive
Los Altos, CA 94024
415 948-6833

Contact: David Crockett, General Partner
Typical Size of Investment: $500,000-$3M
Industry Preferences: Software, communications, multimedia
Sample Investments: Cornerstone Imaging, Net Frame, Media Vision, Broadband Technologies, Clarity Software

ASSET MANAGEMENT COMPANY

275 East Bayshore Road, Suite 150
Palo Alto, CA 94303
415 494-7400

Contact: Franklin P. Johnson or Craig C. Taylor
Typical Size of Investment: $1M-$5M
Industry Preferences: Information technology, biological sciences, physical sciences
Sample Investments: Natural Language (software), Latitude Communications, 50/50 Micro, Intelligence

ATLAS VENTURE

222 Berkeley Street
Boston, MA 02116
617 859-9290
(Other offices in Amsterdam, Munich, and Paris)

Contact: Eileen Richardson, Analyst or Barry Fidelman
Typical Size of Investment: $500,000-$1M plus
Industry Preferences: Varied; communications; computer related electronics; geographic preference for Northeast or West Coast of United States
Sample Investments: Dr. T's Musical Software, Vermeer Technologies

AT&T VENTURES CORP.

3000 Sand Hill Road, Bldg. 4-235
Menlo Park, CA 94025
415 233-0617
Contact: Allessandro Piol or Neal Douglas
Typical Size of Investment: Medium to large investments
Industry Preferences: Multimedia communications software
Sample Investments: Knowledge Adventure, Sierra On-Line, Imagination Network, Digital Generations Systems, General Magic, 3DO, Redgate, Enter Television, BNN Planet, First Virtual

AUSTIN VENTURES

114 West Seventh Street
1300 Norwood Tower
Austin, TX 78701
512 479-0055

Contact: John D. Thorton
Typical Size of Investment: $1M-$7M
Industry Preference: Various communications and computer services and applications
Sample Investments: Human Code, Inc.

AVI MANAGEMENT PARTNERS

One First Street, Suite 12
Los Altos, CA 94022
415 949-9855

Contact: Peter Wolken, Partner
Typical Size of Investment: $100,000-$1.5M
Industry Preferences: High technology
Sample Investments: Maspar, Photon Dynamics, Accel Graphics, S3

BACCHARIS CAPITAL, INC.

2420 Sand Hill Road, Suite 100
Menlo Park, CA 94025
415 324-6844

Contact: Stephen P. Monticelli, Mary Bechmann
Typical Size of Investment: $500,000-$1M plus
Sample Investmens: Stella Interactive

BANKAMERICA CAPITAL/ BANKAMERICA VENTURES

950 Tower Lane, Suite 700
Foster City, CA 94404
415 358-6000

Contact: Jess Marzak, Inv. Officer; James McCall, Inv. Officer
Typical Size of Investment: $1M-$10M

BASS ASSOCIATES

436 Tasso Street, Suite 325
Palo Alto, CA 94301
415 323-3655

Contact: Charles Bass
Sample Investments: Starlight Networks, Macromedia, Authorware, Fluent

BATTERY VENTURES

200 Portland Street
Boston, MA 02114
617 367-1011

Contact: Richard D. Frisbie
Typical Size of Investment: $750,000-$1.5M
Industry Preferences: Various communications and computer services
Sample Investments: Pro CD

BAY PARTNERS

10600 North De Anza Blvd.
Cupertino, CA 95014-2031
408 725-2444

Contact: John Freidenrich, W. Charles Hazel
Typical Size of Investment: $500,000-$1M
Industry Preferences: Various data communications, software applications
Sample Investments: International Catalogue Corp., E-Mu Systems, Macromedia, Barney Scan, By Video, Everest Solutions, H. Square, Optigraphics, Parallax Graphics, Paracomp, Vitel Communications, Interactive Catalogue Corp., Raster Graphics

BERENSON MINELLA VENTURES

667 Madison Avenue
New York, NY 10021
212 935-7676

Contact: Jeffrey Wolf
Typical Size of Investment: Prefers over $2.5 M, but will consider smaller opportunities
Industry Preferences: Ground floor funding (seed and growth stage) in cutting-edge technologies and innovative concepts with strong commercial potential; health care services, medical devices, environmental technology and services, telecommunications, multimedia and health care information systems. They are a newly-formed division of Berenson Minella & Company, a merchant banking firm.

BESSEMER VENTURE PARTNERS

3000 Sand Hill Rd., Suite 225
Menlo Park, CA 94025
415 854-2200

Contact: Neil Brownstein, President
Typical Size of Investment: $1M+
Industry Preferences: Software, chip and communications technology, retail
Sample Investments: Versant Object Technology, Worldtalk

BRENTWOOD ASSOCIATES

2730 Sand Hill Road Rd., Suite 250
Menlo Park, CA 94025
415 854-7691

Contact: John Walecka, General Partner
Typical Size of Investment: $500,000-$3M
Industry Preferences: Communications, software, multimedia, medical devices, biotechnology
Sample Investments: Cirrus Logic, Imaginarium, Media Vision, Agile Networks, Sybase

BURR, EGAN, DELEAGE & CO.

One Embarcadero Center, Suite 4050
San Francisco, CA 94111
415 362-4022

Contact: Garrett Gruener
Typical Size of Investment: $1M-$10M
Industry Preferences: Electronics information technology, software, medical and biotechnology, communications, health, cable TV, radio, computer
Sample Investments: Accent, Baycom Partners, Broderbund, Auravision Corp., Premisys Communications Holdings, Berkeley Systems, New Media Graphics

CANAAN PARTNERS

2884 Sand Hill Road, Suite 115
Menlo Park, CA 94025
415 854-8092

Contact: Alan Salyman, Eric Young, General Partners
Typical Size of Investment: $500,000-$15M
Industry Preferences: Information industry, medical technology, health care, financial and distribution services (formerly, this firm was GE Venture Capital)
Sample Investments: Latitude Communications, Productivity Solutions, Palladium Interactive

CHARTER VENTURES

525 University Avenue, Suite 1500
Palo Alto, CA 94301
415 325-6953

Contact: A.Barr Dolan, partner; David Lundberg, associate
Typical Size of Investment: $100,000-$1M
Sample Investments: 3D/fx

CIBC WOOD GUNDY CAPITAL

BCE Place
161 Bay Street, Sixth Floor
Toronto, Ontario M5J 2S8
Canada
416 594-8022

Contact: Jill Denham
Typical Size of Investment: $2M-$15M

CORAL GROUP

60 South Sixth St., Suite 3510
Minneapolis, MN 55402
612 335-8666

Contact: Don Lucas, Yural Almog
Typical Size of Investment: $100,000-$1.5 M (various amounts)
Industry Preferences: Medical and computer industries
Sample Investments: Vicarious, Macromedia

CORPORATE VENTURE PARTNERS, L.P.

171 East State Street, Suite 261
Ithaca, NY 14850
607 277-8024

Contact: David Costine, General Partner
Typical Size of Investment: $250,000-$1M
Industry Preferences: Various
Sample Investments: Spectrum HoloByte

DOMINION VENTURES, INC.

44 Montgomery Street, Suite 4200
San Francisco, CA 94104
415 362-4890

Contact: Michael Lee, Managing General Partner
Typical Size of Investment: $500,000-$3M
Industry Preferences: Financial services, telecommunications, health care, software

DRAPER ASSOCIATES

400 Seaport Ct. #250
Redwood City, CA 94063
415 599-9000

Contact: Tim Draper
Typical Size of Investment: $250,000-$500,000 (will go higher and lower)
Industry Preferences: Early-stage investments, software, communications, multimedia, digital media
Sample Investment: Accolade, T/Maker, Three-Sixty, Red Gate, Medior, Vividus

EDISON VENTURE FUND

997 Lenox Drive, #3
Lawrenceville, NJ 08648
609 896-1900

Other Offices:
1500 K Street NW Suite 500
Washington DC 20005
202 347-7901

P.O. Box 749
Harrisburg, PA 17108-0749
717 234-8009

Contact: Thomas A. Smith
Typical Size of Investment: $500,000-$2M plus
Industry Preference: Varied; geographical preference Northeast or Middle Atlantic
Sample Investment: Optical data

EL DORADO

20300 Stevens Creek Blvd., Suite 395
Cupertino, CA 95014
408 725-2474

Contact: Shanda Bahles or Gary Kalbach
Typical Size of Investment: Over $1M
Industry Preference: Commercial communications, micro and minicomputers, office automation
Sample Investments: Drew Pictures, Gold Disk, Wire Networks, Pulse Entertainment

EUCLID PARTNERS CORP.

50 Rockerfeller Plaza, Suite 1022
New York, NY 10020
212 489-1770

Contact: Frederick R. Wilson
Typical Size of Investments: $250,000-$1M
Industry Preferences: Communications, computer related, medical/health related, genetic engineering

FIREWORKS PARTNERS

1510 Page Mill Road
Palo Alto, CA 94304
415 855-4650

Contact: Michael Dolbec, Director
Sample Investments: A $50M fund set up by IBM for strategic investments.

GABELLI MULTIMEDIA PARTNERS

1 Corporate Center
Rye, NY 10580
914 921-5399

Contact: Francine Sommer, General Partner
Typical Size of Investment: $250,000-$15M
Industry Preference: High tech, software, multimedia
Sample Investments: New Fund, Exchange Resources, Pacific Pan Video Limited

GIDEON HIXON FUND

1900 Foshay Tower
821 Marquette Avenue
Minneapolis, MN 55402
612 337-5997

Contact: Benson K. Whitney, Managing General Partner
Typical Size of Investment: $100,000-$500,000
Sample Investments: Medior

GRACE/HORN VENTURE PARTNERS

20300 Stevens Creek Blvd., Suite 330
Cupertino, CA 95014
408 725-0774

Contact: Bob Pedigo
Typical Size of Investments: $500,000-$1M
Industry Preference: Data communications and various software systems
Sample Investments: Image OnLine

GREYLOCK MANAGEMENT

755 Page Mill Road, Suite B-140
Palo Alto, CA 94304
415 493-552

Contact: Mike Dolbec
Typical Size of Investment: Over $1M
Industry Preferences: Commercial communications, computer mainframes, services, biotechnology
Sample Investments: Avid, Media Magic, Tenth Planet Explorations, Raptor Systems

HAMBRECHT & QUIST

One Bush Street
San Francisco, CA 94104
415 576-3300

Contact: Christina Morgan, Standish O'Grady, William R. Hambrecht, Theodore H. Heinrichs
Typical Size of Investment: $500,000-$5M
Industry Preferences: Computer hardware, software, environmental technology, biotechnology
Sample Investments: Transaction Network Services, Network General Acquired Protocols, Mercury Interactive, Crystal Dynamics

HANCOCK VENTURE PARTNERS, INC.

One Financial Center, 44th Floor
Boston, MA 02111
617 348-3707

Contact: Kevin S. Delbridge, General Partner
Typical Size of Investment: $500,000-$1M plus
Sample Investments: Raster Graphics, Net Wise

HIGHLAND CAPITAL

One International Place
Boston, MA 02110
617 330-8765

Contact: Paul Maeder
Typical Size of Investment: $500,000-$1.5M plus
Industry Preferences: High technology
Sample Investments: Avid, Pro CD

HUMMER, WINBLAD VENTURE PARTNERS

5900 Hollis St., Suite R
Emeryville, CA 94068
510 652-8061

Contact: Mark Gorenberg or Ann Winblad
Typical Size of Investment: Under $100,000-$4M
Industry Preferences: Exclusively invests in new and growing software companies
Sample Investments: Arbor Software Corp., Berkeley Systems, Inc., Books That Work, Central Point Software, DeltaPoint, Inc., Escalade, Farallon Computing, Inc., Humongous Entertainment, Pop Rocket, Powersoft Corp., Reference Software, Scopus Techonology, Slate Corp., Soleil Network Technology, T/Maker Co., Watermark Software, Wind River Systems

IAI VENTURE CAPITAL

1100 Dain Tower
Minneapolis, MN 55440
612 376-2825

Contact: Yural Almog
Typical Size of Investment: Over $1M
Industry Preferences: Cable television, software systems, biotechnology
Sample Investments: Authorware, Digital Generation Systems

INDOSUEZ VENTURES

2180 Sand Hill Road, Suite 450
Menlo Park, CA 94025
415 854-0587

Contact: David E. Gold, General Partner; Nancy D. Burrus, General Partner
Typical Size of Investment: $100,000-$1.5M
Geographical Preferences: United States (within two hours of office of West Coast)
Sample Investments: Accel Graphics, Inc.

INNOCAL, L.P.

600 Anton Boulevard, Suite 1270
Costa Mesa, CA 92626
714 850-6784

Contact: James E. Houlihan III, General Partner, H.D. Lambert, General Partner
Minimum Investment: $500,000
Geographical Preferences: United States: West Coast
Sample Investments: Cloud Nine (WannaBe Interactive)

INSTITUTIONAL VENTURE PARTNERS

3000 Sand Hill Road Bldg 2, Suite 290
Menlo Park, CA 94025
415 854-0132

Contact: Geoffrey Yang or Ruthann Quindlen
Typical Size of Investment: Seed to $3M
Industry Preferences: Biotechnology, telecommunications, software, information sciences
Sample Investments: Collabra Software, Nomadic Systems, Objectivity, Storm Technology, Tenth Planet Explorations, Inc., Mpath Interactive, Lightspan Partnership, Digital Access

INTEGRAL CAPITAL PARTNERS

2750 Sand Hill Road
Menlo Park, CA 94025
415 233-0360

Contact: Roger McNamee
Typical Size of Investment: $500,000+ (larger amounts) (80% public sector; 20% private)
Industry Preferences: Life science, information science, telecommunications, cable industries
Sample Investments: Avantos, Performance Systems, Univax

INTERWEST PARTNERS

3000 Sand Hill Road, Bldg 3, Suite 255
Menlo Park, CA 94025
415 854-8585

Contact: Phillip Gianos, Roberto Mornsen, or David Whorton
Typical Size of Investment: $2M-10M; minimum $1M
Industry Preferences: Various communications, software applications and services, information sciences
Sample Investments: Crystal Dynamics, Starlight Networks, Stratacom, Synema, J3 Learning

JAFCO AMERICA VENTURES, INC.

555 California Street, Suite 4380
San Francisco, CA 94104
415 788-0706

Contact: Bill Shelander, General Manager, San Francisco; Michael Colby Orsak, Investment Manager, San Francisco
Typical Size of Investment: $500,000 minimum; preferred investment over $1M; second-stage and mezzanine financing
Industry Preferences: Various
Sample Investments: Sega, C-Cube, HSC Software, Com21, Netware

KLEINER, PERKINS, CAUFIELD & BYERS

2750 Sand Hill Road
Menlo Park, CA 94025
415 233-2750

Contact: Doug MacKenzie, Vinod Khosla, John Doerr, Kevin Compton, or Will Hearst
Typical Size of Investment: $1M-$2M + (larger investments)

Industry Preferences: Information technology, life sciences, health care
Sample Investments: Wireless Access, Photon Dynamics, MNI, Collabra Software, Maspar, Intuit, Macromind, Paracomp, Netscape, America Online, Digital F/X, Spectrum Holobyte, InterActive Partners, 3DO, Preview Media, MNI Interactive, Total Entertainment Network, Lorichel, Inc., Hands On Technology, Lightspan Partnership

LABRADOR VENTURES

400 Seaport Court, Suite 250
Redwood City, CA 94063
415 366-6000

Contact: Larry Kubal, General Partner
Typical Size of Investment: $100,000-$1M
Industry Preferences: Information, software, communications

MATRIX PARTNERS

2500 Sand Hill Road, Suite 113
Menlo Park, CA 94025
415 854-3131

Contact: Andrew Verhalen or Joe Rizzi
Typical Size of Investment: $1M-$1.5M
Industry Preferences: Computer, communications, semiconductor
Sample Investments: Red Pepper Software, Vesitas Software, Aspect Telecommunications, Synema, Vermeer Technologies

MAYFIELD FUND

2800 Sand Hill Road, Suite 250
Menlo Park, CA 94025
415 854-5560

Contact: Mike Leventhal or Yogen Dalal
Typical Size of Investment: $1M-$4M (Mayfield Software Partners, an affiliate, offers investments of smaller sizes)
Industry Preferences: High-tech, biotechnology, computer software and hardware, semiconductors, life sciences
Sample Investments: Silicon Graphics, Aspect Telecommunications, Imaginarium, University Games, Air Communications, MusiNet Interactive, Digital Generations Systems, Knowledge Adventure, Mediashare, Sharevision

MENLO VENTURES

3000 Sand Hill Road
Building 4, Suite 1000
Menlo Park, CA 94025
415 854-8540

Contact: Thomas H. Bradt
Typical Size of Investment: $500,000-$5M
Industry Preferences: Commercial communications, computers, leisure and recreational products

MERRILL, PICKARD, ANDERSON & EYRE

2480 Sand Hill Road, Suite 200
Menlo Park, CA 94025
415 854-8600

Contact: Kathryn Gould, Andy Rachleff, Steve Merril
Typical Size of Investment: $1M-$4M
Industry Preferences: Software, communications, computers, designed automation, medical devices
Sample Investments: Rocket Science, Knowledge Adventure, Macromedia, Red Pepper Software, Palm Computing, Starlight Networks, Supermac, Enter Television, S3

MK GLOBAL VENTURES

2471 E. Bayshore Rd., Suite 520
Palo Alto, CA 94303
415 424-0151

Contact: Michael D. Kaufman or Raymond Chin
Sample Investments: Landbase, Hypermedia Communication, Sharevision

MOHR, DAVIDOW VENTURES

3000 Sand Hill Road, Bldg 1, Suite 240
Menlo Park, CA 94025
415 854-7236
Contact: Jon Feiber or Nancy Shoendorf
Typical Size of Investment: $500,000-$1M
Industry Preferences: Start-ups in biotech and informational sciences
Sample Investments: Rocket Science, Books that Work, Knowledge Adventure, PED Software, Enter Television, S3, Tenth Planet Explorations

MORGAN STANLEY VENTURE PARTNERS

3000 Sand Hill Road, Building 4-250
Menlo Park, CA 94025
415 233-2600

Contact: Robert Loarie, General Partner
Typical Size of Investment: $3M-$12M
Industry Preferences: Information technology, health care

NAZEM & CO.

3000 Sand Hill Road, Bldg 1, Suite 205
Menlo Park, CA 94025
415 854-3010

Contact: Paul Dall
Typical Size of Investment: $1M+
Industry Preferences: High tech, multimedia, health care (also manages Transatlantic Fund)
Sample Investments: Media Vision, Optodigital Design, Digital F/X, StarPress Multimedia

NEW ENTERPRISES ASSOCIATES

235 Montgomery Street
San Francisco, CA 94104
415 986-1579

Contact: Richard Kramlich, Peter Morris
Sample Investments: Silicon Graphics, StarPress Multimedia, The Learning Co., Enter Television, Cottage Software, Hands On Technology

NHL PARTNERS, L.P.

888 Seventh Avenue, 20th Floor
New York, NY 10106
212 649-4900

Contact: Jim Rosenthal, Vice President Business Development
Typical Size of Investment: $500,000-$1M
Industry Preference: A $30M Venture Fund to Invest in "The Development and Production of Interactive Video Game Software and the Distribution and Marketing of all Multimedia Software, Including Interactive Games on a Worldwide Basis." A joint venture of New Line Cinema and the French media conglomerate Havas.
Sample Investments: Anonymous Entertainment, Vision III Imaging

NORWEST VENTURE CAPITAL

3000 Sand Hill Road
Building Three, Suite 105
Menlo Park, CA 94025-7116
415 854-6366

Contact: George J. Still, Jr., Partner
Typical Size of Investment: $1.5M-$5M
Sample Investments: Raster Graphics

OAK INVESTMENT PARTNERS

3000 Sand Hill Road, Bldg. 3-240
Menlo Park, CA 94025
415 854-8825

Contact: Bandel Carano, Fredric Harman, General Partners
Typical Size of Investment: $500,000-$7M
Industry Preferences: Electronics, software, telecommunications, design automation, retail, medical
Sample Investments: Delta Point (graphics software), Nomadic Systems, Endgate Technology, Digital F/X, Proxima, NetWise, daVinci Time & Space, PictureTel

OLYMPIC VENTURE PARTNERS

2420 Carillon Point
Kirkland, WA 98033
206 889-9192

Contact: George H. Clute, General Partner
Typical Size of Investment: $100,000-$1M plus
Sample Investments: Theatrix Interactive

PARAGON VENTURE PARTNERS

3000 Sand Hill Road, Bldg. 2-190
Menlo Park, CA 94025
415 854-8000

Contact: Robert Kibble, General Partner
Typical Size of Investment: $300,000-$3.5M
Industry Preferences: Leading edge technologies
Sample Investments: Synoptics Communications

PARTECH INTERNATIONAL

101 California St., Suite 3150
San Francisco, CA 94111
415 788-2929

Contact: Thomas McKinley, Vincent Worms, Partners
Typical Size of Investment: $500,000-$3M
Industry Preferences: Business services, CATV, communications, computer hardware and software, electronics, data processing, environmental services, health services
Sample Investments: Focal Therapeutics

PATRICOFF & CO VENTURES

445 Park Avenue
New York, NY 10022
212 753-6300

Contact: Robert M. Chefitz, Vice President
Typical Size of Investment: $500,000-$5M
Sample Investments: Digital Pictures, Apple, Cellular Communications

PHOENIX GROWTH CAPITAL CORP.

2401 Kerner Blvd.
San Rafael, CA 94901
415 485-4569

Contact: Norm Nelson, Senior Vice President
Typical Size of Investment: $250,000-$3M
Industry Preferences: High technology, biotechnology, software, communication, computer and peripherals and services
Sample Investments: C-Cube Microsystems, Qualcom

PHOENIX PARTNERS

100 Second Avenue, Suite 36600
Seattle, WA 98104
206 624-8968

Contact: David Johnson, General Partner
Typical Size of Investment: $500,000-$5M
Industry Preferences: New Media, Interactive Hardware and Software
Sample Investments: Splash Studios; Two-Way Media; Conner Peripherals; Media Vision

POINT VENTURE PARTNERS

2970 USX Tower
600 Grant Street
Pittsburgh, PA 15219
412 261-1966

Contact: Kent L. Engelmeier, General Partner
Sample Investments: Galt Technologies

PROVIDENCE VENTURES

The Fleet Center
50 Kennedy Plaza, Suite 901
Providence, RI 02903
401 751-1700

Contact: Paul Salem, Vice President

QUAESTUS

330 East Kilbourn Avenue
Milwaukee, WI 53202
414 283-4500

Contact: Richard W. Weening, Managing Principal
Typical Size of Investments: Minimum investment $500,000; preferred investment over $1M; first-, second-, and third-stage including mezzanine financing
Industry Preferences: Communications, computer related, medical/health related, publishing, business information databases, real time news services
Sample Investments: Connect, Inc.

QUEST VENTURE PARTNERS

555 California Street, Suite 2955
San Francisco, CA 94104
415 989-2020

Contact: Lucien Ruby, Managing General Partner

ROSEWOOD CAPITAL L.P.

Four Embarcadero Center, Suite 1500
San Francisco, CA 94111
415 362-5526

Contact: Howard Rosenberg

SACHAR CAPITAL, LTD.

545 Madison Avenue, 10th Floor
New York, NY 10022

Contact: Laura Sachar, President

SAND HILL VENTURE GROUP

10393 Noel Avenue
Cupertino, CA 95014
408 253-9294

Contact: D. McCrea Graham, II, Partner
Typical Size of Investment: $250,000-$500,000
Industry Preferences: Scanning related software systems, voice processing
Sample Investments: Xenon Microsystems, Sharevision

SEQUOIA CAPITAL

3000 Sand Hill Rd., Bldg. 4-280
Menlo Park, CA 94025
415 854-3927

Contact: Mike Morris, Mark Stevens, Don Valentine
Typical Size of Investment: $500,000+ (wide ranging)
Industry Preferences: Health care, biotechnology, semiconductors, environment, high tech software
Sample Investments: Illustra Info. Tech., Infinity Financial Tech., Storm Tech., Visigenic Software, Maspar, Macromedia, Avid, Authorware, Yahoo, Fast Multimedia, C-Cube

SEVIN ROSEN MANAGEMENT CO.

13455 Noel Road, Suite 1670
Dallas, TX 75240
214 702-1100

550 Lytton Avenue
Palo Alto, CA 94301
415 326-0550

Contact: Stephen M. Dow, Partner
Typical Size of Investment: $500,000-$1M plus
Sample Investments: Silicon Video

SIERRA VENTURES

3000 Sand Hill Road, Bldg. 4-210
Menlo Park, CA 94025
415 854-1000

Contact: Jeffrey M. Prazan
Typical Size of Investment: $1M-$5M
Industry Preferences: Information technology
Sample Investments: Air Communications, Axcis Pocket Information Network, Silicon Video, Intuit

SIGMA PARTNERS

2884 Sand Hill Road, Suite 121
Menlo Park, CA 94025
415 854-1300

Contact: Burgess Jamieson, Partner
Typical Size of Investment: Over $1M
Industry Preferences: Various communications and computer services, semiconductors, industrial automation
Sample Investments: Vermeer Technologies

ST. PAUL VENTURE CAPITAL, INC.

8500 Normandale Lake Boulevard
Suite 1940
Bloomington, MN 55437
612 830-7474

Contact: Rick Boswell, Executive Vice President; Everett Cox, Executive Vice President; Nancy Olson, Executive Vice President
Typical Size of Investment: $500,000-$5M
Sample Investments: J3 Learning

SUMMIT PARTNERS

499 Hamilton Avenue, Suite 200
Palo Alto, CA 94301
415 321-1166

Contact: Gregory M. Avis, Managing Partner; Walter G. Kortschak, General Partner
Typical Size of Investment: From $1.5M-25M
Industry Preferences: Communications, computer related, consumer, distribution, electronic components and instrumentation, high-tech health and specialized serivices and various others
Sample Investments: Diamond Multimedia Systems, Digital Link

SUTTER HILL VENTURES
755 Page Mill Road, Suite A-200
Palo Alto, CA 94304
415 493-5600

Contact: Paul Wythes, General Partner
Typical Size of Investment: $100,000-$3M
Industry Preferences: High technology, software, health care services, medical devices, biotechnology, telecommunications, semiconductors and equipment
Sample Investment: Oasis Healthcare Systems, Palm Computing, Omnicell Technology, Avid Technologies, Digidesign, SuperMac

TA ASSOCIATES
435 Tasso St.
Palo Alto, CA 94301
415 328-1210

Contact: Michael C. Child, Brian J. Conway
Typical Size of Investment: $5M-$30M
Industry Preferences: Information technology, health care services, financial services
Sample Investments: Versant Object Technology; Diamond Multimedia Systems

TECHNOLOGIES FOR INFORMATION AND ENTERTAINMENT FUND

1 Cranberry Hill
Lexington, MA 02173
617 862-8622

Contact: Fred Bamber
Typical Size of Investment: $100,000-$3M
Industry Preferences: Entertainment industry, information and communication technology
Sample Investments: ISD Chip

TECHNOLOGY FUNDING, INC.

2000 Alameda de las Pulgas, Suite 250
San Mateo, CA 94403
415 345-2200
800 821-5323

Contact: Thomas J. Toy, Partner; John R. Tingleff, Partner; Peter F. Bernardoni, Vice President; Gregory T. George, General Partner
Typical Size of Investments: $500,000-$2M

Industry Preferences: Communication, computer related, medical product distribution, electronic components and instruments, medical/health, genetic engineering, industrial products and equipments, energy/natural resources
Sample Investments: Velocity Development, Inc.

TECHNOLOGY PARTNERS FUND

1550 Tiburon Blvd., Suite A
Belvedere, CA 94920
415 435-1935

Contact: Bill Hart
Typical Size of Investment: Up to $2M
Industry Preferences: Interactive multimedia, medical devices, information processing
Sample Investments: 3DO, Crystal Dynamics, Round Book Publishing Group, Inc., Cloud Nine (WannaBe Interactive)

TECHNOLOGY VENTURE INVESTORS

2480 Sand Hill Road, #101
Menlo Park, CA 94025
415 854-7472

Contact: Marc Wilson, General Partner, Robert C. Kagle, General Partner
Typical Size of Investment: $500,000-$5M
Industry Preferences: Computer software and hardware, semiconductor, data communications, telecommunications
Sample Investments: Mediashare, Walker Interactive, Intuit

TGS MANAGEMENT CORP.

100 Congress Avenue, Suite 980
Austin, TX 78701
512 322-3100

Contact: Ron Walsh

THOMPSON CLIVE, INC.

3000 Sand Hill Road, Bldg 1-185
Menlo Park, CA 94025
415 854-0314

Contact: Peter Zeibelman, Partner
Typical Size of Investment: $500,000-$3M
Industry Preferences: Software, communications, computer-related, life sciences
Sample Investments: Walker Interactive, Persistance Software, Applied Imaging

THIRD MILLENIUM VENTURE CAPITAL, LTD.

P. O. Box 1123
Los Altos Hills, CA 94023
415 941-9137

Contact: John Koza

TRANSATLANTIC FUND (NAZEM & CO.)

3000 Sand Hill Road, Bldg. 2-205
Menlo Park, CA 94025
415 854-3010

Contact: Paul Dall
Typical Size of Investment: $1M+
Industry Preferences: High tech, multimedia, health care
Sample Investments: Media Vision, Optodigital Design, Digital F/X, StarPress Multimedia

TRINITY VENTURES

155 Bovet Road, Suite 660
San Mateo, CA 94403
415 358-9700

Contact: Noel Fenton, Managing General Partner
Typical Size of Investment: $250,000-$3M
Industry Preferences: Computer-related, consumer products, communications, industrial automation, health products
Sample Investments: Illustra Information Technologies (data-based management software), Versant Object Technology

US VENTURE PARTNERS

2180 Sand Hill Road, Suite 300
Menlo Park, CA 94025
415 854-9080

Contact: Steven M. Krausz
Typical Size of Investment: $1M-$3M
Industry Preferences: Medical, technology, specialty retail, consumer products
Sample Investments: Imaginarium, Photon Dynamics, 3D/fx, Palladium

VANGUARD VENTURE PARTNERS

525 University Avenue, Suite 600
Palo Alto, CA 94301
415 321-2900

Contact: Kip Myers, Cliff Higgerson
Typical Size of Investment: $2M-$3M
Industry Preferences: Information Technology, Medical Devices, Entertainment
Sample Investments: PF Magic, Image OnLine, Macromedia, Art Search, Adam Software, Outstanding Multimedia

VENROCK ASSOCIATES

755 Page Mill Road, Suite A230
Palo Alto, CA 94304
415 493-5577

Contact: Tony Sun, David Hathaway
Typical Size of Investment: $500,000-$4M
Industry Preferences: Biotechnology, health care, computers, telecommunications
Sample Investments: Apple Computer, Intel, Drew Pictures, Sharevision, Photon Dynamics, 3D/fx

VERTEX MANAGEMENT

1000 Lousiana Street, Suite 1110
Houston, TX 77002
713 659-7870

Contact: Charles Wu
Typical Size of Investment: Over $1M
Industry Preferences: Commercial and data communication, software applications, biotechnology
Sample Investments: Creative Technology, inTouch, RasterOps, Spectrum HoloByte

VIKING CAPITAL

150 Federal Street, 26th Floor
Boston, MA 02110-1745
617 443-9200

Contact: Marcia J. Hooper, General Partner; Walter J. Levison, General Partner
Typical Size of Investment: $500,000-$3M
Sample Investments: Arnowitz Studios

VS&A COMMUNICATIONS PARTNERS

212 935-4990

Contact: Jeffrey Stevenson, President
Sample Investments: Rifkin Acquisition Partners

VULCAN VENTURES, INC.

110 110th Avenue NE, Suite 550
Bellevue, WA 98004
206 453-1940

Contact: William D. Savoy, President
Industry Preferences: Vulcan Ventures is Paul Allen's venture arm and is interested in software and cutting-edge technology investments
Sample Investments: Medio Multimedia, Trilobyte, Storyopolis, 3.D/EYE Inc., Precision Systems; DreamWorks SKG; affiliates have also invested in Asymetrix Corp. and Starwave Corp. (which itself has invested in Jim Henson Interactive).

WALDEN GROUP OF VENTURE CAPITAL FUNDS

750 Battery St., 7th Floor
San Francisco, CA 94111
415 391-7225

Contact: Arthur Berliner, Bil Tal
Typical Size of Investment: $500,000-$2M
Industry Preferences: All industries
Sample Investments: Creative Labs, S3, Macromedia, RasterOps, Creative Technologies, Digital F/X

WARBURG, PINCUS VENTURES, INC.

466 Lexington Avenue
New York, NY 10017
212 878-0600

Contact: Henry Kressel
Typical Size of Investment: $1M plus
Sample Investments: Maxis

WEISS, PECK & GREER VENTURE PARTNERS

555 California St., Suite 4760
San Francisco, CA 94104
415 622-6864

Contact: Phillip Greer, Managing Partner
Typical Size of Investment: $500,000-$4M
Industry Preferences: Computer software, hardware, communications, biotechnology, medical devices, service businesses
Sample Investments: Visigenic Software, Coactive Computing, Electronics for Imaging, Parc Place Systems, CAPS, Theatrix Interactive

WILLIAM BLAIR VENTURE PARTNERS

135 South LaSalle Street
Chicago, IL 60603

Contact: Samuel B. Guren, Ellen Walsh
Sample Investments: Supermac

WOODSIDE FUND

850 Woodside Dr.
Woodside, CA 94062
415 368-5545

Contact: Vincent Occhipinit, General Partner
Typical Size of Investment: $75,000-$300,000
Industry Preferences: Communications, computer-related, consumer electronics, medical devices
Sample Investments: Accel Graphics

XEROX TECHNOLOGY VENTURES

101 Continental Boulevard
El Segundo, CA 90245

Contact: Robert H. Curtin, Vice President
Typical Size of Investment: No minimum-$1M plus
Sample Investments: Netwise

Investment Bankers and Underwriters

This section lists some of the leading investment bankers and underwriters who help put deals together for game development companies. Keep in mind that these professionals don't typically directly invest in companies; they help companies with financing transactions, mergers and acquisitions, private placements, and initial public offerings. "Investment bankers" are somewhat misnamed, since they usually don't make investments, and they are not bankers.

ADAMS, HARKNESS & HILL, INC.

60 State Street
Boston, MA 02109
617 371-3900

ALEX BROWN & SONS

101 California Street
San Francisco, CA 94111
415 544-2800

Contact: Steve Eskenazie
Typical Size of Investment: Varies
Industry Preferences: All industries, including technology, health care and consumer products
Sample Engagements: Electronic Arts

BROADVIEW ASSOCIATES

555 Twin Dolphin Dr., Suite 570
Redwood City, CA 94065-2102
415 802-5900

Contact: Harvel Poppel or Steve Smith
Typical Size of Investment: Larger investments
Industry Preferences: Software and hardware
Sample Engagements: Sterling Software; Reuters, Ltd.

COWEN & CO.

345 California Street, 26th Floor
San Francisco, CA 94104
415 434-7800

Contact: Michael Dorsey, Managing Director
Sample Engagements: Media Vision, S3

COXE CAPITAL

2 Greenwich Plaza, Suite 100
Greenwich, CT 06830
203 622-1319

Contact: Brent Coxe, President
Industry Preferences: Software, emerging growth
Sample Engagements: Sanctuary Woods

D. H. BLAIR INVESTMENT BANKING CORP.

44 Wall Street, 2nd Floor
New York, NY 10005

Contact: Jonathan Turkel, Vice President
Typical Size of Investment: Private financing \$500,000-\$5M; larger placements \$5M-\$25M
Industry Preferences: Software, technology, biotechnology
Sample Engagements: Interactive Flight Technologies; NetVantage

FROST CAPITAL PARTNERS

44 Montgomery Street, 22nd Floor
San Francisco, CA 94109
415 274-2422

Contact: Dean Frost or Ian Berman
Typical Size of Investment: $3M-$15M
Industry Preferences: Entertainment and educational software
Sample Engagements: Ablesoft; Velocity; Software Marketing Corp.; QQP

HAMBRECHT & QUIST

One Bush St.
San Francisco, CA 94104
415 576-3300

Contact: Christina Morgan, Standish O'Grady, Partner
Typical Size of Investment: $500,000-$5M
Industry Preferences: Computer hardware, software, environmental technology, biotechnology (they also manage a VC fund)
Sample Engagements: Transaction Network Services, Network General Acquired Protocols, Mammoth Micro, Apple, NeXT, Softimage

GRIEF & CO.

333 South Grand Ave., 39th Floor
Los Angeles, CA 90071
213 346-9255
213 346-9260 (Fax)

Contact: Lloyd Grief
Typical Size of Investment: $10M-$300M
Industry Preferences: Technology, media entertainment, consumer products, retailing Manufacturing
Sample Engagements: Signs and Glassworks; nu.millenia; MGM Interactive

JEFFRIES & CO., INC.

580 California St., Suite 2080
San Francisco, CA 94104
415 399-4400

Contact: Lee Isgur
Typical Size of Investment: Wide range
Industry Preferences: Various (Mr. Isgur is a much-quoted analyst on multimedia companies)
Sample Engagements: Trans-Texas, Oliander Group

LEHMAN BROTHERS

One Sansome Street, Suite 3200
San Francisco, CA 94104
415 984-6868

MONTGOMERY SECURITIES

600 Montgomery Street
San Francisco, CA 94111
415 627-2000

Contact: Joseph Schell, Managing Officer
Typical Size of Investment: $15M-up
Industry Preferences: Technology, financial services, health care, consumer, specialty retailers, restaurants
Sample Engagements: Media Vision, Macromedia

MORGAN STANLEY & CO.

555 California Street, 22nd Floor
San Francisco, CA 94104
415 576-2000
415 576-2392 (Fax)
415 233-2500 (Menlo Park)

Contact: Mary Meeker
Sample Engagements: Netscape, 3DO, Electronic Arts

NEW MEDIA CAPITAL

575 Lexington Avenue, Suite 410
New York, NY 10022
212 572-0788
212 572-0766 (Fax)

Contacts: Laurent Ohana or Leslie Murdock
Typical Size of Investment: $100,000-$1M
Industry Preferences: New media, CD-ROM, Internet, software, electronic publication
Sample Engagements: Cybersites, Inc.; Hi-D, Inc.

PIPER JAFFRAY, INC.

1200 5th Avenue, Suite 1400
Seattle, WA 98101

Contact: John R. Jacobs, Managing Director of Corporate Finance
Sample Engagements: Accolade, Sierra On-Line, Spectrum HoloByte, Virgin Interactive

REDWOOD SECURITIES GROUP, INC.

600 California Street, Suite 1650
San Francisco, CA 94108-2408
415 954-0663

Contact: Aditya Mukerji, Managing Officer
Typical Size of Investment: $500,000-$50M
Industry Preferences: Utilities, transportation, high technology, private entities

ROBERTSON STEPHENS & CO.

555 California St., Suite 2600
San Francisco, CA 94104
415 781-9700

Contact: John Grillos, David Goldsmith, or J. Misha Petkovich
Industry Preferences: Wide world of digital entertainment, education, media

SMITH BARNEY

350 California Street, 21st Floor
San Francisco, CA 94104
415 955-1675

Contact: Craig Johnson

SOUTHPORT PARTNERS

2425 Post Road, Suite 200
Southport, CT 06490
203 255-1231

Contact: A. Christopher Bulger

UNTERBERG HARRIS

275 Battery Street, Suite 2980
San Francisco, CA 94111
415 399-1500

Contact: Christy DeMartini or Andrew Kessler
Sample Engagements: Activision, Trilobyte, Tsunami

VOLPE, WELTY & CO.

One Maritime Plaza, 11th Floor
San Francisco, CA 94111
415 956-8120

Contact: Thomas Volpe, Managing Officer
Typical Size of Investment: $5M+
Industry Preferences: Communications, software, interactive media, health care information, management, pharmaceuticals, biomedical diagnostics, medical devices, service industries
Sample Engagements: New Media Graphics, Macromedia, Digidesign, SuperMac, Avid Technology, Educational Insights, TRO

Books

The books listed in this section should help you in those difficult moments of getting your business off the ground, managing the development process for your products, and so on.

The Macintosh Way by Guy Kawasaki (Scott Foresman; ISBN 0-673-4615-0)

Selling the Dream by Guy Kawasaki (Harper Collins, New York, NY, 1992; ISBN 0-887-3060-04)

How to Drive Your Competition Crazy by Guy Kawasaki (Little Brown & Company, 1995; ISBN 0-786-86124-X)

Guy was one of Apple's first evangelists and he was just recently named as an Apple fellow putting him in prestigious company with people like Alan Kay. He spent time trying to get companies to produce products for the Macintosh when it first shipped. He later went on to become president of Acius, which makes 4th Dimension—a powerful database product for the Mac.

These books provide neat hybrid marketing advice and anecdotes from the computer business. You'll find a lot of "from the trenches" tips all presented in a humorous style—Guy is somewhat of a closet comedian.

Managing Software Maniacs by Ken Whitaker (John Wiley & Sons, New York, NY, 1994; ISBN 047-10099-70)

If you're a manager, team leader, or producer in the games business, you've got to deal with a lot of different people and technical problems. This book is really a common sense guide about pulling together and motivating a software development team. With over 200 pages of topics like dealing with engineers, managing risk, and scheduling, this is a guide well worth some attention by people who need to manage game projects.

Building a Successful Software Business by Dave Radin (O'Reilly & Associates, Sebastopol, CA, 19994; ISBN 1-56592-064-3)

This book is really about setting up a business with a tailoring of specific advice about selling software. If you need information about selling, pricing, positioning, dealing with bankers, and so on, this is a great resource for you. Being a lone-wolf developer is one thing, but running a development house or successful publishing company involves a completely different set of circumstances that this book can help you with.

Business and Marketing Oriented Publications

There are a number of newsletters, magazines, and online publications designed to help you run a software business. Here is a listing of some of the more useful ones.

Software Publishing
Webcom Communications Corp.
10555 East Dartmouth, Suite 330
Aurora, CO 80014-2633

Phone: 303 745-5711 **Fax:** 303 745-5712
WWW: http://www.infowebcom.com/~softpub
Subscription: $36 **Newsstand:** N/A **Publishes:** BiMonthly **Pages:** 90

This is an excellent magazine for anyone in the software business. The articles detail all sorts of publishing dos, don'ts, how-tos, and news. The adds are jammed packed with duplicators, packaging services, and so on.

The Red Herring

Phone: 415 865-2277 **Fax:** 415 865-2280
WWW: http//www.herring.com
Subscription: $115/yr **Newsstand:** N/A **Publishes:** Monthly **Pages:** N/A

This is a well designed magazine devoted to technology strategy, finance, and investment. It concentrates a lot on the game industry and their Web site is filled with awesome articles from past issues, industry information, and contacts. This is a must-have for anyone looking for financial help (read venture capital) or who is looking to keep up on the high-finance of the games/Internet/multimedia industry.

Upside
Upside Publishing Company
2015 Pioneer Court
San Mateo, CA 94403

Phone: 415 377-0950 **Fax:** 415 377-1962
WWW: http//www.upside.com
Subscription: $48/yr **Newsstand:** $4.95 **Publishes:** Monthly **Pages:** N/A

This is another business magazine that focuses on the software industry. You'll find a number of articles that discuss the business implications of the Web, online gaming, technology management, and techniques for raising capital for high-tech companies.

Retail Oriented Publications

If you are planning to take your products into retail channels, I suggest you do as much reading as you can in any of the following publications.

Computer & Entertainment Retailing
Plesman Publications Ltd.
2005 Sheppard Avenue East, 4th Floor
Willowdale, Ontario M2J 5B1

Phone: 416 497-9562 **Fax:** 416 497-9427
WWW: http://www.plesman.com/main.htm
Subscription: $115/yr **Newsstand:** N/A **Publishes:** Monthly **Pages:** N/A

Computer & Entertainment Retailing is Canada's only monthly newspaper designed to give retailers who sell computer and consumer electronics products the most comprehensive coverage of news, events, and issues that affect their business.

Qualified Canadian subscribers can sign up using the Web site listed above for a free subscription but U.S. subscribers will have to pay $115/yr for the ability to see the pulp version of this magazine. Check out their good Web site for articles, many of which are useful even if you're not selling in Canada.

Computer Dealer News
Plesman Publications Ltd.
2005 Sheppard Avenue East, 4th Floor
Willowdale, Ontario M2J 5B1

Phone: 416 497-9562 **Fax:** 416 497-9427
WWW: http://www.plesman.com/main.htm
Subscription: $250/yr **Newsstand:** N/A **Publishes:** BiWeekly **Pages:** N/A

Computer Dealer News is Canada's only bi-weekly national newspaper about the computer retailing business in Canada.

Qualified Canadian subscribers can sign up using the Web site for a free subscription but U.S subscribers will have to pay $250/yr for the ability to see the pulp version of this magazine.

Computer Reseller News
CMP Publications, Inc.
600 Community Drive
Manhasset, NY 11030

Phone: 516 562-5000
WWW: http://techweb.cmp.com/crn/current/
Subscription: Free **Newsstand:** N/A **Publishes:** Weekly **Pages:** N/A

Computer Reseller News is the number one magazine on anything having to do with the reselling of computer hardware and software.

Computer Retail Week
CMP Publications, Inc.
600 Community Drive
Manhasset, NY 11030

Phone: 516 562-5000
WWW: http://techweb.cmp.com/crw/current/
Subscription: Free **Newsstand:** N/A **Publishes:** Weekly **Pages:** N/A

Since retailing is a major force, this CMP publication focuses more on the consumer and retail business of computers. *Computer Reseller News* publication, the big brother to this covers everything from government sales to VARs to retail. Here you'll find more coverage of issues like games, multimedia, major retail news, and more.

Multimedia Merchandising
1632 Fifth Street, Suite 220
Santa Monica, CA 90401

Phone: 310 458-3102 **Fax:** 310 458-3192
Subscription: Free* **Newsstand:** N/A **Publishes:** Monthly **Pages:**70

Multimedia Merchandising is aimed at retailers, distributors, and producers of across-the-board multimedia titles and gives ample coverage to games.

SMART:Computer & Software Retailing
7025 Albert Pick Road, Suite 2000
Greensboro, NC 27409

Phone: 910 605-0121 **Fax:** 910 605-1143
Subscription: Free **Newsstand:** N/A **Publishes:** 21/Year **Pages:** 45

This is another publication covering the computer and software retailing markets with excellent coverage of consumer markets for computer games, videogames, and educational software.

General Industry News and Market Analysis

One of the best ways to run a growing company and keep yourself out of trouble is to keep a close eye on what your competition is up to. The publications listed in this section provide excellent coverage of news about the games, multimedia, and electronic entertainment industries.

Electronic Gaming News
BRP Publications
1333 H Street NW 2nd Floor
Washington, DC 20005

Phone: 202 842-3022
Subscription: $499 **Newsstand:** N/A **Publishes:** 25/Year **Pages:** 12

From the people who bring you *Multimedia Daily* comes this biweekly newsletter on the game industry.

Interactive Update
17 East 29th Street
New York, NY

Phone: 212 684-2333 **Fax:** 212 684-0291
WWW: http://www.alexassoc.com
Subscription: $395 **Newsstand:** N/A **Publishes:** Bi-weekly **Pages:**10

Interactive Update is a newsletter which concentrates on a wide range of interactive industry issues, from interactive TV to games to the commercial online services and the Internet. Like other publications of this type, it's aimed mostly at managers and executives who need the timely information contained inside as they wheel and deal.

Jupiter Communication Newsletters
594 Broadway, Suite 1003
New York, NY 10012

Phone: 212 941-9252 **Fax:** 212 941-7376
WWW: http://www.jup.com/jupiter/

Jupiter Communications markets an entire line of informative newsletters. While they don't specifically offer a games industry targeted newsletter, the publications listed here do offer lot's of interesting industry information that concerns consumer use of videogames, the Internet, and computers:

Consumer Information Appliance	$475
Online Marketplace	$545
Interactive Content	$499
Interactive Home	$475
The Digital Kids Report	$425

Contact Jupiter either at the listing above or at their Web site to order sample issues which will give you a good idea of their content and worth to your business.

Multimedia Wire
Phone: 301 493-9291 **Fax:** 301 493-8996
WWW: http://www.mmwire.com
Subscription: $445 **Newsstand:** N/A **Publishes:** Daily **Pages:** 2

Multimedia Wire sends out two pages a day by fax or email that summarizes the key news in multimedia, games, and online technology. MMWire's Web site is one of the best around. You can get a weekly recap of news, want ads, information on key organizations, and much more.

Multimedia Daily
BRP Publications
1333 H Street NW 2nd Floor
Washington, DC 20005

Phone: 202 842-3022
Subscription: $495/$595 **Newsstand:** N/A **Publishes:** Daily **Pages:** 5

Delivered either by Fax ($595) or email ($495), this publication offers daily updates on what's going on in the multimedia industry including generous coverage of the games industry.

Video Game Advisor Magazine
Cyberactive Publications, Inc.
64 Danbury Road
Suite 500
Wilton, CT 06897

Phone: 800 295-2718 **Fax:** 203 761-6184
WWW: http://www.vgadvisor.com

Video Game Advisor is provided free of charge to qualified professional buyers within the interactive gaming industry. One year subscription rate for the U.S. is $63.95. The rate in Canada is $67.95. Single copy price is $7.95: Canada $8.95.

Other Sources of Information

It's important to remember that the resources I've profiled earlier are the most relevant sources I could find. However if you are truly serious about the business of promoting products, following trends, and trying to keep up on the industry, there are many other newspapers and magazines that give major coverage to this industry.

Table 33.1 presents a list of the non-game oriented publications I check in on as much as possible (and I used extensively for researching material for this book). Each publication is presented with a brief note of its relevance to the game development industry. I've also included information to show you how to get each publication.

Table 33.1 Useful Publications for Keeping up on the Computer Industry

Publication	Relevance	Where to Get/Access
Business Week	This and *Fortune* both provide a lot of coverage on the electronic entertainment industry. Several front page stories have focused on Sega, Nintendo, and other entertainment software companies.	*Business Week* maintains current issues and past issues online on America On-Line (Keyowrd=Business Week). Their Web site is *http://www.businessweek.com* and of course you can get the printed publication at local newsstands.
Business Wire	Many companies use *Business Wire* to publish their press releases. It's a great way to check in at the end of a day and see what new announcements have been made.	You can find *Business Wire* feeds on AOL and at the Businesswire Web site at *http://www.hnt.com/bizwire/.*
Daily Variety	*Daily Variety* covers of Hollywood and the rest of the entertainment world, which increasingly means games and especially the deals Hollywood studios are cutting in this arena.	You can find *Daily Variety* across the country and also access stories.
Fortune	*Fortune* tends to give its articles more depth about management issues than *Businessweek* (which is more newsy). They recently published a big issue on high-tech which included profiles of companies like Humongous Entertainment.	*Fortune* maintains current and recent issue archives online on CompuServe (GO FORTUNE) and at its Web site is on Time Warner's Pathfinder *http://pathfinder.com/.* You can also get it at your local newsstand.

Table 33.1 Useful Publications for Keeping up on the Computer Industry (Continued)

Publication	Relevance	Where to Get/Access
New York Times	The *New York Times* has the second best daily business coverage of any paper in the country. In addition, the paper's business editors devote more than significant space to the emerging multimedia industry including a bursting scene in New York dubbed Silicon Alley.	The *New York Times* maintains daily archives on America OnLine; they recently got back rights to begin archiving material. You can also visit their Web site at *http://nytsyn.com/cgi-bin/times/lead/go.*The *New York Times* is available almost anywhere on the newsstands.
PRNewswire	PRNewswire is the wirefeed for press releases put out by non news/government oriented entities which features mainly businesses. If you want daily updates about the industry, just check in here and you'll find news announcements from about every major game company in existence.	PRNewswire is accessible from both America Online, as part of it's general news coverage and in a more organized fashion in its own forum on CompuServe (GO PRNewswire) You can access the Web site at *http://www.prnewswire.com.*
San Jose Mercury News	The paper of Silicon Valley has done many interesting articles on the game development/multimedia industry (including an awesome profile of San Frans Multimedia Gulch). Also from time to time they have want ads for companies hiring!	Not everyone lives in San Jose but don't worry because this paper of Silicon Valley was an early online participant complete with archives on AOL and now their Web site: *http://www.sjmercury.com/.*
USA Today	*USA Today* has regular coverage of games in it's life section and in its business section from time to time. *USA Today* is an excellent promotional arena as many *Wall Street* and other PR oriented people read this paper.	*USA Today* had it's own online service but is now on the Web at *http://www.usatoday.com.*

Table 33.1 Useful Publications for Keeping up on the Computer Industry (Continued)

Publication	Relevance	Where to Get/Access
Wall Street Journal	The business journal of record. The *Wall Street Journal* gives games industry coverage just as it would any other major business issue and its marketing section features crisp analysis of business decisions and strategies.	The *Wall Street Journal* just started a Web service at *http://www.wsj.com/* and of course, it is available all around the world.

Online Resources

First and foremost, you should check out the various Web sites of the above listed resources. They alone offer lots of information, news, tips, and analysis. Here are some additional entertainment-specific Web specific sites you should explore.

AIM (Amusement International Magazine)
`http://w3.thegroup.net/~aim/`

This Web site provides a trade journal for the international coin-operated amusement business in Europe and the rest of the world. Although it covers all sorts of coin-op issues like pinball and pool tables, it has extensive coverage of the all important video arcade scene. Pointers exist throughout the site to various local magazines and resources for people involved in the coin-op scene.

Tracking Shipped Titles via Electronics Boutique

Electronics Boutique, the large national reseller of computer and video games, provides as a service to its customers: two mailing lists which send out information two to three times a week of all the new titles which have arrived. These two lists are excellent ways to stay on top of shipped products.

Video Game List
Send an email message to Majordomo@teleport.com. The first line of your message must be:

subscribe ebvgames-l.

You do not need anything else in the message, and your subject line may be anything you like. (That is a lowercase "L" at the end.)

Computer List
Send an email message to Majordomo@teleport.com. In the first line of your message must be:

subscribe ebcmptrs-l

You do not need anything else in the message, and your subject line may be anything you like. (That is a lowercase "L" at the end)

Morph's Daily Spectrum
`http://www.iw.com/netday/morph/daily.htm`

Morph's produces this daily; it's a bible of information. A must read.

EDUPAGE
`listproc@educom.unc.edu`

This is a roundup of news and stuff on the computer industry and the Net in particular. To subscribe to Edupage: send a message to the above address and in the BODY of the message type:

subscribe Edupage Arthur Miller
(assuming that your name is Arthur Miller; if it's not, substitute your own name)

Multimedia Mailing List
`majordomo@case.wsgr.com`

Send email with:
subscribe multimedia-list EMAIL ADDRESS

The law firm of Wilson Sonsini Goodrich & Rosati, specifically Catherine Kirkman, produces a weekly email zine that summarizes news concerning topics covered here. It's free and decent.

Newspage
`http://www.newspage.com/`

To move beyond the abstracts to full access you'll have to subscribe to this service but if you do it's perhaps one of the best news sources on the Web with extensive coverage of everything including computers and games.

***PC WEEK* Magazine**
`http://www.zdnet.com/~pcweek/`

This is the magazine that covers the PC industry inside or not. *PC WEEK* has a great Web site. If you want to keep up with what's going on in the PC world point your browser here.

InfoWorld
`http://www.infoworld.com/`

Along with *PC WEEK*, this is the source for weekly news on the entire PC industry.

Inquiry.Com
`http://www.inquiry.com`

This is a new service which is a free searchable archive for developers of software products. It's a good place to search for information about sales and marketing.

Additional Organizations

AMOA (Amusement and Music Operators Association)
401 North Michigan Avenue
Chicago, IL 60611-4267

Phone: 316 262-3538 **Fax:** 316 262-6200

This is the association made up of companies and individuals involved in the video game arcade scene as well as devices like coin-op pool, pinball, and other location-based amusement devices.

Software Publishers Association
1730 M Street, NW, Suite 700
Washington, DC 20036-4510

Phone: 202 452-1600 **Fax:** 202 223-8756
WWW: http://www.spa.org

The SPA is the leading organization for software publishers. While the IDSA is more targeted at game developers, the SPA still provides useful resources and support for game developers.

APPENDIX A

Choosing a Legal Entity

As mentioned in Chapter 29 on legal issues, a game development venture can be organized in one of several different forms:

- Sole proprietorship
- General partnership
- Limited partnership
- Corporation
- Limited liability company

The choice of entity has substantial tax and liability impact, and may affect the company's ability to raise money from investors. What follows is only a brief summary of the different entities available in most states of the U.S., and a few of the considerations in choosing among them. Before deciding on the form of your game development business, you should consult with your attorney or accountant and consider how the various trade-offs apply to your specific situation.

Sole Proprietorship

In a sole proprietorship, a single individual operates as a business, either under his or her own name or by filing a fictitious business statement (Joe Smith, doing business as "Incredibly Entertaining Software"). Except for filing a fictitious business name statement, no government filing or minimum tax payment is required for a sole proprietorship. You work on your own, hire people as necessary, and deduct your business expenses from your state and federal taxes.

The drawback to a sole proprietorship is that the owner is personally liable for all of the business's financial commitments, including all contracts, leases, and other obligations. This would include obligations that arise if someone is injured by one of your employees on company business. That risk of personal liability is often the motivation for a sole proprietor to form a corporation. Another motivation is that other business entities provide greater flexibility to raise money from investors. As a sole proprietor, you may convince your rich uncle to loan you $100,000 in seed money to start your title. Most investors, however, want to share in the upside appreciation of any start-up, so they want an equity ownership position in a corporation, partnership, or limited liability company.

General Partnership

In some respects, being a partner in a general partnership is like being a sole proprietor. Each partner is personally liable for the obligations of the business. The partners are taxed as individuals, reporting their share of the partnership's income and their share of the partnership's expenses. Forming a partnership does not require any legal formalities or government filings. In practice, however, the issues surrounding partnership are much more complicated than doing business on your own.

Joint Personal Liability

To the outside world, partners are a unified force. Each partner has the authority to make commitments for the partnership by his or her actions alone, and all partners are jointly and personally liable for all of the commitments made by each partner. So, if one day a partner impulsively purchases a graphics package for $40,000, the partnership will be obliged to pay that amount, even if everyone else thought it was a bad move. If the partnership doesn't have the money in the partnership accounts to pay for the software, each partner will be personally liable to the vendor *for the entire amount.* If only one partner has the personal assets to pay the debt, the vendor has the right to collect from that one partner. The partner would have the right to be reimbursed by the partnership, but, as far as the outside world is concerned, the risk and responsibility of *all* partnership actions lies with each individual partner.

Pitfalls in Forming a Partnership

Forming a partnership is very easy—almost scarily so. If two or more people work together for profit as co-owners of a business, they are partners—*whether they explicitly agree to be partners or not.* Partners that don't have a written agreement stating the terms of their deal will have those terms dictated by state law, even where the end result is unfair.

One term that will be imposed in the absence of a written agreement to the contrary is majority control of the partnership. The majority has the power to make business decisions for the partnership and each partner will have to pay his or her share of the cost of the decision, even if some partners disagree.

Another term imposed without a written agreement to the contrary is joint ownership. Joint ownership means each partner owns a pro-rata share of all of the assets of a partnership. Everything contributed by the partners that is used in the business and all of the income the partnership receives is split evenly between the partners, regardless of the value of the assets and services rendered by each individual partner.

Consider this scenario: Mark has owned a game development company (a sole proprietorship) for seven years. He owns a lot of equipment and has nurtured a solid, if small, client base. Edie is a marketing consultant. Mark and Edie agree to work together to expand the company but do not discuss the details of the deal. After one year, both Mark and Edie decide they should go their separate ways. What is Edie entitled to when the company breaks up? Her attorney says: "One-half of the com-

pany. The two were partners. Though Mark may have contributed more, each may be entitled to 50 percent of the company when the partnership ends."

The importance of getting an agreement in writing is covered in the chapter on legal issues, but the point of the story is this: Becoming partners should be a conscious and thoughtful decision. If you agree to be partners, your agreement about how profits, risks, and responsibilities are going to be shared needs to be *in writing* and signed by everyone involved.

For tax purposes, a partnership is thought of simply as a group of individuals, sharing in the profits and losses of the partnership. Each partner reports his or her share of the partnership's income and expenses on his or her individual tax return and pays the tax due on that amount. Though the partnership doesn't pay any tax itself, it has to file an informational return with the Internal Revenue Service, giving the income and loss attributable to each partner. As always, before deciding what contributions will be made by each partner, or how income and losses are going to be divided up, talk to an accountant or lawyer about the tax implications.

Limited Partnership

Limited partnerships are designed to encourage investment in partnerships. Similar to the way the corporation shields shareholders from liability, a *limited* partner's risk won't exceed his or her contribution as long as he or she does not play an active role in the business. But, active involvement may trigger the same personal liability faced by the general partners.

As in general partnerships, income and losses are passed through to both general and limited partners and reported on individual tax returns. Unlike general partnerships, state governments typically require a certificate of limited partnership, disclosing information, including, among other things, the names of each partner and what interests each has in the partnership.

Corporations

A corporation is a distinct legal entity, separate from the individuals who form, own, and run the business. The corporation provides some attractive benefits, but its legal requirements pose certain burdens.

Limited Liability of Shareholders

The main advantage of doing business as a corporation is limited liability. Unlike a general partnership or sole proprietorship, the corporation is solely responsible for its financial obligations, not its owners. The shareholders' only risk is the time and money each has contributed to the corporation.

Of course, every benefit has its price. To have the benefit of limited liability, a corporation must operate as a distinct entity, separate from its founders and managers. "Separateness" is achieved by following certain formalities, including corporate record keeping, annual shareholders and directors meetings with records (known as minutes), and certain shareholder and director voting procedures. Failure to respect these formalities may subject the owners of a corporation to legal liability.

Incorporating and Staying Incorporated

Each state has different requirements when you form a corporation. Generally speaking, the founders file articles of incorporation (often just a one page form) with the Secretary of State and, in many states, pay a yearly minimum corporate tax. The corporation will also need to apply for an employer identification number from the Internal Revenue Service to be used when dealing with the IRS.

Once incorporated, in addition to the internal record keeping that needs to be done, the state government requires yearly informational filings, including the names of the current officers and the address of the business's main office. This information, along with fees, will also be required by states in which the corporation does business, even though the main office is elsewhere.

Tax Issues

Standard "C" type corporations are also separate entities for tax purposes, which creates a potential disadvantage to doing business as a corporation—double taxation. The corporation pays income tax on its net income. If the corporation then pays any dividends to shareholders, that money is treated as income to the shareholders and taxed *again*. Since corporations can't deduct dividends to their shareholders, the effect is to tax the corporation's income twice, once at the corporate level and once at the individual shareholder level.

Typically, in a corporation with just a few shareholders who also work for the company, the double tax isn't a problem. Shareholders can take money from the company in the form of salaries. Since reasonable salaries are deducted by the corporation as a business expense, the income is taxed only at the individual level and the double tax is avoided. Note that, if those salaries are particularly high for the type of job performed, the Internal Revenue Service may decide that the company is avoiding tax and tax the corporation on the amount that exceeds a reasonable salary for the job. Shareholders may also be taxed if they get stock in the company in exchange for work they have done (that's compensation income).

S Corporations

One way to avoid the "double taxation" of a standard C corporation is to elect to be treated as a "S Corporation." (Named after everyone's favorite bedtime reading, subchapter S of the Internal Revenue Code.) An S Corporation pays no income tax at the corporate level. Instead, income or loss of an S Corporation is simply passed on directly to the shareholders to be reported on their individual income tax returns, avoiding double tax on the income. At the same time, like any other kind of corporation, the shareholders in an S Corporation are not personally liable for the company's debts and obligations.

The benefits of the S corporation are not available to every corporation. For example, an S corporation can't have more than 35 shareholders, all of whom have to be individual citizens (or resident aliens) of the United States. Partnerships and corporations cannot be shareholders in an S corporation. An S corporation can only issue one class of stock, meaning that each share of stock has the same right to dividends, and to the company's assets, if it goes out of business.

Also, an S corporation cannot have a subsidiary. Like the restriction on classes of stock, the S corporation has less flexibility in its business planning.

Limited Liability Company

Though a relatively new development, limited liability companies recognized in many states ("LLCs"), are already very popular, largely because they are less restrictive than both S corporations and limited partnerships. LLCs have limited liability like a corporation and the tax benefit of being taxed like a partnership. But LLCs do not have the same restrictions as S corporations: The owners can be any type of entity, not just individuals, and there is no maximum number of members. LLCs do not restrict how the owners' rights to money or liquidation proceeds are divided up. LLCs can own subsidiaries. Unlike general partnerships, the management of the business is not restricted to owners of the business; the owner can either manage the business him or herself or appoint management to handle the day to day operations of the business. Unlike limited partnerships, all of the members can be actively involved in the business without the risk of personal liability.

The downside is this: Forming an LLC entails more effort and expense than other types of companies. State laws typically require both the filing of a document called "articles of organization" and that owners sign an operating agreement establishing such terms as the voting rights of members, sharing of profit and losses, contribution obligations, and restrictions on transfers of interests.

APPENDIX B

Contracts for Game Developers

EMPLOYMENT AGREEMENT

THIS EMPLOYMENT AGREEMENT (this "Agreement") is entered into by and between ______________, a corporation to be organized under the laws of the State of <state> with its principal place of business at ______________________ (the "Company"), and _______________, an individual whose current residence is at _________________ ("Employee").

RECITALS

A. The Company is engaged in the business of producing interactive computer software.

B. The Company desires to hire Employee and Employee desires to be an employee of the Company.

NOW, THEREFORE, for mutual consideration, the receipt and adequacy of which is hereby acknowledged, the parties agree as follows:

1. **Company's Trade Secrets:** In performance of Employee's job duties as may be designated by the Company from time to time, Employee will be exposed to the Company's Trade Secrets. "Trade Secrets" means information or material that is commercially valuable to the Company and not generally known in the industry. This includes:

(a) any and all versions of the Company's proprietary computer software (including source code and object code), hardware, firmware and documentation;

(b) technical information concerning the Company's products and services, including product data and specifications, diagrams, flow charts, drawings, test results, know-how, processes, inventions, research projects and product development;

(c) information concerning the Company's business, including cost information, profits, sales information, accounting and unpublished financial information, business plans, markets and marketing methods, customer lists and customer information, purchasing techniques, supplier lists and supplier information and advertising strategies;

(d) information concerning the Company's employees, including their salaries, strengths, weaknesses and skills;

(e) information submitted by the Company's customers, suppliers, employees, consultants or co-venturers with the Company for study, evaluation or use; and

(f) any other information not generally known to the public which, if misused or disclosed, could reasonably be expected to adversely affect the Company's business.

2. **Nondisclosure of Trade Secrets**: Employee will keep the Company's Trade Secrets (and Trade Secrets of any customer contracting with the Company), whether or not prepared or developed by Employee, in the strictest confidence. Employee will not use or disclose such secrets to others without the Company's written consent, except when necessary to perform Employee's job. Employee agrees that any customer, publisher or other third party who provides confidential information to the Company is an intended third party beneficiary of this provision. However, Employee shall have no obligation to treat as confidential any information which:

(a) was in Employee's possession or known to Employee, without an obligation to keep it confidential, before such information was disclosed to Employee by the Company;

(b) is or becomes public knowledge through a source other than Employee and through no fault of Employee's;

(c) is or becomes lawfully available to Employee from a source other than the Company; or

(d) is disclosed pursuant to a requirement of a governmental agency or as otherwise required by any court of competent jurisdiction.

3. **No Conflicting Obligations**: Employee's performance of this Agreement and as an employee of the Company does not and will not breach any agreement to keep in confidence proprietary information, knowledge or data acquired by Employee prior to Employee's employment with the Company. Employee will not disclose to the Company, or induce the Company to use, any confidential or proprietary information or material belonging to any previous employer or other person or entity. Employee is not a party to any other agreement which will interfere with Employee's full compliance with this Agreement. Employee will not enter into any agreement, whether written or oral, in conflict with the provisions of this Agreement.

4. **Return of Materials:** When Employee's employment with the Company ends, for whatever reason, Employee will promptly deliver to the Company all originals and copies of all documents, records, software programs, media and other materials containing any of the Company's Trade Secrets. Employee will also return to the Company all equipment, files, software programs and other personal property belonging to the Company or to any of its customers.

5. **Confidentiality Obligation Survives Employment:** Employee's obligation to maintain the confidentiality and security of the Company's Trade Secrets continues even after Employee's employment with the Company ends and continues for so long as such material remains a Trade Secret. This Agreement does not in any way restrict Employee's right or the Company's right to terminate Employee's employment at any time, for any reason or no reason.

6. **Computer Programs Are Works Made for Hire:** Company may ask, as part of Employee's job duties, Employee to create, or contribute to the creation of, computer programs, audiovisual works, documentation, artwork and other copyrightable works (collectively called "Work Product"). Employee agrees that any and all Work Product shall be "works made for hire" and that the Company shall own all the copyright rights in such works. IF AND TO THE EXTENT ANY SUCH MATERIAL DOES NOT SATISFY THE LEGAL REQUIREMENTS TO CONSTITUTE A WORK MADE FOR HIRE, EMPLOYEE HEREBY ASSIGNS ALL RIGHT, TITLE AND INTERESTS TO ALL EMPLOYEE'S COPYRIGHT AND OTHER INTELLECTUAL PROPERTY RIGHTS IN THE WORK PRODUCT TO THE COMPANY.

7. **Disclosure of Developments:** While Employee is employed by the Company, Employee will promptly inform the Company of the full details of all Employee's works of authorship, new or useful art, inventions, discoveries, findings, improvements, designs, innovations and ideas (collectively called "Developments") -- whether or not the Developments are patentable, copyrightable or otherwise protectable -- that Employee conceives, completes or reduces to practice (whether individually or in collaboration with others) and which:

(a) relate to the Company's present or prospective business, or actual or demonstrably anticipated research and development; or

(b) result from any work Employee does using any equipment, facilities, materials, Trade Secrets or personnel of the Company; or

(c) result from or are suggested by any work that Employee may do for the Company.

8. **Assignment of Developments**: Employee hereby assigns to the Company or the Company's designee, Employee's entire right, title and interest in all of the following, that Employee conceives or make (whether alone or with others) while employed by the Company:

(a) all Developments;

(b) all copyrights, Trade Secrets, trademarks and mask work rights in Developments; and

(c) all patent applications filed and patents granted on any Developments, including those in foreign countries.

9. **Waiver of Rights**: In the event Employee has any right in and to the Work Product or Developments that cannot be assigned to the Company, Employee hereby unconditionally and irrevocably (a) waives the enforcement of all such rights, and all claims and causes of action of any kind with respect to any of the foregoing against the Company, its distributors and customers, whether now known or hereafter to become known, and (b) agrees, at the request and expense of the Company and its respective successors and assigns, to consent to, and to join in, any action to enforce such rights or to procure a waiver of such rights from the holders of such rights.

10. **License**: In the event Employee has any rights in and to the Work Product or the Developments that cannot be assigned to the Company and cannot be waived, Employee hereby grants to the Company, and its respective successors and assigns, an exclusive, worldwide, royalty-free license during the term of the rights to reproduce, distribute, modify, publicly perform and publicly display, with the right to sublicense and assign such rights in and to the Work Product or the Developments including, without limitation, the right to use in any way whatsoever the Work Product or the Developments. Each of Company's clients, customers and business partners is an intended third party beneficiary of this provision and may independently enforce Employee's obligations hereunder.

11. **No Retention of Rights**: Employee retains no rights to use the Work Product or the Developments and agrees not to challenge the validity of the ownership by the Company of the Work Product or the Developments.

12. **Royalties**: Employee's compensation from the Company may include potential royalty payments, as set forth in any separate letter agreement between the Company and Employee, and if there is currently such an agreement, it will be attached hereto as Exhibit A. Notwithstanding any such agreement, Employee understands that

Employee is an "at will" employee, who may be terminated at any time by Company, and that Employee has no right to be employed for a specific term and no right to insist on specific grounds for termination.

13. **Execution of Documents:** Both while employed by the Company and afterwards, Employee agrees to execute and aid in the preparation of any papers that the Company may consider necessary or helpful to obtain or maintain any patents, copyrights, trademarks or other proprietary rights at no charge to the Company, but at the Company's expense.

14. **Appointment of Attorney-In-Fact:** In the event that the Company is unable for any reason whatsoever to secure Employee's signature to any lawful and necessary document required to apply for or execute any patent, copyright or other applications with respect to any of the Work Product or the Developments (including improvements, renewals, extensions, continuations, divisions or continuations in part hereof), Employee hereby irrevocably appoints the Company and its duly authorized officers and agents as Employee's agents and attorneys-in-fact to execute and file any such application and to do all other lawfully permitted acts to further the prosecution and issuance of patents, copyrights or other rights thereon with the same legal force and effect as if executed by Employee.

15. **Conflict of Interest:** During Employee's employment by the Company, Employee will not engage in any business activity competitive with the Company's business activities.

16. **Noninterference with Company Employees:** While employed by the Company, Employee will not:

(a) induce, or attempt to induce, any Company employee to quit the Company's employ;

(b) recruit or hire away any Company employee; or

(c) hire or engage any Company employee or former employee whose employment with the Company ended less than six months before the date of such hiring or engagement.

17. **Enforcement:** Employee agrees that in the event of a breach or threatened breach of this Agreement, money damages would be an inadequate remedy and extremely difficult to measure. Employee agrees, therefore, that the Company shall be entitled to an injunction to restrain Employee from such breach or threatened

breach. Nothing in this Agreement shall be construed as preventing the Company from pursuing any remedy at law or in equity for any breach or threatened breach.

18. **Assignment**: This Agreement may be assigned by the Company. Employee may not assign or delegate Employee's duties under this Agreement without the Company's prior written approval. This Agreement shall be binding upon Employee's heirs, successors, and permitted assignees.

19. **Governing Law**: This Agreement is made and shall be construed and enforced in accordance with the laws of the State of <state>.

20. **Arbitration**: In the event of any dispute in connection with this Agreement, the Parties agree to resolve the dispute by binding arbitration in <city, state>, under the Commercial Arbitration Rules of the American Arbitration Association ("AAA"), with a single arbitrator familiar with software development disputes appointed by AAA. In the event of any dispute, the prevailing party shall be entitled to its reasonable attorneys' fees and costs from the other party, whether or not the matter is litigated or arbitrated to a final judgment or award.

21. **Choice of Forum**: The parties hereby submit to the jurisdiction of, and waive any venue objections against, the United States District Court for the __________ District of <state>, __________ Division and the Superior and Municipal Courts of the State of <state>, __________ County, in any litigation arising out of this Agreement.

22. **Severability**: If any provision of this Agreement is determined to be invalid or unenforceable, the remainder shall be unaffected and shall be enforceable against both the Company and Employee.

23. **Entire Agreement**: This Agreement supersedes and replaces all prior agreements or understandings, oral or written, between the Company and Employee, except for (a) prior confidentiality agreements, if any, Employee has signed relating to information not covered by this Agreement, and (b) a letter agreement in the form attached hereto as Exhibit A.

24. **Modification**: This Agreement may not be modified except by a writing signed both by the Company and Employee.

25. **Employee Review and Receipt of Agreement**: Employee acknowledges that Employee has carefully read and considered all provisions of this Agreement and agrees that all of the restrictions set forth herein are fair and reasonably required to

protect the Company's interests. Employee acknowledges that Employee has received a copy of this Agreement as signed by Employee.

26. **Notice Pursuant to State Law:** Employee acknowledges that Employee has been notified of its rights, if any, under California Labor Code Section 2870, "Employment Agreements: Assignment of Rights," and that Employee has had a full and fair opportunity to read the provisions of Section 2870, a copy of which is attached hereto as Exhibit B. Employee understands that this Agreement does not apply to any invention that qualifies fully under the provisions of Section 2870. This section shall serve as written notice to Employee as required by California Labor Code Section 2872.

27. **Prior Developments:** As a matter of record, Employee has identified all prior developments ("Prior Developments") that have been conceived or reduced to practice or learned by Employee, alone or jointly with others, before Employee's employment with the Company, which Employee desires to remove from the operation of this Agreement. The Prior Developments are listed on attached Exhibit C. Employee represents and warrants that this list is complete. If there is no such list, Employee represents that it has made no such Prior Developments at the time of signing this Agreement.

[EMPLOYEE]:

Date: ____________________ ______________________________
Employee's Signature

____
Typed or Printed Name

[COMPANY]:

Date: ____________________ ______________________________
Signature

____
Typed or Printed Name

____
Title

EXHIBIT A

[FORM OF COMPENSATION LETTER AGREEMENT]

EXHIBIT B

California Labor Code Section 2870 provides as follows:

(a) Any provision in an employment agreement that provides that an employee shall assign, or offer to assign, any of his or her rights in an invention to his or her employer shall not apply to an invention that the employee developed entirely on his or her own time without using the employer's equipment, supplies, facilities, or trade secret information except for those inventions that either:

(1) Relate at the time of conception or reduction to practice of the invention to the employer's business, or actual or demonstrably anticipated research or development of the employer or

(2) Result from any work performed by the employee for the employer.

(b) To the extent a provision in an employment agreement purports to require an employee to assign an invention otherwise excluded from being required to be assigned under subdivision (a), the provision is against the public policy of this state and is unenforceable.

EXHIBIT C

PRIOR DEVELOPMENTS

[List of all Prior Developments; if blank write "none"]

NON-DISCLOSURE AND CONFIDENTIALITY AGREEMENT

____, together with any and all parents, subsidiaries, affiliates, consultants, employees, agents and all similar persons or entities, (collectively "Recipient") agrees that, with respect to certain Confidential Information (as defined below) furnished to it by the person identified as Discloser on the signature page hereof ("Discloser"): Recipient will maintain such information in confidence in the same manner and to the same extent Recipient protects Recipient's own confidential and/or proprietary information of a similar nature. By way of illustration, and not as a limitation, unless Discloser grants permission, the Confidential Information shall not be disclosed to any person except Recipient's employees (and only on a need-to-know basis where the employee is made aware of the non-disclosure requirement) nor shall the Recipient utilize the Confidential Information for its own purpose except to further the discussions and/or negotiations between the parties and to provide services or materials to Discloser. The individual signing this agreement as Recipient shall be responsible for any breach of this Agreement by any and all parents, subsidiaries, affiliates, consultants, employees, agents and all similar persons or entities.

Recipient agrees to maintain the secrecy of Confidential Information and to prevent its unauthorized dissemination and use; provided, however, that Recipient need not maintain the confidence of Confidential Information that: 1) is generally known or available by publication, commercial use or otherwise through no fault of Recipient; 2) is known by Recipient before the disclosure and is not subject to restriction; 3) is lawfully obtained from a third party who has the right to make such disclosure; 4) is required to be disclosed by law or court order; or 5) is released for publication or disclosure by Discloser in writing.

For the purpose of this Agreement, "Confidential Information" includes any trade secrets, knowledge, data or other proprietary or confidential information relating to products, processes, know-how, designs, developmental or experimental work, computer programs, databases, other original works or authorship, customer lists, business plans, marketing plans and strategies, financial information or other subject matter included in or derived from the document or set of documents identified as Source Document(s) on the signature page hereof or otherwise provided by Discloser to Recipient orally or in further documentation resulting from the parties' discussions and/or negotiations based upon the Source Documents or upon any project that they are working on together.

Recipient understands and agrees that Discloser is providing Confidential Information to Recipient in reliance on Recipient's agreement contained herein, and Recipient will be fully responsible to Discloser for any damage or harm caused to Discloser by any breach of this agreement by Recipient.

Recipient agrees that Discloser is entitled to equitable relief, including injunction and specific performance, in the event of any breach of this Agreement by Recipient, in addition to all other remedies available at law or in equity.

At any time, upon request by Discloser, Recipient will within five (5) business days return all Confidential Information furnished to Recipient, and any copies or extracts thereof, and destroy any notes or analyses which are derived from or contain any Confidential Information.

Recipient's duty to protect Discloser's Confidential Information expires ten (10) years from the date of this Agreement.

This Agreement may only be modified in a writing signed by both parties.

This Agreement shall be governed by and construed in accordance with the laws of the State of <state>.

This Agreement may be executed in counterparts.

RECIPIENT:	DISCLOSER:
By: ______________________	______________________
Title: ______________________	Date: ______________________
Date: ______________________	

SOURCE DOCUMENT(S):____

____

____

____

INDEPENDENT CONTRACTOR AGREEMENT

THIS INDEPENDENT CONTRACTOR AGREEMENT (this "Agreement") is entered into by and between ______________________________, a corporation to be organized under the laws of the State of <state> with its principal place of business at ______________________________________, (hereinafter referred to as "Company") and ______________________________ [with its principal place of business at/currently residing at] ______________________________ (hereinafter referred to as "Independent Consultant").

RECITALS

A. Independent Consultant desires to provide Company services for fees hereinafter agreed to by Independent Consultant and Company.

B. Company is engaged in the business of producing interactive computer software.

C. Company desires to obtain a high level of professional skill from Independent Consultant.

NOW, THEREFORE, for mutual consideration, the receipt and adequacy of which is hereby acknowledged by the parties, the parties agree as follows:

I. INDEPENDENT CONSULTANT

Independent Consultant hereby acknowledges that it is engaged in the independent business of computer programming consulting, and will perform its obligations under this Agreement as an Independent Consultant and not as an employee of Company. Independent Consultant will be solely responsible for all matters relating to payments to any employees Independent Consultant may have, including compliance with workers compensation laws, payment of unemployment, disability insurance, social security, income tax withholding, and all other taxes assessed on Independent Consultant or any of its employees under federal, state, and local laws, rules or regulations governing such matters.

II. COMPENSATION

Independent Consultant is to be compensated pursuant to the terms of a letter agreement between Company and Independent Consultant, in the form attached hereto as Exhibit A.

III. TERM

The term of this Agreement shall run from the date of execution for a period of ______________ (___) months, unless earlier terminated by written notice given by either party, with or without cause, or under other provisions of this Agreement.

IV. INDEMNIFICATION IN GENERAL

Independent Consultant shall indemnify, defend, and hold harmless Company, its employees, officers, directors and agents (collectively, the "Indemnified Parties") from any loss, liability, cost, damage, claim, or expense, including but not limited to liability as a result of the death, personal injury, or emotional injury of any person, or damage to, or loss of or destruction of, any property arising out of, resulting from, or in connection with the breach of Independent Consultant's obligations, representations or warranties set forth in this Agreement, whether such breach was caused by the acts or omissions of Independent Consultant or any of its employees, officers, directors or agents, except to the extent that such loss, liability, costs, damage, claim or expense arises from the gross negligence or willful misconduct of any of the Indemnified Parties. Upon request of any Indemnified Party, Independent Consultant shall, at no cost or expense to such Indemnified Party, defend any claim or suit asserting a claim for any such loss, liability, cost, damage, claim or expense.

V. INDEMNIFICATION FOR PAYROLL TAXES

In the event that Independent Consultant is found to be an employee of Company by any court, state, or federal agency, and as a result thereof Company is assessed any liability for payroll taxes and/or withholding of income and/or social security taxes, Independent Consultant agrees to indemnify and hold harmless Company for the total amount for all sums required to be paid by Company as a result of such liability. Such indemnification includes, but is not limited to, payroll taxes, amounts to be withheld, penalties, and interest. Company may withhold any such sums from amounts due Independent Consultant under Section II above, from and after such time as the Independent Consultant is found to be an employee of Company.

VI. PROPRIETARY RIGHTS OF THE PARTIES

1. Independent Consultant promises and agrees that it will promptly and fully inform and disclose to Company all computer program designs, creations, improvements, and discoveries that Independent Consultant conceives, completes, or reduces to practice during the term of this Agreement which pertain or relate to the business of the Company or to any experimental work carried on by the Company ("Work Product"), whether such Work Product is produced by Independent Consultant alone or with others and whether or not produced during regular working hours.

2. Independent Consultant agrees that any and all intellectual properties, including but not limited to all ideas, concepts, themes, inventions, designs, improvements, and discoveries conceived, developed, or written by Independent Consultant, either individually or in collaboration with others, pursuant to this Agreement which pertain or relate to the business of the Company or to any experimental work carried on by the Company ("Work Product Rights"), shall belong to and be the sole and exclusive property of Company.

3. Independent Consultant agrees that all rights in all intellectual properties as prepared by it pursuant to this Agreement, including, without limitation, patent rights and copyrights applicable to the Work Product or Work Product Rights, and shall belong exclusively to the Company, shall constitute "works made for hire."

4. Independent Consultant hereby irrevocably assigns, conveys and otherwise transfers to Company, and its respective successors and assigns, all rights, title and interests worldwide in and to the Work Product, Work Product Rights and all proprietary rights therein, including, without limitation, all copyrights, trademarks, design patents, trade secret rights, moral rights, and all contract and licensing rights, and all claims and causes of action of any kind with respect to any of the foregoing, whether now known or hereafter to become known. In the event Independent Consultant has any rights in and to the Work Product or Work Product Rights that cannot be assigned to Company, Independent Consultant hereby unconditionally and irrevocably waives the enforcement of all such rights, and all claims and causes of action of any kind with respect to any of the foregoing against Company, its distributors and customers, whether now known or hereafter to become known and agrees, at the request and expense of Company and its respective successors and assigns, to consent to and join in any action to enforce such rights and to procure a waiver of such rights from the holders of such rights and to procure a waiver of such rights from the holders or such rights. In the event Independent Consultant has any rights in and to the Work Product that cannot be assigned to Company and cannot be waived, Independent Consultant hereby grants to Company, and its respective successors and assigns, an exclusive, worldwide, royalty-free license during the term of the rights to reproduce, distribute, modify, publicly perform and publicly display, with the right to sublicense and assign such rights in and to the Work Product including, without limitation, the right to use in any way whatsoever the Work Product. Independent Consultant retains no rights to use the Work Product and agrees not to challenge the validity of the ownership by Company in the Work Product.

5. Independent Contractor acknowledges in the event Independent Contractor is deemed to be an employee of Company, it has been notified of its rights, if any, under California Labor Code Section 2870, "Employment Agreements;

Assignment of Rights," and that it has had full and fair opportunity to read such code attached hereto as Exhibit B.

6. Independent Consultant further agrees to assist Company with regard to intellectual property or rights created under this Agreement in obtaining patents on all inventions, designs, improvements, and discoveries that are patentable or copyright registration on all works of creation that are copyrightable, and to execute all documents and do all things necessary to vest Company with full and exclusive title and protect against infringement by others. In the event that Company is unable for any reason whatsoever to secure signature to any lawful and necessary document required to apply for or execute any patent, copyright or other applications with respect to any Work Product or Work Product Right (including improvements, renewals, extensions, continuations, divisions or continuations in part thereof), Independent Consultant hereby irrevocably designates and appoints Company and its duly authorized officers and agents as its agents and attorneys-in-fact to act for and in its behalf and instead of Independent Consultant, to execute and file any such application and to do all other lawfully permitted acts to further the prosecution and issuance of patents, copyrights or other rights thereon with the same legal force and effect as if executed by Independent Consultant.

7. The other provisions of this Section VI shall not apply to intellectual properties or rights therein derived from Independent Consultant's activities or employment prior to the time it entered into an independent contractor relationship with Company ("Preexisting Rights"). Company agrees that those Preexisting Rights are and shall continue to be the exclusive property of Independent Consultant. However, if Independent Consultant uses such Preexisting Rights in the project on which it is working for Company, Independent Consultant, hereby grants to Company a royalty-free, worldwide, perpetual, irrevocable, non-exclusive license, with the right to sublicense, to reproduce, distribute, modify, publicly perform and publicly display such inventions and copyrighted works or other Preexisting Rights in connection with Company's products.

8. Independent Consultant during the term of this Agreement will have access to and become acquainted with various trade secrets, consisting of devices, secret inventions, computer programs, processes, and compilations of information, records, and specifications, which are owned by Company and which are regularly used in the operation of the business of Company. Independent Consultant shall not disclose any of these trade secrets, directly or indirectly, or use them in any way, either during the term of this Agreement or for a period of five (5) years thereafter, except as required in carrying out its obligations under this Agreement. Each of Company's clients, customers and business partners is an intended third party

beneficiary of this confidentiality provision and may enforce Independent Contractor's obligations hereunder. All files, records, documents, drawings, specifications, equipment and similar items relating to the business of Company, whether prepared by Independent Consultant or otherwise coming into its possession, shall remain the exclusive property of Company and shall not be removed under any circumstances from the premises where the work of Company is being carried on, without the prior written consent of Company.

9. In the course of the duties described herein, Independent Consultant will be handling confidential data of customers of Company. All such data is confidential and shall not be disclosed, directly or indirectly, or used by Independent Consultant in any way, either during the term of this Agreement or at any time thereafter, except as required in the course of carrying out its obligations under this Agreement.

10. Independent Consultant agrees to deliver promptly all of Company's property, and all copies of Company's property or the confidential data of Company's customers in Independent Consultant's possession to Company at any time upon Company's request.

VII. <u>OBLIGATIONS OF INDEPENDENT CONSULTANT</u>

1. Independent Consultant acknowledges and agrees that the sale or unauthorized use or disclosure of any of Company's trade secrets obtained by Independent Consultant during the course of its work under this Agreement, including information concerning Company's current or any future and proposed work, customers, services, or products, the facts that any such work, services or products are planned, under consideration or in production, as well as any descriptions thereof, constitute unfair competition. Independent Consultant promises and agrees not to engage in such unfair competition with Company at any time whether during or following the completion of its work with Company.

2. Independent Consultant acknowledges and agrees that the above-referenced information constitutes valuable trade secrets of Company and that any unauthorized copying, disclosure or use of such information by Independent Consultant, or any of its employees, agents and/or contractors would cause Company irreparable harm for which its remedies at law shall be inadequate. Independent Consultant agrees that Company shall have the right, in addition to any other remedies available to it, to the issuance of immediate injunctive relief, without bond, enjoining any breach or threatened breach of Independent Consultant's obligations set forth in this <u>Section VII</u>. The parties hereto agree that the non-prevailing party shall pay for any and all damages, costs, and expenses, including but not limited to

reasonable fees for any attorneys, incurred by the prevailing party in seeking and/or obtaining injunctive or other relief for the enforcement of any of the provisions of this Section VII subsequent to the expiration of termination hereof.

3. Independent Consultant represents that its performance under this Agreement does not and will not breach any agreement to keep in confidence proprietary information, knowledge or data it acquired before entering into this Agreement. Independent Consultant represents that it is not, and will not become, a party to any other agreement that will interfere with full compliance with this Agreement.

VIII. MODIFICATIONS

The provisions of this Agreement shall not be modified without the express written consent of all parties.

IX. ADDITIONAL EXPENSES

The obligations expressed herein are in addition to the obligations contained in any other agreements between the parties regarding subject matter not covered in this Agreement, including the following, if signed by all parties: joint venture agreement, consulting and non-disclosure agreement, and various letter agreements regarding fees for services rendered. The provisions of said agreements shall remain in effect, except as specifically modified or superseded by the terms of this Agreement.

X. ARBITRATION

In the event of any dispute in connection with this agreement, the parties agree to resolve the dispute by binding arbitration in <city>, <state>, under the Commercial Arbitration Rules of the American Arbitration Association ("AAA"), with a single arbitrator familiar with software development disputes appointed by AAA. In the event of any dispute, the prevailing party shall be entitled to its reasonable attorneys' fees and costs from the other party, whether or not the matter is litigated or arbitrated to a final judgment or award.

XI. VENUE

The proper venue of any action or arbitration arising from this Agreement shall be ______________ <county>, <state>.

XII. GOVERNING LAW

The laws of the State of <state> shall apply to any controversy arising from this Agreement.

XIII. SURVIVAL

Independent Consultant's obligations under Section IV, V, VI, and VII of this Agreement shall, without limitation, survive termination of this Agreement.

XIV. ENTIRE AGREEMENT

This Agreement supersedes and replaces all prior agreements or understandings, oral or written, between Company and Independent Consultant relating to the subject matter hereof, except for prior confidentiality agreements and for the letter agreement regarding compensation in the form attached hereto as Exhibit A.

Dated: ________________ [Company]

By: ________________

Name: ________________

Title: ________________

Dated: ________________ [Independent Consultant]

By: ________________

Name: ________________

Title: ________________

EXHIBIT A

[FORM OF COMPENSATION LETTER AGREEMENT]

EXHIBIT B

California Labor Code Section 2870 provides as follows:

(a) Any provision in an employment agreement that provides that an employee shall assign, or offer to assign, any of his or her rights in an invention to his or her employer shall not apply to an invention that the employee developed entirely on his or her own time without using the employer's equipment, supplies, facilities, or trade secret information except for those inventions that either:

(1) Relate at the time of conception or reduction to practice of the invention to the employer's business, or actual or demonstrably anticipated research or development of the employer or

(2) Result from any work performed by the employee for the employer.

(b) To the extent a provision in an employment agreement purports to require an employee to assign an invention otherwise excluded from being required to be assigned under subdivision (a), the provision is against the public policy of this state and is unenforceable.

WORK FOR HIRE AGREEMENT, RELEASE, AND ASSIGNMENT
[Work on Speculation]

The undersigned, ___________________ , ("Professional"), for good and valuable consideration, receipt of which is hereby acknowledged, hereby agrees with ___________________________, (together with all of their successors and assigns "Developer") as follows:

Professional agrees to perform a minimum of __ hours of services and to deliver the materials identified on Exhibit 1 (the "Materials"), all as a work for hire under the Copyright Act, specially ordered and commissioned by Developer in connection with an audio-visual work (together with all future derivative works, the "Work"). Developer and Professional agree that if Developer is able to secure funding to complete the development of the Work, they will attempt to reach agreement on a mutually satisfactory arrangement to compensate Professional for Professional's efforts in connection with the work after that date. In any event, however, if the parties cannot agree on further compensation arrangements, then if the Work is publicly released, Developer must nevertheless pay Professional $___ for the services performed and the Materials delivered under this Agreement.

Professional assigns to Developer all rights, title and interest, whether now or hereafter existing, and of every kind and character in all media now existing or hereafter coming into existence (collectively, the "Rights") in the Materials or the Work. These Rights include, but are not limited to, the right to worldwide copyright and to renew said copyright as required; the right to incorporate the Material into the Work and all other works of Developer and to make any adaptation, revision, or translation thereof; the right to use or omit, within the discretion of Developer, Professional's name, from and in connection with the Work; and the right to use the Material in any media now known or hereafter developed and in connection with promotion or advertising of the Work or otherwise. These Rights are assignable and otherwise conveyable by Developer in the context of publication, distribution and promotion of the Work or otherwise in whatever form and at whatever time as deemed appropriate by Developer.

Upon reasonable request by Developer, Professional shall execute and deliver such additional instruments of assignment as may be reasonably necessary to carrying out the intent of this Agreement. Professional hereby expressly waives any and all "artist's rights" or "moral rights" he or she might otherwise have in the Materials or the Work. Professional acknowledges that at all times, Professional is an independent contractor and not an agent, employee or representative of Developer.

Date: ________________________ Professional

By: ___________________________

Name: ________________________

Date: ________________________ Developer

By: ___________________________

Name: ________________________

EXHIBIT 1

Materials

APPENDIX C

Conferences and Trade Shows

Otherwise known as deductible "vacations" in great cities, the conferences and trade shows presented in this appendix are significant for their content, geographic location, or the crowd they attract. To further your career as a game developer, you should consider attending one or more of these events during the year.

The Basic Stuff—Costs, Locals, and Dates

Instead of giving you all of the details about each conference, I've provided only the basic contact information and some local information. This is because a lot of these shows vary in pricing, locale, and dates from year to year. The average range in price seems to be $200 to $1,000 depending on the specific show, the time you register (getting in early can save you big bucks), and whether you might be a member or associate of the show's sponsor.

Many of these shows and conferences are closed shows. Thus you should call ahead to check on the requirements for attending. For example, if you show up at a show like CES and you don't have some form of proof you are involved in the consumer electronics industry, you may not be able to get in.

Specific Game Conferences

Computer Game Developers Conference
Contact: Miller Freeman, Inc.
Location: Santa Clara, CA
Phone: 800 441-8826 **Fax:** 415 905-2222

The Computer Game Developers Conference is the major show of its kind anywhere in the world. It was started over ten years ago in game developer's Chris Crawford's house. In 1995, the conference was attended by over 2,500 people—an indication that the game development industry has really expanded.

The conference features speeches, roundtables, and in-depth sessions on artwork, design, programming, management, music, and much more. Also included is an expo featuring many development-related companies such as Intel, Microsoft, SoftImage, SGI, and others. For people looking for a new job, the conference features a jobs expo and many companies take suites to schmooze and talk deals.

This is the single most important conference you can attend as a game developer.

Creating Interactive Entertainment
East Coast Developers Conference
Contact: Alexander & Associates
Location: New York, NY
Phone: 212 622-2333

This show is not affiliated at all with the CGDC or the CGDA. It is produced by the market research firm of Alexander and Associates in New York. It provides a good way for East Coast-based developers to meet and mix, especially those who for one reason or another can't go to the Computer Game Developers Conference.

This show tends to feature not only developers but lots of representatives from the large New York area publishing conglomerates.

Electronic Entertainment Expo (E3)
Contact: Infotainment World, IDSA
Location: Los Angeles, CA
Phone: 617 361-8000 **Fax:** 617 361-3389

The first Electronic Entertainment Expo (E3) was held last spring in Los Angeles with huge success. Created at the behest of Sega, Nintendo, and other console mainstays, this show was born to give consumer game and multimedia companies their own focused trade show instead of the more general, crowded, and expensive Consumer Electronics Show.

E3 is now the new king of the game shows. There's no doubt that it will grow significantly as companies who didn't attend last year realize it can't be missed. With its heavy game focus and lower costs than CES, this is the show we've been waiting for. Now if we could only get the Game Developers Conference and E3 to be held one right after the other all, us non-Californians could save some serious airfare!

GENCON
GenCon Game Festival Headquarters
201 Sheridan Springs Road
P.O. Box 756
Lake Geneva, WI 53147-0756

GENCON is the original gaming convention dating back to the days of pen and paper and board games. Why is this conference of interest to game developers making products for consoles and computers? Well, many games today are still based on the designs and practices employed by their paper-based parents.

If you are creating role-playing based products, this conference may be worthwhile since there is a lot of cross-over and you may pick up some ideas from the people who attend this conference.

Milia 96
Contact: Reed Midem Organization
Location: Cannes France
Phone: 212 689-4220 **Fax:** 212 689-4348

Milia is a major multimedia conference for Europe and the World that brings together developers, rights holders, film, art, book, video, computers, and more. Held on the French Riviera, it's quickly becoming a major event as many different types of media industries continue to converge.

General Computer/Electronic Shows

CES and CES Interactive—The Digital Destination
Contact: Electronic Industries Association
Location: Spring: Orlando, FL; Winter: Las Vegas, NV
Phone: 703 907-7600 **Fax:** 703 907-7601

The Consumer Electronics Show is the biggest electronics trade show of its kind. Until recently, many game-oriented, especially console-oriented, companies would display their products at CES. However, now that the Electronic Entertainment Expo (E3) has become the leading show for game companies, the added costs of the CES show have made some of these companies re-consider attending.

CES is fighting back though and has launched a co-show called CES Interactive to provide an game/interactive outlet that may encourage game developers to attend.

Comdex
Contact: Softbank, Inc.
Location: Winter: Las Vegas; Spring: Atlanta
Phone: 617 449-6600 **Fax:** 617 449-6617

Comdex is the largest computer-oriented trade show of its kind. I've listed it here although it does not have major significance for game developers. You may want to attend it to learn about the latest products, hardware, and peripherals in the computer world. But keep in mind that it is not a place to show off games or schmooze with other game company execs.

Always held in conjunction with Comdex is Microsoft's Windows World, a companion show that was set up to really push the Windows agenda. Again, the only significance this show has for game developers is for learning about the latest and greatest in software and computer hardware—not games.

European Computer Trade Show Autumn
Contact: N/A
Location: London, England (Held twice yearly in the Spring and Fall)
Phone: 800 321-3269 2

The ECTS is the largest computer show in Europe of interest to game developers. Many developers use this show to display their games to retailers and consumers in Europe. Although I have not attended this show myself, my compatriots in Europe tell me it is a great schmoozing event and learning experience.

MacWorld
Contact: MacWorld and Mitch Hall Associates
Location: Summer: Boston, MA; Winter: San Francisco, CA
Phone: 617 440-2729 **Fax:** 617 440-0357

If you're doing anything with or for a Mac, this is the conference and trade show to attend.

Software Development Oriented Shows

SIGGRAPH
Contact: ACM/Siggraph
Location: Varies year to year (Held in the Fall mostly)
For Info: http://www.siggraph.org

Although SIGGRAPH is not a show of direct gaming interests, it is *the* show for graphics and animation. SIGGRAPH has for years been the show for showing off the state of the art in graphic programming, artistry, and technology.

Although it's not a game development show, its graphical focus is essential to the process of game development and game companies are encouraged to attend.

Of specific interest are the presentation of programming papers on real time 3D graphics and animation (many new ideas are first talked about here) and the expo hall filled with the latest and greatest in high-tech graphical production hardware and software. (I remember seeing VR gear here before anywhere else back in 1988.)

Software Development
Contact: Miller Freeman, Inc.
Location: San Francisco, CA (Held in the Spring)
Phone: 415 905-2784 **Fax:** 415 905-2222

This is the big general programming conference and trade show from the group that brings you *Dr. Dobbs Journal.* Software Development features key technical sessions on all sorts of cutting edge topics concerning the crafting of computer software.

Software Development is held once a year in the Spring in San Francisco and recently a European Software Development conference was launched.

Macromedia International User Conference and Exhibition
Contact: Macromedia
Location: San Francisco, CA (Usually held in the Fall)
Phone: 800 287-7141 **Fax:** 203 840-5660

Macromedia's Director product is a major tool for creating software and has grown in use with over 300,000 developers. This conference sponsored in part by Macromedia is a key destination for even casual users of their products.

DV and CD-ROM Expo
Contact: *DV* Magazine, *CD-ROM Professional* Magazine, Mitch Hall Associates
Locations: Various locations (Usually held in the Fall)
Phone: 617 440-2729 **Fax:** 617 440-0357

From two magazines that focus on the creation of cool content for CD-ROMs comes this conference, which covers the CD-ROM industry and digital video in depth. In the past, sessions have been provided for game developers. You'll also find coverage on marketing, digital video production, CD-ROM production, multimedia tools, and more.

VBITTS
Contact: Fawcette Technical Publications and Microsoft
Locations: Worldwide, various locales throughout the year
Phone: 415 833-7100

If you're a working VB programmer, this is the conference for you. While the focus is on corporate development, sessions are provided on multimedia development, Internet programming, and so on—all worth attending if you are a VB game developer.

Internet/Web/VRML Conferences of Note

Online Developers
Contact: Jupiter Communications
Locations: San Francisco, CA (Held in the Fall)
Phone: 212 941-9252 **Fax:** 212 941-7376

Online Developer brings together key online industry folks such as providers, commercial services, publishers, telco executives, and more to discuss the creation of online applications. Last year's conference featured an extensive array of online games, sure to be a major component of future conferences as well.

Web Developer 96
Contact: Mecklermedia
Location: Dallas, Chicago, and other locales; Spring and Fall conferences
Phone: 800 632-5537 **Fax:** 203 226-6976

Meckler's Web Developer conference focuses on Web programming, site design, and all sorts of technical sessions.

Internet World 96
Contact: Mecklermedia
Location: Conferences is held around the world with two in the U.S.
Phone: 800 632-5537 **Fax:** 203 226-2976

This show is more of a general Internet products showcase which is growing as fast as the Internet itself. Meckler is producing Internet World shows in every country imaginable and twice yearly in the U.S. This could easily become the Comdex of the Internet.

Internet World Home Expo
Contact: Mecklermedia
Location: New York, NY
Phone: 913 362-8030

If I had a penny for every Internet-oriented conference Mecklermedia put on, I'd be a rich man. This conference is an attempt by Meckler to create a more consumer Internet-oriented conference and show than its quickly growing general Internet World conference.

Web Design
Contact: Miller Freeman, Inc.
Location: San Francisco, CA
Phone: 415 905-2784 **Fax:** 415 905-2222

Held in conjunction with Miller Freeman's Software Development, this new conference could become one of the hottest Web shows around.

VR World
Contact: Mecklermedia
Location: Location varies year to year. Held twice yearly in the U.S.
Phone: 800 632-5537 **Fax:** 203 226-6976

Mecklermedia has been running VR World for a while and each year it gets bigger and better. With the emergence of VR gaming and VRML, VR is moving from the labs to practical consumer technologies that game developers may want to explore.

Miscellaneous

American Booksellers Association Conference
Contact: American Booksellers Association
Location: Chicago, IL
Phone: 310 372-2732 **Fax:** 310 374-3342

In the past few past years, booksellers have increasingly become resellers of software. In addition, many game companies are looking to successful books for content ideas.

This is the single biggest gathering of book publishers, agents, authors, and distributors in the country and might prove an interesting experience.

Software Publishers Association–Spring Symposium
Contact: SPA
Location: San Francisco, CA
Phone: 202 452-1600 **Fax:** 202 223-8756

The SPA holds a yearly conference to discuss issues affecting the software industry in general. Heads of companies gather and other companies offering services to publishers also attend.

Conference Database
Microsoft Events Page
`http://www.microsoft.com/devonly`

Microsoft holds a number of conferences every year and often they hold special conferences on key topics. Thus, it's a good idea to check in here to keep up on the times Redmond actually lets you know what they're thinking.

Knowledge Web Computer Events Directory
`http://www.kweb.com/`

Are you looking for even more conference information, the latest schedules, locales, and pricing? Check out this incredible database of conferences and trade shows located on the World Wide Web.

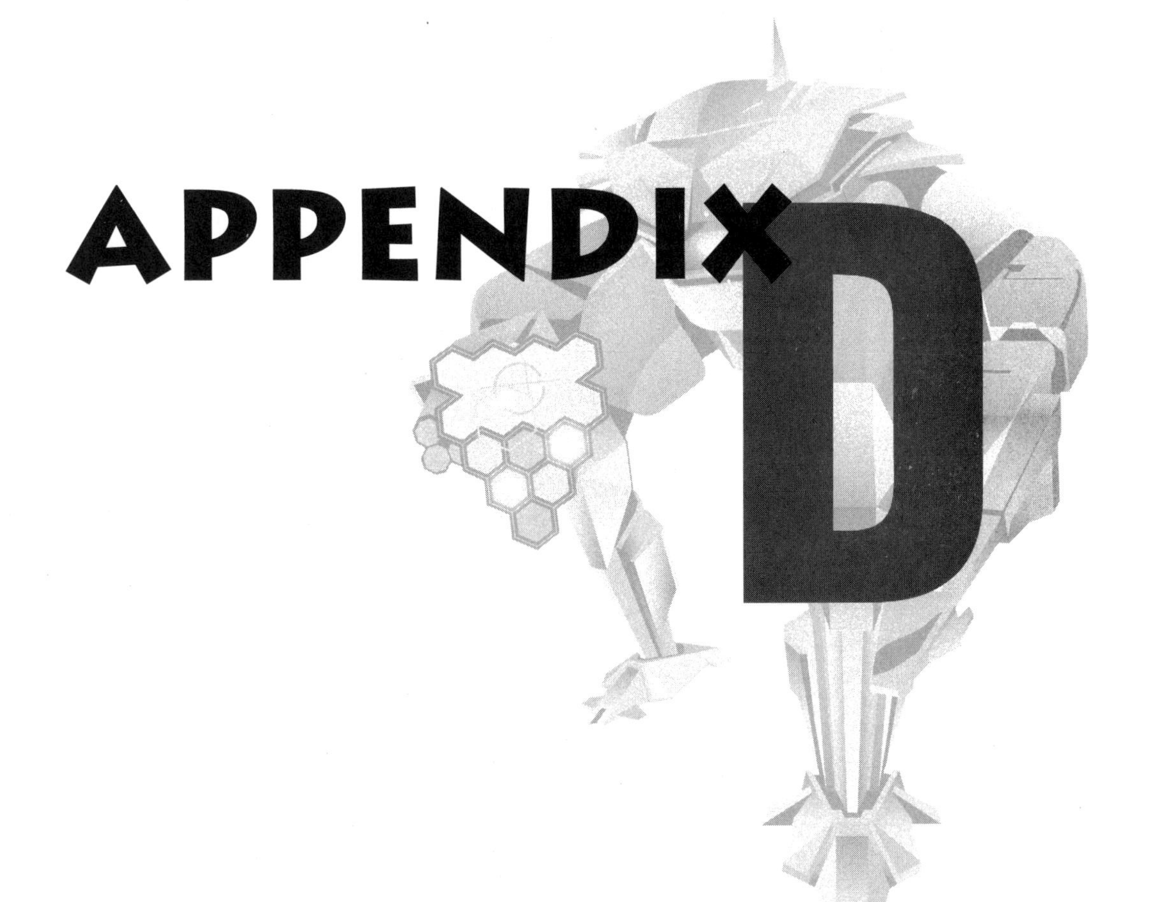

APPENDIX D

Organizations for Game Developers

There are many relevant organizations for game developers to be aware of. As I compiled the list presented in this appendix, I found that there is a wide range of organizations that have a say or stake in the game development arena. Each one is listed here along with a summary explaining its connection to game development.

Professional Organizations of Interest

Computer Game Developers Association
555 Bryant Street Suite 330
Palo Alto, CA
Phone: 415 948-CGDA **Fax:** 415 948-2744

Please note: In order to keep costs down, this phone line is not staffed by anyone. Leave a message and someone from the CGDA will return your call as soon as possible.

The CGDA is an association of interactive entertainment professionals dedicated to serving the careers and interests of its members. It's not a trade association or a union; however, it is the single most important computer game developer organization on the planet. The goals of the CGDA are:

- To foster information exchange among professionals in the industry
- To represent the community of interactive entertainment developers when policy issues arise in industry or government
- To increase artistic and financial recognition for developers
- To enhance the quality of interactive entertainment and educational software

The most important reason for joining the CGDA is that it lets you participate in a community of people with similar interests and concerns. The CGDA will take an active role in helping to set government and industry policy on important issues such as software ratings. In addition, the CGDA offers a variety of services to its members, designed to assist them in their careers. They also publish a newsletter that has all kinds of good information.

Membership will cost $75 for 1996. (Foreign memberships are roughly $10-$20 more to cover extra additional postal costs.)

CGDA has recently begun to launch and support local chapters around the U.S. and the world. As this book went to press, chapters in Austin, New York/New Jersey, Colorado, and two chapters in the San Francisco Bay Area are actively meeting and growing. There is a local chapter file maintained on CompuServe's Game Developers forum (GO GAMDEVS).

Interactive Digital Software Association
Phone: 202 833-4372
Email: IDSA@aol.com

The Interactive Digital Software Association is the "first" organization dedicated to meeting the needs of the interactive entertainment software industry. The IDSA was formed in April, 1994 to represent interactive entertainment software publishers of all sizes and for all platforms, including videogame cartridge, videogame compact disk, and personal computer platforms. Its members comprise some of the biggest and most influential companies like Spectrum Holybyte and Electronic Arts.

The IDSA is also the establishment behind the major ratings board to rate interactive entertainment software and unlike the RSAC, this board is endorsed by the members of Congress pushing for a ratings process for games.

Recreational Software Advisory Council (RSAC)
2067 Massachusetts Avenue, Fourth Floor
Cambridge, MA 02140
Phone: 617 864-5612 **Fax:** 617 864-5740
WWW: http://www.rsac.org/

RSAC is one of the leading ratings agency for computer games. The RSAC ratings process is covered extensively in Chapter 29 so check in there for more detail or contact RSAC for the most up-to-date information.

Women's Interactive Entertainment Association
P.O. Box 1127
San Carlos, CA 94070
Phone: 415 568-1268 **Fax:** 415 802-3297
Email: kdonlon@segaoa.com

The goal of this organization is to get more women both playing and developing interactive entertainment. The WIEA has been brewing for several years, but they held their first public meeting at E3, attracting nearly 200 people. Their second public meeting was at Sega on July 12, 1995. The organization is open to both men and women, and intends to concentrate on issues concerning interactive development, the industry, and women consumers. Specifically, it has outlined the following goals:

- Strengthening the network of relationships among women in the industry
- Encouraging more women to join the industry, particularly in technical positions
- Advocating the development of more gender-neutral and female-specific products
- Encouraging publishers to market their products in gender-neutral ways

- Conducting research on the female market, so as to replace speculation about it with real numbers

They also hope to create a job bank, provide grants, and hold regular seminars and meetings. They already have a newsletter, *WIEA Wave*, which is issued quarterly.

Charter memberships are available now for $75. They will go up to $150 soon. Student memberships are available at $50.

GamePC Consortium
Phone: 408 434-9888 **Fax:** 408 434-0818
Email: 75300.2772@compuserve.com

The GamePC Consortium is a group of hardware and software developers who meet regularly to discuss what to do and how to promote the PC game platform. The consortium is open to all developers interested in helping to define game standards on the PC.

Members are kept up to date on industry news, hold meetings to discuss hardware standards, network, and receive special offers like discounts on conferences and industry newsletters. You can find minutes from meetings and information about the GamePC Consortium on the above listed Web site.

Interactive Multimedia Association
Phone: 410 626-1380 **Fax:** 410 263-0590
WWW: http://www.ima.org

The Interactive Multimedia Association is the oldest, largest, and most active trade association devoted to multimedia. Although this organization attracts more than just game developers, it obviously provides a lot of benefit for game developers who join.

They help members with issues like intellectual property rights, code portability, marketing, multimedia technologies, and more. Specific benefits for members include a subscription to the IMA bi-monthly journal and white papers and documents published or provided by the organization. They also offer a subscription to the *Intellectual Property Project Proceedings*, the journal of the Intellectual Property Project.

The IMA also offers an extensive job bank. They only offer company memberships and the fee is $500 to $10,000 depending on revenues.

Multimedia Roundtable
Phone: 617 497-7090 x3199 **Fax:** 617 868-0577
Email: MMround@aol.com

This organization, which costs $15 to join, is an east-coast multimedia developers organization working to provide a network for east-coast developers. They hold monthly meetings in the Boston area.

The Software Publishers Association
Phone: 202 452-1600 **Fax:** 202 223-8756
Email: membership@spa.org
WWW: http://www.spa.org

The SPA is the major lobbying and organization arm for software developers worldwide. Its members are among the biggest firms in the industry but also include smaller companies too. The benefits of SPA membership include access to market research, industry sales information, market support, and discounts on many major publications of concern to developers.

In addition, the SPA operates an extensive antipiracy campaign and can be extremely helpful in solving world copyright infringement problems.

The folks at MMWire have a great site that lists all sorts of information about software, game, and multimedia oriented organizations. They do a good job of updating and adding organizations as the information becomes available.

MMWIRE's Association Page:

`http://www.mmwire.com`

Talent Organizations

Recently, a large group of major game companies signed agreements regarding professional artistic talent, such as actors and song writers, as it pertains to works in the computer game development field. While most developers are not immediately affected by these contracts, the organizations and the signing of an agreement is something you should be aware of. The other relevant factor is that some of these organizations, especially those like ASCAP, are the ones you must negotiate with concerning reproducing or licensing work based on published work.

ASCAP (Association of Composers, Authors, and Publishers)
7920 Sunset Boulevard, Suite 300
Los Angeles, CA 90046
Phone: 213 883-1000 **Fax:** 212 595-3050

ASCAP, along with BMI and SASAC, is the protector and cataloger of original musical content. Composers use ASCAP as a clearing house to receive royalties for their work.

BMI (Broadcast Music, Inc.)
8730 Sunset Boulevard, 3rd Floor
Los Angeles, CA 90069
Phone: 310 659-9109 **Fax:** 212 586-2000

BMI is the other major music rights organization of note. If you're looking to use professional music in your games, this group and ASCAP are useful organizations to contact.

American Federation of Television & Radio Artists (AFTRA)
National Office
260 Madison Ave.
New York, NY 10016
Phone: 212 532-0800

The Screen Actors Guild (SAG)
National Office
5757 Wilshire Blvd.
Los Angeles, CA 90036-3600
Phone: 213 954-1600

AFTRA and SAG are the two major talent unions for performers. AFTRA and SAG have been active in securing contracts with the multimedia and interactive entertainment industries. Make sure if you plan on using AFTRA or SAG members you are in compliance with potential agreements you or your publisher may need to make or have made.

You can locate local offices for SAG and AFTRA by pointing your Web browser to *http://www.entertainet.com/orgs_uns/dfwactor/locals.htm.*

Directors Guild of America
Phone: 818 785-6321 or 310 289-5330 **Fax:** 818 758-7046
WWW: http://www.dga.org/dga

The Directors Guild may be a useful resource for companies planning on doing extensive digital video sequences for their games. The DGA has begun working to place directors on interactive products and thus has developed some familiarity and guidelines for its members.

Other Potential Organizations and Talent Unions

List of Key Entertainment Industry Unions
`http://www.entertainet.com/orgs_uns/dfwactor/unions.htm`

This site has a comprehensive contact list for key performance-oriented unions like all the other film and theatrical unions that cover people like film editors, cameramen, make-up artists, set builders, and more.

Also be sure to check out the following Web site that presents talent production guides for the film, theater, and video industry. They can be helpful for tracking down key talent along with the above listed organizations:

Lone Eagle Publishing
Phone: 310 471-8066 **Fax:** 310 471-4969
WWW: http://www.loneeagle.com

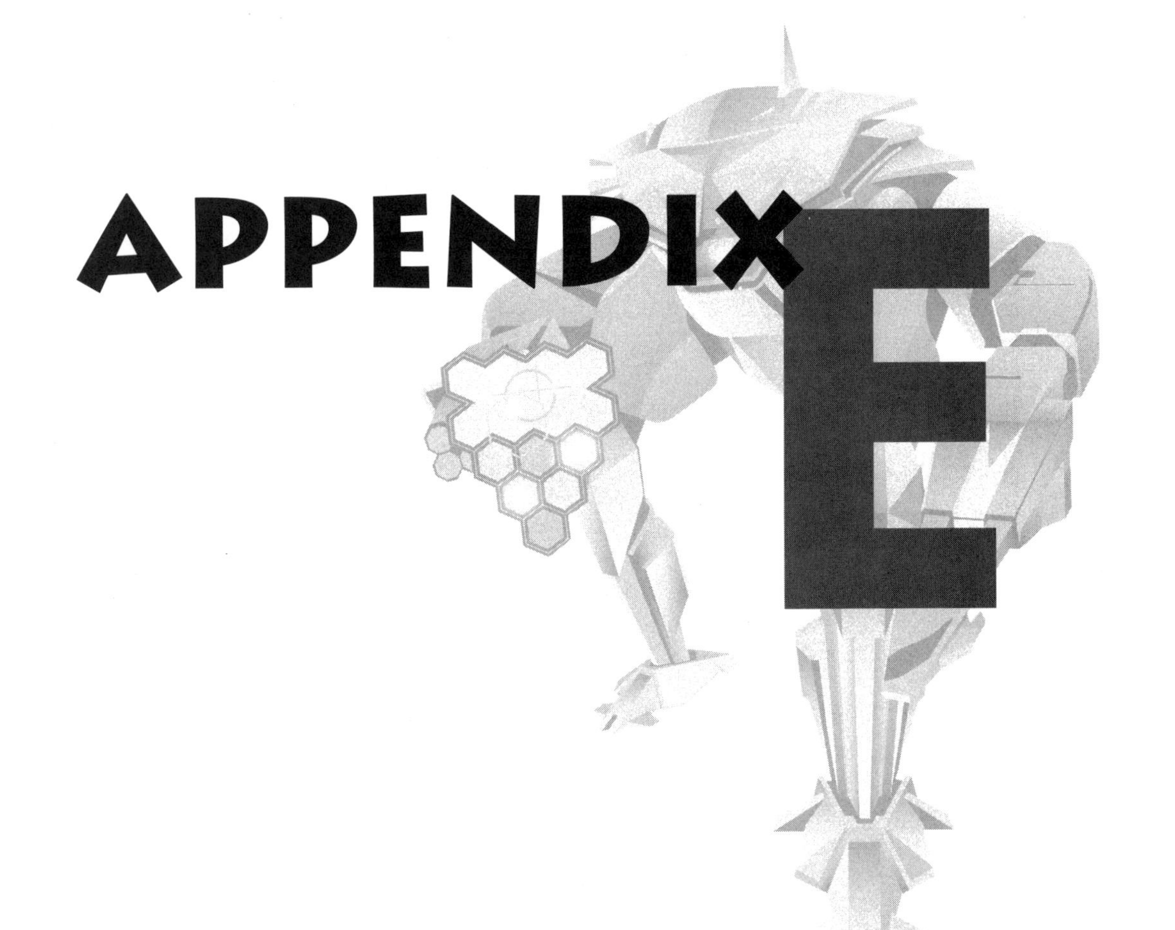

What's on the CD-ROM

In many ways the CD-ROM for the *Ultimate Game Developer's Sourcebook* is just like the book. It's packed with useful resources for graphics production, programming, sound, and more. Many of the programs and demos on the CD-ROM are products that I mentioned in the book, although you will find a few programs on the CD that are not mentioned in the book. The book and the CD make a nice set and I'm glad to have been able to bring you both.

Graphics Production

Truespace 2.0 Working Demo

`\demos\caligari`

Truespace 2.0 is an excellent and affordable 3D graphics and animation package for Windows. It has lots of cool features and you can play with them all in this demo.

NeoPaint

`\utility\imaging\neopaint`

NeoPaint, which I didn't talk about in Chapter 12, is actually a leading shareware paint package. It allows you to paint in 256 colors, and it provides lots of DeluxePaint-like features.

Paint Shop Pro

`\utility\imaging\psp3`

I raved about this shareware art package in Chapter 12. Well here it is. Paint Shop Pro offers you drawing, image processing, and much more. The shareware version is very good and the registration rate is a bargain. Check out this package; it's among the best.

Sound and Music Production

WinJammer!

`\utlity\sound\winjamr`

I love WinJammer; it's a great shareware product. WinJammer is a MIDI sequencing and editing package that's available as shareware. While most programmers don't need a full MIDI sequencing package, they might need something with which to experiment with and use to change MIDI files.

CoolEdit

`\utility\sound\cooledit`

CoolEdit is one of the top shareware sound editing and digization programs around. This version on the CD-ROM will give you an idea of the power this program packs for what is essentially a bargain upgrade price!

Sound Forge Working Demo

`\utility\sound\sndforge`

Sound Forge is a very powerful sound editor used by many developers in the industry. You can see it in action for yourself by checking out this working demo.

Waveform Hold and Modify (WHAM)

`\utility\sound\wham`

For your viewing, demoing, and testing pleasure here is another major shareware sound editing shareware program.

Wav2Voc

`\utility\sound\wav2voc`

VOC files are the native files used by the widely supported and installed SoundBlaster sound cards. This little utility is really handy for converting the many existing Windows WAV files to the VOC format.

Game Engines

The AckNex Toolkit and the Original ACK!

`\demos\acknex`

The AckNex Toolkit is derived from Lary Myers' original ACK-3D engine and is a complete 3D raycasting engine. AckNex is available for license. (You can read more about how to license it in Chapter 21.)

If you are interested in Lary Myers' ACK-3D engine, I suggest you get a copy of Lary's book to go along with the engine provided on the CD-ROM. (The explanations of his code and the tricks he used to put this stuff together are great for those interested in programming 3D raycasting engines.)

Graphic Libraries and Programming Tools

Autodesk FLI Player

`\utility\video\waaplay`

Want to play back FLI\FLC animations in your programs? Look here and check out Autodesk's own programming utilities to help you work with their animation format in your games.

UniVBE

`\utility\video\univbe`

UniVBE from SciTech Software is the Universal VESA 2.0 program. With this display driver you can write for tons of VGA cards that support VESA standards without worrying about the peculiarities of any specific card. Many programmers use this technology and here you'll find the shareware version of it for your own evaluation!

Metagraphics Media!Lab Demo
`\demos\metagrph`

Media!Lab, which was briefly covered in Chapter 16, is a commercially available graphics programming library for Windows. Here you will find some demonstrations and further information of the product's capabilities.

Metagraphics MegaGraphics
`\toolkit\megagraph`

This is a 32-bit graphics programming library from the Metagraphics people who brought you Media!Lab (see above) graphics library. This library is a DOS-based product that handles all kinds of different animation and graphic tasks.

Xsharp Graphics Library
`\toolkit\xsharp`

You might want to check out this graphics library from the author of the Coriolis Groups' *Zen of Graphics Programming* and *Zen of Code Optimization.* Many of the routines provided here are explained in *Zen of Graphics Programming.*

FastGraph Shareware Version
`\toolkit\fastgrph`

This is the shareware version of the top-selling FastGraph graphics library by Ted Gruber Software, who recently shipped a Windows version. If you want to see a number of examples of how this library can be used to create games, check out Diana Gruber's *Action Arcade Adventure Set* published by The Coriolis Group. This book shows you how to use the FastGraph library to create cool side-scrolling arcade games.

WordUp Graphics Toolkit
`\toolkit\wordup`

This library, covered in Chapter 17, is available for testing here. You'll also find a few really simple (meaning easy to understand) demos of some key game graphic engines including a magic carpet style engine.

Demonstration SourceCode

Games with Source
`\games`

This directory contains about 16 or so games, including backgammon, 3D, Tic-Tac-Toe, and so on. Almost all of them have source code available for you to explore.

Iguana Demos

`\demos\iguana`

This directory contains demos and source examples from Iguana, a major development house in Austin, TX. Iguana is now a subsidiary of Acclaim Entertainment—one of the world's biggest game software companies.

Wolfenstein 3D Source Code

`\toolkit\wolfnstn`

Ever wanted to see the source code behind a wildly successful commercial game? Well here's your chance. While Id does not support this code (don't call them) and the code is complex, this sneak peek behind the scenes is a great resource for beginners and professionals alike.

Game Programmers Encyclopedia

`\toolkit\gpe`

The *Game Programmers Encyclopedia* is one of those resources that you just wish you had more of. A bunch of programmers and regulars on the rec.games.programmer Usenet group got together and pooled example code, FAQs, and other programming resources together in this well organized encyclopedia of tricks, tips, and source examples.

Sound Libraries

Diamondware DOS STK

`\toolkit\dwstk`

Diamondware's Windows STK is almost done but just not in time for this CD-ROM. We do, however, have their DOS STK which is a great well-priced solution for DOS developers. Since the Windows STK API is very much like its DOS counterpart, you can become familiar with the API here and translate those skills to the upcoming Windows version when it arrives shortly.

TinyMod

`\toolkit\tinymod`

TinyMod is a DOS programming library for implementing MOD file playback in your games. I described MOD files in detail in Chapter 14 of this book. They can be really cool music files. Game developers and especially demo developers love them. If you want to use MODs in your game, check this out.

Soundblaster Toolkit

`\toolkit\Sb`

In this directory you will find a series of examples and utilities to help you learn about programming Creative's Soundblaster Sound Card in your DOS applications.

Windows Tools

While I and many other book authors would love to have brought you the Windows Game SDK, so far Microsoft hasn't allowed it to be distributed separately from their Developers Level II CD-ROM. However, I have provided older, but still useful, tools from the first generation of Windows game technologies.

WaveMix
`\toolkit\wavemix`

WaveMix, which is described in Chapter 16, is a simple Windows DLL that is still used quite a bit to play back multiple WAV files simultaneously.

WinG
`\windows\system\wing`

WinG was the original graphics enhancement before Microsoft offered DirectDraw. With WinG, programmers can speed graphics and draw to bitmaps in memory much more conveniently. WinG's DisDib features are being merged into the Window95 Graphics API but for many developers still working with Win3.1 for compatibility issues, WinG is the way to go.

Win32S
`\windows\system\win32s`

Just in case you've missed this and are looking to program a 32-bit game that will work with Win 3.1 as well as Windows 95, Win32s will help you bridge the gap between the two major operating systems.

MediaArchitechs MediaKnife
`\demos\medarchs`

This demo is also designed for VB programmers. It is brought to you by Media Architechs and includes MediaKnife, a major custom control for VB users to add sprites, graphics, animations, and palette management to their programs.

Delphi Turbo Sprite Toolkit
`\toolkit\trbosprt`

In Chapter 16 I talked about an entire sprite toolkit developed by a Delphi programming team. Well here it is. If you are using Delphi to make games, this is well worth taking a look at.

InstallSheild Demo

`\utility\instshld`

InstallSheild is the leading installation program that many companies use to properly install Windows Programs. There's a great demo of the program here for you to evaluate on your own.

FOREHelp Help System Authoring

`\utility\forehelp`

Many Windows programs, even games, need a nice help system (however limited) to go along with the product. This product can help you develop a nice help system to go with your programs.

WinDirect from SciTech Software

`\toolkit\windirec`

This demo of WinDirect from SciTech software will show you its power as a substitute system for allowing direct access of video card features from Windows. It's really a competing product to DirectDraw from Microsoft itself and many companies are using it. Check it out for yourself and see if it works for you.

Telecommunications

Compuserve's WinCim

`\utility\cserve`

The Game Developers section on Compuserve is a great daily resource of gaming tools and information. I am including a copy of WinCim for you so you have no excuse not to sign on today to check out and participate on the forum message boards! GO GAMDEV for more information.

Index

B

D

H

M

Q

R

S

T

U

V